THE RULE AGAINST HEARSAY

Contemporary Decisions

* * *

A LandMark Publication

Litigator Series

The Rule Against Hearsay
Contemporary Decisions

Published in the United States of America
by LandMark Publications.
www.landmark-publications.com

Publication Date: February 2017;
Subject Heading: Law of Evidence;
Audience: Law Professionals.

Character Set: ISO 8859-1 (Latin-1);
Language Code: EN;
Interior Type: Text; Monochrome.

Help us serve you better.
Write to landmarkpx@live.com with
your requests, comments and suggestions.

ISBN: 978-1520500515

SUMMARY OF CONTENTS

Federal Rules of Evidence
Article VIII. Hearsay

Rule 801. Definitions That Apply to This Article

(a) Statement. "Statement" means a person's oral assertion, written assertion, or nonverbal conduct, if the person intended it as an assertion.

(b) Declarant. "Declarant" means the person who made the statement.

(c) Hearsay. "Hearsay" means a statement that:

(1) the declarant does not make while testifying at the current trial or hearing; and

(2) a party offers in evidence to prove the truth of the matter asserted in the statement.

Rule 802. The Rule Against Hearsay

Hearsay is not admissible unless any of the following provides otherwise:

- a federal statute;
- these rules; or
- other rules prescribed by the Supreme Court.

FEDERAL RULES OF EVIDENCE

Rule 807. Residual Exception

(a) In General. Under the following circumstances, a hearsay statement is not excluded by the rule against hearsay even if the statement is not specifically covered by a hearsay exception in Rule 803 or 804:

   (1) the statement has equivalent circumstantial guarantees of trustworthiness;

   (2) it is offered as evidence of a material fact;

   (3) it is more probative on the point for which it is offered than any other evidence that the proponent can obtain through reasonable efforts; and

   (4) admitting it will best serve the purposes of these rules and the interests of justice.

(b) Notice. The statement is admissible only if, before the trial or hearing, the proponent gives an adverse party reasonable notice of the intent to offer the statement and its particulars, including the declarant's name and address, so that the party has a fair opportunity to meet it.

FOREWORD

THIS CASEBOOK contains a selection of U. S. Court of Appeals decisions that analyze, interpret and discuss the rule against hearsay and its exceptions. The selection of decisions spans from 2013 to the date of publication.

The residual hearsay exception of Federal Rule of Evidence 807 provides that a hearsay statement is not excluded by the rule against hearsay, even if not covered by an exception in Rule 803 or 804. *US v. Stoney End of Horn*, (8th Cir. 2016).

A proponent of hearsay evidence must establish five elements in order to satisfy Rule 807: "(1) circumstantial guarantees of trustworthiness; (2) materiality; (3) probative value; (4) the interests of justice; and (5) notice." *United States v. Ochoa,* 229 F.3d 631, 638 (7th Cir. 2000) (citing *United States v. Hall,* 165 F.3d 1095, 1110 (7th Cir. 1999)). *US v. Moore, 824 F. 3d 620*, (7th Cir. 2016).

The government seeks to introduce evidence of a phone number the defendant had provided his probation officer. The district judge grants defendant's motion to exclude the probation officer's records as inadmissible hearsay.

Defendant's out of court statements bear markers of reliability that are equivalent to those found in statements specifically covered by Rule 803 or Rule 804. The purpose of Rule 807 is to make sure that reliable, material hearsay evidence is admitted, regardless of whether it fits neatly into one of the exceptions enumerated in the Rules of Evidence. The order of the district court to exclude the probation officer's records as inadmissible hearsay is vacated. *US v. Moore, ibid.*

For the purposes of assessing the trustworthiness of a hearsay statement under Rule 807, this court, in *Snyder,* offered the following list of factors to consider:

> the character of the witness for truthfulness and honesty, and the availability of evidence on the issue; whether the testimony was given voluntarily, under oath, subject to cross-examination and a penalty for perjury; the witness' relationship with both the defendant and the government and his motivation to testify before the grand jury; the extent to which the witness' testimony reflects his personal knowledge; whether the witness ever recanted his testimony; the existence of corroborating evidence; and, the reasons for the witness' unavailability.

United States v. Snyder, 872 F.2d 1351, 1355-56 (7th Cir. 1989). *US v. Moore, ibid.*

This list is "neither exhaustive nor absolute," but it is a helpful guide. *United States v. Doerr,* 886 F.2d 944, 956 (7th Cir. 1989). In this case, the district court's reasoning focused on the first of these factors, to the exclusion of the other five. *US v. Moore, ibid.*

* * *

Rule 807 provides that a hearsay statement is not excluded by the rule against hearsay, even if not covered by an exception in Rule 803 or 804, if the statement (1) has "equivalent circumstantial guarantees of trustworthiness" to statements admitted under the enumerated exceptions, (2) is offered as evidence of a material fact, (3) is more probative on the point offered than any other reasonably available evidence, and (4) will best serve the general purposes of the rules of evidence and the interests of justice. We have said that this exception to the rule against hearsay "was necessary to permit courts to admit evidence in exceptional circumstances where the evidence was necessary, highly probative, and carried a guarantee of trustworthiness equivalent to or superior to that which underlies the other recognized exceptions." *United States v. Renville,* 779 F.2d 430, 439 (8th Cir. 1985). *US v. Stoney End of Horn,* 829 F. 3d 681, (8th Cir. 2016).

Defendant argues that the district court erroneously admitted hearsay evidence. The witness testified: "She told me that she had been drinking, her and Stoney, and she said Stoney beat the shit out of her. " *US v. Stoney End of Horn, ibid.*

The district court is entitled to some deference in applying Rule 807, but the court here did not address why the witness' statement had "circumstantial guarantees of trustworthiness" equivalent to the enumerated hearsay exceptions. *US v. Stoney End of Horn, ibid.*

The record as a whole, excluding the hearsay, shows a convincing case of assault. The hearsay testimony was harmless error. (It "likely did not have more than a very slight effect on the verdict.") The conviction is affirmed. *US v. Stoney End of Horn, ibid.*

* * *

"[P]rior inconsistent statements by a witness are not hearsay and are competent as substantive evidence if the declarant testifies at trial and is subject to cross-examination concerning the statement, and the prior inconsistent statement was given under oath at a 'trial, hearing, or other proceeding.'" *United States v. Wilson,* 806 F.2d 171, 175-76 (8th Cir. 1986) (quoting Fed. R. Evid. 801(d)(1)(A)). "The district court has considerable discretion in determining whether prior statements are inconsistent with trial testimony." *United States v. Matlock,* 109 F.3d 1313, 1319 (8th Cir. 1997) (citing *United States v. Russell,* 712 F.2d 1256, 1258 (8th Cir. 1983) (per curiam); *United States v. Thompson,* 708 F.2d 1294, 1302 (8th Cir. 1983) ("The district court should have considerable discretion to determine whether evasive answers are inconsistent with statements previously given." (citation omitted))). *US v. Dean,* (8th Cir. 2016).

A prior inconsistent statement given by a witness under oath during a grand jury proceeding can be used as substantive evidence. *US v. Dean, ibid.*

At trial, a witness repeatedly testifies on direct examination that she never saw the defendant with a gun the night that he assaulted her. Those statements squarely contradicted her prior grand jury testimony that (1) she saw her father with the firearm, (2) he discharged that firearm, (3) she heard the firearm go off, and (4) the gun that the police recovered from the apartment was the same gun that her father was firing. The prior statements of the witness are admitted at trial. Affirmed. *US v. Dean, ibid.*

In applying Rule 801(d)(1)(A), inconsistency is not limited to diametrically opposed answers but may be found in evasive answers, inability to recall, silence, or changes of position. *US v. Dean, ibid.*

A 911 call and recorded body-microphone statements are admissible as present sense impressions and excited utterances. Affirmed. *US v. Dean, ibid.*

Federal Rule of Evidence 803(1) provides that "[a] statement describing or explaining an event or condition, made while or immediately after the declarant perceived it" is "not excluded by the rule against hearsay." "The underlying rationale of the present sense impression exception is that substantial contemporaneity of event and statement minimizes unreliability due to defective recollection or conscious fabrication. There is no *per se* rule indicating what time interval is too long under Rule 803(1) . . . ." *United States v. Hawkins,* 59 F.3d 723, 730 (8th Cir. 1995) (alteration in original) (quotations and citations omitted), *vacated on other grounds,* 516 U.S. 1168 (1996). *US v. Dean, ibid.*

* * *

Federal Rule of Evidence 801 provides that a statement offered against a party is not hearsay if the statement was "made by the party's coconspirator during and in furtherance of the conspiracy." Fed. R. Evid. 801(d)(2)(E). Statements can further the conspiracy in a number of ways. "Some examples include comments designed to assist in recruiting potential members, to inform other members about the progress of the conspiracy, to control damage to or detection of the conspiracy, to hide the criminal objectives of the conspiracy, or to instill confidence and prevent the desertion of other members." *Johnson,* 200 F.3d at 533. A coconspirator's statement may satisfy the "in furtherance" requirement even if the statement was not "exclusively, or even primarily, made to further the conspiracy." *United States v. Cruz-Rea,* 626 F.3d 929, 937 (7th Cir. 2010). *US v. Elder,* (7th Cir. 2016).

The defendant challenges the district court's decision to admit a witness' testimony about the conversation the witness overheard between two conspirators. *US v. Elder, ibid.*

The challenged statements were made between two conspirators, in the presence of a third conspirator, about a problem that arose during a recent conspiratorial transaction with a fourth conspirator, and that appears to have prompted a decisive remedial change in the conspiracy's structure. Under these circumstances, there was plainly a "'reasonable basis'" to conclude that the statements furthered the conspiracy. Affirmed. *US v. Elder, ibid.*

The Rule Against Hearsay

816 F.3d 479 (2016)

UNITED STATES of America, Plaintiff-Appellee,

v.

Derrick SMITH, Defendant-Appellant.

No. 15-2005.

United States Court of Appeals, Seventh Circuit.

Argued February 26, 2016.

Decided March 11, 2016.

US v. Smith, 816 F. 3d 479 (7th Cir. 2016)

p.480 Michael T. Donovan, Marsha A. McClellan, Office of the United States Attorney, Chicago, IL, for Plaintiff-Appellee.

Derrick Smith, Dolton, IL, pro se.

Samuel E. Adam, Attorney, Victor P. Henderson, Attorney, Henderson Adam, LLC, Chicago, IL, for Defendant-Appellant.

Before POSNER, FLAUM, and EASTERBROOK, Circuit Judges.

EASTERBROOK, Circuit Judge.

In March 2011 Derrick Smith was appointed to the Illinois House of Representatives to complete an unfinished term. He wanted to be elected in his own right, which meant that he had to campaign in his party's primary, set for March 2012. One of his campaign assistants, known to Smith as "Pete," alerted the FBI that Smith might be corrupt. Pete (whose last name has been kept confidential) began recording some of his conversations with Smith. At the FBI's suggestion, Pete told Smith that a woman who lived in his district would provide $7,000 (money that would help Smith pay his campaign staff) if Smith wrote a letter supporting her application for a grant from the state's Capital Development Board for the construction of a daycare center. This was a sting; there was no such woman, and the money would come from the FBI.

Letters of recommendation from one public official to another are common and lawful—unless paid for. The exchange of an official act for money violates federal law, no matter how the recipient uses the cash. See, e.g., *Evans v. United States,* 504 U.S. 255, 112 S.Ct. 1881, 119 L.Ed.2d 57 (1992); *McCormick v. United States,* 500 U.S. 257, 111 S.Ct. 1807, 114 L.Ed.2d 307 (1991); *United States v. Blagojevich,* 794 F.3d 729 (7th Cir.2015). Smith wrote the letter, and Pete handed over $7,000. Smith immediately used some of the money to pay his campaign staff; a search of his home turned up the rest.

At Smith's trial for violating 18 U.S.C. §§ 666(a)(1)(B) and 1951, the prosecutor introduced the recorded conversations with Pete. The jury convicted, and the judge p.481 sentenced Smith to five months' imprisonment and one year's supervised release. Neither side called Pete as a witness: he was a shady character and may have been stealing from the FBI in addition to assisting it. Pete said that he would not testify, asserting his constitutional privilege not to be compelled to incriminate himself. Since the prosecutor did not want Pete's testimony, he did not ask the court to grant use immunity; defense counsel did not call Pete to see whether the district judge would honor his assertion of the privilege. (It is easy to imagine lines of questioning whose answers could not incriminate Pete.)

The sole argument Smith makes on appeal is that, with Pete not in court, the use of his recorded statements violated the Confrontation Clause of the Sixth Amendment. It is unclear why Smith casts this as a constitutional argument rather than as one based on the hearsay doctrine. See *United States v. Walker,* 673 F.3d 649, 659-61 (7th Cir.2012) (concurring opinion). The hearsay rule excludes out-of-court statements offered for their truth. See Fed.R.Evid. 801(c). (There are exceptions, but the United States does not argue that any applies.)

The Confrontation Clause, by contrast, affects only "testimonial" statements. See, e.g., *Ohio v. Clark,* ___ U.S. ___, 135 S.Ct. 2173, 192 L.Ed.2d 306 (2015); *Crawford v. Washington,* 541 U.S. 36, 124 S.Ct. 1354, 158 L.Ed.2d 177 (2004). Indeed it covers only a subset of testimonial hearsay. Statements that would have been admissible at common law in 1793 (in other words, statements that are not hearsay or are covered by longstanding exceptions to the hearsay doctrine) are outside the Sixth Amendment, see *Giles v. California,* 554 U.S. 353, 358-59, 128 S.Ct. 2678, 171 L.Ed.2d 488 (2008), as are all statements by witnesses who are available for cross-examination, see *Crawford,* 541 U.S. at 60 n. 9, 124 S.Ct. 1354. And *Clark* shows that the Court has not yet decided whether the Confrontation Clause covers testimonial statements by one private party to another. Thus if a statement is not hearsay, because not offered for its truth, it also is not "testimonial" for the purpose of the Confrontation Clause.

The district judge admitted Pete's recorded statements after concluding that they helped to put Smith's recorded statements in context. Smith maintains that Pete's statements do more than put his own in context—and that even if just used for context they are inadmissible because Pete said much more on the recordings than Smith did. It is easy to find statements in judicial opinions discussing whether statements have been used for "context" and commenting on the relative length of different speakers' statements, but those observations must not be understood to displace the legal standards—for hearsay whether the out-of-court statement is offered for truth, and for the Confrontation Clause whether the out-of-court statement is testimonial.

To see this, consider a simple hypothetical. "Pete: I will pay you $7,000 in exchange for a letter my client can use to seek a grant for a daycare center. Do you agree? Smith: Yes." In this example, Pete utters 25 words to Smith's one—but there is no hearsay because Pete's statement is not used to show that anyone will pay $7,000. It is used instead to show the meaning of Smith's "yes," which does not depend on whether Pete was speaking truthfully. The "yes" constitutes Smith's agreement to exchange money for an official act. Pete's statements may put Smith's "in context," but that's unimportant. What matters is that, without being used for their truth, they enable the jury to determine the import of Smith's own words. Allowing the jury to hear Pete's p.482 words no more violates the Confrontation Clause than does providing a jury with a dictionary or a translation from a foreign language or an expert on criminal jargon. Talking about "context" does not help to establish whether such an exchange is properly admitted, nor does counting the number of words tell us whether Pete's statement is hearsay under Rule 801 or "testimonial" for constitutional purposes.

Now consider a different example. "Pete: Last week I paid you $7,000 for a letter that my client will use to seek a grant for a daycare center. Do you remember?

Smith: Yes." This has the same 25-to-1 ratio of words, and it too could be said to show the context of Smith's reply. But this statement would be hearsay, because it would be relevant only if Pete spoke the truth—that he had paid $7,000 in exchange for a letter. Once again it would be best to tackle the dispositive questions directly rather than be sidetracked into word counts or a search for "context." Even the briefest testimonial out-of-court statement—e.g., "Smith shot Jones"—can violate Rule 801 and the Confrontation Clause, no matter its effect on the context in which to place hearers' responses.

We looked through the record to determine whether Pete's statements (and those of other persons heard on the recordings) were offered for their truth. Here is one exchange that Smith has selected as an example:

> [Pete]: The broad is fixin' to give.
>
> Smith: I got you, mother fucker. I told your ass, I got you.
>
> [Pete]: For real, look. The broad is gonna give seven thousand, with no problem.
>
> Smith: Okay.

Pete's statements in this exchange are admissible. They were not offered for their truth—that is, to show that someone *was* going to pay Smith. The "broad" did not exist, and the FBI did not plan to let Smith keep the money. Instead Pete's statements were used to show what Smith himself understood the transaction to entail.

Here's another exchange to which Smith objected:

> [Pete]: You ready, you ready to write?
>
> Smith: Yeah I got it.

Once again Pete's statement was not offered for the truth of anything, though it does tend to show the meaning of Smith's "I got it." No hearsay here.

It would not be helpful to run through all of the other exchanges. They are similar to these. Smith has not been convicted on the basis of hearsay, or of out-of-court testimonial statements. Smith's own words and deeds convicted him.

AFFIRMED

818 F.3d 1091 (2016)

UNITED STATES of America, Plaintiff-Appellee

v.

Cameron Taevon JONES, Defendant-Appellant.

No. 15-6119.

United States Court of Appeals, Tenth Circuit.

April 5, 2016.

p.1093 Appeal from the United States District Court for the Western District of Oklahoma; (D.C. No. 5:07-CR-00294-F-1).

Kyle Edward Wackenheim, Research and Writing Attorney (Paul Antonio Lacy, Assistant Federal Public Defender, with him on the briefs), Office of the Federal Public Defender for the Western District of Oklahoma, Oklahoma City, OK, appearing for Appellant.

Timothy W. Ogilvie, Assistant United States Attorney (Sanford C. Coats, United States Attorney, with him on the brief), Office of the United States Attorney for the Western District of Oklahoma, Oklahoma City, OK, appearing for Appellee.

Before TYMKOVICH, Chief Judge, BRISCOE, and MATHESON, Circuit Judges.

MATHESON, Circuit Judge.

The district court revoked Cameron Jones's supervised release. It relied on hearsay evidence from the Government's only witness at the revocation hearing. On appeal, Mr. Jones argues (1) Federal Rule of Criminal Procedure 32.1(b)(2)(C) requires the district court to apply a balancing test to determine whether hearsay evidence may be considered for revocation, (2) the district court abused its discretion because it did not apply the Rule 32.1(b)(2)(C) balancing test, and (3) this error is reversible. Exercising jurisdiction under 28 U.S.C. § 1291, we agree with Mr. Jones and reverse and remand to the district court for a new revocation hearing.

I. BACKGROUND

A. *Factual History*

1. Mr. Jones's Previous Convictions

In 1998, Mr. Jones was convicted of interference with commerce by threat or violence, in violation of 18 U.S.C. § 1951, and of using and carrying a firearm during a crime of violence, in violation of 18 U.S.C. § 924(c)(1). In 2007, he was convicted p.1094 of possession with intent to distribute cocaine in violation of 21 U.S.C. § 841(a)(1) and sentenced to 71 months in prison and five years of supervised release. The court also ordered the prison sentence to run consecutively to the 24-month term of incarceration imposed as a result of the revocation of supervised release in the 1998 case.

The 2007 presentence report stated Mr. Jones was a member of the Rolling 60s Crips gang and goes by the alias C-Rag.

2. The September 27, 2014 Murder

On August 29, 2014, Mr. Jones was released from prison and began serving his five-year term of supervised release for the 2007 conviction. On September 27, 2014, Mr. Miles, a Rolling 60s Crips member, was murdered. Two days after the murder, the United States Probation Office filed a petition to revoke Mr. Jones's supervised release, alleging Mr. Jones violated the following conditions: (1) "[t]he defendant shall not commit another federal, state, or local crime;" (2) "[t]he defendant shall not possess a firearm, destructive device, or any other dangerous weapon;" and (3) "[t]he defendant shall not associate with any persons engaged in criminal activity and shall no[t] associate with any person convicted of a felony unless granted permission to do so by the probation officer." ROA, Vol. I at 18-19. The petition asserted Mr. Jones violated these conditions by murdering Mr. Miles, possessing a firearm, and associating with Mr. Miles, a convicted felon.

B. *Procedural History*

1. The Revocation Hearing

After the Probation Office filed its petition, the district court held a revocation hearing on April 9, 2015. The Government presented one witness: Inspector Benavides, a homicide detective with the Oklahoma City Police Department who investigated the murder. He testified about Ms. Palmore's and Trenton Nguyen's statements given during witness interviews. He also testified about his investigation of the murder, Mr. Jones's arrest, and Mr. Jones's state murder prosecution. He testified as follows.

a. *Ms. Palmore's statements*

Inspector Benavides interviewed Ms. Palmore on the day of the shooting. He testified Ms. Palmore claimed to have seen the shooting and that she provided the following information:

- She "had just gotten out of prison."
- Before the murder, she was at a bar named Slick Willie's with a group of people that included Mr. Jones and Mr. Miles.
- At Slick Willie's, Mr. Miles tried to break up a fight between "some females" and, in the process, had a confrontation with Mr. Jones.
- Following the confrontation, she and the rest of the group left Slick Willie's.
- When she arrived at her apartment, a group that included Mr. Jones was located in a nearby parking lot of a Cricket cell phone store.
- Ms. Palmore saw Mr. Miles walk toward the group accompanied by an "Asian boy," who was later identified as Mr. Nguyen.
- Ms. Palmore went inside her apartment, but at some point heard people in the parking lot yelling.
- She went outside and saw Mr. Jones shooting at the car Mr. Miles was sitting in.
- Mr. Jones was "walking up to the car shooting into the car."

• When Mr. Jones arrived at the driver's side window, he shot into the car.

p.1095 • Mr. Miles was trying to get out of the passenger's side of the car during the shooting.

• An "entire clip" was shot.

• After the shooting, Mr. Jones got into a two-door white Monte Carlo, which sped away from the scene, and "the bottom of the car kind of hit the asphalt and they drove off."

• "She was 100 percent sure" Mr. Jones was the shooter.

• She had known Mr. Jones since she was 15 years old[1] but had not seen him for many years before the night of the murder because she had recently been released from prison.

ROA, Vol. III at 20-23.

During the interview, Inspector Benavides showed Ms. Palmore a photo lineup consisting of six headshots of different African-American men, including Mr. Jones. Ms. Palmore identified someone other than Mr. Jones as the shooter. Inspector Benavides had the following exchange with Mr. Jones's counsel on cross-examination:

Q. And then when you took her to the police department, you did a very controlled photo identification?

A. Yes, sir.

Q. And she identified the wrong person; isn't that correct?

A. She — actually, she identified — for the first time, she identified — for me, she identified two people out of one lineup. And that's the first time that has ever happened to me. So once she did that, I went back inside with her and I verified with her that we were absolutely talking about Cameron Jones. And she was very adamant, 100 percent sure, that Cameron Jones was the shooter.

Q. Right. But the point I'm trying to make here is she's saying it was [Mr. Jones].

A. Yes, sir.

Q. But the picture she identified was not [Mr. Jones].

A. She identified the picture of [Mr. Jones], but she identified him as the person bringing the gun and giving it — the person that she identified as the shooter was a random guy that I had put in the lineup. And once we looked at it, you know, the similarities to him and to [Mr. Jones], I mean, they're similar. And the photo lineup is there, you can look at it, I've given it to you. That's why I went back in there to reaffirm with her who we were talking about.

ROA, Vol. III at 38-39.

Inspector Benavides testified that, although Ms. Palmore misidentified Mr. Jones during the photo lineup, she was adamant that Mr. Jones was the shooter. According to Inspector Benavides, Ms. Palmore told him "[she] could have been mistaken, [she] hadn't seen him in a while, [she] had just gotten out of prison, but she [was] 100 percent sure that [Mr. Jones] was the shooter." *Id.* at 40.

b. *Mr. Nguyen's statements*

Inspector Benavides testified that Mr. Nguyen provided the following information:

• Mr. Jones and Mr. Miles had a confrontation at Slick Willie's.

• After the confrontation, he and Mr. Miles left Slick Willie's and went to Mr. Miles's house.

p.1096 • Mr. Miles said he was going to fight Mr. Jones because Mr. Jones was responsible for the altercation at Slick Willie's.

• Mr. Nguyen and Mr. Miles went to the Cricket parking lot and Mr. Miles "start[ed] calling [Mr. Jones] out in front of everybody."

• Mr. Jones was on the phone when Mr. Miles was "calling him out" and did not respond to Mr. Miles's provocations. Mr. Jones "decided he wasn't going to fight."

• Mr. Nguyen and Mr. Miles walked back to Mr. Miles's house.

• Mr. Nguyen was not present when Mr. Miles went back to the Cricket parking lot and was shot.

Id. at 24-25.

c. *Additional investigation*

Inspector Benavides testified further about his investigation of the shooting. When he arrived at the Cricket parking lot, he was briefed by the law enforcement personnel already on the scene. Mr. Miles's body was "in the parking lot on the passenger side [of the car]." *Id.* at 13. The body was outside the car on the ground because first responders had attempted to administer medical treatment. There were 11 shell casings on the ground on the driver's side of the car. The bullet holes in the car "were from the back to the front, indicating.... the [shooter] was walking up when the shots were fired." *Id.* at 15.

Two additional shell casings were found inside the car on the driver's seat. Inspector Benavides testified the shell casings inside the car indicated the shooter was close, possibly arm's length, to the driver's side window when he fired the shots.

The crime-scene investigator told him "two gentlemen" named "C-Rag and PK" were involved in the shooting. *Id.* at 15. Mr. Jones went by C-Rag; Mr. Jones's brother, Jacara Jones, went by PK.

The additional eyewitnesses who were in the parking lot at the time of the shooting "refused to talk to [the police]." *Id.* at 40-41.

d. *Mr. Jones's arrest*

Inspector Benavides also testified about Mr. Jones's arrest. The police arrested Mr. Jones at his home the morning after the shooting. A white two-door Monte Carlo was parked outside the house. The rear bumper on the passenger's side was damaged and it appeared there was "contact with the asphalt ... you could see the scratches and the scrape." *Id.* at 28.

After receiving a *Miranda* warning, Mr. Jones agreed to make a statement. He denied any involvement in the shooting and stated he arrived home the previous night around 12:30 to 1:00 a.m. He stated he got off work, went to the gym, and helped a friend move furniture in an area across town from Slick Willie's and the Cricket parking lot.

Cell phone records showed Mr. Jones was in the area of Slick Willie's "about the time that the witnesses stated they saw him there. [The records] also indicated he was in the area of the homicide right at the time that the incident occurred." *Id.* at 29-30.

e. *The state prosecution*

Inspector Benavides testified as follows about the state prosecution of Mr. Jones. Mr. Jones was charged with first-degree murder of Mr. Miles in Oklahoma state court, but the prosecutors dropped the charges because Ms. Palmore refused to testify. She was set to be the "main witness on the case." *Id.* at 31. Mr. Miles was a gang member and a convicted felon, Ms. Palmore was listed as a witness on public records associated with the State's p.1097 murder prosecution, and the district attorney could refile the charge against Mr. Jones.

f. *Ms. Palmore and the revocation hearing*

The Government did not subpoena or attempt to contact Ms. Palmore to testify at the revocation hearing.

2. The District Court's Rulings

During the revocation hearing, the district court concluded the Government had proved by a preponderance of the evidence that Mr. Jones had committed supervised-release violations one and two — (1) the prohibition on committing any federal, state, or local crime and (2) the prohibition on possession of firearms. The court further concluded the Government failed to prove violation three — (3) association with a felon.[2] Mr. Jones's counsel objected at the hearing to "all of [Inspector Benavides's] hearsay statements," asserting they violated Mr. Jones's rights under the Due Process Clause, Confrontation Clause, and Federal Rule of Criminal Procedure 32.1.

On April 30, 2015, Mr. Jones filed a post-hearing motion to strike Inspector Benavides's hearsay testimony.[3] On May 21, 2015, the district court denied Mr. Jones's motion, concluding Inspector Benavides's testimony was sufficiently reliable and that a preponderance of evidence established Mr. Jones violated the two conditions of supervised release. The district court relied heavily on the testimony about Ms. Palmore's statements. On June 10, 2015, the court issued a separate order revoking the remainder of Mr. Jones's term of supervised release, resulting in a 36-month term of imprisonment, and imposed 10 years of supervised release.

II. DISCUSSION

Mr. Jones raises three issues on appeal: (1) whether Federal Rule of Criminal Procedure 32.1(b)(1)(C) requires the district court to apply a balancing test to determine whether hearsay evidence may be considered for revocation, (2) whether the district court abused its discretion because it did not apply the Rule 32.1(b)(1)(C) balancing test, and (3) whether such error was harmless. We address these issues in turn and conclude the district court committed reversible error when it failed to apply the Rule 32.1(b)(1)(C) balancing test to the hearsay evidence presented at the revocation hearing. We confine our analysis to Mr. Jones's right to confront Ms. Palmore because Mr. Jones has not argued on appeal that he has a right to confront any other hearsay declarant.

"We review the district court's decision to revoke supervised release for abuse of discretion. Legal questions relating to the revocation of supervised release are reviewed *de novo*. A district court necessarily abuses its discretion when it makes an error of law." *United States v. LeCompte,* 800 F.3d 1209, 1215 (10th Cir.2015) (quotations omitted).

A. *The Rule 32.1(b)(2)(C) Balancing Test Applies*

The first issue is whether Rule 32.1(b)(2)(C) requires a district court to apply the balancing test to determine p.1098 whether hearsay evidence may be considered for revocation. We hold that it does.

Rule 32.1(b)(2)(C) was amended in 2002 to state that a person subject to a revocation hearing "is entitled to," among other things, "an opportunity to appear, present evidence, and question any adverse witness unless the court determines that the interest of justice does not require the witness to appear." Fed.R.Crim.P. 32.1(b)(2)(C).

The advisory committee notes to this provision provide:

Rule 32.1(b)(1)(B)(iii) and Rule 32.1(b)(2)(C) address the ability of a releasee to question adverse witnesses at the preliminary and revocation hearings. Those provisions recognize that the court should apply a balancing test at the hearing itself when considering the releasee's asserted right to cross-examine adverse witnesses. *The court is to balance the person's interest in the constitutionally guaranteed right to confrontation against the government's good cause for denying it.*

Rule 32.1 advisory committee's note to 2002 amendment (emphasis added).

Before the 2002 amendment to Rule 32.1, this court applied a reliability test to determine whether hearsay evidence may be considered at a revocation hearing. The reliability test "allows the admission of hearsay evidence without a showing of cause for the declarant's absence if the evidence is sufficiently reliable." *Curtis v. Chester,* 626 F.3d 540, 545 (10th Cir.2010).[4] Since the 2002 amendment, we have not needed to confront the impact of amended Rule 32.1(b)(2)(C) on our pre-2002 precedent. The closest we have come to addressing that question was in *Curtis,* but we determined both the reliability test and the balancing test would produce the same outcome in that case.

In this case, we resolve the question and hold the Rule 32.1(b)(2)(C) balancing test governs whether hearsay evidence may be used to revoke supervised release. The following discussion provides the background and rationale for this holding.

1. *Morrissey v. Brewer,* 408 U.S. 471 (1972)

In *Morrissey,* the Supreme Court stated, "the revocation of parole is not part of a criminal prosecution and thus the full panoply of rights due a defendant in such a proceeding does not apply to parole revocations." 408 U.S. at 480, 92 S.Ct. 2593. The Court held a supervised releasee facing revocation of parole must receive the "minimum requirements of due process," including "the right to confront and cross-examine adverse witnesses (unless the hearing officer specifically finds good cause for not allowing confrontation)." *Id.* at 489, 92 S.Ct. 2593. Our unpublished decisions recognize that minimum due process extends to releasees facing revocation of supervised release, *United States v. Mullane,* 480 Fed.Appx. 908, 910 (10th Cir. 2012) (unpublished); *United States v. Stevens,* 119 Fed.Appx. 222, 225 (10th Cir. 2004) (unpublished), and we agree.

Although *Morrissey* established a right to confrontation, that right is flexible at revocation hearings. *See Gagnon v. Scarpelli,* 411 U.S. 778, 782 n. 5, 93 S.Ct. p.1099 1756, 36 L.Ed.2d 656 (1973) ("While in some cases there is simply no adequate alternative to live testimony, we emphasize that we did not in *Morrissey* intend to prohibit use where appropriate of the conventional substitutes for live testimony, including affidavits, depositions, and documentary evidence."); *Kell v. U.S. Parole Comm'n,* 26 F.3d 1016, 1020 (10th Cir. 1994) ("Petitioner's right to confront adverse witnesses is not absolute."). And *Morrissey* did not provide a clear test for determining a releasee's confrontation right. *Curtis,* 626 F.3d at 545.

2. The 2002 Amendment to Rule 32.1

Rule 32.1 "codif[ied] due process guarantees that apply to revocation hearings." *Ruby,* 706 F.3d at 1226. The rule was amended and expanded in 2002. Among other things, Rule 32.1(b)(2)(C) grants a releasee facing revocation of supervised release "an opportunity to appear, present evidence, and question any adverse witness unless the court determines that the interest of justice does not require the witness to appear."

The advisory committee notes to the 2002 amendment direct courts to apply a balancing test when considering a releasee's confrontation rights at a revocation hearing under Rule 32.1(b)(2)(C): "The court is to balance the person's interest in the constitutionally guaranteed right to confrontation against the government's good cause for denying it." Rule 32.1 advisory committee's note to 2002 amendment.

3. Circuit Courts' Adoption of the Balancing Test

Every circuit court except ours has adopted the balancing test. Some circuits did so before the 2002 amendment. *United States v. Chin,* 224 F.3d 121, 124 (2d Cir.2000); *United States v. Comito,* 177 F.3d 1166, 1170 (9th Cir.1999); *Barnes v. Johnson,* 184 F.3d 451, 454 (5th Cir.1999); *United States v. Frazier,* 26 F.3d 110, 114

(11th Cir.1994); *United States v. Bell*, 785 F.2d 640, 642 (8th Cir.1986). Other circuits did so after. *United States v. Jordan*, 742 F.3d 276, 279 (7th Cir.2014); *United States v. Doswell*, 670 F.3d 526, 530 (4th Cir.2012); *United States v. Jackson*, 422 Fed.Appx. 408, 410-11 (6th Cir.2011) (unpublished); *United States v. Lloyd*, 566 F.3d 341, 344 (3d Cir.2009); *United States v. Stanfield*, 360 F.3d 1346, 1360 (D.C.Cir. 2004); *United States v. Taveras*, 380 F.3d 532, 536 (1st Cir.2004).

We applied the reliability test in *Kell*, which was decided before the 2002 amendment. 26 F.3d at 1020. In *Curtis*, a 2010 case, we considered whether the balancing test applies at a parole-revocation hearing under Rule 32.1(b)(1)(B)(iii).[5] The appellant urged us to abandon the reliability test and adopt the balancing test based on the amendment and the advisory committee notes. 626 F.3d at 545. We left the question open, concluding the hearsay testimony at issue was admissible under both the balancing and reliability tests. *Id.* at 546-47. In doing so, we acknowledged that the 2002 amendment "cast[s] some doubt on our case law," and that *Kell* is "asynchronous with both the majority of circuit courts and the subsequent amendment to Rule 32.1." *Id.* at 545-46.

4. The Balancing Test Applies

We join the other circuits and conclude the balancing test applies when determining a releasee's confrontation rights at a revocation hearing. Taking the plain language of Rule 32.1(b)(2)(C) and the advisory committee notes together, we must determine whether the "interest of p.1100 justice does not require the witness to appear" by balancing (1) "the person's interest in the constitutionally guaranteed right to confrontation" against (2) "the government's good cause for denying it."[6] Rule 32.1 advisory committee's note to 2002 amendment. We note "reliability is a very important factor in determining the strength of a releasee's confrontation right." *Curtis*, 626 F.3d at 546 (emphasis omitted).

We acknowledge our departure from *Kell*, which applied the reliability test before Rule 32.1 was amended. We may depart from precedent without en banc review when an amendment to an applicable rule or statute creates a new standard. *See United States v. Savani*, 733 F.3d 56, 62 (3d Cir.2013) ("Although we, as a three-judge panel, are generally bound by prior decisions of this Court, we may reevaluate a precedent in light of intervening authority and amendments to statutes or regulations." (quotations omitted)); *Landreth v. C.I.R.*, 859 F.2d 643, 648 (9th Cir.1988) (reexamining precedent in light of intervening amendment to controlling statute). Put differently, we may apply a new governing standard embodied in an amended rule without en banc reversal of pre-amendment precedent applying a different standard.

No panel since the 2002 amendment, including the *Curtis* panel, has adopted the reliability test in favor of the balancing test. Moreover, *Kell* was decided before the 2002 amendment and did not rely on any federal rule of criminal procedure. We therefore adopt the Rule 32.1(b)(2)(C) balancing test without en banc review of *Kell*.

B. *The District Court Abused Its Discretion by Failing to Apply the Balancing Test*

The second issue is whether the district court applied the balancing test. The Government argues that it did. Mr. Jones argues it did not. We agree with Mr. Jones and conclude the court's legal error was an abuse of discretion.

The Government argues the district court applied the balancing test because the court quoted both Rule 32.1(b)(2)(C) and the advisory committee notes and weighed the reliability of the hearsay evidence against the "gravity of the matter." ROA, Vol. I at 43. We disagree. Mentioning the rule and advisory notes is not the same as applying them.

In the order denying Mr. Jones's motion to strike, the district court found Inspector Benavides's testimony reliable and probative of the Government's contention that Mr. Jones murdered Mr. Miles. In particular, due to the corroborating physical evidence, the court found reliable Inspector Benavides's testimony about Ms. Palmore's account of the shooting and gave it "decisive effect." *Id.* at 42. The court also pointed to Inspector Benavides's testimony about Ms. Palmore's insistence that Mr. Jones was the shooter and about Mr. Jones's false alibi.

Although the district court considered reliability and the "gravity of the matter," it did not apply the Rule 32.1(b)(2)(C) balancing test. ROA, Vol. I at 43. Reliability is relevant to determine Mr. Jones's interest in confrontation, *Curtis,* 626 F.3d at 546 — the first part of the balancing test — but the district court did not fully or adequately address Mr. Jones's interest in p.1101 cross-examination or the second part of the balancing test — the Government's explanation for failing to present Ms. Palmore as a witness.

Because the district court failed to apply the balancing test under Rule 32.1(b)(2)(C), it committed legal error and therefore abused its discretion. *LeCompte,* 800 F.3d at 1215 ("A district court necessarily abuses its discretion when it makes an error of law." (quotations omitted)).

C. *The District Court's Error Was Reversible*

The third issue is whether the district court's error was reversible or harmless. We conclude it was reversible.

1. Harmless Error Standard

The harmless error doctrine requires us to disregard preserved trial errors that do not affect substantial rights. *See* 28 U.S.C. § 2111; Fed.R.Crim.P. 52(a). "An error is harmless unless it had a substantial influence on the outcome or leaves one in grave doubt as to whether it had such effect." *United States v. Stiger,* 413 F.3d 1185, 1190 (10th Cir.2005) (quotations omitted). A constitutional error is reversible unless the Government can prove harmlessness beyond a reasonable doubt. *Chapman v. State of California,* 386 U.S. 18, 24, 87 S.Ct. 824, 17 L.Ed.2d 705 (1967). A nonconstitutional error is reversible unless the Government can prove harmlessness by a preponderance of the evidence. *Stiger,* 413 F.3d at 1190.

In this case, we need not determine whether an error in applying Rule 32.1(b)(2)(C) is constitutional or nonconstitutional because the Government cannot show harmlessness under either standard.

2. Analysis

The district court's error is reversible. We have grave doubt as to whether the court would have admitted the testimony under the Rule 32.1(b)(2)(C) balancing test on the record before it. And because Inspector Benavides was the only witness and the court gave his testimony about Ms. Palmore's statements "decisive effect," ROA, Vol. I at 42, it follows that the court's error affected Mr. Jones's substantial rights.

First, Mr. Jones had a strong interest in testing Ms. Palmore's statements to Inspector Benavides. Several textbook bases for cross-examination were present here:

- First, testing Ms. Palmore's ability to perceive — her distance from the parking lot, her angle of vision, any obstructions to her view, the quality of the lighting, and whether she had been drinking at Slick Willie's.

- Second, exploring possible bias — whether her long-term acquaintance with Mr. Jones might have affected her statements to Inspector Benavides.

- Third, examining whether Ms. Palmore's prior conviction might affect her credibility.

- Fourth, asking why Ms. Palmore refused to cooperate in the state prosecution of Mr. Jones, a matter on which the parties and the court could only posit educated guesses without her testimony.

- Fifth, elaborating on Ms. Palmore's misidentification of Mr. Jones in the photo lineup. Despite corroborating evidence that placed Mr. Jones in the parking lot at the time of the shooting, Ms. Palmore pointed to someone else when asked to identify the shooter.

Adding to Mr. Jones's interest in cross-examining Ms. Palmore are the generally recognized concerns with eyewitness testimony even when the witness appears at the evidentiary proceeding. *See, e.g.,* p.1102 *Manson v. Brathwaite,* 432 U.S. 98, 119, 97 S.Ct. 2243, 53 L.Ed.2d 140 (1977) (noting the "high incidence of miscarriage of justice resulting from the admission of mistaken eyewitness identification evidence at criminal trials" (quotation omitted)); *United States v. Wade,* 388 U.S. 218, 228, 87 S.Ct. 1926, 18 L.Ed.2d 1149 (1967) ("The vagaries of eyewitness identification are well-known; the annals of criminal law are rife with instances of mistaken identification."); *United States v. Stevens,* 935 F.2d 1380, 1392, 1407 (3d Cir.1991) (noting concerns with reliability of eyewitness testimony and holding district court erred in excluding expert testimony "about the lack of a correlation between confidence and accuracy in eyewitness identifications"); *United States v. Smith,* 736 F.2d 1103, 1106 (6th Cir.1984) (acknowledging "the dangers of [eyewitness] misperception in criminal cases").

Second, the Government has made only a limited showing of good cause for its failure to produce Ms. Palmore to testify. The Government argues on appeal that Ms. Palmore risked retaliation because she was the only witness to a gang-related shooting, her name was on public records associated with the State's murder prosecution, and she refused to cooperate with the State. The Government further asserts any attempt to subpoena Ms. Palmore would have been futile.

The Government has not adequately supported its argument. It did not even ask Ms. Palmore to attend the revocation hearing. Nor did it issue her a subpoena. Instead, it asks us to infer Ms. Palmore refused to testify at the state court trial based on a fear of reprisal and would have refused to testify at the revocation hearing for the same reason. Although we could reasonably infer as the Government suggests, we could also reasonably infer Ms. Palmore's refusal to testify at the state trial arose out of other reasons. She may have doubted whether Mr. Jones was actually the shooter. Or she may have been lying when she insisted Mr. Jones was the shooter. Or perhaps she did not want to testify against her longtime acquaintance.

Weighing Mr. Jones's strong interest in confrontation and cross-examination against the Government's limited showing of good cause, we are left in grave doubt as to whether the district court would have admitted Inspector Benavides's testimony under the balancing test on the record presented and also as to whether it would have revoked Mr. Jones's supervised release. We therefore conclude the district court's error was reversible because the Government cannot show harmlessness by a preponderance of the evidence, let alone beyond a reasonable doubt.

D. *Sixth Amendment Right to Confrontation*

Mr. Jones also argues his inability to cross-examine Ms. Palmore violated his Sixth Amendment rights. The parties agree our case law holds that the Sixth Amendment does not apply to revocation hearings. *Curtis,* 626 F.3d at 544 ("Sixth Amendment rights are not applicable in parole revocation hearings because those hearings are not criminal prosecutions." (quotation omitted)). Nevertheless, Mr. Jones raises the argument "so as to preserve any future extension of the Sixth Amendment." Aplt. Br. at 26. We agree that our case law forecloses the argument.

III. CONCLUSION

For the reasons stated, we reverse the district court's revocation of Mr. Jones's supervised release and remand for a new p.1103 revocation hearing consistent with this opinion.

[1] On cross-examination, Mr. Jones's counsel asked Inspector Benavides, "You said that Ms. Palmore had known all of these people involved since she was 15. How many years ago was that, approximately?" ROA, Vol. III at 24. Inspector Benavides answered, "I mean, numerous years. She's an older woman now." *Id.*

[2] The Government did not cross appeal from this ruling.

[3] Mr. Jones's in-court objection and motion to strike appeared to challenge all of Inspector Benavides's hearsay testimony — he does not specify any portions of the testimony to which he objects. On appeal, he limits his challenge to Inspector Benavides's testimony about Ms. Palmore's statements. He does not challenge the testimony about Mr. Nguyen's statements or any other out-of-court statements.

[4] "Examples of evidence possessing recognized indicia of reliability include: (1) the conventional substitutes for live testimony (e.g., affidavits, depositions, and documentary evidence), (2) statements falling under an established exception to the hearsay rule, (3) statements corroborated by detailed police investigative reports, and (4) statements corroborated by the releasee's own statements." *Curtis,* 626 F.3d at 545. "Corroborating evidence is often key to determining whether a statement is sufficiently reliable." *United States v. Ruby,* 706 F.3d 1221, 1229 (10th Cir.2013).

[5] The balancing test applies to both Rule 32.1(b)(1)(B)(iii) and Rule 32.1(b)(2)(C). Rule 32.1 advisory committee's note to 2002 amendment.

[6] Courts give weight to the advisory committee notes unless they contradict the plain language of the rule. *See Schiavone v. Fortune,* 477 U.S. 21, 31, 106 S.Ct. 2379, 91 L.Ed.2d 18 (1986) ("Although the Advisory Committee's comments do not foreclose judicial consideration of the Rule's validity and meaning, the construction given by the Committee is of weight." (quotations omitted)).

829 F.3d 681 (2016)

UNITED STATES of America, Plaintiff-Appellee,

v.

STONEY END OF HORN, Defendant-Appellant.

United States of America, Plaintiff-Appellee,

v.

Stoney End of Horn, Defendant-Appellant.

No. 15-2150, No. 15-2151.

United States Court of Appeals, Eighth Circuit.

Submitted: February 12, 2016.

Filed: July 15, 2016.

US v. Stoney End of Horn, 829 F. 3d 681 (8th Cir. 2016)

p.683 Appeals from United States District Court for the District of South Dakota — Aberdeen

Counsel who presented argument on behalf of the appellant was Terry Jay Sutton, of Watertown, SD.

Counsel who presented argument on behalf of the appellee was Troy R. Morley, AUSA, of Pierre, SD.

Before SMITH and COLLOTON, Circuit Judges, and GRITZNER,[1] District Judge.

COLLOTON, Circuit Judge.

Stoney End of Horn was convicted by a jury on four counts of sexual abuse of a minor and one count of assault resulting in serious bodily injury, all occurring in Indian country. The district court[2] sentenced End of Horn to concurrent sentences of 293 months' imprisonment for each count of sexual abuse and another concurrent sentence of 120 months' imprisonment for the assault. End of Horn appeals his convictions and sentences. We affirm.

p.684 **I.**

The evidence on the assault charge, which we recount in the light most favorable to the verdict, concerned an incident that occurred early in the morning on September 27, 2008. The night before, End of Horn was out drinking with his girlfriend, Pauline Brave Crow, in Mobridge, South Dakota, and he agreed to give his cousin (Robert End of Horn) and two of Robert's friends (Quinton Fernandez and Elizabeth Mellette) a ride to Wakpala in Brave Crow's car.

During the drive, End of Horn and Brave Crow got into an argument. The discussion became heated, and Brave Crow attempted to jump out of the moving vehicle. End of Horn stopped the car and continued to argue with Brave Crow. End of Horn hit Brave Crow in the face with his open palm, and the two got out of the car. As the argument carried on, Robert and Fernandez tried unsuccessfully to intervene, and the passengers eventually decided to walk to Wakpala rather than wait longer for a ride. They left Brave Crow and End of Horn at the side of the road.

Some time later, Jackie Little Dog, a childhood friend of Brave Crow, encountered Brave Crow's vehicle on the side of the road to Wakpala. Little Dog testified that when she stopped behind the parked car, she saw End of Horn hitting Brave Crow's head and face. Little Dog left because she was afraid of End of Horn. She did not report the incident to authorities, but later told one of Brave Crow's daughters what she had seen.

Later in the morning of September 27, Officer Tracy Whitaker of the National Park Service was dispatched to the residence of End of Horn's father in Wakpala in response to an assault report. There, she saw an ambulance crew treating Brave Crow for facial injuries. Whitaker asked End of Horn how Brave Crow was hurt, and End of Horn said that he and Brave Crow had been attacked by hitchhikers. Whitaker attempted to locate the site of the alleged attack, but could not find evidence of an assault by hitchhikers.

Brave Crow suffered a serious fracture, known as a LeFort III fracture, in the bones of her face. She sustained broken bones in her upper jaw and face, facial swelling and bruising on the left side of her face, and bruising under both eyes. Brave Crow was "very, very quiet" when interviewed, and she did not identify her assailant when hospitalized. Brave Crow's injuries required multiple surgeries. Her health deteriorated, and she eventually died on June 25, 2010, as a result of complications from injuries caused by the assault.

The evidence concerning sexual abuse centered on the testimony of S.N.H., a relative of Brave Crow and a twelve-year-old minor during the relevant period. S.N.H. lived with End of Horn and Brave Crow in McLaughlin, South Dakota. She testified about an incident that occurred when Brave Crow was in the hospital for a stroke in February 2010. According to S.N.H., she woke up to discover End of Horn rubbing her vagina. End of Horn then pulled up her shirt and bra and licked her nipples before inserting his penis into her vagina.

S.N.H. also testified that End of Horn engaged in vaginal intercourse with her once a month from April through July 2010 while they were staying at the house of End of Horn's father in Wakpala. The sexual contact eventually ended. S.N.H. later reported the sexual abuse in a questionnaire that she filled out at a youth treatment facility.

A grand jury charged End of Horn with second-degree murder and assault resulting in serious bodily injury based on the p.685 attack on Brave Crow. A separate grand jury charged him with multiple counts of sexual abuse of a minor arising from his contact with S.N.H. By agreement of the parties, the cases were consolidated for trial. A jury convicted End of Horn of assault, murder, and four counts of sexual abuse. The district court, relying on *Ball v. United States,* 140 U.S. 118, 11 S.Ct. 761, 35 L.Ed. 377 (1891), and *Merrill v. United States,* 599 F.2d 240, 242 & n. 4 (8th Cir. 1979) (per curiam), concluded that the second-degree murder charge required proof that Brave Crow's death occurred within a year and a day of the assault. Because the interval between assault and death was twenty-one months, the court set aside the verdict on the murder count. The court then sentenced End of Horn on the remaining counts, and he appeals.

II.

End of Horn challenges the sufficiency of the evidence to support the sexual abuse convictions. The governing statutes prescribe criminal punishment for any

Indian in Indian country who "knowingly engages in a sexual act with another person" when the other person "has attained the age of 12 years but has not attained the age of 16 years" and "is at least four years younger than the person so engaging." 18 U.S.C. §§ 1153, 2243(a). The definition of "sexual act" includes "contact between the penis and the vulva or the penis and the anus." 18 U.S.C. § 2246(2)(A).

End of Horn asserts that no reasonable jury could have convicted him because there was no physical evidence of the alleged abuse, and because S.N.H.'s willingness to be alone with him after alleged incidents of abuse conflicted with her claims. No physical evidence was necessary: "a victim's testimony alone can be sufficient to support a guilty verdict." *United States v. Seibel,* 712 F.3d 1229, 1237 (8th Cir. 2013) (internal quotation omitted); *see United States v. Kenyon,* 397 F.3d 1071, 1076 (8th Cir. 2005). S.N.H. explained her continued interaction with End of Horn after the sexual abuse as an effort to protect her younger sister from possible abuse. She testified that she did not report the abuse earlier because she did not want to make her mother unhappy. These were proper areas for cross-examination and argument by the defense, but ultimately S.N.H.'s credibility was a question for the jury. *Kenyon,* 397 F.3d at 1076; *United States v. Kirkie,* 261 F.3d 761, 768 (8th Cir. 2001). S.N.H.'s testimony was sufficient to support the convictions.

End of Horn also challenges the conviction for assault causing serious bodily injury and the concurrent sentence of 120 months' imprisonment. He argues that the district court erroneously admitted hearsay evidence from Brave Crow's former husband, Benjamin Mellette. The court, citing the residual hearsay exception of Federal Rule of Evidence 807, allowed Mellette to testify that Brave Crow told him after the roadside assault that "Stoney beat the shit out of her." Over objection, Mellette testified: "She told me that she had been drinking, her and Stoney, and she said Stoney beat the shit out of her. And then she turned around and said, 'But Ben, you know, that's my personal life.'"

Rule 807 provides that a hearsay statement is not excluded by the rule against hearsay, even if not covered by an exception in Rule 803 or 804, if the statement (1) has "equivalent circumstantial guarantees of trustworthiness" to statements admitted under the enumerated exceptions, (2) is offered as evidence of a material fact, (3) is more probative on the point offered than any other reasonably available evidence, and (4) will best serve the general purposes of the rules of evidence and the interests of justice. We have p.686 said that this exception to the rule against hearsay "was necessary to permit courts to admit evidence in exceptional circumstances where the evidence was necessary, highly probative, and carried a guarantee of trustworthiness equivalent to or superior to that which underlies the other recognized exceptions." *United States v. Renville,* 779 F.2d 430, 439 (8th Cir. 1985). We review the district court's ruling for abuse of discretion. *United States v. Thunder Horse,* 370 F.3d 745, 747 (8th Cir. 2004).

The district court is entitled to some deference in applying Rule 807, but the court here did not address why Mellette's statement had "circumstantial guarantees of trustworthiness" equivalent to the enumerated hearsay exceptions. The government defends the ruling by pointing to other evidence at trial that supports a finding that End of Horn assaulted Brave Crow. But corroborating evidence does not provide the circumstantial guarantees of trustworthiness contemplated by the

Rule. Statements admitted under the firmly rooted hearsay exceptions enumerated in Rule 803 and 804 — for example, dying declarations, excited utterances, or statements made for medical treatment — are "so trustworthy that adversarial testing would add little to their reliability." *Idaho v. Wright,* 497 U.S. 805, 821, 110 S.Ct. 3139, 111 L.Ed.2d 638 (1990), *abrogated on other grounds by Crawford v. Washington,* 541 U.S. 36, 124 S.Ct. 1354, 158 L.Ed.2d 177 (2004). According to the theory of the hearsay rule, this trustworthiness must be gleaned from circumstances that "surround the making of the statement and that render the declarant particularly worthy of belief," not by "bootstrapping on the trustworthiness of other evidence at trial." *Id.* at 819, 823, 110 S.Ct. 3139 (citing 5 J. Wigmore, Evidence § 1420, at 251 (J. Chadbourn rev. 1974)); *see United States v. Tome,* 61 F.3d 1446, 1452 & n. 5 (10th Cir. 1995).

To admit Mellette's testimony under the residual exception, there must be a reason why a declarant's statement to her former spouse about an assault by a new intimate partner is inherently trustworthy. When neither the government nor the district court has articulated such a theory, we are not disposed to develop one on our own. We therefore assume that the evidentiary ruling was erroneous, and we consider whether admission of the evidence affected End of Horn's substantial rights. Because statements to friends about abuse are not "testimonial" statements that implicate the Sixth Amendment right to confront witnesses against the accused, *United States v. Wright,* 536 F.3d 819, 823 (8th Cir. 2008); *see Giles v. California,* 554 U.S. 353, 376, 128 S.Ct. 2678, 171 L.Ed.2d 488 (2008), we apply the harmless-error standard for non-constitutional errors. *See* Fed. R. Crim. P. 52(a); *Kotteakos v. United States,* 328 U.S. 750, 764-65, 66 S.Ct. 1239, 90 L.Ed. 1557 (1946). A non-constitutional error is harmless if we are confident that the error did not influence the jury or had only a very slight effect on the verdict. 328 U.S. at 764, 66 S.Ct. 1239. The corroborating evidence cited by the government, of course, is highly relevant to whether an evidentiary error was harmless. *See Wright,* 497 U.S. at 823, 110 S.Ct. 3139.

The record as a whole, excluding the hearsay, shows a convincing case that End of Horn assaulted Brave Crow. Testimony of Robert End of Horn and Quinton Fernandez, passengers in Brave Crow's car, established that they left End of Horn and Brave Crow alone on the side of a road near Wakpala on the morning of the incident. The passengers observed a lengthy argument, inside and outside the car, during which End of Horn was visibly p.687 angry. According to Fernandez, End of Horn struck Brave Crow in the face with his open palm. These witnesses also testified that they heard screams coming from the location of the vehicle as they walked into the distance. Jackie Little Dog, a childhood friend of Brave Crow, testified that she saw End of Horn striking Brave Crow in the head and face when she encountered their car parked on the side of the road to Wakpala. The defense attacked her credibility because she failed to report the incident, but Little Dog had no apparent bias and explained that her fear of End of Horn accounted for her initial silence. Other witnesses observed that End of Horn had abrasions on his right knuckles and swelling on his hands after the incident, thus supporting an inference that he committed the assault.

End of Horn's explanation for the injuries to Brave Crow was plagued by inconsistencies. He informed one officer that hitchhikers (three male and one female) attacked him and Brave Crow when they stopped while driving *from* Mobridge to Wakpala, but told another officer that the attack occurred when he was driving from Wakpala *toward* Mobridge. End of Horn reported to the first officer that he drove away from the attacking hitchhikers but then realized that Brave Crow was not in the vehicle and returned to the original site. Yet he told the second officer that the hitchhikers fled after he hit one of them, and that he searched for Brave Crow when he saw that she was not in the car before leaving the scene. When End of Horn spoke to a physician's assistant at the emergency room of the hospital, he reported that he and Brave Crow encountered an apparently disabled vehicle on the highway and pulled over to help, at which point two men grabbed Brave Crow and dragged her out into a field. But when speaking with Brave Crow's daughter Miranda, End of Horn claimed that he and Brave Crow stopped to pick up hitchhikers when a group of four men and a woman knocked him out, and that he could not find Brave Crow when he regained consciousness. Brave Crow declined to identify her attacker for law enforcement or for her own daughters — unlikely behavior if she had been assaulted by strangers on the roadway. End of Horn's claim that hitchhikers brutally beat Brave Crow while leaving him virtually unscathed strained credulity.

Harmless-error analysis necessarily requires a prediction about what would have occurred if the record were different. Our assessment is that the evidence of guilt was strong and that the hearsay testimony from Mellette likely did not have more than a very slight effect on the verdict. Without that testimony, a guilty verdict was still highly likely based on testimony about the heated argument that preceded the assault, the eyewitness account of Little Dog, circumstantial evidence of End of Horn's injured hands and Brave Crow's refusal to identify her attacker, and the implausibility of End of Horn's shifting explanations for an attack by unidentified strangers. We therefore conclude that the erroneous evidentiary ruling did not affect End of Horn's substantial rights. End of Horn also challenges the sufficiency of the evidence, but the evidence discussed amply supported the verdict.

III.

End of Horn next challenges his sentence of 293 months' imprisonment on the sexual abuse convictions. He first contends that the district court committed procedural error in calculating an advisory sentencing range when it added four levels because S.N.H. was "in the custody, care, or supervisory control" of the defendant. p.688 *See* USSG § 2A3.2(b)(1).[3] The probation office recommended this adjustment based on evidence at trial that S.N.H. lived with Brave Crow and End of Horn, and that she considered End of Horn a "father figure." At sentencing, End of Horn intentionally withdrew his objection to application of the four-level adjustment. S. Tr. 28. His claim of error is therefore waived. *United States v. Thompson*, 289 F.3d 524, 526-27 (8th Cir. 2002).

End of Horn also disputes the district court's decision to depart upward from the advisory guideline range of 151 to 188 months to a sentence of 293 months. The district court cited four separate provisions in support of its upward departure: USSG § 4A1.3 (inadequacy of criminal history category), § 5K2.1 (conduct resulting in death), § 5K2.8 (extreme conduct), and § 5K2.21 (dismissed and uncharged conduct). End of Horn challenges the court's reliance on §§ 4A1.3 and 5K2.1. We review the district court's decision to depart upward for abuse of discretion. *United States v. Shillingstad,* 632 F.3d 1031, 1037 (8th Cir. 2011).

Section 4A1.3(a)(1) provides that a district court may depart upward when "reliable information indicates that the defendant's criminal history category substantially under-represents the seriousness of the defendant's criminal history or the likelihood that the defendant will commit other crimes." Here, the district court cited five convictions in state court for which End of Horn received no criminal history points, six convictions in tribal court that were not counted, and a larceny offense while serving in the military. Tribal offenses are a proper basis for departure, USSG § 4A1.3(a)(2)(A), and although many of the uncounted offenses in state and tribal courts were driving offenses, "even offenses which are minor and dissimilar to the instant crime may serve as evidence of the likelihood of recidivism if they evince the defendant's incorrigibility." *United States v. Agee,* 333 F.3d 864, 867 (8th Cir. 2003). The district court thus did not abuse its discretion in relying on § 4A1.3 and End of Horn's criminal history as a factor in support of its upward departure.

Section 5K2.1 authorizes a departure if death resulted from the defendant's offense conduct. The district court, addressing End of Horn's assault on Brave Crow, found that "[t]he medical evidence was conclusive that this vicious assault that the Defendant perpetrated was the cause of her death." This finding was not clearly erroneous in light of substantial evidence showing that End of Horn committed the assault, the coroner's classification of Brave Crow's death as homicide caused by blunt force trauma, and a surgeon's description of the amount of force required to cause Brave Crow's injuries. The degree of force used against Brave Crow supported an inference that the perpetrator intended to cause death or knowingly risked that result. The court thus did not abuse its discretion in relying on § 5K2.1 and Brave Crow's death as a factor supporting an upward departure.

* * *

The judgments of the district court are affirmed.

[1] The Honorable James E. Gritzner, United States District Judge for the Southern District of Iowa, sitting by designation.

[2] The Honorable Charles B. Kornmann, United States District Judge for the District of South Dakota.

[3] The presentence report mistakenly cited USSG § 2A3.1(b)(1) rather than § 2A3.2(b)(1), but the report correctly identified § 2A3.2 as the applicable guideline, PSR ¶ 24, and the reference to § 2A3.1(b)(1) apparently was a typographical error.

UNITED STATES OF AMERICA, Plaintiff-Appellee,

v.

MATTHEW ELDER, Defendant-Appellant.

No. 15-2584.

United States Court of Appeals, Seventh Circuit.

Argued September 9, 2016.

Decided October 25, 2016.

US v. Elder, (7th Cir. 2016)

Michael C. Keating, for Defendant-Appellant.

Thomas W. Patton, for Defendant-Appellant.

Johanna M. Christiansen, for Defendant-Appellant.

Lauren Wheatley, for Plaintiff-Appellee.

Bob Wood, for Plaintiff-Appellee.

Kyle Matthew Sawa, for Plaintiff-Appellee.

Brian L. Reitz, for Plaintiff-Appellee.

Appeal from the United States District Court for the Southern District of Indiana, Evansville Division, No. 13-cr-00017, Richard L. Young, Chief Judge.

Before POSNER, MANION, and WILLIAMS, Circuit Judges.

MANION, Circuit Judge.

Matthew Elder was convicted for conspiracy to distribute methamphetamine and sentenced to a mandatory term of life imprisonment. He now appeals his conviction and sentence. For the reasons that follow, we affirm Elder's conviction but vacate his sentence and remand for resentencing.

I. BACKGROUND.

A. Trial and Conviction

In 2013 Matthew Elder ("Elder") and seven codefendants, including his father Bill Elder ("Bill"), were charged in a superseding indictment with conspiring to traffic large quantities of methamphetamine from Arizona to southwest Indiana. Elder and Bill pleaded not guilty and went to trial, while the remaining codefendants all pleaded guilty.

At trial, Elder's coconspirators testified in detail about his involvement in the conspiracy. Perhaps the most important testimony came from coconspirator Michael Curinga, who first met Elder in Arizona in the summer of 2012. Curinga began supplying Elder with methamphetamine for personal use, though it wasn't long before Elder expressed an interest in buying "large quantities" of methamphetamine to transport to Indiana.[1] To that end, Elder introduced Curinga to Bill around October 2012, and the three met at a restaurant a few days later to exchange drugs. The deal went off without a hitch. Elder gave Curinga a cooler with money inside. Curinga took the cooler to his supplier, replaced the money with methamphetamine, then returned to the restaurant and gave the cooler back to Bill and Elder. Curinga charged Bill and Elder $33,000 for the drugs.

Elder and Curinga continued to deal on very similar terms over the next several months. Each time, Elder gave Curinga a cooler packed with money; Curinga brought the cooler to his supplier, replaced the money with several pounds of methamphetamine, and then returned the cooler to Elder. On one occasion in December 2012, Curinga noticed that Elder's payment for the drugs came up short. Elder insisted that the money was all there, and Curinga eventually decided to "eat the difference" because the deal was still profitable. But Curinga was not the only one concerned about Elder's malfeasance; a few months later, Bill called Curinga and complained that Elder was "getting his hands in the money" and was bad for business. As a result, Bill and Curinga agreed to cut Elder out of the next delivery, which took place in February 2013.

The jury also heard from a coconspirator named Michael Clark, who testified that he purchased methamphetamine from Bill and Elder at a Phoenix hotel in December 2012. Clark arrived at the hotel with a bag of money, Bill and Elder counted the money, and Elder left with the money and returned a few hours later with methamphetamine. (Clark explained that he knew the substance brought by Elder was methamphetamine because he had been using that drug for the past twenty years and so was very familiar with it, and because the substance produced the same effect as methamphetamine when he tried it.) Bill and Elder then distributed the methamphetamine among the three of them, and Clark transported his share of the drugs back to Indiana as usual.

Further evidence against Elder came from coconspirators Lauri Cupp and Terry Ward, who were dating and lived together at Ward's house in Indiana during the conspiracy. Ward used to travel to Phoenix with Bill to buy methamphetamine and then bring it back to Ward's house for further distribution among the conspirators. A portion of the drugs would go to Cupp, who used some for herself and sold the rest to her customers. On one particular drug run in December 2012, Bill and Ward took longer than usual. Cupp testified that when they returned, she heard them angrily complaining that their trip was delayed because Elder gave them only part of the methamphetamine that he owed them. Defense counsel objected to Cupp's testimony as hearsay, but the court admitted the testimony under the coconspirator exclusion to the hearsay rule. *See* Fed. R. Evid. 801(d)(2)(E).

Following trial, the jury found Elder guilty of conspiring to distribute 50 grams or more of methamphetamine and 500 grams or more of a mixture or substance containing a detectable amount of methamphetamine, in violation of 21 U.S.C. §§ 841 and 846.

B. Sentencing

Before sentencing, the government filed an information under 21 U.S.C. § 851 indicating that Elder had two prior Arizona drug convictions: a 1999 conviction for possession of equipment or chemicals for the manufacture of dangerous drugs, and a 1997 conviction for possession of drug paraphernalia. The government argued that Elder's two prior convictions were "felony drug offenses" under 21 U.S.C. § 841(b)(1)(A), which requires a defendant to be sentenced to life if he is convicted of a serious drug offense after having previously been convicted of two or more drug-related felonies. The district court reluctantly agreed, explaining that it believed a life sentence was overly harsh and unjust, but that it had no discretion to issue a lesser sentence under the statute. Based on its finding that Elder's prior convictions qualified as felony drug offenses, the court sentenced Elder to a mandatory term of life imprisonment in July 2015.

II. DISCUSSION.

Elder raises three arguments on appeal. First, he argues that the district court erred by allowing Cupp to testify about the conversation she overheard concerning his involvement in the conspiracy. Second, he argues that the jury's verdict must be overturned because it is not supported by sufficient evidence. Third, he argues that the district court erroneously imposed a mandatory term of life imprisonment. We address each argument in turn.

A. Statements of Coconspirators

Elder challenges the district court's decision to admit Cupp's testimony about the conversation she overheard between Bill and Ward when they returned from Arizona in December 2012. In particular, he contends that the coconspirator exclusion does not apply because the conversation was not "in furtherance of the conspiracy." *See* Fed. R. Evid. 801(d)(2)(E). We review the district court's ruling for an abuse of discretion and its underlying factual findings for clear error. *United States v. Johnson,* 200 F.3d 529, 532 (7th Cir. 2000).

Federal Rule of Evidence 801 provides that a statement offered against a party is not hearsay if the statement was "made by the party's coconspirator during and in furtherance of the conspiracy." Fed. R. Evid. 801(d)(2)(E). Statements can further the conspiracy in a number of ways. "Some examples include comments designed to assist in recruiting potential members, to inform other members about the progress of the conspiracy, to control damage to or detection of the conspiracy, to hide the criminal objectives of the conspiracy, or to instill confidence and prevent the desertion of other members." *Johnson,* 200 F.3d at 533. A coconspirator's statement may satisfy the "in furtherance" requirement even if the statement was not "exclusively, or even primarily, made to further the conspiracy." *United States v. Cruz-Rea,* 626 F.3d 929, 937 (7th Cir. 2010) (internal marks omitted).

We see no error in the district court's conclusion that the challenged statements in this case were made in furtherance of the conspiracy. Cupp testified that she heard Bill and Ward saying that Elder did not give them the agreed-upon amount of drugs to be distributed in Indiana as planned. Bill and Ward's statements directly related to the conspiracy's progress and were clearly part of the ordinary "information flow" among conspirators designed to "help each perform his role." *See United States v. Alviar,* 573 F.3d 526, 545 (7th Cir. 2009) (internal marks omitted). The statements also worked to undermine confidence in Elder as a reliable drug source, and they alerted Cupp to a deficiency in her supply chain (recall that Ward got the drugs from Elder, while Cupp got her drugs from Ward) that resulted in an appreciable delay in business as well as an unanticipated reduction in supply. Far from mere "narrative declarations" of past events, *Johnson,* 200 F.3d at 533, the statements also betokened the conspiracy's impending reorganization: shortly after complaining about Elder's misconduct, Bill called Curinga to exclude Elder from future transactions because he was bad for business.

In sum, the challenged statements were made between two conspirators, in the presence of a third conspirator, about a problem that arose during a recent conspiratorial transaction with a fourth conspirator, and that appears to have prompted a decisive remedial change in the conspiracy's structure. Under these circumstances, there was plainly a "'reasonable basis'" to conclude that the statements furthered the conspiracy. *See Cruz-Rea,* 626 F.3d at 937. Accordingly, the district court did not abuse its discretion in admitting Cupp's testimony under Rule 801(d)(2)(E).

B. Sufficiency of the Evidence

Elder next contends that the government presented insufficient evidence to convict him of conspiracy. In considering the sufficiency of the evidence, "[w]e view the evidence in the light most favorable to the government and will overturn a conviction only if the record contains no evidence from which a reasonable juror could have found the defendant guilty." *United States v. Longstreet,* 567 F.3d 911, 918 (7th Cir. 2009); *see also United States v. Jones,* 222 F.3d 349, 352 (7th Cir. 2000) ("[A]s long as *any* rational jury could have returned a guilty verdict, the verdict must stand."). When challenging a conviction for insufficiency of the evidence, the defendant bears a "heavy" burden that is "'nearly insurmountable.'" *United States v. Moses,* 513 F.3d 727, 733 (7th Cir. 2008).

To prove a conspiracy charge, "the government must show both that a conspiracy existed and that the defendant knowingly agreed to join it." *United States v. Pagan,* 196 F.3d 884, 889 (7th Cir. 1999). The essence of a conspiracy is "an agreement to commit an unlawful act." *United States v. Baker,* 40 F.3d 154, 160 (7th Cir. 1994) (internal marks omitted).

Here, the government introduced ample evidence establishing that Elder knowingly agreed with others to unlawfully distribute methamphetamine as charged in the superseding indictment. Curinga testified that he and Elder negotiated several high-volume deals to further the drug ring's operations in Indiana, and that Elder successfully introduced him to Bill to expand the drug ring and increase supply. Additional testimony showed that, around December 2012, Elder supplied methamphetamine to coconspirators Clark, Bill, and Ward, who then delivered the drugs to Indiana according to plan. Viewed in the light most favorable to the government, the uncontroverted testimony of Elder's coconspirators was more than sufficient to enable a rational jury to find Elder guilty of the charged conspiracy beyond a reasonable doubt.

Elder's arguments to the contrary are easily disposed of. He first argues that the evidence was insufficient because it "came from almost entirely biased witnesses." As we have said time and again, however, "[i]t is for the jury—not the court of appeals—to judge the credibility of witnesses, and attacks on witness credibility are insufficient to sustain a challenge to the sufficiency of the evidence." *United States v. Griffin,* 84 F.3d 912, 927 (7th Cir. 1996); *see also United States v. Curry,* 79 F.3d 1489, 1497 (7th Cir. 1996) (noting that arguments challenging witness credibility are "wasted on an appellate court" because "questions of credibility are solely for the trier of fact"). Indeed, "a conviction for conspiracy may be supported by testimony that is 'totally uncorroborated and comes from an admitted liar, convicted felon, large scale drug-dealing, paid government informant.'" *United States v. Pulido,* 69 F.3d 192, 206 (7th Cir. 1995). The testimony of Elder's coconspirators supports the verdict, and we will not secondguess the jury's assessment of their credibility. *See United States v. Rollins,* 544 F.3d 820, 835 (7th Cir. 2008).

Elder further argues that the evidence at trial was deficient because, when questioning Curinga on direct examination, the prosecution made a reference to "3.5 pounds" of methamphetamine in response to Curinga's testimony that Elder asked him for "3.5 ounces." Elder argues that this discrepancy cast "enormous doubt" over Curinga's subsequent testimony that he regularly supplied Elder with multiple-pound shipments of methamphetamine. Once again, this argument fails at the outset because it was distinctly within the province of the jury to weigh the consistency of Curinga's testimony and assess his overall credibility. *See United States v. Muthana,* 60 F.3d 1217, 1223 (7th Cir. 1995) ("Assessing a witness'[s] credibility 'is a matter inherently within the province of the jury.'"). Elder also exaggerates the supposed inconsistency in Curinga's testimony. Notwithstanding his initial reference to "3.5 ounces," Curinga consistently testified, without prompting from the government, that he and Elder negotiated the sale of "large quantities" of methamphetamine; that, on several occasions, he supplied Elder with shipments of methamphetamine weighing more than three pounds each; that the drugs were carefully packaged in "one pound bricks" before being placed in the cooler; and that a single deal was worth tens of thousands of dollars.

Finally, Elder challenges Clark's testimony about the December 2012 drug exchange at the Phoenix hotel, arguing that Clark's identification of the exchanged substance as methamphetamine was based on "pure speculation." This argument borders on the frivolous. Clark testified that he had been using methamphetamine for the previous twenty years; that he routinely traveled to Arizona to buy methamphetamine from his coconspirators; and that, when he did so in December 2012, the substance he obtained from Elder looked like methamphetamine and produced the same effect as methamphetamine when he tried it. Clark's testimony, viewed in the light most favorable to the prosecution, supports a reasonable inference that the substance supplied by Elder was methamphetamine. *See United States v. Bradley,* 165 F.3d 594, 596 (7th Cir. 1999) (noting that it is "common sense" that those who use, buy, and sell illegal drugs are the "real experts" on what those drugs are).

All in all, the government presented substantial evidence showing that Elder procured, possessed, trafficked, and distributed large amounts of methamphetamine, and that he did so in furtherance of the conspiracy charged in the superseding indictment. Elder's conviction is supported by sufficient evidence, and the jury's verdict must stand.

C. Mandatory Life Sentence

As discussed earlier, the district court in this case reluctantly imposed a mandatory life sentence after concluding that Elder's prior two Arizona convictions (one in 1997 and one in 1999) qualified as "felony drug offenses" under 21 U.S.C. §

841. On appeal, Elder argues that his 1997 conviction was not a conviction for a felony drug offense because it was not punishable by more than one year imprisonment. Elder did not raise this argument at sentencing, so our review is for plain error only. *See United States v. Gray*, 332 F.3d 491, 492 (7th Cir. 2003); Fed. R. Crim. P. 52(b).

Under § 841's "three strikes" provision, a person who conspires to distribute 50 grams or more of methamphetamine must be sentenced to life in prison if he has previously been convicted of two or more felony drug offenses. 21 U.S.C. § 841(b)(1)(A). For purposes of § 841, a prior offense is a "felony drug offense" only if, among other things, it is "punishable by imprisonment for more than one year." 21 U.S.C. § 802 (44). Although Elder's 1997 offense of conviction—possession of drug paraphernalia in violation of Ariz. Rev. Stat. Ann. § 13-3415(A)—is presently punishable by imprisonment for more than one year, the offense carried a one-year maximum sentence at the time of Elder's conviction in 1997. *Compare* Ariz. Rev. Stat. Ann. § 13-702(D) (effective Jan. 1, 2009), *with* Ariz. Rev. Stat. Ann. § 13-701(C) (amended Jan. 1, 2009). As a consequence, Elder's 1997 conviction was not a conviction for a felony drug offense within the meaning of § 841, and the district court's finding to the contrary was plainly erroneous. The government agrees and correctly concedes that the mandatory life sentence was improper. We therefore vacate Elder's sentence and remand for a complete resentencing in conformity with this opinion.[2]

III. CONCLUSION.

For the foregoing reasons, we affirm Elder's conviction but vacate his sentence and remand for resentencing consistent with this opinion.

AFFIRMED IN PART; VACATED AND REMANDED IN PART.

[1] Curinga initially testified that Elder asked him for 3.5 ounces of methamphetamine, but he later clarified that the two exchanged numerous pounds of methamphetamine during the conspiracy.

[2] Elder also challenges the district court's finding that his 1999 Arizona conviction qualified as a felony drug offense. Because we conclude that Elder's sentence must be vacated based solely on the district court's erroneous finding regarding the 1997 conviction, we do not reach this additional argument. The parties are free to address the significance of the 1999 conviction on remand.

823 F.3d 422 (2016)

UNITED STATES of America, Plaintiff-Appellee

v.

Terrence Anthony DEAN, Defendant-Appellant.

No. 15-2359.

United States Court of Appeals, Eighth Circuit.

Submitted: January 15, 2016.

Filed: May 16, 2016.

US v. Dean, 823 F. 3d 422 (8th Cir. 2016)

p.423 Appeal from United States District Court for the Southern District of Iowa — Des Moines

Timothy S. Ross-Boon, AFPD, of Des Moines, IA, for Appellant.

Bradley Price, AUSA, of Des Moines, IA, for Appellee.

Before MURPHY, SMITH, and BENTON, Circuit Judges.

PER CURIAM.

A jury convicted Terrence Anthony Dean of being a felon in possession of a firearm, in violation of 18 U.S.C. §§ 922(g)(1), 924(a), and 924(d). The district court[1] sentenced Dean to 72 months' p.424 imprisonment. Dean appeals his conviction and sentence, arguing that the district court erred in admitting prior statements of a witness at trial and in applying a four-level enhancement under U.S.S.G. § 2K2.1(b)(6)(B) for possession of a firearm in connection with another felony. We affirm.

I. *Background*

On the evening of December 27, 2013, Dean, a felon, was drinking alcohol at the apartment that he shared with his daughter, Myishia Maxwell. Maxwell and her friend, Tiffany Bass, were present at the apartment, caring for seven minor children. Maxwell was seven months pregnant. Maxwell and Bass both saw Dean, who was drunk, shoot a handgun outside. Maxwell, Bass, and Dean then went to the grocery store together, but Dean returned to the apartment separately. When Dean returned to the apartment, Maxwell was cooking. Dean began playing music loudly in the living room. Maxwell complained about the noise level, and a fight ensued between the two. Dean entered the kitchen and cursed in Maxwell's face. Maxwell threw a handful of shredded cheese at Dean, and Dean responded by grabbing Maxwell's skillet and hitting her with it. Bass witnessed the altercation.

Maxwell, who was bleeding, left the apartment and called 911. She reported that Dean had struck her in the face with a skillet, had been waving a gun around, and had the gun in his pocket. When police arrived, Maxwell was outside of the apartment. Visibly upset and injured, Maxwell told officers that Dean had a gun and that they would find the gun if they searched for it. Police performed a consent search of the home and located a loaded Cobra .32 caliber handgun wrapped in a white towel, hidden under aluminum cans inside a garbage can. Officers also observed taco meat — the skillet's contents — splattered against the kitchen walls.

Maxwell provided a written statement indicating that Dean "[h]ad a gun [and] sh[o]t 2 time[s] [i]n [the] air" and also "[p]icked up a pot [and] hit [Maxwell] [i]n

[her] head," resulting in "food [going] all over [Maxwell's] kitchen." She also stated that Dean "then h[e]ld [the] gun in [the] air," making her "feel like he could have h[ur]t the kids or [Maxwell]." Officers arrested Dean without incident. Maxwell subsequently appeared before the grand jury pursuant to a subpoena, where she testified consistently with her written statement and recorded statements to officers. She further stated that the gun that police seized was the same gun that Dean had been waving around and shooting earlier that night.

Dean was detained at the Polk County Jail pending trial. While there, he called his sister and instructed her to influence the testimony of Maxwell and Bass. In some of the calls, Dean told his sister to make sure that Maxwell convinced Bass not to testify at all. In others, Dean coached his sister about what she and Maxwell should say if they were to testify.

Trial began on April 6, 2015.[2] When the jury was unable to reach a verdict, the court declared a mistrial. A second trial began on April 20, 2015. During the second trial, Dean called Maxwell as a defense witness after the government rested. On direct examination, she stated multiple times that she never saw Dean with a gun on the night in question. On cross-examination, the government established that Maxwell's statements at trial were inconsistent p.425 with her prior statements in the 911 call, her prior recorded oral statements to officers, her prior written statement to police, and her prior grand jury testimony. The government used these prior statements to impeach Maxwell. On redirect, Maxwell was again asked whether she "saw [her] father with a gun that night," and she shook her head. When Dean's counsel instructed her to answer yes or no, Maxwell replied, "I don't remember." Dean's counsel then attempted to introduce as prior consistent statements Maxwell's statements from the *first* trial in which she testified that she did not see her father with a gun. The government objected, arguing that "[t]he timing of the statement makes it problematic, ... as it was not made before there was improper influence or motive to fabricate." After a sidebar conference, the court denied Dean's request, concluding that the statements did not pre-date Maxwell's motive to fabricate as required by Federal Rule of Evidence 801(d)(1)(B)(i).

The court later clarified that the 911 call, the grand jury transcript, and Maxwell's statements at the scene, as recorded by an officer's body microphone, were admissible as substantive evidence pursuant to Rule 801(d)(1)(A). Maxwell's written statement was not formally admitted during the trial but was instead used solely for impeachment purposes. Over the government's objection, the court instructed the jury regarding Maxwell's prior testimony at the first trial and

> t[ook] judicial notice of the fact that on April 6th of 2015, after taking an oath and testifying under penalty of perjury in another proceeding, Myishia Maxwell testified that she did not see a gun on December 27th of 2013 and did not ever see her father in possession of a gun on that day. You may consider this evidence along with everything else in the case.

The jury returned a guilty verdict.

Prior to sentencing, the probation office prepared a presentence investigation report (PSR). The PSR recommended application of a four-level enhancement under U.S.S.G. § 2K2.1(b)(6)(B) for the use or possession of a firearm in connection with another felony offense. Dean objected to application of the enhancement, denying the presence of a firearm and denying that an assault occurred. The parties agreed that Dean did not directly threaten Maxwell with the firearm and was not brandishing the gun at the moment that he hit Maxwell with the skillet.

At sentencing, the district court found by a preponderance of the evidence that Dean committed an aggravated misdemeanor assault, which is a felony under federal law, when he struck Maxwell with the skillet. The district court relied on "the grand jury testimony which came in substantively of Myishia Maxwell; the written statement to the police that she made on December 27th of 2013 which came in and was used for impeachment purposes ...; as well as the 911 call which came in at both trials." The district court found that this trial evidence established that

> Mr. Dean grabbed a hot, heavy, cast iron skillet full of hot taco meat off the stove, used it to hit his very pregnant daughter in the head, caused her a head injury, then ripped the telephone out of the wall so she couldn't call for law enforcement. And while that's going on, he's got a gun in his pocket, and she knows it, and she reports it within, you know, seconds or minutes of the assault happening and while she's still bleeding. She flees the house. She's clearly worried about the gun and reports it immediately to the police.

p.426 The district court concluded that the gun was "present and known" during "an aggravated misdemeanor level assault" and therefore "either facilitat[ed] or could have facilitated that assault." Specifically, the court noted "that Ms. Maxwell kn[ew] of [the gun], kn[ew] her father ha[d] it on him, and kn[ew] the violent nature of her dad, who[] tr[ied] to prevent her from calling for help and who ha[d] just hit her in the head with a cast iron skillet." The court found that Dean had brandished and discharged the same gun earlier in the night, "mak[ing] those facts even more complicated." Finally, the district court noted that Maxwell's written statement indicated that Dean "was waving a gun in the air at the time of the assault in the kitchen." Based on this evidence, the district court found that a four-level enhancement pursuant to U.S.S.G. § 2K1.2(b)(6)(B) was applicable. After calculating the applicable Guidelines range and discussing the factors in 18 U.S.C. § 3553(a), the district court sentenced Dean to 72 months' imprisonment.

II. *Discussion*

Dean argues that the district court erred in admitting Maxwell's prior statements and in applying the four-level enhancement under U.S.S.G. § 2K2.1(b)(6)(B) for possession of a firearm in connection with another felony.

A. *Prior Statements*

The district court admitted Maxwell's grand jury testimony, 911 call, and statements at the scene, as recorded by an officer's body microphone, as substantive evidence. "We review a district court's ruling on the admissibility of evidence for abuse of discretion." *United States v. Thetford*, 806 F.3d 442, 446 (8th Cir.2015) (citation omitted).

1. *Grand Jury Testimony*

At trial, Maxwell repeatedly testified on direct examination that she never saw Dean with a gun the night that he assaulted her. Those statements squarely contradicted her prior grand jury testimony that (1) she saw her father with the firearm, (2) he discharged that firearm, (3) she heard the firearm go off, and (4) the gun that the police recovered from the apartment was the same gun that her father was firing.

"[P]rior inconsistent statements by a witness are not hearsay and are competent as substantive evidence if the declarant testifies at trial and is subject to cross-examination concerning the statement, and the prior inconsistent statement was given under oath at a 'trial, hearing, or other proceeding.'" *United States v. Wilson,* 806 F.2d 171, 175-76 (8th Cir.1986) (quoting Fed.R.Evid. 801(d)(1)(A)). "The district court has considerable discretion in determining whether prior statements are inconsistent with trial testimony." *United States v. Matlock,* 109 F.3d 1313, 1319 (8th Cir.1997) (citing *United States v. Russell,* 712 F.2d 1256, 1258 (8th Cir.1983) (per curiam); *United States v. Thompson,* 708 F.2d 1294, 1302 (8th Cir.1983) ("The district court should have considerable discretion to determine whether evasive answers are inconsistent with statements previously given." (citation omitted))).

"In *Wilson,* we held a prior inconsistent statement given by a witness under oath during a grand jury proceeding could be used as substantive evidence." *United States v. Cervantes,* 646 F.3d 1054, 1060 (8th Cir.2011) (citing *Wilson,* 806 F.2d at 175-76). *Wilson* controls. At trial, Maxwell confirmed that she testified before the grand jury "under oath subject to penalty of perjury."

p.427 Despite *Wilson,* Dean argues that her testimony on *redirect* examination that she *could not remember* whether Dean had a gun on the night of the assault is not inconsistent with her grand jury testimony. This argument fails. The district court had already properly admitted the grand jury testimony on cross-examination because it directly contradicted Maxwell's testimony on direct examination. Moreover, Maxwell's testimony on redirect examination that she did not remember whether Dean had a gun on the night of the assault *is inconsistent with* her prior grand jury testimony that he did have a gun. "In applying Rule 801(d)(1)(A), 'inconsistency is not limited to diametrically opposed answers but may be found in evasive answers, *inability to recall,* silence, or changes of position.'" *Matlock,* 109 F.3d at 1319 (emphasis added) (quoting *Russell,* 712 F.2d at 1258 ("Polin's statement on the stand that he could not recall having any contact with Russell around the time he cashed the forged postal money orders is sufficiently inconsistent with his grand jury testimony for the trial court to admit the previous testimony.")).

Accordingly, we hold that the district court did not err in admitting Maxwell's prior grand jury testimony as a prior inconsistent statement pursuant to Rule 801(d)(1)(A).

2. *911 Call and Recorded Body-Microphone Statements*

The district court initially ruled that the 911 call was admissible as a present sense impression and excited utterance but that the recorded body-microphone statements could be used only for impeachment purposes; however, the court ultimately ruled that both categories of evidence could be admitted as substantive evidence under the present-sense-impression and excited-utterance exceptions to the hearsay rule.

Federal Rule of Evidence 803(1) provides that "[a] statement describing or explaining an event or condition, made while or immediately after the declarant perceived it" is "not excluded by the rule against hearsay." "The underlying rationale of the present sense impression exception is that substantial contemporaneity of event and statement minimizes unreliability due to defective recollection or conscious fabrication. There is no *per se* rule indicating what time interval is too long under Rule 803(1)...." *United States v. Hawkins,* 59 F.3d 723, 730 (8th Cir.1995) (alteration in original) (quotations and citations omitted), *vacated on other grounds,* 516 U.S. 1168, 116 S.Ct. 1257, 134 L.Ed.2d 206 (1996).

In *Hawkins,* the defendant argued that the district court abused its discretion in admitting the victim's "911 call because the contents of the tape are inadmissible hearsay" and contended that the victim had time to fabricate her story. *Id.* at 730. We held that the victim's "statements from the 911 tape were admissible as a 'present sense impression' under Rule 803(1)." *Id.* We explained that the victim's "911 call was placed with sufficient contemporaneity to the underlying events to be admissible under Rule 803(1)." *Id.* Specifically, we noted that the occupants of the apartment adjacent to the victim's apartment placed a 911 call prior to the victim's call, complaining about a disturbance in the victim's apartment. *Id.* The victim then placed her 911 call seven minutes later from a nearby store, stating that "'my husband *just* pulled a gun out on me.'" *Id.* (citation omitted). We pointed out that "[o]ther courts have held in similar circumstances that statements on 911 tapes are admissible as a present sense impression." *Id.* (citing *United States v. Mejia-Valez,* 855 p.428 F.Supp. 607 (E.D.N.Y.1994) (holding that tapes of two 911 calls, the first 2 to 3 minutes after the shooting and the other approximately 16 minutes after shooting, were sufficiently contemporaneous with the event and therefore admissible as present sense impressions); *United States v. Campbell,* 782 F.Supp. 1258, 1260-61 (N.D.Ill.1991) (holding statements on 911 tape admissible as present sense impression where call was made almost immediately after the defendant left the store after a shooting incident); *Bemis v. Edwards,* 45 F.3d 1369, 1372 (9th Cir.1995) (holding that, under certain circumstances, statements on a 911 tape may be admissible as a present sense impression)). Additionally, we determined that the victim's statements were reliable based on the victim's ability to describe details during her call; specifically, "she was able to describe the gun in some detail" and "stated that there was someone else in the apartment with her husband." *Id.*

Similar to the victim in *Hawkins,* Maxwell described the assault in detail during the 911 call, reporting that Dean had struck her in the face with a skillet, had been waiving a gun around, and currently had the gun in his pocket. Also, Maxwell's "911 call was placed with sufficient contemporaneity to the underlying events," *see id.,* as she made the call while she was still bleeding from the assault. Likewise, Maxwell made her subsequent statements in the officer's body microphone immediately after hanging up from the 911 call during a time when she was visibly upset and injured. In the statements captured by the body microphone, Maxwell, consistent with the 911 call, reported that Dean had a gun and that the officers would find the gun if they searched for it.

Because Maxwell's 911 call and recorded statements occurred with sufficient contemporaneity to the assault and evidence reliability, we hold that the district court did not err in admitting them under the present-sense-impression exception to the hearsay rule pursuant to Rule 803(1).[3]

B. *U.S.S.G. § 2K2.1(b)(6)(B)*

Dean argues that the district court procedurally erred in finding that a four-level sentencing enhancement pursuant to U.S.S.G. § 2K2.1(b)(6)(B)[4] applied for Dean's purported use or possession of a firearm in connection with another felony offense. Dean contends that the evidence was insufficient to establish that another felony occurred. Alternatively, he argues that even if another felony occurred, insufficient evidence exists that the firearm facilitated or had the potential to facilitate the felony.

We need not resolve whether the district court clearly erred in applying the four-level enhancement pursuant to § 2K2.1(b)(6)(B). *See United States v. Holm,* 745 F.3d 938, 940 (8th Cir.2014) p.429 (reviewing for clear error whether the evidence supported the district court's finding that a firearm was possessed "in connection with" a felony). On this record, any error in applying the enhancement was harmless.

"We have held that it is permissible for sentencing courts to offer alternative explanations for their sentencing decisions and that, in some circumstances, such explanations may serve to prove other identified sentencing errors harmless." *United States v. Sayles,* 674 F.3d 1069, 1072 (8th Cir.2012) (citing *United States v. Straw,* 616 F.3d 737, 742-43 (8th Cir.2010) ("Where the record clearly ... show[s] not only that the district court intended to provide an alternative sentence, but also that the alternative sentence is based on an identifiable, correctly calculated guidelines range, any error in applying an enhancement for number of victims is harmless." (alterations in original) (quotations and citations omitted))). Relevant to the present case, "we have found harmless sentencing error when a court specifically identifies the contested issue and potentially erroneous ruling, sets forth an alternative holding supported by the law and the record in the case, and adequately explains its alternative holding." *Id.* (citing, *inter alia, Straw,* 616 F.3d at 742 ("Incorrect application of the Guidelines is harmless error where the district court specifies the resolution of a particular issue did not affect the ultimate determination of a sentence." (citation omitted))).

That is precisely what the district court did here. In imposing Dean's sentence, the district court explained that it had considered all of the factors under § 3553(a), including the instant offense, Dean's history and characteristics, and its determination of "a fair and reasonable sentence in light of all of the circumstances of the case." The district court cited "a number of troubling aspects" in Dean's case, such as Dean's "violent assault" against Maxwell, who was pregnant, while minor children were present. The court also referenced Dean's ripping the phone out of the wall to prevent Maxwell from calling for help, his waving around of the gun, and his discharging of the gun earlier in the day when he was intoxicated. After discussing these "serious matters," the court then discussed Dean's "obstructive efforts" to influence Maxwell's testimony. Thereafter, the court noted Dean's "long history of alcoholism and at one point ... very heavy crack use and ... dabbl[ing] in other drugs here and there." Finally, the court discussed Dean's extensive criminal history.

"[H]aving considered all of those factors," the district court sentenced Dean to 72 months' imprisonment. After imposing sentence, the court made clear that it would have imposed the same sentence even without the four-level enhancement under § 2K2.1(b)(6)(B), stating:

> I will tell you that had I ruled differently on these adjustments or on the criminal history point category, *I would likely have varied upward, in fact would have varied upward to that same sentence.* When this case originally came to me and I started looking at it, the reason I rejected the 24 months [in the original plea agreement] was because I just didn't see it as appropriate given the facts of the case, and I still don't see 24 months as an appropriate sentence in this case. *I do think six years is the appropriate sentence in this case, no matter whether we reach it through the guidelines or we reach it through the statute.*

(Emphases added.)

In summary, "even assuming [that the court erred in applying the four-level enhancement under § 2K2.1(b)(6)(B)], any p.430 such error was harmless. The district court clearly identified the contested ... issue, sought and discussed facts as necessary to support its broader sentencing decision, and adequately explained its overall sentence applying 18 U.S.C. § 3553(a)." *See Sayles*, 674 F.3d at 1072.

III. *Conclusion*

Accordingly, we affirm the judgment of the district court.

[1] The Honorable Stephanie M. Rose, United States District Judge for the Southern District of Iowa.

[2] Dean went to trial after the district court rejected a plea agreement.

[3] Because we hold that the district court did not err in admitting the evidence under Rule 803(1), we need not address whether the evidence was likewise admissible under the excited-utterance exception pursuant to Rule 803(2).

[4] Section 2K2.1(b)(6)(B) provides:

(6) If the defendant —

* * *

(B) Used or possessed any firearm or ammunition in connection with another felony offense; or possessed or transferred any firearm or ammunition with knowledge, intent, or reason to believe that it would be used or possessed in connection with another felony offense,

increase by 4 levels. If the resulting offense level is less than level 18, increase to level 18.

824 F.3d 620 (2016)

UNITED STATES of America, Plaintiff-Appellant,

v.

Maurice Dimitrie MOORE, Defendant-Appellee.

No. 15-1785.

United States Court of Appeals, Seventh Circuit.

Argued January 6, 2016.

Decided May 27, 2016.

US v. Moore, 824 F. 3d 620 (7th Cir. 2016)

Appeal from the United States District Court for the Northern District of Indiana, South Bend Division, No. 3:14-CR-68, Hon. Jon E. DeGuilio, Judge.

p.621 David E. Hollar, Attorney, Office of the United States Attorney, Hammond, IN, for Plaintiff-Appellant.

H. Jay Stevens, Attorney, Indiana Federal Community Defenders, Inc., South Bend, IN, for Defendant-Appellee.

Before POSNER and WILLIAMS, Circuit Judges, and PALLMEYER, District Judge.[1]

PALLMEYER, District Judge.

Marcus Hayden, a federal probationer, engaged in an armed battle with police on April 9, 2012. One officer was injured in the gun fight, and Hayden himself was shot and killed. The government recovered the firearm Hayden used and has charged Defendant Maurice Moore with selling that weapon to Hayden, a known felon, and falsely reporting that the weapon was stolen. In Moore's upcoming trial, the government seeks to introduce evidence of a phone number Hayden had provided his probation officer. Moore made several calls to that number in the hours surrounding the purported theft of the firearm. The district judge has granted Moore's motion to exclude the probation officer's records as inadmissible hearsay. We conclude, however, that the records are admissible under the residual hearsay exception, Fed. R. Evid. 807, and therefore vacate the district court's order.

I.

Law enforcement officers attempted to serve a warrant on federal probationer Marcus Hayden on April 9, 2012. A gun fight ensued, leaving Hayden dead and one officer injured. Using the serial number of the gun they recovered from Hayden, officers quickly identified the firearm as registered to Defendant Maurice Moore. Moore had reported the gun, a Glock, stolen from his car on March 2, 2012. In an interview with agents from the Bureau of Alcohol, Tobacco, Firearms, and Explosives on April 10, 2012, Moore acknowledged that he knew Hayden but said the two were not at all close.

According to the government, additional investigation revealed that Moore had a stronger connection to Hayden than he let on. At approximately 4:30 p.m. on March 2, 2012, Moore purchased a new gun (this one a Ruger) from a store in Fort Wayne, Indiana. Roughly thirty minutes later, he claims to have discovered his older weapon, the Glock, had been stolen. He called the Fort Wayne police department to report the theft at 5:30 p.m. Shortly thereafter, he filed a stolen-property report at a nearby precinct, but could not recall the Glock's serial number. He called the station at approximately 8:00 p.m. to provide the number. Before, during, and after these events on March 2, Moore's phone placed and received numerous calls to and from a number ending in 9312 ("the 9312 number").

The government believes Hayden was on the other end of those calls. The government seeks to offer evidence that Hayden identified the 9312 number as his cell phone number on a supervision report he filed with his probation officer in February 2012.[2] The report notes, as well, that Hayden admitted to having recently smoked marijuana. In signing the form, Hayden "certif[ied] that all information furnished is complete and correct." There is no evidence that any probation officials ever p.622 reached Hayden using the 9312 number, but other circumstances support the conclusion that it was his: Hayden supplied his probation officer with a new cell number, this one ending in 6466 ("the 6466 number"), on March 22, 2012. A Deputy United States Marshal reached Hayden at this number sometime before his death. Phone records indicate that Moore's phone ceased communicating with the 9312 number on March 7, 2012. Mere hours after the final call between the two, Moore's phone received a text from the 6466 number for the first time. Many more calls between Moore's phone and the 6466 number occurred in the weeks that followed.

A grand jury returned a three-count indictment against Moore in July 2014. Shortly before the scheduled trial date, the government notified Moore of its intent to introduce Hayden's monthly supervision reports and notes kept by Hayden's probation officer (collectively, "the Reports"). Moore moved to exclude the Reports on hearsay grounds. Over the government's objection, the court sided with Moore and excluded the Reports for the purpose of "establish[ing] that the numbers actually belonged to Hayden." This timely interlocutory appeal followed.

II.

On appeal, the government argues that Hayden's telephone number is admissible on three separate theories: (1) as hearsay admissible under the business-records exception, Fed. R. Evid. 803(6); (2) as hearsay admissible under the so-called "residual exception," Fed. R. Evid. 807; and (3) as non-hearsay for the limited purpose of establishing a connection between Hayden and Moore.[3] We turn first to the government's Rule 807 argument, as it proves dispositive. *See United States v. Dumeisi*, 424 F.3d 566, 577 (7th Cir. 2005).

We review the district court's decision to exclude evidence for an abuse of discretion, but we review its interpretation of the rules de novo. *United States v. Rogers*, 587 F.3d 816, 819 (7th Cir. 2009). Trial courts have a "considerable measure of discretion" in determining whether evidence should be admitted under Rule 807. *United States v. Sinclair*, 74 F.3d 753, 758 (7th Cir. 1996) (quoting *Doe v. United States*, 976 F.2d 1071, 1076 (7th Cir. 1992)). Accordingly, we will reverse "only where the trial court committed a clear and prejudicial error." *Id.* at 758 (internal quotation marks omitted).

A proponent of hearsay evidence must establish five elements in order to satisfy Rule 807: "(1) circumstantial guarantees of trustworthiness; (2) materiality; (3) probative value; (4) the interests of justice; and (5) notice." *United States v. Ochoa*,

229 F.3d 631, 638 (7th Cir. 2000) (citing *United States v. Hall*, 165 F.3d 1095, 1110 (7th Cir. 1999)). Moore concedes that the evidence in question is material and has never objected that he was given insufficient notice or that Hayden's statements are not highly probative. The district court's determination that the Reports would not serve the interests of justice relied exclusively on its conclusion that the statements contained therein were not trustworthy.

For the purposes of assessing the trustworthiness of a hearsay statement under Rule 807, this court, in *Snyder*, offered the following list of factors to consider:

> the character of the witness for truthfulness and honesty, and the availability of p.623 evidence on the issue; whether the testimony was given voluntarily, under oath, subject to cross-examination and a penalty for perjury; the witness' relationship with both the defendant and the government and his motivation to testify before the grand jury; the extent to which the witness' testimony reflects his personal knowledge; whether the witness ever recanted his testimony; the existence of corroborating evidence; and, the reasons for the witness' unavailability.

United States v. Snyder, 872 F.2d 1351, 1355-56 (7th Cir. 1989).

This list is "neither exhaustive nor absolute," but it is a helpful guide. *United States v. Doerr*, 886 F.2d 944, 956 (7th Cir. 1989). In this case, the district court's reasoning focused on the first of these factors, to the exclusion of the other five. Although the supervision report form signed by Hayden included a warning that any false statements could lead to criminal penalties, the district judge doubted that the specter of prosecution would motivate Hayden to be truthful, because "Hayden apparently had little interest in abiding by the law." Thus, the court concluded, Hayden's statements memorialized in the Reports lacked sufficient guarantees of trustworthiness to be admitted under Rule 807.

Hayden's criminal record, though predominately one of violent crimes rather than deception, is troublesome. Apart from that history, however, the other *Snyder* factors weigh decisively in favor of the admission of the Reports.

Several of the factors are uncontroversial: Hayden had personal knowledge of his cell phone number; he is not available to testify due to his death in 2012, not because of any impropriety by the government; and he never recanted the sworn statement that his phone number in February 2012 was (___) ___-9312. But the most important factor here is Hayden's motivation — or lack thereof — to lie about his phone number. The district court concluded that Hayden's criminal history casts doubt on his motivation to tell the truth. Hayden's apparent willingness to break the law does not explain why he would lie in this instance, however. When Hayden identified his phone number as (___) ___-9312, he knew not only that he could be punished for lying but that probation officers would use that number to contact him. He knew that they would call him because they had done so with a number he had previously reported.[4] Furthermore, at the time he gave his probation officer the 9312 number, Hayden had no reason to believe that his phone number would be integral in the criminal prosecution of another man. In short, he had no obvious reason to lie. *Cf. United States v. Burge*, 711 F.3d 803, 815 (7th Cir. 2013) (approving district court's decision to exclude hearsay testimony offered under Rule 807 where the out-of-court declarants "had a motive to testify falsely to exculpate themselves").

Other circumstances militate in favor of admission of the phone number Hayden reported. Most notably, we know that he confessed to smoking marijuana in his February 2012 report and that he accurately conveyed a change in his contact information in the report filed on March 22, 2012. In the latter report, he listed a new phone number, the 6466 number, which a Deputy United States Marshal did use to contact him. And the 6466 number is also corroborative in another respect: p.624 Moore's phone was in frequent contact with the 9312 number throughout the first few months of 2012. But that correspondence ended abruptly on March 7, 2012. Hours later, Moore's phone commenced an equally prolific exchange with the 6466 number, a powerful indication that the person who owned that number was previously using the 9312 number.

We have warned against the liberal admission of evidence under Rule 807, *see Akrabawi v. Carnes Co.*, 152 F.3d 688, 697 (7th Cir. 1998) (cautioning against the frequent utilization of Rule 807, lest the residual exception become "the exception that swallows the hearsay rule"), but in the circumstances of this case, the exception is particularly apt. Hayden's statements in the Reports bear markers of reliability that are equivalent to those found in statements specifically covered by Rule 803 or Rule 804. The purpose of Rule 807 is to make sure that reliable, material hearsay evidence is admitted, regardless of whether it fits neatly into one of the exceptions enumerated in the Rules of Evidence. That purpose is served by admitting the Reports, and the district court erred in excluding them from Moore's trial. *See Dumeisi*, 424 F.3d at 577 (affirming the admission of foreign intelligence documents under Rule 807 in the trial of defendant accused of acting as an agent of the Iraqi government); *Huff v. White Motor Corp.*, 609 F.2d 286, 295 (7th Cir. 1979) (vacating district court's order excluding testimony that recounted statements made by plaintiff's deceased husband regarding the car accident that gave rise to the suit because the statements had circumstantial guaranties of trustworthiness equivalent to the other hearsay exceptions).

III.

For the foregoing reasons, we vacate the district court's order excluding Hayden's probation records and the notes of his probation officer and remand the case for further proceedings consistent with this opinion.

[1] The Honorable Rebecca R. Pallmeyer, United States District Court for the Northern District of Illinois, sitting by designation.

[2] That number is officially registered to one Tara Wilson, but Wilson claims that she is not familiar with the 9312 number and that she knows neither Hayden nor Moore.

[3] The government raised a fourth theory below — that the documents were admissible as public records under Federal Rule of Evidence 803(8) — but it has abandoned that argument on appeal.

[4] Upon his release from prison, Hayden initially provided his probation officer with his mother's phone number as his contact number. The officer used that number multiple times to contact Hayden.

810 F.3d 913 (2016)

In re C.R. BARD, INCORPORATED, MDL. No. 2187, PELVIC REPAIR SYSTEM PRODUCTS
LIABILITY LITIGATION.

Donna Cisson; Dan Cisson, Plaintiffs-Appellees,

v.

C.R. Bard, Incorporated, Defendant-Appellant,

Samuel S. Olens, Attorney General of the State of Georgia, Intervenor.

Federation Of Defense & Corporate Counsel; Product Liability Advisory Council, Incorporated; Cook
Biotech Incorporated; Chamber of Commerce of the United States of America; Cook Incorporated;
Cook Medical LLC, Amici Supporting Appellant,

Public Justice; National Center for Health, Amici Supporting Appellees.

In Re: C.R. Bard, Incorporated, MDL. No. 2187, Pelvic Repair System Products Liability Litigation.

Donna Cisson; Dan Cisson, Plaintiffs-Appellants,

v.

C.R. Bard, Incorporated, Defendant-Appellee,

Samuel S. Olens, Attorney General of the State of Georgia, Intervenor.

Federation of Defense & Corporate Counsel; Chamber of Commerce of the United States of America;
Product Liability Advisory Council, Incorporated, Amici Supporting Appellee,

Public Justice; National Center for Health, Amici Supporting Appellants.

Nos. 15-1102, 15-1137.

United States Court of Appeals, Fourth Circuit.

Argued: September 16, 2015.

Decided: January 14, 2016.

In Re CR Bard, Inc., 810 F. 3d 913 (4th Cir. 2016)

p.917 ARGUED: Elliot H. Scherker, Greenberg Traurig, P.A., Miami, Florida, for Appellant/Cross-Appellee. Anthony J. Majestro, Powell & Majestro, PLLC, Charleston, West Virginia, for Appellees/Cross-Appellants. Julie Adams Jacobs, Office Of The Attorney General Of Georgia, Atlanta, Georgia, for Intervenor. ON BRIEF: Lori G. Cohen, R. Clifton Merrell, II, Sean P. Jessee, Atlanta, Georgia, Daniel I.A. Smulian, Greenberg Traurig, LLP, New York, New York; Brigid F. Cech Samole, Jay A. Yagoda, Greenberg Traurig, P.A., Miami, Florida; Melissa Foster Bird, Nelson Mullins Riley & Scarborough, Huntington, West Virginia, for Appellant/Cross-Appellee. Allison Van Laningham, Turning Point Litigation, Greensboro, North Carolina; Henry G. Garrard, III, Josh B. Wages, Blasingame, Burch, Garrard, Ashley PC, Athens, Georgia, for Appellees/Cross-Appellants. Samuel S. Olens, Attorney General, W. Wright Banks, Jr., Deputy Attorney General, Office of the Attorney General of Georgia, Atlanta, Georgia, for Intervenor. Debra Tedeschi Varner, McNeer, Highland, McMunn & Varner LC, Clarksburg, West Virginia; Stacy A. Broman, Meagher & Geer PLLP, Minneapolis, Minnesota, for Amicus Federation of Defense & Corporate Counsel. Chilton Davis Varner, Stephen B. Devereaux, Madison H. Kitchens, Atlanta, Georgia, Jeffrey S. Bucholtz, Paul Alessio Mezzina, King & Spalding LLP, Washington, D.C., for Amici Product Liability Advisory Council, Inc. and Chamber of Commerce of the United States; Hugh F. Young, Jr., Product Liability Advisory Council, Inc., Reston, Virginia, for Amicus Product Liability Advisory Council, Inc.; Kathryn Comerford Todd, Sheldon Gilbert, National Chamber Litigation Center, Inc., Washington, D.C., for Amicus Chamber of Commerce of the United States. Douglas B. King, Wooden & McLaughlin LLP, Indianapolis, Indiana, for Amici Cook Incorporated, Cook Medical LLC, and Cook Biotech Incorporated. Michael J. Quirk, Esther E.

Berezofsky, Joseph Alan Venti, Williams Cuker Berezofsky, LLC, Philadelphia, Pennsylvania, for Amici Public Justice, P.C., and National Center for Health Research.

Before GREGORY, AGEE, and DIAZ, Circuit Judges.

Affirmed by published opinion. Judge GREGORY wrote the opinion, in which Judge AGEE and Judge DIAZ joined.

GREGORY, Circuit Judge:

On August 15, 2013, a jury awarded Donna Cisson $250,000 in compensatory damages on a design defect and failure to warn claim against C.R. Bard, Inc. ("Bard"), and awarded an additional $1,750,000 in punitive damages. The punitive damages award was split pursuant to a Georgia statute, with seventy-five percent going to the State of Georgia and twenty-five percent going to Cisson. This was the first jury verdict arising from multi-district litigation involving more than 70,000 cases against the proprietors of transvaginal mesh medical devices used to treat pelvic organ prolapse and other pelvic issues, of whom Bard is one.

We address several issues on appeal. The first issue raised by Bard is the district court's refusal to admit evidence relating to Bard's compliance with the Food and Drug Administration's ("FDA") Section 510(k) product safety process ("510(k) process"). Second, Bard challenges the denial of its motion *in limine* asking the district court to exclude evidence and argument pertaining to a material data safety sheet ("MSDS") produced for polypropylene, a key material in the Avaulta Plus surgical mesh. Bard argues that the p.918 MSDS relied on by Cisson was hearsay outside any exception. Third, Bard appeals the district court's jury instruction on causation, arguing that under controlling Georgia law the court should have told jurors that causation must be demonstrated by expert testimony stated to a reasonable degree of medical probability. Bard also argues that, as a matter of law, the evidence Cisson presented to prove causation was insufficient to meet this more rigorous standard. Bard's final challenge on appeal is to the constitutionality of the punitive damages award, which it argues is excessive and in violation of the Due Process Clause. In a cross-appeal, Cisson argues that the district court committed constitutional error by failing to find that the Georgia split-recovery statute violates the Takings Clause. For the reasons that follow, we affirm the district court on all issues.

I.

Cisson was implanted with the Avaulta Plus, a transvaginal mesh medical device developed and marketed by Bard, on May 6, 2009, to address pelvic organ prolapse and stress urinary incontinence. The surgery was performed by Dr. Brian Raybon, a physician who had provided input to Bard during the development of the Avaulta Plus and who trained other physicians to use the device. Prior to her procedure, Cisson received warnings about a number of risks that could result from the surgical implant and signed a consent form acknowledging these warnings. Three months after the surgery, Cisson's doctor diagnosed "an adhesion band" of scar tissue running across her vagina that was taut like a "banjo string" and was causing Cisson pain. Dr. Raybon resected the mesh, which involved cutting out a thick band of scar tissue and mesh encased in the tissue. Three weeks after the resection surgery, Cisson returned to Dr. Raybon who said she was healing well and should return in a year. Instead, a few months later, Cisson went to a different doctor who referred her to Dr. John Miklos. Dr. Miklos explanted the Avaulta Plus from Cisson's body, although complete removal of the mesh was not possible.

Complaining that the surgical mesh marketed by Bard caused ongoing "loss of sexual feeling" and "severe pain with intercourse and otherwise," Cisson filed a lawsuit against Bard in March 2011 in the Northern District of Georgia. Bard already faced suits from other claimants dating back to 2009, and the Judicial Panel for Multidistrict Litigation had begun transferring these cases to the Southern District of West Virginia in 2010. *In re Avaulta Pelvic Support Sys. Prods. Liab. Litig.,* 746 F.Supp.2d 1362 (J.P.M.L. 2010). Cisson's suit was added to these and would later become the first to reach a jury verdict.

On June 4, 2013, Bard won summary judgment on Cisson's claims for negligent inspection, marketing, packaging and selling, manufacturing defect, and breach of warranty. The district court allowed claims for design defect, failure to warn, and loss of consortium to proceed to trial. During the trial, Cisson focused both her design defect and failure to warn claims on several alleged dangers presented by the Avaulta Plus. Expert witnesses were brought to testify that the design of the device's arms, used to anchor the Avaulta Plus inside a patient's body, resulted in ongoing pain to a patient as long as the device was implanted. Experts also testified that the pores in the mesh component of the Avaulta Plus were too small and that the mesh was subject to shrinking after implantation, with the result being a rigid scar plate and increasing tension on p.919 internal tissue. Cisson's experts further testified that polypropylene, from which the monofilament used in the Avaulta Plus mesh was made, may be attacked by the patient's body, causing inflammation of the tissue and degradation of the mesh. Slides were presented to the jury that Cisson's expert, Dr. Bernd Klosterhalfen, testified showed the polypropylene of the Avaulta Plus in Cisson's body was being attacked, causing a scar plate to form.

Beyond presenting evidence that the Avaulta Plus had caused her injuries, Cisson also painted a picture of Bard as ignoring, and at times hiding from others, the warning signs that its product could cause injuries. There was substantial argument regarding a MSDS Bard received from Phillips Sumika Polypropylene Company ("Phillips"), the corporation that manufactured the polypropylene pellets used to extrude the Avaulta Plus mesh. The MSDS contained an explicit warning that polypropylene should not be used in short — or long-term human implantations. Internal e-mails showed that Bard executives knew about the MSDS, and that they sought to prevent their monofilament suppliers from learning of the warning. In addition to raising its hearsay objection to the MSDS, Bard countered that polypropylene had been used for decades in clinical settings and that the warning was with respect to polypropylene pellets, not to the extruded monofilament used in the Avaulta Plus.

Bard argued to the jury that its product was similar to the Avaulta Classic — a predecessor surgical mesh device that Bard contended had been safely used for years — and that it had taken appropriate steps to ensure biocompatibility and product safety. Bard argued to the judge (on evidentiary motions) that it was unfair to allow Cisson to attack its product's safety while Bard was prevented from presenting evidence that it complied with the FDA's 510(k) process.

The jury ultimately credited Cisson's evidence, awarding damages for the design defect and failure to warn claims. The jury returned a verdict for Bard on the consortium claim. Bard timely noted this appeal.

II.

Bard's first claim on appeal is that the district court abused its discretion by granting Cisson's motion *in limine* asking the court to exclude all evidence that Bard had complied with the FDA's 510(k) process. Bard sought to admit the evidence to show that its conduct was reasonable. Bard argued that this was relevant to its defense to the design defect claim under Georgia's product liability case law, as well as to the question of punitive damages. The district court excluded the evidence under Federal Rule of Evidence 402 for lack of relevance, and under Rule 403 for being substantially more prejudicial than probative. We affirm the court's ruling based on Rule 403 and therefore need not address its reliance on Rule 402.[1]

p.920 A.

Although Rule 403 will "generally favor admissibility," *United States v. Wells*, 163 F.3d 889, 896 (4th Cir.1998), district courts are granted "broad discretion" to decide "whether the probative value of evidence is substantially outweighed by the danger of unfair prejudice, misleading the jury, or confusion of the issues," *Minter v. Wells Fargo Bank, N.A.,* 762 F.3d 339, 349 (4th Cir.2014). "[E]xcept under the most 'extraordinary' of circumstances, where that discretion has been plainly abused," this Court will not overturn a trial court's Rule 403 decision. *United States v. Simpson*, 910 F.2d 154, 157 (4th Cir.1990) (quoting *United States v. Heyward*, 729 F.2d 297, 301 n. 2 (4th Cir.1984)) (internal quotation marks omitted).

Cisson's claim for design defect is controlled by Georgia product liability law. Georgia uses a "risk-utility" test for product liability claims, requiring the trial court to "evaluate design defectiveness under a test balancing the risks inherent in a product design against the utility of the product so designed." *Banks v. ICI Americas, Inc.,* 264 Ga. 732, 450 S.E.2d 671, 674 (1994). This test includes some reliance on "negligence principles," and "incorporates the concept of 'reasonableness,' i.e., whether the manufacturer acted reasonably in choosing a particular product design, given the probability and seriousness of the risk ..., the usefulness of the product in that condition, and the burden on the manufacturer to ... eliminate the risk." *Id.* at 673-74. Bard argues that compliance with the 510(k) process was important to its design defect defense because it shows that the company's conduct was reasonable.

Assuming without deciding that the 510(k) compliance evidence is relevant, under Georgia's risk-utility test the probative value of that evidence must depend on the extent to which the regulatory framework safeguards consumer safety. The 510(k) process allows some medical devices to avoid the strict safety testing requirements imposed by the Medical Device Amendments ("MDA") to the Federal Food, Drug, and Cosmetic Act, so long as the device is "substantially equivalent" to a pre-1976 device already in use at that time. *See Medtronic, Inc. v. Lohr,* 518 U.S. 470, 493, 116 S.Ct. 2240, 135 L.Ed.2d 700 (1996). Thus, devices approved under the 510(k) process "may be marketed without premarket approval" as would be required by the MDA, although they "are subject to 'special controls ... that are necessary to provide adequate assurance of safety and effectiveness.'" *Talley v. Danek Med., Inc.,* 179 F.3d 154, 160 (4th Cir.1999) (quoting 21 U.S.C. § 360c(a)(1)(B)). In this respect, although the process is certainly not a rubber stamp program for device approval, it does operate to exempt devices from rigorous safety review procedures.

While some courts have found evidence of compliance with the 510(k) equivalence procedure admissible in product liability cases, the clear weight of persuasive and controlling authority favors a finding that the 510(k) procedure is of little or no evidentiary value. The Supreme Court has p.921 regarded product clearance accomplished through the 510(k) process as "a qualification for an exemption rather than a requirement." *Riegel v. Medtronic, Inc.,* 552 U.S. 312, 322, 128 S.Ct. 999, 169 L.Ed.2d 892 (2008). This is in part because the "process impose[s] no requirements with respect to the design of the device." *Duvall v. Bristol-Myers-Squibb Co.,* 103 F.3d 324, 329 (4th Cir.1996). "Thus, even though the FDA may well examine 510(k) applications ... with a concern for the safety and effectiveness of the device," the agency's clearance rests only on whether the device is "substantially equivalent to one that existed before 1976" before allowing it "to be marketed without running the gauntlet of the [MDA premarket approval] process." *Lohr,* 518 U.S. at 493-94, 116 S.Ct. 2240.

Bard points out that much of this precedent stems from the Supreme Court's decision in *Lohr,* and argues that the case and its progeny should not be controlling here. Bard argues that because *Lohr* held only that state common law claims were not preempted by the MDA and the 510(k) process, *id.,* and not that compliance with the 510(k) process was inadmissible as evidence to refute such claims, it is an inapposite precedent. However, the Supreme Court held that state law product liability claims were not preempted because the 510(k) does not amount to a safety regulation requiring device producers to meet any established design standards. *Id.* The entire analysis turned on the Court's finding that "the § 510(k) exemption process was intended to ... maintain the status quo with respect to the marketing of existing medical devices and their substantial equivalents," not impose new regulatory requirements on devices. *Id.* at 494, 116 S.Ct. 2240. Numerous courts, including this one, have relied on that reasoning in cases over the past two decades, and at a minimum the Supreme Court's statements about the 510(k) process (repeated most recently in 2008) are very persuasive as to whether and how compliance speaks to the relative safety of a device.

Nor is Bard helped by FDA statements claiming that "the principles of safety and effectiveness underlie the substantial equivalence determination" that is the heart of the 510(k) review process. 2014 Guidance for Industry and Staff: The 510(k) Program: Evaluating Substantial Equivalence in Premarket Notifications 6. Such statements merely show that the FDA believes an equivalence determination is sufficient to "provide a reasonable assurance of safety and effectiveness," *id.* at 7, but this was also the case when the Supreme Court found the 510(k) process insufficiently tied-up with safety to preempt state tort actions, *Lohr,* 518 U.S. at 493-94, 116 S.Ct. 2240, and again when the Court called the process an "exemption" and not a safety "requirement," *Riegel,* 552 U.S. at 322, 128 S.Ct. 999. Bald assertions by the FDA do little to alter the analysis of the basic question: How much information does 510(k) clearance provide a jury about the safety of the underlying product, and is the value of this information substantially outweighed by the possibility of prejudice in a particular case?

Turning, then, to the district court's ruling, it is clear that the court did not abuse its discretion by excluding Bard's evidence of 510(k) clearance. In one of several related rulings, the court stated that bringing in such evidence would result in a "mini-trial" about (1) the strengths and weaknesses of the process and (2) whether Bard had in fact made all of the disclosures it should have made during the process. Bard's evidence would have initiated a battle of experts: Bard was prepared to characterize the review process as "thorough" and "robust" p.922 and the FDA's clearance of the Avaulta Plus as "an affirmative safety ... decision" based on "specific safety and efficacy findings." JA 613-15. Cisson was prepared to argue, as she has done before this Court, that these characterizations wildly inflate the significance of the process, and that in any event Bard failed to make necessary disclosures to the FDA.

All of this, the district court reasoned, presented "the very substantial dangers of misleading the jury and confusing the issues." JA 1251. The court expressed concern that subjecting the jury to many hours, and possibly days, of complex testimony about regulatory compliance could lead jurors to erroneously conclude that regulatory compliance proved product safety. In other words, having a "minitrial" could easily inflate the perceived importance of compliance and distract the jury from the central question before it — whether Bard's design was unreasonable based on any dangers it posed versus the costs required to avoid them. While 510(k) clearance might, at least tangentially, say something about the safety of the cleared product, it does not say very much that is specific. The vast majority of courts have said so, and having been thoroughly briefed not only by the parties but by several amici, we say so again today. As such, the district court did not abuse its discretion when it determined that allowing the 510(k) evidence in on the question of design defect would be substantially more prejudicial than probative.

B.

Bard also argues that evidence of 510(k) compliance would have been particularly relevant on the question of punitive damages. Under Georgia law, punitive damages are available where there is "clear and convincing evidence" of "willful misconduct, malice, fraud, wantonness, oppression, or that entire want of care which would raise the presumption of conscious indifference to consequences." Ga.Code Ann. § 51-12-5.1(b). And Georgia courts have noted that regulatory "compliance does tend to show" this high willfulness standard has not been met. *Barger v. Garden Way, Inc.*, 231 Ga.App. 723, 499 S.E.2d 737, 743 (1998).

Although the question remains one of federal, not state, evidentiary law, federal courts are not likely to disagree with the Georgia courts that evidence regarding regulatory compliance (or non-compliance) is often relevant to the willfulness inquiry. *See* Restatement (Third) of Torts, Prod. Liab. § 4. Nevertheless, Bard's argument is ultimately unpersuasive. While such evidence may be relevant, the compliance at issue in this case was, at most, minimally so. Again, the 510(k) process has been repeatedly characterized as something less than a safety requirement, gaining the applicant an exemption from regulation rather than subjecting the applicant to regulation. *Riegel,* 552 U.S. at 322, 128 S.Ct. 999; *see also Almy v. Sebelius,* 679 F.3d 297, 308 (4th Cir.2012); *Rodriguez v. Stryker Corp.,* 680 F.3d 568, 574 (6th Cir. 2012) ("The 510(k) process does not comment on safety."). Thus, the decision to pursue 510(k) clearance was a choice to minimize the burden of compliance, potentially cutting in favor of punitive damages. *See Anastasi v. Wright Med. Tech., Inc.,* 16 F.Supp.3d 1032, 1036-37 (E.D.Mo.2014) (finding that defendant chose the FDA 510(k) process to "avoid the safety reviews, including clinical trials, required for premarket approval under FDA regulations"). As such, the district court is entitled to put 510(k) evidence before the jury, but it is not obligated to do so. The court was within its discretion to determine that the value of putting the controversy over the 510(k) process, and Bard's compliance or p.923 non-compliance with that process, before the jury was substantially outweighed by the likelihood of confusing the issues and misleading the jury.

C.

This Court does not reach the district court's ruling that the 510(k) evidence could be excluded as irrelevant under Rule 402 because the evidence was properly excluded under Rule 403. The district court's Rule 403 ruling implicitly indicates that even if the evidence is relevant, it is insufficiently relevant to warrant admission. We agree that the district court was within its discretion in denying admission of the evidence using the lower standard in Rule 403, and therefore decline to address the more difficult question presented by the Rule 402 ruling.

III.

The second issue on appeal is whether the district court erred when it overruled Bard's hearsay objections to the admission of a MSDS pertaining to polypropylene, a material used in the construction of the Avaulta Plus implanted in Cisson's body. There is, of course, a presumption that hearsay will not be admitted into evidence in federal courts. Fed.R.Evid. 802. The MSDS in question in this case read in pertinent part as follows:

> MEDICAL APPLICATION CAUTION: Do not use this ... material in medical applications involving permanent implantation in the human body.... Do not use this ... material in medical applications involving brief or temporary implantation in the human body or contact with internal body fluids or tissues, unless the material has been provided directly from [Phillips] under an agreement which expressly acknowledges the contemplated use.

JA 4826.

The district court accepted Cisson's argument that the MSDS could come in as non-hearsay for the limited purpose of showing that the statement was made and that Bard was aware of it. The court also ruled, *sua sponte,* that the MSDS was admissible for its truth under the hearsay exceptions contained in Federal Rules of Evidence 803(17), 803(18), and 807.

We review the district court's applications of the hearsay rules, like applications of all Federal Rules of Evidence, for abuse of discretion, and its interpretations of such rules *de novo*. *Precision Piping & Instruments, Inc. v. E.I. du Pont de Nemours & Co.*, 951 F.2d 613, 619 (4th Cir. 1991). Doing so, we reverse the district court's rulings as to the hearsay exceptions. However, we affirm the decision to admit the evidence as non-hearsay, finding that any use of the evidence by the plaintiff that went beyond the limited purpose for which it was admitted as non-hearsay resulted in harmless error and was not prejudicial to Bard's defense.[2]

A.

Rule 803(17), titled "Market Reports and Similar Commercial Publications," creates an exception to the prohibition p.924 on hearsay for "market quotations, lists, directories, or other compilations that are generally relied on by the public or by persons in particular occupations." Fed. R.Evid. 803(17). The district court ruled that the MSDS qualified as an "other compilation" within this exception. We disagree.

The district court's ruling relied on its interpretation of the term "other compilation" in Rule 803(17). A question of interpretation going to the scope of the rule is reviewed *de novo*. *See Precision Piping*, 951 F.2d at 619. Our analysis is guided by *ejusdem generis*, a statutory canon of interpretation holding that where a statute contains an exemplary list of objects to which it applies, a general term that follows specific ones will be limited in its meaning by the more specific terms that preceded it. *Circuit City Stores, Inc. v. Adams*, 532 U.S. 105, 114-15, 121 S.Ct. 1302, 149 L.Ed.2d 234 (2001). The district court's reliance on the general term — "other compilations" — concluding Rule 803(17)'s exemplary list makes the canon applicable.

The narrower terms listed by the rule — "market quotations, lists, directories" — are items that recite established factual information. In general, a MSDS might contain similarly factual information. But in this case, Cisson sought to use a portion of the MSDS that was not factual but rather operated as a warning and disclaimer of liability for the self-interested issuing party. The warning from Phillips that polypropylene should not be used in human implants was an opinion the company issued within the MSDS for self-interested reasons, and it therefore bears no resemblance to the factual, list-type documents enumerated in Rule 803(17).

An advisory note to Rule 803(17) states that "[t]he basis of trustworthiness" for evidence admitted under the exception should be "the motivation of the compiler to foster reliance by being accurate." Fed.R.Evid. 803(17), advisory comm. note (1972). Disclaimers of the sort in the MSDS are not typically so motivated, being intended instead to prevent any use of a product that might create a liability. Cisson has offered no proof or argument that the disclaimer warrants the same presumption of reliability afforded to market quotations and directories, and a disclaimer clearly lacks the hallmarks of reliability that make market reports an exception. The district court therefore erred in holding the MSDS admissible for its truth under Rule 803(17).

B.

Rule 803(18), titled "Statements in Learned Treatises, Periodicals, or Pamphlets," creates an exception to the prohibition on hearsay when a statement in such publications is (1) "called to the attention of an expert witness on cross-examination or relied on by the expert on direct examination"; (2) the reliability of that statement is established "by the expert's admission or testimony, by another expert's testimony, or by judicial notice"; and (3) the statement is read into evidence rather than being received as an exhibit. Fed.R.Evid. 803(18). The district court ruled, again *sua sponte,* that the MSDS could come in for the truth of the matter asserted as a "pamphlet" within the exception. Again, we disagree. We review this application of Rule 803(18) for abuse of discretion.

The MSDS, as used in this case, does not meet any of the rule's three facial requirements. First, it was not "relied on by [an] expert on direct examination," nor was it "called to the attention of an expert witness on cross-examination": Cisson's expert witnesses did not address the MSDS, and Bard's witnesses attacked the p.925 MSDS on direct examination. Second, the publication was not "established as a reliable authority" for the same reasons — because Cisson's witnesses did not address the MSDS and Bard's witnesses attacked it, no witness testifying at trial ever sought to demonstrate the reliability of the MSDS.[3] Finally, Cisson introduced the MSDS as an exhibit rather than having it read into evidence as required by the rule. Fed.R.Evid. 803(18). Therefore, without addressing whether the MSDS presented in this case could have qualified as a "pamphlet," we find that the district court abused its discretion by admitting it under Rule 803(18) because the reliability of the evidence was not established according to the rule's requirements.

C.

Rule 807, titled the "Residual Exception," creates a hearsay exception for certain statements not covered by any exceptions in Rule 803 or 804. Fed.R.Evid. 807. For a statement to come under this exception it must contain "circumstantial guarantees of trustworthiness," be used to prove "a material fact," and be "more probative on the point for which it is offered than any other evidence" available through "reasonable efforts." *Id.* We review the district court's application of the rule here for an abuse of discretion, noting however that the residual hearsay exception "was meant to be invoked sparingly." *Heyward,* 729 F.2d at 299 (quotation marks omitted).

As discussed in more detail below, the MSDS was hardly the best evidence available that polypropylene was potentially dangerous for human implantation. The relative dangers of polypropylene in pellet and monofilament form was an issue that received substantial attention from both parties' experts who themselves relied on studies, reports, empirical evidence, and tissue sample slides evidencing Ms. Cisson's particular pathology. The warning in the MSDS, on the other hand, was nothing more than an assertion made by the self-interested manufacturer of polypropylene that the product should not be implanted in humans. The MSDS made no attempt to explain why polypropylene might be dangerous or how Phillips had come to this conclusion. Because there was ample other evidence available to address polypropylene's viability as a material for surgical implants, we find that the district court abused its discretion in finding, again *sua sponte,* that the MSDS could come in for its truth under Rule 807.

D.

Having reviewed and reversed the district court's several *sua sponte* rulings that the MSDS could come in for its truth under various hearsay exceptions, we now turn to Cisson's original rationale for offering the MSDS: that it was not offered as hearsay. Cisson argued, and the district court agreed, that the warning in the MSDS would not be hearsay if it was offered to show only that Phillips made, and Bard received, the warning statement. Bard does not dispute this on appeal, but argues instead that Cisson used the MSDS for its truth during the trial and that it was therefore offered as hearsay without an exception. Having thoroughly reviewed the record we have found no reversible error, and we therefore affirm the district court's admission of the MSDS.

"Out-of-court statements constitute hearsay only when offered in evidence p.926 to prove the truth of the matter asserted." *Anderson v. United States,* 417 U.S. 211, 219, 94 S.Ct. 2253, 41 L.Ed.2d 20 (1974). A statement that would otherwise be hearsay may nevertheless be admissible if it is offered to prove something other than its truth, and this includes statements used to charge a party with knowledge of certain information. *Gardner v. Q.H.S., Inc.,* 448 F.2d 238, 244 (4th Cir.1971) (finding out-of-court statements admissible "to show defendants' knowledge of the harm their product could inflict, provided only that [the statements] were brought to the attention of the defendants"); *see United States v. Macias-Farias,* 706 F.3d 775, 781 (6th Cir.2013). "[W]hether an out-of-court assertion is hearsay depends on its *use"* at trial. David F. Binder, Hearsay Handbook § 1:9 (4th ed.2015).

Cisson originally sought to introduce the MSDS to show that Bard had received the warning from Phillips, one of many safety-related "red flags" she argued demonstrated Bard's knowledge that its product might be unsafe. This was used to support Cisson's argument that the company should have further investigated the safety of the Avaulta Plus rather than marketing the product immediately. Cisson insists that during the trial she did not rely on the MSDS to show that polypropylene was unsafe or to prove causation. Bard argues, however, that "[h]aving secured ... a ruling that the MSDS was admissible for its truth, Plaintiffs took full advantage of the rulings" by using the document to show that polypropylene was unsuitable for implantation and contributed to Cisson's injuries. Appellant's R. Br. 30. Cisson's position ultimately proves more convincing for two reasons. First, throughout the trial Cisson consistently limited use of the MSDS to establishing that Bard received the warning and then responded either by ignoring it or withholding it from other parties. Second, even if Cisson did at any time use the MSDS for its truth, she did so in a way that did not prejudice the defendant.

Roger Darois, Bard's Vice President of Research and Advanced Technology, was the key witness Cisson used to establish that Bard had received, and then ignored and withheld, the MSDS warning regarding human implantation. Throughout that testimony, Cisson's attorney pressed Darois on Bard's response to the warning, pointing out that (1) the company did not reach out to Phillips to clarify why the warning had been added to the MSDS in 2007 after decades of polypropylene production, (2) Bard's supplier of monofilament refused to continue supplying processed polypropylene for medical applications after it learned of the MSDS warning, and (3) Darois told Bard staff members to take steps that would prevent Phillips from learning that Bard was implanting medical devices made with polypropylene into human patients.

As Bard pointed out in its appeal on the 510(k) issue, Georgia product liability law incorporates reasonableness principles, *ICI Americas,* 450 S.E.2d at 673-74, and the punitive damages standard in Georgia requires a jury to find the defendant was willful and wanton in its disregard for the safety of others, Ga.Code Ann. § 51-12-5.1(b). It seems clear that Cisson used the MSDS, at least with regard to the Darois testimony (which again was the most significant exchange involving the MSDS), to show Bard's conduct was not only unreasonable but "would raise the presumption of conscious indifference to consequences." Id. None of the questions to Darois went to proving the actual truth of the MSDS warning, that is, the testimony did not address whether polypropylene was actually dangerous or could have caused Cisson's injuries.

p.927 Bard argues that Cisson relied on the MSDS as substantive evidence of causation not only during the Darois testimony, but throughout the trial, claiming that "Plaintiffs' counsel went so far as to tell the jury that it could ... find for Plaintiffs based solely on the MSDS." Appellant's R. Br. 30. It is first worth noting that this assertion stands in stark contrast to Bard's characterization of the MSDS testimony in its closing argument at trial:

> The MSDS sheet. Think about it. Go back to your notes. Think about it. Not a single witness for the plaintiff talked about the MSDS sheet. Nobody[.].... [T]heir experts, Dr. Brennan and Dr. Klosterhalfen and Dr. Hoyte, they didn't talk about it. Nobody linked it up. Nobody linked this issue up.

JA 6578. At that time, Bard apparently felt that the MSDS simply had not been used in a way that could support causation, but on appeal it argues Cisson ubiquitously abused the district court's mistaken ruling that the MSDS could be used for its truth, causing an incurable prejudice to Bard. At oral argument Bard's counsel called the MSDS the "centerpiece" of Cisson's case to the jury. Oral Argument 15:05. Having reviewed a great deal of the more than 7000 pages of record before us (not only the portions cited by Bard to support its contentions, but many more pages of testimony, transcripts, exhibits, and rulings), we find Bard's characterization generally overwrought. We tend to agree instead with their earlier statements to the jury that Cisson never sought to link the MSDS to the question of causation.

There is, however, one statement made by Cisson's counsel that has given us some pause. After bringing up the MSDS during closing arguments, Cisson's trial counsel said, "Now, the interesting thing about that is you can dismiss all the experts. You can say, well, this expert is biased and that expert is biased. But Phillips Sumika, they don't have a dog in the hunt." JA 6537. On its face, the statement appears to instruct the jury that the MSDS is more reliable than the experts and can therefore establish causation. But we need not decide whether the statement was an attempt to use the MSDS to overcome adverse expert testimony on the question of causation, because that single stray comment was not enough to prejudice Bard and require a new trial. Federal courts of appeal review the fairness of district court proceedings "without regard to errors or defects which do not affect the substantial rights of the parties." 28 U.S.C. § 2111; *McDonough Power Equip., Inc. v. Greenwood,* 464 U.S. 548, 553-54, 104 S.Ct. 845, 78 L.Ed.2d 663 (1984). To find the alleged error harmless, "we need only be able to say 'with fair assurance, after pondering all that happened without stripping the erroneous action from the whole, that the judgment was not substantially swayed by the error.'" *United States v. Heater,* 63 F.3d 311, 325 (4th Cir.1995) (quoting *United States v. Nyman,* 649 F.2d 208, 211 (4th Cir.1980)).

The alleged error in this case was harmless for three reasons. First, Bard has pointed to only one actually problematic statement from Cisson's counsel over the course of a ten day trial. Although Bard cites several parts of the record it claims show the MSDS being used for its truth, the only one that is at all convincing is the "dismiss all the experts" statement. For example, Bard argues that the MSDS was used as substantive evidence of causation in Cisson's opening argument, citing JA 2358-60. That portion of the transcript, however, shows Cisson's attorney explaining to jurors that the MSDS was produced by the polypropylene manufacturer, that it contained a warning that material should not be used in implants, that the MSDS p.928 (and its warning) was in Bard's possession, and that Bard should have taken the warning seriously by verifying that the material was safe for its medical device. None of that goes to causation, and all of it supports Cisson's contention that the MSDS was being used to show Bard was warned about *potential* dangers and acted irresponsibly in response to that warning. Bard cites other parts of the opening argument, but these show Cisson's attorney referring to the MSDS, not as scientific proof that polypropylene is unsafe, but rather as a "red flag" and a "safety alert" that should have put Bard on notice to investigate further.

Bard also points to a portion of the Darois testimony at JA 4424-27 (and a related exhibit at JA 4652-54), but the questions and answers on those pages demonstrate only that Bard was attempting to keep Phillips in the dark about polypropylene being used in the Avaulta Plus after Phillips added the implantation warning to the MSDS in 2007. Again, this evidence tended to show that Bard's reaction to the warning was unreasonable, not that polypropylene caused Cisson's injuries. The MSDS simply was not being used for its truth. The same is true of all Bard's citations to the record on this point, with the exception of the one statement we have noted. The fact that there was only one such instance during ten days of evidence cuts strongly in favor of finding the alleged error harmless.

Second, Cisson presented substantive evidence showing that the polypropylene implanted in her body was degraded, providing the jury with a much more compelling reason to conclude that polypropylene contributed to her injuries than simple reliance on a warning in a MSDS. Had Cisson's "dismiss all the experts" statement been repeated, particularly on separate occasions and thereby developed into a theme, we might be more persuaded that there was error and that it was not harmless. After all, taken on its face and without context, the statement can be interpreted to tell the jurors that they can ignore both Cisson's experts, who testified that polypropylene can degrade in the body and cause injuries, and Bard's experts, who testified this was undemonstrated and unlikely.

However, the jury in this case heard substantial evidence to support the conclusion that the polypropylene in Cisson's Avaulta Plus degraded and harmed her. Cisson presented three separate experts who testified on this point: Dr. Anthony Brennan, a biomedical engineer; Dr. Bernd Klosterhalfen, a pathologist; and Dr. Brian Raybon, the physician who implanted the Avaulta Plus into Cisson's body. Dr. Brennan provided the jury with an opinion that fluids in the human body can degrade polypropylene, Dr. Raybon testified that the polypropylene in Cisson's implant had degraded, and Dr. Klosterhalfen reviewed Cisson's pathology and told the jury she had an inflammatory reaction and scar plate, symptoms consistent with polypropylene degradation. In order for us to reverse the district court, Bard must show that its "substantial rights" were affected, *Greenwood,* 464 U.S. at 553-54, 104 S.Ct. 845, or that the jury was "substantially swayed by the error," *Heater,* 63 F.3d at 325, but the fact that the jury had substantial expert testimony on one side and a single stray comment by Cisson's attorney on the other again cuts strongly in favor of finding the alleged error harmless.

Finally, Cisson's causation evidence linked three other design defects to her injuries in *addition* to the alleged polypropylene defect. Bard therefore cannot meet its burden without some showing that the jury was unpersuaded by these p.929 alternative theories of causation, or at least that the polypropylene theory was sufficiently central to its damages award that Bard's substantial rights were affected. *See id.* (assuming an evidentiary ruling was erroneous and then considering all of the evidence adduced at trial to determine the likelihood of prejudice). Specifically, Cisson's evidence included expert testimony to the effect that the mesh in the Avaulta Plus was subject to shrinking post-implantation, that the pores in the mesh were too small and therefore likely to result in the formation of rigid scar tissue, and that the arms used to hold the Avaulta Plus in place in the body were defectively designed and contributed to Cisson's pain. Bard fails to demonstrate, or even argue, that the jury based its conclusions on the polypropylene degradation evidence rather than these theories, which were central to her case. Cisson, on the other hand, presented multiple experts in support of each causation theory and linked them to her injuries.

Bard has failed to demonstrate that the one problematic statement regarding the MSDS it has managed to identify in the record had a significant effect on the jury's decision. Given the very significant evidence Cisson presented on causation, and given that the problematic statement was, at most, addressed to one of Cisson's four theories of causation, we cannot find that Bard's substantial rights were affected. We therefore find the alleged error harmless and affirm the district court's admission of the MSDS.

IV.

The third issue raised by Bard on appeal is whether the district court erred in its instruction to the jury on causation, as well as in its subsequent ruling upholding the jury's causation finding pursuant to its denial of Bard's renewed motion for judgment as a matter of law. Bard charges that it was prejudiced because the court's causation instruction did not reflect Georgia law.

Rulings on jury instructions are reviewed for abuse of discretion, but where there is an error of law we review *de novo. Emergency One, Inc. v. Am. FireEagle, Ltd.,* 228 F.3d 531, 538 (4th Cir.2000). We review to ensure that the "charge [was] accurate on the law and [did] not confuse or mislead the jury." *Hardin v. Ski Venture, Inc.,* 50 F.3d 1291, 1294 (4th Cir. 1995). Because the court's instruction met this standard, and because the jury had ample evidence on which to base its causation finding, we affirm the district court.

Bard's position is that Georgia law requires injury causation be proved by "expert testimony stated to a reasonable degree of medical probability or certainty," that the court was wrong to deny its request for an instruction reflecting that standard, and that Cisson failed to offer expert testimony on two alleged design defects sufficient under the standard to prove they caused her injuries. But Bard's characterization of Georgia law incorrectly states the standard of proof applicable here, inserting the standard for medical malpractice cases into this product liability case.

The district court charged the jury using Georgia's pattern jury instructions for strict liability tort cases, which defines the burden of proof for proximate cause as a preponderance of the evidence. *See* Ga. Suggested Pattern Jury Instructions, Vol. I: Civil Cases §§ 60. 200 & 62.610 (5th ed.2015). It is also established under Georgia law that plaintiffs in medical implant cases "may present medical as well as non-medical evidence to show causation." *Allison v. McGhan Med. Corp.,* 184 F.3d 1300, 1320 (11th Cir.1999).

p.930 Bard cannot point to a single Georgia case (or any case applying Georgia law) stating that the standard in the pattern jury instruction is incorrect. Instead, Bard points to an inapposite Georgia Supreme Court case, *Zwiren v. Thompson,* 276 Ga. 498, 578 S.E.2d 862 (2003), a comparison that suffers from multiple problems. First, *Zwiren* was a medical malpractice case, not a product liability case. Second, while the *Zwiren* court did indeed adopt the "reasonable medical probability or certainty" standard Bard advocates, the thrust of the opinion was to *reduce* the standard from "reasonable medical certainty" to "reasonable medical probability." *Id.* at 867. This lower standard "is the functional equivalent of preponderance of the evidence" — the same standard expressed by the pattern jury instruction. *Allison,* 184 F.3d at 1320. Thus, even in malpractice cases, "Georgia case law requires only that an expert state an opinion regarding proximate causation in terms stronger than that of medical possibility." *Zwiren,* 578 S.E.2d at 867. In medical implant cases the need for exclusively medical evidence is abrogated. *Allison,* 184 F.3d at 1320.

Cisson presented ample expert and non-expert testimony for a jury to find that the design defects caused her injuries. In addition to the evidence already described in Part III of this opinion, Cisson presented the following testimony to the jury: Dr. Lennox Hoyte, a urogynecologist, and Dr. John Miklos, one of Cisson's treating physicians, respectively testified that the arms on the Avaulta Plus constituted a design defect and caused Cisson's pain; Dr. Bernd Klosterhalfen, a pathologist, and Dr. Jim Ross testified that inadequate pore size can cause the implanted mesh to shrink and can lead to inflammatory reactions and rigid scarification inside the body; and Dr. Anthony Brennan, a professor and expert in material sciences and biomedical engineering, Dr. Klosterhalfen, and Dr. Brian Raybon, another of Cisson's treating physicians, testified that polypropylene can degrade in the human body, degradation can cause internal inflammation, and that Ms. Cisson's mesh was degraded. This and the other evidence presented at trial was more than enough for the jury to conclude that the alleged defects caused Cisson's injuries. Although Bard argues that Cisson's burden was to show precisely how each alleged defect caused particular injuries, under Georgia product liability case law "it is not necessary for the plaintiff to specify precisely the nature of the defect"; a plaintiff need only show that "the device did not operate as intended and this was the proximate cause of [the plaintiff's] injuries." *Trickett v. Advanced Neuromodulation Sys., Inc.,* 542 F.Supp.2d 1338, 1345 (S.D.Ga.2008) (emphasis removed) (quoting *Williams v. Am. Med. Sys.,* 248 Ga.App. 682, 548 S.E.2d 371, 373 (2001)) (quotation marks omitted).

We therefore find that the district court did not err in giving the Georgia pattern jury instruction, in denying Bard's request for a modified instruction, or in upholding the jury's causation finding.

V.

The jury awarded Cisson $250,000 in compensatory damages and $1.75 million in punitive damages.[4] "The Due Process Clause of the Fourteenth Amendment prohibits the imposition of p.931 grossly excessive or arbitrary punishments on a tortfeasor" in the form of punitive damages. *State Farm Mut. Auto. Ins. Co. v. Campbell,* 538 U.S. 408, 416, 123 S.Ct. 1513, 155 L.Ed.2d 585 (2003). As such, Bard argues that the punitive award in this case was constitutionally excessive. We review this constitutional question *de novo, id.* at 418, 123 S.Ct. 1513, and affirm the award.

The Supreme Court has articulated three "guideposts" for reviewing the constitutionality of a punitive damages award: "(1) the degree or reprehensibility of the defendant's misconduct, (2) the disparity between the harm (or potential harm) suffered by the plaintiff and the punitive damages award, and (3) the difference between the punitive damages awarded by the jury and the civil penalties authorized or imposed in comparable cases." *Cooper Indus., Inc. v. Leatherman Tool Group, Inc.,* 532 U.S. 424, 440, 121 S.Ct. 1678, 149 L.Ed.2d 674 (2001) (citing *BMW of N. Am., Inc. v. Gore,* 517 U.S. 559, 574-75, 116 S.Ct. 1589, 134 L.Ed.2d 809 (1996)). The Court also noted that the first of these factors, reprehensibility, is the most important. *Campbell,* 538 U.S. at 419, 123 S.Ct. 1513 (quoting *Gore,* 517 U.S. at 575, 116 S.Ct. 1589). Bard, however rests its challenge entirely on the second guidepost, asserting only that the punitive award "is constitutionally impermissible, as it is seven times the $250,000 compensatory damages award." Appellant's Br. 58.

Bard's argument is based principally on the *Campbell* Court's observation that "an award of more than four times the amount of compensatory damages might be close to the line of constitutional impropriety." 538 U.S. at 425, 123 S.Ct. 1513. However, Bard apparently failed to realize that the Court went on to say "these ratios are not binding" and to conclude that "[s]ingle-digit multipliers are more likely to comport with due process ... than awards with ratios in range of 500 to 1." *Id.*

Bard effectively urges this court to adopt a bright line rule against punitive damages exceeding a ratio of four-to-one, despite the Supreme Court itself "declin[ing] again to impose a bright-line ratio which a punitive damages award cannot exceed" in *Campbell. Id.* The district court found that "here, the compensatory damages and punitive damages against Bard both arose from its misconduct that resulted in Ms. Cisson's injuries," JA 7139-40 n. 8, and grounded its refusal to overturn the award in reprehensibility of Bard's conduct, JA 7138-43. We therefore find that the seven-to-one ratio was not constitutionally excessive in this case and affirm the district court.

VI.

The final issue before us comes from Cisson who challenges, by cross-appeal, the district court's ruling that a Georgia split-recovery statute garnishing seventy-five percent of any punitive damages award arising from a product liability judgment, O.C.G.A. § 51-12-5.1(e), does not violate the Takings Clause of the Fifth Amendment of the United States Constitution. Cisson asserts that Georgia created a property interest in such punitive damages awards when it codified them in O.C.G.A. § 51-12-5.1, and that enforcement of the state's subsequently enacted split-recovery statute violates the Takings Clause. The district court rejected that argument, and we review its decision *de novo*. To succeed, Cisson must first show she has "a constitutionally protected property interest" in the punitive damages award at issue. *See Washlefske v. Winston*, 234 F.3d 179, 184 (4th Cir.2000). Cisson contends that she has a vested property interest in the entire punitive damages award, but, in the scant briefing p.932 she has provided to this Court on the issue, she has failed to articulate a viable theory in support of that contention.

Cisson makes no claim that her right to punitive damages arises from the common law or is otherwise fundamental, so we need not address the opinions of some courts which have found that no such right is cognizable under the Takings Clause. *E.g. Engquist v. Oregon Dep't of Agric.*, 478 F.3d 985, 1002-04 (9th Cir. 2007). Instead she argues that her property interest was created by Georgia statute. Appellee's Br. 92. But Cisson does not explain how Georgia exceeds its authority by defining the contours of the right it has allegedly created. *Washlefske*, 234 F.3d at 184; *see Cheatham v. Pohle*, 789 N.E.2d 467, 473 (Ind.2003) (holding that the legislature could define a plaintiff's interest in a statutorily created property right). "[I]f a statute creates a property right ..., the property interest so created is defined by the statute...." *Washlefske*, 234 F.3d at 184. As such, under Cisson's own theory "the legislature may lawfully regulate the amount of punitive damages which can be awarded," *Mack Trucks, Inc. v. Conkle*, 263 Ga. 539, 436 S.E.2d 635, 639 (1993), and she has therefore provided no basis for us to find the state's actions unconstitutional.

As such, we affirm the judgment of the district court.

VII.

For the foregoing reasons, the judgment of the district court on all issues raised in this appeal is

AFFIRMED.

[1] We also need not address Bard's contention that state law, rather than federal, controls the question — at least not at any great length. Because this is a diversity case, the "general rule" is that federal courts apply state substantive law and federal

procedural law. *Hottle v. Beech Aircraft Corp.,* 47 F.3d 106, 109 (4th Cir.1995). As procedural rules, the Federal Rules of Evidence control over conflicting state evidentiary rules in diversity cases. *Id.* Only where a state evidentiary rule is "bound-up" with substantive state policy will it control over the federal rule. *Id.* at 110. This is not such a case.

First, Bard fails to point to a state evidentiary rule contradicting Rule 403. Instead, Bard argues that regulatory compliance has been ruled relevant in numerous Georgia product liability cases. But the rulings Bard points to are just that — rulings, not rules. Bard does not demonstrate that Georgia law requires evidence of regulatory compliance to be admitted in all cases regardless of probative value or prejudicial effect, so there is no competing rule.

Second, Bard fails to demonstrate that the alleged rule is sufficiently "bound-up" with substantive state policy. Regulatory compliance is one of at least thirteen non-exclusive factors Georgia courts consider under the risk-utility test — hardly a cornerstone of the state's product liability jurisprudence. Ga. Suggested Pattern Jury Instruction, Vol. I: Civil Cases § 62.650 (5th ed.2015).

[2] Cisson argues that Bard waived its right to attack the MSDS rulings on appeal by failing to continually object. Bard, however, was relieved of this obligation by Rule 103(b) once the court had "definitively" ruled on the matter. Fed.R.Evid. 103(b). Cisson also argues that Bard waived this attack by introducing earlier versions of the MSDS for discussion by its witnesses, but this, of course, was in response to the district court overruling Bard's several objections to admission of the MSDS. Once a court has definitively decided evidence can come in, the opposing party must be allowed to defend against that evidence without losing its otherwise well-preserved objection.

[3] Nor did the district court invoke judicial notice to establish the reliability of the MSDS. The reliability of the MSDS warning was clearly in dispute at trial, and judicial notice would have been improper.

[4] The punitive damages were subject to a split-recovery statute, dividing the award between the plaintiff and the State of Georgia. As a result, Cisson only received twenty-five percent of the award, while Georgia received the remaining seventy-five percent. *See* Part VI. *infra.*

828 F.3d 1098 (2016)

JL BEVERAGE COMPANY, LLC, Plaintiff-Counter-Defendant-Appellant,

v.

JIM BEAM BRANDS CO.; Beam Suntory Inc., Defendants-Counter-Plaintiffs-Appellees.

No. 13-17382.

United States Court of Appeals, Ninth Circuit.

Argued and Submitted January 8, 2016 San Francisco, California.

Filed July 14, 2016.

JL Beverage Company v. Jim Beam Brands, 828 F. 3d 1098 (9th Cir. 2016)

p.1101 Appeal from the United States District Court for the District of Nevada; Miranda M. Du, District Judge, Presiding, D.C. No. 2:11-cv-00417-MMD-CWH.

Colin Christopher Holley (argued), Jeremy T. Katz, and George L. Hampton, Hampton Holley, Corona Del Mar, California; Ryan R. Gile, Weide & Miller, Las Vegas, Nevada; for Plaintiff-Counter-Defendant-Appellant.

Mark J. Liss (argued), Claudia Stangle, and Angela Baylin, Leydig, Voit & Mayer, Chicago, Illinois; Jonathan Fountain and Michael McCue, Lewis Roca Rothgerber, Las Vegas, Nevada; for Defendant-Counter-Plaintiff-Appellee.

Before: J. Clifford Wallace, John T. Noonan, and Marsha S. Berzon, Circuit Judges.

OPINION

WALLACE, Senior Circuit Judge:

JL Beverage Company, LLC (JL Beverage) appeals from the district court's summary judgment in favor of Jim Beam Brands Company (Jim Beam) on JL Beverage's trademark infringement, false designation of origin, and unfair competition claims. We have jurisdiction pursuant to 28 U.S.C. § 1291. Because genuine issues of material fact remain, we reverse and remand for further proceedings consistent with this opinion.

I.

This dispute centers on two alcoholic beverage manufacturers, JL Beverage and Jim Beam, which sell competing lines of flavored vodkas. JL Beverage manufactures, sells, and promotes a line of flavored and unflavored vodka called "Johnny Love Vodka." Restaurant owner and bartender Johnny Metheny created the Johnny Love line of vodkas around 2003-2004. To promote the new line, Metheny enlisted a friend to design a unique logo, and Metheny quickly adopted the proposed lips image. He believed the lips were "definitely sexy" and could "impart the flavor" of the vodka if colored to denote the flavor in the bottle of vodka. The lips were colored red for unflavored, purple for passionfruit, yellow for aloha, orange for tangerine, and green for apple. In 2005, Metheny sold the Johnny Love Vodka line to JL Beverage.

Since July 2005, JL Beverage has used the following two trademarks in connection with its sale of the Johnny Love Vodka products:

p.1102 The first mark, called "Johnny Love Vodka" or the "JLV mark," was registered on August 16, 2005, with the United States Patent and Trademark Office (USPTO) as Registration No. 2, 986,519 in International Class 33-Vodka. JL Beverage registered the second mark, called the "JL Lips Mark," with USPTO on October 25, 2011 under Registration No. 4,044,182 in International Class 33-Distilled Spirits. Both images appear on the Johnny Love line of vodkas and flavored vodkas:

The JL Lips Mark is imprinted on the top of the bottle and on the back label, and is incorporated into the JLV Mark as the "o" in "Love." The mark color on the back label also corresponds to the flavor in the bottle:

The Johnny Love Vodka bottles come in four different sizes.

After acquiring Johnny Love Vodka and the two trademarks, JL Beverage expended substantial resources developing, advertising, and marketing Johnny Love Vodkas throughout the United States. JL Beverage at one point had distributors in twenty states, and it holds a Federal Basic Alcohol Permit for national use. JL Beverage's nationwide marketing campaign included print-media advertisements, third-party publications, and the development of its own website. Although in recent years its sales have been substantially reduced, its overall marketing efforts resulted in millions of dollars in sales of Johnny Love products throughout the country.

In 2010, Jim Beam entered the flavored vodka market with a new line of flavored p.1103 vodkas called "Pucker Vodka." Jim Beam purchased the Pucker brand from Koninklijke De Kuyper, B.V. (KDK). KDK had marketed a line of liqueurs and cordials under the "Pucker" brand, and, in its original design, used lips images in connection with its labeling and logos. After Jim Beam purchased KDK's flavored vodka line, it decided to redesign and rebrand Pucker to "expand on the equity of the Pucker brand and lips" into flavored vodka." To that end, Jim Beam hired the design firm of Libby, Perszyk, Kathman, Inc. (LPK) to independently "develop a new and unique look and feel" for its Pucker vodka product that would communicate "[i]ntense flavor and [i]ntense fun" in connection with the brand.

The redesigned Pucker Vodka bottle contains a prominent lips image on the center of its label. Like the Johnny Love Vodka labels, the lips image varies in color depending on the vodka flavor in the bottle:

Jim Beam instructed LPK to use both the Pucker name and lips as part of any design it developed for Pucker's new label. After LPK provided Jim Beam with several possible design options, Jim Beam's project team made final selections of the proposed Pucker Vodka products and sent their choices to the company's legal department for clearance. Jim Beam instructed its legal counsel to perform a clearance search for lips designs. The legal department found 40 references to lips for alcohol-related products. JL Beverage's JLV Mark was in the search report. Although JL Beverage's Lips Mark is incorporated into the JLV Mark, it did not separately appear in the search report because JL Beverage had not yet filed its registration application for the standalone lips mark. Based on its research, Jim Beam's legal department approved the Pucker brand's bottle shape and label.

Emily Johnson, a former Jim Beam employee, worked for Jim Beam as a financial and business analyst during the development of the Pucker Vodka product. Prior to her employment at Jim Beam, Johnson met JL Beverage's president, T.J. Diab, and learned about JL Beverage's products. In March 2010, during her employment at Jim Beam, she sent an email to Diab from her home account, which stated "I was reading through some reporting on vodka flavors and saw Aloha on the list!"

Jim Beam attempted to register the Pucker lips design around March 2011, filing applications for trademarks in the bottle and cap, the stylized Pucker wording, and the lips design. After the registration process began, an official in Jim p.1104 Beam's legal department discovered that the lips mark that LPK had selected to be featured in the center of the Pucker Vodka label was "stock art" from iStockphoto LP. Because Jim Beam could not claim ownership in the lips image, it withdrew its USPTO application for the lips design.

Prior to withdrawal, Jim Beam also received notice from the USPTO that it had rejected Jim Beam's registration application. In the rejection letter, the USPTO cites JL Beverage's Lips Mark as a basis for refusing the registration.

Jim Beam officially relaunched its newly-designed Pucker Vodka products in March and April 2011. Jim Beam advertises Pucker Vodka products nationally through television and cable commercials, digital advertising, print advertisements in national magazines, and in-store and onpremise promotions at restaurants and bars.

Shortly after the Pucker Vodka launch, Shaun Robertson, a JL Beverage broker for Johnny Love Vodka, began receiving phone calls and messages concerning the similarities between the two vodkas. Robertson provided, in a declaration to the court, a summary of in-person conversations, text messages, and phone calls he had with friends and acquaintances in which those individuals confused a different flavored vodka product for Johnny Love.

JL Beverage delivered a cease and desist letter to Jim Beam on March 18, 2011. Jim Beam responded that it did not believe its Pucker Vodka logo infringed JL Beverage's mark. JL Beverage filed a complaint in the United States District Court for the District of Nevada in July 2011, alleging trademark infringement, false designation of origin, and unfair competition. JL Beverage moved for preliminary injunction, which the district court denied. JL Beverage and Jim Beam then filed cross-motions for summary judgment. The district court denied JL Beverage's motion and granted Jim Beam's motion. The district court subsequently denied JL Beverage's motion for reconsideration.

II.

We review the district court's summary judgment de novo, including its decision on cross-motions for summary judgment. *Szajer v. City of L.A.,* 632 F.3d 607, 610 (9th Cir.2011); *Guatay Christian Fellowship v. Cty. of San Diego,* 670 F.3d 957, 970 (9th Cir.2011). Viewing the evidence in the light most favorable to the nonmoving party, we determine whether there are any genuine issues of material fact. *Olsen v. Idaho State Bd. of Med.,* 363 F.3d 916, 922 (9th Cir.2004). We review the district court's conclusions of law de novo, and its factual findings for clear error. *Id.*; *Lahoti v. VeriCheck, Inc.*, 586 F.3d 1190, 1195-96 (9th Cir.2009). "[W]here it is unclear whether the district court relied on proper law, we may vacate the judgment and remand with instructions to apply the correct legal standard." *Lahoti*, 586 F.3d at 1196 (citing *United States v. Pintado-Isiordia*, 448 F.3d 1155, 1158 (9th Cir.2009)).

This appeal turns in large part on whether the district court correctly applied the standard for deciding a motion for summary judgment. The success of each of JL Beverage's claims turns on the same issue: whether there was a genuine dispute of material fact as to the likelihood of consumer confusion. JL Beverage asserts the following claims: (1) federal trademark infringement under the Lanham Act, 15 U.S.C. § 1114; (2) false designation of origin and unfair competition under the Lanham Act, 15 U.S.C. § 1125(a); and (3) Nevada common law trademark infringement and unfair competition. The likelihood of consumer confusion is central to each claim. *See* 15 U.S.C. § 1114(1)(a) p.1105 (providing that a person is liable for trademark infringement where he or she "use[s] in commerce any reproduction, counterfeit, copy, or colorable imitation of a registered mark in connection with the sale, offering for sale, distribution, or advertising of any goods or services on or in connection with which such use *is likely to cause confusion,* or to cause mistake, or to deceive") (emphasis added); *A.L.M.N. v. Rosoff,* 104 Nev. 274, 277, 281, 757 P.2d 1319 (1988) (holding that Nevada's common law trademark infringement and unfair competition claims mirror their federal counterparts, and plaintiffs need only prove that (1) they own a protectable right in the marks, and (2) the defendant's use of the mark is likely to "confuse, cause mistake, or deceive an 'appreciable number' of reasonable customers" with respect to the marks).

In its summary judgment ruling, the district court used the standard applicable to preliminary injunctions instead of the standard for summary judgment rulings. The district court, having already ruled on JL Beverage's motion for preliminary injunction, continued to apply the standard it used at that stage when it ruled on the parties' cross-motions for summary judgment. In its summary judgment order, the district court concluded: "[f]or reasons articulated in the Order denying the Preliminary Injunction, the Court determines that no issues of material fact remain which could provide Plaintiff a basis for success on any of its claims. Defendant's Motion for Summary Judgment is accordingly granted."

The district court's failure to apply the correct standard is significant: on motion for preliminary injunction, the plaintiff — as the moving party — bears the burden of establishing the merits of its claims. *See Winter v. Nat. Res. Def. Council, Inc.,* 555 U.S. 7, 20, 129 S.Ct. 365, 172 L.Ed.2d 249 (2008). In contrast, on a defendant's motion for summary judgment, not only does the movant carry the burden of establishing that no genuine dispute of material fact exists, but the court also views the evidence in the light most favorable to the non-moving party. *See, e.g., Olsen,* 363 F.3d at 922. The defendant-movant must demonstrate that, even viewing the evidence in the light most favorable to the plaintiff, the plaintiff cannot satisfy its burden to prove its claims. *See Celotex Corp. v. Catrett,* 477 U.S. 317, 322-23, 106 S.Ct. 2548, 91 L.Ed.2d 265 (1986).

But in its summary judgment order, the district court ignored the important distinctions between the two standards, and, when ruling on the defendant's motion for summary judgment, ultimately placed the burden on JL Beverage, the plaintiff, to prove the merits of its claims. Moreover, it failed to view the evidence in the light most favorable to JL Beverage, and never analyzed whether a genuine dispute of material fact existed.

While the district court must apply the correct standard in any case, the necessity to do so is heightened in cases turning on the likelihood of consumer confusion. Because the determination is based on a non-exhaustive, multi-factor, fact-intensive inquiry, we have cautioned against granting summary judgment in these cases. *Rearden LLC v. Rearden Commerce, Inc.*, 683 F.3d 1190, 1210 (9th Cir.2012) ("Given the open-ended nature of this multi-prong inquiry, it is not surprising that summary judgment on 'likelihood of confusion' grounds is generally disfavored"); *Au-Tomotive Gold, Inc. v. Volkswagen of Am., Inc.*, 457 F.3d 1062, 1075 (9th Cir.2006) ("Because the likelihood of confusion is often a fact-intensive inquiry, courts are generally reluctant to decide this issue at the summary judgment stage"); *Thane Int'l, Inc. v. Trek Bicycle Corp.*, 305 F.3d 894, 901-02 (9th Cir.2002) ("We have cautioned p.1106 that district courts should grant summary judgment motions regarding the likelihood of confusion sparingly, as careful assessment of the pertinent factors that go into determining likelihood of confusion usually requires a full record"), *superseded by statute on other grounds*, 15 U.S.C. § 1125. Where, as here, conflicting facts render it unclear whether there was a likelihood of consumer confusion, summary judgment is inappropriate.

III.

To determine whether a likelihood of consumer confusion exists, our court relies on the eight-factor *Sleekcraft* test, which reviews: (1) the strength of the mark; (2) proximity or relatedness of the goods; (3) similarity of the marks; (4) evidence of actual confusion; (5) marketing channels used; (6) type of goods and the degree of care likely to be exercised by the purchaser; (7) the defendant's intent in selecting the mark; and (8) the likelihood of expansion of the product lines. *AMF Inc. v. Sleekcraft Boats*, 599 F.2d 341, 348-49 (9th Cir.1979), *abrogated in part on other grounds by Mattel, Inc. v. Walking Mountain Prods.*, 353 F.3d 792, 810 (9th Cir.2003). The factors are non-exhaustive and applied flexibly; the *Sleekcraft* factors are not intended to be a "rote checklist." *Rearden*, 683 F.3d at 1209. "A determination may rest on only those factors that are most pertinent to the particular case before the court, and other variables besides the enumerated factors should also be taken into account based on the particular circumstances." *Id.*

Utilizing the eight-factor test, plaintiffs may establish a likelihood of consumer confusion as a result of either (1) forward confusion, or (2) reverse confusion. *Survivor Media, Inc. v. Survivor Prods.*, 406 F.3d 625, 630 (9th Cir.2005). JL Beverage alleges both forward and reverse trademark confusion. "Forward confusion occurs when consumers believe that goods bearing the junior mark came from, or were sponsored by, the senior mark holder." *Id.* Reverse confusion, on the other hand, "occurs when consumers dealing with the senior mark holder believe that they are doing business with the junior one." *Id.*

In its order denying a preliminary injunction, the district court determined that factors two, five, and six of the *Sleekcraft* test favor JL Beverage and a finding of a likelihood of confusion. Jim Beam does not dispute that these factors favor JL

Beverage. Rather, Jim Beam contends that there is no genuine dispute of material fact concerning factors one, three, four, and seven, and, accordingly, no genuine dispute of material fact concerning a likelihood of confusion. So the issue before us is whether, viewing the evidence in the light most favorable to JL Beverage, there is a genuine dispute of material fact concerning whether factors one, three, four, and seven favor JL Beverage, and, accordingly, a genuine dispute of material fact as to the likelihood of consumer confusion.

A.

JL Beverage contends that there is a factual dispute as to the strength of its standalone lips logo (Lips Mark) and composite mark consisting of the lips logo and the words "Johnny Love Vodka" (JLV Mark). We examine the strength of JL Beverage's mark to determine the scope of trademark protection to which the mark is entitled. *Surfvivor*, 406 F.3d at 631 (citing *Entrepreneur Media, Inc. v. Smith*, 279 F.3d 1135, 1141 (9th Cir.2002)). As the uniqueness of the mark increases, so too does the degree of protection. *Id.* A mark's strength is "evaluated in terms of its conceptual strength and commercial strength." *GoTo.com, Inc. v. Walt Disney Co.*, 202 F.3d 1199, 1207 (9th Cir.2000).

p.1107 A mark's conceptual strength "depends largely on the obviousness of its connection to the good or service to which it refers." *Fortune Dynamic, Inc. v. Victoria's Secret Stores Brand Mgmt., Inc.*, 618 F.3d 1025, 1032-33 (9th Cir.2010). To determine a mark's conceptual strength, we classify a mark along a spectrum of five categories ranging from strongest to weakest: arbitrary, fanciful, suggestive, descriptive, and generic. *Network Automation, Inc. v. Advanced Sys. Concepts, Inc.*, 638 F.3d 1137, 1149 (9th Cir.2011). Arbitrary and fanciful marks, which employ words and phrases with no commonly understood connection to the product, are the two strongest categories, and "trigger the highest degree of trademark protection." *Surfvivor*, 406 F.3d at 631. In the middle of the spectrum are suggestive marks, which suggest a product's features and require consumers to exercise some imagination to associate the suggestive mark with the product. *Fortune Dynamic*, 618 F.3d at 1033, (citing *Zobmondo Entm't, LLC v. Falls Media, LLC*, 602 F.3d 1108, 1114 (9th Cir.2010)). Descriptive and generic marks, at the other end of the spectrum, are the two weakest categories. Descriptive marks define a particular characteristic of the product in a way that does not require any imagination, while generic marks describe the product in its entirety and are not entitled to trademark protection. *Surfvivor*, 406 F.3d at 632.

After identifying whether a mark is generic, descriptive, suggestive, arbitrary, or fanciful, the court determines the mark's commercial strength. *Miss World (UK) Ltd. v. Mrs. Am. Pageants, Inc.*, 856 F.2d 1445, 1449 (9th Cir.1988), *abrogated in part on other grounds by Eclipse Assocs. Ltd. v. Data Gen. Corp.*, 894 F.2d 1114, 1116 n. 1 (9th Cir.1990). Commercial strength "is based on actual marketplace recognition." *Network Automation*, 638 F.3d at 1149 (citation omitted). As a result, advertising expenditures, which increase marketplace recognition, offer evidence of commercial strength and "can transform a suggestive mark into a strong mark." *Id.* (citation omitted).

JL Beverage has alleged both forward and reverse confusion claims. The JLV and Lips Marks' conceptual and commercial strength plays a different role in each type of claim. "In the usual [forward] infringement case," the court "determine[s] whether the junior user is palming off its products as those of the senior user." *Dreamwerks Prod. Grp., Inc. v. SKG Studio,* 142 F.3d 1127, 1129-30 (9th Cir. 1998). Consequently, for JL Beverage's claim of forward confusion, we evaluate the conceptual and commercial strength of the JLV and Lips Marks to determine whether a customer interested in purchasing vodka would be confused into thinking that JL Beverage produces Jim Beam's Pucker Vodka, or that Johnny Love Vodka is the same product as Pucker Vodka. In contrast, in claims of reverse confusion, the question is "whether consumers doing business with the senior user might mistakenly believe that they are dealing with the junior user." *Id.* at 1130. As a result, the court evaluates the conceptual strength of JL Beverage's marks and compares it to the commercial strength of Jim Beam's mark. *Id.* at 1130 n. 5.

1.

We turn first to analyzing the JLV and JL Lips Marks' conceptual strength. Jim Beam contends the JLV Mark is descriptive because it contains the word "vodka," and therefore describes the product. Jim Beam, however, ignores the color-coordinated feature of the JLV Mark. Instead of just labeling the bottle "vodka," the JLV Mark has color-coordinated lips that match a particular flavor. Reasonable jurors, viewing the Mark in its entirety, could conclude that the Mark is p.1108 suggestive because they must use their imaginations to connect the color of the lips to the vodka flavor.

Jim Beam also contends that the Lips Mark has weak conceptual strength. Jim Beam overlooks that the salient feature of the Lips Mark — the lips — have no commonly understood connection with the alcohol product it represents. As a result, a fact-finder could reasonably conclude that the Lips Mark is arbitrary, garnering the highest degree of trademark protection.

Jim Beam counters that the Lips Mark is part of a "crowded field" of similar lips logos, and thus there is less likelihood of consumer confusion. Jim Beam argues that JL Beverage waived its right to contest this issue on appeal because it failed to raise it before the district court. However, because the district court considered this issue, it is not waived on appeal. *Cmty. House, Inc. v. City of Boise,* 490 F.3d 1041, 1054 (9th Cir.2007) ("[E]ven if a party fails to raise an issue in the district court, we generally will not deem the issue waived if the district court actually considered it"). Returning to the issue, when "the marketplace is replete with products using a particular trademarked" symbol, it "indicates not only the difficulty in avoiding its use but also, and directly, the likelihood that consumers will *not* be confused by its use." *Entrepreneur Media, Inc. v. Smith,* 279 F.3d 1135, 1144 (9th Cir.2002). Jim Beam has provided several examples of lips marks used on product labels for different types of alcohol. The lips logos Jim Beam presents, however, lack the crucial feature of the Lips Mark: unlike the Lips Mark, they are not color-coordinated by flavor for an entire line of flavored vodkas.

In addition, the vast majority of the products on which lips are used are not liquor products, but rather beer, wine, or non-alcoholic beverages. In that regard, the parties dispute how broadly the relevant market should be characterized for the purposes of evaluating whether the field is crowded with lips uses. In other words, there are genuine disputes of material fact as to what constitutes the relevant "field," whether the field is "crowded," and the effect of the foregoing on the likelihood of confusion analysis. *See also Maker's Mark Distillery, Inc. v. Diageo N. Am., Inc.,* 679 F.3d 410, 420-21 (6th Cir.2012) (agreeing with the district court that, in a trademark dispute between a bourbon maker and a tequila maker, the relevant market was not "all distilled spirits," but rather a narrower field); *Fleischmann Distilling Corp. v. Maier Brewing Co.,* 314 F.2d 149, 159-60 (9th Cir.1963) (calling, in a pre-*Sleekcraft* case, scotch whiskey and beer "related" for purposes of the likelihood of confusion). Perhaps most importantly, the impact of a "crowded field" of lips logos is not dispositive in determining a mark's conceptual strength; rather, it is but one factor a court considers in evaluating the overall strength of the mark. *See Entrepreneur Media,* 279 F.3d at 1143-44.

Here, the district court failed to construe the evidence concerning the JLV and Lips Marks' conceptual strength in the light most favorable to JL Beverage to determine whether a genuine dispute of material fact exists. Had the district court applied the correct standard, it may well have concluded that the Marks' conceptual strength placed the Marks in a category that warranted a higher degree of protection.

2.

We now turn to the second step of our inquiry: the Marks' commercial strength. Jim Beam argues that JL Beverage has a "relatively weak" market presence, while it maintains a "relatively strong" market presence.

JL Beverage concedes that Jim Beam has a strong market presence. JL Beverage p.1109 correctly points out, however, that this finding supports its reverse confusion claim: evidence that Jim Beam's junior mark, the Pucker Vodka lips, is wellknown suggests a greater likelihood that consumers will confuse JL Beverage's senior mark for the Pucker Vodka line. *See Walter v. Mattel, Inc.,* 210 F.3d 1108, 1111 n. 2 (9th Cir.2000) ("In a reverse confusion case ... the inquiry focuses on the strength of the junior mark because the issue is whether the junior mark is so strong as to overtake the senior mark"). The national recognition of the Jim Beam mark increases the likelihood that consumers will believe they are doing business with Jim Beam, not JL Beverage, when they purchase Johnny Love Vodka. *See Cohn v. Petsmart, Inc.,* 281 F.3d 837, 842 (9th Cir.2002) (explaining that, in reverse confusion cases, the junior mark holder's commercial strength "creates a potential that consumers will assume that" the senior holder's mark refers to the junior holder's mark, "and thus perceive that the businesses are somehow associated").

To support its forward confusion claim, JL Beverage argues in the alternative that it too has a strong market presence. JL Beverage submitted evidence that it sold its products nationally, and that it spent considerable resources on marketing through print media, third-party publications, and internet advertising.

Viewing the evidence in the light most favorable to JL Beverage, there is a genuine dispute of material fact as to the commercial strength of JL Beverage's Johnny Love Vodka in the marketplace. Moreover, the determination as to whether the evidence demonstrates that JL Beverage has robust commercial strength will lend support to JL Beverage whatever the fact-finder decides, as JL Beverage has raised both forward and reverse confusion claims.

B.

We now address factor three of the *Sleekcraft* test, the similarity of the marks. JL Beverage contends that the similarity of shape and color in the competing lips designs renders the marks similar.

Similarity of the marks "has always been considered a critical question in the likelihood-of-confusion analysis." *GoTo.com,* 202 F.3d at 1205. Three principles guide a court in determining whether marks are similar. *Fortune Dynamic,* 618 F.3d at 1032. First, "similarity is best adjudged by appearance, sound, and meaning." *Id.* (citation and alteration omitted). "Second, the marks must be considered in their entirety and as they appear in the marketplace." *Id.* (citation omitted). "Third, similarities are weighed more heavily than differences." *Id.* (quoting *GoTo.com,* 202 F.3d at 1206).

In viewing the competing JL Beverage and Jim Beam marks in their entirety, there are numerous similarities in their appearance: both have puckered, human lips as the focal point of their design; the lips have a similar angle and shape; and the lips are color-coordinated with the flavor of the vodka. In addition to the photos of the marks, which suggest a similar appearance, JL Beverage offered evidence from officials who concluded that the marks are similar. First, JL Beverage relies upon the Chief Administrator of the North Carolina Alcoholic Beverage Control Commission's (NCABCC) statement that the Jim Beam mark "looks a lot like" JL Beverage's design. Second, it provided evidence that a USPTO Examiner stated, in his initial review of Jim Beam's application to register its lips, that the Jim Beam and JL Beverage "marks are highly similar lip designs oriented at a similar angle. Consequently, the marks create an overall similar commercial impression." The entirety p.1110 of the marks' appearances, coupled with documented statements stating that the marks appear similar, establishes a genuine dispute of material fact concerning their similarity.

In response, Jim Beam first argues that the marks are "dramatically different" because the bottle shapes are distinct, the product labeling is not similar, and both products prominently feature their house marks. While a fact-finder may ultimately conclude that these factors render the marks dissimilar, Jim Beam's competing factual analysis does nothing to alleviate the existence of a dispute of material fact concerning the marks' similarity.

Jim Beam next contends that the USPTO Examiner's statement is unpersuasive as it was only a preliminary assessment for determining whether its lips design would be trademarked. Regardless of whether the statement was the result of a preliminary assessment, it suggests that others found the marks similar.

C.

The fourth factor of the *Sleekcraft* test looks to evidence of actual consumer confusion. *Surfvivor,* 406 F.3d at 633. JL Beverage contends that there is evidence of actual consumer confusion through Shaun Robertson, a manager of one of JL Beverage's product brokers, who submitted a declaration with an attached email in which he lists instances of confusion about which individuals informed him. The district court, although it did not ultimately rule on the admissibility of the statements in Robertson's declaration, concluded in its preliminary injunction order that factor four favored neither party because the evidence was hearsay, and unreliable, and because many of the cited instances actually showed a lack of consumer confusion.

Robertson's declaration presents a smattering of statements that JL Beverage alleges serve as evidence of actual consumer confusion. For instance, Robertson reported that a woman named Missy Giblin contacted Robertson stating that she saw JL Beverage's new commercial for Johnny Love Vodka, when in fact JL Beverage was not running commercials at that time; a man named Sam Mills told Robertson that he mistakenly purchased Pucker Vodka, having thought it was Johnny Love Vodka; and Micheal C. Herring, the Chief Administrator of the NCABCC, sent Robertson an email that stated "see attached. This is Jim Beam's new line of vodka. Looks a lot like Johnny Love."

Jim Beam argues, and the district court correctly concluded, that the statements contained in Robertson's declaration and email are hearsay. *See Japan Telecom., Inc. v. Japan Telecom, Am. Inc.*, 287 F.3d 866, 874 n. 1 (9th Cir.2002) (concluding that statements made by the declarant that the declarant knows of others who were confused by similar trademarks are inadmissible hearsay). Almost all of the instances that Robertson recounts are statements that he gathered from others via email, telephone calls, or text messages. At times, Robertson even fails to specify where or how some of the alleged conversations took place.

We note, however, that at summary judgment a district court may consider hearsay evidence submitted in an inadmissible form, so long as the underlying evidence could be provided in an admissible form at trial, such as by live testimony. *See Fraser v. Goodale*, 342 F.3d 1032, 1036-37 (9th Cir.2003). But here, JL Beverage has not argued that the hearsay declarants would be available to testify at trial, or that its hearsay evidence would be admissible at trial in some other form. We address, therefore, only the district court's conclusion that the statements discussed in Robertson's declaration are hearsay, not subject to an exception.

p.1111 In addition to being hearsay, some of the reported statements were provided to Robertson by friends and acquaintances. For example, Diab testified that while he personally did not know Missy Giblin, he believed that she was a friend of Robertson and his co-worker. In addition, text messages Robertson received on his personal cell phone, which suggested consumer confusion, showed that Robertson and the sender had a high level of familiarity, as the messages contained phrases such as "hey babes," "dude," and "call me back hun." Evidence from such "partial source[s] possesses very limited probative value." *Filipino Yellow Pages v. Asian Journal Publ'ns, Inc.*, 198 F.3d 1143, 1152 (9th Cir.1999).

JL Beverage acknowledges that the statements submitted in Robertson's declaration are hearsay, but alleges that at least some of the statements are admissible under the "state of mind" exception to the hearsay rule. Federal Rule of Evidence 803(3) allows admission of "[a] statement of the declarant's then-existing state of mind ... or emotional, sensory, or physical condition."

To support its argument, JL Beverage relies heavily on *Lahoti v. Vericheck, Inc.,* 636 F.3d 501, 509 (9th Cir.2011) (*Lahoti II*), which admitted hearsay statements regarding consumer confusion under the state of mind exception. In *Lahoti II,* the court admitted testimony from Vericheck company representatives who received telephone calls from confused customers who could not find information about Vericheck on the website www.Vericheck.com, which the defendant had created. *Id.* The statements in Robertson's declaration differ from the testimony in *Lahoti II* in two important ways. First, many of the alleged conversations Robertson had were not with customers calling because they were currently confused and seeking information about JL Beverage; rather, the individuals were reporting, after the fact, that they had mistaken two products. Second, unlike the spontaneous calls of confusion that company representatives received in *Lahoti II,* Robertson received some of the reports of confusion from possible biased sources: his friends and acquaintances. Accordingly, JL Beverage's reliance on *Lahoti II* is of little help.

Finally, some of the statements included in the declaration, including Herring's, state only that the Johnny Love Vodka and Pucker Vodka products "look alike." Statements that the products look alike do not necessarily demonstrate consumer confusion: consumers who identify products as "looking alike" recognize the products' similarities, but the question is whether they have mistaken one product for another.

Whether JL Beverage may be able to supplement its evidence of actual consumer confusion through further discovery is not known. However, as it now stands, this evidence of actual consumer confusion does not weigh in JL Beverage's favor. Nevertheless, as we have previously held, "[b]ecause of the difficulty in garnering" evidence of actual confusion, "the failure to prove instances of actual confusion is not dispositive." *Sleekcraft,* 599 F.2d at 353.

D.

We turn last to factor seven of the *Sleekcraft* test, which assesses the defendant's intent in selecting the mark. JL Beverage contends that Jim Beam knew of the registered JLV and Lips Marks, yet proceeded to use a colored lips logo on its Pucker Vodka bottles.

Factor seven favors the plaintiff "where the alleged infringer adopted his mark with knowledge, actual or constructive, that it was another's trademark." *Brookfield Comnc'ns, Inc. v. W. Coast Entm't* p.1112 *Corp.,* 174 F.3d 1036, 1059 (9th Cir.1999). When "an alleged infringer knowingly adopts a mark similar to another's, courts will presume an intent to deceive the public." *Official Airline Guides, Inc. v. Goss,* 6 F.3d 1385, 1394 (9th Cir.1993).

JL Beverage has set forth evidence to create a genuine dispute of material fact as to whether Jim Beam knew of JL Beverage's registered trademarks, yet proceeded to use its colored-lips logo anyway. JL Beverage provided the following: (1) as a result of a trademark search that Jim Beam's legal team performed, Jim Beam was aware of JL Beverage's JLV trademark; (2) Jim Beam employee Emily Johnson, who worked with a Pucker flavored-vodka team, was aware of Johnny Love Vodka prior to joining Jim Beam; and (3) Jim Beam continued its nationwide rollout of Pucker Vodka even after the USPTO denied its trademark application; as a basis for that denial, the USPTO identified the similarity of Jim Beam's proposed marks to JL Beverage's.

Jim Beam contends that we should nonetheless conclude that factor seven weighs in its favor because there is no evidence that Jim Beam intended to infringe JL Beverage's trademarks. Unfortunately for Jim Beam, "[a]bsence of malice is no defense to trademark infringement." *Dreamwerks*, 142 F.3d at 1132 n.12. The relevant inquiry is not Jim Beam's intent, but rather whether it adopted the colored lips logo with the knowledge that the mark already belonged to JL Beverage. Viewing the evidence in the light most favorable to JL Beverage, there is a dispute of material fact concerning what Jim Beam knew when it launched the Pucker Vodka line.

IV.

In ruling on the parties' cross-motions for summary judgment, the district court does not appear to have viewed the evidence in the light most favorable to JL Beverage and to determine whether a genuine dispute of material fact existed. Balancing the *Sleekcraft* factors as a whole, we conclude there is a genuine dispute of material fact as to the likelihood of consumer confusion. A reasonable fact-finder could conclude that: the JLV Mark has conceptual strength because the Mark's salient feature, the color-coordinated lips, requires consumers to use their imagination to connect the color to the vodka flavor; the Lips Mark has conceptual strength because the lips have no commonly understood connection to the vodka product; Johnny Love Vodka does or does not have commercial strength (because a finding of either would support one of JL Beverage's theories of confusion- reverse or forward); Johnny Love and Pucker Vodka are related flavored-liquor products sold to the same customers and distributors; the products are similar given their use of color-coordinated, puckered human lips as the focal point of their bottle designs; consumers purchasing the vodka products are not likely to exercise a high degree of care in distinguishing between the two; and Jim Beam was aware of JL Beverage's trademarks prior to rolling out its Pucker Vodka line. Accordingly, we reverse and remand for further proceedings consistent with this opinion.

REVERSED and REMANDED.

820 F.3d 979 (2016)

UNITED STATES of America, Plaintiff-Appellee

v.

Jerry GOLLIHER, Defendant-Appellant.

No. 15-1586.

United States Court of Appeals, Eighth Circuit.

Submitted: November 20, 2015.

Filed: April 28, 2016.

US v. Golliher, 820 F. 3d 979 (8th Cir. 2016)

p.981 Appeal from United States District Court for the District of South Dakota — Rapid City.

Jeffrey Robert Connolly, Rapid City, SD, Bian L. Gardner, Michael S. Weinstein, p.982 New York, NY, for Plaintiff-Appellee.

Kevin Koliner, AUSA, Sioux Falls, SD, for Defendant-Appellant.

Before SMITH, BYE, and BENTON, Circuit Judges.

SMITH, Circuit Judge.

Jerry Golliher was convicted by a jury of attempted commercial sex trafficking of a minor. He appeals, arguing that his counsel was ineffective and that the district court[1] should have admitted certain e-mails, provided the trial transcript to the jury in response to a jury question, and stricken the prosecutor's allegedly improper statements. We affirm.

I. *Background*

Law enforcement placed the following advertisement on a website: "Here for the [Biker] Rally with 2 younger girls that are down for most anything. Age makes no difference so don't be afraid to ask." Golliher responded to that Internet ad by e-mail, not knowing that law enforcement had placed it as part of a sex-trafficking sting operation. The officer who received Golliher's e-mail responded, "Bobbi is 13 almost 14 and Toni is 12. They both have experience and are good to go. Let me know what you [think]." After an interchange that included age-regressed photos and a discussion of price and a meeting location, Golliher, expecting to pick up Bobbi, met undercover law enforcement. Golliher got out of his car and got into the car of the undercover officer, whom Golliher believed to be Bobbi's pimp. When the officer asked Golliher what he wanted, Golliher indicated that he was willing to pay the discussed $150 for half an hour with Bobbi. The officer promptly arrested Golliher. Golliher was charged with one count of attempted commercial sex trafficking of a minor, in violation of 18 U.S.C. §§ 1591(a)(1), 1591(b)(1), and 1594(a).

Before trial, the government sought to prohibit Golliher from introducing at trial e-mails that he had previously exchanged with purported prostitutes in which he rebuffed their services upon learning that they were underage. Golliher asserts that the e-mails would have impacted the jury's deliberations significantly because they showed that he was not interested in underage sex. The court excluded the e-mails as hearsay. But the court and the prosecution recognized that Golliher might be permitted to introduce the e-mails as a prior consistent statement should the prosecution call into question whether the events took place. Golliher never recounted the events surrounding those e-mails during his voluntary testimony nor offered the e-mails for admission into evidence.

During the prosecutor's closing argument, he discussed the law of entrapment and the elements of the crime of attempt. The prosecutor explained the entrapment defense this way:

> Let's flip over to the next instruction, ladies and gentlemen. Instruction number 3. Entrapment. What ... you have to decide is was the defendant willing to do this or did somebody have to talk him into it? Did somebody have to twist his arm? In this case, the evidence showed two things. The government proved beyond a reasonable doubt that the defendant was willing [on] August 2, 2013, to go out on to the Internet to try to obtain a young girl for sex in exchange for $150. The government proved beyond a p.983 reasonable doubt that nobody forced him to do it. Nobody forced him to do it. The government has to prove one of these two things. Not both, but the evidence shows that he willingly did it and the evidence shows that nobody forced him to do it. He did it all on his own. He knew what he was doing and he took those steps all on his own.

The prosecutor made the following statements about the crime of attempt:

> The other issue is whether or not there was a substantial step and whether or not he took that step. Ladies and gentlemen, we don't have to prove that he had sex, obviously, but we also don't have to prove that he would have had sex. It is up to you to decide whether a substantial step was made. And I would focus you on the section down here which is that it not be incompatible with innocence, yet it must be necessary to the consummation of the crime and to be of such a nature that a reasonable observer, viewing it in context, could conclude beyond a reasonable doubt that it was undertaken in accordance with a design to violate the statute. We don't have to prove that he would have done it; we have to prove that he took a substantial step to engage in commercial sex trafficking, not that at the end of the day that was what he wanted. That's not what we have to prove.

The prosecutor also said the following on the same topic:

> And then the next story was, you know, I wouldn't have gone through with it; I was pushed into it. And then he agreed that he showed up, that he was the one who was chatting, that he showed up, and then he said, "But I didn't agree to it. I was just looking into it. I hadn't decided." Ladies and gentlemen, that is not a defense. If you decide that he took a substantial step enough at the moment that he was arrested, if that at that moment the substantial step had been made, then this case is done. It doesn't matter whether or not he was going — what he was going to do at his house.

Also during closing argument, the prosecutor used the first-person pronouns *we* and *I* in asking the jury to convict Golliher. The prosecutor concluded his summation with the following:

> The government has proved [its] case, all of these elements that it was [not] an entrapment, beyond a reasonable doubt. And we ask that as you deliberate, we are confident as you deliberate, that you will agree the defendant is guilty

beyond a reasonable doubt of going on to the Internet and attempting to solicit a minor for sex for $150 on August 2, 2013. Thank you.

And the prosecutor ended his rebuttal this way:

He's guilty of attempted commercial sex trafficking. Of every element that we are required to prove, he's guilty beyond a reasonable doubt and I ask you to find him as such. Thank you.

After the jury retired to deliberate, the jury foreperson sent a note to the court expressing confusion about the evidence:

We have confusion on the age of Bobbi — being 13 or 14. There was an e-mail that stated she was 13 and the court proceedings stated Bobbi as 14.

The court responded:

As a judge, I cannot comment on the evidence. It is your job as the jury to determine the facts. You need to rely on your own recollection of the evidence and unanimously agree beyond a reasonable doubt.

This instruction should be taken together with the instructions I previously p.984 gave to you. The instructions must be considered as a whole.

After the jury returned a guilty verdict, the district court entered a final judgment of conviction. Golliher appeals. We have jurisdiction to review the conviction pursuant to 28 U.S.C. § 1291.

II. *Discussion*

On appeal, Golliher argues that (A) his trial counsel provided ineffective assistance of counsel; (B) the district court abused its discretion by not admitting Golliher's e-mails under the residual exception to the hearsay rule; (C) the district court plainly erred by not providing the trial transcript to the jurors in response to their question; and (D) the district court plainly erred by not striking certain statements that the prosecutor made to the jury.

A. *Ineffective Assistance of Counsel*

Golliher argues that it is "readily apparent" that his trial counsel was ineffective by not seeking to admit the allegedly exculpatory e-mails through the business records exception to the hearsay rule under Rule 803(6) of the Federal Rules of Evidence. He asserts that these e-mails contain conversations showing that he stopped communicating with any purported prostitute once he learned that she was a minor. Golliher used a Yahoo e-mail account. He reasons that these e-mails are Yahoo's business records. As such, he argues that his attorney should have sought their admission with the help of a records custodian from Yahoo. He contends that his attorney's failure to do so constituted ineffective assistance of counsel. We decline to address this argument.

"[W]e review claims of ineffective assistance of counsel on direct appeal only in 'exceptional cases.'" *United States v. Sanchez-Gonzalez*, 643 F.3d 626, 628 (8th Cir.2011) (citation omitted); *see also United States v. Soriano-Hernandez*, 310 F.3d 1099, 1105 & n. 9 (8th Cir.2002). One such exceptional case exists when "the alleged error of trial counsel is 'readily apparent.'" *Sanchez-Gonzalez*, 643 F.3d at 628-29 (citation omitted). We decline to consider Golliher's argument because he has not shown that his case is exceptional, warranting our examination of his claim of ineffective assistance of counsel on direct appeal rather than through a collateral attack in a habeas corpus action. It is not readily apparent that the e-mails would have been admissible in the manner that Golliher contends. On this record, we are unwilling to address Golliher's ineffective-assistance claim.

B. *Residual Exception to the Hearsay Rule*

The district court concluded that Golliher's e-mails, which allegedly show him rebuffing underage sex, were inadmissible under the residual exception to the hearsay rule, Rule 807 of the Federal Rules of Evidence. Golliher argues that the e-mails are admissible under the residual exception because they would have been more probative than any other form of evidence on the matter. Because Golliher has failed to provide us with any information with which to evaluate the probative quality of the e-mails, we affirm.

Rule 28(a)(8)(A) of the Federal Rules of Appellate Procedure requires an appellant's argument section to include "citations to the ... parts of the record on which the appellant relies." "We have in the past ... refused to consider arguments not supported by proper [record] citations." *Minn. Ass'n of Nurse Anesthetists v. Allina Health Sys. Corp.,* 276 F.3d 1032, 1055 n. 14 (8th Cir.2002) (citation omitted). We may therefore refuse to consider a challenge to a district court's decision p.985 to exclude evidence when the appellant fails to direct us to the part of the record that contains the substance of the excluded evidence, especially when the substance is necessary to evaluate admissibility under the Federal Rules of Evidence. *See Cody v. Harris,* 409 F.3d 853, 860-61 (7th Cir.2005) (declining to evaluate defendant's Rule 807 challenge because he had "not provided enough information to evaluate whether [the Rule 807] criteria have been met").

In this case, Golliher seeks to have certain e-mails admitted under the residual exception to the hearsay rule. That exception provides as follows:

> Under the following circumstances, a hearsay statement is not excluded by the rule against hearsay even if the statement is not specifically covered by a hearsay exception in Rule 803 or 804:
>
> (1) the statement has equivalent circumstantial guarantees of trustworthiness;
>
> (2) it is offered as evidence of a material fact;
>
> (3) *it is more probative on the point for which it is offered than any other evidence that the proponent can obtain through reasonable efforts;* and
>
> (4) admitting it will best serve the purposes of these rules and the interests of justice.

Fed.R.Evid. 807(a) (emphasis added). We are unable to evaluate whether Golliher's e-mails satisfy these requirements because Golliher has not presented their actual substance in any manner, either by reproducing them in the briefs or appendix or by providing record citations to them. The only record citation that Golliher provides is to the pretrial conference where he asked the court to admit the e-mails and the court excluded them. Golliher should have, at that time, complied with Rule 103(a)(2) of the Federal Rules of Evidence by "inform[ing] the court of [the e-mails'] substance by an offer of proof." Without an offer of proof to preserve in the record the substance of the excluded evidence, Golliher's arguments are left unsupported and unpersuasive. For example, Golliher asserts without any citation to the record that these e-mails are more probative than other evidence under the third prong of Rule 807. But we have no way of evaluating whether they are probative at all, let alone whether their probative character outweighed other forms of available evidence such as Golliher's own voluntary testimony. Accordingly, we decline to overturn the district court's exclusion of these e-mails because Golliher has failed to adhere to the requirements of Rule 28(a)(8)(A) of the Federal Rules of Appellate Procedure.

C. *The Jury's Question*

During jury deliberations, the foreperson sent a note to the court expressing confusion about whether the evidence showed that Bobbi was 13 or 14. In the note, the foreperson observed that documentary evidence showed that she was 13 but testimony had indicated that she was 14. The court replied, instructing the jurors to rely upon their own recollection. Golliher argues that it was plain error for the court not to offer the jurors the opportunity to review the relevant portions of the trial transcript during their deliberations as part of its supplemental instruction. We disagree.

Because Golliher did not object to the court's supplemental instruction, we review for plain error. *United States v. Hansen,* 791 F.3d 863, 870 (8th Cir.2015) (citing Fed.R.Crim.P. 30(d), 52(b)). Under this standard, Golliher must show "(1) an error, (2) that was plain, (3) [that] affects substantial rights, and (4) the error seriously affects the fairness, integrity or public p.986 reputation of judicial proceedings." *Id.* (quotations and citations omitted).

We have held that "[o]nly if it can be demonstrated that the failure to permit the reading of requested testimony created unfairness to the defendant is the defendant entitled to have the jury informed as a matter of right." *United States v. Bassler,* 651 F.2d 600, 603 (8th Cir.1981) (citation omitted). Golliher alleges that the importance of the subject matter about which the jury expressed confusion renders the court's failure to offer the transcript to the jury unfair. There is no doubt that the jury's conclusion that Bobbi was 13 instead of 14 had a significant impact on his sentence.[2] But that does not make the district court's failure to offer the trial transcript to the jury somehow erroneous or prejudicially unfair. Golliher has presented no evidence from the trial transcript indicating that Bobbi was actually 14. The government's brief quotes seven examples of trial testimony suggesting that Bobbi was 13, not 14. Put simply, Golliher has failed to make the required showing that the court's supplemental instruction constituted an error — plain or otherwise.

D. *Prosecutorial Misconduct*

Lastly, Golliher argues that the district court plainly erred by failing to strike alleged prosecutorial misconduct in the prosecutor's statements to the jury. First, he argues that the prosecutor misstated the law of entrapment by repeatedly using the phrase "nobody forced him to do it." Second, he argues that the prosecutor told the jury that the government did not have to prove that Golliher intended to commit the crime. Third, he argues that the prosecutor improperly vouched for Golliher's guilt by using the personal pronouns *I* and *we.* Our review is for plain error because Golliher did not object to any of these statements. *See Hansen,* 791 F.3d at 870 (citing Fed.R.Crim.P. 30(d), 52(b)).

1. *Misstatement of the Law of Entrapment*

Golliher first argues that the prosecutor misstated the law of entrapment by equating persuasion with force. During his closing argument, the prosecutor said, "The government proved beyond a reasonable doubt that nobody forced him to do it.... The government has to prove one of these two things. Not both, but the evidence shows that he willingly did it and the evidence shows that nobody forced him to do it." Golliher reasons that the prosecutor's statements were improper. We agree. Nevertheless, we affirm because these statements were harmless in light of the court's correct instructions to the jury.

The district court gave the following jury instruction on the law of entrapment:

> One of the issues in this case is whether the defendant was entrapped. The prosecution has the burden of proving beyond a reasonable doubt that the defendant was not entrapped [because] either:
>
> 1. The defendant was willing to commit the crime of sex trafficking of a child before he was approached or contacted by law enforcement agents or someone acting for the government.
>
> Or 2. The government or someone acting for the government did not *persuade or talk the defendant into committing the crime* of sex trafficking of a child.
>
> p.987 If you find that the prosecution proved at least one of these two things beyond a reasonable doubt, then you must reject the defendant's claim of entrapment. If you find the prosecution failed to prove at least one of these two things beyond a reasonable doubt, then you must find the defendant not guilty.

(Emphasis added.) There is a discrepancy between the law of entrapment as instructed by the court and as represented by the prosecutor. The second prong of the entrapment instruction required the government to prove that it did not "persuade or talk the defendant into committing the crime." But the prosecutor equated this standard with something akin to arm twisting or force. The prosecutor said, "The government has to prove one of these two things," "that the defendant was willing" or "that nobody forced him to do it." Such a discrepancy amounts to more than inartful recitation of the standard; it eroded the presumption of innocence by lowering the government's burden of proof. *See Kellogg v. Skon,* 176 F.3d 447, 451 (8th Cir.1999).

But improper statements alone do not warrant a new trial under plain-error review. "In determining whether the prosecutor's argument rendered the trial unfair, we consider the totality of the circumstances." *Id.* (citations omitted). Where the court properly instructs the jury, defense counsel reinforces the court's instruction, and there is no objection at trial, an improper statement of the law by the prosecutor does not undermine the fairness of the trial. *Id.* In this case, Golliher has not asserted that the court improperly instructed the jury. Indeed, his trial counsel openly approved of the instructions, describing them as "just wonderful." And he admonished the jury not to "underestimate the work that went into that by the Court and everybody else .... [T]his is not a talking points memo. This is the law and the only way this system works is if you follow the law and follow that oath."

Moreover, the evidence in this case shows that Golliher was not persuaded or talked into obtaining 13-year-old Bobbi for sex. Golliher drove to the predetermined location, where he expected to meet Bobbi's pimp. He got out of his car and into the undercover officer's car. The undercover officer asked Golliher what he was looking for. Golliher replied, "Probably half [an hour]." When the undercover officer asked Golliher if he had the money, Golliher pulled cash out of his pocket. Finally, Golliher told the undercover officer, "I am not going to hurt her. I am not going to scare her. I am a real gentle guy." In short, the prosecutor's improper statement of the law was harmless because the evidence indicates that Golliher needed no persuasion. He did not need to be talked into anything; he willfully sought to obtain 13-year-old Bobbi for sex.

2. *Intent*

Golliher next argues that the prosecutor removed intent from the elements of the crime. He points to two statements by the prosecutor. First, the prosecutor said, "We don't have to prove that he would have done it; we have to prove that he took a substantial step to engage in commercial sex trafficking, not that at the end of the day that was what he wanted." Second, the prosecutor said, "It doesn't matter whether or not he was going — what he was going to do at his house." Golliher argues that these statements are a misstatement of the law. We disagree.

The context of these statements makes clear that the prosecutor was discussing the substantial step required to find attempt. In that context, these statements p.988 were not plainly improper. And because the court properly instructed the jury with respect to the required element of intent, any impropriety was harmless. *See Kellogg,* 176 F.3d at 451.

3. *Vouching*

Golliher finally argues that the prosecutor improperly vouched for Golliher's guilt. He points to the closing lines of the prosecutor's summation and rebuttal where the prosecutor made the following two statements using the first-person pronouns we and *I:* "[W]e are confident as you deliberate, that you will agree the defendant is guilty beyond a reasonable doubt." And, "I ask you to find him" guilty. Golliher argues that these statements show that the prosecutor "clearly inject[ed] personal beliefs into the process." We disagree.

"Although the use of [the first person by a prosecutor during arguments] has been often criticized (and discouraged) by this court and others, it is not always improper." *United States v. Bentley,* 561 F.3d 803, 811 (8th Cir.2009) (citations omitted). "It is only improper when it suggests that the government has special knowledge of evidence not presented to the jury, carries an implied guarantee of truthfulness, or expresses a personal opinion about credibility." *Id.* at 812 (citations omitted). Moreover, we have held that passing use of the first person "is not plain error if it is used 'to refer the jury to the government's evidence and to summarize the government's case against the defendants.'" *Id.* (citation omitted).

In this case, the statements of which Golliher complains do not indicate anything about the personal belief of the prosecutor. In both cases, the prosecutor is urging the jury to consider the evidence and the elements of the crime and to find Golliher guilty. Accordingly, these statements were not plainly improper.

III. *Conclusion*

For these reasons, we affirm Golliher's conviction.

[1] The Honorable Karen E. Schreier, United States District Judge for the District of South Dakota.

[2] The government charged Golliher with violation of 18 U.S.C. § 1591. Under that section, a defendant's minimum sentence increases from 10 years to 15 years if the minor was below age 14.

FEDERAL CIRCUIT DECISIONS

The Rule Against Hearsay

No cases were selected for publication.

DC Circuit Decisions

The Rule Against Hearsay

752 F.3d 470 (2014)

UNITED STATES of America, Appellee

v.

Morris B. FAHNBULLEH, Appellant.

Nos. 11-3045, 11-3047.

United States Court of Appeals, District of Columbia Circuit.

Argued October 16, 2013.

Decided June 13, 2014.

US v. Fahnbulleh, 752 F. 3d 470 (DC Cir. 2014)

p.473 Barbara E. Kittay, appointed by the court, argued the cause and filed the briefs for appellant Morris B. Fahnbulleh.

Charles B. Wayne, appointed by the court, argued the cause and filed the briefs for appellant Joe O. Bondo.

David P. Saybolt, Assistant U.S. Attorney, argued the cause for appellee. With him on the brief were Ronald C. Machen, Jr., U.S. Attorney, and Elizabeth Trosman and Elizabeth H. Danello, Assistant U.S. Attorneys.

Before GARLAND, Chief Judge, SRINIVASAN, Circuit Judge, and SENTELLE, Senior Circuit Judge.

Opinion for the Court filed by Senior Circuit Judge SENTELLE.

SENTELLE, Senior Circuit Judge:

Joe Bondo and Morris Fahnbulleh were charged with and convicted of several counts of fraud in connection with their work on a humanitarian aid program in Africa funded by an agency of the United States government. They seek reversal of their conviction, or failing that, vacation of their sentences, alleging various errors made by the district court in the trial proceedings. For the reasons stated herein, we affirm the judgment of the district court.

p.474 BACKGROUND

The United States Agency for International Development ("USAID") initiated a food aid program, known as a Food-for-Work program, for the African country of Liberia. Under the program, Liberian communities would provide labor to perform community projects such as digging wells and repairing roads, and laborers would receive food for their services. To implement the program, the USAID contracted with humanitarian organization Catholic Relief Services ("CRS"). CRS in turn subcontracted with another humanitarian organization, World Vision, which administered the program in three counties in Liberia through its federated organization, World Vision International (hereinafter collectively referred to as "World Vision"). Appellants Morris Fahnbulleh and Joe Bondo worked for World Vision on the USAID subcontract from 2005 to 2007. Bondo was a food monitor and Food-for-Work officer, and Fahnbulleh was the World Vision commodities manager in Liberia.

In 2009 Bondo and Fahnbulleh were arrested and charged with fraud allegedly committed on the Liberia Food-for-Work program. In particular, they were each charged with one count of conspiracy to defraud the United States (18 U.S.C. §§

371, 2), one count of conspiracy to commit mail and wire fraud (18 U.S.C. §§ 1349, 2), four counts of mail fraud (18 U.S.C. § 1512(b)(1)), two counts of wire fraud (18 U.S.C. §§ 1343, 2), and four counts of false claims (18 U.S.C. §§ 287, 2). Bondo was further charged with two counts of witness tampering (18 U.S.C. § 1512(b)(1)). Fahnbulleh and Bondo were tried together by a jury. Fahnbulleh was convicted on all counts, while Bondo was acquitted on the conspiracy to commit mail fraud and wire fraud count, but convicted on the other charges. Both were sentenced by the district court to 142 months imprisonment.

Bondo and Fahnbulleh now appeal their convictions and sentences.

DISCUSSION

Between them, Bondo and Fahnbulleh make five main arguments on appeal: 1) they were denied a speedy trial; 2) the district court lacked subject matter jurisdiction and venue; 3) the district court erred by admitting two government exhibits into evidence; 4) the district court erred in denying a motion by Bondo for a mistrial; and 5) the district court improperly calculated Fahnbulleh's and Bondo's sentencing guidelines range. We discuss each argument below.

A. Speedy Trial

After investigating allegations that fraud had been committed by World Vision employees during the Liberia Food-for-Work program, federal authorities arrested Fahnbulleh and Bondo. Bondo was held for approximately seven months and Fahnbulleh approximately five months before being indicted. Both Bondo and Fahnbulleh argue that their cases should have been dismissed under the Speedy Trial Act ("STA"), 18 U.S.C. § 3161 *et seq.*

Appellants correctly point out that 18 U.S.C. § 3161(b) requires that "[a]ny information or indictment charging an individual with the commission of an offense shall be filed within thirty days from the date on which such individual was arrested...." However, the STA provides for exclusion of certain periods from this 30 day limit. At the time of Bondo's and Fahnbulleh's arrests (two months apart) in mid-2009, the government filed motions seeking to exclude periods of delay from the 30 day limit. In particular, the government requested delays pursuant to p.475 § 3161(h)(8) of the STA, which excludes a period of time, "not to exceed one year," from the 30-day period if the government has requested assistance in obtaining evidence from a foreign country. In support of its motions, the government attached a letter sent in early 2009 from the U.S. Department of Justice ("DOJ") to the Liberian government, seeking documents relating to the alleged fraud in the Liberia Food-for-Work program. The district court granted the motions. In late 2009 Bondo and Fahnbulleh were indicted.

Fahnbulleh asserts that § 3161(h)(8)'s directive that the exclusion "not ... exceed one year" suggests that before an exclusion is granted the district court must determine on the record what time period would be in the interest of justice and how that would outweigh the interest of the defendant and the public in a speedy trial. Fahnbulleh argues that the district court undertook no such review, making it appear that any length of time, not exceeding one year, requires no further examination. He contends that he was seriously prejudiced in his long wait for indictment, including loss of employment and financial resources, and the anxiety, physical illness, and humiliation associated with prolonged detention. Fahnbulleh further contends that the balance of this prejudice against the government's alleged need to await additional foreign evidence was not considered or addressed by the district court. Bondo makes arguments similar to Fahnbulleh's, contending that the district court was obligated to look behind the reasons for the government's exclusion-of-time motion, requiring the government to set forth specific facts to warrant further extension, including detailed information about the status of the foreign evidence request, what actions the government had taken in the intervening months, what additional efforts it would make, and why an indictment could not be returned without the foreign evidence.

"We review a district court's Speedy Trial Act determination de novo as to matters of law, and for clear error as to findings of fact." *United States v. Stubblefield,* 643 F.3d 291, 294 (D.C.Cir.2011) (internal citation, quotation marks, and alteration brackets omitted). Here, the government requested, and the district court granted, an extension of time under the STA pursuant to 18 U.S.C. § 3161(h)(8), which provides:

> Any period of delay, not to exceed one year, ordered by a district court upon an application of a party and a finding by a preponderance of the evidence that an official request ... has been made for evidence of any such offense and that it reasonably appears, or reasonably appeared at the time the request was made, that such evidence is, or was, in such foreign country.

We agree with the government that § 3161(h)(8) sets out only two requirements: (1) that a request for foreign evidence be made; and (2) that it reasonably appears that the evidence is in the foreign country. Referencing the early 2009 letter sent by DOJ to the government of Liberia requesting documents relevant to its investigation, the district court found by a preponderance of the evidence that a request had been made to Liberia for documents and that it reasonably appeared that these documents were in Liberia. The district court consequently granted the government's requests for a period of delay. We conclude that the district court did not clearly err in granting the § 3161(h)(8) delay periods.

B. Subject Matter Jurisdiction and Venue

Prior to trial, the district court denied Fahnbulleh's motion for dismissal p.476 of his case for lack of subject matter jurisdiction and improper venue. Pursuant to 18 U.S.C. § 3231, "[t]he district courts of the United States shall have original jurisdiction... of all offenses against the laws of the United States." "[I]f an indictment or information alleges the violation of a crime set out in Title 18 or in one of the other statutes defining federal crimes, that is the end of the jurisdictional inquiry." *United States v. George,* 676 F.3d 249, 259 (1st Cir.2012) (internal quotation omitted). Fahnbulleh and Bondo were charged with and found guilty of numerous crimes set out in Title 18. No more is necessary to establish subject matter jurisdiction.

Nevertheless, Fahnbulleh (and Bondo by adoption) argues that the district court should have granted his motion to dismiss his case for lack of subject matter jurisdiction because the evidence failed to demonstrate any agreement to defraud the United States, as opposed to an agreement to defraud private parties. Because that argument rests on the evidentiary proof at trial, it does not in fact impugn the district court's subject matter jurisdiction. Instead, it sounds in the nature of a claim that the evidence was insufficient to establish any conspiracy to defraud the United States. So understood, we find the argument unpersuasive. Fahnbulleh's argument on this proposition proceeds as follows: in implementing the Food-for-Work program, the USAID contracted with Catholic Relief Services, which in turn contracted with Fahnbulleh's employer World Vision to administer the program in three counties in Liberia. World Vision had no privity with the United States. If World Vision did commit a crime, it was against CRS and not the United States, and disputes between private parties do not provide a basis for subject matter jurisdiction. While Fahnbulleh's argument is orderly, it is not ultimately persuasive.

A similar argument was rejected by the Supreme Court in *Tanner v. United States,* 483 U.S. 107, 107 S.Ct. 2739, 97 L.Ed.2d 90 (1987). In that case, a Florida corporation — Seminole Electric Cooperative, Inc. ("Seminole") — received a bank loan for a power plant construction project which included an access road. The loan was guaranteed by the Rural Electrification Administration ("REA"), a credit agency of the United States Department of Agriculture. One of the defendants, Conover, was the procurement manager at Seminole; the other defendant, Tanner, was a friend of his who owned a limerock mine. During construction of the power plant, Conover's department at Seminole prepared two contracts favorable to Tanner to use Tanner's limerock in constructing the access road. At about this same time Tanner made payments to Conover for thousands of dollars, allegedly on their personal transactions. During performance of the two contracts, Conover made misrepresentations to Tanner's bonding company on the access road's state of completion. Conover and Tanner were subsequently indicted for and convicted of, *inter alia,* conspiracy to defraud the United States in violation of 18 U.S.C. § 371. *Id.* at 110-13, 107 S.Ct. 2739. They argued that if they were guilty of a conspiracy to defraud, the target of the conspiracy was Seminole and not the United States. *Id.* at 129, 107 S.Ct. 2739. The Supreme Court disagreed, stating that "[i]f the evidence presented at trial was sufficient to establish that petitioners conspired to cause Seminole to make misrepresentations to the REA, then petitioners' convictions may stand." *Id.* at 132, 107 S.Ct. 2739. So too here.

Evidence presented at trial of this case showed that pursuant to its contract with CRS, World Vision was to follow U.S. grant regulations and to provide U.S.-mandated reports on implementation of the p.477 Food-for-Work program. These reports were generated from the collection of raw data on eight forms. Many of the raw data forms referenced the USAID funding; Bondo signed and verified many of these forms; and Fahnbulleh verified their accuracy. Included among the U.S.-mandated reports were recipient status reports ("RSRs") and commodity status reports ("CSRs"), to be provided monthly to CRS, as well as financial reports and narrative reports, to be provided quarterly. CRS in turn reformatted these reports and sent them on to USAID. Furthermore, the evidence showed that Fahnbulleh was involved in sending the CSRs, RSRs, and narrative reports to Washington, D.C., at times emailing the reports to Washington himself. As in *Tanner,* "the evidence presented at trial was sufficient to establish that [Fahnbulleh and Bondo] conspired to cause [CRS] to make misrepresentations to [USAID] ... [Fahnbulleh's and Bondo's] convictions may stand."

* * * * * *

Fahnbulleh goes on to argue that the district court erred in denying his motion to dismiss his case for lack of venue. He further argues that the court again erred when it denied his request for a jury instruction on venue. According to Fahnbulleh, venue was not proper here because none of the alleged co-conspirators ever stepped foot into the District of Columbia. He claims that any acts committed within D.C. constituted only innocent acts of U.S. government employees, paying claims submitted by CRS. First, we note that venue for a conspiracy prosecution lies anywhere an overt act is committed. *United States v. Rosenberg*, 888 F.2d 1406, 1415 (D.C.Cir.1989). As noted in our subject matter jurisdiction discussion above, Fahnbulleh and Bondo caused fraudulent reports to be sent to Washington in furtherance of the conspiracy. For the same reason, venue was proper for the substantive offenses. Pursuant to 18 U.S.C. § 3237(a), mail fraud "may be inquired of and prosecuted in any district ... into which such commerce [or] mail matter moves." Also, pursuant to 18 U.S.C. § 3732(a), venue for wire fraud lies in any jurisdiction to or from which the communication was transmitted. Finally, venue for false claims is properly laid where, *inter alia*, the claim is received. *See United States v. Leahy*, 82 F.3d 624, 633 (5th Cir.1996).

As to the failure of the district court to deliver the proffered instruction on venue to the jury, we perceive no reversible error. It is established law in this circuit with respect to venue instructions that a venue "instruction is necessary only when the question of venue is genuinely in issue." *United States v. Haire*, 371 F.3d 833, 840 (D.C.Cir.2004). Various courts have dealt differently with the question of when venue is at issue so as to require an instruction. *See United States v. Perez*, 280 F.3d 318, 333-35 (3d Cir.2002) (collecting cases). In *Haire*, we expressly adopted and followed the Third Circuit's analysis in *Perez*, concluding "that the instruction is necessary only when the question of venue is genuinely in issue." 371 F.3d at 840. The *Perez* holding establishes that

> Even if a defendant properly objects to venue ... it does not become a fact question for the jury unless and until the defendant also places it in issue by establishing a genuine issue of material fact with regard to venue. 280 F.3d at 335.

The unrebutted evidence discussed above clearly established that there is no genuine issue of material fact with reference to venue, and the refusal of the district judge to offer the venue instruction is not error.

p.478 C. Admission of Government Exhibits 100 and 104

Over objection of defense counsel, the trial judge admitted into evidence Government Exhibits 100 and 104. Exhibit 100 consisted of 36 binders containing over 10,000 pages of raw data collected, using eight different forms, on the Liberia Food-for-Work program. The government called to the witness stand Eric Fullilove, Chief Financial Officer of World Vision International, to authenticate the contents of Exhibit 100. It was admitted into evidence under Fed.R.Evid. 803(6), the business records exception to the hearsay rule. That rule provides for the admission of

> [a] memorandum, report, record, or data compilation, in any form, of acts, events, conditions, opinions, or diagnoses, made at or near the time by, or from information transmitted by, a person with knowledge, if kept in the course of a regularly conducted business activity, and if it was the regular practice of that business activity to make the memorandum, report, record or data compilation, all as shown by the testimony of the custodian or other qualified witness ... unless the source of information or the method or circumstances of preparation indicate lack of trustworthiness.

Fahnbulleh and Bondo both argue that the district court erred in allowing into evidence Government Exhibit 100. Fahnbulleh contends that the government did not demonstrate authenticity or trustworthiness as required by Rule 803(6), because Fullilove had no personal familiarity with the documents as he did not work at World Vision until after the project was completed; he reviewed but did not conduct the audit of the records; and he had never been to Liberia. For his part, Bondo argues that Fullilove's testimony to admit Exhibit 100 failed in fulfilling Rule 803(6)'s requirement that the information in the records be transmitted by a person with knowledge. According to Bondo, the district court admitted the 36 binders comprising Exhibit 100 on nothing more than Fullilove's conclusory statement that the records were maintained by World Vision in the ordinary course of business. Since these records were the "guts of the government's documentary evidence against" him, argues Bondo, their admission into evidence without a proper foundation affected his substantial rights.

We review the district court's admission of business records for abuse of discretion. *United States v. Gurr,* 471 F.3d 144, 151 (D.C.Cir.2006). As Fahnbulleh correctly notes, under Fed. R. of Evid. 803(6), records of a regularly conducted activity are to be admitted at trial as an exception to the rule against hearsay if: (A) the records were made at or near the time by someone with knowledge; (B) the records were kept in the course of a regularly conducted activity of, *inter alia,* a business or organization; (C) making the records was a regular practice of that activity; (D) all these conditions are shown by the testimony of the custodian or another qualified witness; and (E) neither the source of information nor the method or circumstances of preparation indicate a lack of trustworthiness.

We conclude that the district court did not abuse its discretion in admitting Exhibit 100. Even assuming the evidence was admitted for the truth of the matters asserted, *but see Anderson v. United States,* 417 U.S. 211, 220, 94 S.Ct. 2253, 41 L.Ed.2d 20 (1974) (statements are not hearsay if "the point of the prosecutor's introducing those statements was simply to prove that the statements were made so as to establish a foundation for later showing... that they were false"), all of the requirements for admission of the evidence as business records were met. First, Fullilove p.479 testified that the forms making up Exhibit 100 were prepared by World Vision employees as part of their job responsibility throughout the course of the Food-for-Work program. Second, Fullilove testified that all the forms were maintained in the ordinary course of business. Third, Fullilove testified that these forms were similar to the forms regularly maintained in its other branches. Fourth,

Fullilove was World Vision International's Chief Financial Officer, and as such was familiar with the forms and circumstances of their creation. Furthermore, he testified that he had supervised and reviewed the forensic audit of World Vision International that had collected and analyzed the forms. We have held that the "custodian [of the records] need not have personal knowledge of the actual creation of the document." *United States v. Adefehinti,* 510 F.3d 319, 325 (D.C.Cir.2007) (internal citation and quotation marks omitted). Finally, there was no evidence that the documents presented in court were not reliable reports of the data that had been entered.

＊ ＊ ＊ ＊ ＊ ＊

Exhibit 104 consisted of a summary of the forms in Exhibit 100. It was admitted pursuant to Fed.R.Evid. 1006, through Fullilove. Rule 1006 permits admission of an exhibit summarizing "[t]he content of voluminous writings ... that cannot be conveniently examined in court." For a summary of documents to be admissible, the documents must be so voluminous as to make comprehension by the jury difficult and inconvenient; the documents themselves must be admissible; the documents must be made reasonably available for inspection and copying; the summary must be accurate and nonprejudicial; and the witness who prepared the summary should introduce it. *United States v. Hemphill,* 514 F.3d 1350, 1358 (D.C.Cir. 2008).

Bondo (and Fahnbulleh by adoption) argues that the district court erred in admitting the Government's Exhibit 104 because its admission failed to satisfy the requirements of Rule 1006. In particular, Bondo asserts, again, that the raw data of Exhibit 100 was not itself admissible, and furthermore that the summary was not prepared by the witness who introduced it, Fullilove. We have already rejected the argument that Exhibit 100 was not itself admissible. And although Fullilove did not prepare Exhibit 104 himself, he testified that he supervised a team of auditors who reviewed the raw data and prepared the summary, and that he then reviewed the summary. We have previously approved introduction of summary testimony when the witness supervised others who prepared the summary. *United States v. Lemire,* 720 F.2d 1327, 1349 (D.C.Cir.1983). We conclude that the district court did not err in admitting Exhibit 104.

D. Denial of Mistrial

During closing arguments, the government in its rebuttal made seven references to "taxpayers" and their expectations of the Food-for-Work program. Counsel for both Bondo and Fahnbulleh objected. The district court agreed that these comments were improper and, as a remedy, instructed the jury to disregard the prosecutor's comments about taxpayers. On appeal, Bondo (and Fahnbulleh by adoption) argues that the district court erred in not declaring a mistrial, and that as a result his convictions should be reversed.

We review the district court's denial of a motion for mistrial for alleged prosecutorial impropriety in closing argument for abuse of discretion. *United States v. Becton,* 601 F.3d 588, 598 (D.C.Cir.2010). In *United States v. Gartmon,* we noted:

p.480 This court has used a relatively consistent set of criteria for evaluating the potential prejudice of closing argument errors. We have generally looked to three factors in determining whether improper remarks by the prosecutor sufficiently prejudiced a defendant: the closeness of the case, the centrality of the issue affected by the error, and the steps taken to mitigate the effects of the error.

146 F.3d 1015, 1026 (D.C.Cir.1998) (internal quotation marks and citations omitted). Bondo argues that these three factors tilted in his favor. First, he contends that the closeness of his case was shown by his acquittal of conspiracy to commit mail and wire fraud. Second, he asserts that the value of the alleged misappropriations was inextricably bound up within the entirety of the case, and that there was no way to extricate the government's characterization of the alleged loss as one that was personal to each juror. Finally, he argues that the prosecutor's "taxpayer" argument was so improper that the district court's instruction could not ameliorate the unfair prejudice the argument caused.

We do not find these arguments persuasive. First, the case against Bondo (and Fahnbulleh) was not close: numerous documents and several witnesses all pointed to their guilt. Second, the "taxpayer" remarks by the prosecutor were not central to the issue of whether the defendants were guilty of fraud in submitting false documents. Third, the district court told the jury to "disregard the comments that were made about the taxpayers," and further instructed them that "[t]his is a case of the United States versus the two defendants. It's not a case of the taxpayers against the defendants. That's not what this case is about." We conclude that the improper remarks by the prosecutor did not prejudice the defendants, especially in light of the judge's curative instruction. The district court thus did not abuse its discretion in not declaring a mistrial.

E. Sentencing

At sentencing, the district court determined that under the United States Sentencing Guidelines ("USSG" or "Guidelines") both Fahnbulleh's and Bondo's base offense level was 7. The district court then enhanced each offense level: by 16 points pursuant to USSG § 2B1.1(b)(2)(C) for a calculated loss of $1.9 million; by 6 points pursuant to USSG § 2B1.1(b)(1)(I) for 250 or more victims; and by 4 points pursuant to USSG § 3B1.1(a) for being an organizer or leader of a criminal activity involving five or more people.[1]

Fahnbulleh and Bondo argue that their cases should be remanded for re-sentencing, contending that the district court improperly calculated their Guidelines ranges. Fahnbulleh contends that the district court's finding of a loss of $1.9 million was in error because the jury's verdict demonstrated that the only misconduct unanimously found involved falsification of documents and some work done at personal residences. Second, Fahnbulleh claims that the district court's finding of 250 or more victims was in error because this number was never submitted to the jury, and in finding this number the district court relied solely on sentencing letters submitted by individuals who distributed food. Third, he argues that he was not an organizer or leader of any criminal activity because the evidence showed that it was not he but his co-conspirators who gave the instructions regarding the falsification p.481 of documents and the work done at personal residences.

Bondo argues that the government failed to satisfy its burden of establishing through reliable, specific evidence any amount of loss, much less a $1.9 million loss. The only evidence proffered to support the figure, according to Bondo, were the unsworn hearsay statements of 258 village leaders from the communities covered by the food distribution program. Bondo contends that the district court merely speculated that the actual loss was equal to the amount World Vision agreed to pay for reimbursement. Consequently, Bondo argues, the district court's $1.9 million loss calculation is unsupportable and unreasonable. And concerning the number of victims calculated by the district court, Bondo argues that because the government failed to satisfy its burden of establishing an amount of loss with reliable and specific evidence, the district court was precluded from finding that there were any victims because victims are only those who sustain any actual loss.

At sentencing, the district court may make findings of fact under a preponderance-of-the-evidence standard. *See United States v. Bras,* 483 F.3d 103, 107-08 (D.C.Cir.2007). The district court may even rely on evidence that would be inadmissible at trial, as long as that evidence has "sufficient indicia of reliability to support its probable accuracy." *Id.* at 109 (internal quotation marks and citation omitted). In reviewing a sentencing decision, this court reviews for clear error factual findings made by the district court, and gives "due deference" to the district court's application of the Guidelines to the facts. *United States v. Saani,* 650 F.3d 761, 765 (D.C.Cir.2011).

As noted, both Fahnbulleh and Bondo argue that the district court erred in enhancing their offense levels by 16 points pursuant to USSG § 2B1.1(b)(2)(C) for a calculated loss of $1.9 million. The district court did not clearly err in finding a loss of $1.9 million. At sentencing, the district court stated that the evidence clearly showed a loss of $1.9 million. In support of this statement, the court made reference to an internal audit of the Liberia Food-for-Work program conducted by World Vision showing this amount of loss. Furthermore, the court noted that evidence presented at trial supported this amount. That evidence included testimony presented by the government that World Vision International repaid $1.9 million to the United States government in compensation for the conspirators' fraud. *See United States v. Bisong,* 645 F.3d 384, 398 (D.C.Cir.2011) ("For sentencing, the loss amount need only be a reasonable estimate of the loss based on the available information."). We conclude that the district court made a reasonable estimate of loss.

Both Bondo and Fahnbulleh also argue that the district court erred in enhancing their offense levels by 6 points pursuant to USSG § 2B1.1(b)(1)(I) for 250 or more victims. Prior to sentencing, the government submitted to the court a summary exhibit detailing the amount of lost food as calculated by World Vision International examiners; the summary was based on interviews conducted by the examiners of leaders in 258 towns in which food was claimed to have been distributed. The district court at sentencing made reference to three of these interviews, all three of which contained references to more than 100 people who performed work but did not receive food. The court stated that consequently by a preponderance of the evidence the number of victims who had worked for the

Food-for-Work program was in excess of 250. We conclude that it was reasonable for the district court p.482 to rely on the three interviews, which was more than sufficient to put the number of victims over the 250 required by USSG § 2B1.1(b)(1)(I).

Finally, Fahnbulleh argues that the district court erred in enhancing his offense level by 4 points pursuant to USSG § 3B1.1(a) for being an organizer or leader of a criminal activity involving five or more people. At Fahnbulleh's sentencing the district court stated that the evidence presented at trial showed that Fahnbulleh held "a position of hierarchy" in the conspiracy, and that "at least five people were acting at his behest." That evidence consisted of testimony from five witnesses who admitted to committing fraud during the Food-for-Work program and testified that they were supervised by Fahnbulleh (and Bondo, among others). We conclude that the district court did not clearly err in finding that Fahnbulleh was an organizer or leader of a criminal activity involving five or more people.[2]

CONCLUSION

We have carefully considered all of defendants' arguments. For the reasons stated above, the judgment of the district court is affirmed.

[1] An additional two point enhancement, not at issue here, was added to Bondo's offense level pursuant to USSG § 3C1.1 for obstructing the investigation.

[2] We have given full consideration to other arguments raised by the appellants and find none require separate discussion.

FIRST CIRCUIT DECISIONS

The Rule Against Hearsay

786 F.3d 92 (2015)

UNITED STATES of America, Appellee,

v.

Edison BURGOS-MONTES, Defendant, Appellant.

No. 13-2305.

United States Court of Appeals, First Circuit.

May 13, 2015.

US v. Burgos-Montes, 786 F. 3d 92 (1st Cir. 2015)

p.98 Rachel Brill, for appellant.

Francisco A. Besosa-Martínez, Assistant United States Attorney, with whom Rosa Emilia Rodríguez-Vélez, United States Attorney, and Nelson Pérez-Sosa, Assistant United States Attorney, Chief, Appellate Division, were on brief, for appellee.

Before LYNCH, Chief Judge, HOWARD and KAYATTA, Circuit Judges.

KAYATTA, Circuit Judge.

Edison Burgos-Montes ("Burgos") appeals from his conviction for two counts of drug conspiracy and two counts of murder. The latter stem from the disappearance of Burgos' girlfriend Madelin Semidey-Morales ("Semidey") shortly after Burgos learned that she had been acting as a government informant. Although the government sought the death penalty, the jury sentenced Burgos to life in prison. Burgos now challenges his conviction on a large number of grounds. For the reasons described in this opinion, we affirm the district court in full.

I. Background

In this appeal, Burgos challenges the sufficiency of the evidence supporting p.99 his conviction, the denial of several pretrial motions to suppress evidence, and a number of other district court actions before and during trial. We typically recite those facts relevant to sufficiency claims and challenges to a denial of a motion to suppress in the light most favorable to the verdict or to the district court's ruling. *See United States v. Bayes,* 210 F.3d 64, 65-66 (1st Cir.2000) (sufficiency); *United States v. Soares,* 521 F.3d 117, 118 (1st Cir.2008) (suppression). For other issues, such as claims of prejudicial error, we offer a "balanced" treatment, *see United States v. Felton,* 417 F.3d 97, 99 (1st Cir. 2005), in which we "objectively view the evidence of record." *United States v. Nelson-Rodríguez,* 319 F.3d 12, 23 (1st Cir. 2003).[1] Given that we cannot simultaneously recite the facts in both manners, we limit our initial summary of this lengthy record to those details essential to framing the issues on appeal. We then offer the key facts relevant to each issue as part of our discussion of that issue, recited in the appropriate form. We do the same for the standard of review for each issue.

In October 2004, Semidey agreed to work with agents of the federal Drug Enforcement Administration ("DEA") to inform on Burgos. Semidey had begun dating Burgos while her husband was in jail, and she continued to do so after her husband was released. Over the next nine months, Semidey moved in with Burgos and provided information to the DEA, arranged a meeting in which undercover officers negotiated a cocaine sale with Burgos (although the sale was never consummated), and recorded conversations between herself and Burgos. In these conversations, Burgos described, among other things, techniques for importing cocaine from the Dominican Republic to Puerto Rico, and the prices he generally charged for kilogram-quantities of cocaine. According to trial testimony, sometime around June 2005, one of Burgos' employees told Burgos that Semidey was an informant, a claim that Burgos investigated and confirmed. Semidey also told her handlers (according to her handlers) that Burgos had threatened to kill her over this rumor, and suggested that if she ever disappeared, agents should look for her body on a "farm" that Burgos owned. On July 4, 2005, Semidey disappeared after telling her handler that she had returned to Burgos' house. A witness at trial testified that she last saw Semidey getting into Burgos' car on the night Semidey disappeared. Two days later, law enforcement agents observed Burgos supervising an employee as the employee cleaned the inside of Burgos' car during a rainstorm.

After efforts to locate Semidey proved unsuccessful, DEA agents sought and received p.100 the authorization to wiretap Burgos' cell phone in September 2005. In December, DEA agents also recruited a co-conspirator named Neftalí Corales-Casiano ("Corales") to work as an informant. He recorded a number of telephone calls between himself and Burgos between December 20 and 28. Most incriminating was a December 28 conversation in which Corales said he was concerned that Semidey's body would be found, to which Burgos replied, "It won't appear." On December 29, the government sought and received authorization to search Burgos' farm, as well as the car that agents had observed Burgos having an employee clean two days after Semidey disappeared. The search of the car revealed traces of blood that DNA analysis suggested was Semidey's. Semidey never reappeared, and her body was never found.

In January 2006, Burgos was indicted for conspiring to import and conspiring to possess with intent to distribute controlled substances in violation of 21 U.S.C. §§ 846, 841(a), 963, and 952. The indictment described a conspiracy lasting from 1998 to 2005, and described a number of acts in furtherance of the conspiracy that took place primarily between January and June 2005, including discussions with unindicted co-conspirators about arrangements to purchase between one and ten kilograms of cocaine, and stealing a boat. A May 2006 superseding indictment added two murder counts, stemming from Semidey's disappearance. The indictment charged that Burgos had murdered Semidey to prevent her from communicating with law enforcement and to retaliate against her for communicating with law enforcement in violation of 18 U.S.C. §§ 1512(a)(1)(A) and (C), and 1513(a)(1)(B).[2] The government also notified Burgos that it would seek the death penalty.

In the lead-up to trial, Burgos filed a number of motions seeking to strike the death penalty, all of which were denied. He also filed numerous motions to suppress evidence. Although the district court granted some of his motions to suppress, it denied both a motion to suppress the evidence obtained through the wiretap, *United States v. Burgos Montes,* No. 06-009-01(JAG), 2010 WL 5184844, at *13 (D.P.R. Dec. 20, 2010), and a motion to suppress evidence from the search of Burgos' car and farm. *United States v. Burgos Montes,* No. Crim. 06-009 JAG, 2011 WL 1743420, at *1 (D.P.R. May 2, 2011).

After hearing thirty days of evidence, the jury convicted Burgos on all four counts. During the penalty phase of the trial, Burgos raised allegations of possible juror bias. The district court held an in camera meeting with the juror in the presence of counsel and determined that there was no bias, so the juror returned to the box and the penalty phase continued. On the basis of this episode, Burgos filed a motion for acquittal or new trial. He also moved for acquittal or new trial on the basis that the evidence fell short of the minimum sufficient to convict.[3] The court denied both motions in a sealed order. Because the jury could not reach a unanimous verdict on the death penalty, Burgos was sentenced to life imprisonment.

Burgos filed a timely notice of appeal challenging: (1) the denial of the motion to p.101 suppress evidence from the wiretap, (2) the denial of the motion to suppress evidence from the search of the car and farm, (3) the denial of the motion for acquittal or new trial on the basis of alleged jury bias, (4) the denial of the motions to strike the death penalty, (5) the denial of the motions to acquit or for a new trial based on the sufficiency of the evidence, and (6) various evidentiary rulings.

II. Analysis

A. Motion To Suppress Wiretap Evidence

Burgos challenges the district court's denial, after an evidentiary hearing, of his motion to suppress a number of conversations recorded through a wiretap of his cell phone after Semidey disappeared. The wiretap was authorized under Title III of the Omnibus Crime Control and Safe Streets Act of 1968, 18 U.S.C. §§ 2510-22, which imposes a set of statutory requirements on top of the constitutional requirements applicable to ordinary search warrants. *See United States v. Nelson-Rodríguez,* 319 F.3d 12, 32 (1st Cir.2003). Burgos advances four primary challenges to the wiretap, which we address in turn.

1. "Omitted" Information About Semidey

Burgos' first argument is that in the affidavit in support of their wiretap application, the DEA agents omitted information about Semidey that, had it been included, would have precluded a finding of probable cause under the Fourth Amendment of the United States Constitution. In assessing such an argument (assuming the omitted information was intentionally or recklessly withheld), we ask whether the application, had it contained the omitted information, would still have provided a "sufficient" basis for authorizing the wiretap.[4] *United States v. Young,* 877 F.2d 1099, 1102-03 (1st Cir.1989) (citing *Franks v. Delaware,* 438 U.S. 154, 171-72, 98 S.Ct. 2674, 57 L.Ed.2d 667 (1978)).

The government's application for authorization to conduct a thirty-day wiretap of Burgos' cell phone was supported by a thirty-seven-page affidavit filed by DEA Agent Jacobsen, with the participation of Agent Iglesias, who was the lead agent on the case. The affidavit described the investigation as being led by the DEA and involving the FBI, the Puerto Rico Police Department, and two Puerto Rico investigative units, the Hacienda and the NIE. In addition to Burgos, one of the five targeted individuals was Corales, whom the affidavit described as a former police officer who was fired for corruption allegations in 1997, and who had multiple felony arrests and convictions between 1995 and 1998.

The evidence supporting the affidavit consisted of information from three confidential sources, including Semidey (through her reports submitted prior to her disappearance). The first two sources described the activities of named individuals believed to be lower-level members of a drug trafficking conspiracy that brought cocaine into Puerto Rico from the Dominican Republic. The evidence connecting Burgos to drug trafficking came from or p.102 through Semidey. According to the affidavit, she described conversations in which Burgos said he could procure large amounts of cocaine. She also helped arrange a meeting between Burgos and undercover officers, which was recorded, and in which the officers arranged a cocaine purchase. Toll registers confirmed that Burgos was in contact with the people that Semidey said he called to discuss the planned sale to the officers. Burgos never delivered any drugs, however.

The application also described Semidey's statements that Burgos suspected the undercover officers were officers and that he had confronted her with a rumor that she was cooperating. According to the affidavit, Burgos threatened to make her "disappear from the earth." It also described Semidey's disappearance on July 4, 2005, and agents' observations of Burgos supervising as an employee "rigorously" washed the interior of Burgos' car during a rainstorm on July 6.

The affidavit described Semidey as a paid informant who was cooperating for personal reasons. It then described her observations of Burgos' drug activities, her role in helping to arrange a failed buy-bust, the fact that Burgos had threatened her, and her disappearance. "Omitted" from the affidavit were the facts that Semidey was in a relationship with Burgos, that she was married to another man who had been released from prison shortly before she agreed to inform on Burgos, and that she may have been trying to avoid prosecution on unrelated charges.[5]

Nothing in these omitted facts materially undercuts the affidavit's ample demonstration of probable cause. The omitted information furnishes, at best, grist for a somewhat conjectural and by no means strong argument that one might make to discredit Semidey. None of this grist is so probative as to make its omission particularly notable. *See Young*, 877 F.2d at 1103 ("The law does not require an officer swearing out an affidavit for a warrant to include all possible impeachment material. It need only explain that the officer has found the informant to be reasonably reliable."). We note, too, that key portions of Semidey's statements in the affidavit were corroborated within the affidavit itself. The affidavit reflects that after Semidey introduced Burgos to undercover agents, Burgos himself spoke with undercover agents on at least three occasions regarding a potential cocaine sale. Moreover, toll records corroborated Semidey's descriptions of Burgos' telephone communications about this potential sale.

In sum, even had the affidavit included the omitted information, the affidavit would easily have contained a sufficient basis for concluding that a wiretap would produce evidence that Burgos was involved in a drug conspiracy or murder. Burgos' challenge to the wiretap based on this "omission" of information concerning Semidey therefore fails.[6] *Young*, 877 F.2d at 1102.

2. "Omitted" Information About Corales

Burgos' next argument trains on the so-called "necessity" requirement of 18 U.S.C. § 2518(1)(c). This subsection provides that wiretaps are generally only p.103 available when the government shows with a "full and complete statement ... whether or not other investigative procedures have been tried and failed or why they reasonably appear to be unlikely to succeed if tried or to be too dangerous." *Id.*

According to Burgos, the affidavit's claim that a wiretap was necessary was deficient because it did not provide "full and complete" information about Corales. Specifically, Burgos argues that the affidavit did not give any indication that Corales had sometimes worked as an informant and could potentially be used as one in this investigation. Burgos argues that a wiretap could not have been necessary until the government first tried to use Corales as an informant.

In considering a claim that improperly omitted facts undermine the necessity of a wiretap, we use a similar approach to that which we use to assess a claim that such omissions undermine probable cause: we ask whether, had the omitted information been included, there would still have been a "minimally adequate" basis for determining that the wiretap was necessary.[7] *See United States v. Cartagena*, 593 F.3d 104, 109-11 (1st Cir.2010).

The answer to this question is "yes." The affidavit explained why normal investigative techniques were not expected to yield results. In particular, agents had twice tried and failed to arrange a buy-bust, and using other informants was dangerous, given what appeared to have happened to Semidey. That explanation provides more than adequate support for a conclusion that the exigencies did not warrant further delay in order to try to recruit yet another confidential informant, much less for what appeared to be an exceedingly dangerous mission. *See* 18 U.S.C. § 2518(1)(c) (recognizing that some investigative techniques may be "too dangerous"). Whether Corales could have been recruited as an informant (or even the fact that he later acquired his own reasons to volunteer as an informant, as discussed in footnote 10 of this opinion) is therefore beside the point.

3. Sealing Of The Wiretap Recordings

We now turn to Burgos' argument that the wiretap application failed to comply with certain procedural requirements under 18 U.S.C. § 2518(8)(a). That subsection provides that "[i]mmediately upon the expiration of the period of the order" authorizing a wiretap, "such recordings shall be made available to the judge issuing such order and sealed under his directions." *Id.* It further provides that "[t]he presence of the seal provided for by this subsection, or a satisfactory explanation for the absence thereof" is a prerequisite for any use of the evidence. *Id.*

Burgos makes two arguments: (1) that the records were not sealed "immediately," because the government ended the wiretap on September 30 but the recordings were not sealed until October 7, and (2) that they were not sealed by the same judge who had issued the order. The government does not dispute these deviations from the statutory requirements. It argues, however, that because it has offered a "satisfactory explanation" for the late sealing, and because the use of a different judge is immaterial, the recordings need not be suppressed. After an evidentiary hearing to consider the issue of sealing, the district court denied Burgos' motion to suppress the wiretap evidence on these p.104 grounds. *Burgos Montes,* 2010 WL 5184844, at *5-8.

Before turning to the substance, we must first address the threshold issue of the proper standard of review. Neither party points us to a standard of review for the question of whether the government's explanation for the absence of a seal that complies with the requirements of section 2518(8)(a) is "satisfactory." It appears that this circuit has never expressly articulated one. Other circuits are split, with some employing a clearly erroneous standard, *see, e.g., United States v. Coney,* 407 F.3d 871, 874 (7th Cir.2005), and others applying plenary review to the question of whether the explanation is satisfactory, even though subsidiary factual questions are reviewed for clear error, *see, e.g., United States v. Sawyers,* 963 F.2d 157, 159 (8th Cir.1992). In *United States v. Mora,* 821 F.2d 860, 869-70 (1st Cir.1987), which articulated the factors that define a "satisfactory explanation" in this circuit, we accepted the district court's supported subsidiary factual findings, but applied de novo review to whether those facts were satisfactory under the newly announced test. We will follow in those footsteps.

In assessing the ramifications of an untimely sealing, *Mora* established that the key inquiry was whether the government had proven "by clear and convincing evidence that the integrity of the tapes ha[d] not been compromised." *Id.* at 867. Sealing helps ensure and demonstrate a lack of tampering. To the extent that there is any delay in sealing, the field may open more widely for the defendant to question and explore what happened to the records pre-sealing.

Here, the district court concluded that Iglesias was credible in his testimony that the "recordings were kept in a manner that sufficiently excludes the possibility of tampering," and noted that Burgos had not even argued that they had been tampered with. *Burgos Montes,* 2010 WL 5184844, at *7. On appeal, Burgos again offers no allegations of tampering. While the burden of proof is on the government, this does not mean the government must prove a negative when the defendant does not even allege that tampering has taken place. Burgos also does not offer any facts speaking to the other factors in *Mora,* particularly indications of bad faith by law enforcement personnel or prejudice to him—his argument simply turns on the bare fact that seven days is not "immediately." However, in *Mora* itself, the court found that delays of twenty and forty-one days, while concerning, did not automatically require suppression in light of the other factors. *Id.* at 869. We conclude the same here regarding the seven-day delay, given the lack of any evidence of tampering or other possible prejudice, and the lack of evidence of bad faith.

We can also quickly dispense with Burgos' objection to the sealing of the recordings by a judge other than the one who approved the wiretap. When Iglesias took the recordings to the issuing judge, he was told that the judge was unavailable and was sent to a different judge, who sealed them. Burgos cites no case where recordings have been suppressed under such circumstances. Few cases have addressed the issue at all, although the Second Circuit has suggested in dictum that when the issuing judge's unavailability would result in a delay, sealing by a non-issuing judge is permissible. *United States v. Poeta,* 455 F.2d 117, 122 (2d Cir.1972). As a purely textual matter, the agents appear to have complied with the statute in that they "made [the recordings] available to the [issuing] judge" and followed her "direction[ ]" to take them to a different judge for sealing. Thus, this argument also fails.

p.105 4. Miscellaneous Shots At The Warrant

Burgos lobs a number of other arguments at the substance of the affidavit, none of which give us significant pause. He argues that the affidavit was not full and complete because some statements were too vague, and because it includes a one-sentence disclaimer that the affidavit included only information relevant to the wiretap application and not all of the information from the entire investigation. These arguments fail on the grounds that an affidavit need not include the "minutiae" of an investigation. *See Cartagena,* 593 F.3d at 110; *see also United States v. Yeje-Cabrera,* 430 F.3d 1, 9-10 (1st Cir. 2005).

Burgos also complains that the affidavit's authorization to include individuals "yet unknown" violates the requirement that the application include "the identity of the person, if known, committing the offense and whose communications are to be intercepted." 18 U.S.C. § 2518(1)(b)(iv). He argues that the government knew the names of certain other individuals that would eventually be recorded and failed to include them. In *United States v. Donovan,* 429 U.S. 413, 97 S.Ct. 658, 50 L.Ed.2d 652 (1977), the Court held that this requirement to identify individuals extends to those whose conversations the government has probable cause to believe would be intercepted. Although it is typically the unnamed individuals who challenge a wiretap under such circumstances, *see id.* at 428, 97 S.Ct. 658; *see also United States v. Chiarizio,* 525 F.2d 289, 291-93 (2d Cir. 1975), we will assume without deciding that a named individual can also bring such a challenge because it does not affect the outcome here.[8] Nevertheless, Burgos offers no facts establishing that the government had probable cause to believe that the other individuals would be intercepted on the targeted telephone, so this argument also fails.

B. Motion To Suppress Evidence From Burgos' Car And Farm

Burgos next challenges on a number of grounds the denial of his motion to suppress evidence seized from his car and farm pursuant to a search warrant. As with the wiretap warrant, Burgos argues that the application for the warrant was deficient because of omissions and inaccuracies in the application. In considering such a challenge, our approach is similar to the one we used with regard to the wiretap: "we excise the offending inaccuracies and insert the facts recklessly omitted, and then determine whether or not the 'corrected' warrant affidavit would establish probable cause." *Burke v. Town of Walpole,* 405 F.3d 66, 82 (1st Cir.2005) (quoting *Wilson v. Russo,* 212 F.3d 781, 789 (3d Cir.2000)).[9] Burgos also argues that the application did not satisfy the "particularity" requirement of the Fourth Amendment. In reviewing the denial of a motion to suppress based on such a claim, we review the district court's fact-finding for clear error, and conclusions of law de novo. *United States v. Kuc,* 737 F.3d 129, 132 (1st Cir.2013).

p.106 1. "Omitted" Information About Corales and Semidey

A warrant application must include sufficient information to establish probable cause both that a crime has been committed, and that evidence of the crime will be found in the place to be searched. *United States v. Hicks,* 575 F.3d 130, 136 (1st Cir.2009). Burgos argues that the application for the warrant was deficient because it omitted material information undermining the credibility of Semidey and Corales, whose statements comprised much of the information in the affidavit. Burgos again argues that the affidavit did not explain the nature of Semidey's relationship with Burgos or her potential motivations for serving as an informant, nor the fact that Corales was a disgraced former cop with a history of perjury and multiple felony convictions.

The affidavit provided the following as a basis for probable cause:

• Semidey's statements to a DEA agent that Burgos had confronted her with a rumor that she was an informant, and had threatened to kill her;

• Semidey's statements that if she ever disappeared, law enforcement should look for her on Burgos' farm;

• Observations of Burgos having an employee "rigorously" wash the interior of his car in the rain two days after Semidey disappeared and shortly after the police contacted him with questions about Semidey;

• High call volume from Burgos' phone to Semidey's that stopped the night of her disappearance, followed by a single call to her number after the police contacted him about her disappearance;

• Visual observations by Iglesias of "what appeared to be a newly turned area of earth in the approximate dimensions of a grave" on the farm;

• A recording of a call between Burgos and co-conspirator Radamés Castillo-Martinez ("Castillo") in which Castillo said he was concerned that something might have happened to Burgos because of "this girl";

• Statements by Corales and Castillo that Burgos knew Semidey was an informant;

• Several statements by Corales, identified in the affidavit as "CS # 2," recounting conversations in which Burgos said he was not concerned to hear that co-conspirator Castillo had been arrested because he was confident that the police were not going to find Semidey; that the DEA would have arrested him by then if it could; and that he didn't understand how Semidey could have "cause[d] damage" to him after he had paid her bills and her children's living expenses;[10]

• A conversation between Corales and Burgos in which Burgos said that Semidey's body "won't appear" and that "[t]hey can look for her in Yauco, Ponce, and Mayaguez and they're not going to find her." In the conversation, Burgos and Corales also made plans to bury a stolen boat on the farm. (This conversation was recorded, although the affidavit does not make that clear.);

• Corales' statement that he believed Semidey may be buried on the farm.

This evidence clearly suffices to establish probable cause, even considering the affidavit in light of the omitted information about Semidey and Corales. In particular, the credibility of Semidey's statements that Burgos had threatened p.107 her are not undercut by the kind of information that might cast doubt on her credibility with regard to Burgos' drug activities. When informant Jane reports that target John threatened to kill her because John learned that Jane is an informant, and Jane then disappears after last being seen getting into John's car, after which John is seen washing the car in a rainstorm, it almost goes without saying that there exists probable cause to conduct further investigations into John no matter what one thinks about Jane's motives for serving as an informant. *See United States v. Hibbard,* 963 F.2d 1100, 1101-02 (8th Cir.1992) (upholding a warrant authorizing the search of defendant's residence for the whereabouts of a missing person based entirely on the fact that the defendant had threatened the victim and that the victim was last seen in the defendant's presence). Whatever additional corroboration such statements might need is amply provided for by the recorded conversation between Burgos and Corales in which Burgos stated that Semidey was not going to appear. In short, nothing in the omitted evidence cast any material doubt on Semidey's statements relevant to the warrant application.

As for Corales, the corroborating information not dependent on his credibility is sufficient to establish a nexus to the car and the farm. The search of the car was based primarily on agents' observations of Burgos having the car's interior washed in the rain two days after Semidey disappeared, and shortly after law enforcement went to Burgos house to attempt to question him. As for the farm, the affidavit established a nexus based on Semidey's statements that law enforcement should look for her body on the farm if she disappeared, as well as the recorded conversation in which Burgos and Corales agreed to bury a boat on the farm. Thus, even considering the affidavit in light of Corales' potential unreliability, there is a sufficient basis for probable cause.

2. Other Probable Cause Arguments

Burgos makes several other arguments for why the warrant failed to establish probable cause. First, he points to certain inaccuracies in the warrant's description of events. In particular, he argues that Iglesias' trial testimony regarding his observations of disturbed earth on the farm appear to vary from his description in the affidavit. As discussed above, however, probable cause existed even without the observation of the disturbed earth, so we need not delve into this argument. As for the car, Burgos attempts to build a probable cause challenge based on the fact that the affidavit described Burgos washing the inside of his vehicle with an employee, while testimony in the suppression hearing made clear that Burgos was actually supervising the employee and did not participate in the washing himself. Burgos argues that having a third party wash the car is inconsistent with an attempt to remove evidence of a crime, where one would expect great secrecy. However, the description of the car-washing in the affidavit does indicate that a third party, who seemed to be Burgos' employee, was involved, so this minor difference in how Iglesias described the event is not material.

Finally, Burgos makes a staleness argument based on the passage of time between Semidey's disappearance in July 2005 and the government's application for a search warrant in December, after Corales agreed to cooperate. Burgos argues that even if there was probable cause to believe that there had once been evidence in the car, the affidavit did not include any reason to believe that it would have still remained six months later. An allegation p.108 of staleness is evaluated not merely on how old the information is, but circumstances including the nature of the suspected crime, the character of the items to be seized, the habits of the suspect, and the nature of the premises to be searched. *United States v. Bucuvalas,* 970 F.2d 937, 940 (1st Cir.1992), *abrogated on other grounds by Cleveland v. United States,* 531 U.S. 12, 18, 121 S.Ct. 365, 148 L.Ed.2d 221 (2000). Burgos cites no case where evidence was suppressed on the basis of a failure to state the common-sense notions that bodies often stay where they are disposed of, and that DNA evidence can last longer than six months, and we decline to announce such a rule here—particularly given that the passage of time without Semidey's reappearance made foul play appear increasingly more likely.

3. Particularity

Burgos next argues that the search warrant violates the Constitutional requirement that a warrant must "particularly describ[e] ... [the] things to be seized." U.S. Const. amend. IV. The warrant authorizes a search for "[e]vidence and trace evidence relevant to the homicide of Madelin Semidey-Morales in violation of Title 18, *United States Code,* Section 1513. See also the attached affidavit, which is hereby incorporated and made part hereof." Burgos argues that "evidence and trace evidence" is insufficiently particular, and that the failure to define the kind of "trace evidence" sought was particularly egregious because Iglesias admitted that he used the broad term precisely to avoid limiting the forensic analysis.

Although federal courts do not generally uphold warrants authorizing the search for "evidence of crime X" unless that statement follows a list of illustrative examples, *see United States v. Bithoney,* 631 F.2d 1, 2-3 & n. 1 (1st Cir.1980), Burgos' argument fails because the warrant incorporates by reference the affidavit, which describes the target of the search as "the person, or remains, of Madelin Semidey-Morales, evidence of the manner of her death and her personal effects." Affidavit language expressly incorporated by the warrant can satisfy the particularity requirement. *See Rivera Rodríguez v. Beninato,* 469 F.3d 1, 5 (1st Cir.2006); *cf. Groh v. Ramirez,* 540 U.S. 551, 557-58, 124 S.Ct. 1284, 157 L.Ed.2d 1068 (2004) (collecting circuit cases allowing incorporation by reference and leaving open the possibility of incorporation). While there still exists some generality in terms like "evidence of the manner of her death" and "her personal effects," this is a situation in which the "circumstances of the crime make an exact description of the fruits and instrumentalities a virtual impossibility." *United States v. Timpani,* 665 F.2d 1, 5 (1st Cir.1981) (quoting *Spinelli v. United States,* 382 F.2d 871, 886 (8th Cir.1967)). In such cases, "the searching officer can only be expected to describe the generic class of items he is seeking." *Id.* (quoting *Spinelli,* 382 F.2d at 886).

4. Compliance With Rule 41(e)

Burgos next attacks the warrant on the grounds that the issuing magistrate failed to fill in two of the spaces on the preprinted warrant form: one for the date by which the warrant was to be executed, and one for the judge to whom the warrant should be returned. (The space on the form for the return date is followed by the parenthetical "not to exceed 10 days.") Burgos argues that these omissions violate Federal Rule of Criminal Procedure 41(e)(2)(A) (2009), which required the warrant to "command the officer ... to execute the warrant within a specified time p.109 not longer than 10 days" and to "return the warrant to the magistrate judge designated in the warrant," and that such violation mandates suppression.[11]

In *United States v. Bonner,* 808 F.2d 864 (1st Cir.1986), we considered a different subdivision of Rule 41, one providing that officers must leave a copy of the warrant at the place to be searched. *See* Fed.R.Crim.P. 41(f)(1)(c).[12] We held that because the subdivision is "ministerial," a violation does not require suppression unless the defendant can demonstrate prejudice. *Bonner,* 808 F.2d at 869. Prejudice means being "subjected to a search that might not have occurred or would not have been so abrasive" had the rules been followed. *Id.* (internal quotation marks omitted). Other circuits have held the same applies to all the prerequisites of Rule 41. *See United States v. Schoenheit,* 856 F.2d 74, 76-77 (8th Cir.1988); *United States v. Burke,* 517 F.2d 377, 386-87 (2d Cir.1975).

We have little trouble concluding that the prejudicial error rule of *Bonner* should extend to the failure by the issuing magistrate to define the time period of the search when the form itself provides that the search is to be completed within the time frame specified by the rule, and to the failure to designate a magistrate to whom the form should be returned. "The exclusionary rule should be limited to those situations where its remedial objectives are best served, i.e., to deter illegal police conduct, not mistakes by judges and magistrates." *Bonner,* 808 F.2d at 867 (citing *United States v. Leon,* 468 U.S. 897, 908, 916, 104 S.Ct. 3405, 82 L.Ed.2d 677 (1984)). Burgos does not suggest why he was prejudiced by the warrant's technical failings. Absent a showing of prejudice, there is no basis for suppressing the evidence.[13]

5. Fruit Of The Poisonous Tree

While serving as an informant, Semidey (against her handlers' instructions) took a number of documents—including some pertaining to the farm—from Burgos' residence. The physical evidence of this unconstitutional search was suppressed. Burgos now argues that any evidence from the farm should be suppressed as the fruit of the poisonous tree. The district court denied the motion to suppress on the grounds that a search of the farm was inevitable. *See United States v. Scott,* 270 F.3d 30, 42-45 (1st Cir.2001) (explaining the inevitable discovery doctrine). On appeal, Burgos argues in a single conclusory sentence that the government has not met its burden of proving by a preponderance of the evidence that the farm would have been discovered by lawful means. He does not challenge the specific evidence from which the district court concluded that discovery was inevitable: DEA agents' conversations with Semidey and Corales, as well as an instance where local police seized some stolen containers from the property. This argument, even if not waived for perfunctory briefing, *see United States v. Zannino,* 895 F.2d 1, 16 (1st Cir.1990), fails in the face of the evidence found persuasive by the district court.

p.110 C. Juror Bias

We now turn to Burgos' claim that the district court abused its discretion when it first failed to hold an evidentiary hearing to investigate allegations of juror bias, and then failed to grant a new trial on account of that alleged bias, all in violation of Burgos' Sixth Amendment right to a trial by impartial jury. U.S. Const. amend. VI. This claim arises out of an incident during the sentencing phase of trial in which a juror appeared to slump in his chair when a man we will call Juan walked into the room. Juan was married to one of the witnesses who testified for the defense in the penalty phase. At the next break, Juan told defense counsel that he was a second cousin of the juror (their grandmothers were sisters). Defense counsel told the judge that the juror was appearing to hide from Juan.

The judge held an in camera meeting in which he asked the juror if he recognized anyone in the court room that day. The juror said he had not recognized anyone "involved in the case," and stressed that if he recognized anyone, he would speak up.[14] The district court asked several more times (e.g., "So far in the case, you haven't recognized anybody?"). To each question, the juror responded that he had not, and that "[i]f I ... recognize somebody, I will tell the Court. But I didn't." He also explained that he slumped because he was uncomfortable, and that although he had grown up the part of Puerto Rico where the events at issue had taken place, he had moved away from his hometown more than two decades before, and rarely returned to visit. The court also asked specifically if he recognized the name "Juan," and the juror responded that he did not.

Satisfied with the juror's credibility, the district court continued the penalty phase of the trial. Based on this episode, Burgos filed a motion for acquittal or new trial and requested an evidentiary hearing. His motion also raised the new argument that a defense witness from the guilt phase was also related to the juror (her father was the juror's mother's cousin).[15] The district court denied this motion on the grounds that the juror was credible when he said he didn't recognize anyone in the proceedings, and that moreover there hadn't been even a suggestion that he had recognized the witness during the guilt phase. Burgos now appeals the denial of this motion.

Burgos can hardly complain now that the district court failed to remove the juror. After all, the only jury finding made after Burgos raised the issue favored Burgos by rejecting the death penalty. So he must train his argument on a claim that the district court abused its discretion by failing to grant a new trial because of later-discovered bias relevant to the guilt phase. All Burgos has to go on is his belated complaint that a witness he himself had called was a distant cousin of the juror. Because the district court took as credible the juror's statement that he did not recognize anyone in the proceedings, Burgos instead makes an argument based on implied bias: that either the bare fact of a blood relationship, or the fact that the juror lied about the existence of a blood relationship, is sufficient to imply bias as a matter of law. See *Amirault v. Fair,* 968 F.2d 1404, 1406 (1st Cir.1992) (per curiam).

Neither argument prevails. First, the district court concluded that the juror did not lie about not recognizing anyone in the p.111 proceedings, and nothing suggests that finding was clearly erroneous. See *id.* at 1405 (stating that a court's findings of juror credibility merit "great deference"). As for the bare fact that the juror and the witness were distant cousins, implied bias requires "exceptional" or "extreme" circumstances, *id.* at 1406 (quoting *Smith v. Phillips,* 455 U.S. 209, 222, 102 S.Ct. 940, 71 L.Ed.2d 78 (1982) (O'Connor, J., concurring)), and we cannot conclude that the district court erred in finding the situation fell well short of this mark, given that the familial connections were so attenuated that no one during the guilt phase seems to have even noticed that the witness and the juror were distant cousins.

Burgos' alternative argument challenges the procedure employed by the district court. He says that the court erred by investigating the claim of juror bias through an in camera discussion, rather than an evidentiary hearing. The case law suggests otherwise. While a district court must make an "adequate inquiry" into non-frivolous claims of juror bias or misconduct, *United States v. Ortiz-Arrigoitia,* 996 F.2d 436, 442 (1st Cir.1993), the district court has "broad discretion to determine the type of investigation which must be mounted." *United States v. Boylan,* 898 F.2d 230, 258 (1st Cir.1990). The court "may, but need not, convene a full-blown evidentiary hearing." *Id.* We review the district court's determination of how to investigate such claims for patent abuse of discretion. *Id.*

The district court certainly did not patently abuse that broad discretion here. The relevant question is not whether the juror was actually related to anyone in the proceedings; it is whether such a relationship, if it exists, biased the juror against the defendant. Indeed, the district court accepted that the juror may have been related to the witness, but it credited the juror's testimony that he did not recognize anyone, let alone harbor any bias against the defendant as a result of that unrecognized relationship with a witness for the defense. Thus, while an evidentiary hearing could conceivably have proven the relationships if they were at issue, they were not at issue. The district court did not patently abuse its discretion.

D. Trial Before A Death-Qualified Jury

Prior to trial, Burgos filed a number of motions challenging the government's decision to seek the death penalty. The district court denied them all. Burgos was tried before a death-qualified jury, and sentenced to life in prison. He now argues that because he never should have faced the death penalty, his trial before a death-qualified jury violated his Sixth Amendment rights.

For his argument that he never should have faced the death penalty in the first place, Burgos simply incorporates by reference his pre-trial motions, offering no arguments for why the district court erred in dismissing those motions. Arguments incorporated into a brief solely by reference to district court filings are deemed waived. *See Exec. Leasing Corp. v. Banco Popular de P.R.,* 48 F.3d 66, 67-68 (1st Cir.1995). As such, Burgos has waived his argument that the district court erred when it rejected his various motions to strike the death penalty.

Given a proper death penalty charge, it is well established that using a death-qualified jury for the guilt phase does not violate a defendant's Sixth Amendment rights. *Buchanan v. Kentucky,* 483 U.S. 402, 414-16, 107 S.Ct. 2906, 97 L.Ed.2d 336 (1987). Here, Burgos faced charges of murdering Semidey to prevent her from, or in retaliation for, p.112 communicating with law enforcement in violation of 18 U.S.C. §§ 1512(a)(1)(A) and (C), and 1513(a)(1)(B), and the death penalty is available for these violations as a matter of law. *Id.* §§ 1111(b), 1512(a)(3)(A), 1513(a)(2)(A). Thus, there has been no Sixth Amendment violation.

E. Sufficiency Of The Evidence

Burgos next appeals from the order denying his motion for acquittal or new trial on the basis of insufficient evidence to convict. This court reviews a denial of a Rule 29 motion for acquittal based on insufficiency of the evidence de novo, examining the evidence in the light most favorable to the verdict, *United States v. Troy,* 583 F.3d 20, 24 (1st Cir. 2009), and asking whether a rational jury could find guilt beyond a reasonable doubt, *United States v. Andujar,* 49 F.3d 16, 20 (1st Cir.1995). A district court's denial of a motion for a new trial is reviewed for manifest abuse of discretion. *United States v. González-González,* 136 F.3d 6, 12 (1st Cir.1998).

Burgos argues that the government presented insufficient evidence that he killed Semidey with the intent to prevent her attendance or testimony in an official proceeding, 18 U.S.C. § 1512(a)(1)(A), to "prevent a communication about the commission or possible commission of a federal offense to a federal law enforcement officer," *id.* § 1512(a)(1)(C), or to "retaliate" for providing such information, *id.* § 1513(a)(1)(B). As Burgos would have it, the evidence at worst established two equally plausible reasons for him to have killed Semidey: he killed her in a domestic dispute because they had an argument three days before her disappearance that, according to trial testimony, did not seem to have anything to do with her being an informant,[16] or he killed her because of her informing. Alternatively, he says that it was equally plausible that another member of the conspiracy killed her.

We agree with the district court that these other theories were not equally plausible. The jury heard testimony that Burgos tried several times to confirm whether or not Semidey was an informant, that he concluded that she was, and that he had threatened to kill her and "make her disappear from the face of the earth" if he ever found out that she was cooperating with the government. The jury heard, too, evidence of Burgos' drug-related activities and Semidey's knowledge of those activities, providing him with ample motive to make sure she never testified against him. If Burgos was merely unhappy with his non-marital relationship, he had numerous options for ending that relationship. If he was unhappy because Semidey was a government informant clearly possessed of knowledge sufficient to convict him, he had fewer reliable options available to him other than murder, or so the jury could reasonably have concluded.

F. Prejudicial Variance

Burgos then argues that the evidence presented at trial regarding the duration of the drug conspiracy constituted a fatal variance from that charged in the indictment.[17] Burgos was charged with one p.113 count of conspiracy to possess cocaine with intent to distribute, and one of conspiracy to import cocaine, both of which were charged to have extended from 1998 to 2005. Burgos argues that because the only evidence of the conspiracy in the 1998-99 time frame came from Corales, who was in prison for six months starting in 2001, and who also testified as a witness for the government in an unrelated murder case, there could not have been a continuous 1998-2005 conspiracy to import and distribute cocaine. He argues that at best, the government has presented evidence of two distinct conspiracies (a distribution conspiracy in 1998-99, and a conspiracy to import and distribute in 2004-05[18]), creating a fatal variance from the 1998-2005 conspiracy charged in the indictment.

To determine whether a variance exists, we "review the record to determine whether the evidence and reasonable inferences therefrom, taken as a whole and in the light most favorable to the prosecution, would allow a rational jury to determine beyond a reasonable doubt that a single conspiracy existed." *United States v. Mangual-Santiago,* 562 F.3d 411, 421 (1st Cir.2009) (internal quotation marks omitted). "Although conflicting inferences may arise, so long as the evidence is adequate to permit a reasonable trier of fact to have found a single conspiracy beyond a reasonable doubt, the jury's finding will not be disturbed on appeal." *Id.* Even if we find a variance, it "does not warrant reversal unless it is prejudicial." *United States v. Yelaun,* 541 F.3d 415, 419 (1st Cir.2008). We review de novo the question of whether a variance was prejudicial. *United States v. Wihbey,* 75 F.3d 761, 774 (1st Cir.1996).

The record contains sufficient evidence to support the jury's finding that Burgos participated in a conspiracy from 1998 to 2005. Corales testified that he met Burgos in 1998. At the time, both had their own drug points and were involved in unrelated drug activities, although they knew people in common. After their meeting, he and Burgos began selling each other kilogram-quantities of cocaine. Corales went to jail, but only for six months in 2001, during which time the two remained in contact (for example, Burgos provided the ice cream for an inmate party Corales organized), and when Corales was released, Burgos gave him a job in his construction company. Sometime around 2003 or 2004, the two developed the plan to import drugs from the Dominican Republic, which only got as far as stealing a boat. When the government asked whether the exchange of drugs between Corales and Burgos lasted throughout their seven-year relationship (meaning 1998 to 2005), Corales answered in the affirmative.[19]

p.114 The government presented no evidence that other people were involved in the conspiracy with Corales and Burgos until they began planning to import drugs sometime around 2003 or 2004. Thus, there is no evidence of a 1998-2005 conspiracy unless Corales remained a member for the entire time. Burgos argues that the gap in the government's evidence and the bare fact that Corales went to prison means that the conspiracy ended in 1999 and re-started several years later. A six-month hiatus, however, does not necessarily mean the conspiracy ended. *See United States v. Alejandro-Montañez,* 778 F.3d 352, 359-60 (1st Cir.2015). Nor does the imprisonment of conspiracy members necessarily require a finding of withdrawal or abandonment. *See Mangual-Santiago,* 562 F.3d at 422-23.

Burgos points to two additional points that could suggest Corales withdrew from the conspiracy: the fact that he gave up his own drug points; and the fact that in 1999 he agreed to testify for the government in unrelated cases. (Although defense counsel pushed Corales to admit he was "working for" or an "informant" for the government, Corales insisted that all he agreed to do was show up in court and testify.) On balance, though, while the evidence could have allowed the jury to infer that Corales withdrew from the conspiracy with Burgos and began a new conspiracy with Burgos out of the blue around 2003, it is also sufficient to support an inference that Corales never withdrew from the original conspiracy. Thus, there is no variance.

G. Evidentiary Rulings

Finally, Burgos challenges a number of the district court's evidentiary rulings, both individually and for their cumulative impact. As a general matter, this circuit reviews evidentiary rulings for abuse of discretion. *Baker v. Dalkon Shield Claimants Trust,* 156 F.3d 248, 251-52 (1st Cir.1998). However, if the evidentiary ruling rests on an interpretation of law, we review it de novo, with subsidiary fact-finding reviewed for clear error. *Id.*

Even if a district court errs, such error does not require reversal if it was harmless—i.e., if it can be said that "'the judgment was not substantially swayed by the error.'" *United States v. Meserve,* 271 F.3d 314, 329 (1st Cir.2001) (quoting *Kotteakos v. United States,* 328 U.S. 750, 765, 66 S.Ct. 1239, 90 L.Ed. 1557 (1946)). The government generally bears the burden of persuasion on whether an error was harmless, although an appellate court may also consider sua sponte whether an error was harmless. *United States v. Rose,* 104 F.3d 1408, 1414-15 (1st Cir. 1997) (holding that a court may hold that an error was harmless even if the government does not make that argument, because of the seemingly mandatory text of Fed.R.Crim.P. 52(a) and the policy interest in conserving judicial resources).

For claims that an evidentiary ruling violated the Sixth Amendment's Confrontation Clause, the error must be harmless beyond a reasonable doubt. *United States v. Cameron,* 699 F.3d 621, 652 (1st Cir.2012). Cumulative errors may merit a reversal if they achieve a "critical mass" that "cast[s] a shadow upon the integrity of the verdict." *United States v. Sepulveda,* 15 F.3d 1161, 1196 (1st Cir. 1993).

1. Semidey's Hearsay Statements

Burgos argues that the district court erred in admitting Semidey's statements under the "forfeiture by wrongdoing" exception to the rule against hearsay. Fed.R.Evid. 804(b)(6). That exception allows the admission of hearsay statements p.115 "against a party that wrongfully caused—or acquiesced in wrongfully causing—the declarant's unavailability as a witness, and did so intending that result." *Id.* We review for clear error the question of whether the government has demonstrated that Burgos had the requisite intent for this exception to apply. *See Baker,* 156 F.3d at 252; *see also United States v. Scott,* 284 F.3d 758, 762 (7th Cir.2002) (question of whether Rule 804(b)(6) applies turns on fact-finding). This circuit has not defined the standard of evidence necessary to establish the requisite intent, although for the closely analogous claim that a defendant has waived his Sixth Amendment right to confront a potential witness by murdering that witness, this circuit requires the government to prove waiver by a preponderance of the evidence, *see United States v. Houlihan,* 92 F.3d 1271, 1280 (1st Cir.1996), and the majority of circuits seem to apply this standard to Rule 804(b)(6), *see Davis v. Washington,* 547 U.S. 813, 833, 126 S.Ct. 2266, 165 L.Ed.2d 224 (2006). We do the same here.

Our finding that the evidence was sufficient to convict Burgos of murdering Semidey to make sure she did not share further her knowledge of his criminal activity readily disposes of this evidentiary challenge. The only wrinkle Burgos seeks to introduce is a claim that, for purposes of Rule 804(b)(6), the prosecution must prove that charges had been filed at the time he killed Semidey. This circuit has previously held that the analogous exception to the Confrontation Clause applies to the murder of witnesses in criminal investigations even before charges have been brought. *Houlihan,* 92 F.3d at 1280. The reasoning of that case is just as applicable here, as the rule that Burgos advocates would simply create an incentive to "murder suspected [witnesses] sooner rather than later." *Id.* Thus, the forfeiture-by-wrongdoing exception is available for statements by a witness who was murdered before charges were brought if it was "reasonably foreseeable that the investigation [would] culminate in the bringing of charges." *Id.* Here, the district court did not clearly err in concluding that Burgos intended to prevent Semidey from testifying at a trial that, had she continued working with the government, was reasonably foreseeable to occur.

Burgos' attempt to rely on *Giles v. California,* 554 U.S. 353, 128 S.Ct. 2678, 171 L.Ed.2d 488 (2008) is misplaced. That case merely established that Rule 804(b)(6) and the analogous Confrontation Clause provision do not apply without an intent to prevent testimony—i.e., the exception is not available for statements by murder victims simply because the defendant made them unavailable. *Giles,* 554 U.S. at 367-77, 128 S.Ct. 2678. It did not announce a rule that the murder must actually follow the filing of charges.

2. Hearsay References To Burgos Being Under Investigation

At trial, Burgos pursued lines of attack that made relevant whether law enforcement had a preexisting investigation of or interest in Burgos prior to Semidey becoming an informant. A DEA supervisor therefore testified that he already knew Burgos as a person of interest before Semidey came into his office. Two other agents so agreed. None of the witnesses testified about what it was that caused the agents to initially become suspicious of Burgos.

Burgos now claims that all of this was somehow inadmissable hearsay. We think not. Having placed at issue the chronology of the investigation, Burgos can hardly complain that the government put on direct witnesses who could say when they started looking at Burgos. The fact that p.116 such testimony may have implied that other persons told the agents something that caused them to focus on Burgos hardly causes their first-hand, relevant testimony concerning the investigation's status to become hearsay. None of them even related the substance of what unnamed others may have said, let alone offered it for its truth.[20] *See* Fed.R.Evid. 801(c)(2).

3. *Daubert* Challenge To Testimony Of Dog Handlers

At trial, the government introduced the testimony of several law enforcement officers that one of two so-called "cadaver dogs" "alerted" when led by an area on Burgos' property where one of the officers had identified a possible grave site approximately six months before. Because no human remains were discovered, the sole purpose of this testimony was to suggest that, because the dog alerted, the jury could conclude that the location had, at one point, concealed a human cadaver.

Burgos objected to this testimony on several grounds, in particular that the testimony constituted, under Federal Rule of Evidence 702, an expert opinion that the cadaver dog could reliably locate a spot in which human remains had been buried, and that the government had failed to lay a proper basis for its reliability under *Daubert v. Merrell Dow Pharmaceuticals, Inc.,* 509 U.S. 579, 113 S.Ct. 2786, 125 L.Ed.2d 469 (1993). The district court nevertheless allowed the testimony, and Burgos now challenges that ruling on appeal.

Upon reviewing the record, we tend to agree with Burgos that the government did not lay out much of a case that a dog could reliably identify a spot in which there had been (presumably months earlier) a human cadaver, as opposed to simply responding to animal remains or to the leash-holding handler's conscious or unconscious cues. It is one thing to use a dog to identify a place in which one might look to see if human remains are present. It is quite another to use a dog to identify dirt that was once exposed to a human cadaver. The prosecution witnesses offered virtually no evidence that the scientific reliability of such a use had been established, or that their investigation protocols were generally accepted for such a use. Burgos' experts, in turn, provided easy-to-follow testimony explaining numerous basic defects in the use of the dogs for the purpose for which they were used here. They also offered much common sense, noting, for example, that the officer using the dog on a leash that alerted was the officer who had previously identified the suspected spot.

Ultimately, however, we need not determine whether the admission of the testimony was an abuse of discretion because it is plain that, for two reasons, any possible error was harmless. First, the government presented a large amount of much more compelling circumstantial evidence that Burgos was responsible for Semidey's death. That evidence included testimony from Semidey's brother-in-law that Burgos had repeatedly tried to confirm, and then said he had confirmed, a rumor that Semidey was an informant; testimony from Semidey's handlers that Semidey told them that Burgos had threatened to make her disappear if he found out she was working for the government; testimony from another witness that Burgos had threatened to kill that witness if he told anyone that Burgos p.117 knew that Semidey was an informant; testimony by Corales that after Burgos learned that Semidey was an informant, Burgos had asked Corales for a gun and said that Semidey was going to disappear; and testimony that Semidey was last seen in Burgos' car. The jury heard the recorded conversation between Corales and Burgos in which Burgos said that Semidey would not be found. They also heard testimony that Burgos had choked Semidey during a fight, which—even if the fight did not have to do with Semidey being an informant—demonstrated (assuming the jury found it credible) that Burgos was capable of violence. Finally, trace DNA evidence was found in the trunk of Burgos' car.

It is no doubt true that Burgos offered evidence to the contrary. Among other things, Burgos pointed out a number of inconsistencies in the testimony of the DEA agents investigating him; established that Corales' credibility is, to put it mildly, questionable; and offered evidence that the suspicious car-washing and the DNA evidence recovered from the trunk may have had innocent explanations. On balance, though, we conclude that the evidence other than the dog alert, while circumstantial, pointed quite forcefully at Burgos.

Our second reason for this conclusion is that the testimony about the dog alert carried very little incremental probative force because its limitations would be almost certainly apparent to any reasonable jury. Even though the dog handlers' testimony was "scientific, technical, or other specialized knowledge," *see* Fed.R.Evid. 702, it was at the non-technical end of the spectrum. Indeed, the prosecution did not even propose it as expert testimony, and the witnesses offered no technical or jargon-laden support for their claims. The defense exposed the limitations in the handlers' claims through easy-to-follow cross-examination and persuasive testimony from an expert clearly more knowledgeable on the matter than the officers. We expect the jurors were well able to understand and evaluate these types of arguments that a dog may not be able to distinguish soil that once contained a decomposed human from soil that once contained a decomposed animal, or that a handler walking the dog on a leash might cause the dog to alert. In short, the testimony about the alert of a cadaver dog that found no cadaver added little to the case.

This is not to say that the district court does not have a responsibility to exercise its gatekeeper role under Rule 702 with regard to such testimony. Indeed, in other contexts in which the government seeks to offer dog alerts as substantive evidence (for example, of the presence of an accelerant in an arson case), courts routinely test the reliability of such testimony under *Daubert. See, e.g., United States v. Marji,* 158 F.3d 60, 62-63 (2d Cir.1998) (per curiam). It is, rather, to say that failure to conduct such an analysis, assuming it is error, is more likely to be harmless in a case such as this, in which the prosecution witnesses cited no studies or reports to buttress their experience-based observations, nor claimed any special scientific expertise, and in which the defense gave the jury ample evidence from which to judge for themselves whether a cadaver dog alert that revealed no cadaver was anything more than a false alert.

4. Prior Bad Acts

At trial, the government introduced as evidence a number of recordings that Semidey had made of conversations with Burgos. One of those recordings reveals Burgos' involvement with drug trafficking in a time frame that supports the prosecution's claim that Burgos had been involved in p.118 such activity for a long time. A portion of that recording also includes a statement that, as part of that drug trafficking conspiracy, he had served as a lookout for a murder.

Burgos objected to the evidence on two grounds: (1) that the government failed to comply with Fed.R.Evid. 404(b)(2), which requires that, upon request, the government must give notice of the evidence of prior bad acts that it seeks to offer; and (2) that the evidence was in any event inadmissible as propensity evidence prohibited by Fed.R.Evid. 404(b). The district court allowed the recording to be played, but also instructed the jury that the statements about the murder may be false and should be ignored.[21]

We begin with the notice issue. The wrinkle in Burgos' argument is that the government had provided the recordings to defense several years before trial. What it did not do was specifically call attention to the fact that they contained Rule 404(b) material, even though the defense sent an e-mail specifically requesting such information. We do not reject the distinct possibility that a large bulk production may well be, without more, deficient notice. However, we need not decide whether it is so here, because even if the notice was deficient, the error was harmless.

Burgos makes no argument at all that the lack of clear notice caused him any prejudice at all. Indeed, he does not even argue that his counsel did not know beforehand that the government would seek to play the recordings. We also have not identified for ourselves any way that the defense strategy was hampered by lack of specific notice, and therefore conclude that the lack of specific notice was harmless.[22]

That leaves the question of whether the evidence was admissible on its merits. On that question, Burgos argues both that the district court erred in determining the evidence to be admissible as offered for something other than propensity, and that the admission of the evidence was not harmless. On the question of admissibility, our review is for abuse of discretion. *United States v. Rivera-Rivera*, 477 F.3d 17, 20 (1st Cir.2007).

We cannot find that the district court abused its discretion in allowing the recording as evidence relevant to an issue other than propensity. Although the government offered the recording for purposes of dating the conspiracy, the district court also stated that it was admissible as evidence of "motive" or "opportunity." The recording confirms in Burgos' own voice that he told Semidey things to which he would certainly not want her to testify. That fact was relevant to his motive to kill her. And it also corroborated her general claim that he confided in her in that matter. p.119 To the extent that the evidence might nevertheless have been excluded as unfairly prejudicial under Rule 403, given that the government had presented other evidence of Burgos' motive, the trial court's limiting instruction to the jury tilted the balance enough to trigger our deference to such a balancing.

5. Cell Phone Records

Semidey owned and used a cell phone. Her telecommunications carrier was a company named Centennial, which has since been acquired by AT & T Puerto Rico. In the regular course of its business, Centennial maintained in its computer files data for each call made by each user, including Semidey. The data included the phone numbers dialed on Semidey's phone or from which it received calls; the dates, times, and durations of the calls; whether each call was incoming or outgoing; and the particular cell tower that connected the phone to the network during the call.

During trial, the government introduced as an exhibit a print-out of Centennial's data concerning Semidey's phone's activity on various dates. The government also introduced a record maintained by Centennial showing the locations of its cell towers, including those cell towers to which its records show Semidey's phone connected on the pertinent dates. Centennial's records were accompanied by a certification of the custody of Centennial's records in compliance with Fed.R.Evid. 803(6)(D) and 902(11). The government also presented testimony from a

Centennial employee describing Centennial's record-keeping practices and explaining the data in the actual exhibits. The employee who testified was not the same employee who had queried Centennial's database to compile the print-out used at trial.

Burgos raised below (in connection with a motion in limine and a voir dire examination of the Centennial witness) and now presses on appeal three objections to the cell phone records.

First, Burgos contends that because the print-out of Semidey's phone records "was a highly specific document prepared pursuant to a request from law enforcement, containing only information requested by the agency," it did not qualify as an exception to the hearsay rule under Fed.R.Evid. 803(6)(B) and (D). That exception applies to documents "kept in the course of a regularly conducted activity of a business," and for which "making the record was a regular practice of that activity." *Id.* Burgos devotes one sentence to this contention in a 127-page brief and cites no precedent.

Burgos' complaint about the Centennial exhibits could apply to virtually any print-out of data stored in computerized business records. This circuit has previously held that exhibits showing selected data pulled from records that a company keeps in the ordinary course of business fall under the business records exception, even if the physical exhibits themselves were made to comply with a request from law enforcement. *United States v. Cameron,* 699 F.3d 621, 641-42 (1st Cir.2012) (holding that exhibits showing internet providers' records of when the defendant logged in and out of his account and the IP address from which he had logged in fell into the business records exception even though the exhibits themselves were created in response to a search warrant). Other circuits have directly held that phone records fall into the business records exception. *See, e.g., United States v. Yeley-Davis,* 632 F.3d 673, 678-79 (10th Cir. 2011); *United States v. Green,* 396 Fed. Appx. 573, 575 (11th Cir.2010) (per curiam). We see no reason to disagree here.

Burgos argues, second, that the admission of the records "failed the Confrontation p.120 Clause standard set in *Melendez-Diaz v. Massachusetts,* 557 U.S. 305, 325, 129 S.Ct. 2527, 174 L.Ed.2d 314 (2009)." Why this is so, Burgos does not explain. *Melendez-Diaz* held that business records, although not usually testimonial for purposes of triggering the Confrontation Clause, may be testimonial if the regularly conducted business activity is the creation of evidence for trial, such as analyzing substances at a forensic lab. *See id.* at 321-24, 129 S.Ct. 2527. In this case, however, the exhibits contained no data or analysis created for trial. Rather, they were simply print-outs of data created and stored by Centennial in the course of running a phone company.

Again, *Cameron* is instructive. There, even though the court concluded that records the company made in the regular course of providing internet service were not testimonial for purposes of triggering the Confrontation Clause, it held that records of the company's reports to a child pornography tip line were. It reasoned that even though company employees made such reports as part of the regular course of business, the purpose of reviewing and reporting suspected child pornography was to facilitate law enforcement.[23] *Id.* at 647-48. "[T]o create each Report, someone at Yahoo! analyzed Yahoo!'s data, drew conclusions from that data, and then made an *entirely new* statement [the tip line Report] reflecting those conclusions.... This means that someone at Yahoo! analyzed Yahoo!'s business records and concluded that (1) a crime had likely been committed and (2) a particular user likely committed that crime." *Id.*

Here, Centennial responded to a request for data that it had previously gathered and maintained for its own business purposes. The fact that the print-out of this data in this particular format was requested for the litigation does not turn the data contained in the print-out into information created for litigation. Rather, the physical manner in which the exhibit was generated simply reflects the fact that the business records were electronic, and hence their production required some choice and offered some flexibility in printing out only the requested information. *See, e.g., Yeley-Davis*, 632 F.3d at 678-79.

Third, Burgos challenges a statement by the Centennial witness that Semidey's phone was "in or around" the cell tower listed as connecting the phone during a call. She then expanded on this statement by responding in the affirmative when the government asked whether the cell tower that connected the call "was closest to the cell phone being used" when the call was initiated. Burgos argues that the witness was not qualified under Fed.R.Evid. 702 to offer testimony on the technical matter of how cell phone calls are routed through a company's towers. It does seem that the witness's responses exceeded her knowledge —nothing on the exhibit indicated that the connecting cell tower was always the closest cell tower, and the witness explained on voir dire that she did not have the knowledge or expertise to opine that the connecting cell tower was actually closer than any other cell tower.

However, we conclude that the witness's gloss was of no apparent material affect. The prosecution used the evidence to argue that Semidey must not have had her phone on July 2, shortly before she disappeared: testimony established that at around eight o'clock in the morning she was in Guánica, but the connecting tower for a call received at 7:50 a.m. was in Levittown, more than sixty miles away on p.121 the other side of the island. (This, in turn, lent indirect support to testimony by Semidey's brother-in-law that Burgos said that he had confirmed Semidey was an informant because he had her phone, and had seen that she had used it to call the DEA.) Whether or not a phone necessarily connects to the "closest" tower, any juror could have easily concluded that a cell phone would not be sixty miles away from its connecting tower. The custodian's assertion that the connecting tower is the one closest to the phone was of no significance at all in that context.

Moreover, it is not even clear who the records helped most. Burgos' counsel chose to avoid cross-examining the Centennial witness in front of the jury, and then used the exhibits in closing to make several exculpatory points, one of which involved the location of the phone. While this approach did not waive Burgos' objection to the exhibits, it does support our conclusion that the Centennial witness's opinion about which tower a phone connects to did not do real damage to Burgos' defense, and may even have helped it.

6. Bolstering DNA Evidence With Hearsay

At trial, the government introduced DNA evidence that traces of Semidey's blood were found in Burgos' car. Burgos raised a number of concerns about the analyst's methodology. The government was allowed to elicit testimony that the department protocol was to have each analyst's work reviewed by a second analyst, and if they disagreed, then a third analyst was called. It also elicited testimony that a third analyst was not called in this case. Burgos argues that this constitutes de facto testimony by the second analyst that he was in agreement with the first. Burgos argues that this violates the Confrontation Clause under *Melendez-Diaz,* 557 U.S. at 310-11, 129 S.Ct. 2527, because Burgos was unable to cross-examine the second analyst.

Burgos points to no case prohibiting the introduction of testimony that internal review protocols had been followed unless the reviewer is available to testify. We again have difficulty identifying this non-statement as hearsay, and also note that such a rule would create a disincentive to this sort of internal control mechanisms in forensic investigations. As such, we decline to announce such a rule, and hold that if there was error, any error was harmless beyond a reasonable doubt because Burgos had ample opportunity to cross-examine the primary analyst.

Because we have disposed of several issues on harmless error grounds, we have also considered whether all such possible errors cumulatively were harmless. We find that they were, given how tangential the challenged evidence in question was, as compared to the strong body of plainly admissible evidence supporting the verdict.

III. Conclusion

For the reasons stated above, we *affirm.*

[1] In doing so, we note that this circuit has been inconsistent in its approach to reciting the facts of the case when considering a challenge other than the sufficiency of the evidence to support a conviction. *See United States v. Rodríguez-Soler,* 773 F.3d 289, 290 (1st Cir.2014) (discussing the inconsistency). Generally, though, the nature of the question on appeal and the applicable standard of review should make self-evident whether an appellate court should present the record largely in equipoise (for example, when it is assessing how an added or omitted item may have tipped the balance, *see Felton,* 417 F.3d at 99), or present the evidence as if the factfinder favored the prosecution's side of any factual disputes (to ascertain, for example, whether the evidence was sufficient to sustain the conviction, *see United States v. Ayala-García,* 574 F.3d 5, 8 (1st Cir.2009)), or assume that the jury could well have been persuaded by the defendant's side of such disputes (to ascertain, for example, whether the failure to submit an element of the offense to the jury requires reversal in the absence of any objection to the failure, *see United States v. Georgacarakos,* 988 F.2d 1289, 1294-97 (1st Cir.1993), *abrogated on other grounds by United States v. Scott,* 270 F.3d 30, 35 (1st Cir. 2001)).

[2] The indictment also included a forfeiture count that is not at issue in this appeal.

[3] Burgos argued that there was insufficient evidence that Burgos intended to kill Semidey because she was an informant, as opposed to for some other reason. He also argued that the evidence presented at trial constituted a fatal variance from that charged in the indictment. The latter argument was also the basis of a mistrial motion that the district court denied in open court.

[4] *Young* used several terms to describe the standard it was applying to the reformed affidavit, including "adequate," "sufficient," and whether the omissions were "material" to a finding of probable cause. 877 F.2d at 1102-04 There is nothing to suggest the court intended the terms to convey different meanings; indeed, its reliance on *Franks* makes clear it was applying a sufficiency standard. *Franks,* 438 U.S. at 171-72, 98 S.Ct. 2674 (asking whether a reformed affidavit contained "sufficient content ... to support a finding of probable cause").

[5] While there was trial testimony by Semidey's mother and sister that Semidey agreed to be an informant to avoid possible prosecution in another matter, the DEA agents involved denied this.

[6] Our conclusion that the affidavit contained a sufficient basis to establish probable cause for the wiretap at the time of the Title III application also disposes of Burgos' argument that the information contained in the affidavit was "stale."

[7] We do not read the "minimally adequate" standard to differ substantively from the sufficiency standard applied to a challenge that omissions undermine probable cause. *See* footnote 4, *supra.*

[8] While this would make little sense in the Fourth Amendment context, where the named individual would be asserting the unnamed individual's rights, in this context the named individual is claiming that his conversations were recorded pursuant to a statutorily deficient wiretap, even though it is difficult to see how the deficiency could be prejudicial.

[9] While the rule applies to omissions made with intentional or reckless disregard for the truth, *see Burke,* 405 F.3d at 81-82, we need not decide whether or not the omissions here were reckless or intentional, because either way, they do not undermine probable cause.

[10] Corales volunteered to serve as an informant in December 2005, after he learned that co-conspirator Castillo had been arrested on charges related to their preparations to import cocaine from the Dominican Republic.

[11] In 2009, Congress amended Rule 41(e), increasing to 14 days the time to execute the warrant.

[12] At the time *Bonner* was decided, the subdivision was numbered 41(d).

[13] The warrant was executed in compliance with the 10-day statutory maximum in effect at the time, and Burgos does not argue it was not. The warrant was issued on December 29, 2005; the search of the farm took place on December 30 and 31, 2005, and the search of the car took place on January 5, 2006.

[14] "I'm telling the truth, if in any case I would recognize anybody of the persons involved in the case, it would come from me to tell the Court.... I haven't."

[15] In the motion, Burgos also raised a number of even more attenuated connections.

[16] Semidey's mother testified that the fight began when Burgos said he wouldn't sell a kilogram of cocaine to a certain person and Semidey said she would have sold the drugs. Her mother then responded affirmatively to defense counsel's characterizing the fight as being about the fact that Burgos didn't like that Semidey was "acting like a drug dealer." Agent Iglesias also testified that Semidey told him that the fight had to do with Burgos' reluctance to sell drugs to a certain person.

[17] Burgos preserved this objection below through a mistrial motion that the district court denied in open court.

[18] Burgos' view of the events could arguably be characterized as three or four conspiracies: separate importation and distribution conspiracies in both 2004-05 and 1998-99, although as we discuss below, he argues that there was no evidence of an importation conspiracy in 1998-99. However, because his primary complaint turns on two distinct periods of time, we follow his lead in referring to only "two" conspiracies.

[19] The exchange followed a discussion in which Corales was unable to estimate how many kilograms of cocaine had changed hands between him and Burgos during their relationship. It consists of:

Q: Well, is it fair to say that this relationship went on for close to seven years?

A: Yes.

Q: And throughout that time period, were there exchanges of drugs, either from you to him or from him to you in kilo quantities of cocaine?

A: Yes.

[20] Semidey's husband's testimony that he had heard of the investigation from the supervisor, even if it was hearsay, was harmless because it was cumulative of the admissible testimony.

[21] The district court instructed the jury as follows: "These statements by Mr. Burgos are uncorroborated and, as I mentioned to you before lunch, for all we know he may have been huffing and puffing to impress his girlfriend. Okay? You must not consider the statements regarding those incidents for the truth of those events. In other words, you must not take those things as proof that the events actually occurred or that Mr. Burgos was in any way involved in them, neither may you hold them against Mr. Burgos in any other manner."

[22] Burgos offers two cases that he argues stand for the proposition that the failure to provide notice of Rule 404(b) evidence cannot be harmless. Both involve surprise testimony that hampered the defense strategy in identifiable ways. *United States v. Carrasco,* 381 F.3d 1237, 1240-41 (11th Cir.2004) (undermining a defense based on a lack of intent); *United States v. Vega,* 188 F.3d 1150, 1155 (9th Cir.1999) (surprise witness prevented defense from preparing for cross-examination on the prior acts).

[23] Because the records triggered the Confrontation Clause, the court did not analyze whether they satisfied the business records exception.

784 F.3d 11 (2015)

UNITED STATES of America, Appellee,

v.

Jorge CORREA-OSORIO; Denise Shepard-Fraser, Defendants, Appellants.

Nos. 12-1300, 12-2220.

United States Court of Appeals, First Circuit.

April 22, 2015.

US v. Correa-Osorio, 784 F. 3d 11 (1st Cir. 2015)

p.13 Alejandra Bird López, for appellant Jorge Correa-Osorio.

p.14 Claudia Leis Bolgen, with whom Bolgen & Bolgen was on brief, for appellant Denise Shepard-Fraser.

John A. Mathews II, Assistant United States Attorney, with whom Rosa Emilia Rodríguez-Vélez, United States Attorney, and Nelson Pérez-Sosa, Assistant United States Attorney, Chief, Appellate Division, were on brief, for appellee.

Before THOMPSON, LIPEZ, and BARRON, Circuit Judges.

THOMPSON, Circuit Judge.

OVERVIEW

Jorge Correa-Osorio and Denise Shepard-Fraser stand convicted of cocaine offenses. Both ask us to reverse, though for different reasons. Correa, for example, thinks the judge quadruply erred—first by admitting identification evidence (because a witness made him off a highly suggestive and unreliable procedure), next by admitting key statements under the coconspirator exception to the hearsay rule (because the government showed neither that he was in on the conspiracy nor that the statements furthered the conspiracy's aim), then by admitting evidence of a cocaine-filled suitcase (because the evidence was irrelevant, prejudicial, and confusing), and finally by committing cumulative error (because the net effect of what the judge did made his trial fundamentally unfair). He is wrong. Shepard, for her part, thinks the judge doubly erred—first by finding the evidence sufficient to support her convictions (because the government did not prove guilty knowledge) and then by giving her a 128-month prison term (because the sentence was procedurally and substantively unreasonable). But she is wrong too. We will explain our thinking shortly, right after we set out the case's background.

BACKGROUND

This case should seem familiar to any regular reader of the Federal Reporter, given that it concerns yet another major cocaine conspiracy involving a creative distribution network, a large cast of coconspirators (some with colorful nicknames), and a turncoat who became the government's star witness.

(1)

The Conspiracy at a Glance

Running from June 2006 to June 2008, the conspiracy—led by a man named Manuel Santana-Cabrera (also known as "El Boss")—operated like this. Recruited couriers took commercial flights from San Juan to mainland cities, including Philadelphia and New York. Before boarding, they would check luggage filled with old clothes, pillows, blankets, *etc.*—stuff that could get through security without incident. Other conspirators working at the airport would switch the checked luggage with luggage packed with cocaine. Couriers would then fly to their destinations, claim their checked bags, and hand them off to a taxi driver—known to some as "Manopla"—who was in on the conspiracy too. Couriers would make $3,000 a trip.

(2)

The Conspiracy's Unraveling

In September 2006 DEA agents in Philadelphia heard from their colleagues in San Juan that there was something fishy about the flight itineraries of José Vega-Torres and two others, who were flying from San Juan to New York after a layover in Philly.[1] The Philadelphia agents p.15 looked for and found the trio's bags. After a drug-detecting dog alerted to the odor of drugs, agents got a search warrant. Their search struck pay dirt: each bag had at least 13 brick-shaped objects wrapped in a blanket, and the objects field-tested positive for cocaine.

Agents arrested Vega and his two sidekicks in New York. Vega initially told a pack of lies about why he had cocaine in his luggage, who had given it to him, who had asked him to go to New York, and who had chauffeured him to the airport. But he eventually agreed to come clean and cooperate in exchange for the government's promise not to indict his wife on conspiracy-related charges too (she was with him on one of his smuggling trips to New York). His cooperation later led to the arrest of Correa and Shepard (plus others) and to much of the evidence the government used at trial (Correa and Shepard were tried together).

(3)

The Case Against Correa

At trial Vega identified Correa, calling him by a nickname, "El Don." And he testified about the times that he saw him in 2006, apparently (he did not recall the exact dates).

The first time, Vega had gone to leader Santana's house with a conspirator named Israel Martes-Canales (nicknamed "Shaq"). While there, he and Martes helped load six suitcases into the trunk of Correa's car. The suitcases were similar in size and weight to drug luggage Vega had picked up in New York. Correa told Santana that he was actually using his wife's car and that he would "get in trouble" if she found out what he was up to. And after Correa left, Santana told Vega that "Don" was "in charge of taking bags into the airport and putting them inside the plane."

Vega later saw Correa working at the San Juan airport. About to jet off to New York to deliver more cocaine, he spotted Correa on the tarmac, loading bags onto a plane.

As for the last occasion, Vega went one time with Martes and another conspirator named Ricardo Soler-Rivera to drop a bag off at Correa's house. Soler said the bag had $90,000, just before he gave it to Correa.

Seeking to undermine his credibility, Correa's lawyer extensively cross-examined Vega on a number of topics. Vega, for example, testified about the inducements he received for cooperation, the big one being the government's pledge not to go after his wife if he played ball. Beyond that, he confessed to not telling agents about "El Don" during an early debriefing, even though other conspirators' names easily rolled off his tongue. And despite saying how a conspirator told him that the mainland-bound suitcases contained cocaine, he admitted to not personally knowing whether that was in fact true. He also admitted to never seeing Correa handle any of his checked luggage. What is more, he said that "El Don" had braided hair—something the defense played up because Correa later testified that he did not have braids in 2006.

On redirect Vega said that he personally knew Correa was part of the Santana-drug-trafficking cabal. But the government did not just rely on Vega's testimony to help tell the conspiracy's story. As part of its case-in-chief, the government, for example, also presented (over defense objections) evidence concerning the seizure of a cocaine-filled suitcase at the San Juan airport on October 4, 2007. The prosecution's theory was that evidence about the suitcase constituted overt-act evidence p.16 linking the defendants to the conspiracy. Here is what you need to know.

Marionel Báez-Peña—an airport-worker-turned-convict—testified that he loaded drug luggage onto planes for two people: kingpin Santana and a person named Maximo Bencosme-Aybar (also known as "Phantasma"). Báez had done two jobs for Santana. And he was set to do one for Bencosme on October 4.[2] But he was not feeling well that day, so he asked airport-worker Miguel Ramos-Santi to help out. Another airport worker, Luis del-Valle-Febres, testified that early on the morning of October 4, Ramos asked him to put a tag on a suitcase left on a cart. And del-Valle did just that.

Unfortunately for those involved, DEA-agent Hector Tapia-Gerena—a member of the team investigating Santana's drug doings—got (according to his testimony) a tip that day about a suspicious suitcase at the San Juan airport. Springing into action, he headed for the airport's baggage carousel and spied an unattended suitcase on a cart. The bag's tag read September 23. A drug-sniffing dog detected the presence of contraband. And x-rays of the suitcase showed—in outline—block-shaped items. Agents opened the bag and saw pillows, towels, and t-shirts, plus 13 bricks of powder that tested positive for cocaine. One thing led to another, and agents arrested Báez, Ramos, and del-Valle.

Testifying in his own defense, Correa denied important elements of the accusations against him. For example, he said that until his arrest, he had never met Santana. And he added that the first time he laid eyes on Vega was in court. He also painted a picture of himself as an educated, intelligent person of strong character who lived a very simple lifestyle—one incompatible with a criminal way of life. He insisted too that he did not have access to some areas while working at the airport and so could not have snuck drug bags in as alleged.

(4)

The Case Against Shepard

The case against Shepard essentially rests on a single event—her flying from San Juan to New York on September 9 and back again on September 10. The crucial testimony came from Vega, who had known her for about 20 years and who had what he described as a "friendly" relationship with her in 2006. This is what he had to say.

Already in New York, Vega and Martes went with cabbie Manopla to a New York airport to pick up Shepard and two others. Vega saw the threesome walking from the airport to the cabstand, each carrying two suitcases. Vega and Martes helped put the bags in the taxi's trunk. Manopla then dropped everyone off at a hotel and sped off with the luggage. The accommodations were a little tight—the five from the cab (Vega, Martes, Shepard, and her two companions) stayed with four or five others in a single room a conspirator (the record does not say who) had booked for what ended up being Shepard's one night there. Everyone—except for Vega—came from the same housing project in Puerto Rico.

At some point (the record does not indicate exactly when), Santana called Martes and ordered him to pick up a cash-filled bag at another locale and get the money back to Puerto Rico. So Martes and Vega hopped in a cab, grabbed a bag of $261,000 p.17 in cash, and headed back to the hotel. They paid each person in the room—including Shepard—$3,000 for helping get the suitcases to New York. Then they rolled up the rest of the money in socks and crammed the rolls into their cohorts' luggage. Vega, however, did not say who else was there when he and Martes rolled and packed the cash—most importantly for present purposes, he did not say whether Shepard saw the "show."

Martes flew back to San Juan, apparently to handle a pressing matter (it is unclear just when he left). Vega stayed behind, bought the others—including Shepard—tickets to San Juan, and jetted back with them on September 10 (their flight left New York at 9:00 p.m. on September 10 and landed in San Juan at 12:55 a.m. the next day). Martes and Soler rendezvoused with the group at the San Juan airport and drove them to Santana's house. Only Vega and Martes went inside, however. And there they gave Santana the cash.

Looking to score some points on cross-examination (she presented no evidence in her defense), Shepard's lawyer got Vega to talk about his run-ins with the law. Her attorney also got him to repeat that he had lied to federal agents a bunch of times before. And her lawyer got him to admit that he could not look Shepard in the eye in court (other than when he pointed to her sitting at counsel table). But the prosecution's redirect brought out that he personally knew that she was a member of the Santana-drug-trafficking syndicate (a damning bit of evidence when it comes to one of her arguments on appeal, *i.e.,* that she hadn't a clue what was in the suitcases; more on this later).

(5)

Verdicts and Sentences

After hearing all the evidence, the jury convicted Correa and Shepard each on two counts: conspiring to distribute cocaine and possessing with intent to distribute cocaine. *See* 21 U.S.C. §§ 841(a)(1), 841(b)(1)(A), and 846. The judge then handed out stiff prison sentences, with Correa and Shepard getting concurrent terms of 132 months and 128 months, respectively.

Which takes us to today's appeals.[3]

CORREA'S APPEAL

Correa believes that the judge slipped by admitting Vega's in-court identification of him. He also thinks that the judge stumbled by admitting three "hearsay" statements under the coconspirator exception: Vega's statement calling him "El Don," Santana's statement calling "El Don" the go-to guy for getting drug bags on planes, and Soler's statement saying a bag for "El Don" had $90,000. On top of that he thinks that the judge blundered by admitting evidence concerning the suitcase seized on October 4. And lastly he believes that the judge's errors—even if harmless on their own—cumulatively violated his fair-trial rights. Though passionately argued, these points do not get him the reversal he seeks.

(1)

In-Court Identification

Leading things off is Correa's claim that Vega identified him at trial under unduly-suggestive conditions—an identification, he adds, that was not otherwise reliable. He never raised this objection below, limiting us to plain-error review—a standard that requires him to prove four p.18 things: (1) an error, (2) that is clear or obvious, (3) which affects his substantial rights (*i.e.,* the error made him worse off), and which (4) seriously impugns the fairness, integrity, or public reputation of the proceeding. *See, e.g., United States v. Olano,* 507 U.S. 725, 734-37, 113 S.Ct. 1770, 123 L.Ed.2d 508 (1993); *United States v. Kinsella,* 622 F.3d 75, 83 (1st Cir.2010). Applying that not-so-defendant-friendly standard, *see United States v. Williams,* 717 F.3d 35, 42 (1st Cir. 2013)—and knowing too that we must fight off any "reflexive inclination" to reverse unpreserved errors, *see Puckett v. United States,* 556 U.S. 129, 134, 129 S.Ct. 1423, 173 L.Ed.2d 266 (2009)—we see no way to reverse here.

First, some context. Vega testified for the government over three days. During the first day or so he talked at length about a number of things, including: his personal life (he is married with three children), how and why he joined the Santana-commanded conspiracy (a friend told him about it, knowing he needed money), what he did for the conspiracy (helping get cocaine to New York and cash back to Puerto Rico), and the fallout from his arrest in New York (pleading guilty to drug crimes, agreeing to cooperate with authorities, and getting benefits for his cooperation).

On the second day Vega brought up Shepard (explaining, for example, how he had known her for two decades and was "friendly" with her in 2006). And he identified her for the jury.[4] That afternoon—following a lunch break—the prosecutor asked Vega about his visiting Santana's house. On one of those occasions, Vega said, a "person known as 'the Don' was there." Responding to a question from the judge, Vega clarified that Santana and "El Don" were different people. And if "El Don" is in the "courtroom," the prosecutor said to Vega, "can you describe him or her?" "Yes," Vega replied, "[t]he gentleman with the long-sleeved shirt." Correa's lawyer "concede[d] that [Vega] is referring to my client."

Kicking off cross-examination, Correa's counsel asked Vega if he had met with DEA agents and prosecutors to "discuss what you were going to testify" to. "Yes," Vega answered. Counsel (as we said) then later tried to chip away at the in-court identification, getting Vega to say that "El Don" had braided hair (reminiscent of a look favored by a Puerto Rican rapper known as "Don Omar") and eliciting from Correa that he (Correa) did not have braids in 2006 (which again is around the time Vega supposedly saw him). And counsel repeated this misidentification theory in his closing argument, telling the jury that Vega simply "confus[ed] my client with somebody else." Vega had an obvious motive to lie, counsel also stressed, because his wife's freedom was at stake.

Now back to Correa's newly-minted argument. He believes that because he was the only male defendant at defense table, Vega obviously knew whom he should single out—any watcher of TV crime dramas can surely tell which person in the courtroom is the defendant, he adds. And this procedure, he says, was so unnecessarily suggestive that it raised a very serious likelihood of misidentification—meaning the judge should have barred the evidence on due-process grounds, even without an objection from counsel. We see things differently.

p.19 The Constitution, caselaw holds, guards against convictions tied to evidence of questionable reliability—not by banning the evidence's admission, but by giving defendants the tools to convince jurors the evidence is not belief-worthy. *See Perry v. New Hampshire,* ___ U.S. ___, 132 S.Ct. 716, 723, 181 L.Ed.2d 694 (2012). There is, however, a small exception for police-arranged identifications—think photo arrays, showups, and lineups. *See id.* at 724. Due process, we see, bars trial courts from admitting such evidence "if the ... identification procedure was so impermissibly suggestive as to give rise to a very substantial likelihood of irreparable misidentification"—irreparable because trial mechanisms would not help a jury distinguish between reliable and unreliable identifications. *See Neil v. Biggers,* 409 U.S. 188, 197, 93 S.Ct. 375, 34 L.Ed.2d 401 (1972) (quoting *Simmons v. United States,* 390 U.S. 377, 384, 88 S.Ct. 967, 19 L.Ed.2d 1247 (1968)); *see also Manson v. Brathwaite,* 432 U.S. 98, 116, 97 S.Ct. 2243, 53 L.Ed.2d 140 (1977). Based on the *Biggers* line of cases, courts confronted with a challenge to a police-run identification process must ask, first, whether the process was unduly suggestive, and, if yes, whether the identification was still reliable given the totality of the circumstances.[5] *See, e.g., United States v. Arthur,* 764 F.3d 92, 99-100 (1st Cir.2014); *United States v. Jones,* 689 F.3d 12, 17 (1st Cir.2012). Deterring police misuse of identification procedures is the key principle animating what we will call the *Biggers* test. *See Perry,* 132 S.Ct. at 726.

The deterrence rationale falls away, obviously, if the police did not arrange the identification. And thus, our judicial superiors tell us, the *Biggers* test does not apply and an altogether different method of analysis takes center stage: if a witness identifies the defendant under circumstances that are not police-rigged, any dispute about the identification's reliability is for the jury, with the defendant protected by ordinary criminal-trial safeguards—the right to an effective counsel who can try to poke holes in the witness's identification, the right to be presumed innocent and be convicted by a jury of one's peers only by proof beyond a reasonable doubt, *etc. See id.* at 723, 728-30 (abrogating *United States v. Bouthot,* 878 F.2d 1506, 1516 (1st Cir.1989), among other cases).

A key question is: In cases like ours—involving a prosecutor's securing an in-court identification under supposedly suggestive circumstances—which approach applies, *Perry's* or *Biggers's?*[6] One could argue either way.

On the one hand: In a recent case bearing an uncanny resemblance to Correa's—involving as it does in-court identifications of a male defendant seated at counsel table, with the police playing no part in his getting picked out—the Eleventh Circuit (by a 2-1 vote) read *Perry* as holding that the *Biggers* test applies only if the complained-of suggestion arose from improper police conduct. *See United States v. Whatley,* 719 F.3d 1206, 1215-17 (11th Cir. 2013). And staying with *Perry,* that Circuit rebuffed the defendant's due-process challenge, concluding that he got the same p.20 process "identified in *Perry* as constitutionally sufficient" for persons not identified through police-rigged procedures. *Id.* at 1216-17.

On the other hand: The Seventh Circuit (by a 2-1 vote)—after citing *Perry*—more recently used the *Biggers* test to reject a due-process attack on an in-court identification of a black male seated at defense table. *See Lee v. Foster,* 750 F.3d 687, 691-92 (7th Cir.2014). Because nothing in the record showed that the witness had made the identification "solely on the basis of [the defendant's] race" or that the prosecutor had asked the witness to point to the black male at counsel table, that Circuit found no undue suggestion. *Id.*

We need not choose sides in this debate today. And that is because Correa's identification argument fails under either *Perry* or *Biggers.*[7]

(a)

Applying *Perry*

Assuming without deciding that *Perry* governs our situation, we note the following. The jurors had ring-side seats for Vega's identification. Hearing him speak and reading his facial expressions and body language, they were best positioned to detect any hint of unsureness when he singled-out Correa. They also had an up-close look at Vega during the defense's cross-examination of him—and counsel cross-examined him with gusto, getting him to say, for example, that "El Don" had braided hair when Correa testified that he did not wear his hair that way in 2006. Plus, the jurors heard counsel's attack on Vega's credibility during summation, with counsel arguing (among other things) that Vega had "confus[ed] my client with somebody else" and that he had every incentive to tell agents whatever they wanted to hear (keeping his wife out of jail was incentive number one). And of course the jury found Correa guilty despite the presumption of innocence and the beyond-a-reasonable doubt burden of proof.

Correa protests that the identification does not square with due process because he was seated at the defense table when Vega fingered him. But the government did not put him there. Also keep in mind that he had a constitutional right to be present at trial, *see Illinois v. Allen*, 397 U.S. 337, 338, 90 S.Ct. 1057, 25 L.Ed.2d 353 (1970), and defendants (who have to sit somewhere, clearly) usually sit at counsel table to assist in their defense.

Simply put, Correa received all the safeguards *Perry* stamped sufficient to protect a defendant's due-process rights in this context. *See Perry*, 132 S.Ct. at 728-30 (explaining that the way to handle unreliable evidence is through the adversary system, which includes the assistance of counsel, the ability to confront witnesses, the right to introduce evidence, and the presumption of innocence). Which is why his argument loses under *Perry*.

(b)

Applying the *Biggers* Test

Alternatively, assuming without deciding that the *Biggers* test holds sway, we have p.21 this to say. Sure, every in-court identification has "some element of suggestion." *Perry*, 132 S.Ct. at 727.[8] What matters is whether there was *undue* suggestion (words like "unnecessary" and "impermissible" can substitute for "undue," by the way). And that is where Correa gets tripped up.

An in-court identification may be unduly suggestive if, for example, the prosecutor drew the witness's attention to the defendant (say, by pointing to him) or asked questions that suggested the hoped-for result,[9] or if the defendant looked different from others in the courtroom or at counsel table when the identification occurred (say, by being the only black person present).[10] These are constitutional danger zones, for sure. Yet the record reveals no such problems here, however. And Correa does not argue otherwise—these special problems do not appear in his brief and so any argument along those lines is waived. *See, e.g., United States v. Zannino*, 895 F.2d 1, 17 (1st Cir.1990).

Instead he basically says that he had a huge "pick me" sign on him because (again) he was the only male defendant at counsel table, and it was that—and that alone—which made the situation unduly suggestive.[11] But he does not cite—and we could not find—any federal-appellate case supporting his position (our court has not addressed the issue), though we did spy a case from another circuit undercutting his claim. *See United States v. Bush*, 749 F.2d 1227, 1232 (7th Cir.1984) (noting that "[t]he only suggestive circumstance identified by defendant is that he sat at counsel table" and holding that "[t]his circumstance alone is not enough to establish a violation of due process").[12] Simply put, p.22 he never gets to first base under the *Biggers* test.

(c)

Summing up so Far

The plain-error standard is "extremely" difficult to prove. *United States v. Vigneau,* 187 F.3d 70, 82 (1st Cir.1999). And rightly so, since the standard's central aim is "to encourage timely objections," *see United States v. Dominguez Benitez,* 542 U.S. 74, 82, 124 S.Ct. 2333, 159 L.Ed.2d 157 (2004)—a goal that (hopefully) deters unsavory sandbagging by lawyers (*i.e.,* their keeping mum about an error, pocketing it for later just in case the jury does not acquit) and gives judges the chance to fix things without the need for appeals and new trials, *see Puckett,* 556 U.S. at 134, 140, 129 S.Ct. 1423. But what happened to Correa was not plain error, because it was not error when measured against either *Perry* or *Biggers.*

(d)

Responding to the Dissent[13]

The dissent thinks we are all wrong on the *Biggers* issue, insisting that the prosecutor so clearly manipulated the in-court identification—using an unnecessarily-suggestive process—that the judge should have found a *Biggers* violation without help from counsel. *See United States v. Frady,* 456 U.S. 152, 163, 102 S.Ct. 1584, 71 L.Ed.2d 816 (1982) (explaining that plain error means an error so obvious that a judge is "derelict in countenancing it, even absent the defendant's timely assistance in detecting it"). But nothing the dissent says points to plain error—*i.e.,* an "indisputable" slip up on the judge's part, given controlling precedent. *See United States v. Jones,* 748 F.3d 64, 70 (1st Cir.2014) (citing *United States v. Marcus,* 560 U.S. 258, 262, 130 S.Ct. 2159, 176 L.Ed.2d 1012 (2010)); *see also United States v. Caraballo-Rodriguez,* 480 F.3d 62, 70 (1st Cir. 2007); *United States v. Diaz,* 285 F.3d 92, 97 (1st Cir.2002).

Here is the essence of the dissent's undue-suggestion thesis: The prosecutor's prepping Vega, having him testify for over a day (which gave him plenty of time to eye Correa at counsel table), and then (and only then) having him pick Correa out infracted due process—an in-your-face infraction that should have spurred the judge to strike the identification. The prosecutor, the dissent adds, should have done one of two things instead—first, relied on an identification Vega made pretrial through non-suggestive means (no pretrial ID appears in the record, though), or, second, relied on an in-court lineup (we will call these his alternative-identification methods). But in our experience nothing odd went down here—certainly nothing amounting to a clear-cut constitutional violation.

Prosecutors (like other lawyers) prep witnesses (even if just to tell them to testify truthfully). And there is no hint in the record that the prosecutor crossed any line in prepping Vega (for example by coaching him to pick Correa). Importantly too, the dissent cites no law (let alone binding law)—and we know of none—saying that routine witness prep equals undue suggestion.

As for the identification's timing, even the dissent admits that prosecutors can (within wide margins) present their case in p.23 the order they wish. And the prosecutor did what any lawyer would do, eliciting background info from Vega—

about how the Santana-controlled conspiracy ran (who did what, with whom, for whom, where, and when), for instance—which helped establish a foundation for identifying Correa.[14] Regardless, the dissent again cites no settled law—and we are aware of none—holding a prosecutor acts in an unduly-suggestive way simply by having a witness testify (here, for a day and a half) before identifying the accused.[15]

What is left is the dissent's talk of alternative-identification methods. Once again the dissent cites no controlling authority—and we found none—requiring out-of-court identifications or in-court lineups over the "usual practice" of having a witness identify the defendant from the stand (again, assuming the usual practice does not stray into the constitutional danger zone most recently referenced in footnote 15).[16]

Concluding, as we do, that the dissent's undue-suggestion critique does not add up to plain error (or, indeed, to error of any kind), we turn to Correa's other claims.[17]

(2)

"Hearsay" Statements

Correa does not contest the sufficiency of the evidence against him. Rather he next complains that much of the government's case depended on hearsay statements not admissible under the coconspirator exception, which exempts from the hearsay rule comments made by a coconspirator during and in furtherance of the conspiracy. *See* Fed.R.Evid. 801(d)(2)(E). This is how that exception works. If a defendant contests the admissibility of an alleged coconspirator statement, p.24 the judge may conditionally admit the evidence and put off ruling until the close of all the evidence. *See, e.g., United States v. Ciresi,* 697 F.3d 19, 25-26 (1st Cir.2012) (discussing *United States v. Petrozziello,* 548 F.2d 20 (1st Cir.1977)). Prosecutors must then prove by a preponderance of the evidence (apart from the statements themselves) the elements of admissibility under the exception—that the defendant and the speaker were coconspirators and that the speaker made the statement during the course and in furtherance of the conspiracy. *See id.* at 25; *see also United States v. Piper,* 298 F.3d 47, 52 (1st Cir.2002). A judge's ruling on this score is called a *"Petrozziello* ruling." *Ciresi,* 697 F.3d at 25. If prosecutors fall short, the defendant can ask the judge to declare a mistrial or strike the statements. *See, e.g., United States v. Mangual-Garcia,* 505 F.3d 1, 8 (1st Cir.2007).

Correa gripes about three statements admitted through Vega's testimony: Vega's statement pinning the "El Don" nickname on him, Santana's statement tagging "El Don" as the person in charge of getting drug bags on planes, and Soler's statement saying a bag handed to "El Don" had $90,000. In making this pitch, he does not deny being nicknamed "El Don."[18] Nor does he question Santana's and Soler's membership in the conspiracy. He just thinks that the prosecutors did not show it more likely than not (the usual preponderance standard) that he was *the* "El Don" who coconspired with the speakers or that the challenged comments furthered the conspiracy.

We typically give abuse-of-discretion review to the question of whether a statement is in fact hearsay. *See, e.g., United States v. Brown,* 669 F.3d 10, 22-24 (1st

Cir.2012); *United States v. Colón-Díaz,* 521 F.3d 29, 33 (1st Cir.2008). And we usually review objections to a judge's Petrozziello ruling for clear error, *see, e.g., Ciresi,* 697 F.3d at 26, knowing a party cannot show clear error if there are competing views of the evidence, *see, e.g., United States v. Dowdell,* 595 F.3d 50, 73 (1st Cir.2010).

Right off the bat, the parties fight over whether Correa did enough below to preserve the nickname argument for review (they agree he preserved the other arguments, however). We can sidestep that issue, though, because it is easier to decide the argument on the merits. *See United States v. Murphy,* 193 F.3d 1, 5 (1st Cir. 1999) (taking a similar tack in a similar situation).

Correa helpfully concedes one thing—that Vega was not at all clear on how he learned about the "El Don" moniker that he stuck Correa with. That is a very big deal because we need not worry about the coconspirator exception unless the contested comment constituted hearsay. *See id.* at 6. Correa speculates that Vega "could only have learned" about the "El Don" sobriquet "through hearsay"— *i.e.,* that Vega must have heard about the nickname from someone other than Correa. But the evidence does not foreclose the possibility that Vega did indeed hear about the "El Don" handle from Correa. True, Vega did testify that he did not chat with Correa the time he saw him at Santana's house. Yet that hardly means that Vega did not catch Correa introduce himself to another there as "El Don." And because no one can possibly know—based on what is before us—whether Vega got the nickname info via hearsay, Correa has not shown an abuse of discretion on this threshold issue.

p.25 Moving to the *Petrozziello* issue, Correa has not shown clear error with the judge's handling of the other statements—Santana's comment that "El Don" was the point man for getting the drug bags on planes, and Soler's remark that a bag for "El Don" had $90,000. For one thing, the record—even leaving aside the hearsay statements themselves—demonstrates that Correa more probably than not was a coconspirator of the speakers. Recall Vega's testimony about seeing Correa with conspiracy-chief Santana at Santana's home. They had suitcases that resembled the ones Vega smuggled into New York. The bags—which Vega helped load into the trunk of the car—weighed about the same too. And after putting the bags into the auto, Vega heard Correa tell Santana that the car was his wife's and that this could land him in hot water with her if she knew what he was up to. The evidence of Correa's conspiracy membership might not be overwhelming, but it suffices on a preponderance standard.[19] Or at least the judge did not clearly err in so concluding. Also, the "in furtherance" requirement can be satisfied (among other ways) by statements identifying other conspirators, explaining how the conspiracy works, or updating members on the conspiracy's doings. *See, e.g., Ciresi,* 697 F.3d at 29, 30; *United States v. Díaz,* 670 F.3d 332, 348-49 (1st Cir.2012). And using the preponderance test, the contested statements fit the bill. Or so the judge was entitled to conclude without clearly erring.[20]

Two sets of issues down, two to go.

(3)

Evidence Concerning the Suitcase Seized on October 4

Correa's penultimate argument—made and lost below, meaning abuse-of-discretion review is called for—is simple enough. Prosecutors, he reminds us, presented evidence about the suitcase seized on October 4 to help establish the existence of the Santana-led conspiracy. Yet, he insists, other evidence already in the record showed a Santana-run conspiracy, and no evidence tied this suitcase to that conspiracy. Yes, he stresses, Báez did testify that he himself helped sneak drug bags onto planes for both Santana *and* Bencosme. But, he notes, Báez made it crystal clear that he and others did the October 4 caper only for *Bencosme,* and there is zero evidence (to quote his brief) that Bencosme "ever worked for or with" Santana. So, his argument continues, evidence of the October 4 seizure was wholly irrelevant, unfairly prejudicial, and potentially confusing, given that it could have distracted the jury's attention from a material issue—namely, the existence (or not) of a Santana-headed conspiracy. *See* Fed. R.Evid. 403. His theory has a certain bite. But we need not decide whether he is right because any error—if error there was—was harmless and so not reversible.

Errors in admitting evidence are "harmless" unless the evidence "likely affected" the trial's outcome. *See United States v. Landrón-Class,* 696 F.3d 62, 71 (1st Cir.2012) (parenthetically quoting *United States v. Dunbar,* 553 F.3d 48, 59 (1st Cir.2009)); *see also United States v. Adams,* 375 F.3d 108, 113 (1st Cir.2004). p.26 And as for whether a Santana-captained conspiracy was a real thing—the *raison d'être* for the suitcase evidence's presentation, Correa says—plenty of evidence showed that it was. Just remember all the testimony about how conspirators stashed drug bags aboard chosen planes in San Juan bound for New York, then dropped the drugs off in New York for sale, and then shipped cash back to San Juan, with Santana—a/k/a "El Boss"—pulling the strings. Compared with all this, the suitcase evidence is a drop in the bucket. So we can say with "fair assurance" that the disputed evidence did not sway the jury's verdict, meaning Correa's second-to-last argument—like his others—goes nowhere.[21] *See Landrón-Class,* 696 F.3d at 71.

(4)

Cumulative Error

That leaves us with Correa's protest that, even if his claimed errors do not justify reversal individually, they do when taken cumulatively. But because we have espied only *one* assumed error that is harmless at that, the cumulative-error doctrine cannot help him. *See United States v. DeSimone,* 699 F.3d 113, 128 (1st Cir. 2012).

Enough said about Correa's appeal. Now on to Shepard's.

SHEPARD'S APPEAL

Shepard attacks the sufficiency of the evidence to convict her and the reasonableness of her sentence. Though skillfully presented, her arguments do not persuade.

(1)

Adequacy of the Evidence

Sufficiency challenges rarely succeed, *see United States v. Moran,* 984 F.2d 1299, 1300 (1st Cir.1993), and this one is no exception. The gist of Shepard's argument—below and on appeal—is that prosecutors failed to prove beyond a reasonable doubt that she knew the bags she grabbed at the New York airport had drugs in them, as opposed to some other form of contraband. And so, the theory goes, her conspiracy and substantive-possession convictions cannot stand.[22] The judge disagreed. We of course assess her claim *de novo,* viewing the evidence—including all fair inferences—in the light most agreeable to the verdict and asking whether a sensible jury could have convicted beyond a reasonable doubt. *See, e.g., United States v. Seng Tan,* 674 F.3d 103, 107 (1st Cir.2012). Critically too, even if she has a plausible innocent explanation for her actions, we must affirm if—after viewing the record from the prosecution's p.27 vantage point—there was adequate evidence of her guilt. *See, e.g., United States v. George,* 761 F.3d 42, 48 (1st Cir.2014).

What sinks Shepard's sufficiency claim is Vega's testimony that he *personally knew* that she was a member of Santana's drug-trafficking enterprise.[23] From that evidence a clear-eyed jury could readily infer that members like Shepard know that drug smuggling is a drug enterprise's lifeblood and that handling drugs is what members do. *See United States v. Ortiz,* 966 F.2d 707, 712 (1st Cir.1992) (explaining that "jurors are neither required to divorce themselves from their common sense nor to abandon the dictates of mature experience"). And a wide-awake jury could then go on to infer that Shepard knew from the suspicious happenings surrounding her New York trip—her getting $3,000 simply for jetting there on someone else's dime, grabbing a couple of suitcases from the airport's luggage carousel, and passing them off to others almost immediately, never to see the bags again, *etc.*—that the suitcases contained drugs. *See id.*

Wait a minute, says Shepard, holes remain in the record—for example, there is no direct evidence that (1) she ever saw even a speck of drugs in Puerto Rico or in New York, that (2) she and Vega were anything more than mere acquaintances (Vega's cell phone had several conspirators' contact info, but not Shepard's), that (3) either Vega or anyone else ever so much as hinted that she would be lugging drug bags to a waiting taxi, or that (4) she was present when Vega and Martes rolled and packed the cash for the trip back to Puerto Rico. Even assuming that these are plausible theories of innocence, she gains nothing, "because the issue is not whether a jury rationally could have acquitted but whether it rationally could have found guilt beyond a reasonable doubt." *Seng Tan,* 674 F.3d at 107. Granted, the government's case may not have been "airtight"—most are not, we know. *See Leftwich v. Maloney,* 532 F.3d 20, 28 (1st Cir.2008). But taking all the evidence—direct and circumstantial—in the light most flattering to the verdict, we think a levelheaded jury had enough to make a guilty-knowledge inference required to convict. *See also United States v. Sawyer,* 85 F.3d 713, 733 (1st Cir.1996).

(2)

Reasonableness of the Sentence

That takes us to the dispute over Shepard's 128-month prison term—a sentence 8 months above the 10-year statutory mandatory minimum but 23 months below the bottom of the 151-188 month recommended guidelines range. She does not question the correctness of either the mandatory minimum or the guidelines range. But she does contest the procedural and substantive reasonableness of her sentence, offering lots of reasons why she should get a 120-month term after a sentencing do-over. We review preserved arguments for abuse of discretion and unpreserved ones for plain error. *See, e.g., United States v. Tavares,* 705 F.3d 4, 24 (1st Cir.2013). Ultimately, though, none of her arguments succeed.

(a)

Procedural Reasonableness

Shepard first accuses the judge of not considering every sentencing factor p.28 listed in 18 U.S.C. § 3553(a).[24] But after listening to her lawyer argue for leniency (a plea that—among other things—referenced her pre-arrest rehabilitative efforts and stressed how a heavy sentence would hurt her family) and after hearing her statement (an "allocution," in legal lingo), the judge said that he had considered "all the factors." And his comment "is entitled to some weight"—that is particularly true when a judge issues a within-guidelines sentence, *see United States v. Clogston,* 662 F.3d 588, 590 (1st Cir.2011) (internal quotation marks omitted), and here (don't forget) we have a *below*-guidelines sentence. But the judge said much more. For example, he touched on the seriousness of her crimes ("hundreds of kilograms of cocaine were transported in this conspiracy" and "nothing" could have happened without her and other couriers like her), talked about her difficult family circumstances (she is a "widowed mother of five children"), highlighted her lack of criminal record, alluded to societal-protective concerns ("how many children are affected by drugs ...?"), stressed the need to avoid unwarranted disparities between her sentence and Correa's (he had gotten 132 months). And he concluded that a 128-month sentence—a term far lower than the 151-188 month guidelines range— served the purposes reflected in § 3553(a). We see nothing resembling an abuse of discretion here.

Trying a different tack, Shepard argues that the judge put too much weight on one factor (eliminating unjustified sentencing disparities) and too little weight on others (her history and characteristics, as well as guidelines policy statements dealing with downward departures for things like family responsibilities).[25] Over and over again we have said that judges are not required to "give each factor equal billing," noting that because sentencing outcomes "turn mostly on 'case-specific and defendant-specific'" nuances, "'[t]he relative weight of each factor will vary with the idiosyncratic circumstances of each case'"—and thus judges can tweak "'the calculus accordingly.'" *United States v. Denson,* 689 F.3d 21, 28-29 (1st Cir.2012) (quoting *United States v. Dixon,* 449 F.3d 194, 205 (1st Cir.2006)). The judge did what the caselaw permits. So again we find no abuse of discretion.

Shepard also contends—for the first time on appeal, though—that the judge did not adequately explain his reasoning for her sentence. But what we have already written shows she is wrong. A judge must say enough for us to meaningfully review p.29 the sentence's reasonableness. *See United States v. Fernández-Cabrera,* 625 F.3d 48, 53 (1st Cir.2010) (adding that a judge's explanation need not be "precise to the point of pedantry"). And the judge's explanation was up to snuff—which is another way of saying that he committed no error in this respect, much less plain error.

(b)

Substantive Reasonableness

Not only is Shepard's sentence procedurally reasonable—it is substantively reasonable too, which is to say not too harsh under the "totality of the circumstances." *Gall v. United States,* 552 U.S. 38, 51, 128 S.Ct. 586, 169 L.Ed.2d 445 (2007). Her arguments otherwise—that her family circumstances and pre-arrest rehabilitation call for a 120-month term instead of a 128-month stretch, and that the judge placed too much emphasis on minimizing unjust sentencing disparities— are essentially a rebranding of her failed procedural-unreasonableness theories. When all is said and done, a claim like hers is a tough sell—more so when the sentence comes within a correctly-calculated guidelines range, *see Clogston,* 662 F.3d at 592-93, and here (as we have said, hopefully without trying the reader's patience) we have a *below*-guidelines term! For every case there is a range of reasonable punishment. *See, e.g., United States v. Walker,* 665 F.3d 212, 234 (1st Cir.2011). And because Shepard's sentence (backed by the judge's plausible explanation) does not fall outside "the expansive universe" of acceptable outcomes, we spot no abuse of discretion—which leads straight to affirmance. *See United States v. King,* 741 F.3d 305, 308 (1st Cir.2014).

FINAL WORDS

Our work over, we *affirm* Correa's and Shepard's convictions, and we *affirm* Shepard's sentence too.

BARRON, Circuit Judge, concurring in part and dissenting in part.

I fully join the majority's treatment of Denise Shepard-Fraser's challenges to the sufficiency of the evidence and the reasonableness of her sentence. I cannot join, however, the majority's treatment of Jorge Correa-Osorio's challenge to the in-court identification. In my view, that challenge has merit, and, accordingly, I would reverse the judgment of conviction on the ground that the District Court plainly erred in allowing the jury to weigh that evidence.

I.

Eyewitness testimony is undeniably powerful. That testimony is all the more powerful when the eyewitness identifies the defendant right in front of the jury.

Ordinarily, we let juries weigh such testimony, just as they may weigh any other admissible evidence. But in certain circumstances, concerns about the reliability of an in-court identification—with all the persuasive force that comes from the witness identifying "that man" as the person who committed the crime—require more than faith in the jury's capacity to evaluate what is reliable and what is not. *See, e.g., Kampshoff v. Smith,* 698 F.2d 581, 585 (2d Cir.1983) ("[D]oubts over the strength of the evidence of a defendant's guilt may be resolved on the basis of the eyewitness' seeming certainty when he points to the defendant and exclaims with conviction that veils all doubt, '[T]hat's the man!'" (second alteration in original) (quoting *United States v. Wade,* 388 U.S. 218, 235-36, 87 S.Ct. 1926, 18 L.Ed.2d 1149 (1967))).

One such circumstance arises when the government elicits the identification in court after having used suggestive out-of-court p.30 means to prompt the witness to make an earlier identification. *See Simmons v. United States,* 390 U.S. 377, 382, 88 S.Ct. 967, 19 L.Ed.2d 1247 (1968); *see also Manson v. Brathwaite,* 432 U.S. 98, 97 S.Ct. 2243, 53 L.Ed.2d 140 (1977). The classic out-of-court, government-designed, suggestive means are a stacked lineup, *see Foster v. California,* 394 U.S. 440, 442-43, 89 S.Ct. 1127, 22 L.Ed.2d 402 (1969), a highly suggestive photo array, *see Simmons,* 390 U.S. at 382, 88 S.Ct. 967, or, perhaps even worse, a show-up—in which the government brings the suspect before the witness in a one-to-one confrontation, *see Stovall v. Denno,* 388 U.S. 293, 295, 87 S.Ct. 1967, 18 L.Ed.2d 1199 (1967).

When the government uses such out-of-court prompts unnecessarily, due process bars the jury from weighing the in-court identification unless it survives review under the so-called *Biggers* factors. *See Neil v. Biggers,* 409 U.S. 188, 199-200, 93 S.Ct. 375, 34 L.Ed.2d 401 (1972); *see also United States v. Maguire,* 918 F.2d 254, 264-65 (1st Cir.1990) ("The Supreme Court has declared generally the same test for the admissibility of an in-court identification subsequent to a suggestive out-of-court identification as it has employed for admission of an allegedly suggestive pretrial out-of-court identification."). Courts use those factors to decide whether the in-court identification arises from the witness's prior encounters with the person identified rather than from the influence of the out-of-court suggestive prompt the government has used. *See United States v. Castro-Caicedo,* 775 F.3d 93, 97 (1st Cir.2014). And when those factors indicate a substantial risk that the suggestive prompt did corrupt the in-court identification—say because the witness encountered the person identified years before and never since, and then only in conditions not likely to make the memory stick with any accuracy—then the jury may not consider the in-court identification. *Biggers,* 409 U.S. at 198, 93 S.Ct. 375.

Correa does not argue to us that an out-of-court suggestive prompt preceded this in-court identification. He instead argues that what happened in the courtroom was alone so suggestive as to necessitate review under *Biggers.* And I conclude that, on these facts, Correa is right.

In reaching this conclusion, I recognize courtroom identifications are a traditional feature of criminal trials. But tradition should not distract from what to me seems obvious and what I do not understand the majority to deny. A prosecutor who orchestrates an in-court identification does at least risk exposing the jury to a very misleading form of unusually powerful and prejudicial testimony. For that reason, judges must be on the lookout for the case in which that risk is realized—even if it is realized through means other than the government's prior use of egregious out-of-court suggestive prompts.

Here, we confront government-selected, in-court means for prompting that, though subtle, were plenty suggestive-and unnecessarily so. So much so, in my view, that even on plain error review, an inspection of the identification's reliability under *Biggers* is required. *See United States v. De León-Quiñones,* 588 F.3d 748, 753 (1st Cir.2009) ("To establish plain error, a defendant 'must show an error that was plain, (i.e., obvious and clear under current law), prejudicial (i.e., affected the outcome of the district court proceedings), and seriously impaired the fairness, integrity, or public reputation of the judicial proceedings.'" (quoting *United States v. Griffin,* 524 F.3d 71, 76 (1st Cir.2008))). And, after undertaking that inspection, I further believe that due process demands a greater degree of assurance that Correa was "that man" than this identification can possibly p.31 supply. For that reason, I cannot agree that this in-court identification—on which the government's case almost entirely rests—may be the cause of Correa's long-term loss of liberty.[26]

II.

To begin, I must first explain why *Perry v. New Hampshire,* ___ U.S. ___, 132 S.Ct. 716, 181 L.Ed.2d 694 (2012), does not shield from *Biggers* review any in-court identification that is untainted by a prior suggestive out-of-court prompt—the seemingly categorical position the Eleventh Circuit takes. *See United States v. Whatley,* 719 F.3d 1206, 1216 (11th Cir.2013). But the explanation is not hard to give. Simply put, *Perry* did not involve an in-court identification at all. *Perry* thus cannot set the standard for how we should treat one.

Perry concerned only whether a prior out-of-court identification should have been subjected to review under the *Biggers* factors. And *Perry* concluded that due process did not require such review in that case because the government did not orchestrate the out-of-court identification. *See Perry,* 132 S.Ct. at 725-27. Rather, as *Perry* explained, the witness had made a spontaneous out-of-court identification of the suspect while the suspect stood next to a police officer in a parking lot. *Id.* at 721-22. The Court noted that defense counsel—in briefing and in argument—explicitly conceded that the government "did not arrange the suggestive circumstances surrounding [the] identification," *id.* at 725, and that defense counsel did "not allege any manipulation or intentional orchestration by the police," *id.* (citing Tr. of Oral Arg. 5). There was, as the New Hampshire Supreme Court found, "a complete absence of improper state action." *New Hampshire v. Perry,* No. 2009-0590, 2010 WL 9105720, at *1 (N.H. Nov. 18, 2010) (quoting *New Hampshire v. Addison,* 160 N.H. 792, 8 A.3d 118, 125 (2010)). Thus, notwithstanding that the circumstances of the identification may have been suggestive, the Court concluded that the deterrence rationale that underlies the whole *Biggers* line had no application. *Perry,* 132 S.Ct. at 726.

In my view, therefore, *Perry* is no per se bar to finding plain error here. *Perry* is instead best read to affirm what the Court had said before about when the *Biggers* test must be applied. Due process requires the *Biggers* review for reliability "when law enforcement officers use an identification procedure that is both suggestive and unnecessary." *Id.* at 724. For it is only when the government is responsible for the suggestiveness that due process requires an inquiry into the reliability of the identification.

III.

With *Perry* out of the way, the issue reduces to the following. When, if ever, should an in-court identification be subject to *Biggers* review by virtue of the suggestive attributes of what happened in the courtroom itself? Substantial precedent shows that a government-orchestrated, in-court identification may, in some circumstances, be so suggestive as to trigger *Biggers* review, even absent a prior, out-of-court suggestive prompt. *See, e.g., United States v. Greene,* 704 F.3d 298, 307-08 (4th p.32 Cir.2013); *United States v. Rogers,* 126 F.3d 655, 657-58 (5th Cir.1997) ("[I]t is obviously suggestive to ask a witness to identify a perpetrator in the courtroom when it is clear who is the defendant."); *United States v. Hill,* 967 F.2d 226, 232 (6th Cir.1992); *United States v. Rundell,* 858 F.2d 425, 426 (8th Cir.1988); *see also United States v. Beeler,* 62 F.Supp.2d 136, 140-45 (D.Me.1999) (suppressing, in advance of trial, in-court identification because it would be impermissibly suggestive and unreliable). And the government does not argue otherwise.

The majority contends, however, that such review is required only when the in-court identification involves special features of concern. The majority then notes that, here, the prosecutor's in-court questions or comments did not expressly draw the witness's attention to the defendant or directly suggest the hoped-for result. *See Greene,* 704 F.3d at 307-08. Nor was the defendant in this case of a different race or gender from all other persons in the courtroom or at counsel table. *See United States v. Archibald,* 734 F.2d 938, 941 (2d Cir.1984). But, as I will explain, the government still orchestrated this identification to occur in circumstances that clearly were unnecessarily suggestive—at least when the circumstances are considered in their totality.

As to orchestration, the challenged in-court identification did not just happen. Instead, the prosecutor brought it about through a cooperating witness, José Vega-Torres, who had been prepped and promised (according to his own testimony) that his cooperation would protect his wife from prosecution. And Vega was asked to provide testimony that was—the government concedes—the whole of the case against Correa.

As to suggestiveness, the prosecutor asked Vega to identify Correa only on Vega's second day of testifying, after the lunch break. Thus, the prosecutor asked Vega to make the identification only after Vega had spent a day and a half on the stand, with Correa—the only male defendant—seated before him at counsel table. And during Vega's day-plus time on the stand, defense counsel rose to object at numerous points. By the time of the identification, then, the object of the prosecution would have been obvious.

The majority points out that the government did not put Correa at counsel table. He took that seat on his own, as it was his right to do. But the government still chose to seek the identification from Vega fully aware that the defendant was so positioned—and thus fully aware that Vega would be asked to identify Correa at a moment when he was at that table and after Vega had observed him there at substantial length. Indeed, it is fair to say the longest look that Vega—by his own account—ever had of Correa was during the time the government had asked Vega to appear on the stand prior to asking him to make the identification. *Cf. United States v. Montgomery,* 150 F.3d 983, 992 (9th Cir.1998) ("permitting [the witness] to view [the defendant] in the courtroom the day before the witness was scheduled to testify" found to be a "suggestive procedure[]").

In these circumstances, I do not believe Correa is overstating things in contending that the government's presentation of the identification was "the functional equivalent of the one person show-up, a classically suggestive method of identification in which an eyewitness is confronted with only one option to cho[o]se from." *See Greene,* 704 F.3d at 307-08 (4th Cir.2013); *Hill,* 967 F.2d at 232; *Beeler,* 62 F.Supp.2d at 144-45; *Commonwealth v. Crayton,* 470 Mass. 228, 21 N.E.3d 157, 166 (2014) ("Where, as here, a prosecutor asks a witness p.33 at trial whether he or she can identify the perpetrator of the crime in the court room, and the defendant is sitting at counsel's table, the in-court identification is comparable in its suggestiveness to a showup identification."). And, for that reason, I believe it clear that the identification's reliability must be tested under the *Biggers* factors.

After all, the government cannot show that these suggestive means were somehow "necessary." *See Perry,* 132 S.Ct. at 724 (finding "[c]rucial" to the Court's allowance of a suggestive procedure in *Stovall* that it was a "necessity"); *Stovall,* 388 U.S. at 302, 87 S.Ct. 1967 (finding a suggestive encounter necessary because "[n]o one knew how long [the hospitalized witness] might live" and thus "the police followed the only feasible procedure"); *United States ex rel. Kirby v. Sturges,* 510 F.2d 397, 403-04 (7th Cir.1975) (Stevens, J.) (concluding, despite there being "no evidence of bad faith or excessive zeal to obtain a conviction," that a showup was "unnecessarily suggestive" because it was "not justified by any exigent circumstances, or even by any minimal showing of inconvenience"). True, as a general matter, the prosecution is entitled to present its case in the order it thinks best. But that standard feature of the way that we organize criminal trials does not mean it was necessary for the government to elicit the identification of Correa in the highly suggestive way that it chose.

The government could have relied on an identification by Vega that he made out of court through a non-suggestive means. In fact, the government introduced photo arrays showing that Vega had made out-of-court identifications of other alleged conspirators. Yet the government chose not to pursue that same approach at trial in Correa's case. And, even if the government wished to proceed with an in-court identification, the government acknowledged at oral argument that there were mitigating measures that could have been taken in court but were not. *See Beeler,* 62 F.Supp.2d at 144-45 (noting "that a number of courts have reasoned that the preferred remedy for a suggestive in-court identification is not, necessarily, the suppression of the identification but an in-court lineup or some other protective measure to ensure the fairness of the identification and cross-examination of the eyewitness"); *see also Kirby,* 510 F.2d at 405-06 (describing "unanimity among scholars" that "evidence of, or derived from, a showup identification should be inadmissible unless the prosecutor can justify his failure to use a more reliable identification procedure").

I recognize that, in one respect, the situation is different when, unlike here, an in-court identification is made only after a prior, suggestive out-of-court identification.

In that type of case, the jurors do not have the opportunity to witness the complained of suggestive circumstance themselves. Here, by contrast, the jurors did, as they obviously watched what happened in court. But, that does not show that an in-court identification of this sort must be left to the jury to weigh. For while in theory the jurors were well-positioned to evaluate the suggestiveness of what they saw, in fact the jurors were exposed to a seemingly certain identification made in a very suggestive setting. In other words, the fact that the jury witnessed this particular identification does not solve the problem. It potentially is the problem. *See Kampshoff,* 698 F.2d at 585 ("There can be no reasonable doubt that inaccurate eyewitness testimony may be one of the most prejudicial features of a criminal trial. Juries, naturally desirous to punish a vicious crime, may well be unschooled in the effects that the subtle compound of suggestion, anxiety, and forgetfulness p.34 in the face of the need to recall often has on witnesses." (footnote omitted)).

In light of the "obvious[] suggestive[ness]" of the circumstances in which the government chose to elicit the identification, I conclude—as the Fifth Circuit did more than a decade ago in considering an unobjected-to, in-court identification— that even on plain error review, the *Biggers* test applies. *See Rogers,* 126 F.3d at 658. In that case, the Fifth Circuit confronted circumstances not unlike those at issue here and undertook such reliability review because the witness had been asked to make the identification "when it [was] clear who [was] the defendant." *Id. Rogers* explained that the witness initially provided testimony without making any identification but was then called back to the stand the next day to identify the defendant, the only black man at counsel table, as the culprit.[27] *Id.* at 657-58 & n. 1. And while the Fifth Circuit noted that the concern about suggestiveness was "heightened" in that case because the witness was of a different race from the defendant, *id.* at 658, here that same concern is heightened by the duration of the witness's pre-identification testimony and the gender of the defendant relative to the other defendant at counsel table.

In both cases, therefore, the key fact is the ultimate one that the *Biggers* line suggests to me should matter: each time, it was obvious who the defendant was when the prosecution asked the witness to make the in-court identification. So although I grant that there is no case finding plain error on facts exactly like these, it seems to me that the relevant inquiry into suggestiveness that *Biggers* requires yields an answer no less obvious in Correa's case than the Fifth Circuit found in *Rogers.* And given that "the 'plainness' of [an] error can depend on well-settled legal principles as much as well-settled legal precedents," *United States v. Brown,* 352 F.3d 654, 664 (2d Cir.2003) (emphasis omitted), I do not believe counsel's failure to object at trial should shield this in-court identification from the scrutiny that *Biggers* plainly requires in comparably suggestive circumstances.

IV.

In consequence of the unnecessarily suggestive means that the government used, I believe we must apply the *Biggers* factors to test whether Vega's identification was corrupted by the suggestiveness of the setting. *See* 409 U.S. at 199-200, 93 S.Ct. 375.[28] And it is plain to me that, after doing so, we should have no confidence that

Vega's identification rested on his recollection p.35 of Correa's appearance from prior encounters—to the extent they qualified as "encounters"—rather than from the suggestive circumstances in which the prosecutor asked Vega to make his choice.

Vega testified to viewing Correa, known to him in the conspiracy as "El Don," on only three occasions, each of which occurred long ago. The only physical interaction was brief, at most lasting a matter of minutes. And the encounters between the two men could be described, at best, as indirect: putting luggage in a car, a sighting through a car window, and finally, Vega's glimpse of "El Don" handling baggage on the tarmac while Vega waited in the airport from what must have been a substantial distance. The witness never purported to have had a personal relationship with the defendant. Nor did Vega offer any previous description that matched Correa's.

Furthermore, Vega claimed to have interacted with Correa only in 2006, while Vega's in-court identification of Correa occurred five years later, in 2011. *Biggers* suggested, however, that a far shorter, seven-month gap between sighting and identification counted against the identification's reliability. *Id.* at 201. And while we have sometimes permitted lengthy time gaps, we have not been so forgiving when the encounters were as fleeting and indirect as these. *See, e.g., United States v. Flores-Rivera*, 56 F.3d 319, 331 (1st Cir. 1995) (excusing seven-year time gap when "other reliability criteria were sufficiently persuasive").

Vega did not appear to hesitate in identifying Correa from the stand. But certainty on the part of the witness does not reveal much. *See United States v. Jones,* 689 F.3d 12, 18 (1st Cir.2012) ("[L]ack of confidence is certainly a reliable warning sign, while the presence of confidence is probably closer to a neutral factor."). Such apparent certainty may result from the suggestive circumstances, and certainty after suggestive prompting cannot show reliability. *See, e.g., Raheem v. Kelly,* 257 F.3d 122, 139 (2d Cir.2001) (finding it "difficult to view [a witness's] certainty as an indicator of reliability independent of the suggestive lineup").

Not surprisingly, therefore, the government does not argue that the *Biggers* factors support the identification's reliability. This identification, which should have triggered the *Biggers* test, clearly cannot survive it.

V.

That leaves the issue of prejudice. *See United States v. Delgado-Marrero,* 744 F.3d 167, 184 (1st Cir.2014) (describing the "infrequent case[] in which reversal is warranted" under the plain error standard of review); *see also Rogers,* 126 F.3d at 658-60 (finding error in the admission of an obviously suggestive and unreliable in-court identification, but holding error harmless in light of overwhelming evidence of guilt). But here, the prejudice is clear.

The government conceded that Vega's testimony provided the only direct evidence that linked Correa to this conspiracy. And a review of the record also reveals many—in some cases, inexplicable—weaknesses in the government's case. These weaknesses include: the inability of the testifying investigative agent to explain how and why Correa was identified as a member of the conspiracy; the evidence suggesting Correa worked for a different baggage handling company than any of the other coconspirators tasked with the same alleged role in the conspiracy; the testimony suggesting Vega made out-of-court identifications of many of the co-conspirators without apparently making an out-of-court identification of Correa; another testifying p.36 co-conspirator's non-recognition of Correa; and the failure of the government to call any co-conspirators—despite having entered into plea agreements with them—who had dealt personally with Correa.

There is some corroborating evidence of Correa's involvement in the conspiracy: a resume listing his email address as including the words "El Don" and his wife's ownership of the same car Vega testified that "El Don" had at Vega's one interaction with him. But that evidence itself traces back only to Vega's testimony. Thus, the other evidence against Correa gives no assurance that, even absent the identification by Vega, the jury would have convicted. *See, e.g., United States v. Casas*, 356 F.3d 104, 123-24 (1st Cir.2004) (vacating conviction of defendant Cunningham when—apart from improper testimony—only evidence of involvement with conspiracy was his identification by three coconspirators with whom he had few contacts).

This case, then, is like those that have given courts the most pause about the due process implications of admitting in-court identifications. The problematic identification here was essential to the government's case. *See Raheem*, 257 F.3d at 142 ("The identification testimony of [the witnesses] clearly bore on an essential issue, the identity of the shooter. And that testimony was crucial to the prosecution's case, for the State presented no evidence other than the testimony of [the witnesses] to tie [the defendant] to the events."); *Kampshoff*, 698 F.2d at 588 ("[A]ll told, absent the identification testimony, the evidence against Kampshoff is simply not overwhelming."); *cf. United States v. Williams*, 436 F.2d 1166, 1168 (9th Cir. 1970) ("[W]here the question of guilt or innocence hangs entirely on the reliability and accuracy of an in-court identification, the identification procedure should be as lacking in inherent suggestiveness as possible.").

Still, to succeed on plain error review, the defendant must make one more showing. He must demonstrate that the error "seriously impaired the fairness, integrity, or public reputation of the judicial proceedings." *De León-Quiñones*, 588 F.3d at 753 (quoting *Griffin*, 524 F.3d at 76). But that additional requirement poses no obstacle for Correa. When the government introduces an unnecessarily suggestive in-court identification on which nearly the whole of the prosecution depends, it seems to me clear that this last part of the plain error test is met.

VI.

I recognize the concern about opening the door to other successful attacks on in-court identifications. But not every in-court identification is similarly staged, with the cooperating witness prepped to testify, brought to the stand, and then prompted to give an identification of the one male defendant at counsel table and then only after having provided a day and a half of testimony. Not every in-court identification rests on minimal contacts that occurred long ago and thus plainly lacks sufficient indicia of reliability to survive the *Biggers* test. Not every prosecution rests so heavily on an in-court identification this shaky. And fewer still are the prosecutions that are so dependent on in-court identifications that share these concerning attributes. I thus do not think it too much to require the government to make the case against Correa on evidence less likely to mislead the jury in this needless way. And, in my view, the Due Process Clause requires that same conclusion.

I respectfully dissent.

[1] DEA stands for Drug Enforcement Administration.

[2] Responding to the prosecutor's request that he "[t]ell the jury what happened in October of 2007," Báez said, "[w]ell, in October of 2007 I had a job with [Bencosme] on that day." The "job," Báez explained, was to stow a drug bag on a departure-bound plane.

[3] We will fill in more details as we go along.

[4] "If you see [Shepard]," the prosecutor said, "could you describe what he or she is wearing for the jury"? "She is wearing a blue jacket," Vega replied. Shepard's lawyer said he had no objection "whatsoever" to the in-court identification.

[5] Reliability typically turns on (1) the witness's opportunity to look at the person, (2) his degree of attention, (3) the accuracy of his prior description, (4) how sure he was when he made the identification, and (5) the amount of time between the crime and the identification. *See, e.g., Biggers,* 409 U.S. at 199-200, 93 S.Ct. 375.

[6] The Supreme Court handed down *Perry* after Correa's trial. But we consider the law as it exists on appeal in deciding whether a judge's action was plain error. *See Henderson v. United States,* ___ U.S. ___, 133 S.Ct. 1121, 1126, 185 L.Ed.2d 85 (2013).

[7] *United States v. Espinal-Almeida* does not say which case rules supreme in our situation. Quoting *Perry,* we noted that "due process 'does not require a preliminary judicial inquiry into the reliability of an eyewitness identification when the identification was not procured under unnecessarily suggestive circumstances *arranged by law enforcement.*'" 699 F.3d 588, 603 n. 16 (1st Cir.2012) (quoting *Perry,* 132 S.Ct. at 730) (emphasis added by *Espinal-Almeida*). *Espinal-Almeida* focused on police conduct (specifically, whether something an officer had done meant an identification was police-arranged), not on prosecutorial conduct. So we can put that case to one side. Also, and interestingly, neither side has briefed the issue— both assume *Biggers* controls.

[8] The sainted Judge Friendly, *see* David M. Dorsen, *Henry Friendly: Greatest Judge of His Era* (2012), once called in-court identifications—"where the defendant is sitting at the counsel table"—"perfunctory," labeled their effect "weak[]," and said "only" their "weakness..., along with [their] traditional character, saves [them] from condemnation as being [themselves] impermissibly suggestive." *Brathwaite v. Manson,* 527 F.2d 363, 367 n. 6 (2d Cir.1975), *rev'd on other grounds,* 432 U.S. 98, 97 S.Ct. 2243, 53 L.Ed.2d 140 (1977). "[T]here is always the question how far in-court identification is affected by the witness' observing the defendant at the counsel table," he also said. *United States ex rel. Phipps v. Follette,* 428 F.2d 912, 915 (2d Cir.1970). But he noted too that "[m]ere statement" of this problem "indicates what great weight must be given to the determination of the judge who saw and heard the witness." *Id.*

[9] *See, e.g., United States v. Greene,* 704 F.3d 298, 307-08 (4th Cir.2013).

[10] *See, e.g., United States v. Rogers,* 126 F.3d 655, 657-58 (5th Cir.1997); *United States v. Murdock,* 928 F.2d 293, 297 (8th Cir.1991); *United States v. Archibald,* 734 F.2d 938, 942-43 (2d Cir.), *modified & reh'g denied,* 756 F.2d 223 (2d Cir.1984). *But see United States v. Curtis,* 344 F.3d 1057, 1063 (10th Cir.2003) (agreeing that identifying a "[d]efendant as the robber, when the robber was a black man and [d]efendant was the only black man in the courtroom, might be somewhat suggestive, but it is not unconstitutionally so").

[11] His trial lawyer was a man, we note in passing.

[12] A few months back Massachusetts's highest court—the Supreme Judicial Court ("SJC")—said that when "a prosecutor asks a witness at trial whether he or she can identify the perpetrator of the crime in the court room, and the defendant is sitting at counsel's table, the in-court identification is comparable in its suggestiveness to a showup identification." *Commonwealth v. Crayton,* 470 Mass. 228, 21 N.E.3d 157, 166 (2014). But the SJC's opinion turned on state common-law principles, not on federal (or even state) constitutional ones. *See id.* at 169 n. 16. And the SJC acknowledged that other courts hold that "'[t]he inherent suggestiveness in the normal trial setting does not rise to the level of constitutional concern.'" *Id.* at 172 n. 21 (quoting *Byrd v. State,* 25 A.3d 761, 767 (Del. 2011)). Clearly then this case is not enough for Correa to prevail on plain error. *See, e.g., United States v. Marcano,* 525 F.3d 72, 74 (1st Cir.2008) (per curiam) (emphasizing "that plain error cannot be found in case law absent clear and binding precedent").

[13] We use "dissent" to refer to Judge Barron's separate opinion concurring in part and dissenting in part.

[14] One of Correa's counsel's favorite objections was lack of foundation.

[15] We say "simply" because we three judges agree that certain circumstances not present here—(1) a prosecutor's drawing a witness to the defendant or asking questions directly suggesting the desired-for result, or (2) a defendant's looking different from others in the courtroom—might make the in-court identification process unduly suggestive.

[16] *See United States v. Brien,* 59 F.3d 274, 278 (1st Cir.1995) (mentioning the "usual practice"). Staying with the in-court lineup issue, we see that a defendant can ask for—but has no right to—one or "other particular procedure[s]." *United States v. Pérez-González,* 445 F.3d 39, 48 (1st Cir.2006); *Brien,* 59 F.3d at 279 (noting that to change the usual practice, it was "up to" defense counsel to offer a plan, which the judge could reject if he offers a "plausible justification" for doing so). Often a defendant does not want an in-court lineup, fearing that if a "fairly staged" one "would still likely result" in his identification, the lineup "would strengthen" the eyewitness's "credibility" and "undermine" the defense's "misidentification argument to the jury." *Brien,* 59 F.3d at 279. But again—and at the risk of repeating ourselves—we detect no settled caselaw allowing a prosecutor to force a defendant into an in-court lineup to get an identification.

[17] Although we need not reach the issue, we are also unpersuaded by the dissent's claim that Vega's identification of Correa was too unreliable for the jury to consider. To highlight just one problem with the dissent's claim: The dissent worries that Vega's previous encounters with "El Don" were indirect, brief, and occurred five years before the in-court identification. But these are usually matters

for the jury to sort out. *See Jones*, 689 F.3d at 18 (stressing that "it is only in extraordinary cases that identification evidence should be withheld from the jury") (internal quotation marks omitted); *see also Perry*, 132 S.Ct. at 727 (indicating that a jury should consider—among other things—how much time passed "between exposure to and identification of the defendant, whether the witness was under stress when he first encountered the suspect, how much time the witness had to observe the suspect, how far the witness was from the suspect, ... and the race of the suspect and the witness").

[18] FYI: Correa's résumé (admitted as an exhibit) listed his email addresses as (emphases ours) "eldon0789@hotmail.com" and "eldon 0789@gmail.com."

[19] This is, after all, one of the lowest standards of proof on the books. *See United States v. Volungus*, 730 F.3d 40, 46 (1st Cir. 2013).

[20] Clear error means the judge's action was "wrong with the force of a 5 week old, unrefrigerated, dead fish...." *Toye v. O'Donnell (In re O'Donnell)*, 728 F.3d 41, 46 (1st Cir. 2013) (quoting *S Indus., Inc. v. Centra 2000, Inc.*, 249 F.3d 625, 627 (7th Cir.2001)).

[21] Correa sometimes calls the October 4 suitcase evidence "cumulative." But cumulative evidence is usually dismissed as harmless, *see, e.g., United States v. Savarese*, 686 F.3d 1, 14 (1st Cir.2012), and again we have no reason to question the evidence's harmlessness here.

[22] The conspiracy charge required prosecutors to prove a knowing and intentional agreement between her and another to violate the drug laws, *see United States v. Ramos-Mejía*, 721 F.3d 12, 14 (1st Cir.2013), while the substantive charge required them to prove her knowing possession of drugs with intent to distribute, *see United States v. García-Carrasquillo*, 483 F.3d 124, 130 (1st Cir.2007). We oversimplify slightly, but you get the picture. Because the two charges required the government to prove that she acted knowingly, we examine her knowledge as a whole, rather than breaking it down for each count. One other thing. "'[K]nowledge' can be established by showing that a defendant was 'wilfully blind' to facts patently before [her]." *United States v. Rivera-Rodríguez*, 318 F.3d 268, 271 (1st Cir.2003). The judge did not give a willful-blindness instruction, however. Consequently we consider only whether the government proved her actual knowledge.

[23] Here are the money quotes from the prosecution's redirect examination of Vega: "Mr. Vega-Torres," the prosecutor began, "based on your own personal knowledge, we want you to tell the jury who were the members of the Manuel Santana drug trafficking organization at the time that you were involved." "Denise Shepard" and El "Don," Vega replied, though he named other members too.

[24] There are seven factors. Factor one is "the nature and circumstances of the offense and the history and characteristics of the defendant." 18 U.S.C. § 3553(a)(1). Factor two is

the need for the sentence ... (A) to reflect the seriousness of the offense, to promote respect for the law, and to provide just punishment for the offense; (B) to afford adequate deterrence to criminal conduct; (C) to protect the public from further crimes of the defendant; and (D) to provide the defendant with needed educational or vocational training, medical care, or other correctional treatment in the most effective manner."

Id. § 3553(a)(2). Factor three is "the kinds of sentences available." *Id.* § 3553(a)(3). Factor four is the guidelines. *Id.* § 3553(a)(4). Factor five is "any pertinent policy statement... issued by the Sentencing Commission." *Id.* § 3553(a)(5). Factor six is "the need to avoid unwarranted sentence disparities." *Id.* § 3553(a)(6). And factor seven is "the need to provide restitution to any victims." *Id.* § 3553(a)(7).

[25] A quick word about sentencing disparities: sentencers can consider disparities between codefendants, we have noted—even though § 3553(a)(6) chiefly addresses disparities among defendants nationwide. *See, e.g., United States v. Ayala-Vazquez,* 751 F.3d 1, 32 (1st Cir.2014).

[26] Correa received a prison sentence of eleven years. That term, I might add, is greater than the sentences received by all other members of the conspiracy, save for the leader, who received a sentence of 135 months—only three months longer than Correa's. Correa and his co-defendant in this trial, Denise Shepard-Fraser, were the only alleged conspirators who went to trial. All others listed in the indictment, with the exception of one individual against whom charges were dismissed, entered into plea agreements.

[27] The prosecutor identified "something odd" in the witness's demeanor during her initial testimony and afterwards had the FBI case agent approach her. *Rogers,* 126 F.3d at 657. The witness told the agent during that conversation that she recognized the defendant as the culprit and the government then asked—and was granted permission—to recall her to the stand. *Id.* And while the defendant's counsel objected to the witness being recalled, counsel did not object to her identification after she took the stand. *Id.* at 657-58.

[28] The factors to consider in evaluating whether the identification is reliable despite the unnecessary suggestiveness of the identification procedure include "the opportunity of the witness to view the criminal at the time of the crime, the witness' degree of attention, the accuracy of the witness' prior description of the criminal, the level of certainty demonstrated by the witness at the confrontation, and the length of time between the crime and the confrontation." *Biggers,* 409 U.S. at 199-200, 93 S.Ct. 375. Of course, as the majority notes, courts need not apply these factors to test the reliability of an identification not orchestrated by the government to occur in an unnecessarily suggestive way. *See* Maj. Op. 23 n. 17.

Second Circuit Decisions

The Rule Against Hearsay

747 F.3d 111 (2014)

UNITED STATES of America, Appellee,

v.

Rajat K. GUPTA, Defendant-Appellant.

Docket No. 12-4448.

United States Court of Appeals, Second Circuit.

Argued: May 21, 2013.

Decided: March 25, 2014.

US v. Gupta, 747 F. 3d 111 (2nd Cir. 2014)

p.115 Richard C. Tarlowe, Assistant United States Attorney, New York, NY (Preet Bharara, United States Attorney for the Southern District of New York, Damian Williams, Edward B. Diskant, Justin S. Weddle, Assistant United States Attorneys, New York, NY, on the brief), for Appellee.

Seth P. Waxman, Wilmer Cutler Pickering Hale & Dorr, Washington, D.C. (Paul R.Q. Wolfson, Megan Barbero, Daniel Aguilar, Wilmer Cutler Pickering Hale & Dorr, Washington, D.C.; Gary P. Naftalis, David S. Frankel, Alan R. Friedman, Robin M. Wilcox, Kramer Levin Naftalis & Frankel, New York, NY; Peter G. Neiman, Alan E. Schoenfeld, Wilmer Cutler Pickering Hale & Dorr, New York, NY, on the brief), for Defendant-Appellant.

Before: NEWMAN, KEARSE, and POOLER, Circuit Judges.

KEARSE, Circuit Judge:

Defendant Rajat Gupta ("Gupta") appeals from a judgment entered in the United States District Court for the Southern District of New York on November 9, 2012, following a jury trial before Jed S. Rakoff, *Judge,* convicting him on three counts of securities fraud, in violation of 15 U.S.C. §§ 78j(b) and 78ff, and one count of conspiracy to commit securities fraud, in violation of 18 U.S.C. § 371. Gupta was sentenced principally to 24 months' imprisonment, to be followed by a one-year term of supervised release, and was ordered to p.116 pay a fine of $5,000,000. In an amended judgment entered in February 2013, Gupta was also ordered to pay restitution in the amount of $6,218,223.59, an order that is the subject of a separate appeal that has been held in abeyance pending decision of the present appeal. In the present appeal, Gupta challenges his conviction, contending principally that he is entitled to a new trial on the grounds that the trial court erred (1) by admitting statements of a coconspirator, recorded in wiretapped telephone conversations to which Gupta was not a party, and (2) by excluding relevant evidence offered by Gupta. For the reasons that follow, we conclude that Gupta's contentions lack merit, and we affirm the judgment.

I. BACKGROUND

At the times pertinent to this prosecution, Gupta was a member of the board of directors of The Goldman Sachs Group, Inc. ("Goldman Sachs" or "Goldman"), the global financial services firm headquartered in New York. Gupta was also involved in several financial ventures with Raj Rajaratnam (or "Raj"), founder of The Galleon Group ("Galleon"), a family of hedge funds that invested billions of dollars for its principals and clients. The present prosecution arose out of a multiyear government investigation of insider trading at Galleon which included court-authorized wiretaps of Rajaratnam's cell phone, *see United States v. Rajaratnam,* 719 F.3d 139, 144-45 (2d Cir.2013).

During its investigation, the government discovered evidence indicating, *inter alia,* that Rajaratnam was receiving inside information about Goldman Sachs from Gupta and trading on that information. Eventually, Gupta was charged with six counts of securities law violations. Count One of the superseding indictment on which Gupta was tried (the "Indictment") alleged, *inter alia,* that Gupta, Rajaratnam, "and others ... conspire[d] ... to commit ... securities fraud" (Indictment ¶ 30); that "GUPTA disclosed ... Inside Information" about Goldman Sachs "to Rajaratnam, with the understanding that Rajaratnam would use the Inside Information to purchase and sell securities" (*id.* ¶ 12(b)); and that Rajaratnam, knowing the information he received from Gupta was confidential, "shared the Inside Information with other coconspirators at Galleon and caused the execution of transactions in the securities of Goldman Sachs" (*id.* ¶ 12(c)). The object of the conspiracy was the "purchase and sale of securities" in order to "receive illegal profits and/or illegally avoid losses" (*id.* ¶¶ 31 and 32(b)) based on "GUPTA['s] disclos[ure of] Inside Information obtained from Goldman Sachs" to Rajaratnam, which information "Rajaratnam shared ... with other coconspirators at Galleon" (*id.* ¶¶ 32(a) and (d)). Gupta was convicted on the conspiracy count and on three substantive counts of securities fraud (Counts Three, Four, and Five), all relating to trades of Goldman Sachs stock by Rajaratnam based on confidential inside information Rajaratnam received from Gupta in the fall of 2008.

A. *Evidence Supporting the Counts of Conviction*

All of the government's evidence that Gupta passed confidential information about Goldman Sachs to Rajaratnam, on the basis of which Rajaratnam made purchases or sales of Goldman stock, was circumstantial. Most of the evidence described below was presented through testimony from employees of Galleon or Goldman, wiretapped telephone calls between Rajaratnam and other Galleon employees, records of calls made to or from telephones used by Gupta or Rajaratnam, and p.117 records as to the timing of trades by Galleon in Goldman Sachs stock.

1. *Galleon Trades of Goldman Sachs Stock on September 23, 2008*

At 3:15 p.m. on September 23, 2008, Goldman Sachs held a special meeting of its board of directors. The purpose of the meeting was to approve an investment of $5 billion in Goldman by Warren Buffett. The imminent investment was highly confidential, as it was likely to have "a meaningful impact" on Goldman's stock price. (Trial Transcript ("Tr.") 1590.) It was to be announced to the public after the 4 p.m. close of trading on the New York Stock Exchange.

Gupta, a former managing director of the consulting firm McKinsey & Company ("McKinsey"), participated in the Goldman Sachs board meeting via telephone from a conference room at McKinsey's New York office. Telephone records indicated that Gupta was on the Goldman Sachs conference call from 3:13 p.m. until 3:53 p.m.

At approximately 3:54 p.m., Gupta's assistant, Renee Gomes, dialed Rajaratnam's direct line; the McKinsey conference room telephone from which Gupta had participated in the Goldman Sachs board meeting was then connected to the call to Rajaratnam's line. The connection between Rajaratnam's line and the telephone Gupta used lasted approximately 30 to 35 seconds.

Caryn Eisenberg, Rajaratnam's assistant in 2008-2009, testified that on September 23, 2008, she answered a call on his direct line at about 10 minutes before the 4:00 p.m. market close. As a general rule Eisenberg was not to put calls through to Rajaratnam near the end of the trading day, but she put the caller on hold, located Rajaratnam, and put the call through. Although at the time of trial Eisenberg no longer remembered the name of the man who was on the line, she testified that she put this call through because his name was on the short list of persons whose calls Rajaratnam would accept near the end of the trading day; she recognized his voice as that of a frequent caller; and the man said it was "urgent" that he "speak to Raj." (Tr. 238-39.)

Rajaratnam took the call in his office and was on the telephone only briefly. Eisenberg testified that Rajaratnam thereafter summoned Galleon co-founder Gary Rosenbach into his office and the two had a closed-door conversation. Rosenbach then "went back to his desk," picked up his telephone, "and started saying buy Goldman Sachs." (*Id.* at 254.)

Galleon trader Ananth Muniyappa testified that at approximately 3:56 p.m. on September 23, Rajaratnam, as he was hanging up his telephone, instructed Muniyappa, who was at his own desk nearby, to purchase 100,000 shares of Goldman Sachs stock. When Muniyappa determined that he would probably be unable to buy as many as 100,000 shares before the market's close (he managed to buy only a total of 67,200 shares), he quickly informed Rajaratnam, who promptly instructed Rosenbach to buy Goldman stock.

Rosenbach proceeded to buy 200,000 shares of the stock, 150,000 for Rajaratnam's portfolio — which specialized in technology stocks — and 50,000 for Rosenbach's own portfolio. Rosenbach also bought 1.5 million shares (1,000,000 for Rajaratnam's portfolio and 500,000 for his own) of a financial-sector index fund made up of stocks of several institutions, including Goldman. Each of these trades was made in the final "three to four minutes" of the trading day (Tr. 401), *i.e.,* between approximately 3:56 p.m. and 4:00 p.m. In all, the Goldman Sachs stock purchased by Muniyappa and Rosenbach at the behest of p.118 Rajaratnam in the final minutes of the trading day on September 23 — excluding the shares of the index fund — cost more than $33 million.

Warren Buffett's $5 billion investment in Goldman Sachs was announced at approximately 6:00 p.m. on September 23. The next morning, Goldman's stock price rose to a high nearly 7% above its September 23 closing price. A government witness testified that the profits on the above Galleon purchases of Goldman stock at the end of the trading day on September 23 exceeded $1 million.

Eisenberg testified that after Rajaratnam took the urgent call near the close of trading on September 23 he was smiling more than usual. (*See* Tr. 259.) But not everyone at Galleon was happy. Leon Shaulov was a Galleon trader and portfolio manager. Muniyappa did not buy any Goldman Sachs stock for Shaulov on

September 23. Muniyappa testified that that evening, shortly after Goldman announced the Warren Buffett investment, Shaulov sent Rosenbach an email saying, "Thanks for the heads up, by the way. I'm short 170 million in financials. Not one word from anyone. Thank you very much. All I get is sick dilution. Zero help. Zero." (*Id.* at 441-42; *see also id.* at 439 (a "short" position is one speculating that the market price will go down).)

On the morning of September 24, 2008, before the stock markets opened, Rajaratnam placed two calls from his cell phone (which was wiretapped) to Ian Horowitz, his principal trader. In the first call, at 7:09 a.m., Rajaratnam began to tell Horowitz about the events of the previous afternoon:

RAJ RAJARATNAM: .... So, big drama yesterday, but I have to ....

IAN HOROWITZ: Yeah, I, I, I heard.

RAJ RAJARATNAM: Hum.

IAN HOROWITZ: I heard a little, um, you mean the last three minutes of the day?

RAJ RAJARATNAM: No. *I got a call at 3:58,* right?

IAN HOROWITZ: Yeah.

RAJ RAJARATNAM: *Saying something good might happen to Goldman.* Right?

IAN HOROWITZ: So it is what it is. Everything's, everyone's fine, I saw it cross the board....

RAJ RAJARATNAM: No I saw, I, *so, I told Ananth [Muniyappa] to buy some,* he was fucking around, he can't, you know. *So I went to Gary [Rosenbach] and said just buy me.* right?

IAN HOROWITZ: Mm hmm.

RAJ RAJARATNAM: *Because you were not there.* It happens all the fucking time, you know you're there every day of the year, right? ....

(Government Exhibit ("GX") 21-T ("First Rajaratnam-Horowitz Call"), at 1-2 (emphases added).)

Rajaratnam called Horowitz again at 7:56 a.m. After asking how much Goldman Sachs stock Galleon currently owned, Rajaratnam continued his report on the previous afternoon's events:

RAJ RAJARATNAM: Okay, yeah, let me tell you what happened, honestly, right?

IAN HOROWITZ: Yeah, no, I looked at our price, I looked at our price, and I looked at what happened.

RAJ RAJARATNAM: Yeah.

IAN HOROWITZ: Someone had this before us, someone, whatever went on, something happened, someone, they ...

RAJ RAJARATNAM: *I got a call right saying something good's gonna happen.*

p.119 IAN HOROWITZ: We'll talk about, how 'bout this, we'll talk when you come in.

RAJ RAJARATNAM: Okay.

IAN HOROWITZ: We'll talk when you come in, okay?

RAJ RAJARATNAM: But I didn't do anything, *you were not there, I asked Ananth to buy some.*

IAN HOROWITZ: You did nothing.

RAJ RAJARATNAM: *Then I went to Gary* ... and ...

IAN HOROWITZ: You did nothing wrong.

RAJ RAJARATNAM: *Yeah at 3:58,* I can't, I can't yell out in the fucking halls.

IAN HOROWITZ: No. You did nothing wrong, we'll talk about it when you come in, nothing's wrong.

RAJ RAJARATNAM: It is, I guess, *Leon [Shaulov] was very upset. You know, fuck him, look, I've kept my mouth shut when he gave me WaMu, right?*

IAN HOROWITZ: Get, get upset about what? You got nothing, *this is at 3:58.*

RAJ RAJARATNAM: *Yeah, if it was, one o'clock, I always am good with him, I always call him in, I tell him everything, you know? AMD, IBM, everything,* right?

IAN HOROWITZ: He's not in, so I'm, he hasn't said anything. Listen, if something comes in, I'll let you know.

(GX 22-T ("Second Rajaratnam-Horowitz Call"), at 2-3 (emphases added).)

2. *Galleon Trades of Goldman Sachs Stock on October 24, 2008*

On October 23, 2008, more than halfway through the fourth quarter of Goldman Sachs's fiscal year, Goldman's chairman convened an unofficial board meeting by conference call to bring the directors up-to-date on company events. At that time, Wall Street analysts were projecting that Goldman — which, since becoming a public company, had never reported a quarterly loss — would continue to report profits. In the conference call, which began at 4:15 p.m., Goldman's management informed the board that the company's fourth-quarter result would be a loss.

Records were introduced to show that Gupta, on a telephone in his home office, participated in the Goldman Sachs conference call for approximately 33 minutes and disconnected at 4:49 p.m. At 4:50 p.m., a call was placed from the telephone of Gupta's assistant Renee Gomes to the direct office line of Rajaratnam; Gupta's home office line was conferenced in to that call, and Gomes's line was disconnected. Gupta's home office telephone was connected to Rajaratnam's direct line for some 12½ minutes, until 5:03 p.m.

The next morning, October 24, 2008, in three transactions, Rajaratnam sold a total of 150,000 shares of Goldman Sachs stock. The first 50,000 shares were sold at 9:31 a.m., one minute after the stock market opened — the first opportunity to trade in Goldman shares since the board meeting the previous day. Another 50,000 shares were sold at 10:09 a.m.; and the final 50,000 shares were sold at 10:37 a.m. Goldman Sachs's fourth-quarter losses were not announced to the public until December 16. Based on the decline in Goldman's stock price after that announcement, the government introduced calculations showing that Rajaratnam, by selling his shares on October 24, avoided a loss of more than $3.8 million.

At 12:12 p.m. on October 24, Rajaratnam returned a call to David Lau, a Singapore-based portfolio manager for Galleon International, one of Galleon's hedge funds. Lau had sought to reach Rajaratnam for general investment advice. Galleon International p.120 invested in non-U.S. securities primarily (*see* Tr. 1467), but not exclusively (*see id.* at 2415); and it had in the past owned stock in Goldman (*see* GX 90). The conversation began with Rajaratnam advising that, as a general matter, it would be safer to invest in United States companies than in emerging market countries:

> RAJARATNAM: Hey David, you called?
>
> DAVID LAU: Yeah, just to give me, give me a, find the pulse because we are quite shocked overseas and uh long bonds, I mean quite shocked in relative for the VAR ... because VAR broke out, blew out and our positions are the same so I just want to find out what you guys are thinking.
>
> RAJ RAJARATNAM: Yeah, I mean, I think, ah we think that *the U.S. is umrelatively the safe haven,* right.
>
> DAVID LAU: Um.
>
> RAJ RAJARATNAM: Because all of these um emerging market ah countries, many of them have to reduce interest rates, which is bad for their currencies, right.
>
> DAVID LAU: Um um um.
>
> RAJ RAJARATNAM: And, I mean today for example there is a reasonable calmness in the market you know the market is only down 2 or 3%, right.
>
> DAVID LAU: Yeah, that's why I'm surprised. I thought it would go nuts.
>
> RAJ RAJARATNAM: Yeah I mean our risk here is ah hedge fund redemption risk, right Citadel I hear is in trouble, you know, and things like that but I think generally, not that I want to be long equities, but generally I think one trade in equities would be, you know, buy the Spiders and short the EEMs or something, you know.
>
> DAVID LAU: Hmm Hmm.
>
> RAJ RAJARATNAM: But it looks like here the most cyclical companies the semi equipment companies, and the home builders are the ones that are leading the way out right.
>
> DAVID LAU: Right.
>
> (GX 29-T ("Rajaratnam-Lau Call"), at 1-2 (emphasis added).)

Rajaratnam then proceeded to describe to Lau the confidential negative information he had received the previous day "from somebody who's on the Board of Goldman Sachs," which "they don't report until December." (GX 29-T, at 2.) Rajaratnam noted the current optimistic view of Wall Street analysts of Goldman Sachs's likely profits, and he described the potential for selling the stock short:

> RAJ RAJARATNAM: *Um, now I, I heard yesterday from somebody who's on the Board of Goldman Sachs, that they are gonna lose $2 per share. The Street has them making $2.50.*
>
> DAVID LAU: Really?
>
> RAJ RAJARATNAM: You know. Yeah. *Now I can get that number,* you know, one, *they don't report until December,* they, I think their quarter ends in November, but (UI [*i.e.,* unintelligible]) one more, but you know they have these huge marks in ICBC and all of that stuff right. That uh is getting absolutely clobbered. You know.

DAVID LAU: Right.

RAJ RAJARATNAM: *So what he was telling me was that uh, Goldman, the quarter's pretty bad.* They have zero revenues because their trading revenues are offset by asset losses, and *to date they have lost $2 per share,* they just announced a 10% cut and uh you know, the basic business is ok but uh you know this is uh tough for them. *I don't think that's built into Goldman Sachs stock price. So if it gets to $105,* p.121 *I'm gonna, it's $99 now, it was at $102. I was looking for $105, I'm gonna whack it you know.*

DAVID LAU: (Laughs) Okay. Okay. Okay (UI) ...

RAJ RAJARATNAM: Okay, *I don't think it makes sense to take longer term views right now....*

(GX 29-T, at 2 (emphases added).)

3. *The Relationship Between Gupta and Rajaratnam*

The government also presented evidence that Gupta and Rajaratnam had a close relationship. Gupta described Rajaratnam as a "close friend[]" (GX 1905) — indeed, "a very close friend" (GX 1922) — and was in frequent communication with him. Rajaratnam's address book noted Gupta as a "Good friend." (Tr. 223.) Rajaratnam had instructed Eisenberg that there were only five people she was authorized to connect with him near the end of the trading day; Gupta was one of them. (*See id.* at 210, 213-14; *see also id.* at 273 (during the two years when Eisenberg was Rajaratnam's assistant, the list was expanded to about 10 names).)

Gupta and Rajaratnam were also involved in several business ventures together. In 2005, they, along with a third partner, formed Voyager Capital Partners Ltd. ("Voyager"), an investment fund capitalized with $50 million, $5 million of which was contributed by Gupta and $40 million by Rajaratnam; Gupta later borrowed $5 million from Rajaratnam in order to buy out the third partner's share (*see* Tr. 1858-59), giving Gupta a $10 million stake in Voyager. Other collaborations were discussed in a July 29, 2008 call from Gupta to Rajaratnam (*see* GX 9-T ("Gupta-Rajaratnam Call")) — the only call between these two that was captured in the wiretaps. In 2007, Gupta, Rajaratnam, and two others launched another investment fund, New Silk Route, in which Rajaratnam invested $50 million (*see id.* at 8); Gupta was the chairman (*see* GX 2164). Gupta was also heavily involved in Galleon itself. He had invested several million dollars in Galleon funds; he was involved in the planning of a new Galleon fund called Galleon Global (which ultimately was not created); he had a keycard allowing him access to Galleon's New York offices; and he regularly worked on Galleon's behalf in seeking potential investors (*see* GX 9-T, at 13-14). In early 2008, Gupta was made chairman of Galleon International, which, as of April 2008, managed assets totaling some $1.1 billion and could earn "performance fees" (Tr. 1696). Gupta was given a 15 percent ownership stake. (*See, e.g., id.;* GX 9-T, at 6; *id.* at 13 (Gupta: "you've given me ... a position in Galleon International").)

In the July 2008 Gupta-Rajaratnam Call, Rajaratnam asked Gupta about a rumor that Goldman Sachs might seek to buy a commercial bank. Gupta responded that there had been "a big discussion" of that possibility, in particular with respect to "Wachovia," as well as of the possibility of buying an insurance company, in particular "AIG." (GX 9-T, at 2-3.) Gupta said the Goldman board was divided and that such purchases were unlikely to be "imminent," but that if certain banks were "a good deal ... it's quite conceivable they'd come and say let's go buy" one. (*Id.* at 3-4.) The board's discussions were confidential. (*See, e.g.,* Tr. 856-58.) Even the matter of whether or not a subject had been discussed at a Goldman board meeting was confidential. (*See, e.g., id.* at 2048.)

B. *The Defense Case*

Gupta called several witnesses in his defense. Most were character witnesses who testified that they believed Gupta to p.122 be an honest person; Gupta also sought to have them testify that he had "integrity" and thus would not have been inclined to share inside information with Rajaratnam. Gupta's daughter Geetanjali Gupta ("Geetanjali") testified about certain conversations Gupta had with her about Rajaratnam, and sought to indicate that Gupta would not have been inclined to share inside information with Rajaratnam because Gupta believed Rajaratnam had cheated him out of money with respect to the Voyager investment. Gupta also sought to introduce documentary evidence suggesting that a different Goldman Sachs insider was giving Rajaratnam confidential information about Goldman Sachs, and that Gupta contemplated leaving a substantial portion of his wealth to charity. As discussed in greater detail in Part II.B. below, the trial judge imposed limitations with respect to each category of Gupta's proposed evidence.

C. *The Verdict*

The jury found Gupta guilty on four of the six counts against him: Count One, conspiracy to commit securities fraud in violation of 18 U.S.C. § 371, and three substantive counts of securities fraud in violation of 15 U.S.C. §§ 78j(b) and 78ff The substantive securities fraud convictions were on Count Three, based on Rosenbach's purchase of 150,000 shares of Goldman Sachs stock for Rajaratnam on September 23, 2008; Count Four, based on Muniyappa's purchase of 67,200 shares of Goldman Sachs stock for Rajaratnam on September 23, 2008; and Count Five, based on Rajaratnam's sale of 150,000 shares of Goldman Sachs stock on October 24, 2008.

Gupta was sentenced principally to 24 months' imprisonment and ordered to pay a $5 million fine. This Court granted his motion for bail pending appeal.

II. DISCUSSION

On appeal, Gupta argues principally that Rajaratnam's wiretapped conversations with Horowitz and Lau were inadmissible hearsay; that the trial court erred in curtailing evidence proffered by Gupta in his defense; and that the errors, either singly or in combination, entitle him to a new trial. For the reasons that follow, we disagree.

A. *The Wiretap Evidence*

Preliminarily, we note that Gupta's brief on appeal challenged the admission of any wiretapped conversations, including the conversation between Rajaratnam and

Gupta himself, on the ground that the wiretap authorizations were obtained in violation of Title III of the Omnibus Crime Control and Safe Streets Act of 1968, *see* 18 U.S.C. §§ 2510-2522, and the Fourth Amendment to the Constitution. Rajaratnam, who was prosecuted and convicted on multiple counts of securities fraud and conspiracy, had raised such challenges in his case; and Gupta's brief on appeal stated that Gupta was raising the same issues as Rajaratnam and was adopting the challenges made in Rajaratnam's appeal. Rajaratnam's challenges were rejected in *United States v. Rajaratnam,* 719 F.3d at 151-57, 160. Gupta's Title III and constitutional challenges are thus foreclosed.

With respect to Rajaratnam's statements in his two conversations with Horowitz and in his conversation with Lau, Gupta also objected to their admission on the ground that they were hearsay. The government contended that Rajaratnam's statements either were nonhearsay because they were statements in furtherance of a conspiracy of which Rajaratnam and Gupta were members, *see* Fed.R.Evid. 801(d)(2)(E), or were hearsay statements within the exception for declarations p.123 against penal interest *see* Fed.R.Evid. 804(b)(3), or within the residual hearsay exception, *see* Fed.R.Evid. 807.

The district court found that the government had sufficiently established the existence of a conspiracy among Gupta, Rajaratnam, and others (*see* Tr. 430-31, 434-35, 440), and that Rajaratnam's statements in each of the three conversations were in furtherance of the conspiracy. The court thus ruled that all three conversations were admissible under Rule 801(d)(2)(E). (*See* Tr. 633-35, 695; *see also* Hearing Transcript, May 16, 2012 ("Hearing Tr."), at 4, 24-25.)

The district court rejected outright the government's contention that Rajaratnam's statements were admissible under the residual hearsay exception. And the court stated that it was "dubious" as to whether the statements could be admitted as statements against penal interest but that it need not resolve that issue in light of its ruling that they were admissible as nonhearsay statements in furtherance of a conspiracy of which Rajaratnam and Gupta were members. (Hearing Tr. 4.)

Gupta challenges the rulings that Rajaratnam's statements to Lau and Horowitz were in furtherance of a conspiracy of which Gupta was a member. He contends that Lau was not alleged to be a coconspirator and that Rajaratnam's statements to Horowitz were in furtherance only of a separate conspiracy between Rajaratnam and Shaulov. The government defends the court's admission of the Rajaratnam statements as coconspirator statements in furtherance of a conspiracy of which Rajaratnam and Gupta were not the only members; in addition, it argues that Rajaratnam's statements could properly have been admitted as statements against his penal interest. We conclude that, under Rules 801 and 804 of the Federal Rules of Evidence, Rajaratnam's statements in all three conversations were admissible both as nonhearsay statements in furtherance of the Rajaratnam-Gupta conspiracy and under the exception for statements against penal interest. We address these issues separately with respect to the statements to Horowitz and those to Lau.

1. *Statements in Furtherance of a Conspiracy*

Under Rule 801(d), an out-of-court statement offered for the truth of its contents is not hearsay if "[t]he statement is offered against an opposing party and" it "was

made by the party's coconspirator during and in furtherance of the conspiracy."
Fed.R.Evid. 801(d)(2)(E). Thus, "[i]n order to admit a statement under this Rule,
the court must find (a) that there was a conspiracy, (b) that its members included
the declarant and the party against whom the statement is offered, and (c) that the
statement was made during the course of and in furtherance of the conspiracy."
United States v. Maldonado-Rivera, 922 F.2d 934, 958 (2d Cir.1990), *cert. denied*, 501 U.S.
1233, 111 S.Ct. 2858, 115 L.Ed.2d 1026 (1991). In determining the existence and
membership of the alleged conspiracy, the court must consider the circumstances
surrounding the statement, as well as the contents of the alleged coconspirator's
statement itself. *See* Fed. R.Evid. 801(d)(2); *see also Bourjaily v. United States*, 483 U.S.
171, 176-81, 107 S.Ct. 2775, 97 L.Ed.2d 144 (1987).

"To be in furtherance of the conspiracy, a statement must be more than 'a merely
narrative' description by one co-conspirator of the acts of another." *United States v.
SKW Metals & Alloys, Inc.*, 195 F.3d 83, 88 (2d Cir.1999) ("*SKW Metals*") (quoting
United States v. Beech-Nut Nutrition Corp., 871 F.2d 1181, 1199 (2d Cir.) ("*Beech-Nut*"),
cert. denied, 493 U.S. 933, 110 S.Ct. 324, 107 L.Ed.2d 314 (1989)).

> p.124 While idle chatter between co-conspirators does not further a conspiracy,
> *see United States v. Paone*, 782 F.2d 386, 390 (2d Cir.). *cert. denied*, 479 U.S. 882,
> 107 S.Ct. 269, 93 L.Ed.2d 246 (1986), we have recognized that "[s]tatements
> between conspirators which provide reassurance, serve to maintain trust and
> cohesiveness among them, or inform each other of the current status of the
> conspiracy, further the ends of [a] conspiracy."

United States v. Simmons, 923 F.2d 934, 945 (2d Cir.) (quoting *United States v. Rahme*,
813 F.2d 31, 35-36 (2d Cir.1987) (other internal quotation marks omitted)), *cert.
denied*, 500 U.S. 919, 111 S.Ct. 2018, 114 L.Ed.2d 104 (1991); *see, e.g., United States v.
Maldonado-Rivera*, 922 F.2d at 958-59.

"A finding as to whether or not a proffered statement was made in furtherance of
the conspiracy should be supported by a preponderance of the evidence, and such
a finding will not be overturned on appeal unless it is clearly erroneous." *United
States v. Thai*, 29 F.3d 785, 814 (2d Cir.), *cert. denied*, 513 U.S. 977, 115 S.Ct. 456, 130
L.Ed.2d 364 (1994); *see, e.g., United States v. James*, 712 F.3d 79, 105-06 (2d Cir.),
petition for cert. filed, No. 13-632 (U.S. Nov. 22, 2013). "'Where there are two
permissible views of the evidence, the factfinder's choice between them cannot be
clearly erroneous.'" *Beech-Nut*, 871 F.2d at 1199 (quoting *Anderson v. Bessemer City*,
470 U.S. 564, 574, 105 S.Ct. 1504, 84 L.Ed.2d 518 (1985)). The court's ultimate
decision to admit or exclude a proffered statement is reviewed for abuse of
discretion. *See, e.g., United States v. Persico*, 645 F.3d 85, 99 (2d Cir.2011), *cert. denied*,
___ U.S. ___, 132 S.Ct. 1637, 182 L.Ed.2d 246 (2012); *SKW Metals*, 195 F.3d at 87-
88.

a. *Rajaratnam's in-Furtherance Statements to Horowitz*

We see no error or abuse of discretion in the district court's admission of the
statements by Rajaratnam in his two telephone conversations with Horowitz.
Although Gupta insists that Rajaratnam had a "separate conspiracy with Shaulov"
(*e.g.,* Gupta brief on appeal at 38, 39), that Rajaratnam's statements to Horowitz
were "focus[ed] on placating Shaulov" (*id.* at 37), and that "Rajaratnam's

conversation with Horowitz was not 'in furtherance' of the alleged Rajaratnam/Gupta conspiracy" (*id.* at 36; *see id.* at 37 ("placating Shaulov had nothing to do with furthering the alleged conspiracy between Rajaratnam and Gupta")), that argument suffers from multiple flaws. First, the Indictment did not allege a conspiracy only between Rajaratnam and Gupta; it alleged that the conspiracy also encompassed "other coconspirators at Galleon" (Indictment ¶¶ 12(c), 32(d)). Second, so long as a coconspirator statement was in furtherance of the conspiracy, there is no requirement that it have been in furtherance of the interests of the defendant himself or of any particular coconspirator. Third, there was ample evidence that the conspiracy of which Gupta and Rajaratnam were members included Horowitz, Rosenbach, and Shaulov.

For example, after receiving the September 23 call at 3:54 p.m. from Gupta, Rajaratnam had a closed-door conversation with Rosenbach; Rosenbach immediately began buying Goldman Sachs stock and shares of an index fund that included Goldman stock; Rosenbach made those purchases not only for Rajaratnam's portfolio but for his own portfolio as well; and after the market closed, Rosenbach returned to Rajaratnam's office for another closed-door conversation (*see* Tr. 254-55). That evening, when Shaulov bitterly complained that he had not been given a p.125 "heads up" on the Buffett investment, he complained to Rosenbach. (*Id.* at 441-42.) The next morning, Rosenbach sent Rajaratnam an email stating "I spoke to Leon and believe I diffused [*sic*] him." (GX 1632.) Rajaratnam, in his conversations with Horowitz that morning, explained why he had not immediately informed Horowitz and Shaulov upon receipt of the September 23 Goldman Sachs information. In his first call, Rajaratnam pointed out that Horowitz, who was the head of the Galleon trading desk and the trader principally responsible for executing trades for Rajaratnam (*see* Tr. 205, 361), had not been in the office when the call came in. The district court found that this conversation was in furtherance of the conspiracy of which Gupta was a member because Rajaratnam needed to explain to Horowitz, his trader, why the purchases of Goldman stock were made (*see* Hearing Tr. 19-20); and the court found that the ensuing conversation between Rajaratnam and Horowitz "reeks of knowledge, intent, and the need of Mr. Rajaratnam to explain to his lieutenant why in his absence the significant trade occurred" (*id.* at 21). In that second conversation, Rajaratnam told Horowitz that Shaulov was upset but should not have been because the call about Goldman Sachs came in late, at "3:58"; had it come in at "one o'clock," Rajaratnam would have informed Shaulov because he "always" relayed "everything" to Shaulov. (GX 22-T, at 3.)

Thus, there was ample evidence to support findings (1) that the members of the conspiracy in which Gupta passed confidential Goldman Sachs information to Rajaratnam included not only Gupta and Rajaratnam but also Rosenbach, Horowitz, and Shaulov, and (2) that Rajaratnam's statements and explanations to Horowitz served to further the conspiracy by informing Horowitz, and eventually Shaulov, of the status of that conspiracy, reassuring them of its continuity, and preserving trust and cohesiveness among the coconspirators. Rajaratnam's statements in his telephone calls to Horowitz were properly admitted under Rule 801(d)(2)(E).

b. *Rajaratnam's in-Furtherance Statements to Lau*

Although the government concedes that Lau was not a member of the alleged conspiracy, the district court admitted under Rule 801(d)(2)(E) Rajaratnam's statements to Lau as well. While that Rule "'requires that both the declarant and the party against whom the statement is offered be members of the conspiracy, *there is no requirement that the person to whom the statement is made also be a member.*'" *In re Terrorist Bombings of U.S. Embassies in East Africa,* 552 F.3d 93, 139 (2d Cir.2008) (*"Terrorist Bombings"*) (quoting *Beech-Nut,* 871 F.2d at 1199) (emphasis ours), *cert. denied,* 558 U.S. 1137, 130 S.Ct. 1050, 175 L.Ed.2d 928 (2010). Statements designed to induce the listener's assistance with respect to the conspiracy's goals satisfy the Rule's infurtherance requirement. *See, e.g., Terrorist Bombings,* 552 F.3d at 139; *Beech-Nut* 871 F.2d at 1199 ("Coconspirator statements may be found to be 'in furtherance' of the conspiracy within the meaning of Rule 801(d)(2)(E) if they 'prompt the listener to respond in a way that facilitates the carrying out of criminal activity.'" (quoting *United States v. Rahme,* 813 F.2d at 35)).

Applying these principles, we conclude that there was no clear error in the district court's finding that Rajaratnam's statements to Lau were in furtherance of a conspiracy of which Gupta and Rajaratnam were members. Lau was a portfolio manager for Galleon International, seeking to make profitable investment decisions for p.126 his portfolio. The Rajaratnam-Lau Call resulted from Lau's solicitation of Rajaratnam's view of "the pulse" of the market. (GX 29-T, at 1.) The conversation took place on October 24, 2008, shortly after Rajaratnam had sold his Goldman Sachs stock in the wake of Gupta's call to Rajaratnam, a call placed one minute after the end of the Goldman Sachs board of directors conference call in which Gupta learned that Goldman in December would report a quarterly loss. Rajaratnam responded to Lau's request for guidance on the market by advising that "the U.S. is... relatively the safe haven" and providing his opinion with respect to specific sectors (*id.* at 1-2); but Rajaratnam went on to say that he had nonpublic information that, contrary to the prevailing view of market analysts, Goldman's current quarter would not be profitable (*see id.* at 2 ("I heard yesterday from somebody who's on the Board of Goldman Sachs, that they are gonna lose $2 per share. The Street has them making $2.50.")). Rajaratnam noted that Goldman would not report its quarterly results until December; stated that if the stock price reached a certain level, he would sell short (*see id.* ("whack it")); and concluded, "I don't think it makes sense to take longer term views right now" (*id.*).

We see no error in the district court's finding that Rajaratnam's statements to Lau, "an important colleague and subordinate who had the ability to execute further trades in Galleon International" (Hearing Tr. 22), were in furtherance of the conspiracy of which Rajaratnam and Gupta were members. Although Gupta argues that in connection with these statements the government was required to "pro[ve] ... not merely that Lau was theoretically capable" of trading in Goldman Sachs stock but that Rajaratnam's "purpose was to induce Lau to trade" (Gupta brief on appeal at 33 (emphasis omitted)), this argument ignores the allegation and the proof that one of the goals of the conspiracy was to use inside information to avoid losses — a goal clearly pursued by Rajaratnam in dumping his Goldman Sachs shares as quickly as possible after learning that Goldman would later publicly announce a quarterly loss. Gupta had a 15 percent ownership stake in Galleon International, which was entitled to fees based on its performance. (*See* Tr. 1696.) Although Galleon International invested principally in securities of non-United States companies (*see id.* at 1467), it was not precluded from investing in domestic securities (*see id.* at 2415); and, indeed, it had in the past owned stock in Goldman (*see* GX 90). In light of this evidence, Rajaratnam's statements to Lau could have prompted Lau not to purchase Goldman shares for Galleon International in October 2008. This supports the district court's conclusion that such statements were in furtherance of the conspiracy of which Gupta was a member.

Although Gupta argues that Rajaratnam was simply "bragging" about his sources (Gupta brief on appeal at 35), this was at best an argument for the jury. Further, to the extent that it could be permissible to view the conversation as Gupta urges, *i.e.,* that it was merely a "casual conversation about past events," not one in which Rajaratnam's statements were in furtherance of the conspiracy (Gupta brief on appeal at 35-36 (citing *United States v. Lieberman,* 637 F.2d 95, 102 (2d Cir. 1980))), the clear-error standard for reversal has not been met. To the extent that there may be more than one permissible view as to Rajaratnam's purpose in making the October 24, 2008 statements to Lau, the district court's determination that the statements about Goldman shares were made in furtherance of the conspiracy was a choice between or among permissible inferences and hence cannot be deemed p.127 clearly erroneous, *see Anderson,* 470 U.S. at 574, 105 S.Ct. 1504. Gupta's contentions provide no basis for overturning the district court's finding that Rajaratnam's statements to Lau were in furtherance of the insider-trading, loss-avoidance conspiracy of which Gupta was a member and by which Gupta sought to profit, and thus were admissible.

2. *Statements Against Penal Interest*

Rule 804(b)(3) allows the admission of statements against a declarant's proprietary, pecuniary, or penal interest if the declarant is unavailable as a witness. A statement is against such an interest if it is a statement that:

(A) *a reasonable person in the declarant's position would have made only if the person believed it to be true because, when made, it* was so contrary to the declarant's proprietary or pecuniary interest or *had so great a tendency* to invalidate the declarant's claim against someone else or *to expose the declarant to civil or criminal liability;* and

(B) is supported by corroborating circumstances that clearly indicate its trustworthiness, if it is offered in a criminal case as one that tends to expose the declarant to criminal liability.

Fed.R.Evid. 804(b)(3) (emphases added). This Rule "is founded on the commonsense notion that reasonable people, even reasonable people who are not especially honest, tend not to make self-inculpatory statements unless they believe them to be true." *Williamson v. United States,* 512 U.S. 594, 599, 114 S.Ct. 2431, 129 L.Ed.2d 476 (1994).

In assessing whether a statement is against penal interest within the meaning of Rule 804(b)(3), the district court must first ask whether "a reasonable person in the declarant's shoes would perceive the statement as detrimental to his or her own penal interest," *United States v. Saget*, 377 F.3d 223, 231 (2d Cir.2004) ("*Saget*"), *cert. denied*, 543 U.S. 1079, 125 S.Ct. 938, 160 L.Ed.2d 821 (2005), a question that can be answered only "in light of all the surrounding circumstances," *Williamson*, 512 U.S. at 604, 114 S.Ct. 2431; *see also Saget*, 377 F.3d at 231 (an "adequately particularized analysis" is required). The proffered statement "[need] not have been sufficient, standing alone, to convict [the declarant] of any crime," so long as it would have been "probative" in a criminal case against him. *United States v. Persico*, 645 F.3d at 102.

If the court finds that the statement is against the declarant's penal interest, the court must then determine whether there are corroborating circumstances indicating "both the declarant's trustworthiness and the truth of the statement." *United States v. Lumpkin*, 192 F.3d 280, 287 (2d Cir.1999). Further, "the inference of trustworthiness from the proffered 'corroborating circumstances' must be strong, not merely allowable." *United States v. Salvador*, 820 F.2d 558, 561 (2d Cir.), *cert. denied*, 484 U.S. 966, 108 S.Ct. 458, 98 L.Ed.2d 398 (1987). In the context of assessing whether a statement against penal interest was sufficiently reliable to satisfy the Confrontation Clause of the Constitution, we have noted that

> [a] statement incriminating both the declarant and the defendant may possess adequate reliability if ... the statement was made to a person whom the declarant believes is an ally, and the circumstances indicate that those portions of the statement that inculpate the defendant are no less reliable than the self-inculpatory parts of the statement.

Saget, 377 F.3d at 230 (internal quotation marks omitted).

p.128 The trial court's ultimate decision to admit such evidence is reviewed for abuse of discretion. *See, e.g., United States v. Williams*, 506 F.3d 151, 155 (2d Cir.2007), *cert. denied*, 552 U.S. 1223, 128 S.Ct. 1329, 170 L.Ed.2d 138 (2008); *Saget*, 377 F.3d at 231; *United States v. Salvador*, 820 F.2d at 562.

a. *Rajaratnam's Self-Incriminating Statements to Horowitz*

Even if Rajaratnam's statements in his conversations with Horowitz on the morning after his September 23 purchases of Goldman Sachs stock were not in furtherance of the Rajaratnam-Gupta conspiracy, the pertinent statements were contrary to Rajaratnam's penal interest and therefore could properly have been admitted pursuant to Rule 804(b)(3). In the First Rajaratnam-Horowitz Call, Rajaratnam said, "I got a call at 3:58.... [s]aying something good might happen to Goldman.... [S]o, I told Ananth to buy some" and "I went to Gary and said just buy me" (GX 21-T, at 1-2). In the Second Rajaratnam-Horowitz Call, Rajaratnam's statements included the following:

- I got a call, right, saying something good's gonna happen.
- I asked Ananth to buy some.
- Then I went to Gary ....
- Yeah at 3:58, I can't, I can't yell out in the fucking halls.
- Leon was very upset. You know, fuck him, look, I've kept my mouth shut when he gave me WaMu ....

• [I]f it was, one o'clock, I always am good with him, I always call him in, I tell him everything, you know? AMD, IBM, everything ....

(GX 22-T, at 2-3.)

The corroborating evidence included proof that Rajaratnam did receive a call minutes before the close of trading on September 23; that the call was from Gupta, who had said it was "urgent"; that Gupta was a Goldman Sachs board member who had just received confidential Goldman information; and that something quite good for Goldman did in fact happen and was announced after the close of trading that very day. And Rajaratnam's reference to having shared information with respect to "AMD" provided additional corroboration of Rajaratnam's knowing wrongdoing, as Anil Kumar — who was on Rajaratnam's list of five people to whom he would speak near the close of trading (*see* Tr. 210, 213-14) — testified at trial that he had "pled guilty to one count of securities fraud for giving insider information to Mr. Rajaratnam about a company called ATI and AMD's acquisition of it in 2006" (*id.* at 1767). Thus, it would have been well within the bounds of discretion for the district court to conclude that the statements by Rajaratnam were contrary to his penal interest because they exposed him to criminal liability for trading on the basis of inside information, and that they were sufficiently reliable to be admitted in evidence under Rule 804(b)(3).

b. *Rajaratnam's Self-Incriminating Statements to Lau*

We reach the same conclusion with respect to Rajaratnam's statements about his inside information on Goldman Sachs to Lau. In his conversation with Lau, Rajaratnam's statements included the following:

• I heard yesterday from somebody who's on the Board of Goldman Sachs, that they are gonna lose $2 per share. The Street has them making $2.50.

• [T]hey don't report until December....

• So what he was telling me was that uh, Goldman, the quarter's pretty bad.... I don't think that's built into Goldman p.129 Sachs stock price. So if it gets to $105, I'm gonna, it's $99 now, it was at $102. I was looking for $105, I'm gonna whack it you know.

(GX 29-T, at 2.)

Given that this conversation occurred on October 24, 2008, less than two hours after Rajaratnam unloaded his Goldman Sachs stock — beginning one minute after the market opened — Rajaratnam's statement that he had "heard yesterday" from a Goldman board member that Goldman would lose money and would not report its losses until December clearly exposed him to criminal liability for trading on inside information. Moreover, Rajaratnam's statement that if the stock reached a certain level he planned to sell it short was an admission of a plan to engage in additional unlawful insider trading in the future.

Although Gupta argues that these statements were not sufficiently reliable to satisfy the statement-against-penal-interest exception, we disagree. The evidence as to the timing of the Goldman Sachs board's after-hours conference call on October 23, which ended at 4:49 p.m. and was followed by a 4:50 p.m. call from Goldman board member Gupta to Rajaratnam, coupled with Rajaratnam's commencing to dump his Goldman stock one minute after the market opened the next morning, provided ample corroboration for the October 24 statement that Rajaratnam had received information "yesterday" of Goldman's yet-to-be-announced "$2 per share" losses from "somebody who's on the Board of Goldman Sachs."

Again, Gupta argues that Rajaratnam was merely attempting to impress Lau. That was a contention that could be argued to the jury; but as "reasonable people, even reasonable people who are not especially honest, tend not to make self-inculpatory statements unless they believe them to be true." *Williamson,* 512 U.S. at 599, 114 S.Ct. 2431, it would have been within the district court's discretion to find that Rajaratnam, as founder and head of Galleon, would have had no need to attempt to impress his subordinates and that he would not have made these self-incriminating statements without a foundation of truth.

B. *Limitations on Gupta's Defense Evidence*

Gupta also contends that he is entitled to a new trial on the ground that the district court unduly limited evidence proffered by the defense to show that any communication by Gupta of inside information to Rajaratnam in the fall of 2008 was improbable. For the reasons that follow, we conclude that none of the challenged rulings constituted an abuse of the court's discretion and that a new trial is unwarranted.

1. *Testimony by Gupta's Daughter*

The "linchpin" of the defense (Gupta brief on appeal at 46) was the proposition that in mid-September 2008, Gupta was angry with Rajaratnam for having withdrawn $25 million from the Voyager fund (in which Gupta had invested $10 million and Rajaratnam had invested $40 million) without informing Gupta of the withdrawal and without alerting Gupta to withdraw some of his own capital — so angry that Gupta would not have shared inside information about Goldman Sachs with Rajaratnam. To establish Gupta's state of mind — and to suggest that his September 23 and October 23 calls to Rajaratnam were merely efforts to obtain information about Voyager — the defense proffered testimony from Gupta's daughter Geetanjali that on September 20 Gupta was angry with Rajaratnam, believing that Rajaratnam had cheated him. Gupta argues that

p.130 [s]pecifically, Geetanjali would have testified:

> He told me that he was upset about Voyager. He told me that he was worried about the performance of the fund and that *he was frustrated that he couldn't get information from Raj about it.*
>
> He also told me *he was angry that Raj had taken money out of the fund without telling him* and that he thought that that — he didn't understand why he had taken the money out of the fund, and why if he had taken money out of the fund, he had not gotten any of it.

(Gupta brief on appeal at 47 (quoting Tr. 3079 (Geetanjali's statement in response to questioning by the court outside the presence of the jury) (emphases in brief)).)

The government objected that this testimony would be hearsay; Gupta argued that it was admissible under Rule 803(3)'s "state of mind" exception to the hearsay rule. After exploring Geetanjali's proposed testimony in the absence of the jury and hearing arguments from both sides (*see* Tr. 2971-74, 3071-89), the district court ruled that Geetanjali could testify to Gupta's "attitude towards Rajaratnam" with respect to Voyager, "at a given point or maybe two or three points" in time, but that Geetanjali could not testify to the "substantive" details of what Gupta said, *i.e.,* that Gupta stated that he believed Rajaratnam had cheated him (*id.* at 3087; *see id.* at 3086-89).

Accordingly, Geetanjali testified that on September 20, 2008, she had a "conversation with [her] father relating to an investment that [he] had with Mr. Rajaratnam called Voyager" (*id.* at 3093) and in that conversation Gupta expressed "significant concern" about his investment in Voyager (*id.* at 3094). Geetanjali continued as follows:

> THE COURT: And in relating this to you, what was his demeanor?
>
> THE WITNESS: He was upset. He was stressed. He was running his hands through his hair, which he often does when he's stressed. He was walking about. He was quite upset. He's normally a very calm and collected person.
>
> THE COURT: Was it your understanding, if you had one, that this was because of how the investment was doing or because of how Mr. Rajaratnam was treating the investment or what?
>
> THE WITNESS: It was more because of how Mr. Rajaratnam was treating the investment. My father had been very upset that —
>
> THE COURT: No. You've answered the question.

(Tr. 3094.) Geetanjali also testified that Gupta was frustrated by the difficulty he was having in getting information from Rajaratnam about Voyager. (*See id.* at 3095; *see also id.* at 3100 (testifying that at Thanksgiving Gupta was still upset at Rajaratnam about the Voyager investment).) The court instructed the jury that Geetanjali's testimony was to be considered "only on the issue of what bearing it has, if at all, on Mr. Gupta's attitude toward Mr. Rajaratnam during the period of time in question" (*id.* at 3095), and that "the limited purpose for which" Geetanjali's testimony was admitted was "not for... whatever may or may not have been going on at Voyager, but only for what Mr. Gupta's state of mind was with respect to Mr. Rajaratnam at this particular time" (*id.* at 3100).

Gupta contends that the district court erred in preventing Geetanjali from testifying that Gupta believed Rajaratnam had cheated him, because

> p.131 Gupta did not seek to introduce Geetanjali's testimony to prove that Rajaratnam had in fact stolen from him (a point that was undisputed anyway); rather, he wanted to show that he *believed* Rajaratnam had stolen from him at a particular point in time.

(Gupta brief on appeal at 48 (emphasis in original); *see id.* at 49 ("Gupta sought to establish that he *believed at the time* that Rajaratnam was defrauding him" (emphasis in original)).) Gupta argues that Rule 803(3) provides an exception to the hearsay rule for a declarant's then-existing state of mind and that "Geetanjali's testimony — that on September 20, Gupta told her 'he was angry that Raj had taken money out of the fund without telling him' [Tr. 3079] — was classically *admissible* evidence establishing Gupta's state of mind, and directly relevant to his motive for calling Rajaratnam." (Gupta brief on appeal at 48-49 (emphasis added); *see id.* at 49 ("his statement was *admissible* as evidence of [his] belief" that Rajaratnam was defrauding him" (emphasis added)).)

We disagree with the thrust of Gupta's arguments, as we think it clear from the record that the court's limitation on Geetanjali's testimony was not based on a view that the testimony was being offered for its truth but rather was based on its view that the jury would likely be unable to comprehend that the statement could be considered only to show Gupta's belief and not to show the truth of what he believed. For the reasons that follow, we conclude that the limitation imposed was within the court's discretion, and that, in any event, if it was error to have thus limited Geetanjali's testimony, the error was harmless.

a. *The Exercise of Discretion Under Rule 403*

Generally, a statement made by a person while not testifying at the current trial, offered by that person to prove the truth of the matter asserted in his statement, is hearsay. *See* Fed.R.Evid. 801(a)(c). Hearsay generally is inadmissible if it does not fall within an exception provided by Rule 803 or 804. *See* Fed.R.Evid. 802. Rule 803 provides an exception for "[a] statement of the declarant's then-existing state of mind (such as motive, intent, or plan) or emotional, sensory, or physical condition (such as mental feeling, pain, or bodily health), *but not including a statement of memory or belief to prove the fact remembered or believed.* ..." Fed.R.Evid. 803(3) (emphasis added).

However, the fact that a statement falls within an exception to the hearsay rule does not mean that the statement is not to be classified as hearsay; nor does it mean that the statement is automatically admissible. It means simply that the statement — assuming that the criteria specified in the exception are met — is "not *excluded by the rule against hearsay,*" Fed.R.Evid. 803, 804(b) (emphasis added); *see, e.g., Li v. Canarozzi,* 142 F.3d 83, 88 (2d Cir.1998). "The court retains its normal discretion to exclude the evidence on other grounds such as lack of relevance, *see* Fed.R.Evid. 402, improper purpose, *see, e.g.,* Fed. R.Evid. 404, or undue prejudice, *see* Fed. R.Evid. 403." *Li v. Canarozzi,* 142 F.3d at 88; *cf. United States v. Detrich,* 865 F.2d 17, 21 (2d Cir.1988) (for admissibility, it is not sufficient that a proffered statement is not hearsay: "To be admissible it must also be relevant.").

Under Rule 403, even if proffered evidence is relevant, it may be excluded "if its probative value is substantially outweighed by a danger of one or more of the following: unfair prejudice, confusing the issues, misleading the jury, undue delay, wasting time, or needlessly presenting cumulative evidence." Fed.R.Evid. Rule 403; *see, e.g., Huddleston v. United p.132 States,* 485 U.S. 681, 687-88, 108 S.Ct. 1496, 99 L.Ed.2d 771 (1988); *United States v. Reifler,* 446 F.3d 65, 91 (2d Cir.2006); *United States v. Salameh,* 152 F.3d 88, 122-23 (2d Cir.1998) ("*Salameh*"), *cert. denied,* 525 U.S. 1112, 119 S.Ct. 885, 142 L.Ed.2d 785 (1999).

> In reviewing Rule 403 challenges, we "accord great deference" to the district court's assessment of the "relevancy and unfair prejudice of proffered evidence, mindful that it sees the witnesses, the parties, the jurors, and the attorneys, and is thus in a superior position to evaluate the likely impact of the evidence."

United States v. Quinones, 511 F.3d 289, 310 (2d Cir.2007) (quoting *United States v. Paulino,* 445 F.3d 211, 217 (2d Cir.), *cert. denied,* 549 U.S. 980, 127 S.Ct. 446, 166 L.Ed.2d 317 (2006)), *cert. denied,* 555 U.S. 910, 129 S.Ct. 252, 172 L.Ed.2d 190 (2008). "A district judge's" ruling following a "Rule 403 analysis is reversible error only when it is a clear abuse of discretion." *Salameh,* 152 F.3d at 122. "To find such abuse, we must conclude that the challenged evidentiary rulings were arbitrary and irrational." *United States v. Quinones,* 511 F.3d at 307-08 (internal quotation marks omitted); *see, e.g., United States v. Scott,* 677 F.3d 72, 83-84 (2d Cir.2012); *Salameh,* 152 F.3d at 110.

We see no arbitrariness or irrationality in the present case. In limiting Geetanjali's testimony, the trial court made a Rule 403 assessment that the admission of testimony that Gupta believed Rajaratnam had cheated him — which the court observed would be "cumulative," given that the court had (as discussed in Part II.B.1.b. below) admitted other evidence to the same effect (Tr. 3085) — would be unduly prejudicial. Noting that, unlike the other witnesses whose similar testimony had been admitted, Geetanjali had no personal knowledge about Voyager, the court reasoned the jury would have undue difficulty in distinguishing between the aspect of Geetanjali's testimony that could be considered for its truth as to Gupta's state of mind and the aspect that indicated that Gupta had been cheated. When Gupta's counsel argued that the defense would be prejudiced if it could not have Geetanjali testify that Gupta thought Rajaratnam had cheated him, the court responded.

I think the prejudice is the other way.

The jury is going to, I think, draw from this, because the government can't cross-examine the witness in any meaningful way, that Rajaratnam, in fact, cheated Gupta, that Gupta knew it and that Gupta, therefore, was completely outraged; and, hence, it carries a danger here that no other witness carries for the reasons that I've already elaborated on the record.

(Tr. 3086 (emphasis added); *see, e.g., id.* at 2972-73 ("[T]here is *no way the jury can make th[e] distinction*" between the belief and the substance of what was said to have been believed. "They are going to inevitably think if they accept this testimony at all that he is telling the truth to his own daughter, and *they will be taking it for its truth,* and I don't see how *under 403* that gross violation of the hearsay rule can be avoided." (emphases added)).) Thus, the court limited Geetanjali's testimony not on the ground that it was offered to prove that Rajaratnam had in fact cheated Gupta but rather because the court's view was that, if admitted, the jury would likely be unable to comprehend that it was not admitted for that purpose. We see no basis for second-guessing the district court's view as to the likely effect on the jury. Although it would have been within the court's discretion to admit the proposed Geetanjali testimony along with a clear and detailed limiting instruction to the p.133 jury if it believed such an instruction would be effective, we see no abuse of discretion in the court's decision to limit the testimony in light of its conclusion that there was "no way" such an instruction in this case would be effective.

We note that although Gupta perhaps would have us classify the court's ruling as arbitrary on the ground that Geetanjali was not allowed to state that Gupta was "angry" (Gupta brief on appeal at 22), the record does not support that contention. The court ruled that she would be allowed to testify to Gupta's "attitude" toward Rajaratnam; the record does not indicate that the court placed any restriction on the words she could use to describe his attitude. Geetanjali described Gupta as "quite upset" (Tr. 3094) and "frustrated" (*id.* at 3095) by his inability to get information from Rajaratnam about Voyager — descriptions likely sufficient to imply anger; and there was no ruling barring her from expressly describing him as "angry."

Gupta's additional contention that the limitation on Geetanjali's testimony made it seem "only that Gupta was upset in September 2008 about the *performance* of the Voyager investment." (Gupta brief on appeal at 22 (emphasis in original)) is belied by the testimony itself. The court asked whether Gupta was upset "because of how the investment was doing or because of how Mr. Rajaratnam was treating the investment or what"; Geetanjali responded "It was more because of how Mr. Rajaratnam was treating the investment." (Tr. 3094.)

Finally, Gupta suggests that allowing Geetanjali to testify that Gupta believed Rajaratnam had cheated him by taking money out of Voyager without alerting Gupta also to withdraw some of his capital from that venture would have been no more prejudicial than similar evidence that the court had previously admitted, because "the excluded statement did no more than confirm undisputed facts" (Gupta reply brief on appeal at 21). But this very argument substantiates the district court's view that this aspect of the Geetanjali testimony, with its potential for the jury to infer that Gupta had in fact been cheated, would have been cumulative. We cannot conclude that the court abused its discretion in viewing the potential for jury confusion and undue prejudice as substantially outweighing the cumulative evidence's probative value.

b. *Harmless Error*

The fact that "the excluded statement did no more than confirm undisputed facts" (Gupta reply brief on appeal at 21) also contributes to our conclusion that, if the limitation on Geetanjali's testimony was error, the error was harmless. A party may gain relief for an "error in a ruling to admit or exclude evidence only if," *inter alia*, "the error affect[ed] a substantial right of the party." Fed.R.Evid. 103(a); *see, e.g.,* Fed.R.Crim.P. 52(a) ("Any error ... that does not affect substantial rights must be disregarded."). Thus, "[u]nder harmless error review, we ask whether we can conclude with fair assurance that the errors did not substantially influence the jury." *United States v. Oluwanisola,* 605 F.3d 124, 133 (2d Cir.2010) ("*Oluwanisola*") (internal quotation marks omitted); *see, e.g., Kotteakos v. United, States,* 328 U.S. 750, 764-65, 66 S.Ct. 1239, 90 L.Ed. 1557 (1946). If defense evidence has been improperly excluded by the trial court, we normally consider such factors as

> (1) the importance of ... unrebutted assertions to the government's case; (2) whether the excluded material was cumulative; (3) the presence or absence of evidence corroborating or contradicting the government's case on the factual questions at issue; (4) the extent to p.134 which the defendant was otherwise permitted to advance the defense; and (5) the overall strength of the prosecution's case.

Oluwanisola, 605 F.3d at 134; *see also United States v. Miller,* 626 F.3d 682, 690 (2d Cir.2010) (focusing principally on the overall strength of the prosecution's case), *cert. denied,* ___ U.S. ___, 132 S.Ct. 379, 181 L.Ed.2d 239 (2011); *United States v. Song,* 436 F.3d 137, 139-40 (2d Cir.2006) (focusing principally on the extent to which the defendant was otherwise able to present the defense and on the presence of evidence corroborating the government's case); *United States v. Lawal,* 736 F.2d 5, 9

(2d Cir.1984) (focusing principally on the overall strength of the prosecution's case and on the cumulative nature and marginal probative value of the excluded evidence).

All five of the factors set out in *Oluwanisola* lead us to conclude that, if there was error, it was harmless. First, as to the assertions in the government's case that Gupta sought to rebut, he pointed to testimony by Kumar suggesting that Gupta did not learn of Rajaratnam's withdrawal of capital from Voyager until 2009 (*see* Tr. 1858-64); Gupta argued that the singular importance of the proposed evidence as to his conversation with Geetanjali was its timing — *i.e.,* that Gupta told her he was upset with Rajaratnam on September 20 (several days prior to his September 23 call to Rajaratnam upon learning of the imminent Buffett investment) rather than not becoming upset until 2009. (*See, e.g., id.* at 3086 ("Your Honor, this proof is pretty critical and crucial because they put Kumar on there to try and move the date to fit their theory."); *see also* Gupta brief on appeal at 46-47.) Thus, "Geetanjali's statement that Gupta told her he was angry that Rajaratnam had impermissibly and covertly redeemed money from the Voyager fund ... was offered to prove *when* Gupta formed his belief about the redemptions." (Gupta reply brief on appeal at 20 (emphasis in original).) "The importance of this timing question cannot be overstated." (*Id.* at 19.)

But the court placed no restriction at all on the defense's ability to bring out the timing of Gupta's conversation with Geetanjali. Geetanjali testified amply that the conversation occurred on September 20, 2008. She testified that she remembered the date because, *inter alia,* it was her 30th birthday, and it occurred on a trip to Connecticut to celebrate both her birthday and her mother's birthday which was the next day. (*See* Tr. 3092-93.) Further, after Geetanjali proceeded to describe Gupta's being upset with Rajaratnam on account of Rajaratnam's treatment of the Voyager investment, the court highlighted the fact that that testimony was relevant to the "time" of Gupta's anger at Rajaratnam: It instructed the jury that Geetanjali's testimony was to be considered "only on the issue of what bearing it has, if at all, on Mr. Gupta's attitude toward Mr. Rajaratnam *during the period of time in question*" (*id.* at 3095 (emphasis added)), and that "the limited purpose for which" Geetanjali's testimony was admitted was "not for ... whatever may or may not have been going on at Voyager, but only for what Mr. Gupta's state of mind was with respect to Mr. Rajaratnam *at this particular time*" (*id.* at 3100 (emphasis added)). The government's assertions as to the timing of Gupta's animus toward Rajaratnam thus did not go unnoticed or unchallenged.

Second, the testimony that the basis for Gupta's attitude toward Rajaratnam was that Rajaratnam had made a concealed withdrawal from Voyager was plainly cumulative. The government had introduced the testimony of Kumar that Gupta told him that Gupta had discovered that Rajaratnam had withdrawn some of Rajaratnam's p.135 capital from Voyager, and that Gupta said that this was "just plain wrong" and wanted to sue Rajaratnam (Tr. 1863). In addition, Gupta had introduced the deposition testimony of Ajit Jain that Gupta had told him "that he had $10 million invested with Raj in some venture and he had been gipped [*sic*], swindled or cheated by Raj and he had lost his entire 10 million that he had invested with Rajaratnam." (Jain Deposition at 6; *see* Tr. 2722-24, 2775.)

As to the third *Oluwanisola* factor, "the presence or absence of evidence corroborating or contradicting the government's case *on the factual question[] at issue*," 605 F.3d at 134 (emphasis added), which was the timing of Gupta's anger at Rajaratnam, plainly Geetanjali's testimony contradicted the government's theory that Gupta was not angry about Rajaratnam's treatment of Voyager until early 2009. But there was also evidence corroborating the government's contention that Gupta was on friendly terms with Rajaratnam through the fall of 2008. The government introduced a voice mail message from Gupta to Rajaratnam on October 10, 2008, well after the September 20 conversation with Geetanjali, saying "Hey Raj, Rajat here. Just, uh, calling to catch up. I know it must be an awful and busy week. I hope you are holding up well. Uh, and I'll, uh, try to give you a call over the weekend to just catch up. Uh, all the best to you, talk to you soon. Buh-bye," (GX 25-T; *see also* GX 2128-MCK (a January 2009 email from Gupta to Rajaratnam wishing him a "Happy New Year" and "a restful week," forwarding information about a possible Galleon hiree, and concluding "Let's catch up soon").)

Fourth, the record easily establishes that Gupta was able, based on the evidence that was introduced, to advance his defense. The explicit testimony of Kumar and Jain that Gupta believed Rajaratnam had cheated him, along with documentary evidence that Rajaratnam had in fact withdrawn $25 million from Voyager and a tape-recorded conversation in which Rajaratnam stated he had not told Gupta about the withdrawal, were highlights of Gupta's summation to the jury, cited by his counsel Gary P. Naftalis as among Gupta's "badges of innocence" (Tr. 3266; *see id.* at 3270).

> [A] second badge of innocence.... is Rajaratnam's defrauding of Mr. Gupta about the Voyager investment.... Remember Mr. Gupta invested $10 million in this Voyager investment, and ultimately — and it's kind of undisputed — he lost all of his $10 million.... We have heard testimony from a variety of sources about how Mr. *Gupta was very upset about how he was treated with that investment not only losing the money, but the conduct that he came to learn about which Rajaratnam engaged in which consisted of not giving him information.*

(*Id.* at 3270 (emphasis added).) Naftalis argued:

> *[Kumar's] testimony is supportive of the fact that we were swindled, Mr. Gupta was swindled by Mr. Rajaratnam in his Voyager investment.* If you remember, Mr. Gupta made this investment, put a lot of money, $10 million in Voyager, and it turned out that he lost every dime in that investment, every dime. He lost $10 million, and we also established, if you recall, that there was a schedule....
>
> .... *This is what Government Exhibit 2105 shows, unbeknownst to Rajat Gupta, behind the back of Rajat Gupta, concealed from Rajat Gupta, that Raj Rajaratnam put his hands into the cookie jar and took $25 million out.* ...
>
> p.136 ... *[Y]esterday we put in evidence, an October 2nd tape, wiretap conversation* that the government captured of Rajaratnam speaking on October 2nd with one of his colleagues, Mr. Santhanam, and in this conversation *[Rajaratnam] admitted that he never told Rajat Gupta he had taken the equity out.*

(Tr. 3258-59 (emphases added).)

> MR. NAFTALIS: (Continued) Can you stop [the tape] for a second there? Go back to "I told him I didn't take the equity out."

"I didn't tell him, I didn't tell Rajat Gupta that I took the equity out. I didn't tell him I took the $25 million out."

You recall that Mr. Kumar told us... in October he had conversations, *he is one of the many witnesses who testified on this subject about how Rajat Gupta was very upset because he had lost his money and indeed came to learn that he had been swindled by Mr. Rajaratnam who took the money out, concealed it from him.*

(Tr. 3260 (emphases added); *see also id.* at 3272 ("As we know, because we've just played it a few minutes ago, we know that Mr. Rajaratnam had taken $25 million out of the fund and concealed it from Mr. Gupta.").) Counsel also cited the deposition of Jain:

He told us, Mr. Jain, he testified by videotape, that on January 12, 2009, he had lunch with *Mr. Gupta, and Mr. Gupta told him that he had $10 million invested with Rajaratnam, and he had been gypped, swindled and mistreated by Raj* and lost his entire $10 million.

(*Id.* at 3276 (emphasis added).)

Counsel also emphasized that "we learned that Mr. Gupta ... was very upset about how he had been treated by Mr. Rajaratnam" with respect to Voyager "as early as September 20." (Tr. 3271.) He argued that Geetanjali "told you that on the 20th she had [the] conversation with her father" in which Gupta showed he was quite upset, and counsel pointed out, *inter alia,* that "that is a date that stuck in [Geetanjali's] mind" because she was "celebrating on September 20, 2008 her 30th birthday" and "her mother's birthday ... was on the 21st of September." (*Id.*)

In sum, the evidence "from a variety of sources," as defense counsel said (*id.* at 3270), including an exhibit, a wiretapped conversation, and testimony from three witnesses, was clearly sufficient to enable Gupta to present his main defense.

Finally, the government's circumstantial evidence that Gupta in fact passed confidential information to Rajaratnam on September 23 and October 23 was strong. The timing of Gupta's calls to Rajaratnam — each placed approximately one minute after Gupta received extraordinary news about Goldman Sachs's finances — and the timing and nature of Rajaratnam's large trades in Goldman Sachs stock, *i.e.,* purchases within minutes of the first such call in the wake of Gupta's receipt of favorable information, and sales a month later within the first possible minute of trading after the call following Gupta's receipt of unfavorable information, were powerful evidence that Rajaratnam was given the confidential information by Gupta. And that evidence was supported by Rajaratnam's statements, in the wake of those trades, to Horowitz and Lau.

We see no basis for a conclusion that, if Geetanjali had been allowed to testify that Gupta believed Rajaratnam's actions with respect to Voyager had cheated him — rather than to testify (as she was allowed to) that Gupta was quite upset over Rajaratnam's treatment of the Voyager investment — that testimony would have had any substantial influence on the jury. If it was p.137 error for the court to limit Geetanjali's testimony as it did pursuant to Rule 403, we conclude that the error was entirely harmless.

2. Evidence To Suggest an Alternative Tipper

Gupta's "second defense" at trial was to suggest that Rajaratnam had received the confidential Goldman Sachs information from a person other than Gupta. (Gupta brief on appeal at 53.) The person specified was David Loeb, a Goldman vice president who was "one of the sales guys who would call" Rajaratnam "a lot" (Tr. 274-75). Gupta sought to make this showing by proffering two taped telephone conversations and several dozen emails between Loeb and Rajaratnam (collectively the "documents" or "Loeb documents") that Gupta contended showed that Loeb had obtained inside information about technology companies including Intel Corporation and Apple Inc. and immediately attempted to reach Rajaratnam to pass that information to him. (*See, e.g., id.* at 2982, 2999.)

The district court refused to admit the Loeb documents on grounds of hearsay, relevance, lack of foundation, and, given the absence of a proper foundation, the likelihood that the documents would cause jury confusion. On appeal, Gupta argues that the trial court's exclusion of these documents was error because "'the accused may introduce any legal evidence tending to prove that another person may have committed the crime with which the defendant is charged'" (Gupta brief on appeal at 54 (quoting *Holmes v. South Carolina*, 547 U.S. 319, 327, 126 S.Ct. 1727, 164 L.Ed.2d 503 (2006))), and that the proffered documentation showing "Loeb's history of providing Rajaratnam with inside information was sufficient to place an alternative-perpetrator theory before the jury" (Gupta brief on appeal at 53-54). Although Gupta's legal premise is sound, we disagree with his contention that his proffer was sufficient.

"Evidence is relevant if ... it has any tendency to make a fact" that is "of consequence in determining the action" "more or less probable than it would be without the evidence." Fed.R.Evid. 401. The assessment of the relevance of evidence for the purpose of its admission or exclusion is committed to the sound discretion of the district court. *See, e.g., George v. Celotex Corp.,* 914 F.2d 26, 28 (2d Cir. 1990). The trial court also has considerable discretion in deciding whether an adequate foundation has been laid for the introduction of relevant documents. *See, e.g., Kirsch v. Fleet Street, Ltd.,* 148 F.3d 149, 166 (2d Cir.1998). We accord particular deference to the trial court's rulings as to foundation and relevance, and we will not overturn those rulings except for abuse of discretion. *See, e.g., Krieger v. Gold Bond Building Products,* 863 F.2d 1091, 1097 (2d Cir.1988) (relevance); *LaForest v. Former Clean Air Holding Co.,* 376 F.3d 48, 58 (2d Cir.2004) (foundation).

At trial, in response to the government's contention that the Loeb documents were hearsay, Gupta argued that the information in the documents was "not being offered for the truth. It is being offered for the fact that Loeb is saying I have information for you urgently or information that is important, please give me a call or may I call you." (Tr. 2986.) The government pointed out, however, that Gupta was seeking to introduce the documents without calling any witness to provide a foundation indicating that the information was in fact confidential. The government argued that to the extent that the documents themselves portrayed the information as confidential, they were, in the absence of other evidence to show confidentiality, necessarily being offered for the truth of that p.138 portrayal; otherwise the documents were not relevant to indicate that Rajaratnam received confidential information about Goldman finances from Loeb, and their admission could only confuse the jury. Likewise, as to documents in which Loeb referred to information characterized as important without stating that it was confidential, there was, in the absence of other evidence to establish confidentiality, no foundation for a finding that the documents — none of which related to information concerning Goldman Sachs — were relevant. (*See id.* at 2994-95.)

Although Gupta argued that "[t]here [wa]s substantial evidence that supports the argument that Mr. Loeb could well have been the source of the alleged tips[,] if they happened[,] relating to Goldman Sachs" (*id.* at 2998-99), he proffered no evidence to show that Loeb had access to the confidential information about Goldman finances that triggered Rajaratnam's trading following the September 23 and October 23 calls. To the contrary, there was evidence that Goldman kept its "securities division [of] salespeople and traders that interacted with investors" physically and technologically separated from its equity capital markets division (*id.* at 1588-89); the latter division was "privy to a lot of confidential information" (*id.* at 1589) and developed the Buffett investment, which was "extremely confidential" because of its potential impact on Goldman's share price (*id.* at 1590; *see id.* at 1588-95). Loeb was in the securities division, not the equity capital markets division. (*See id.* at 2873-75 ("Loeb was an institutional salesperson," whose job it was to attempt to sell securities based on research done by Goldman analysts).) And although there was evidence that Loeb was on Rajaratnam's list of 10 important persons (*see, e.g., id.* at 273-75) — Loeb was in charge of Galleon's securities account at Goldman (*see id.* at 2875) — and that he called Rajaratnam "a lot" (*id.* at 274-75), Eisenberg, Rajaratnam's assistant, testified that the man who called asking "urgent[ly]" to speak to Rajaratnam near the close of the market on September 23 (*id.* at 238-39) was not Loeb (*see id.* at 327).

The district court concluded that the Loeb documents were replete with inadmissible hearsay (*see* Tr. 3000, 3065); that they "suffer[ed] from," *inter alia,* a "lack of foundation" (*id.* at 3000); and that in the absence of explanatory testimony by a witness the jury would be unable to understand the documents without representations by counsel or speculation, either of which would be improper (*see id.* at 3065). As Gupta insisted on relying solely on the documents themselves, choosing not to call a witness or to present other evidence to lay a foundation for his contention that the information referred to in the Loeb documents was "inside" information (Gupta brief on appeal at 54), we see no error in the trial court's rulings. *See generally United States v. Harwood,* 998 F.2d 91, 97 (2d Cir.) (a "statement [that] is irrelevant unless it was true ... would be hearsay[] and inadmissible"), *cert. denied,* 510 U.S. 971, 114 S.Ct. 456, 126 L.Ed.2d 388 (1993).

3. *Evidence of Proposed Charitable Giving*

During the government's case, a portion of the notes taken by Gupta's financial advisor during an April 2008 meeting with Gupta was admitted in evidence to show that Gupta had an ownership interest in Galleon International. Pursuant to the rule of completeness, *see* Fed.R.Evid. 106, the court allowed Gupta to introduce other parts of those notes concerning other sources of his wealth. The court rejected, however, Gupta's attempt to introduce still other portions of the notes that read, in part, "want to give to charity while alive" p.139 and "? 80% to charity

& 20% to extended family? perhaps" (GX 5517) (the "wealth distribution notes"). The court ruled that, as offered by Gupta, the wealth distribution notes were inadmissible hearsay, that they would be unduly confusing and prejudicial, and that their admission was not justified under Rule 106. Gupta challenges this ruling, arguing that the portion of the notes that "recorded Gupta's intent to donate most of his wealth to charity" (1) "was not hearsay, as it went to Gupta's state of mind," and (2) in any event "should have been admitted to ensure a fair and impartial understanding of the admitted portion." (Gupta brief on appeal at 50-51.) Neither contention has merit.

Gupta's first argument is doubly flawed. To the extent that the above text reflected statements by Gupta, it was plainly hearsay when offered by Gupta. It did not become nonhearsay even if it reflected his state of mind; if it did so reflect, it merely had the potential to fall within an exception to the general rule that hearsay evidence is to be excluded. More importantly, as discussed in Part II.B.1.a. above, the fact that a hearsay statement falls within an exception does not make the statement admissible. It must meet the requirements of, *inter alia,* relevance, and it must not be excludable on the grounds of undue confusion or prejudice under Rule 403. Even if the wealth distribution notes — which were surrounded by question marks and followed by the word "perhaps" — reflected Gupta's actual intent to give 80 percent of his wealth to charity, such intentions were irrelevant to whether Gupta had achieved (or was about to achieve) some of his wealth unlawfully.

Nor were the wealth distribution notes admissible under Rule 106 for purposes of completeness. That Rule provides: "If a party introduces all or part of a writing or recorded statement, an adverse party may require the introduction, at that time, of any other part — or any other writing or recorded statement — *that in fairness ought to be considered at the same time.*" Fed.R.Evid. 106 (emphasis added). "The completeness doctrine does not, however, require the admission of portions of a statement that are neither explanatory of nor relevant to the admitted passages." *United States v. Johnson,* 507 F.3d 793, 796 (2d Cir.2007) (internal quotation marks omitted), *cert. denied,* 552 U.S. 1301, 128 S.Ct. 1750, 170 L.Ed.2d 549 (2008). We see no abuse of discretion, *see, e.g., id.,* in the ruling that the wealth distribution notes were not necessary for completeness here. The notes as to Gupta's ownership interest in Galleon International were relevant to show that Gupta had a financial stake in the profitability of Galleon International; that stake was relevant to show that Rajaratnam's advising Lau in October 2008, just after learning that Goldman would report a quarterly loss, not to buy shares of Goldman was in furtherance of the conspiracy among Rajaratnam, Gupta, and others to profit and avoid losses by trading on the basis of inside information. Whatever thought Gupta may have had as to how to distribute his wealth was not relevant to whether or not he had a stake in Galleon International.

4. *Character Evidence*

At trial, Gupta called several character witnesses who testified to their opinions that Gupta was an honest person. Gupta also sought to have the witnesses testify to their opinions that he had "integrity" (Tr. 2331). The government objected to the giving of opinions on "integrity" to the extent that the defense wanted to elicit testimony "that [Gupta] obeys the law." (*Id.*) The court noted that there were several dictionary definitions of integrity (*see* p.140 *id.* at 2331-32) and asked what, other than honesty, Gupta expected the jury to understand by the word "integrity" (*id.* at 2333). Defense counsel responded with the dictionary definition that read "moral soundness, honesty, uprightness." (*Id.*) The court upheld the government's objection, concluding that moral soundness and uprightness themselves were unduly ambiguous and would convey concepts not pertinent to the present case. The court allowed Gupta's character witnesses to give their opinions only as to Gupta's honesty — the relevant aspect of the dictionary definition cited by defense counsel.

Gupta contends that the district court erred in not allowing him to question witnesses about his "integrity," arguing that his honesty was not at issue in the case because he was not charged with making any false statement. We reject his contention.

The trial court has broad discretion in its rulings on the admissibility of character testimony, and such decisions "will be reversed only upon a clear showing of prejudicial abuse." *United States v. Morgan,* 554 F.2d 31, 33-34 (2d Cir.1977). We see no abuse of discretion in the court's conclusion that, other than honesty itself, the aspects of the "integrity" definition cited by defense counsel were not pertinent to this case.

Gupta also argues that the district court should have instructed the jury that "character testimony may in and of itself raise a reasonable doubt" as to a defendant's guilt of the charges against him (Tr. 3039). The district court declined to give such an instruction because it "artificially singles out one aspect of the proof and gives it sort of prominence above all others by implication," and noted that, although such an instruction is "commonly given," no case law required him to give it. (*Id.* at 3039-40.)

The district court's understanding of the law of this Circuit was correct. We have held that an instruction that character testimony may by itself raise a reasonable doubt is not required. *See United States v. Pujana-Mena,* 949 F.2d 24, 27-28 (2d Cir.1991) ("*Pujana-Mena*"). Although Gupta asks us to "reconsider" *Pujana-Mena,* arguing, in part, that it is "contrary" to two Supreme Court cases (Gupta brief on appeal at 60-61), we decline to do so. Both of the Supreme Court cases cited by *Gupta* — *Edgington v. United States,* 164 U.S. 361, 17 S.Ct. 72, 41 L.Ed. 467 (1896), and *Michelson v. United States,* 335 U.S. 469, 69 S.Ct. 213, 93 L.Ed. 168 (1948) — preceded *Pujana-Mena* and were cited in and distinguished by *Pujana-Mena, see* 949 F.2d at 28-30. Gupta has cited no intervening change in the law suggesting that *Pujana-Mena* was wrongly decided; and even if this panel had the authority to overturn a prior panel decision in another case, we would see no basis for concluding that *Pujana-Mena*'s interpretation of those Supreme Court precedents was incorrect.

CONCLUSION

We have considered all of Gupta's arguments on this appeal and have found them to be without merit. The judgment of the district court is affirmed.

722 F.3d 94 (2013)

Randolph PORTER, Plaintiff-Appellant,

v.

Andrea QUARANTILLO, District Director, New York District of the U.S. Citizenship and Immigration Services, United States Citizenship and Immigration Services, Defendants-Appellees.

Docket No. 13-119-cv.

United States Court of Appeals, Second Circuit.

Argued: April 5, 2013.

Decided: July 8, 2013.

Porter v. Quarantillo, 722 F. 3d 94 (2nd Cir. 2013)

p.95 Zoe Salzman, Emery Celli Brinckerhoff & Abady LLP, New York, NY, for Plaintiff-Appellant Randolph Porter.

Margaret M. Kolbe (Varuni Nelson, Scott Dunn, on the brief), Assistant United States Attorneys, of Counsel, for Loretta E. Lynch, United States Attorney for the Eastern District of New York, New York, NY, for Defendants-Appellees Andrea Quarantillo and United States Citizenship and Immigration Services.

Before: B.D. PARKER, CARNEY, Circuit Judges, and RAKOFF,[*] District Judge.

BARRINGTON D. PARKER, Circuit Judge:

Plaintiff-Appellant Randolph Porter, a naturalized United States citizen, sought a p.96 declaratory judgment from the district court (E.D.N.Y., Irizarry, J.) that he was entitled to derivative United States citizenship as of his birth. Porter's brother was killed on Pan Am Flight 103 by Libyan terrorists in December 1988, and if Porter were able to prove derivative citizenship, he ostensibly would be entitled to compensation from a settlement fund established by the governments of Libya and the United States. His argument below for derivative citizenship rested in large part on the assertion that his mother, Mary Diamond, herself a United States citizen, had remained in this country for over a year following her birth before she moved to St. Vincent and the Grenadines. Lacking other evidence, Porter attempted to show his mother's age at the time of her move by reference to a number of affidavits from his mother, other family members, and a family friend. The district court, determining that these statements were inadmissible hearsay, granted summary judgment in favor of Defendants-Appellees United States Citizenship and Immigration Services ("USCIS") and the agency's New York District Director Andrea Quarantillo. Porter appeals from that decision, and we are called on to decide whether the district court abused its discretion by not admitting the statements under the family history exceptions to the hearsay rule. See Fed.R.Evid. 803(19), 804(b)(4). We conclude that the district court did not abuse its discretion.

BACKGROUND

Porter's brother died on Pan Am Flight 103, which was destroyed over Lockerbie, Scotland by Libyan terrorists on December 21, 1988. Under a settlement reached between the United States and Libya, Porter may have been entitled to compensation for his brother's death if he could show that he, Porter, was a U.S. citizen at the time of the Lockerbie bombing. See Libyan Claims Resolution Act,

Pub. L. No. 110-301, 122 Stat. 2999 (2008); Decision No. LIB-I-001, at 5-6 (Foreign Claims Settlement Commission 2009) (limiting compensation to claimants who were United States nationals "at the time of loss" (internal quotation marks omitted)), *available at* http://www.justice.gov/fcsc/ readingroom/lib-i-001.pdf.

Porter was born in St. Vincent in 1955 and became a naturalized U.S. citizen in 1995. He argued to the USCIS in 2011, however, that he was entitled to derivative U.S. citizenship as of the time of his birth because his mother Mary Diamond was a U.S. citizen (as a consequence of having been born in this country) and had been present here for at least one continuous year before relocating to St. Vincent. *See* 8 U.S.C. § 1409(c) (1952) (establishing requirements for derivative citizenship).[1] Whether Porter, with derivative citizenship, would be eligible to claim from the settlement fund is not at issue in this litigation. The USCIS denied Porter a certificate of citizenship, and Porter sued in district court seeking a declaratory judgment pursuant to 8 U.S.C. § 1503(a) and 28 U.S.C. § 2201(a) that he was a citizen at birth.

Porter relied on several affidavits to support his claim. One of these affidavits, submitted by his mother, Mary Diamond, stated that she was born in Brooklyn in 1929 and moved to St. Vincent in 1930 when she was "between one year old and two years old." App. 136. Diamond's p.97 childhood friend in St. Vincent, Thomas Brown, also submitted an affidavit stating that when they were children, Mary Diamond told him that she moved from New York to St. Vincent "when she was about one and a half years old." App. 142. According to Brown, it was "common knowledge" among people who knew Diamond during her childhood that she left the United States "when she was about one and a half years old." *Id.* Finally, affidavits from Diamond's third cousin, Porter's siblings, and from Porter himself all stated, in substance, that it was Diamond's "reputation" among her family members that she arrived in St. Vincent from the United States when she was approximately one and a half years old.

The parties cross-moved for summary judgment. The district court ruled that the affidavits submitted by Porter were inadmissible hearsay assertions, not subject to the personal or family history exceptions in Rules 803(19) and 804(b)(4). The court reasoned that Diamond's statement concerning her *age* at relocation (as opposed to the fact of relocation) and her reputation for being a certain age at relocation were not inherently reliable enough to fall within those exceptions. The court then held that Porter had failed to prove that his mother had been present in the United States for at least one year before his birth, as required by § 1409(c), and that, consequently, he was not entitled to derivative citizenship. The court granted the government's motion, and this appeal followed.

DISCUSSION

When a party challenges a district court's evidentiary rulings underlying a grant of summary judgment, we undertake a two-step inquiry. First, "we review the trial court's evidentiary rulings, which define the summary judgment record." *LaSalle Bank Nat'l Ass'n v. Nomura Asset Capital Corp.,* 424 F.3d 195, 211 (2d Cir.2005). Because the "principles governing admissibility of evidence do not change on a motion for summary judgment," *Raskin v. Wyatt Co.,* 125 F.3d 55, 66 (2d Cir.1997), we review the district court's decision to exclude evidence as hearsay for abuse of discretion, *see United States v. Coplan,* 703 F.3d 46, 84 (2d Cir. 2012). "[O]nly admissible evidence need be considered by the trial court in ruling on a motion for summary judgment," and a "district court deciding a summary judgment motion has broad discretion in choosing whether to admit evidence." *Presbyterian Church of Sudan v. Talisman Energy, Inc.,* 582 F.3d 244, 264 (2d Cir.2009). A district court abuses its discretion when it bases its ruling "on an erroneous view of the law or on a clearly erroneous assessment of the evidence, or render[s] a decision that cannot be located within the range of permissible decisions." *Sims v. Blot (In re Sims),* 534 F.3d 117, 132 (2d Cir.2008). At the second stage of our inquiry, "with the record defined, we review the trial court's summary judgment decision *de novo,*" construing all evidence in the light most favorable to the nonmoving party. *LaSalle Bank,* 424 F.3d at 205, 211.

Hearsay is any out-of-court statement offered to prove the truth of the matter asserted in the statement. *See* Fed. R.Evid. 801(c). Rule 802 provides that hearsay is inadmissible unless made admissible by a federal statute, the Federal Rules of Evidence, or other rules prescribed by the Supreme Court.

Porter contends that his mother's declaration satisfies the hearsay exception permitting admission of certain statements "of personal or family history" when the declarant p.98 is unavailable.[2] *See* Fed.R.Evid. 804(b)(4). This provision exempts from the rule against hearsay statements about "(A) the declarant's own birth, adoption, legitimacy, ancestry, marriage, divorce, relationship by blood, adoption, or marriage, *or similar facts of personal or family history,* even though the declarant had no way of acquiring personal knowledge about that fact...." *Id.* (emphasis added).

Diamond's sworn statement — "[w]hen I was between one year old and two years old, I moved to St. Vincent and the Grenadines" — does not relate to her "birth, adoption, legitimacy, ancestry, marriage, divorce, [or] relationship by blood, adoption, or marriage." Instead, Porter argues that his mother's age at the time of her relocation from the United States is a "similar fact[] of personal or family history," within the meaning of Rule 804(b)(4)(A). We disagree.

The exception for statements of family history, like the other exceptions to the hearsay rule, is premised on the view that certain categories of statements are "'free enough from the risk of inaccuracy and untrustworthiness'" such that "the test of cross-examination would be of marginal utility." *Idaho v. Wright,* 497 U.S. 805, 819-20, 110 S.Ct. 3139, 111 L.Ed.2d 638 (1990) (quoting 5 Wigmore on Evidence § 1420, p. 251 (J. Chadbourn rev. 1974)). Rule 804(b)(4) assumes that statements of family history "are likely to be informed by knowledge shared in common among family members on the basis of customs and understandings that are likely to be true." 5 Mueller & Kirkpatrick, Federal Evidence § 8:133, p. 224 (3d ed.2007).

Neither the Rules nor the Advisory Committee Notes define the scope of "similar facts of personal or family history," but the Supreme Court has instructed that "absent express provisions to the contrary," we may presume that the drafters of the Rules intended to "adhere to the common law in the application of evidentiary principles." *Tome v. United States,* 513 U.S. 150, 160-61, 115 S.Ct. 696, 130 L.Ed.2d 574 (1995). At common law, the scope of the exception for "declarations of family history" was defined by the following question: "Were the circumstances named in the statement such a marked item in the ordinary family history and so interesting to the family in common that statements about them in the family would be likely to be based on fairly accurate knowledge and to be sincerely uttered?" 5 Wigmore on Evidence § 1502, p. 400 (J. Chadbourn rev. 1974).

The Diamond affidavit does not meet this test. The affidavit fails satisfactorily to explain how the precise date of relocation was sufficiently significant or interesting or unusual such that it ever became — much less remained for more than eighty years — a subject of presumptively accurate family lore. The affidavit was offered not simply to prove that Diamond left the United States at an early age. The affidavit was offered to prove many years after the event a very narrow range of dates for her travel — a range about which she, because of her age, lacked personal knowledge. We do not believe that family members would ordinarily be so interested in Mary's exact age at relocation as to afford Diamond's imprecisely described but definitely bounded statement the level of inherent reliability required by Rule 804. In other words, although a change in one's country of residence or in one's citizenship might, like the date of one's birth, death, p.99 or marriage, be a matter of interest within a family, the district court was properly skeptical that generalized discussions of family history would include statements of age so precise as to foreclose the possibility that Mary was eleven months old but allow the possibility that she was thirteen months old at the time of her relocation, especially when, insofar as the record reflects, nothing appears to have turned on that precise date for the intervening several decades prior to Porter's pursuit of derivative citizenship status. Accordingly, we find no abuse of discretion in the district court's decision to exclude Diamond's affidavit.

Porter asserts that the other affidavits satisfy the parallel exception for statements about "reputation concerning personal or family history," a hearsay exception for which the declarant's availability is immaterial. Fed.R.Evid. 803(19). This provision exempts from the hearsay rule statements concerning a "reputation among a person's family by blood, adoption, or marriage — or among a person's associates or in the community — concerning the person's birth, adoption, legitimacy, ancestry, marriage, divorce, death, relationship by blood, adoption, or marriage, *or similar facts of personal or family history*." *Id.* (emphasis added). Statements are sufficiently trustworthy, and thus satisfy this exception, "when the topic is such that the facts are likely to have been inquired about and that persons having personal knowledge have disclosed facts which have thus been discussed in the community." Fed.R.Evid. 803(19)-(21) advisory committee's note.

For the same reasons as those discussed above, we conclude that the district court did not abuse its discretion by ruling that statements of Diamond's family members and friend, concerning Diamond's precise age at relocation, were inadmissible hearsay. We see no reason for concluding that, without more, a statement about a child's age — precise to a range of months as to a time of relocation more than eighty years ago — is as inherently reliable as the types of statements that Rule 803 permits. *See* 5 Jack B. Weinstein & Margaret A. Berger, Weinstein's Federal Evidence § 803.21[1], p. 803-140 (J. McLaughlin ed., 2013) ("[A] false reputation as to birth, death, or marriage is not likely to arise at any time. However, there is a greater possibility of inaccuracy concerning other aspects of family history, such as an ancestor's travels."). Because Porter submitted no sufficient admissible evidence establishing his mother's age at relocation, we conclude that the district court correctly determined that Porter was not entitled to derivative citizenship.

CONCLUSION

The judgment of the district court is AFFIRMED.

[*] The Honorable Jed S. Rakoff, United States District Judge of the United States District Court for the Southern District of New York, sitting by designation.

[1] "[T]he applicable law for transmitting citizenship to a child born abroad when one parent is a United States citizen is the statute that was in effect at the time of the child's birth." *Drozd v. INS,* 155 F.3d 81, 86 (2d Cir. 1998) (internal quotation marks and alteration omitted). Porter was born in 1955.

[2] The parties agree that, because Mary Diamond passed away after this litigation began, she is "unavailable" for purposes of Rule 804. *See* Fed.R.Evid. 804(a)(4).

706 F.3d 131 (2013)

UNITED STATES of America, Appellant,

v.

Courtney DUPREE, Defendant-Appellee,

Thomas Foley, Rodney Watts, Defendants.

No. 11-5115-cr.

United States Court of Appeals, Second Circuit.

Argued: August 30, 2012.

Decided: January 28, 2013.

US v. Dupree, 706 F. 3d 131 (2nd Cir. 2013)

p.133 Michael Yaeger (Peter A. Norling, on the brief), Assistant United States Attorneys, on behalf of Loretta E. Lynch, United States Attorney for the Eastern District of New York, Brooklyn, N.Y., for Appellant.

Meena Sinfelt (Roscoe C. Howard, Jr., Leasa W. Anderson, on the brief), Andrews Kurth LLP, Washington, D.C., for Defendant-Appellee.

Before: WINTER, RAGGI, and LIVINGSTON, Circuit Judges.

DEBRA ANN LIVINGSTON, Circuit Judge:

The government appeals from a November 23, 2011 order of the United States District Court for the Eastern District of New York (Matsumoto, J.) denying its motion *in limine* to admit a state court temporary restraining order as evidence against Defendant-Appellee Courtney Dupree. The government argues that it is not seeking to admit the order for the truth of any assertion it may contain, but only as evidence that Dupree knew of, and intended to violate, a contractual obligation to maintain funds at Amalgamated Bank when he executed a series of withdrawals and money transfers that deprived the Bank of property to which it was entitled in alleged violation of 18 U.S.C. § 1344.

Because the government is seeking to admit the state court order for a non-hearsay purpose and because the district court's analysis pursuant to Federal Rule of Evidence 403 did not account for the order's probative value if offered to show knowledge, we vacate the district court's order and remand for the district court to conduct a Rule 403 analysis consistent with this opinion.

BACKGROUND

Defendant-Appellee Courtney Dupree ("Dupree") is the former Chief Executive Officer and President of GDC Acquisitions ("GDC"), a holding company which owns several subsidiary companies. In 2008, Dupree negotiated a Credit Agreement between Amalgamated Bank ("Amalgamated"), GDC, and three GDC subsidiaries. The Credit Agreement provided the GDC subsidiaries a term loan and revolving lines of credit worth $21 p.134 million in total. The loans were secured in part with the subsidiaries' accounts receivable and bank deposits. The accompanying Security Agreement included the accounts receivable and deposits in its definition of collateral, and the Credit Agreement itself required the subsidiaries to maintain operating accounts at Amalgamated and to deposit their revenues into those accounts.

On July 23, 2010, Thomas Foley, GDC's Chief Operating Officer and outside counsel, Rodney Watts, GDC's Chief Financial Officer and Chief Investment Officer, and Dupree were arrested for bank fraud in connection with the 2008 Credit Agreement. The government alleged that Dupree and his codefendants fraudulently secured credit loans from Amalgamated by intentionally inflating the subsidiaries' accounts receivable. The government also alleged that defendants further defrauded Amalgamated by having GDC covertly purchase another company in violation of the Credit Agreement.

On the day of the arrests, Amalgamated sent Dupree a letter informing him that it considered the loan to be in default, and that it was exercising its right under the Credit Agreement to accelerate the loan and demand payment in full of the roughly $18 million outstanding balance. Not convinced that GDC would adhere to the terms of the Credit Agreement, including the requirement that the subsidiaries maintain their accounts at the Bank, Amalgamated brought suit for breach of the Credit Agreement and sought a temporary restraining order in New York County Supreme Court that would, *inter alia,* enjoin GDC, Dupree, and the subsidiaries, among others, from removing any assets required to be maintained at the Bank other than in the ordinary course of business.

On August 4, 2010, New York Supreme Court Justice Shirley Kornreich issued the requested restraining order ("the Order" or "the August 4 Order"). In relevant part, the Order "temporarily restrained and enjoined [GDC, Dupree, and the three subsidiaries, among others] from moving, removing, transferring, encumbering or otherwise taking any further action to the detriment of plaintiffs with respect to any assets of [GDC and its subsidiaries], including the Collateral ... other than in the ordinary course of business."[1] The Order also required "[a]ll collection" to be deposited into an account at Amalgamated Bank.

As relevant here, the grand jury returned a superseding indictment on March 25, 2011. While the first four counts of this indictment stemmed from material misrepresentations made on the loan application and actions taken prior to Dupree's arrest, the fifth count was directed solely at Dupree and arose from his course of conduct after the August 4 Order issued. The government alleges that Dupree knew that the Credit Agreement provided Amalgamated a security interest in the subsidiaries' deposits and that he knowingly and intentionally executed a scheme to defraud Amalgamated of this interest in violation of 18 U.S.C. § 1344. Dupree's alleged fraudulent scheme consisted of converting one of the subsidiary company's revenues for his own personal use, either by withdrawing money in cash from the subsidiary's funding account or by transferring money from that funding account to his personal accounts, all without giving notice to Amalgamated. All told, the government alleges that Dupree converted approximately $331,000 to his personal use in the p.135 period after his arrest, using the funds to pay for rent, a car lease, various mortgages, and other expenses.

Dupree moved to dismiss Count Five of the superseding indictment, arguing that the government relied on an alleged violation of the August 4 Order in asserting that he had committed bank fraud, which was not a proper basis on which to ground Section 1344 liability. The district court agreed, concluding that bank fraud "cannot be premised solely on a violation of a state court order" and that because Count Five "allege[d] only that defendant Dupree defrauded Amalgamated via the state court's order," the Count was insufficiently pled. The district court dismissed Count Five without prejudice and with leave to refile, indicating that a bank fraud charge could properly be premised on a scheme to evade the Credit Agreement's provision obligating the subsidiaries "to maintain operating accounts with, and deposit all of their revenue with Amalgamated." The government did not appeal the dismissal of Count Five, but rather sought and obtained a second superseding indictment in which Count Five was modified specifically to reference this provision in the Credit Agreement.

On October 3, 2011, the government filed a motion *in limine* seeking, *inter alia,* to admit the August 4 Order as evidence that Dupree had knowledge of his obligations under the Credit Agreement and that he intended to evade these obligations and to defraud Amalgamated when he executed his withdrawals and transfers. The district court denied this motion, holding the Order was inadmissible hearsay because the government was seeking to introduce the Order for its truth — in the district court's view, to show that the Order created an independent obligation to maintain the accounts at Amalgamated. The district court also noted that even if the August 4 Order were admissible under a hearsay exception, the court would still exclude it under Federal Rule of Evidence 403 on the ground that the dangers of unfair prejudice and confusion of issues from its admission substantially outweigh its probative value. The government timely filed this interlocutory appeal pursuant to 18 U.S.C. § 3731, divesting the district court of its jurisdiction over the fifth count of the second superseding indictment. The case proceeded to trial as to Dupree on the remaining four counts and he was convicted on each of them.

Because we conclude that the August 4 Order is not hearsay and is probative of Dupree's state of mind at the time he allegedly diverted funds the Credit Agreement required to be maintained at Amalgamated, we vacate the district court's order and remand for the district court to conduct a Rule 403 balancing inquiry consistent with this opinion.

DISCUSSION

We review a district court's evidentiary rulings deferentially, reversing only for abuse of discretion. *United States v. Quinones,* 511 F.3d 289, 307 (2d Cir.2007). A district court abuses its discretion when "(1) its decision rests on an error of law (such as application of the wrong legal principle) or a clearly erroneous factual finding, or (2) its decision — though not necessarily the product of a legal error or a clearly erroneous factual finding — cannot be located within the range of permissible decisions." *Zervos v. Verizon N.Y., Inc.,* 252 F.3d 163, 169 (2d Cir.2001).

1. Waiver

As a threshold matter, Dupree contends that the government failed to argue that the August 4 Order is admissible non-hearsay evidence before the district p.136 court, thereby waiving this claim on appeal. As a general rule, we will not consider matters raised for the first time on appeal. *See Thomas E. Hoar, Inc. v. Sara Lee Corp.,* 900 F.2d 522, 527 (2d Cir.1990). Here, however, the government's motion *in limine* asserted that it was seeking to admit the August 4 Order "to prove Dupree's knowledge," and not for its truth. While the government also cited Federal Rule of Evidence 803(8), which provides a hearsay exception for some public records, and its motion papers are not a model of clarity in assessing the Rule 803(8) argument in the alternative, the government's papers specifically cite those portions of the district court's opinion dismissing Count Five as originally pled that note the August 4 Order "is potentially relevant to show defendant Dupree's knowledge and intent to violate the Agreement to maintain all operating accounts at the Bank and deposit all of the subsidiaries' revenue at Amalgamated." While it is perhaps understandable that the government's position might have been misconstrued, we conclude that the argument was not waived. The government properly raised the issue below, and Dupree's waiver argument fails.

2. Hearsay

Dupree next argues that, in any event, the August 4 Order constitutes inadmissible hearsay under the Federal Rules of Evidence, and thus the district court's order excluding it should be affirmed. We disagree.

The Federal Rules of Evidence define hearsay as a declarant's out-of-court statement "offer[ed] in evidence to prove the truth of the matter asserted in the statement." Fed.R.Evid. 801(c). Hearsay is admissible only if it falls within an enumerated exception. *Id.* 802. However, "[i]f the significance of an offered statement lies solely in the fact that it was made, no issue is raised as to the truth of anything asserted, and the statement is not hearsay." *Id.* 801(c) advisory committee's note. Thus, a statement offered to show its effect on the listener is not hearsay. *Id.; see also George v. Celotex Corp.,* 914 F.2d 26, 30 (2d Cir.1990) ("To be sure, an out of court statement offered not for the truth of the matter asserted, but merely to show that the defendant was on notice of a danger, is not hearsay.").

Here, the Order consists primarily of imperative statements and provides in relevant part as follows:

> The Borrower Defendants and the Individual Defendants, and all persons or entities controlled by any of them, directly or indirectly, are temporarily restrained and enjoined from moving, removing, transferring, encumbering or otherwise taking any further action to the detriment of [Amalgamated Bank] with respect to any assets of the Borrower Defendants, including the Collateral... other than in the ordinary course of business...."

The Order identifies GDC and its various subsidiaries as the "Borrower Defendants" and Dupree as one of the four "Individual Defendants." It also specifically requires "[a]ll collection" to be deposited into Amalgamated Bank.

Dupree contends that the August 4 Order is proffered "for its truth" — in his view, to show that the Order created an obligation on his part to maintain and deposit funds into the accounts at Amalgamated, independent of his obligations under the Credit Agreement. He contends, further, that such evidentiary use of the Order would require the jury to determine whether he violated its terms and that "a jury should not be allowed to stand in the place of the state court judge to make such p.137 a finding." Appellee's Br. at 16. We disagree.

At the start, whether the August 4 Order imposed legal obligations on Dupree is not a question directly presented here since, pursuant to the government's theory, the Order's relevance lies not in its legal effect (the Credit Agreement having created the Amalgamated interest allegedly defrauded by Dupree), but in the fact that the Order issued in connection with Amalgamated's suit against Dupree and in the fact that Dupree had knowledge of the Order. Even if the Order's relevance *did* lie in its legal effect, moreover, no hearsay problem would ensue, as the question whether a court's command imposes legal obligations on a party is outside the hearsay rule's concerns. *See* Fed.R.Evid. 801(c) advisory committee's note (explaining that verbal acts, meaning statements affecting the legal rights of parties, are excluded from the definition of hearsay); *see also United States v. Boulware,* 384 F.3d 794, 806 (9th Cir.2004) ("A prior judgment is not hearsay ... to the extent that it is offered as legally operative verbal conduct that determined the rights and duties of the parties.").

Even assuming, moreover, that the August 4 Order, as a series of imperative commands, *could* be offered for the truth of some assertion that it implies — as might be the case, for instance, if the Order were offered to show that Amalgamated Bank exists — the government here does not proffer the August 4 Order for any such assertion. Instead, as the government aptly argues, the significance of the Order lies in the fact that it issued — making it less likely that Dupree, aware of the August 4 Order, could be *unaware* of relevant provisions in the Credit Agreement on which it was premised and that he allegedly disregarded in diverting funds to his personal use. The government maintains that given the Order's timing — coming on the heels of Dupree's arrest and Amalgamated's acceleration of the loan — and the Order's posture — resulting from Amalgamated's suit to enforce its rights under the Credit Agreement — a jury could infer that its issuance served as a reminder to Dupree of his obligations under the Credit Agreement to "maintain all [the subsidiaries'] operating accounts at the Bank" and to "deposit all of [the subsidiaries'] revenue, upon receipt, into an operating account at the Bank." The government argues that such a reminder, coming two years after Dupree signed the Credit Agreement, makes it less likely that Dupree's conduct with regard to the allegedly diverted funds could be an innocent mistake — a line of reasoning, it contends, that does not rely on the truth of any matter asserted in the Order. We agree.

We have repeatedly held that a statement is not hearsay where, as here, it is offered, not for its truth, but to show that a listener was put on notice. *See George,* 914 F.2d at 30; *see also United States v. Ansaldi,* 372 F.3d 118, 130 (2d Cir.2004) (holding that an FDA document describing conversion of drug when ingested was not hearsay and was properly admitted to show defendants knew they were selling a controlled substance). Here, a jury could infer that given the August 4 Order's timing, posture, and language, Dupree knew of his obligations under the Credit Agreement and further knew that he was depriving Amalgamated of its property interests when he allegedly withdrew and transferred money for his personal use in violation of the Credit Agreement's terms. Moreover, a jury could draw this inference without deciding whether the August 4 Order itself created any obligations that Dupree subsequently violated, and without relying on the truth of any assertion that p.138 the August 4 Order might contain.[2] Such use of the August 4 Order does not implicate the hearsay rule, and the district court erred in concluding to the contrary.

3. Rule 403

The district court also determined that it would exclude the August 4 Order pursuant to Rule 403 even if, as we have concluded, the Order is proffered for a non-hearsay purpose. A district court may exclude relevant evidence pursuant to Rule 403 only "if its probative value is substantially outweighed by a danger of one or more of the following: unfair prejudice, confusing the issues, misleading the jury, undue delay, wasting time, or needlessly presenting cumulative evidence." Fed.R.Evid. 403. A court should consider the possible effectiveness of a jury instruction and the availability of other means of proof in making a Rule 403 determination. *Id.* advisory committee's note. We defer to a district court's decision to exclude or admit evidence under this rule and reverse only for abuse of discretion. *United States v. Awadallah,* 436 F.3d 125, 131 (2d Cir.2006).

Here, in conducting its Rule 403 balancing inquiry, the district court failed to consider the probative value of the August 4 Order on the question whether Dupree was aware of his obligations to Amalgamated under the Credit Agreement when he improperly withdrew and diverted money from the Amalgamated accounts. Instead, the district court understandably misconstrued the government's position. The court concluded that the Order was proffered to show that the Order itself imposed a legal obligation on Dupree to deposit the relevant funds at Amalgamated, and that such use of the Order is of little probative worth, since "it is not necessary for the jury to find a violation of the August 4 Order to convict Dupree of Count Five." This was error, requiring the district court's order to be set aside.

As already noted, the August 4 Order is offered to show Dupree's knowledge and intent at the time he obtained the relevant funds. Dupree has never conceded that he was aware that Amalgamated had an interest pursuant to the Credit Agreement in the funds he allegedly diverted to his own use. Dupree's knowledge and intent may thus play a central role in the trial, and the August 4 Order may be of significant importance by "tend[ing] to show that the defendant's conduct was not merely a technical oversight but ... a deliberate theft." Appellant's Br. at 25. The district court committed legal error in not considering the Order's probative value on Dupree's state of mind. *Cf. United States v. Pepin,* 514 F.3d 193, 207-08 (2d Cir.2008) (holding that the district court abused its discretion under Rule 403 when it excluded evidence of postmortem dismemberment probative of defendant's state of mind). Given its relevance, the August 4 Order may properly be excluded only if its probative value in shedding light on Dupree's state of mind is substantially outweighed by the dangers of which Rule 403 warns. *See* Fed.R.Evid. 403 (listing as possible dangers "unfair prejudice, confusing the issues, misleading the jury, undue delay, wasting time, or needlessly presenting cumulative evidence"). The district court noted that a jury might place undue p.139 emphasis on the Order simply because a judge issued it, and that introducing the Order might confuse the issues and mislead the jury. However, we have noted that such dangers can often be cured by careful limiting instructions, *see, e.g., United States v. Mercado,* 573 F.3d 138, 142 (2d Cir.2009) (affirming decision to admit potentially prejudicial evidence where the district court "gave several careful instructions to the jury regarding what inferences it could draw from the admitted evidence"); *see also United States v. Snype,* 441 F.3d

119, 129 (2d Cir.2006) ("[T]he law recognizes a strong presumption that juries follow limiting instructions."), and we see no basis on the present record for concluding that such instructions would be ineffective here. Nevertheless, because it is for the district court in the first instance to consider this question, we vacate and remand so that the district court can conduct a Rule 403 analysis consistent with this opinion.

CONCLUSION

For the foregoing reasons, we vacate the district court's order and remand the case for further proceedings.

[1] The state court action was subsequently stayed. The temporary restraining order remains in effect.

[2] Given this conclusion, we need not address Dupree's contentions that a jury "should not be allowed" to determine whether he violated the terms of the August 4 Order. We note, however, that to the extent Dupree relies on *United States v. Barnett,* 376 U.S. 681, 697-700, 84 S.Ct. 984, 12 L.Ed.2d 23 (1964) (concerning the scope of an alleged contemnor's right to jury trial in the adjudication of his contempt) to argue that jury consideration of this issue would be improper, the citation is inapposite.

THIRD CIRCUIT DECISIONS

The Rule Against Hearsay

No cases were selected for publication.

Fourth Circuit Decisions

The Rule Against Hearsay

742 F.3d 104 (2014)

UNITED STATES of America, Plaintiff-Appellee,

v.

Mohammad Omar Aly HASSAN, Defendant-Appellant.

United States of America, Plaintiff-Appellee,

v.

Ziyad Yaghi, Defendant-Appellant.

Nos. 12-4067, 12-4063, 12-4061.

United States Court of Appeals, Fourth Circuit.

Argued: September 19, 2013.

Decided: February 4, 2014.

US v. Hassan, 742 F. 3d 104 (4th Cir. 2014)

p.110 ARGUED: Robert Joseph Boyle, Robert J. Boyle, Attorney at Law, New York, New York; Robert Daniel Boyce, Nexsen Pruet, Raleigh, North Carolina; John Clark Fischer, Randolph & Fischer, Winston-Salem, North Carolina, for Appellants. Jason Michael Kellhofer, Office of the United States Attorney, Raleigh, North Carolina, for Appellee. ON BRIEF: Kirsten E. Small, Nexsen Pruet, PLLC, Raleigh, North Carolina, for Appellant Mohammad Omar Aly Hassan. Thomas G. Walker, United States Attorney, Jennifer P. May-Parker, Kristine L. Fritz, Assistant United States Attorneys, Office of the United States Attorney, Raleigh, North Carolina, for Appellee.

Before WILKINSON and KING, Circuit Judges, and Samuel G. WILSON, United States District Judge for the Western District of Virginia, sitting by designation.

Affirmed by published opinion. Judge KING wrote the opinion, in which Judge WILKINSON and Judge WILSON joined.

KING, Circuit Judge:

The appellants in these consolidated proceedings, Mohammad Omar Aly Hassan, Ziyad Yaghi, and Hysen Sheriff, were tried jointly in the Eastern District of North Carolina and convicted of several offenses arising from terrorism activities. On appeal, the trio presents myriad challenges to their convictions and sentences. As explained below, we reject the appellants' various contentions of error and affirm.

I.

A.

On July 22, 2009, the federal grand jury in eastern North Carolina returned an indictment against the appellants and five others, alleging multiple terrorism conspiracies and related offenses. Bench warrants were issued for all eight defendants on July 23, 2009, and, four days later, seven were arrested. In September 2009, a superseding indictment was returned, followed on November 24, 2010, by the operative second superseding indictment (the "Indictment"). The Indictment alleged the following offenses that are particularly relevant to these appeals:

• Count One charged the eight defendants with conspiring to violate 18 U.S.C. § 2339A, that is, to provide material support and resources for violations of 18 U.S.C. § 956 (the "Count One conspiracy");

p.111 • Count Two charged the eight defendants with the conspiracy offense of violating 18 U.S.C. § 956(a), i.e., to commit outside the United States acts that would constitute murder, kidnapping, and maiming if committed within the United States (the "Count Two conspiracy");

• Counts Four and Eight charged conspiracy ringleader Daniel Boyd ("Boyd"), his son Zakariya, and appellant Hysen Sherifi with possessing firearms in furtherance of a crime of violence — particularly, the Count Two conspiracy — in contravention of 18 U.S.C. § 924(c); and

• Count Eleven charged Boyd and Sherifi with conspiring to kill members of the uniformed services of the United States in attacks on military personnel and installations in Virginia and elsewhere, in violation of 18 U.S.C. § 1117 (the "Count Eleven conspiracy").

None of the other charges in the Indictment were lodged against any of the appellants. Count Three charged Boyd with receiving a firearm and ammunition in interstate commerce, with knowledge that the offenses set forth in Counts One and Two would be committed therewith, in contravention of 18 U.S.C. § 924(b). Counts Five, Nine, and Ten charged Boyd (and in Count Five, Boyd's son Dylan) with knowingly selling firearms and ammunition to a felon, in violation of 18 U.S.C. §§ 922(d)(1) and 924. Counts Six and Seven charged Boyd with making false statements to the government by misrepresenting his plans to meet others — including appellants Mohammad Omar Aly Hassan and Ziyad Yaghi — when Boyd travelled to the Middle East in 2007, in contravention of 18 U.S.C. § 1001(a)(2). In Counts Twelve and Thirteen, defendant Anes Subasic was charged with knowingly making false statements to procure his naturalization as a citizen, in violation of 18 U.S.C. § 1425(a).

On February 9, 2011, Boyd pleaded guilty to the Count One and Count Two conspiracies, and, pursuant to his plea agreement with the government, Counts Three through Eleven were dismissed as to him. Dylan and Zakariya Boyd each pleaded guilty to the Count One conspiracy, and, in exchange, the other charges against them were dismissed. Boyd was sentenced to 216 months in prison, and his sons Dylan and Zakariya were sentenced to 84 months and 93 months, respectively. Subasic was tried separately from the appellants, convicted of the four offenses alleged against him, and sentenced to 360 months. As for the appellants, Hassan was convicted of the Count One conspiracy and sentenced to 180 months; Yaghi was convicted of the Count One and Count Two conspiracies and sentenced to 380 months; and Sherifi was convicted of the Count One, Count Two, and Count Eleven conspiracies, plus Counts Four and Eight, and he was sentenced to 540 months.[1]

B.

The parties and the trial court were in substantial agreement on the essential elements of the offenses tried before the jury.[2] First, to obtain a conviction under p.112 18 U.S.C. § 2339A for the Count One conspiracy, the government was required to prove as to each appellant: (1) that he entered into a conspiracy; (2) that the objective of the conspiracy was to provide material support or resources; and (3) that he then knew and intended that the provision of such material support or resources would be used in preparation for, or in carrying out, a violation of 18 U.S.C. § 956. *See United States v. Chandia*, 675 F.3d 329, 332 n. 1 (4th Cir.2012). "[M]aterial support or resources," as used in § 2339A, includes currency and other property, training, weapons, expert advice or assistance and personnel. *See* § 2339A(b)(1). To prove the Count Two conspiracy alleged under 18 U.S.C. § 956(a), the government was obliged to show as to each appellant: (1) that he entered into a conspiracy; (2) knowing and intending that the objective of the conspiracy was murder, kidnapping, or maiming outside the United States; (3) that the conspiracy was entered into within the United States; and (4) that a conspirator, not necessarily a defendant or an appellant, committed an overt act in furtherance of the conspiracy within the jurisdiction of the United States.[3]

The Indictment identified the purposes and objects of the Count One and Count Two conspiracies, which were generally to advance violent jihad, support and participate in terrorist activities outside the United States, and commit acts of murder, kidnapping, and maiming outside the United States. The manner and means by which the conspiratorial objects were to be accomplished by the defendants and their conspirators included the following:

- To prepare to become "mujahideen" and die "shahid" — that is, as martyrs in furtherance of violent jihad;

- To radicalize others, mostly young Muslims or converts to Islam, to believe in "fard'ayn," the idea that violent jihad is a personal obligation on the part of every good Muslim;

- To offer financing and training in weapons, and to assist in arranging overseas travel and contacts so that others could wage violent jihad;

- To raise money to support efforts in training and equipping personnel, and to disguise the destination of such monies from the donors; and

- To obtain assault weapons such as the AK-47, and to develop familiarity and skills with the weapons of choice used by mujahideen in Afghanistan and elsewhere.

Multiple overt acts were specifically alleged in the Indictment that relate to the p.113 Count One and Count Two conspiracies, including, inter alia:

- In late 2006, Yaghi travelled to Jordan to engage in violent jihad;

- In late 2006, Boyd purchased a Bushmaster carbine rifle and magazine;

- In early 2007, Boyd purchased a Ruger mini 14 long gun;

- In early 2007, Boyd purchased airline tickets to Israel from the United States for himself and his sons;

- In early 2007, plane tickets were purchased for Yaghi and Hassan to travel from the United States to Israel;

- In June 2007, Boyd, his son Zakariya, Yaghi, and Hassan departed Raleigh, North Carolina, for Israel. Having failed in their attempts to engage in violent jihad, the four men returned to the United States in late July 2007;

• Upon his arrival back in the United States, Boyd lied to federal agents by denying that he had intended to meet Hassan and Yaghi in Israel;

• In February 2008, Boyd solicited money to fund the travel of "brothers" overseas to engage in violent jihad;

• In June 2008, Boyd accepted $500 in cash from Sherifi to help fund violent jihad;

• In June 2008, Boyd showed Sherifi how to use a Kalashnikov AK-47;

• In June 2008, Sherifi departed North Carolina for Kosovo to engage in violent jihad;

• In November 2008, Boyd purchased a Mossburg rifle, a .357 revolver, and a Century Arms rifle;

• In early 2009, Boyd purchased an Ishmash SAGA .308 rifle, three Century Arms rifles, a Ruger 5.56 rifle, and a Smith & Wesson .223 rifle;

• In April 2009, Sherifi returned from Kosovo to the United States for the purpose of soliciting funds and personnel to support the mujahideen; and

• In June and July 2009, Boyd, Sherifi, and Zakariya Boyd trained in military tactics and the use of weapons in Caswell County, North Carolina.

With respect to the essential elements of Counts Four and Eight — which were tried against Sherifi alone — the government was required to establish: (1) that Sherifi knowingly possessed a firearm on or about June 10, 2009, and again on or about July 7, 2009; and (2) that he did so to further the crime of violence alleged in Count Two. *See* 18 U.S.C. § 924(c).[4] Those charges arose from the weapons training sessions conducted by Boyd and others in 2009 in Caswell County.

Finally, to secure Sherifi's conviction under 18 U.S.C. § 1117 on the Count Eleven conspiracy, the government was required to demonstrate: (1) that Sherifi entered into a conspiracy; (2) the object thereof was to kill or attempt to kill officers and employees of the executive branch of the federal government (here, members of the uniformed services), on account of — or while such officers and employees were engaged in — the performance of their official duties; and (3) that at least one overt act was committed in furtherance of the conspiracy.[5] Count Eleven identified several p.114 overt acts, including the following: In June 2009, Sheriff's coconspirator Boyd conducted reconnaissance at the Quantico, Virginia Marine Corps Base; also in June 2009, Boyd reviewed maps of Quantico, intending the maps to be used to plan and coordinate an attack on the base; and, in July 2009, Boyd possessed weapons and ammunition that would be used at Quantico, asserting that they were for the base and to attack Americans.

C.

During the post-Indictment period leading to the trial, the appellants filed multiple pretrial motions in the district court, several of which sought to curtail the government's case. For example, the appellants challenged the government's expert witness and moved to exclude evidence obtained pursuant to the Foreign Intelligence Surveillance Act ("FISA"). The district court disposed of some of the appellants' evidentiary challenges prior to trial. First, after conducting a *Daubert* hearing, the court authorized the trial testimony of the government's expert, Evan

Kohlmann, subject to specified limitations. *See Daubert v. Merrell Dow Pharm., Inc.,* 509 U.S. 579, 113 S.Ct. 2786, 125 L.Ed.2d 469 (1993). Second, the court considered and rejected the appellants' challenges to the government's FISA-derived evidence. After conducting an in *camera* and *ex parte* review of relevant materials, the court ruled that such evidence was admissible. Finally, the court considered several other evidentiary challenges, holding some of them in abeyance pending the trial proceedings.

Before trial, the prosecution moved to preclude the appellants from arguing to the jury that their alleged unlawful conduct was protected by the First Amendment. Although the trial court agreed with the government "that there is no First Amendment defense to the crimes with which [the appellants] are charged," the court determined "that granting the government's motion would go too far." *See United States v. Boyd,* No. 5:09-cr-00216, slip op. at 8-9 (E.D.N.C. July 12, 2011), ECF No. 1222. The court further explained:

> While the government correctly points out that the First Amendment provides no constitutional right to actively support violent crime, the wording of the government's motion would suggest that defendants should not be allowed to mention the First Amendment at all at trial, a restriction that strikes the court as inappropriate. As defendants note, it is the government's burden at trial to prove that defendants engaged in unlawful conduct. Based on defendants' briefs, it seems that defendants intend to challenge exactly what "conduct" the government contends is unlawful. This is a permissible argument to make. However, in making opening and closing arguments and in questioning witnesses, defendants may not invite jury nullification by suggesting that the First Amendment is a defense to the crimes charged. Both sides may submit proposed jury instructions regarding the First Amendment, and such proposals will be considered by the court at the appropriate time.

Id. at 9 (footnotes omitted).

II.

During the trial itself — which was conducted in New Bern over a three-week period in September and October of 2011 — the government presented approximately forty witnesses. Of those, about twenty-two were law enforcement officers, including FBI agents and employees. Other prosecution witnesses included expert Kohlmann, three informants, and three named coconspirators (Boyd and his sons Dylan and Zakariya), as well as former friends and associates of the defendants.[6] Of the three appellants, only Sherifi presented evidence. During his trial presentation, Sherifi called three witnesses, including himself.

A.

Our description of the trial evidence is provided in the light most favorable to the government. *See United States v. Burgos,* 94 F.3d 849, 862-63 (4th Cir.1996) (en banc). That evidence established a series of conspiratorial activities centering on Boyd, who, after pleading guilty to two of eleven charges, became the prosecution's chief trial witness.

1.

A citizen of the United States who converted to Islam as a child, Boyd had, as a young adult, spent time in Pakistan and Afghanistan in the 1980s and early 1990s. While living abroad, Boyd participated in the Afghan resistance against the Soviet occupation and received the nickname "Saifulla," which, in Arabic, means "Sword of God." Boyd later learned that he had been in a training camp operated or funded by the notorious al-Qaida leader Osama bin Laden. Boyd returned to the United States in the early 1990s, and, after another trip to Pakistan, settled with his family near Raleigh.

Boyd thereafter grew increasingly radicalized in his religious beliefs and, by 2004, began to espouse a violent ideology, including the view that the killing of non-Muslims was a "fard," or "fard'ayn," that is, a religious obligation imposed by Islam. As Boyd became more extreme, he disassociated himself from the Islamic community in the Raleigh area. Boyd then began to meet and discuss his violent religious views with others at his Raleigh home and at the Blackstone Halal Market, a grocery store he owned and operated for about a year in nearby Garner. The appellants met and talked with Boyd on numerous occasions during the course of the conspiratorial activities, during which they often discussed violent jihad. Boyd explained that, to him, jihad required "doing something to fulfill [his] obligation in Islam," and was "suggestive of [men] actually involving [themselves] with going and physically helping with the resistance or fighting against ... the NATO forces in Afghanistan or Iraq, or anyplace, really." J.A. 1549.[7] Boyd and the appellants "were at a point of agreement or a meeting of the minds" as to this ideology and understanding of violent jihad. *Id.* at 1549-50.

2.

a.

About 2005, the FBI initiated a criminal investigation into Boyd's activities. By mid-2006, the FBI had introduced its first informant, Abdullah Eddarkoui, into the p.116 Boyd investigation. In that capacity, Eddarkoui grew close to Boyd and his family, eventually interacting with Boyd on a daily basis. In 2007, the FBI introduced a second confidential informant, Alvin Harris, into its investigation. Harris obtained a job with another Boyd business, a construction company called Saxum Walls. Like informant Eddarkoui, Harris became a close friend of the Boyd family. Harris generally spent several days a week with Boyd. Boyd eventually helped Harris obtain a passport so that Harris could travel abroad to engage in violent jihad.

Appellant Yaghi met Boyd in 2006 when Yaghi, then eighteen years old, approached Boyd at an Islamic center in Durham. The two men initially spoke about Boyd's experiences in Afghanistan, after which Yaghi obtained Boyd's phone number. That same year, the FBI also opened an investigation into Yaghi, which was eventually merged into the Boyd investigation.

In the months that followed their first meeting in 2006, Boyd and Yaghi had several conversations, primarily at Islamic centers in the Raleigh area and in Boyd's home. The men discussed various topics, including Boyd's experiences overseas, plus his views on Islam and violent jihad. Yaghi also sought Boyd's advice about Jordan, because Yaghi wanted to travel in that country to visit relatives and study Islam. Yaghi explicitly asked Boyd where in Jordan he would find the "best brothers." J.A. 1548. This inquiry referred to Muslim men who were "going to pray" and maintain "the bonds of fellowship and Islam," and those who "understood [the] obligation of jihad" and could help Yaghi "gain access" to violent resistance movements. Id. at 1550-51. In response, Boyd told Yaghi about a mosque in Jordan where he could find the "best brothers."

In October 2006, Yaghi travelled to Jordan. Shortly before Yaghi left the United States, Boyd and several others — who understood and shared Boyd's violent and extremist ideology — met in a parking lot outside a Durham Islamic center to wish Yaghi well. Boyd described this as a "joyous send-off," during which Boyd and the others gave Yaghi gifts, including an Afghan blanket and a "traditional Pashtun hat." J.A. 1561-62. The men wished Yaghi well, sending him off with the valediction "may we meet again in heaven," which conveyed their hope that Yaghi would make his way to the battlefield, and, if he died, find his way to heaven. Id. at 1555, 1562. According to Boyd, the terms "battlefield" and "battlefront" were used to refer to locations where Muslims were then actively waging violent jihad against the "kuffar," including wars in Afghanistan, Iraq, Kosovo, Chechnya, Somalia, Palestine, and Kashmir. As Boyd and others explained to the jury, "kuffar" is a derogatory term, commonly used by violent Muslims to refer to non-Muslims. See id. at 989-90, 1399-1400, 1557. Boyd and his coconspirators shared the view that getting to the jihadist battlefield and fighting against the kuffar was a necessary and laudable aspiration.

While in Jordan in 2006, Yaghi remained in touch with Boyd by phone and email. In November 2006, Yaghi sent Boyd an email explaining that it was "getting more and more obvious that the true believer[s]" of Islam — such as Yaghi and Boyd — were "under attack by the kuffar and by 'muslims.'" J.A. 4000. As Boyd explained, Yaghi's reference to "muslims" in that email meant those who claimed to be believers but who were not actually "true believers." Id. at 1556-57. Boyd recalled a "shared understanding amongst a lot of the rhetoric online and some of the people in the community" that those who shared his beliefs were "under attack ... physically in the different battlefields," as well as "under p.117 attack ideologically from the ... naysayers of our religion," who did not believe that Muslims had an obligation to defend those fighting on the jihadist battlefields. Id. at 1557.

Prior to his departure for Jordan, Yaghi told Boyd that he hoped to find a wife overseas. While abroad, Yaghi wrote Boyd that Yaghi was waiting to see how his "marriage" would go before planning to "make [his] next move," concluding by advising Boyd that they would "meet in a far better place than this earth." J.A. 4000. It was understood by Boyd and his associates that the phrases "getting married" and "finding a wife" were code for seeking to reach the battlefield to engage in violent jihad. Id. at 1592.[8] During some of their exchanges while Yaghi was abroad, Boyd recalled Yaghi seeming "frustrated" that Boyd "wasn't able to fulfill any real helpful role for [Yaghi] to, you know, get inside somewhere to a battlefield." Id. at 1560-61.

While in the Middle East in 2006, Yaghi also posted numerous statements and copious information on Facebook concerning his adherence to the violent jihadist ideology. Yaghi consistently praised the teachings of Anwar al-Awlaki, an imam and cleric who was born in the United States and later became an al-Qaida militant in Yemen. Al-Awlaki was well known as an al-Qaida leader who espoused violent and radical jihadist views.[9] While overseas, Yaghi also kept in touch with appellant Hassan, who had been his good friend for some time. Yaghi and Hassan corresponded with one another largely through Facebook. In their Facebook postings, Hassan and Yaghi discussed the teachings of al-Awlaki and posted rap songs and poems about their animosity towards the non-Muslim kuffar. One of Yaghi's Facebook postings included the following:

> [F]eds tried ta get at me but im quick wit the trickery thas how I stay slippery/kuffar get smoked like hickory/dickery dock i pull the glock so fast the clock dont have chance ta tock/or tick let the shots rip then I stop the shit/pop my wrists I don't give uck if cops exist/im above the law already explained how im quick on the draw/heard the battle in fallujahs ferocious/niggas runnin out of ammo but they stay strapped wit explosives/rpg 7s I aint worried if all them niggas die cuz inshallah they all going ta heaven[.]

J.A. 4395. Hassan also posted violent rhymes, including the following:

> I used to smoke tree/but I dont do that shit no more that shits far/only thing I p.118 smoke now is fuckin kuffar/getting high off their deaths/fuck buryin them, let the animals eat their flesh/leave their bones for weapons or for conditioning my shins[.]

Id. at 4388. Hassan and Yaghi actively promoted the violent views and teachings of al-Awlaki by providing literature and videos to others, both within and outside the conspiracies.

In 2007, after Yaghi returned to North Carolina from Jordan, he continued his friendship with Boyd. The two men met on a substantial number of occasions throughout 2007. Yaghi also introduced Hassan to Boyd and accompanied Hassan to Boyd's home at least twice.[10] During their visits with Boyd, the three men discussed the "obligation of jihad," which Boyd explained as the need "to go and actually defend against the specific wars in Iraq and Afghanistan that were taking place," and to fight in other wars that were "going on in the Muslim world," such as in Chechnya and Palestine. J.A. 1653-64.

b.

In February 2007, Yaghi learned that Boyd would be travelling to Israel and Palestine with his sons. Yaghi asked to accompany Boyd to the Middle East and asked if Hassan could join them as well. Because the Boyds were taking a family trip, Boyd told Yaghi that he and Hassan could not travel with the Boyds. Boyd agreed, however, to facilitate the purchase of plane tickets for Yaghi and Hassan to fly to Israel. Yaghi and Hassan then gave Boyd money for their tickets, and Boyd arranged through a travel agency for a wire transfer of the necessary funds. Boyd believed that Hassan and Yaghi wanted to travel overseas in an effort to "get to a battlefront somewhere." J.A. 1587. Boyd also told informant Eddarkoui that he had asked Yaghi and another boy (whom Boyd did not specifically identify) to "go somewhere overseas for jihad." *Id.* at 780. In the months leading to their June 2007 trip, Hassan and Yaghi sought Boyd's advice about travelling in Israel and Palestine, and about the locations they should visit. Hassan and Yaghi also told Boyd that they hoped "to get married" and find wives while they sojourned in the Middle East. *Id.* at 1571.

Hassan and Yaghi discussed being familiar with firearms and assault weapons, as well as the need for training in their use, both with one another and with Boyd. Hassan and Yaghi knew that Boyd maintained a large stockpile of such weapons. Boyd had built his weapons arsenal over the years, and it included numerous assault rifles and handguns. The Boyd sons were also familiar with such weapons. Prior to 2006, for example, Dylan Boyd showed an AK-47 to a high school friend. Hassan and Yaghi discussed the need to obtain such weapons to use in implementing their beliefs in violent jihad. In early 2007, Hassan wrote on Yaghi's Facebook page, "[Y]o, theres an AK in Garner for sale — only 250 dollar ... us 3 could get it for real." J.A. 4383. Hassan also posted a link to a YouTube video concerning the basics of shooting and marksmanship. In March 2007, Hassan purchased a small caliber rifle from a sporting goods store in North Carolina. Several months later, Hassan and Yaghi gave Boyd a car ride from a mosque in Durham where the three men had been attending religious services. During the ride, Hassan and Yaghi showed Boyd the small rifle, explaining that they p.119 had purchased it for "training" and "target practice." *Id.* at 1796.

c.

Boyd and his son Zakariya departed for Israel on June 12, 2007, and Hassan and Yaghi left the very next day. Boyd and Zakariya were denied entry into Israel, however, and they instead went to Jordan via France. The Boyds toured Jordan, staying with a friend, and they concluded their Jordanian trip in the town of Salt, where they were joined by Dylan Boyd. Like the Boyds, Yaghi and Hassan were denied entry into Israel; they instead detoured to Jordan via Germany.

While abroad, Hassan and Yaghi repeatedly sought to contact Boyd by email and telephone. They received no responses from Boyd, however, notwithstanding that Boyd had email access during his travels. Hassan and Yaghi also attempted to reach Boyd by calling his home in North Carolina, but they were unable to make contact. Boyd later told the FBI that, as the trips were originally planned, he was to meet Hassan and Yaghi when they arrived in Israel and "hook them up" with persons who would assist their travels in Israel and Palestine. J.A. 1584. Hassan and Yaghi were to "go on their way from there," *id.*, that is, they would ultimately find their way to the battlefield and participate in violent jihad.

While the four men were travelling in the Middle East, rumors circulated in Raleigh that Boyd had sent Hassan and Yaghi overseas to go to the battlefield — specifically to engage in violent jihad. Boyd learned that Aly Hassan, Hassan's father in North Carolina, was upset by those rumors. Boyd called the senior Hassan from Jordan, and the two men had a heated discussion about the younger Hassan's travel plans. Boyd told the senior Hassan that Boyd was not in touch with either Hassan or Yaghi, and he could not get a message to them.

d.

After Boyd and his sons, on the one hand, and Hassan and Yaghi, on the other, returned from their 2007 trips to the Middle East, Hassan and Yaghi remained close friends. Their contacts with Boyd, however, diminished substantially. Hassan and Yaghi neither emailed nor phoned Boyd, but they visited him at the Blackstone Halal Market in Garner on at least two occasions, in the fall of 2007 and again in the spring of 2008. During one of those visits, Yaghi introduced Boyd to defendant Jude Kenan Mohammad.

Mohammad had been raised in the United States, though his father was from Pakistan and still lived there. Boyd and Mohammad became good friends, often discussing such matters as Boyd's experiences fighting in Afghanistan, Mohammad's relatives in Pakistan, and their shared radical and violent religious views. Mohammad also spoke of the evils of westernized living. In the fall of 2008, Mohammad talked of travelling to Pakistan to "go back with his people," which Boyd "assumed was to eventually try to get to the battlefield." J.A. 1605-06. Mohammad also stayed at the Boyd home when the Boyds were on vacation. While in Boyd's home, Mohammad reviewed Boyd's materials on violent jihad and extremist Islamic ideology. Mohammad passed along some of those jihadist materials to others, including Yaghi. His mother recalled dramatic changes in Mohammad's behavior during 2008, after he began to espouse Boyd's violent jihadist ideology. In October 2008, Mohammad went to Pakistan. Following his departure, Mohammad's mother confronted Yaghi — who had moved into Mohammad's apartment — about the changes in her son. Yaghi advised her p.120 that Mohammad was "in the same place" that Yaghi had been "a year prior." *Id.* at 1904-05. Boyd explained that being in the "same place" metaphorically referred to Mohammad having the understanding and beliefs that Yaghi espoused with respect to violent jihad. *Id.* at 1744.

e.

Aside from the aforementioned encounters at the Blackstone Halal Market, Boyd had little contact with either Hassan or Yaghi after their return from the 2007 trip to the Middle East. In January 2009, Yaghi and Hassan were arrested on unrelated charges.[11] While detained, Hassan asked his then paramour to email al-Awlaki directly to seek advice on Hassan's behalf. Hassan also asked her to remove from Facebook some of Hassan's postings, messages, and videos, specifically those relating to violent jihad. In March 2009, Boyd contacted Yaghi, seeking to ascertain what, if anything, Yaghi may have discussed with law enforcement officers while he was in custody. In that conversation with Boyd, Yaghi denied being a snitch. Otherwise, Hassan and Yaghi failed to keep in touch with Boyd, and the government has conceded that they were not part of Boyd's inner circle after late 2007.

Although the defense lawyers for both Hassan and Yaghi emphasized their clients' termination of communications with Boyd, the evidence — viewed in the proper light — established a "parallel set of initiatives" that the prosecution proved were being carried on by Hassan and Yaghi in 2008 and 2009. *See United States v.*

Boyd, No. 5:09-cr-00216, slip op. at 19 (E.D.N.C. Oct. 10, 2011), ECF No. 1494 ("Sufficiency Opinion I"). As the district court explained, after his return from the 2007 trip to the Middle East, Yaghi gave a speech at the Islamic Association of Raleigh promoting jihad and the corresponding moral obligation to commit violence against non-Muslims. Hassan and Yaghi regularly communicated with one another through email and Facebook about jihadist ideology and continued to discuss and engage in weapons training. Hassan espoused increasingly violent and extremist jihadist views during that period, as demonstrated by his Facebook postings. The trial court emphasized that Hassan was highly proficient in using technology to disseminate his beliefs and in seeking to recruit others to his violent ideology. *See id.* at 25. Hassan also became progressively fervent in his support of al-Awlaki.

Hassan befriended an individual named Jamar Carter in late 2006 or early 2007, first meeting Carter at a UPS store where Carter worked near Raleigh. Hassan and Yaghi introduced Carter to the Islamic religion, and shared with Carter their beliefs in violent jihad and appreciation for the teachings of al-Awlaki. At one point, Hassan showed Carter videos depicting car bombings and expressed his view that such actions were permissible. Carter, having decided that his views of Islam varied dramatically from those of Hassan and Yaghi, eventually ceased associating with them.

Boyd's lack of contact with Hassan and Yaghi after 2007 was attributed by the prosecution to several factors, including Boyd's concern that Hassan and Yaghi talked too much and drew unwanted attention to Boyd and his family. As the trial court observed, Boyd was questioned by FBI agents twice in the summer of 2007, once in July and again in August, and Boyd thus grew ever more concerned that p.121 he was under FBI surveillance. *See* Sufficiency Opinion I at 18. During his meetings with the FBI, the agents asked Boyd about his travels abroad and his contacts with Hassan and Yaghi. Boyd misled the FBI concerning the extent of his contacts with Hassan and Yaghi, initially failing to reveal that he had planned to meet Hassan and Yaghi in 2007 while they were travelling abroad in the Middle East.

3.

a.

In March 2008, a mutual friend introduced Boyd to appellant Sherifi, who was then about twenty-three years old. Sherifi and Boyd became close friends, and Sherifi often visited the Blackstone Halal Market where he and Boyd discussed their shared views advocating a violent jihadist ideology.[12] Boyd and Sherifi believed that dying "shahid" — as a martyr — was an important goal for a good Muslim. In the spring of 2008, Sherifi introduced Boyd to defendant Subasic.

Sherifi, Boyd, Dylan, and Zakariya made regular efforts to raise money to support jihadist causes — that is, to fund their own travels or to send money to other "brothers" to further violent jihadist efforts overseas. In June of 2008, Sherifi gave Boyd $500 cash for the "sake of Allah." J.A. 1657. Boyd explained "that this money was to be used to either help get somebody over there to the battlefield or get it to the people who were already there fighting." *Id.* On July 21, 2009, shortly before his arrest, Sherifi received a $15,000 check from a man named Elbaytam, who lived in Raleigh and attended the same mosque as Sherifi. Elbaytam may have intended the funds for charity, consistent with the Muslim custom of "zakat," i.e., charitable giving based on accumulated wealth. Sherifi advised informant Eddarkoui, however, that the money would instead be used to support jihadist efforts. On July 23, 2009, Sherifi deposited $5,000 cash into his bank account.

Sherifi also spoke with Boyd about his desire to travel abroad to join in violent jihad. In June 2008, Sherifi told Boyd about the challenges that Sherifi faced in obtaining the necessary travel documents. Sherifi also speculated that when "there was Shari'ah" he could travel anywhere. J.A. 4035.[13] Boyd suggested that if Sherifi could not travel, he should "make jihad" in the United States. *Id.* Sherifi promptly responded in the affirmative, intoning "Inshallah," or "God willing." *Id.*

In July of 2008, Sherifi was finally able to travel, and he departed for Kosovo. Sherifi advised some friends in Raleigh that he would be visiting family, while telling others that he was "looking for a way to go somewhere to make Jihad." J.A. 765-66. Boyd and Sherifi thereafter remained in close contact, continuing their discussions about violent jihad. Boyd advised Sherifi about getting to the "battlefield" and finding others who adhered to his and Boyd's extremist Islamic views. Boyd and Sherifi also discussed Sherifi's plans while he was abroad. Sherifi hoped ultimately to travel to Jerusalem, and he also considered travelling to Chechnya or Syria to aid in violent jihadist movements. In January 2009, Sherifi wrote Boyd that he had obtained travel documents to a location that, though not his planned destination, was "a good place to seek the greatest pleasure of Allah." *Id.* at 4011. p.122 Sherifi also remained in contact with informant Eddarkoui, advising him of efforts to obtain weapons and participate in weapons training with likeminded persons in Kosovo. In November of 2008, Sherifi wrote to Eddarkoui that "Allah ha[d] opened a way for [him]." *Id.* at 4009. Zakariya explained that opening or finding a way, in the context of violent jihad, meant that Allah had provided a "safe route that you wouldn't get in trouble through to reach a current battlefield." *Id.* at 2468-69.

In January 2009, the FBI introduced a third confidential source into its investigation: Melvin Weeks, a Staff Sergeant in the United States Army at Camp Bondsteel, Kosovo. After meeting at a local mosque, Sherifi and Weeks soon became good friends. Sherifi, who believed that jihad meant "to fight physically with weapons against the enemies of Islam, wherever they are at and whoever they might be," J.A.1947, thereafter began to discuss his violent jihadist beliefs with Weeks and made efforts to convert him. As Weeks explained, jihad, to Sherifi, was not "the jihad of the Prophet Mohammad," but rather "just murderous acts against innocent soldiers and civilians." *Id.* at 2018. Over the next few months, Sherifi provided Weeks with literature and videos, including a video of a beheading, coupled with the explanation that it was "[w]hat happens to the one who leaves the din," i.e., one who leaves the religion of Islam. *Id.* at 1973. Sherifi also introduced Weeks to the teachings of al-Awlaki, providing him with an al-Awlaki writing entitled "44 Ways to Support Jihad," in which the Imam explained how devoted "brothers" could assist violent jihadist causes by providing money and translating extremist texts, among other things. Weeks testified that Sherifi believed the "whole point of governance" was to impose Shari'ah law, and that Sherifi did not respect any other form of government. *Id.* at 2001-02. According to Weeks, Sherifi viewed everyone who did not share Sherifi's beliefs in violent ideology to be an enemy of Islam, including "[e]verybody that America [or its allies were] fighting against." *Id.* at 1949.

While Sherifi was abroad in Kosovo, he also spent time with some like-minded individuals who agreed with Sherifi and advocated violent jihad. As a prime example of such contacts, Sherifi spoke with Bajram Asllani, also known as Abu Hatab, who was a native of Kosovo. Asllani, at the time of trial, was "wanted by the United States government" on "charges of material... support to terrorism and conspiracy to kill, maim and injure overseas." J.A. 2897. Asllani was also wanted in Serbia, where he had been tried and convicted in absentia for his involvement in a "conspiracy to blow up several buildings." *Id.* After Sherifi returned to the United States from Kosovo, he maintained contact with Asllani, speaking with him at least once using a video camera on a computer. According to Sherifi's own testimony, he spoke with Asllani several times and translated documents for him, though Sherifi claimed never to have met Asllani in person. Sherifi also wired Asllani money so that Asllani, who was still in Kosovo, could obtain travel documents.

b.

During the course of his conspiratorial activities, Boyd secured and maintained an extensive firearm and weapons arsenal, which he kept in and about his home and vehicles. Boyd and his sons generally carried firearms on their persons, and Boyd regularly purchased large quantities of ammunition. Zakariya explained that Boyd focused on obtaining armor-piercing ammunition as well as deadly hollow-point handgun ammunition. Beginning in 2008, Boyd voiced an interest in relocating his family overseas and talked about moving p.123 to Jordan. Boyd even began to sell his personal property, including some of his firearms, in preparation for such a move. Boyd was concerned that he would not be able to travel with his entire arsenal and, as a result, built a weapons bunker beneath his back porch and deck, where he planned to store some of the firearms. In July 2009, Boyd, Sherifi, and Harris spent several days working on the weapons bunker. The weapons bunker consisted of an entrenchment roughly six feet deep and was lined with sandbags for protection and stability.

c.

In May 2009, Sherifi returned to the United States from Kosovo, leaving his wife in that Balkan country. Sherifi told friends in Raleigh that he had returned to North Carolina to save money to buy a family farm in Kosovo. Sherifi advised others that he planned for the farmland in Kosovo to be used by his jihadist "brothers" en route to the "battlefield."

That spring, Boyd and Sherifi discussed and developed a scheme to attack the Quantico Marine Corps Base in eastern Virginia. While abroad, Sherifi had identified Camp Bondsteel in Kosovo as a potential target for attack, because the "brothers" hated the presence of American soldiers in Kosovo. After returning to this country, Sherifi worked delivering medical supplies to various locations, including the Fort Bragg Army Post in North Carolina. Sherifi boasted to Boyd about how easy it was, as a delivery truck driver, to access such military facilities. Boyd and Sherifi then identified Quantico as a target, in part because Boyd was already familiar with Quantico, having lived there as a child. As a result, Boyd travelled to Quantico to get a closer look, supplementing his reconnaissance efforts with online research on Google and other websites. Following his visit to Quantico, Boyd reported to Sherifi that it was easy to access the base.

On several occasions, Boyd and Sherifi discussed their planned attack on Quantico, and, at least once talked about kidnapping a Marine officer, "a general or someone of high rank." J.A. 1697. Boyd proposed holding the officer for ransom, seeking in return the release of an Islamic scholar being imprisoned by the United States. As part of this scheme, Boyd suggested cutting off the Marine's ring finger and "sen[ding] his finger with one of his rings" to Marine officials so that the Marines would "know it was him" and that he was Boyd's prisoner. *Id.*

d.

In the summer of 2009, Sherifi participated in two weapons training sessions in Caswell County, North Carolina. Those sessions involved Boyd and others, including informants Harris and Eddarkoui. The first session occurred on June 10, 2009, and the second was conducted about a month later, on July 7, 2009. The sessions took place on a rural property that Harris had obtained for weapons training, telling the group that it belonged to one of his relatives. The property was actually, however, under government control and FBI surveillance. Boyd organized the "practice" sessions with the "idea ... that they would use this [training] in furtherance if they were to go to try and fight somewhere." J.A. 1820. During the sessions, Boyd instructed his trainees on military tactics and weapons skills, showing them how to use a variety of firearms. At the second session, Boyd taught the trainees more about military maneuvers. Boyd also had his trainees practice their firearms skills while he fired automatic weapons, so that they would become accustomed to using weapons while being p.124 subjected to the sound of gunfire. Sherifi attended and participated in both training sessions, and he sought to recruit others to the second session.

On July 22, 2009, soon after the second training session, the initial indictment was returned in these proceedings. Boyd and his coconspirators had planned a third session for July 27, 2009, the very date on which they were arrested. After the arrests, the FBI seized Boyd's weapons arsenal from his home, together with various and sundry gas masks, computers, cell phones, and cash.[14] Fifteen of the firearms were loaded at the time of their seizure. A corresponding search of the North Carolina home of Sheriff's parents resulted in the seizure of packed suitcases and a money belt containing $10,000 in cash.

B.

During the trial, the appellants raised a number of evidentiary objections and reiterated various First Amendment arguments, some related to the court's jury instructions. On October 7, 2011, at the close of the government's case, the appellants moved for judgments of acquittal. The trial court denied each of the acquittal requests, explaining that the evidence, viewed in the light most favorable to the prosecution, was sufficient for the jury to find each of the appellants guilty of the charged offenses. The appellants renewed their acquittal motions — again on sufficiency grounds — at the close of all the evidence, and then again after the jury returned its verdicts. The acquittal motions were all denied.

The prosecution's closing argument reiterated the key evidence linking each of the appellants to the charged conspiracies, focusing on the covert and secretive nature of the appellants' plans. The prosecution sought to underscore the violent tendencies of the appellants and their coconspirators, as evidenced by their fascination with weapons, postings on Facebook, and day-to-day communications with one another. The prosecutors also explained the government's view of the evidence, particularly Boyd's testimony, plus that of expert Kohlmann concerning home-grown terrorism cells. Conversely, the defense lawyers focused on what they characterized as the scattered and vague evidence supporting the conspiracy allegations, contending that the prosecution had failed to establish any concrete object thereof, resulting in a fatal deficiency in its case. Moreover, the defense lawyers attacked the credibility of Boyd and his sons, arguing that their potential to receive life sentences had been substantially reduced by their testimony against the appellants. The defense also asserted that the FBI informants were not credible, emphasizing that all had been paid for their testimony. Finally, the lawyers stressed that, under the First Amendment, the appellants should not be convicted because the evidence against them consisted primarily of protected speech and, in any event, failed to prove the charged conspiracies.

On October 13, 2011, after the closing arguments and instructions, the jury deliberated and returned its separate verdicts. On January 13, 2012, the court sentenced each appellant, and it thereafter filed three p.125 sentencing opinions explaining the sentences imposed. These consolidated appeals followed. We possess jurisdiction pursuant to 28 U.S.C. § 1291 and 18 U.S.C. § 3742(a).[15]

III.

By their appeals, the appellants challenge their convictions in multiple respects. First, they contend that their convictions cannot stand because the trial court committed reversible error in its First Amendment analysis. Second, the appellants pursue recognition of several evidentiary errors, seeking relief by way of a new trial. Finally, they maintain that their motions for judgments of acquittal were erroneously denied, in that the trial evidence was legally insufficient to sustain any of their convictions. We begin with the First Amendment, followed by other issues.

A.

The appellants contend that the trial court committed reversible error in its handling of the argument that their speech espousing violent jihad was protected by the First Amendment. Concomitantly, the appellants assert that they never agreed to take action in connection with their beliefs and expressions, and thus were prosecuted purely for their offensive discourse. Of course, their argument ignores that the jury found — as it was required to do in order to convict — that the appellants had, in fact, agreed to take action in furtherance of violent jihad.

1.

The First Amendment provides that "Congress shall make no law ... abridging the freedom of speech." U.S. Const. amend. I. The Supreme Court has explained that, "as a general matter, the First Amendment means that government has no power to restrict expression because of its message, its ideas, its subject matter, or its content." *United States v. Stevens,* 559 U.S. 460, 468, 130 S.Ct. 1577, 176 L.Ed.2d 435 (2010) (internal quotation marks omitted). Notwithstanding the foregoing, the First Amendment's protections are not absolute, and the Court has approved government "restrictions upon the content of speech in a few limited areas, ... including obscenity, defamation, fraud, incitement, and speech integral to criminal conduct." *Id.* (citations and internal quotation marks omitted). Moreover, the Court has been clear that prohibited conduct cannot "be labeled 'speech' whenever the person engaging in the conduct intends thereby to express an idea." *Wisconsin v. Mitchell,* 508 U.S. 476, 484, 113 S.Ct. 2194, 124 L.Ed.2d 436 (1993) (internal quotation marks omitted).

The statutes underlying the appellants' various convictions serve, inter alia, to criminalize providing, and conspiring to provide, material support for terrorism, *see* 18 U.S.C. § 2339A; conspiring to murder, kidnap, or maim outside the United States, *id.* § 956(a); and conspiring to kill a federal officer or employee, *id.* § 1117. Often, those offenses involve speech. For example, the § 2339A convictions in *United States v. Stewart* were premised on evidence that the defendants provided material support — personnel — to a § 956(a) p.126 conspiracy by communicating to the conspirators the messages of "'spiritual' leader" Abdel Rahman that were intended to induce "criminal acts of violence." *See* 590 F.3d 93, 112-16 (2d Cir.2009). The Second Circuit rejected the defendants' First Amendment argument that, because "the government established only that they provided the underlying conspiracy with Abdel Rahman's 'pure speech,'" the defendants "did not provide 'personnel' within any constitutional interpretation of section 2339A." *Id.* at 115. In so doing, the *Stewart* court determined that the issue was one of protected speech, rather than pure speech, and that Rahman's "call to arms" was not protected. *Id.* The court explained that "[w]ords that instruct, solicit, or persuade others to commit crimes of violence violate the law and may be properly prosecuted." *Id.* (alteration and internal quotation marks omitted).

The appellants' First Amendment contention is somewhat different than that of the *Stewart* defendants. As the appellants would have it, their convictions unconstitutionally rest on their own protected speech, i.e., mere expressions of belief in violent jihad. The appellants invoke *Holder v. Humanitarian Law Project,* 561 U.S. 1, 130 S.Ct. 2705, 177 L.Ed.2d 355 (2010), wherein the Supreme Court recently entertained a First Amendment challenge to 18 U.S.C. § 2339B (making it a federal crime to knowingly provide material support or resources to "a foreign terrorist organization" designated as such by the Secretary of State).[16] The *Humanitarian Law Project* plaintiffs "claimed that they wished to provide support for the humanitarian and political activities of [foreign terrorist organizations in Turkey and Sri Lanka] in the form of monetary contributions, other tangible aid, legal training, and political advocacy, but that they could not do so for fear of prosecution under § 2339B." 130 S.Ct. at 2714. Although the Supreme Court concluded that, "in prohibiting the particular forms of support that plaintiffs seek to provide to foreign terrorist groups, § 2339B does not violate the freedom of speech," *id.* at 2730, the Court emphasized "that Congress has [not] banned [the plaintiffs'] pure political speech," *id.* at 2722 (internal quotation marks omitted). That is,

> [u]nder the material-support statute, plaintiffs may say anything they wish on any topic. They may speak and write freely about the [foreign terrorist organizations], the governments of Turkey and Sri Lanka, human rights, and international law. They may advocate before the United Nations.... The statute does not prohibit independent advocacy or expression of any kind. Section 2339B also does not prevent plaintiffs from becoming members of the [organizations] or impose any sanction on them for doing so. Congress has not, therefore, sought to suppress ideas or opinions in the form of "pure political speech." Rather, Congress has prohibited "material support," which most often does not take the form of speech at all. And when it does, the statute is carefully drawn to cover only a narrow category of speech to, under the direction p.127 of, or in coordination with foreign groups that the speaker knows to be terrorist organizations.

Id. at 2722-23 (alteration and internal quotation marks omitted); *see also Stewart,* 590 F.3d at 115 ("The government does not deny that section 2339A may not be used to prosecute mere advocacy or other protected speech, but contends that the defendants were prosecuted for criminal actions that did not amount to protected speech.").

The appellants rely on *Humanitarian Law Project* for the proposition that they could not be convicted under § 2339A for simply speaking, writing about, or even joining a terrorist organization. That proposition, however, does not undermine any of the appellants' convictions. Their convictions rest not only on their agreement to join one another in a common terrorist scheme, but also on a series of calculated overt acts in furtherance of that scheme. For example, each of the appellants travelled abroad seeking to reach locations considered to be jihadist battlefields, with the hope and intent of engaging in violent jihad. To prepare themselves for jihad, the appellants trained with weapons and took instruction from Boyd. Moreover, Sherifi and Yaghi endeavored to recruit others into the conspiracies: Sherifi through explicit efforts to recruit Sergeant Weeks, and Yaghi by introducing Mohammad and Hassan to Boyd.

Furthermore, it was entirely consistent with the First Amendment to make "evidentiary use of [the appellants'] speech to establish the elements of [their] crime[s] or to prove motive or intent." *See Mitchell,* 508 U.S. at 489, 113 S.Ct. 2194. Indeed, because "the essence of a conspiracy is an *agreement* to commit an unlawful act," *United States v. Jimenez Recio,* 537 U.S. 270, 274, 123 S.Ct. 819, 154 L.Ed.2d 744 (2003) (emphasis added) (internal quotation marks omitted), the supporting evidence may necessarily include a defendant's speech. *See United States v. Rahman,* 189 F.3d 88, 117 (2d Cir.1999) (including conspiracy in list of offenses that "are characteristically committed through speech"). Such is the case here, where the appellants engaged in extensive conversations with Boyd and others about the necessity of waging violent jihad and their shared goal of reaching the jihadist battlefield. Meanwhile, evidence such as Sherifi's discussions with Weeks about the religious obligation to engage in jihad, as well as Sherifi's statements to Eddarkoui about plans to recruit Weeks for violent jihad in Somalia, allowed the jury to attach nefarious intent to what otherwise might have been considered innocent acts. As further examples, Hassan's and Yaghi's Facebook postings advocating violent jihad, as well as their conversations with Boyd to that effect, serve as compelling support for the jury's finding that Hassan and Yaghi travelled abroad with the hope of acting on their beliefs by engaging in jihad and fighting against the "kuffar."

As the Sixth Circuit explained with regard to another terrorism prosecution under 18 U.S.C. § 2339A, "[f]orming an agreement to engage in criminal activities — in contrast with simply talking about religious or political beliefs — is not protected speech." *United States v. Amawi,* 695 F.3d 457, 482 (6th Cir.2012). In that case, "although the conspiracy was closely related to, and indeed proved by, many of the defendants' conversations about political and religious matters, the conviction was based on an agreement to cooperate in the commission [of] a crime, not simply to talk about it." *Id.* The *Amawi* analysis is readily applicable here. Put succinctly, the First Amendment was no bar to the government's use of the appellants' speech p.128 to demonstrate their participation in the charged conspiracies.

2.

In any event, the appellants contend that the jury was not fully instructed — and thus misled — on the scope of the First Amendment's protections. The trial court's First Amendment instruction advised the jury as follows:

> I turn your attention now to the First Amendment to the United States Constitution, which establishes certain rights which accrue to each defendant. The First Amendment provides, in part, that Congress shall make no law respecting an establishment of religion or prohibiting the free exercise thereof or abridging the freedom of speech or of the press or the right of the people to be peaceably assembled. The right of freedom of speech and to engage in peaceful assembly extends to one's religion and one's politics. Having instructed you concerning rights of each defendant pursuant to the First Amendment, I also instruct you that the First Amendment is not a defense to the crimes charged in the indictment.

J.A. 3567-68. Although the appellants offered eleven other First Amendment instructions, their appeal focuses on just three of those proposals. Specifically, they argue that their proposed instructions 37, 40, and 45 were erroneously excluded from the court's charge to the jury.[17] Those proposed instructions were as follows:

> *Number 37:* [Each appellant's] right to exercise religion guarantees his right to believe and profess whatever religious doctrine he desires.

> *Number 40:* The First Amendment protects speech that encourages others to commit violence, unless the speech is capable of producing imminent lawless action. Speech that makes future violence more likely, such as advocating for illegal action at some indefinite time in the future, is protected. Thus, speech may not be punished just because it makes it more likely that someone will be harmed at some unknown time in the future.

> *Number 45:* The First Amendment right to free speech protects the right of an individual or group to advocate for the use of force or advocate for the

violation of law so long as the speech is: 1) not directed to incite or produce imminent lawless action and 2) is not likely to incite or produce imminent lawless action. The First Amendment even protects an individual's right to praise groups or persons using terrorism as a means of achieving their ends. Advocacy is pure speech protected by the First Amendment.

See id. at 453-460.[18]

We review for abuse of discretion a trial court's decision to either give or p.129 refuse to give a proposed instruction. *See United States v. Lighty,* 616 F.3d 321, 366 (4th Cir.2010) (internal quotation marks omitted). In assessing a claim of instructional error, "we do not view a single instruction in isolation; rather we consider whether taken as a whole and in the context of the entire charge, the instructions accurately and fairly state the controlling law." *United States v. Passaro,* 577 F.3d 207, 221 (4th Cir.2009) (internal quotation marks omitted). Thus, "[a] district court commits reversible error in refusing to provide a proffered jury instruction only when the instruction (1) was correct; (2) was not substantially covered by the court's charge to the jury; and (3) dealt with some point in the trial so important, that failure to give the requested instruction seriously impaired the defendant's ability to conduct his defense." *Lighty,* 616 F.3d at 366 (internal quotation marks omitted).

Even if the three rejected instructions correctly recite the legal principles espoused therein, the appellants nevertheless fail in two essential respects. That is, they have not shown (1) that their proposals were not substantially covered by the court's jury charge, or (2) that their proposals dealt with points so important that the court's failure to give them seriously impaired the appellants' ability to conduct their defenses. The court's First Amendment instruction substantially covered the appellants' right to freely exercise and express their religious beliefs, echoing proposed instruction 37. Proposals 40 and 45, encompassing the First Amendment protections extended to speech advocating violence, are of no import in this case. Put simply, the appellants were not prosecuted for inciting violence, *cf., e.g., Stewart,* 590 F.3d at 115, nor would the instructions have permitted any convictions on that ground. Accordingly, the court did not abuse its discretion by declining to give — *in haec verba* — proposed instruction 37, 40, or 45.[19]

B.

We turn now to the various evidentiary issues presented by the appellants. First, they assert that the trial court erred in admitting the opinion evidence of Evan Kohlmann, the government's expert witness. Next, Hassan and Yaghi maintain that the admission of their Facebook pages and certain videos was erroneous. Hassan and Yaghi also challenge selected evidence against them as being inadmissible lay p.130 opinion and improper hearsay. Finally, Yaghi contends that the court erred in admitting evidence that the prosecution obtained improperly pursuant to FISA court orders.

We assess challenges to a trial court's evidentiary rulings for abuse of discretion. *See United States v. Hornsby,* 666 F.3d 296, 307 (4th Cir.2012). In reviewing an evidentiary ruling under that standard, "we will only overturn [a] ruling that is arbitrary and irrational." *United States v. Cole,* 631 F.3d 146, 153 (4th Cir. 2011) (internal quotation marks omitted). With those principles in mind, we address the various evidentiary challenges.

1.

The appellants first contend that the expert testimony of Evan Kohlmann was inadmissible under Federal Rule of Evidence 702 because it was irrelevant and failed to satisfy the foundational requirements established by the Supreme Court in *Daubert v. Merrell Dow Pharmaceuticals, Inc.,* 509 U.S. 579, 113 S.Ct. 2786, 125 L.Ed.2d 469 (1993). The appellants also maintain that, even if Kohlmann's evidence was admissible under Rule 702, it was yet inadmissible under Rule 403 because its probative value was outweighed by the potential for unfair prejudice.

a.

As the Supreme Court has explained, Rule 702 "imposes a special obligation upon a trial judge to ensure that any and all scientific testimony is not only relevant, but reliable." *Kumho Tire Co., Ltd. v. Carmichael,* 526 U.S. 137, 147, 119 S.Ct. 1167, 143 L.Ed.2d 238 (1999) (internal quotation marks omitted).[20] In *Daubert,* the Court identified five factors for use in evaluating the reliability of proposed expert testimony:

> (1) whether the particular scientific theory "can be (and has been) tested"; (2) whether the theory "has been subjected to peer review and publication"; (3) the "known or potential rate of error"; (4) the "existence and maintenance of standards controlling the technique's operation"; and (5) whether the technique has achieved "general acceptance" in the relevant scientific or expert community.

See United States v. Crisp, 324 F.3d 261, 265-66 (4th Cir.2003) (quoting *Daubert,* 509 U.S. at 593-94, 113 S.Ct. 2786). The *Daubert* test is flexible; "[r]ather than providing a definitive or exhaustive list, *Daubert* merely illustrates the types of factors that will bear on the inquiry." *Id.* at 266, 113 S.Ct. 2786.

On April 30, 2010, the government alerted the appellants that it intended to call Kohlmann as an expert witness with respect to various aspects of Islamic extremism. Specifically, it was anticipated that Kohlmann would testify about the "meaning and context of various words and phrases used by the defendants which are commonly used by persons practicing extreme Islam"; the "structure and leadership of groups adhering to the principles of Islamic extremism"; and the "manner and means employed by extremist Islamic groups to recruit individuals and the process p.131 of radicalization which occurs within such groups." J.A. 204-07. The appellants sought to bar Kohlmann's testimony, asserting, inter alia, that the prosecution was unable to satisfy the *Daubert* test.

The trial court — after conducting a *Daubert* evidentiary hearing and allowing ample opportunity for cross-examination of Kohlmann — denied the pretrial exclusion motion by written opinion. *See United States v. Boyd,* No. 5:09-cr-00216 (E.D.N.C. Sept. 16, 2011), ECF No. 1443 (the "*Daubert* Opinion"). The court therein determined that Kohlmann's proposed testimony was both reliable and relevant, thus satisfying Rule 702's requirements. To its credit, the court did not rule broadly that all of Kohlmann's potential testimony was relevant. The court instead made clear that it would not "allow testimony on all of the information included in Kohlmann's very lengthy expert reports," *id.* at 6, explaining that "the government is on notice that only expert testimony relevant to the case is admissible and it should tailor its examination of Kohlmann accordingly," *id.* at 11. The trial court also noted that questions about Kohlmann's credentials and opinions were "ideal fodder for vigorous cross examination." *Id.* at 8.

The trial court did not abuse its discretion in deciding that Kohlmann's proposed evidence satisfied Rule 702. The court heard and considered testimony about Kohlmann's credentials and techniques and was convinced that he possessed "the requisite knowledge, skill, experience, training, and education to testify on various aspects of the trend of decentralized terrorism and homegrown terrorism." *Daubert* Opinion 7. In so ruling, the court gave particular attention to the *Daubert* factors, including thorough assessments of whether Kohlmann's methods were subject to peer review, his "consultation with others in the field," and "whether or not his research findings [were] based in a sound methodology." *Id.* at 9.

The trial court's assessment of Kohlmann's credentials fulfilled its gatekeeping obligation under *Daubert,* and the court did not err in deciding that Kohlmann's testimony was reliable as well as relevant to the issues to be presented. Notably, we have previously approved of Kohlmann's expertise in terrorism matters, ruling that his testimony would "assist the trier of fact to understand the evidence or to determine a fact in issue." *See United States v. Benkahla,* 530 F.3d 300, 309 (4th Cir.2008) (internal quotation marks omitted).[21] There, the trial evidence was also "complicated, touching by necessity on a wide variety of ideas, terms, people, and organizations connected to radical Islam." *Id.* at 309. We thus ruled that the trial court had not abused its discretion in deeming "lengthy testimony about various aspects of radical Islam ... appropriate, and indeed necessary, for the jury to understand the evidence and determine the facts." *Id.* at 310 (internal quotation marks and punctuation omitted). That reasoning applies equally today, because the evidence in this case was similarly complex, involving the testimony of multiple coconspirators and informants. The evidence in each case also involved terminology and concepts that were likely to be unfamiliar to jurors. In such settings, the relevance of expert testimony is quite evident.

b.

The appellants also challenge the trial court's failure to exclude Kohlmann's p.132 testimony under Rule 403, maintaining that its probative value was substantially outweighed by the risk of unfair prejudice.[22] We apply a "highly deferential" standard of review to such an issue, and a trial court's "decision to admit evidence over a Rule 403 objection will not be overturned except under the most extraordinary circumstances, where that discretion has been plainly abused." *United States v. Udeozor,* 515 F.3d 260, 265 (4th Cir.2008) (internal quotation marks omitted). We have emphasized that relevant evidence should only be excluded under Rule 403 "when there is a genuine risk that the emotions of a jury will be excited to irrational behavior, and this risk is disproportionate to the probative value of the offered evidence." *United States v. Siegel,* 536 F.3d 306, 319 (4th Cir.2008).

Here, the district court carefully balanced — both before and during trial — the relevance of Kohlmann's testimony against the potential prejudice arising therefrom. Although linking the appellants to extremist jihadist groups was undoubtedly prejudicial, it was not unfairly so. Indeed, the charges that were lodged against the appellants meant that the prosecution would necessarily seek to establish that link. *See Benkahla,* 530 F.3d at 310 (rejecting Rule 403 challenge to Kohlmann's testimony, despite potential prejudice, where relevance could not be doubted and trial judge could decide that probative value outweighed any prejudicial risk); *United States v. Williams,* 445 F.3d 724, 730 (4th Cir.2006) (explaining that, though prejudicial, "as is all evidence tending to show a defendant's guilt," the challenged evidence was nevertheless admissible because the risk of *unfair* prejudice did not "*substantially* outweigh the probative value of the evidence" (emphasis added)). In these circumstances, the court did not abuse its discretion in overruling the appellants' Rule 403 objections.[23]

2.

Next, Hassan and Yaghi contend that several prosecution exhibits consisting of Facebook pages and the files embedded therein — including videos hosted on YouTube (and maintained by Google) — were not properly authenticated. Hassan also challenges, on hearsay and other grounds, two videos used against him by the prosecutors. First, he maintains that the court erred in admitting a physical training video that he had posted on a website called RossTraining.com. Second, Hassan claims that a video seized from his cell phone by the FBI was also erroneously admitted.

a.

The trial court ruled that the Facebook pages and YouTube videos were self-authenticating under Federal Rule of Evidence 902(11), and thus that they were admissible as business records. That the Facebook pages and YouTube videos were self-authenticating business records was not, however, the end of the trial court's inquiry. The court also required the government, pursuant to Rule 901, to prove p.133 that the Facebook pages were linked to Hassan and Yaghi.

Rule 902(11) authorizes the admission in evidence of records that satisfy the requirements of Rule 803(6)(A)-(C), "as shown by a certification of the custodian... that complies with a federal statute or a rule prescribed by the Supreme Court." Rule 803(6), in turn, provides that business records are admissible if they are accompanied by a certification of their custodian or other qualified person that satisfies three requirements: (A) that the records were "made at or near the time by — or from information transmitted by — someone with knowledge"; (B) that they were "kept in the course of a regularly conducted activity of a business"; and (C) that "making the record was a regular practice of that activity."[24] Turning to Rule 901, subdivision (a) thereof provides that, to "establish that evidence is authentic, the proponent need only present 'evidence sufficient to support a finding that the matter in question is what the proponent claims.'" *See United States v.*

Vidacak, 553 F.3d 344, 349 (4th Cir.2009) (quoting Fed. R.Evid. 901(a)). Importantly, "the burden to authenticate under Rule 901 is not high — only a prima facie showing is required," and a "district court's role is to serve as gatekeeper in assessing whether the proponent has offered a satisfactory foundation from which the jury could reasonably find that the evidence is authentic." *Id.*

Hassan's and Yaghi's Facebook pages were captured via "screenshots," taken at various points in time and displaying Hassan's and Yaghi's user profiles and postings. The screenshots of the Facebook pages also included photos and links to the YouTube videos. On the Facebook pages, Hassan and Yaghi had posted their personal biographical information, as well as quotations and listings of their interests. Each Facebook page also contained a section for postings from other users, on what is called a "wall." Meanwhile, the videos in question were retrieved from Google's server. In establishing the admissibility of those exhibits, the government presented the certifications of records custodians of Facebook and Google, verifying that the Facebook pages and YouTube videos had been maintained as business records in the course of regularly conducted business activities. According to those certifications, Facebook and Google create and retain such pages and videos when (or soon after) their users post them through use of the Facebook or Google servers.[25]

After evaluating those submissions, the trial court ruled that the requirements of Rule 902(11) had been satisfied. The court then determined that the prosecution had satisfied its burden under Rule 901(a) by tracking the Facebook pages and Facebook accounts to Hassan's and Yaghi's mailing and email addresses via internet protocol addresses. In these circumstances, there was no abuse of discretion p.134 in the admissions of any of the Facebook pages and YouTube videos.

b.

Turning to the physical training video uploaded by Hassan to RossTraining.com, Hassan maintains that the trial court's refusal to admit his own related postings contravened the evidentiary "rule of completeness." The rule of completeness has its origins at common law, and is codified in Rule 106 of the Federal Rules of Evidence. Pursuant thereto, "[w]hen a writing or recorded statement or part thereof is introduced by a party, an adverse party may require the introduction at that time of any other part or any other writing or recorded statement which ought in fairness to be considered contemporaneously with it." *United States v. Moussaoui,* 382 F.3d 453, 481 (4th Cir. 2004) (internal quotation marks omitted). As we have explained, a trial court, in applying the rule of completeness, may allow into the record "relevant portions of [otherwise] excluded testimony which clarify or explain the part already received," in order to "prevent a party from misleading the jury" by failing to introduce the entirety of the statement or document. *See United States v. Bollin,* 264 F.3d 391, 414 (4th Cir.2001). Nevertheless, the rule of completeness does not "render admissible... evidence which is otherwise inadmissible under the hearsay rules." *United States v. Lentz,* 524 F.3d 501, 526 (4th Cir.2008) (internal quotation marks omitted). Nor does the rule of completeness "require the admission of self-serving, exculpatory statements made by a party which are being sought for admission by that same party." *Id.*

The physical training video posted by Hassan on RossTraining.com depicted Hassan in a series of physical training workouts. It opened with a series of quotations on the video screen, such as "[t]here is no God but ALLAH and Muhammad is his Messenger," the "strong Muslim is better than the weak Muslim," and "[l]et's please ALLAH and train hard." Trial Ex. 399; J.A. Vol. XIV. The training video concluded with the words "support our troops," which appeared on the screen above an Arabic phrase and an image of an assault rifle. *Id.* After Hassan had uploaded the training video to RossTraining.com, other users of the website posted various comments and questions, some of which were critical of Hassan. Hassan responded to them with postings of his own, including an apology for any controversy his training video had caused. Hassan then posted additional statements about his beliefs and his support of those troops fighting "for the truth." J.A. 2377. In one of those subsequent postings, Hassan said that he "do[es] not support terrorists." *Id.*[26] Hassan's defense lawyer thus sought to introduce into evidence — under the rule of completeness — the follow-up statements posted by Hassan. The court, however, sustained the hearsay objection interposed by the prosecution and excluded those statements.

p.135 Hassan's excluded statements, though possibly exculpatory, do not fall within any hearsay exception that would authorize their admission into evidence. Nor was the jury likely to have been confused or misled by their exclusion. The court simply ruled that Hassan's follow-up postings on RossTraining.com could not be used to establish the truth of any matter asserted — specifically, to show that Hassan did not support terrorists. That ruling was not an abuse of the court's discretion.

c.

Hassan next challenges the prosecution's use against him of the video that the authorities had seized from his personal cell phone. The cell phone video showed Hassan firing a rifle at an outdoor location near the Islamic Center in Raleigh. Hassan maintains that the cell phone video was irrelevant to the prosecution's case because it was not created until early 2009, two years after he stopped having regular contact with Boyd. Hassan also contends that, even if relevant, the cell phone video was unduly prejudicial under Rule 403, because it shows Hassan using a firearm and thereby could have caused the jury to improperly associate Hassan with Boyd's weapons arsenal.

Because the cell phone video was relevant to Hassan's weapons training with Yaghi, it was also relevant to whether Hassan was yet involved — even in 2009 — in the ongoing Count One conspiracy. As for Hassan's claim of prejudice, "[t]he mere fact that the evidence will damage the defendant's case is not enough — the evidence must be *unfairly* prejudicial, and the unfair prejudice must *substantially* outweigh the probative value of the evidence." *See Williams,* 445 F.3d at 730. Put simply, the cell phone video of Hassan firing a rifle did not present a sufficient "danger of unfair prejudice" to warrant its exclusion under Rule 403. Indeed, at least one government witness admitted that there was no reason to believe that

Hassan's mere possession or firing of the rifle was illegal. Moreover, there was no suggestion that Hassan or Yaghi had participated in the weapons training sessions of 2009 or in the creation and preservation of Boyd's weapons arsenal. In these circumstances, the trial court did not err in its ruling with respect to Hassan's cell phone video.

3.

Hassan and Yaghi next contend that three witnesses gave improper lay opinion evidence when they testified to their understandings of what Hassan and Yaghi meant by certain statements or on particular occasions. The following are challenged as erroneously admitted: (1) Boyd's understanding of what Hassan and Yaghi meant in statements to Boyd during face-to-face conversations and in email exchanges; (2) Dylan Boyd's understanding of why Hassan and Yaghi wanted to accompany the Boyds on their 2007 trip to the Middle East; and (3) Jamar Carter's testimony regarding his understanding of Yaghi's use of the phrase "jihad."

Pursuant to Federal Rule of Evidence 701, a lay witness may testify to opinions when such evidence is "(a) rationally based on the witness's perception; (b) helpful to clearly understanding the witness's testimony or to determining a fact in issue; and (c) not based on scientific, technical, or other specialized knowledge within the scope of Rule 702." Rule 701 thus "allows testimony based on the person's reasoning and opinions about witnessed events." *United States v. Offill*, 666 F.3d 168, 177 (4th Cir.2011). Lay witnesses are not entitled to opine broadly or generally; rather, "lay opinion testimony *must* be based on personal knowledge." p.136 *United States v. Johnson*, 617 F.3d 286, 292 (4th Cir.2010). In contrast to Rule 702, which governs expert testimony, Rule 701 "permits lay testimony relating to a defendant's hypothetical mental state." *Offill*, 666 F.3d at 177. Applying those principles, we have ruled that testimony regarding a witness's understanding of what the defendant meant by certain statements is permissible lay testimony, so long as the witness's understanding is predicated on his knowledge and participation in the conversation. *See, e.g., United States v. Min*, 704 F.3d 314, 325 (4th Cir.2013); *Offill*, 666 F.3d at 177-78.

Having evaluated the trial court's admission of the challenged lay opinion testimony, we are satisfied that none of its rulings constituted an abuse of discretion. In each instance, the lay testimony stemmed directly from the witness's conversations with Hassan and Yaghi, and was therefore based on that witness's perceptions. Furthermore, the testimony clearly assisted the jury in understanding the appellants' conversations and statements. Lay opinion testimony is particularly useful when, as here, the terms and concepts being discussed, such as "kuffar," "best brothers," finding "the battlefield," and "shahid," are likely to be unfamiliar to the jury. In particular, the government introduced a substantial amount of evidence relating to the coded and convoluted communications between the conspirators. In such circumstances, the witnesses were entitled, under Rule 701, to explain their understandings and impressions of Hassan's and Yaghi's statements and actions. As a result, the court's rulings with respect to the lay evidence were not an abuse of its discretion.

4.

Hassan and Yaghi next maintain that certain evidence admitted by the trial court constituted inadmissible hearsay. Rule 801 of the Federal Rules of Evidence defines hearsay as any statement that a "declarant does not make while testifying at the current trial," and that is offered "in evidence to prove the truth of the matter asserted in the statement."

First, Hassan contends that Boyd's testimony regarding a conversation between Boyd and a shared acquaintance (the "mutual contact") of Hassan's father and Boyd constituted multi-level hearsay. Boyd explained that the "mutual contact" advised him that Hassan's father "*believed* both [Hassan and Yaghi] had travelled with [Boyd] to ... try to get to a battlefield." J.A. 1760 (emphasis added). Hassan maintains that this statement was admitted to establish that he had, in fact, travelled with Boyd to the Middle East with the hope and intention of making it to the battlefield. The government contends to the contrary: that such testimony was not admitted for the truth of the matter asserted, but simply to establish Boyd's understanding of why Hassan's father was angry with Boyd, thus providing context for a phone call between the two men.

Boyd's testimony about his phone conversation with Hassan's father was not inadmissible hearsay. Assessed in the context of the other evidence, the prosecution elicited the testimony in order to show the basis for Boyd's belief that Hassan's father was angry with Boyd. As the prosecution demonstrated, Boyd's interactions with the elder Hassan, as well as Boyd's understanding of rumors in the Raleigh Islamic community about the travel of Hassan and Yaghi to the Middle East in 2007, were relevant at trial, in that they offered a plausible explanation for the cessation of Boyd's relationship with Hassan and Yaghi.

Second, turning to a specific hearsay challenge interposed by Yaghi, he maintains p.137 that a police detective's testimony that law enforcement began to investigate Yaghi in 2006 after "receiv[ing] information from the Muslim community that [he] was traveling to Jordan ... with the intent to participate in jihad in Iraq," J.A. 2256, constituted inadmissible hearsay. As with Boyd's testimony about the elder Hassan, the prosecution contends that the detective's testimony was simply used as relevant background, and to explain the origins of the Yaghi investigation. Because Yaghi did not object at trial to the detective's testimony concerning the origins of the investigation, we review Yaghi's hearsay challenge solely for plain error. *See United States v. Smith,* 441 F.3d 254, 262 (4th Cir.2006).

Under plain error review, an appellate court may only correct an error when: "(1) there is an error; (2) the error is plain; (3) the error affects substantial rights; and (4) the court determines, after examining the particulars of the case, that the error 'seriously affect[s] the fairness, integrity, or public reputation of judicial proceedings.'" *United States v. Williamson,* 706 F.3d 405, 411 (4th Cir.2013) (quoting *United States v. Olano,* 507 U.S. 725, 732, 113 S.Ct. 1770, 123 L.Ed.2d 508 (1993)). The plain error standard is thus a high bar that is difficult to clear. To establish that an error affected his substantial rights, an appellant must demonstrate that "the error actually affected the outcome of the proceedings." *Id.* (internal quotation marks omitted). Even if the first three prongs of plain error review have been satisfied, an appellant must convince the reviewing court that the error "seriously affect[s] the fairness, integrity, or public reputation of judicial proceedings." *Olano,* 507 U.S. at 732, 113 S.Ct. 1770.

Put simply, the trial court did not plainly err in admitting the detective's testimony. In context, his statement concerning the inception of the Yaghi investigation was presented as background to explain how the law enforcement officer became involved in the case. The detective's statement also supports the inference, however, that some members of the Muslim community of Raleigh believed that Yaghi had travelled abroad with the hope of engaging in jihad, and that some in the law enforcement community likewise thought that Yaghi had done so. Nevertheless, the government introduced a vast amount of other trial evidence to that effect. Thus, even if the detective's statements would have been subject to a hearsay objection, the court's admission thereof would not satisfy either of the final two prongs of plain error review.

5.

On July 27, 2009, well before trial, the government gave notice that it intended to use evidence it had collected pursuant to FISA. The appellants moved to suppress the FISA evidence, or, alternatively, for disclosure of the FISA materials.[27] The district court, after an *in camera* and *ex parte* review of the FISA materials, denied the appellants' motion and explained its reasoning. *See United States v. Boyd,* No. 5:09-cr-00216 (E.D.N.C. June 22, 2011), ECF No. 1174 (the "FISA Opinion"). Yaghi challenges the rulings embodied in the FISA Opinion, asserting that the electronic surveillance orders were not supported by probable cause because, when the orders were issued in June 2007, there was no evidence that Yaghi was an agent of a p.138 foreign power, as required by FISA. Yaghi seeks disclosure of the FISA materials to support his contentions or, in the alternative, asks that we review those materials de novo to assess whether probable cause existed.

FISA established a detailed framework whereby the executive branch "could conduct electronic surveillance for foreign intelligence purposes without violating the rights of citizens." *United States v. Hammoud,* 381 F.3d 316, 332 (4th Cir.2004) (en banc), *vacated on other grounds,* 543 U.S. 1097, 125 S.Ct. 1051, 160 L.Ed.2d 997 (2005). Subject to certain exceptions not relevant here, "electronic surveillance of a foreign power or its agents may not be conducted unless the FISA Court authorizes it in advance," and "[e]ach application to the FISA Court must first be personally approved by the Attorney General." *United States v. Squillacote,* 221 F.3d 542, 553 (4th Cir.2000) (internal quotation marks omitted). Where, as here, the target of electronic surveillance is a "United States person," the FISA Court

> may issue an order authorizing the surveillance only if the FISA judge concludes that there is probable cause to believe that the target of the surveillance is a foreign power or agent of a foreign power, that proposed minimization procedures are sufficient under the terms of the statute, that the certifications required by [50 U.S.C.] § 1804 have been made, and that the certifications are not clearly erroneous.

Id. (internal quotation marks omitted).[28]

FISA identifies several requirements for the government's use of information obtained pursuant to a FISA order, as well as the essential procedures for challenging a prosecutor's use of such information. *See* 50 U.S.C. § 1806. Under those procedures, a defendant may move to suppress evidence that was "obtained or derived from such electronic surveillance," where the information was "unlawfully acquired" or "the surveillance was not made in conformity with an order of authorization or approval" under FISA. *Id.* § 1806(e). When faced with such a suppression motion, "if the Attorney General files an affidavit under oath that disclosure or an adversary hearing would harm the national security of the United States," *id.* § 1806(f), "the district court must review *in camera* and *ex parte* the FISA application and other materials necessary to rule," *Squillacote,* 221 F.3d at 553.

FISA provides that a district court may only divulge "portions of the application, order, or other materials relating to the surveillance ... where such disclosure is necessary to make an accurate determination of the legality of the surveillance." 50 U.S.C. § 1806(f); *see United States v. Rosen,* 447 F.Supp.2d 538, 546 (E.D.Va.2006). We have emphasized that, where the documents "submitted by the government [are] sufficient" to "determine the legality of the surveillance," the FISA materials should not be disclosed. *Squillacote,* 221 F.3d at 554.

Because the Attorney General filed an appropriate affidavit in this case, in response to the appellants' motion to suppress, the district court conducted an *in camera* and *ex parte* review of the FISA materials and determined that there was probable cause to support the FISA orders. The court then articulated and correctly applied the principles established by FISA and our precedent, reviewing the FISA materials "de novo with no deference p.139 accorded to the ... probable cause determinations, but with a presumption of validity accorded to the certifications." FISA Opinion 15. Moreover, as the court recognized, because the statutory application was properly made and approved by a FISA judge, it carried a strong presumption of veracity and regularity. *Id.* at 14-15; *see United States v. Pelton,* 835 F.2d 1067, 1076 (4th Cir.1987).

We have conducted an independent review of the FISA materials and likewise conclude that the FISA applications demonstrated probable cause to believe that Yaghi was an agent of a foreign power when the FISA orders were issued. Having conducted that review, we are satisfied that the materials submitted to the court by the government were sufficient to show that the FISA surveillance was proper. We therefore decline to order any further disclosure of the FISA materials.[29]

C.

Having resolved the appellants' evidentiary challenges that bear on admissibility, we turn to their principal contention on appeal: that the evidence was insufficient to support their various convictions. At the close of the prosecution's case-in-chief, at the conclusion of the trial evidence, and after the jury's return of its verdicts, the appellants challenged the sufficiency of the evidence. The district court ruled that each of their challenges was without merit, as articulated in the court's opinions of October 10 and December 1, 2011. *See* Sufficiency Opinion I; *United States v. Boyd,* No. 5:09-cr-00216 (E.D.N.C. Dec. 1, 2011), ECF No. 1558 ("Sufficiency Opinion II").

We review de novo a trial court's denial of a motion for judgment of acquittal. *See United States v. Osborne,* 514 F.3d 377, 385 (4th Cir.2008). Applying that standard, it is well settled that "[t]he verdict of a jury must be sustained if there is substantial evidence, taking the view most favorable to the [g]overnment, to support it." *Glasser v. United States,* 315 U.S. 60, 80, 62 S.Ct. 457, 86 L.Ed. 680 (1942). As we have explained, "substantial evidence" is that which "a reasonable finder of fact could accept as adequate and sufficient to support a conclusion of a defendant's guilt beyond a reasonable doubt." *United States v. Moye,* 454 F.3d 390, 394 (4th Cir.2006) (en banc) (internal quotation marks omitted). We examine "circumstantial as well as direct evidence," and remain mindful that "a conviction may rely entirely on circumstantial evidence." *United States v. Bonner,* 648 F.3d 209, 213 (4th Cir.2011). In so doing, we accord deference to "the jury's resolution of all evidentiary conflicts and credibility determinations." *Id.* Simply put, "[a] defendant challenging the sufficiency of the evidence faces a heavy burden." *Id.* (internal quotation marks omitted).

After our independent and de novo review of the voluminous trial record, we are satisfied that the evidence presented was sufficient to sustain the appellants' various convictions. The evidence, though largely circumstantial, was nevertheless substantial. p.140 That evidence readily supports the determination that a rational finder of fact could (and in fact did) deem the evidence adequate to support each conviction beyond a reasonable doubt.

1.

We turn first to Yaghi, who challenges the sufficiency of the evidence on the Count One and Count Two conspiracies, maintaining in particular that none of the evidence supports an inference that he agreed to participate therein. Yaghi emphasizes that Boyd and his sons denied under oath entering into any agreements with him, and he argues that it was not otherwise proved that he had entered into even a tacit conspiratorial agreement.

To convict Yaghi on Count One, the government was obliged to prove: (1) that he entered into a conspiracy; (2) that the objective thereof was to provide material support or resources; and (3) that he then knew and intended that such support or resources would be used in preparation for, or in carrying out, a separate conspiracy to murder, kidnap, or maim outside of the United States. *See* 18 U.S.C. § 2339A; *United States v. Chandia,* 514 F.3d 365, 372 (4th Cir.2008).[30] With respect to the first element, the government was obliged to prove a conspiracy — that is, an agreement between two or more persons to engage in illegal activity. *See United States v. Burgos,* 94 F.3d 849, 857-58 (4th Cir.1996) (en banc).[31] Yaghi's involvement in such a conspiracy was adequately demonstrated if the evidence showed "a slight connection between [him] and the conspiracy." *United States v. Kellam,* 568 F.3d 125, 139 (4th Cir.2009) (internal quotation marks omitted).[32] Furthermore, the "existence of a tacit or mutual understanding is sufficient to establish a conspiratorial agreement, and proof of such an agreement need not be direc — it may be inferred from circumstantial evidence." *Id.* (internal quotation marks omitted).[33]

On the second element of the Count One conspiracy, "material support or resources" p.141 is defined as "any property, tangible or intangible, or service," including "currency," "training," "expert advice or assistance," "weapons," or "personnel." 18 U.S.C. § 2339A(b)(1).[34] The third element required the government to establish that Yaghi acted "*with the knowledge or intent*" that such material support or resources would be used to commit a specific violent crime, in this instance a violation of 18 U.S.C. § 956. *See Stewart,* 590 F.3d at 113.

Turning to the Count Two conspiracy, the government was obliged to show that: (1) Yaghi entered into a conspiracy; (2) knowing and intending that the objective thereof was murder, kidnapping, or maiming outside the United States; (3) the conspiracy was entered into within the United States; and (4) a conspirator committed an overt act in furtherance thereof within the jurisdiction of the United States. *See* 18 U.S.C. § 956(a); *United States v. Wharton,* 320 F.3d 526, 538 (5th Cir.2003).

After our de novo assessment of the evidentiary record, we, like the trial court, are satisfied that there was sufficient evidence to support each of Yaghi's conspiracy convictions. That evidence includes the following:

• In 2006, Yaghi sought out Boyd at an Islamic center in Durham to ask about Boyd's experiences in Afghanistan. Yaghi and Boyd became friends, and Yaghi shared Boyd's beliefs in the necessity of violent jihad;

• In the fall of 2006, Yaghi travelled to Jordan, seeking to reach the battlefield. Yaghi maintained contact with Boyd during the trip;

• Prior to and during his 2006 trip to Jordan, Yaghi discussed violent jihad with Boyd. Before his departure, Yaghi asked Boyd how and where he could find the "best brothers," and mentioned "finding a wife." Those terms were coded references for seeking others who shared Yaghi's beliefs in violent jihad and could help Yaghi make his way to the battlefield;

• After returning from his 2006 trip to Jordan, Yaghi brought Hassan to Boyd's home, thus recruiting another man to the terrorism conspiracies;

• Yaghi thereafter again sought Boyd's assistance in travelling to the Middle East, and Boyd purchased plane tickets for Yaghi and Hassan to fly to Israel in the summer of 2007;

• In 2007, as he prepared to travel to the Middle East with Hassan, Yaghi indicated a "readiness to join" Boyd in waging violent jihad;

• Yaghi flew to the Middle East with Hassan in 2007 with the hope of engaging in violent jihad. Yaghi and Hassan were denied entry into Israel and were unable to reach the battlefield. The men thereafter returned to the United States;

• Yaghi and Hassan made unsuccessful efforts to contact Boyd while they were in the Middle East in 2007;

• Yaghi facilitated an introduction between Boyd and defendant Jude Kenan Mohammad in 2008. Coupled with Mohammad's subsequent departure for Pakistan and his "insistence" on finding "a way to the battlefield," this evidence shows that Yaghi recruited Mohammad into both conspiracies. *See* Sufficiency Opinion I at 17;[35]

p.142 • Yaghi posted messages on Facebook promoting his radical and violent jihadist beliefs. Those postings continued after Yaghi's contacts with Boyd diminished, justifying the jury's finding that Yaghi and Hassan — independent of Boyd — continued to engage in initiatives in furtherance of the conspiracies; and

• In late 2007, Yaghi made a speech to an Islamic group in Raleigh, advocating that its members consider violent jihad. From such statements, and from Yaghi's efforts to convert others to his beliefs in violent jihad, the jury was entitled to find Yaghi's continuing participation in the conspiracies.

The trial evidence fully supports the jury's finding that Yaghi believed in violent jihad and acted on those beliefs in concert with coconspirators. Yaghi understood and acquiesced in the objectives of the Count One and Count Two conspiracies, i.e., providing material support and resources for, and committing acts of murder outside the United States. Moreover, numerous overt acts were undertaken in furtherance of each conspiracy, including Yaghi's 2007 trip to the Middle East and his efforts to recruit others into the conspiracies. The verdict against Yaghi must therefore be sustained.

2.

Sherifi challenges each of his five convictions, maintaining that, at best, the trial evidence reflected only his religious and political beliefs, and perhaps his approval of the misdeeds of others. In addition to proving that Sherifi's conduct fulfilled the elements of the Counts One and Two conspiracies, the government was required to satisfy the elements of the other charges lodged against Sherifi. With respect to Sherifi's fifth offense of conviction, the Count Eleven conspiracy, the government was obliged to show that Sherifi entered into a conspiracy to kill federal employees engaged in the performance of their official duties, and a conspirator committed an overt act in furtherance thereof. *See* 18 U.S.C. § 1117. As to Counts Four and Eight — the firearms charges — the prosecution was required to "present evidence indicating that the possession of a firearm furthered, advanced, or helped forward a crime of violence." *United States v. Khan*, 461 F.3d 477, 489 (4th Cir.2006) (internal quotation marks omitted). Count Four alleged that Sherifi possessed a firearm on June 10, 2009, in furtherance of the Count Two conspiracy, and Count Eight alleged that he possessed a firearm on July 7, 2009, also in furtherance of the Count Two conspiracy.

Substantial evidence supports each of Sherifi's five convictions, beginning with the following that relates to his involvement in the Count One and Count Two conspiracies:

• In 2008, Sherifi grew close to Boyd, visiting in Boyd's home and spending time with Boyd's family. In discussions with Boyd, Sherifi confirmed his adherence to the violent jihadist ideology he shared with Boyd, plus the need to act in accordance therewith;

• Sherifi openly advocated his disdain for the laws and government of the United States, believing Shari'ah to be the true law;

• In 2008, Sherifi travelled to Kosovo, advising associates in Raleigh that he was going there to be closer to the battlefield;

p.143 • Sherifi talked with Boyd and others in Raleigh about his efforts to join violent jihadist efforts abroad, as well as his attempts to radicalize and recruit Sergeant Weeks;

• While in Kosovo, Sherifi participated in firearms training with like-minded individuals. At one point, Sherifi was in contact with persons who were considering Camp Bondsteel — where Weeks was stationed — as a target for jihad;

• Sherifi believed that jihad "was just murderous acts against innocent soldiers and civilians";

• After returning to the United States, Sherifi assisted Boyd in preparing a bunker under Boyd's home to conceal Boyd's weapons arsenal;

• Sherifi participated in Boyd's efforts to raise money to support violent jihadist causes, and gave Boyd $500 in cash to that end; and

• While back in the United States, Sherifi made efforts to raise funds to purchase "farmland in Kosovo from which to launch off to the battlefield" in Kosovo, Syria, and elsewhere. *See* Sufficiency Opinion I at 21.

The foregoing evidence readily satisfies the elements of the Count One and Count Two conspiracies as to Sherifi. Sherifi wilfully partook in those conspiracies, and sought to provide money and personnel to support violent jihadist causes, in this country and abroad. Even more so than Yaghi and Hassan, Sherifi advocated his extreme and violent beliefs to Boyd and other members of the conspiracy, demonstrating his intention to act on those beliefs. The evidentiary record shows that a multitude of overt acts were committed in furtherance of the conspiracies, including the weapons training sessions, the construction of Boyd's weapons bunker, travel abroad, and consistent efforts to join violent jihadist battlefields. The verdict against Sherifi on Counts One and Two must therefore be sustained.

The evidence supporting Sherifi's conviction on the Count Eleven conspiracy included the following:

• In June 2008, Sherifi expressed to Boyd his willingness to wage violent jihad in the United States if unable to do so abroad;

• While in Kosovo, Sherifi discussed the possibility of targeting the American military post at Camp Bondsteel for violent jihad;

• In 2009, Boyd shared his plans to attack the Marine Corps Base at Quantico with Sherifi, who readily agreed to participate;

• Sherifi told Boyd about his experiences delivering goods to Fort Bragg, explaining how a person could easily gain entry into an American military facility as a truck driver; and

• Boyd proposed kidnapping a Marine officer and took steps in connection with the Count Eleven plot, including touring Quantico and conducting research about the base.

As with the Count One and Count Two conspiracies, the evidence of Sherifi's agreement with Boyd to participate in an attack on Quantico is sufficient to support his Count Eleven conviction. *Cf. In re Terrorist Bombings of U.S. Embassies in E. Africa,* 552 F.3d 93, 113 (2d Cir.2008) (deeming evidence sufficient to sustain § 1117 conviction). The evidence is more than adequate to support a rational factfinder's determination that Sherifi knowingly joined Boyd in a plot to target Quantico for an attack, and that overt acts were committed in furtherance thereof. Sherifi's conviction on the Count Eleven conspiracy must therefore also be sustained.

p.144 Turning to Sheriff's convictions on the firearms charges, those too must be upheld, given the prosecution's evidence that Sherifi participated in weapons training sessions in North Carolina on June 10 and July 7, 2009, where Boyd taught military tactics and weaponry skills in preparation for violent jihad. There was substantial evidence to support a finding that Sherifi, on both of those occasions, possessed and used at least one firearm for training purposes, in furtherance of the Count Two conspiracy. Sherifi's convictions on Counts Four and Eight are therefore also sustained.

3.

Hassan, who was convicted of the Count One conspiracy only, maintains that there was a dearth of evidence, testimonial or otherwise, showing that he entered into a conspiratorial agreement with anyone. Hassan emphasizes that he was not involved in any of the audio recordings introduced into evidence, and that the FBI informants neither interacted with Hassan nor heard Boyd mention him.

Reviewing the evidence de novo and acknowledging that the evidence against Hassan is not as overwhelming as that implicating the other appellants, there was nevertheless substantial evidence proving that Hassan was involved in the Count One conspiracy.[36] The evidentiary support for his conviction includes the following:

- Beginning in 2006 and continuing through mid-2007, Hassan maintained regular contact with Boyd, often meeting at the Blackstone Halal Market;

- In 2006 and 2007 Boyd was stockpiling weapons and surrounding himself with like-minded individuals called "good brothers." Those brothers shared the view that the killing of non-Muslims was a prescribed obligation. Yaghi and Hassan shared Boyd's beliefs in the necessity of violent jihad;

- Seeking a jihadist battlefield, Yaghi travelled to Jordan in the fall of 2006. While there, Yaghi maintained contact with Hassan, all the while expressing the hope that Hassan would make it to the battlefield. Hassan also "offered veiled encouragement to defendant Yaghi while he was on this expedition" overseas. *See* Sufficiency Opinion I at 12;

- In early 2007, Yaghi and Hassan sought Boyd's assistance in obtaining plane tickets to travel to the Middle East;

- Before departing for the Middle East in 2007, Hassan and Yaghi sought Boyd's advice, including methods of overseas travel to avoid detection. Boyd had discussions with Hassan "about killing and maiming." *Id.* at 13;

- Hassan and Yaghi trained with weapons prior to their 2007 trip overseas as "part of their continued training" for violent jihad. *Id.* at 20.

- During a drive with Boyd in 2007, Hassan brandished a .22 caliber rifle, which Hassan and Yaghi said they had purchased for training and target practice;

• In 2007, exchanges between Yaghi and Boyd indicated that Boyd, who was
p.145 experienced on the battlefield, validated the like-mindedness of Yaghi
and Hassan. As the trial court related, a "readiness to join" Boyd "reasonably
could be concluded" on Hassan's part. *Id.* at 12;

• Using plane tickets purchased through Boyd, Hassan travelled with Yaghi in
2007 to the Middle East, and sought to enter Israel and Palestine;

• Boyd advised his associates in Raleigh that he had asked Hassan and Yaghi
to go overseas to engage in violent jihad;

• After arriving in the Middle East, Hassan and Yaghi sought on several
occasions to contact Boyd;

• Following his return from the 2007 Middle East trip with Yaghi, Hassan's
contacts with Boyd diminished substantially. Another set of initiatives was
then undertaken by Yaghi and Hassan that, as the trial court explained,
"subscribed to [tenets] of violent jihad espoused by Daniel Boyd." *Id.* at 19;

• Hassan's postings on Facebook and other social media confirmed his beliefs
in violent jihad and demonstrated his desire to further the violent causes and
ideology espoused by Boyd and others;

• The physical training video that Hassan posted on RossTraining.com
showed his determination to train physically for violent jihad;

• Hassan showed Jamar Carter videos of car bombings and offered praise for
the people fighting in such a manner. Hassan's view of jihad "deemed suicide
bombings righteous." *Id.* at 19;

• Hassan's nefarious intentions were substantiated when, in January 2009, he
"instructed his paramour to remove his postings on his Facebook page" as
well as "postings on 'Muslim Gangsta For Life,'" which endorsed his radical
ideology. *Id.* at 23;

• Hassan had ties to Anwar al-Awlaki and sought al-Awlaki's counsel in early
2009 on an important matter; and

• Hassan's connection to al-Awlaki, coupled with Kohlmann's explanation of
al-Awlaki's far-reaching influence in the "development of home-grown
terrorists," *id.* at 23-24, show that Hassan "endorsed, collected and distributed
preachings [that] repeatedly called for Jihad against the United States." *Id.* at
25.

In these circumstances, there was substantial evidence proving that Hassan joined
and agreed to participate in the Count One conspiracy and that, in fact, he
participated in multiple overt acts in furtherance thereof. As a result, the trial
evidence supports Hassan's conviction on the Count One conspiracy, and his
contention to the contrary is rejected.

D.

Before turning to the various sentencing issues presented here, I will exercise a
point of personal privilege with respect to the investigation and prosecution of this
important case. The trial record reveals that the appellants strove to conceal their
nefarious activities from outsiders uncommitted to violent revolution around the
world, habitually congregating in secret to discuss their plans and to reinforce, in

the manner of zealots, each other's resolve. That the conspiracy was infiltrated and almost all of its cohorts arrested before they could bring their criminal schemes to fruition should in no way inspire the conclusion that the appellants have been prosecuted for merely harboring ideas, convicted of nothing more than an Orwellian "thoughtcrime."

p.146 To the contrary, the evidence reveals that the appellants are dangerous men who freely and frequently exercised their constitutional right to speak, to be sure, but who also demonstrated a steadfast propensity towards action. Before the appellants' actions could escalate to visit grievous harm upon the government, other countries, or innocent civilians, the FBI and its associates timely intervened. The laudable efforts of law enforcement and the prosecutors have ensured that, on this occasion at least, we will not be left to second-guess how a terrorist attack could have been prevented.

Absent the long reach of the federal conspiracy statutes, the government would have been forced to pursue the appellants with one hand tied behind its back. No such constraint served to hinder the investigation and prosecution of the appellants, however, and we are reminded once more that the charge of conspiring to commit a federal crime has yet to relinquish its well-earned reputation as — in the words of Learned Hand — the "darling of the modern prosecutor's nursery." *Harrison v. United States,* 7 F.2d 259, 263 (2d Cir. 1925). Judge Hand's profound observation is as true now as it was nearly ninety years ago.

Over the course of the modern legal era, the pursuit of federal conspiracy convictions has doubtlessly been a boon to United States Attorneys. And it is eminently fair and reasonable to say that the implementing statutes — particularly those that dispense with the commission of an overt act as an element of the crime — sometimes paint with a broad brush. *Cf. Krulewitch v. United States,* 336 U.S. 440, 450, 69 S.Ct. 716, 93 L.Ed. 790 (1949) (Jackson, J., concurring) ("[T]he conspiracy doctrine will incriminate persons on the fringe of offending who would not be guilty of aiding and abetting or of becoming an accessory, for those charges only lie when an act which is a crime has actually been committed."). But our system of government and law reposes great and solemn trust in federal prosecutors to exercise their discretion as instruments of right and justice, and it is therefore "for prosecutors rather than courts to determine when to use a scatter gun to bring down the defendant." *Id.* at 452, 69 S.Ct. 716.

Indeed, the societal utility of conspiracy prosecutions as a weapon against evildoers is manifest not merely in the substantive elements of the offense, but also in the procedural mechanisms enabling its ready proof, even against those only marginally involved. *See, e.g.,* Fed.R.Evid. 801(d)(1)(E) ("A statement ... is not hearsay [that] was made by the party's coconspirator during and in furtherance of the conspiracy."). A person intending to only be "in for a penny," with the slightest connection to an established conspiracy, actually risks being "in for a pound." It is somewhat unique in this case that Boyd, the prosecution's star witness, was also the ringleader of the conspiracies. This was thus a top-down prosecution of conspiracy offenses, with Boyd and his sons — having departed the dock and ascended the witness stand — implicating others more peripherally involved. That fact matters not, however, in the context of the criminal culpability of these appellants. Put succinctly, the specter of federal criminal liability cannot help but serve as an intense deterrent to those who otherwise would be bent on violence.

We have faithfully applied the well-settled principles of conspiracy law in this case, both in letter and in spirit. In so doing, we have come to the ineluctable conclusion that the government legitimately and appropriately charged the appellants, and the convictions it thereby obtained are without infirmity.

p.147 IV.

Finally, having rejected all challenges to the appellants' convictions, we turn to their contentions concerning the sentences imposed by the district court. The court announced those sentences during a January 13, 2012 hearing, and thereafter filed a sentencing opinion as to each appellant. *See United States v. Boyd*, No. 5:09-cr-00216 (E.D.N.C. Jan. 18, 2012), ECF No. 1653 (the "Sherifi Sentencing Opinion"); *United States v. Boyd*, No. 5:09-cr-00216 (E.D.N.C. Jan. 18, 2012), ECF No. 1654 (the "Hassan Sentencing Opinion"); *United States v. Boyd*, No. 5:09-cr-00216 (E.D.N.C. Jan. 18, 2012), ECF No. 1655 (the "Yaghi Sentencing Opinion").

A.

Hassan, who was convicted of solely the Count One conspiracy, had a base offense level of 33 under the 2011 edition of the Sentencing Guidelines. Because the district court deemed Hassan to be subject to the enhancement for a "federal crime of terrorism" under Guidelines section 3A1.4 (the "terrorism enhancement"), his offense level increased by twelve levels to 45. The court then applied two additional enhancements to Hassan — a three-level adjustment for having selected victims on the basis of their religion, ethnicity, or national origin, *see id.* § 3A1.1(a) (the "hate crime enhancement"), and a two-level adjustment for attempting to obstruct justice by asking his paramour to delete Facebook and other internet postings, *see id.* § 3C1.1 — resulting in a total offense level of 50. The court declined to grant Hassan's request for a four-level "minimal participant" reduction under Guidelines section 3B1.2. With the offense level of 50 and the terrorism enhancement's automatic criminal history category of VI, Hassan's advisory Guidelines range was life in prison. Nevertheless, § 2339A(a) of Title 18 provides for a maximum penalty of only fifteen years. Thus, Hassan's advisory range fell to 180 months (fifteen years), which was the very sentence imposed.

After applying both the terrorism enhancement and the hate crime enhancement to Yaghi, the sentencing court determined that his adjusted offense level was 48 and his criminal history category was VI. The resulting advisory Guidelines ranges were 180 months for the Count One conspiracy and life imprisonment for the Count Two conspiracy. The court sentenced Yaghi to 180 months on Count One and to a concurrent sentence of 380 months on Count Two, for an aggregate sentence of 380 months.

Sherifi, who was convicted of the Count One, Two, and Eleven conspiracies, plus the Count Four and Eight firearm offenses, received the terrorism enhancement, the hate crime enhancement, and a three-level enhancement for targeting government officers or employees as victims, *see* USSG § 3A1.2(a). The court calculated Sherifi's advisory Guidelines ranges as follows: 180 months (the statutory maximum) on Count One; life in prison on Count Two; 60 months (consecutive to any other sentence) on Count Four; 300 months (consecutive to any other sentence) on Count Eight; and life in prison on Count Eleven. Rather than a life sentence, the court imposed an aggregate sentence of 540 months.[37]

On appeal, each of the appellants challenges the sentencing court's application of the terrorism enhancement. In addition, Hassan contends that the court erred in p.148 refusing to grant his request for a minimal participant reduction. Meanwhile, Yaghi and Sherifi challenge the substantive reasonableness of their sentences.

B.

1.

The primary sentencing issue pursued by the appellants relates to the district court's application of the terrorism enhancement. More specifically, each appellant contends that the court clearly erred in finding that he possessed the specific intent necessary for application of that enhancement. In assessing whether a court committed procedural error by improperly calculating the advisory Guidelines range, we review its "legal conclusions de novo and its factual findings for clear error." *United States v. Lawing,* 703 F.3d 229, 241 (4th Cir.2012).

The terrorism enhancement has two components. The first bears upon a defendant's offense level: If the offense of conviction "is a felony that involved, or was intended to promote, a federal crime of terrorism," the applicable offense level increases by twelve levels or to a minimum of level 32. *See* USSG § 3A1.4(a). The second component of the terrorism enhancement results in a criminal history category of VI — the maximum under the Guidelines. *Id.* § 3A1.4(b). For purposes of the enhancement, the phrase "federal crime of terrorism" has the meaning specified in 18 U.S.C. § 2332b(g)(5). *Id.* § 3A1.4 cmt. n. 1. Thus, a "federal crime of terrorism" is an offense that

(A) is calculated to influence or affect the conduct of government by intimidation or coercion, or to retaliate against government conduct; and

(B) is a violation of [an enumerated statute].

18 U.S.C. § 2332b(g)(5). In this case, the statutes of conviction for Count One (18 U.S.C. § 2339A) and Count Two (18 U.S.C. § 956(a)) are among those enumerated in § 2332b (g)(5)(B) and, as a result, satisfy the second prong of the definition of a "federal crime of terrorism." Thus, only the first prong of the definition — § 2332b (g)(5)(A)'s specific intent requirement is implicated here.

As we explained in our series of *Chandia* decisions, a court deciding whether to impose the terrorism enhancement must "resolve any factual disputes that it deems relevant to application of the enhancement," and then, if it finds the requisite intent, "should identify the evidence in the record that supports its determination." *United States v. Chandia,* 514 F.3d 365, 376 (4th Cir.2008) ("*Chandia I*"); *see also United States v. Chandia,* 395 Fed. Appx. 53, 56 (4th Cir.2010) ("*Chandia II*") (unpublished); *United States v. Chandia,* 675 F.3d 329, 331 (4th Cir.2012) ("*Chandia III*"). In his first appeal, we affirmed Chandia's convictions but vacated his sentence, remanding for fact finding as to whether he possessed the intent required for application of the terrorism enhancement. *See Chandia I,* 514 F.3d at 376. We also vacated and remanded in Chandia's second appeal, explaining that the sentencing court had "again concluded that Chandia deserved the terrorism enhancement... without resolving relevant factual disputes ... and without explaining how the facts it did find related to Chandia's motive." *Chandia II,* 395 Fed.Appx. at 54. The court complied with our mandate in the subsequent resentencing proceedings, finally prompting our affirmance in Chandia's third appeal. *See Chandia III,* 675 F.3d at 331-32. Here, abiding by our directives in *Chandia I* and *Chandia II,* the district court resolved the relevant factual disputes and identified, as to each appellant, the evidence that supported an p.149 individualized application of the terrorism enhancement. *See* Hassan Sentencing Opinion 8 n. 5; Yaghi Sentencing Opinion 4 n. 5; Sherifi Sentencing Opinion 3 n. 5.[38]

Beginning with the sentencing court's determination that Hassan possessed the intent necessary for application of the terrorism enhancement, the issue is whether the court erred in ruling that Hassan's actions were "calculated to influence or affect the conduct of government by intimidation or coercion, or to retaliate against government conduct." *See* 18 U.S.C. § 2332b(g)(5)(A). The court found that Hassan had built relationships with Yaghi and Boyd "based on their shared view of Islam, including the goal of waging violent jihad in various parts of the world." Hassan Sentencing Opinion 8 n. 5. The court explained that Hassan "became part of a loose group of conspirators whose goal was to kill non-Muslims, specifically those they believed were living unjustly in Muslim lands." *Id.* To further support its finding on specific intent, the court turned to the record, identifying, in particular, the following: that Hassan shared Boyd's view that jihad imposed an obligation on Muslims of "physically helping with the resistance or fighting against ... the NATO forces in Afghanistan or Iraq, or anyplace, really," J.A. 1549; Hassan's 2007 trip to the Middle East with Yaghi, for the purpose of finding "those who could assist him and defendant Yaghi to join the mujahideen," Hassan Sentencing Opinion 8 n. 5; that Hassan and Yaghi, in advance of their 2007 trip to the Middle East, "brandished a firearm to Daniel Boyd in veiled reference to their shared goals," *id.;* Hassan's role in advancing "jihadist propaganda including the teachings of Anwar al-Awlaki," as well as Hassan's efforts to create and disseminate "his own rhetoric" on the internet, *id.;* and that Hassan was "trying to offer himself as a fighter" and supporting terrorism and extremism by "attempting to be a part of it on the battlefield, and supporting those who would," J.A. 3794. Premised on that evidence, the court properly found that Hassan possessed "the motive and intent to influence or affect the conduct of the government by intimidation or coercion or retaliate against government conduct." *See id.*

In its sentencing of Yaghi, the district court also conducted a detailed analysis, finding by clear and convincing evidence that he possessed the specific intent necessary for the terrorism enhancement. The court observed that Yaghi had initiated a corrupt relationship with Boyd when he "sought out" Boyd at an Islamic center in Durham "to learn more about ... Boyd's time in Afghanistan and presumably to learn more about traveling abroad to commit violent jihad." Yaghi Sentencing Opinion 4 n. 5. As further proof that Yaghi's conduct was calculated to influence or affect the conduct of government by intimidation or coercion, the court relied on his travels in 2006 and 2007 to the Middle East, each time seeking, in the court's words, "to engage in violent jihad." *Id.* The court determined that Yaghi's communications to Boyd, as well as his postings on Facebook, "evidence[d] his intent to wage violent jihad and acceptance of radical Islam." *Id.* Moreover, Yaghi's travels in the Middle East, his relationships with Boyd and Hassan, and his advocacy p.150 of violent jihad on the internet "through raps and other postings," convincingly demonstrated his intent to participate in conduct calculated to influence or affect government. *Id.* During Yaghi's sentencing hearing, the court observed that his conduct had gone "beyond words to actions," and that, despite Yaghi's "very limited resources, [he still went] back over and he trie[d] to go to Israel." J.A. 3901. In these circumstances, application of the terrorism enhancement to Yaghi was supported by a preponderance of the evidence.

As with Hassan and Yaghi, the district court made detailed factual findings with respect to the application of the terrorism enhancement to Sherifi. In assessing Sherifi's motives, the court found particular importance in his "return to the United States [from Kosovo] in 2009 with the intent to solicit funds and personnel" to support the mujahideen. *See* J.A. 3853. The court explained that Sherifi hoped "that he would be able to secure farmland from which to launch various challenges against military occupation or intervention." *Id.* Like Hassan and Yaghi, Sherifi had developed a relationship with Boyd on the basis of their shared "goal of waging violent jihad." Sherifi Sentencing Opinion 3 n. 5. Sherifi also developed relationships with coconspirator Subasic and the notorious Serbian terrorist Asllani. The court credited each of those relationships, as well as Sherifi's participation in the firearms training conducted in Caswell County, his receipt of $15,000 to support the mujahideen, and his "efforts to convert [Sergeant] Weeks," as evidence of Sherifi's specific intent to intimidate, coerce, or retaliate against government. *See id.* Those findings, which are not clearly erroneous, support the court's application of the terrorism enhancement to Sherifi.

2.

The only other sentencing challenge lodged by Hassan, who insists that he was the least culpable of the defendants, relates to the district court's refusal to award him a four-level minimal participant reduction under Guidelines section 3B1.2(a). We have evaluated Hassan's contention of error on that point, and we are satisfied that the court did not clearly err in denying Hassan's request. *See United States v. Powell,* 680 F.3d 350, 358 (4th Cir.2012). In a conspiracy prosecution, a minimal participant reduction is not automatically awarded to the least culpable conspirator. To be entitled to the reduction, a defendant must show by a preponderance of the evidence that his role in the offense of conviction "makes him substantially less culpable than the average participant." *See id.* at 358-59 (internal quotation marks omitted). Although Hassan may have been less active than many of his coconspirators, he has failed to establish that he was a minimal participant. Thus, the court's ruling to that effect was not clearly erroneous, and is not to be disturbed.

3.

Turning to Yaghi and Sherifi's contentions that their sentences were substantively unreasonable, we review for abuse of discretion a challenge to the reasonableness of a sentence. *See United States v. Susi,* 674 F.3d 278, 282 (4th Cir. 2012). If, as here, there is "no significant procedural error, then we consider the substantive reasonableness of the sentence imposed, taking into account the totality of the circumstances, including the extent of any variance from the Guidelines range." *Id.* (internal quotation marks omitted). As a general rule, "[w]e apply a presumption of reasonableness to a sentence within or below a properly calculated guidelines p.151 range." *United States v. Yooho Weon,* 722 F.3d 583, 590 (4th Cir.2013).

Yaghi maintains that his aggregate sentence of 380 months is unreasonably harsh, and particularly so in light of his difficult childhood and his peaceful nature. Before sentencing Yaghi, the court considered the contents of his Presentence Report, resolved his objections thereto, and properly calculated his advisory Guidelines range. The court then carefully evaluated each of the 18 U.S.C. § 3553(a) factors. In so doing, the court weighed the nature and circumstances of Yaghi's offenses of conviction, the need for the sentence imposed, and his history and characteristics. The court emphasized the seriousness of Yaghi's conspiracy convictions and his "escalating contact with the state criminal justice system," explaining that such conduct showed his "disregard for liberty and property rights of others," and his readiness to "resort to force." *See* Yaghi Sentencing Opinion 8. In these circumstances, the court did not act unreasonably, nor did it abuse its discretion. Yaghi's challenge to the substantive reasonableness of his aggregate sentence of 380 months is therefore rejected.

Finally, like Yaghi, Sherifi maintains that his aggregate sentence of 540 months is substantively unreasonable. Notably, Sherifi does not challenge the reasonableness of the consecutive sentence of 360 months imposed on his two firearms offenses — Counts Four (60 months) and Eight (300 months). Rather, he contends that, because 360 months for those two convictions is adequate punishment and serves as a sufficient deterrent, the court should not have imposed any additional consecutive sentences on his conspiracy convictions. Prior to sentencing Sherifi, the court properly calculated the advisory Guidelines ranges for each of his offenses of conviction. Then, after assessing Sherifi's background and his role in the offenses, the court imposed sentences on the conspiracy offenses that were substantially below those authorized by statute and recommended by the Guidelines. In these circumstances, the court did not abuse its discretion in its sentencing of Sherifi, and we are unable to disturb its sentencing decisions on the basis of substantive unreasonableness.

V.

Pursuant to the foregoing, we reject the various contentions of error presented by the appellants and affirm the judgments of the district court.

AFFIRMED.

[1] Although seven of the eight defendants were apprehended and successfully prosecuted, the eighth, Jude Kenan Mohammad, apparently remains at large. Mohammad was charged solely with the Count One and Count Two conspiracies. Other than Mohammad, each of the defendants was convicted of the Count One conspiracy. Boyd, Yaghi, Sherifi, and Subasic were convicted of the Count Two

conspiracy. Hassan was acquitted of the Count Two conspiracy, and that charge was dismissed as to Zakariya and Dylan Boyd.

[2] At trial, there was debate over whether Count One required, as an essential element of the offense, the commission of an overt act. The trial court ruled that no overt act was necessary. On appeal, the appellants have abandoned any issue in that regard.

[3] Section 2339A of Title 18 criminalizes "provid[ing] material support or resources ... knowing or intending that they are to be used in preparation for, or in carrying out, a violation of [certain enumerated statutes]." 18 U.S.C. § 2339A(a). Importantly, one of the statutes listed in § 2339A(a) is 18 U.S.C. § 956. Section 956 provides, in pertinent part, that

[w]hoever, within the jurisdiction of the United States, conspires with one or more other persons, regardless of where such other person or persons are located, to commit at any place outside the United States an act that would constitute the offense of murder, kidnapping, or maiming if committed in the ... United States shall, if any of the conspirators commits an act within the jurisdiction of the United States to effect any object of the conspiracy, [be guilty of an offense against the United States].

18 U.S.C. § 956(a)(1). The appellants have not challenged the grand jury's decision to charge the Count One and Count Two conspiracies as separate offenses. As a result, we need not examine whether Counts One and Two were merged for any purpose.

[4] Pursuant to 18 U.S.C. § 924(c), a "crime of violence" is a felony offense that, "by its nature, involves a substantial risk that physical force against the person or property of another may be used in the course of committing the offense." Section 956(a) of Title 18 — the Count Two conspiracy statute — falls within that definition.

[5] Section 1117 of Title 18 provides, in pertinent part, that "[i]f two or more persons conspire to violate [certain sections] of this title, and one or more of such persons do any overt act to effect the object of the conspiracy, each shall be [guilty of an offense against the United States]." Section 1114 is among the enumerated sections, and makes it a crime to "kill[] or attempt[ ] to kill any officer or employee of the United States ... while such officer or employee is engaged in or on account of the performance of official duties." 18 U.S.C. § 1114.

[6] During the course of the terrorism investigation resulting in the Indictment and prosecution, the government collected the FISA-derived evidence, as well as other audio recordings, such as those made by informants wearing recording devices. The prosecution used computer records and a number of those recordings in evidence plus materials seized from social media and other internet sites.

[7] Citations herein to "J.A. ___" refer to the contents of the Joint Appendix filed by the parties in these appeals.

[8] Kohlmann, the prosecution's expert, explained to the jury that speaking in a coded manner is common in jihadist cells: "Frequently, in communications, individuals will talk about getting married as a euphemism for engaging in a violent extremist act, often a suicidal act, the idea being that you will be married to the virgins of paradise after the act is completed." J.A. 379.

[9] Al-Awlaki grew to prominence in the United States during the late 1990s as a cleric and activist. Following the September 11, 2001 terrorist attacks, al-Awlaki came under suspicion for his associations with two of the 9/11 hijackers. Al-Awlaki was thereafter linked to other terrorist activities within the United States, often communicating with the perpetrators via email. In 2003, al-Awlaki departed this country for Yemen and never returned, eventually becoming an active high-ranking member of al-Qaida. Al-Awlaki published his extreme views — particularly that violent jihad against America was a binding obligation on Muslims — through speeches and writings, which were widely disseminated on the internet. As Kohlmann explained, al-Awlaki's teachings "have proven extraordinarily popular among extremists living in western countries," and have "regularly surfaced" in cases of "homegrown terrorists." J.A. 299. In 2011, al-Awlaki was killed by a drone strike in Yemen.

[10] Although Hassan had been "peripherally known to the Boyd family during his teenage years," J.A. 3071, Hassan did not meet Boyd until 2007, when Hassan was approximately twenty years old.

[11] According to court records, Hassan, Yaghi, and another man were charged with kidnapping and restraining a student at North Carolina State University during a robbery. Hassan pleaded guilty to false imprisonment, and Yaghi pleaded guilty to felonious restraint.

[12] The Blackstone Halal Market closed in approximately mid2008. Thereafter, several of the coconspirators met regularly in Boyd's home.

[13] Shari'ah is a term used to generally describe the moral and religious rules of Islam, as well as its teachings.

[14] At the time of the initial indictment and during his ongoing conspiratorial activities, Boyd possessed more than forty weapons. Boyd's arsenal included assault weapons, sniper rifles, handguns, shotguns, and tens of thousands of rounds of ammunition. See J.A. 4274-79 (cataloging Boyd's arsenal). Boyd had at least ten assault weapons, including several Bushmasters and AK-47s; at least twenty rifles and shotguns; and more than a dozen handguns.

[15] We are appreciative of the extensive efforts rendered in this case by our district court colleague, who patiently addressed the various issues presented. The record convincingly demonstrates her diligence, reflected in nearly a dozen written opinions, plus innumerable orders and oral rulings. We also commend defense counsel for ably and robustly representing the appellants.

[16] The *Humanitarian Law Project* decision concerned the constitutionality of § 2339B, rather than § 2339A. Section 2339A(a) prohibits the provision of "material support or resources" while "knowing or intending that they are to be used in preparation for, or in carrying out," violations of certain terrorism statutes. Meanwhile, § 2339B(a)(1) prohibits "knowingly provid[ing] material support or resources" to an organization that has been designated as a "foreign terrorist organization" by the Secretary of State. Thus, both § 2339A and § 2339B criminalize the provision of "material support," but they have some different elements. See *United States v. Chandia*, 514 F.3d 365, 372 (4th Cir.2008).

[17] The appellants also challenge on First Amendment grounds the trial court's rejection of proposed instruction 28. Rather than pertaining to any protections

accorded by the First Amendment, however, that proposal reflects the appellants' (incorrect) interpretation of the elements of the Count One conspiracy.

The appellants have further suggested that the trial court's charge was not just deficient but also incorrect, because the court affirmatively instructed that the First Amendment was not a defense to the crimes charged. The appellants failed to adequately address that claim in their opening brief, however, and therefore have abandoned it. *See Edwards v. City of Goldsboro*, 178 F.3d 231, 241 n. 6 (4th Cir.1999) ("Failure to comply with the specific dictates of [Federal Rule of Appellate Procedure 28(a)] with respect to a particular claim triggers abandonment of that claim on appeal.").

[18] Pursuant to Rule 30(d) of the Federal Rules of Criminal Procedure, "[a] party who objects to any portion of the instructions or to a failure to give a requested instruction" is required to "inform the court of the specific objection and the grounds for the objection before the jury retires to deliberate." A "failure to object in accordance with this rule" will, in most instances, preclude appellate review. *See United States v. Ebersole*, 411 F.3d 517, 526 (4th Cir.2005). The appellants made arguments in favor of their proposed instructions — including numbers 37, 40, and 45 — *prior to* the court's charge to the jury. The record reveals, however, that the appellants only identified instructions 37, 47, and 48 in their post-charge objections. Nevertheless, the government does not, however, raise any contention of waiver for failure of the appellants to properly object under Rule 30(d). More importantly, we discern no error in the court's refusal of the three instructions at issue.

[19] Additionally, Hassan raises the trial court's failure to instruct on the Second Amendment insofar as it "protects an individual right to possess a firearm unconnected with service in a militia, and to use that [weapon] for traditionally lawful purposes, such as self-defense within the home." *See* J.A. 463 (further specifying that mere possession of a firearm "does not in and of itself make a defendant guilty of a crime"). Notably, Hassan was neither charged with nor convicted of any offense involving his possession of a firearm, and he cannot show that the lack of a Second Amendment instruction prejudiced his defense.

[20] Pursuant to Rule 702, "[a] witness who is qualified as an expert by knowledge, skill, experience, training, or education may testify in the form of an opinion or otherwise" if the following requirements are satisfied:

(a) the expert's scientific, technical, or other specialized knowledge will help the trier of fact to understand the evidence or to determine a fact in issue; (b) the testimony is based on sufficient facts or data; (c) the testimony is the product of reliable principles and methods; and (d) the expert has reliably applied the principles and methods to the facts of the case.

Fed.R.Evid. 702.

[21] Our *Benkahla* analysis focused largely on the relevance of Kohlmann's testimony because, as Judge Wilkinson explained, Kohlmann's "qualifications were obviously substantial and the district court acted well within its discretion in determining that they were sufficient." *See Benkahla*, 530 F.3d at 309 n. 2.

[22] Pursuant to Rule 403, a trial court "may exclude relevant evidence if its probative value is substantially outweighed by a danger of... unfair prejudice, confusing the issues, [or] misleading the jury."

[23] The appellants also assert that Kohlmann's testimony was irrelevant under Rules 401 and 402 because "[c]riminal behavior must be judged by the conduct of individual defendants applied to the particularized elements of the pertinent criminal statute, not the characteristics of any class of defendants 'as a whole.'" Br. of Appellant Sherifi 16. To the extent that assertion constitutes a distinct relevancy challenge to Kohlmann's testimony, it is rejected.

[24] The current version of Rule 803(6), quoted above, was effective as of on December 1, 2011, several months after completion of the trial. The amendments to Rule 803 were not substantive, however, but were part of a restyling of the Rules of Evidence to make them more readily understandable and consistent.

[25] The appellants' contention that the Facebook and Google certifications are insufficient because they were made for litigation purposes several years after the postings occurred is entirely unpersuasive. It would make no sense to require a records custodian to contemporaneously execute an affidavit attesting to the accuracy of a business record each time one is created or maintained, when there is no pending litigation or need for such a certification.

[26] Hassan's assertion that he "do[es] not support terrorists" was part of a lengthier statement:

The troops I support are the ones who fight for truth, whether he is Arab, American, Spanish, Europe, whatever, it doesn't matter as long as he fights for the truth. PS, I do not support terrorists.

J.A. 2377. In posting his apology, Hassan asserted:

Islam is a religion of peace but when attacked we fight back strong. I will edit the video but will probably keep my religious beliefs ... because part of my religious faith is to become strong and in healthy shape.

Id. at 2377-78.

[27] The FISA applications, as well as the electronic surveillance orders issued by the FISA Court and any returns filed in connection with them, are collectively referred to as the "FISA materials."

[28] The FISA provisions, in pertinent part, define a "United States person" as "a citizen of the United States, [or] an alien lawfully admitted for permanent residence." 50 U.S.C. § 1801(i). Yaghi, as a naturalized citizen of this country, is a United States person.

[29] We have heretofore reviewed de novo a district court's determination that a FISA application established probable cause. *Squillacote,* 221 F.3d at 554; *Hammoud,* 381 F.3d at 331. Some of our sister circuits, however, have utilized a more deferential standard of review. *See, e.g., United States v. El-Mezain,* 664 F.3d 467, 567 (5th Cir.2011) (conducting "independent *in camera* review" and applying abuse of discretion standard); *United States v. Abu-Jihaad,* 630 F.3d 102, 130 (2d Cir.2010) (explaining that "FISA warrant applications are subject to minimal scrutiny by the courts, both upon initial presentation and subsequent challenge" (internal quotation marks omitted)). We are satisfied that probable cause existed in this case under any of these standards.

[30] Although the Indictment alleged a series of overt acts in furtherance of the Count One conspiracy, proof of the commission of an overt act in a § 2339A conspiracy is not required by statute. *See* 18 U.S.C. § 2339A; *see also Stewart,* 590

F.3d at 114-16 (setting out elements of § 2339A without including overt act requirement); *cf. supra* note 2 (observing that appellants asserted at trial that overt act was not required). The Count Two conspiracy, by contrast, requires proof that at least one overt act in furtherance thereof was committed within the United States. *See* 18 U.S.C. § 956(a)(1).

[31] The trial court instructed the jury on the law of conspiracy, explaining that

[i]f a defendant understands the unlawful nature of a plan or scheme and knowingly and intentionally joins in that plan or scheme on one occasion, that is sufficient to convict him for conspiracy, even though the defendant hadn't participated before and even though the defendant played only a minor part.

J.A. 3573-74. The court also instructed that the prosecution had no obligation to "prove that a conspiracy has a discrete, identifiable organization structure." *Id.* at 3573.

[32] The conspiracy instructions emphasized that a defendant can be a coconspirator "without knowing [the conspiracy's] full scope or all of its members, and without taking part in the full range of its activities." J.A. 3573. Moreover, the trial court advised the jury that "[o]nce a defendant willfully joins in a conspiracy," he "is presumed to continue in that conspiracy unless and until he takes affirmative steps to withdraw." *Id.* at 3574.

[33] The court explained to the jury that a conspiracy "may be proved wholly by circumstantial evidence," J.A. 3572, which can consist of "a defendant's relationship" with other conspirators and "the length of this association," as well as "the defendant's attitude and conduct, and the nature of the conspiracy," *id.* at 3573.

[34] The court further defined "training" as "instruction or teaching designed to impart a specific skill as opposed to general knowledge," J.A. 3574-75, and defined "personnel" as "one or more persons, which can include a defendant's own person." *id.* at 3575.

[35] In referencing the opinions of the district court on the sufficiency issues, we do not accord any deference to the court's analysis; we quote those opinions only where we agree that they are supported by the record.

[36] That Hassan was acquitted of the Count Two conspiracy is not accorded any weight in our analysis. Even if that verdict is inconsistent with the guilty verdict on Count One, a jury is permitted to return an inconsistent verdict if it sees fit to do so. *See United States v. Powell,* 469 U.S. 57, 63, 105 S.Ct. 471, 83 L.Ed.2d 461 (1984). The question before us relates solely to the Count One conspiracy and whether — viewed in the light most favorable to the prosecution — that charge was properly proven against Hassan.

[37] Sherifi was sentenced to concurrent 180-month terms on Counts One, Two, and Eleven; a consecutive 60-month term on Count Four; and a consecutive 300-month term on Count Eight.

[38] Because the appellants' sentencing proceedings were conducted prior to the issuance of our *Chandia III* decision, the district court did not have the benefit of our ruling that "a preponderance of the evidence is the appropriate standard of proof for establishing the requisite intent for the terrorism enhancement." *See* 675 F.3d at 339. Being appropriately cautious, the court applied the more stringent "clear and convincing evidence" standard.

711 F.3d 445 (2013)

UNITED STATES of America, Plaintiff-Appellee,

v.

William Leonardo GRAHAM, a/k/a Leo, Defendant-Appellant.

No. 09-5067.

United States Court of Appeals, Fourth Circuit.

Argued: January 31, 2013.

Decided: March 29, 2013.

US v. Graham, 711 F. 3d 445 (4th Cir. 2013)

p.446 ARGUED: Michael Alan Wein, Greenbelt, Maryland, for Appellant. Michael p.447 Clayton Hanlon, Office of the United States Attorney, Baltimore, Maryland, for Appellee. ON BRIEF: Rod J. Rosenstein, United States Attorney, Baltimore, Maryland, for Appellee.

Before TRAXLER, Chief Judge, and AGEE and DAVIS, Circuit Judges.

Affirmed by published opinion. Judge DAVIS wrote the opinion, in which Chief Judge TRAXLER and Judge AGEE joined.

OPINION

DAVIS, Circuit Judge:

A jury convicted Appellant William Leonardo Graham of one count of conspiracy to distribute more than five kilograms of cocaine, in violation of 21 U.S.C. § 846. Pursuant to 21 U.S.C. § 851, the district court imposed a mandatory life sentence. On appeal, Graham asserts reversible error in three respects: (1) an alleged violation of the Court Reporter Act, 28 U.S.C. § 753(b); (2) the admission of statements by coconspirators recorded during wiretapped conversations; and (3) his life sentence contravenes the Constitution. For the reasons set forth below, we reject each of Graham's contentions and we therefore affirm the judgment.

I.

Although several of Graham's codefendants testified against him and thereby provided direct evidence of his participation in the narcotics conspiracy, their trial testimony was significantly bolstered by recordings of their wiretapped conversations which occurred during the existence of the conspiracy. Graham's focus on appeal before us is that (1) the full vindication of his right to appellate review has been denied by the lack of a reliable trial record of the wiretapped conversations; and, in any event, (2) the district court abused its discretion when it admitted the wiretapped conversations. For the reasons explained within, we reject each of these contentions.

A.

On September 11, 2008, Graham was named with seven others in count one of a superseding indictment charging conspiracy to distribute and possess with intent to distribute five kilograms or more of cocaine from March 2006 through August 2008. Graham alone proceeded to trial; his codefendants entered into plea agreements or (as to one) the indictment was dismissed on motion of the government. Prior to trial, Graham's counsel discussed with the prosecuting Assistant United States Attorney ("AUSA") the admissibility of five recordings of wiretap conversations among Graham's codefendants in which Graham was not a participant. The government indicated that it planned to seek admission of the recordings as non-hearsay coconspirator statements and/or pursuant to the present sense impression exception to the hearsay rule.

Trial took place from August 17 through August 24, 2009. During opening statements, the AUSA explained to the jury that the government would present testimony of the case agent regarding the investigation, specifically as to how the government was able to install a wiretap on the cellphone of codefendant Lawrence Reeves, and thereby intercept conversations between Reeves and codefendants Devon Marshall and Justin Gallardo. The government further explained that the jury would hear in the recordings that Reeves, Marshall, and Gallardo were attempting to collect a drug debt from Graham. (Reeves, Marshall, and Gallardo all testified against Graham pursuant to plea agreements with the government.)

The government's first witness, Drug Enforcement Agency ("DEA") Special p.448 Agent Thomas Cindric, testified that investigators recorded approximately 35,000 conversations in the course of the investigation of the conspiracy. Cindric also confirmed that there were no recordings of Graham himself talking on the wire.

Next, Reeves testified. He explained how he and Gallardo were in a partnership: Gallardo received drugs from Arizona, Reeves distributed them to various buyers and sellers, and Gallardo returned the proceeds to the Arizona suppliers. Reeves also described working with Graham to sell drugs, including going to Graham's house to "pick up the money that he owed [him] for [a] [] shipment of drugs that [he] gave him." J.A. 178. Reeves testified that he received a total of six shipments of cocaine from Arizona. At some point, Reeves met Marshall, one of Graham's customers. Reeves testified that Marshall was unhappy with Graham's prices and began to buy directly from Reeves.

Reeves testified that while working with Graham to sell the fourth shipment of narcotics, which was delivered to Graham's home and contained approximately 26 kilograms of cocaine and about 200 pounds of marijuana, they "gave [the drugs] to [Graham] up front and expected to get payment afterwards, after he was done selling." Id. at 191. Graham complained about the quality of the marijuana, however, and told them "he tried to sell" it but could not. Id. at 192. As a result, he owed Reeves and Gallardo money for the marijuana, which resulted in the Arizona suppliers going unpaid. According to Reeves, Graham's debt after that transaction was "about $30,000." Id.

Reeves further testified that Graham had received a portion of four of the six shipments from Arizona, but future supplies had ended "[b]ecause Leo [Graham] owed [them] on the money on the marijuana and he refused to pay. And therefore, [they] cut him off." J.A. 199. Specifically, Reeves explained that the sixth shipment was the last shipment from Arizona:

> There was a huge, basically, beef between myself, Mr. Gallardo, and the
> people in Arizona because of this marijuana, and because of the shortage, how

those [kilos] came short, and the money not come in. So they basically shut us down.

J.A. 199.

Thereafter, Reeves asked Marshall to assist in persuading Graham to pay the debt. Reeves and Marshall planned to tell Graham that "Mexicans" were looking for him in hopes that he would be intimidated into paying the debt. *Id.* at 203. During Reeves's testimony, the government played three recordings[1] of wiretapped phone conversations on Reeves's phone. The jurors were given binders containing transcripts of each recording played during the trial. When a recording was played, the prosecutor referenced the corresponding tab number in the transcript binder for the jury to follow along.

p.449 Justin Gallardo was the second cooperating codefendant to testify. He testified that he transported cocaine from Arizona to Maryland, helped Reeves distribute it in Baltimore, and took the money earned from the sales to Arizona. Gallardo confirmed that Graham received multiple kilograms of each cocaine shipment the group received. He testified that he kept tally sheets, which were seized in August 2008 during the execution of a search warrant issued for his home. Gallardo used the sheets to keep track of the amount and type of drug each customer received and the money paid, and the portion of the money to be returned to Arizona. Gallardo's tally sheets showed that Graham acquired cocaine and marijuana from the group and that he owed or paid money for those drugs.

Marshall was the third cooperating codefendant to testify. He explained that in early 2007 he began selling cocaine that he received from a supplier named "Leonardo." Marshall identified Graham as his supplier, "Leonardo." According to Marshall, he would pick up kilogram quantities of cocaine from Graham at Graham's home. Marshall stated that in October 2007 he began to obtain his supply directly from Reeves.

Marshall testified that Reeves informed him that Graham owed Reeves money,[2] and at Reeves's request, Marshall agreed to talk to Graham. When he did so, Marshall told Graham that Mexican cocaine suppliers were looking for him. In response, Marshall testified, Graham said he refused to give any money to Reeves until he "gets some more product" — "coke." J.A. 385.

After meeting with Graham, Marshall relayed the information to Reeves via telephone. Call 22, which was "tab 12" of the transcript binder, was played to the jury. In that call, Marshall told Reeves that Graham had refused to pay the debt. In this conversation, however, Marshall did not tell Reeves that Graham wanted more drugs, and Marshall explained during his testimony that this was because he (Marshall) did not like to talk about drugs over the phone. Marshall did indicate during the call, however, that Graham had said more, and that he (Marshall) would discuss it with Reeves the next day.

In its rebuttal closing argument, the government replayed the first twenty-three seconds of one of the conversations between Reeves and "Big Moe." *See supra* n. 1.

The district court instructed the jury that the actual recorded conversations constituted the evidence, and not the transcripts, which were simply aids to follow the conversations.

The jury convicted Graham of conspiracy to distribute five kilograms or more of cocaine. The parties entered a stipulation that stated that the exhibits from the trial would be "retained by counsel who offered them, pending appeal." J.A. 503.

Graham was sentenced on November 6, 2009. During the sentencing proceeding, the government reminded the district court that it had filed an information under 21 U.S.C. § 851, "noting that the Defendant had three prior felony drug offenses." J.A. 515. The court asked whether there was a mandatory minimum sentence in the case, and the government confirmed that Graham faced a mandatory life sentence as a result of the § 851 information. In response, the court stated "[f]rankly, if I were applying 3553(a) factors, there is no p.450 way that I would impose that sentence in this case.... [I]t would be a severe sentence, but it would certainly not be a life sentence that I am required to impose in this case." J.A. 516. The court imposed a sentence of life imprisonment. Graham filed a timely notice of appeal.

B.

We appointed appellate counsel for Graham. During his research of appealable issues, counsel discovered that none of the recordings played during trial had themselves been recorded or transcribed by the court reporter during their presentation to the jury. Concerned that, as he had not been present for trial, his incomplete knowledge of the trial record might impede his representation of Graham before us, counsel filed and we granted a consent motion to rescind the briefing order to permit counsel to pursue relief before the district court pursuant to Federal Rule of Appellate Procedure ("FRAP") 10.[3]

Thereafter, in summer 2011, the government provided to counsel a copy of a CD containing the recordings and a copy of the transcript binder. The district court held an evidentiary hearing to determine which recordings were played for the jury during trial. Prior to the hearing, the government submitted two affidavits to the district court. One was of the lead trial prosecutor, a former AUSA. The former AUSA stated that he, his co-counsel, and the case agent, had reviewed the DEA wiretaps in Graham's case, and selected which calls would be played at trial. He stated that he organized the preparation of the transcripts for the calls they planned to play for the jury, and checked the transcripts for errors prior to trial. He stated that, based on his recollection, as refreshed by his review of the trial transcript, the wiretap CD, and examination of the transcript binder, he could "attest that the compact disk provided to [him] by [the current AUSA] contains true and accurate copies of the wiretap recordings played during the trial in [Graham's] case." J.A. 710. He specifically identified which recorded calls from the duplicate CD had been played at each reference in the trial transcript to a tape being played to the jury.

During the hearing, the former AUSA testified consistently with the averments in his affidavit. He stated that he was in the courtroom when all of the recordings were played to the jury. He further testified that in preparation for the hearing, he reviewed each page of the trial transcript which indicated a recorded call had been played and "compar[ed] them to the transcripts and ma[de] sure that the transcripts were the transcripts that related to those calls." J.A. 729.

The second affidavit submitted prior to the hearing was of DEA Task Force Officer Detective William Nickoles. Nickoles stated that he was the case agent on

Graham's case and, in that capacity, he reviewed wiretap recordings and the transcripts of the recordings selected to be used at trial. He asserted that he was present at trial when the calls were played on August 18, 2009, and when the prosecutor p.451 played a portion of a call during his rebuttal closing argument. Nickoles averred that he reviewed the contents of the CD that contained copies of the recordings prepared for trial, and the copy of the transcript binder prepared for the trial, and based on that review and his best recollection of relevant events, he could "attest that the compact disk provided to [him] by [the current AUSA] contains the true and accurate copies of the wiretap recordings played during the trial in [Graham's] case." J.A. 714.

Nickoles also testified at the hearing. He explained that, while working as the case agent on Graham's case, he had reviewed every wiretap call in the case. He also stated that he executed his affidavit after listening to the audio CD and reviewing the transcript binder provided to him, which together led him to conclude that they were accurate copies of the originals used in Graham's trial. Finally, he testified that the transcribed portions of the five phone calls in the five tabs in the transcript binder were played in their entirety, and only the transcribed portions were played to the jury.

On July 25, 2012, the district court issued a Memorandum Opinion and Order Confirming Record on Appeal, which made findings as to which calls, and which portions of the calls, were heard by the jury. Six tapes were played at trial, covering five calls; one recording was replayed during the government's rebuttal argument. The district court "[found] beyond a reasonable doubt that the wiretap recordings played at trial were those indicated by the testimony and affidavits" presented by the government. J.A. 804. Thereafter, the parties resumed their briefing in this appeal.[4]

C.

Graham argues that the court reporter's failure to transcribe the contents of the wiretap conversations played to the jury during trial constituted a violation of the Court Reporter Act ("CRA"), 28 U.S.C. § 753(b), and that the district court lacked sufficient proof at the FRAP 10 hearing to conclude definitively what wiretap recordings were played to the jury. In response, the government argues that the district court's findings and conclusions are sound and that, even if the district court erred in failing to ensure at trial that the wiretap conversations played were recorded or transcribed contemporaneously by the court reporter, the error was resolved by the district court's FRAP 10 conclusions.

We review a district court's compliance with the CRA *de novo*. *United States v. Brown*, 202 F.3d 691, 696 (4th Cir.2000).

The CRA states, in pertinent part:

> Each session of the court and every other proceeding designated by rule or order of the court or by one of the judges shall be recorded verbatim.... Proceedings to be recorded under this section include (1) all proceedings in criminal cases had in open court....

28 U.S.C. § 753(b).

We have not previously addressed the issue whether a district court's failure to ensure the transcription of audio recordings played during a trial constitutes a violation of the CRA. We need not resolve the issue in this case, however, because Graham is not entitled to relief on his claim in any event. In *United States v. Brown,* we held that, although a defendant has a right to a meaningful appeal, with the assistance of a complete transcript, p.452 "omissions from a trial transcript only warrant a new trial if 'the missing portion of the transcript specifically prejudices [a defendant's] appeal.'" 202 F.3d 691, 696 (4th Cir.2000) (quoting *United States v. Gillis,* 773 F.2d 549, 554 (4th Cir.1985)). Thus, "'to obtain a new trial, whether or not appellate counsel is new, the defendant must show that the transcript errors specifically prejudiced his ability to perfect an appeal.'" *Brown,* 202 F.3d at 696 (quoting *United States v. Huggins,* 191 F.3d 532, 537 (4th Cir.1999)). Because we find the district court's FRAP 10 findings were amply supported by the evidence presented at the hearing and enabled Graham to "perfect [his] appeal," we need not and do not address whether the CRA was violated. *Id.*

D.

In reviewing the district court's decision on a FRAP 10 motion, we consider the district court's findings conclusive "unless intentionally false or plainly unreasonable." *United States v. Hernandez,* 227 F.3d 686, 695 (6th Cir.2000) (citing *United States v. Zichettello,* 208 F.3d 72, 93 (2nd Cir.2000); *United States v. Garcia,* 997 F.2d 1273, 1278 (9th Cir.1993); *United States v. Serrano,* 870 F.2d 1, 12 (1st Cir. 1989); *United States v. Mori,* 444 F.2d 240, 246 (5th Cir.1971)).

Graham argues that the evidence presented at the FRAP 10 proceeding was insufficient to correct the lack of transcription of the recordings played to the jury. This is so, he contends conclusorily, because the trial court did not hear enough evidence at the FRAP 10 hearing to find definitively which recordings were played during the trial.

We disagree. The district court's findings were adequately supported by the evidence. First, the district court pointed to the fact that both of the witnesses were closely involved in the actual preparation of the original disc containing the recordings and transcript binder used at the trial. Both were present throughout the trial. The district court also noted that the lead trial prosecutor testified that he "very clearly" recalled which recording was played in his rebuttal closing, and after reviewing the trial transcript, the disc, and the transcript binder, remembered which of the other recordings had been played. J.A. 804-05. Lastly, the district court emphasized the fact that "Graham [who attended the hearing with counsel] presented no contradictory affidavits or testimony," and concluded that the calls that were played were calls 20, 22, 23, 1452 and 1454. *Id.* at 805-06.

Based on the wealth of highly persuasive evidence before the district court, we conclude the court had a sufficient basis to find beyond a reasonable doubt that the copies of the disc and transcript binder were genuine and accurate duplicates of the calls that were played at trial. We have no hesitation in concluding that Graham's counsel has available in this case an appellate record that fully and accurately reflects the pre-trial and trial proceedings before the district court leading to the jury's verdict. *Cf. Hernandez,* 227 F.3d at 695.

E.

Graham next argues that the district court erred in admitting the wiretap conversations of his coconspirators under Federal Rule of Evidence ("FRE" or "Rule") 801(d)(2)(E)[5] because the tapes p.453 merely captured "idle chatter" between them about Graham's past debt for marijuana, and because the conversations were not in the course, or in furtherance, of a conspiracy.

We review a district court's admission of a statement under Rule 801(d)(2)(E) for abuse of discretion. *United States v. Blevins,* 960 F.2d 1252, 1255 (4th Cir.1992). The abuse of discretion standard is highly deferential, and a reviewing court should not reverse unless the ruling is "manifestly erroneous." *Gen. Elec. Co. v. Joiner,* 522 U.S. 136, 142, 118 S.Ct. 512, 139 L.Ed.2d 508 (1997) (quoting *Spring Co. v. Edgar,* 99 U.S. 645, 658, 25 L.Ed. 487 (1879)).

The standard for admission of a coconspirator statement is clear in this Circuit:

> A statement is not hearsay if it is "a statement by a co-conspirator of a party during the course and in furtherance of the conspiracy" and is offered against the party. Fed.R.Evid. 801(d)(2)(E). In order to admit a statement under 801(d)(2)(E), the moving party must show that (i) a conspiracy did, in fact, exist, (ii) the declarant and the defendant were members of the conspiracy, and (iii) the statement was made in the course of, and in furtherance, of the conspiracy. *See, e.g., United States v. Heater,* 63 F.3d 311, 324 (4th Cir.1995). Idle conversation that touches on, but does not further, the purposes of the conspiracy does not constitute a statement in furtherance of a conspiracy under Rule 801(d)(2)(E). *See United States v. Urbanik,* 801 F.2d 692, 698 (4th Cir.1986).

United States v. Pratt, 239 F.3d 640, 643 (4th Cir.2001). "A statement by a co-conspirator is made 'in furtherance' of a conspiracy if it was intended to promote the conspiracy's objectives, whether or not it actually has that effect." *United States v. Shores,* 33 F.3d 438, 443 (4th Cir.1994), *cert. denied,* 514 U.S. 1019, 115 S.Ct. 1365, 131 L.Ed.2d 221 (1995).

The existence of the three prongs of admissibility for coconspirator statements (existence of a conspiracy, membership therein of defendant and declarants, and the statements being made in the course of and in furtherance of that conspiracy) must be supported by a preponderance of the evidence. *See Blevins,* 960 F.2d at 1255. The incorrect admission of a statement under the coconspirator statement exclusion from the definition of hearsay is subject to harmless error review. *United States v. Urbanik,* 801 F.2d 692, 698 (4th Cir.1986).

Graham first contends that the district court erred by not making explicit findings on the existence of a conspiracy prior to admitting the statements. This argument fails, however, because a trial court is not required to hold a hearing to determine whether a conspiracy exists before admitting statements under the rule, and the court need not explain the reasoning behind the evidentiary ruling. *Blevins,* 960 F.2d at 1256. We "may affirm a judgment where the record reveals that the co-conspirator's statements were plainly admissible, whether or not a detailed rationale for admitting the statements had been stated by the trial court." *Id.*

Next, Graham argues that each of the five recordings played for the jury was nothing more than "profanity laden conversation" about collecting a debt from p.454 Graham, but that "[t]here's no way that [conversations about] a 'debt collecting' job" constituted coconspirator statements. Appellant's Br. at 65-66 (brackets added). In other words, Graham contends that the conversations played for the jury were not "in furtherance of a conspiracy" to distribute cocaine.

The government responds that the only issue surrounding the admissibility of the statements is whether the conspiracy continued to exist on June 27, 2008, when the recordings were made. The government points to the efforts of Reeves and Marshall to collect the unpaid sums from Graham so that the money could be used to salvage the relationship with their Arizona-based supplier as indicative that the conspiracy was ongoing at the time of the calls. To the extent Graham is arguing that he withdrew from the conspiracy, the government adds, that claim must fail because it is the defendant who has the burden of establishing withdrawal, and "'[a] mere cessation of activity in furtherance of the conspiracy is insufficient.'" Gov't's Br. at 46-47 (quoting *United States v. Walker*, 796 F.2d 43, 49 (4th Cir.1986)). The government contends that although Graham may have refused to pay the debt, he did not take affirmative action to withdraw from the conspiracy.

Additionally, the government argues the conversations were "in furtherance of the conspiracy," because "it was necessary for members of the conspiracy, Reeves and Marshall, to discuss the status of the conspiracy, the status of its members, and monies owed by one member to another." Gov't's Br. at 57.

The government's position is persuasive. The evidence demonstrates that one of the primary reasons Reeves and Marshall sought to collect the debt from Graham was to gain funds to continue or re-establish their drug supply, which according to their testimony at trial, had been plentiful before Graham's refusal to ante up dislocated their profitable enterprise. Additionally, the evidence shows that Graham himself continued to want to engage in further drug activities with the group by receiving more cocaine. There is, in contrast, no evidence that Graham attempted to disavow the conspiracy and communicate his departure to his coconspirators. *See Smith v. United States*, ___ U.S. ___, 133 S.Ct. 714, 719, 184 L.Ed.2d 570 (2013) (holding that the burden rests with the defendant to establish withdrawal from a conspiracy). What we have said in the context of substantive liability for a conspiracy offense applies with equal force in the context of the admissibility of coconspirator statements: "evidence of an internal conflict between [a defendant] and other members of the conspiracy" is not alone sufficient to undermine proof that coconspirator statements were made in furtherance of and in the course of the conspiracy. *See United States v. Green*, 599 F.3d 360, 369 (4th Cir.), *cert. denied*, ___ U.S. ___, 131 S.Ct. 271, 178 L.Ed.2d 179 (2010).

Even though Graham himself was not captured in a conversation with a coconspirator in any of the 35,000 calls recorded during the investigation of this case, and even though there was adversity between Graham and his coconspirators, each call played at trial contained discussions that rendered them "in furtherance" of the overall conspiracy. The calls all consisted of the speakers exchanging information about the status of their efforts to collect the intra-conspiracy debt owed by Graham. Some included discussions of the plan to give Graham the impression (to intimidate him into paying) that "Esses" or "Mexicans" were looking for him to collect on the debt, and most ended with the speakers planning the next time they would discuss their efforts to persuade Graham to pay up. It is apparent that debt collection was a primary aim of the p.455 conspiracy at the time the calls were made, most likely because recoupment of the unpaid funds had some bearing on the group's ability to receive additional narcotics from their Arizona source.

In short, the district court's admission of the challenged statements was neither erroneous nor, it necessarily follows, an abuse of discretion. *Blevins,* 960 F.2d at 1256.

II.

Finally, invoking the strongly-worded sentiments expressed by the district court at sentencing to the effect that it would not choose to impose a life sentence if it had a choice in the matter,[6] Graham challenges his mandatory life sentence.[7] Although the argument is not made with great clarity, we understand his principal purpose to be that he wishes to preserve the issue in the event the Supreme Court should elect to reexamine its holding in *Almendarez-Torres v. United States,* 523 U.S. 224, 118 S.Ct. 1219, 140 L.Ed.2d 350 (1998).[8] In any event, we are bound by *Almendarez — Torres* unless and until the Supreme Court says otherwise. Accordingly, we reject the challenge to Graham's sentence.

III.

For the reasons set forth, the judgment is

AFFIRMED.

[1] Call number 1452 was played first, and it corresponded to "tab 8" in the binder. During call 1452, Reeves and "Big Moe" spoke about Moe's attempts to locate Graham. "Big Moe" was another associate, and he was offered a portion of the pay-out if he was successful in persuading Graham to pay the debt.

The second call played was call 23, which corresponded to "tab 13" in the binder. It consisted of Reeves talking with Gallardo about Marshall's attempts to get Graham to pay the debt. Reeves told Gallardo that Graham had refused to pay.

The third call played was call 1454, which corresponded to "tab 9" in the binder. The call was between Reeves and "Big Moe." Reeves explained Marshall's attempt to intimidate Graham by telling him "Esses" were looking for him, and that Graham continued to refuse to pay the debt.

[2] Call 20, which corresponded to "tab 11" of the transcript binder, was played for the jury. In that call, Reeves asked Marshall to "pull it off" (i.e., get Graham to pay the debt), and told Marshall that he could "keep the rest" if he could manage to get the debt paid. J.A. 664.

[3] Federal Rule of Appellate Procedure 10(e) provides as follows in pertinent part:

(e) Correction or Modification of the Record.

(1) If any difference arises about whether the record truly discloses what occurred in the district court, the difference must be submitted to and settled by that court and the record conformed accordingly.

(2) If anything material to either party is omitted from or misstated in the record by error or accident, the omission or misstatement may be corrected and a supplemental record may be certified and forwarded:

. . .

(B) by the district court before or after the record has been forwarded ...

FRAP 10(e).

[4] In our summary of the evidence set forth above in section I.A. of this opinion, we have interpreted the record fully in accordance with the district court's findings and conclusions.

[5] Rule 801(d)(2)(E) provides:

(d) Statements That Are Not Hearsay. A statement that meets the following conditions is not hearsay:

(2) An Opposing Party's Statement. The statement is offered against an opposing party and:

(E) was made by the party's coconspirator during and in furtherance of the conspiracy.

The statement must be considered but does not by itself establish ... the existence of the conspiracy or participation in it under (E).

Fed.R.Evid. 801(d)(2)(E).

[6] The district court stated:

In this case, if I did have my discretion, I would impose a harsh sentence. It would be a sentence at the bottom of the guidelines. It would be a 30-year sentence, which I find would be appropriate and would meet the goals of 3553(a), because you certainly deserve, I believe, every day of the sentence within the guidelines, but, as I said, at the bottom of the guidelines. I impose, because I am required to, a sentence of life.

J.A. 528.

[7] The government's timely filing of a 21 U.S.C. § 851 information put Graham on notice of its intent to prove at sentencing three prior felony drug offense convictions, rendering Graham eligible for an enhanced sentence under 21 U.S.C. § 841.

[8] *See, e.g., United States v. Mason,* 628 F.3d 123, 133-34 (4th Cir.2010):

Finally, Mason contends that the fact of his prior convictions needed to be proved to a jury beyond a reasonable doubt. Because that fact was not found by a jury beyond a reasonable doubt, he asserts, the use of the prior convictions to enhance his sentence violated his Sixth Amendment rights. Mason candidly acknowledges that this argument is presented for purposes of preserving the issue for the Supreme Court and that, under the present jurisprudence of *Almendarez — Torres v. United States,* 523 U.S. 224, 118 S.Ct. 1219, 140 L.Ed.2d 350 (1998), such an argument cannot be sustained. We agree. Moreover, we note that since *Almendarez — Torres,* the Supreme Court has repeatedly affirmed the exception, as have we. *See Shepard v. United States,* 544 U.S. 13, 25-26 & n. 5, 125 S.Ct. 1254, 161 L.Ed.2d 205 (2005); *Apprendi v. New Jersey,* 530 U.S. 466, 488-90, 120 S.Ct. 2348, 147 L.Ed.2d 435 (2000); *United States v. Cheek,* 415 F.3d 349, 354 (4th Cir.2005).

714 F.3d 197 (2013)

UNITED STATES of America, Plaintiff-Appellee,

v.

Donald CONE, Defendant-Appellant, and

Chun-Hui Zhao; Richard J. Nelson, Cisco Systems., Inc., Parties-In-Interest.

United States of America, Plaintiff-Appellee,

v.

Chun-Yu Zhao, a/k/a Jessica Smith, a/k/a Chun Yu Zhao, Defendant-Appellant.

Nos. 11-4888, 11-4934.

United States Court of Appeals, Fourth Circuit.

Argued: October 26, 2012.

Decided: April 15, 2013.

US v. Cone, 714 F. 3d 197 (4th Cir. 2013)

p.200 ARGUED: Lisa Hertzer Schertler, Schertler & Onorato, LLP, Washington, D.C., for Appellants. Lindsay Androski Kelly, Office of the United States Attorney, Alexandria, Virginia, for Appellee. ON BRIEF: Justin A. Torres, Gibson, Dunn & Crutcher, LLP, Washington, D.C.; Geremy C. Kamens, Office of the Federal Public Defender, Alexandria, Virginia, for Appellant Donald Cone. Neil H. MacBride, United States Attorney, Jay V. Prabhu, Assistant United States Attorney, Office of the United States Attorney, Alexandria, Virginia, for Appellee.

Before AGEE, WYNN, and FLOYD, Circuit Judges.

Affirmed in part, vacated in part, and remanded by published opinion. Judge AGEE wrote the majority opinion, in which Judge FLOYD joined. Judge WYNN wrote an opinion concurring in part and dissenting in part.

p.201 OPINION

AGEE, Circuit Judge:

Donald Cone and Chun-Yu Zhao were convicted of various charges under an indictment arising out of a scheme to import and resell counterfeit pieces of computer networking equipment, some of which bore the trademark of Cisco Systems, Inc. ("Cisco"). On appeal, they challenge certain evidentiary rulings made at their joint trial and whether some of the criminal acts alleged can support a conviction for criminal counterfeiting under 18 U.S.C. § 2320. Additionally, Cone challenges whether sufficient evidence supports his conviction for conspiracy and Zhao challenges the sufficiency of the evidence on certain substantive counts upon which she was convicted. For the reasons set forth below, we reject Zhao and Cone's attack on the district court's evidentiary rulings and Cone's argument that his conviction was not supported by sufficient evidence. However, the government's theory of prosecution based on a "material alteration" theory of counterfeiting trademarks is not cognizable under the criminal counterfeiting statute based on the facts of this case. Further, the government's evidence on Count 10 was insufficient as a matter of law to sustain Zhao's conviction. We therefore vacate the judgment of the district court on certain counts of conviction, affirm the judgment of the district court in all other respects, and remand for resentencing.

I.

Background and Material Proceedings Below

A. The Factual Background

Zhao, then a recent immigrant from the People's Republic of China ("China"), was recently divorced from Junling Yang, an indicted co-conspirator in this case who remains at large, when she married Cone.[1] While living and working in the United States, Zhao and Cone formed JDC Networking, Inc. ("JDC"), a licensed distributor of products made by and for Cisco. JDC conducted frequent business with a company known as Han Tong Technology ("Han Tong"), a Hong Kong-based business alleged to be operated by members of Zhao's family. As a Cisco "registered partner," JDC was contractually prohibited from purchasing Cisco products for resale from outside of the United States, yet records introduced at trial reflect that, from 2004 through 2010, JDC imported over 200 shipments from Han Tong and companies associated with Han Tong in China containing both genuine Cisco products and fake imitations.

In 2005 and 2006, while Zhao and Cone were living together in Rockville, Maryland, U.S. Customs and Border Patrol ("CBP") agents began intercepting and seizing shipments of highly sophisticated counterfeit computer networking products sent from Han Tong to "Lucy" and "Donald," at addresses in Rockville, Maryland. The investigation went cold, however, when the shipper of the counterfeit goods began declaring a very low value for the goods shipped and using variant spellings of the destination address, thus foiling CBP's tracking techniques.

From 2004 to 2010, JDC marketed computer equipment bearing a Cisco mark to consumers and resale outlets. Several of JDC's customers, however, were dissatisfied with some of the products they purchased from JDC. E-mails introduced at trial from JDC customers revealed that some clients believed they had been sold counterfeit or fake products.

p.202 Zhao filed income tax returns indicating that JDC was struggling and that she was only earning a small salary. In fact, JDC was thriving and producing significant income for her. JDC records reflect that it was purchasing Cisco products (or purported Cisco products) in China for resale at considerably below the expected market price for such products and then reselling the products with a high markup.

As JDC thrived, however, Zhao's marriage to Cone deteriorated. In late 2007, Cone moved out of the couple's home, and Zhao moved into a condominium with her ex-husband Yang. Upset with Zhao over their faltering marriage, Cone sent Zhao a series of e-mails demanding his share of JDC proceeds. In one, he stated "I won't let my life get ruined. I will make sure everyone knows the truth about everything. IRS, DOJ, Customs, Immigration, et cetera.... I have proof of everything." (J.A. 1651.) In another e-mail, Cone indicated that "other companies were returning products to us because they were counterfeit." (J.A. 1653.) Zhao and Cone later divorced.

In 2010, CBP was notified that four pieces of "highly sophisticated, very expensive" counterfeit networking technology ("routers") bearing Cisco marks were seized upon entry from China into the United States, bound for a Parcel Plus retail storefront in Northern Virginia and with an estimated value of thousands of dollars per piece of equipment. CBP agents compared the attributes of this shipment with those in the 2005-06 investigation and concluded that the 2010 shipments were similar and likely related to the same counterfeiting scheme.

Coordinating its efforts with DHL (a shipping company) and Immigration and Customs Enforcement ("ICE"), CBP intercepted the next package sent from China to the address in Virginia. When CBP and ICE agents opened the package, they discovered over 300 labels bearing a Cisco mark that agents suspected to be counterfeit. CBP and ICE forwarded the package to an ICE facility in Washington, where agents coordinated a controlled delivery of the package to the Parcel Plus retail storefront. Agents observed Zhao retrieving the package and followed her to her home. CBP and ICE agents then executed an anticipatory search warrant at the residence.

In the course of searching Zhao's home, federal agents discovered, in addition to the shipment of suspected counterfeit Cisco labels that led them to Zhao, unlabeled transceivers that matched the labels found in the shipment, labeled transceivers, business and financial records, torn labels and label backing, and instructions on how to convert Cisco equipment into different models.

As investigators were executing the search warrant at Zhao's home, a FedEx delivery driver attempted to deliver two packages to her. The delivery driver revealed to the agents executing the warrant that Zhao maintained a storage unit across the street. Although Zhao initially denied the existence of the storage unit (and later provided law enforcement agents with a false unit number and a false entry code to the storage facility), agents were eventually able to gain access. Agents found quantities of boxes filled with equipment bearing a Cisco mark filling "at least half" the storage unit. (J.A. 614.)

After being arrested, Zhao was interviewed by ICE Agent Julie Hilario for approximately 45 minutes. Although Zhao initially denied any involvement with counterfeiting (and even denied receiving the package that was the subject of the controlled delivery), she eventually admitted that she sold "fake" Cisco products to p.203 make a greater profit than with a legitimate product.

As ICE and CBP pursued the investigation, agents interviewed Cone by telephone (he had left the United States and was living in China). Cone admitted that JDC received and resold both real and counterfeit Cisco products from Han Tong (which he described as a "fake" company). (Vol. V J.A. 1990.) With respect to "authentic" Cisco products, Cone informed agents that he and Zhao altered authentic Cisco products obtained from China and sold them to clients, representing that they were higher end products than they actually were. Cone was later arrested when he returned from China in December 2010.

B. District Court Proceedings

Cone and Zhao were both indicted by a grand jury (along with Yang and Chun-Yan Zhao, defendant Zhao's sister) in 2010 in the United States District Court for the Eastern District of Virginia on one count of conspiracy in violation of 18 U.S.C. § 371, with three objects: (1) trafficking in counterfeit goods and labels; (2)

importation and sale of improperly declared goods; and (3) wire fraud (Count 1); and three counts of wire fraud in violation of 18 U.S.C. § 1343 (Counts 16-17, 23).[2]

As relevant to that part of the Count 1 conspiracy charge alleging trafficking in counterfeit goods and labels, the government presented at trial three theories underlying the alleged objects of that conspiracy. First, that some of the products seized from Zhao's residence or sold to end-users were represented to be Cisco products but in fact were "pure" counterfeits (i.e., the products were never made by or for Cisco). Second, other products (acquired from legitimate Cisco resellers in the United States and abroad) were indeed made by or for Cisco, but were converted by Zhao and Cone into a different type of Cisco product and represented to buyers as the original of that item (the "material alteration" theory). Third, other products acquired from China that were originally made by or for Cisco but were relabeled and mislabeled by Zhao and Cone with new serial numbers to deceive customers into believing that the products were eligible for Cisco warranty and services in the United States, when, in fact, such products were not so eligible.[3]

In support of Count 8 (counterfeiting) the government introduced testimony from its expert, Cisco engineer Michael Heidecker, who testified that the four routers seized by CBP in 2010 each contained a unique Cisco "MAC address," but that the MAC addresses found on the routers were p.204 actually assigned to other Cisco products. Thus, Heidecker was able to establish that the four routers were not actually manufactured by Cisco. Furthermore, they were shipped in packaging that, although displaying a Cisco mark, was, according to Heidecker, counterfeit. Defense expert Richard Krebs, however, opined that the routers were manufactured by or for Cisco, because the MAC addresses for each were actually consistent with the MAC addresses assigned to Cisco and because counterfeiters could not have created the switches due to the prohibitive cost.

Craig Grant, a manager at Vology, a Cisco equipment reseller, testified regarding Cisco-marked transceivers that are the subject of Count 10 (counterfeiting). Grant testified that Vology purchased ten Cisco transceivers from JDC, but returned them to JDC because Vology was unable to verify the transceivers' authenticity. Specifically, Grant stated that the Vology inventory team noted that the transceivers were not packaged in standard Cisco packaging. The exact items JDC sold to Vology were not available at trial (having been returned to JDC and resold). Heidecker told the jury that Cisco does not sell unlabeled transceivers and packages them in a certain specific manner not followed in the case of Vology.

During the government's case in chief, Zhao lodged timely objections to several items of evidence. First, Zhao moved to exclude statements made by Cone which she argued incriminated her and therefore required exclusion under *Bruton v. United States,* 391 U.S. 123, 88 S.Ct. 1620, 20 L.Ed.2d 476 (1968) (holding that admission of a statement inculpating a co-defendant in a joint trial violates the co-defendant's rights under the Confrontation Clause). The district court denied the motion, although it did require the government to excise any mention of Zhao's name when Cone's statements were presented to the jury and replace her name with a gender-neutral noun. The court reasoned that "there are multiple individuals involved [in the conspiracy]" and therefore, Zhao's rights under the Confrontation Clause would not be prejudiced by use of a gender-neutral substitute. Accordingly, when

Cone's statements were read into evidence, "another individual" was substituted for Zhao's name.

Zhao also filed a motion in limine to exclude e-mails from JDC customers characterizing certain Cisco products purchased from JDC as "fake" or "counterfeit." She argued that the e-mails constituted inadmissible hearsay. The district court denied the motion on the grounds that the e-mails were to be admitted not for their truth, but rather, as evidence that Zhao and Cone were on notice that the products JDC sold were not authentic. After the e-mails were introduced at trial, Zhao requested a limiting instruction from the court that the e-mail statements were not to be considered by the jury for their truth. The court replied as follows but did not give the requested limiting instruction.

> I believe I've said that multiple times to the jury. I'll say it again. The jury is going to decide what is counterfeit or not. They make up the definition. The e-mails say what they say, and the jury will have to decide if they're believable or not. That's their job.

(J.A. 1673-74.)

At the close of the evidence, Cone moved pursuant to Federal Rule of Criminal Procedure 29 for judgment of acquittal on the charges against him. The district court granted the motion with respect to the wire fraud counts (16-17, 23), granted it in part to the extent that Count 1 (conspiracy) related to wire fraud, but denied the motion for the remainder of Count 1 p.205 charging a counterfeiting and importation of misdeclared goods conspiracy.

Zhao similarly filed a Rule 29 motion as to all of the wire fraud counts, as well as a motion to dismiss Counts 1 through 6 (the conspiracy charge and the improperly declared goods charges). The district court granted the motion with respect to the wire fraud charges and denied it in all other respects.[4]

In denying the Rule 29 motions on the remaining counts, the district court briefly discussed Cone and Zhao's argument that the government's "material alteration" theory exceeded the scope of the federal criminal counterfeiting statute. The court reasoned:

> the issue of whether the marks appear on the serial numbers and the various labels including barcodes are encompassed in the definition [of spurious mark] because labels are being applied to Cisco products to give the end[]user an impression that the goods that were of a higher grade than when they originated from the factory....

> The statute has to be interpreted in the light of the meaning, and the presentation of an item as new when it has been altered under a mark is likely to cause confusion and lead the consumer to believe the product was made by the genuine owner of the trademark in the fashion in which it left the factory even though it was not.

(J.A. 2344.)

The jury returned a mixed verdict, convicting Cone of conspiracy (the only remaining charge against him), convicting Zhao of conspiracy, all four improperly declared goods charges, all four trafficking in counterfeit goods and labels charges, two counts of money laundering, one count of making a monetary transaction with criminally derived proceeds, and three charges not relevant to this appeal. Zhao was acquitted on one false statement to law enforcement charge and one money laundering charge.

The district court imposed a thirty-month sentence upon Cone and a sixty-month sentence upon Zhao. Both noted timely appeals and we have jurisdiction pursuant to 28 U.S.C. § 1291.

II.

A. Counterfeiting Charges

1. "Material Alteration" as Counterfeiting a Mark Under 18 U.S.C. § 2320

Zhao and Cone raise a pointed challenge on appeal to their convictions under Count 1 (conspiracy to counterfeit) and by Zhao on the underlying substantive counterfeit charge in Count 9. Their argument is that material alteration, one of the government's theories of criminal liability under the federal criminal counterfeiting statute, 18 U.S.C. § 2320 (2011, West 2012)[5] is not a crime as defined by that statute.

We emphasize at the outset of our analysis, as we noted earlier, that the government alleged several distinct activities as separate acts of counterfeiting (and similarly types of conspiracies to counterfeit). In Count 7, for example, the government alleged that the Cisco labels found in Zhao's home and storage locker were completely fake, that is, never manufactured by or for Cisco resulting in "pure" counterfeit labels. As we explain below, that act p.206 of counterfeiting is plainly cognizable as violating § 2320. What Zhao and Cone challenge is the government's theory of prosecution for "material alteration" counterfeiting. That is, the government contends § 2320 counterfeiting of marks includes transactions in which a good bears a genuine and authentic mark, but is altered to be a different product than the one to which the mark was originally fixed. Cone and Zhao not surprisingly disagree with the government and argue that "the [criminal counterfeiting] statute eliminates from the universe of 'counterfeit marks' any mark that was placed on a good by its authorized manufacturer and confirms that goods that have been marked in that fashion are not 'counterfeit.'" Opening Br. of Appellants at 25.[6] As the statute is written, we conclude that Cone and Zhao have the better argument.

Where, as here, we are asked to interpret the language of a criminal statute, we are guided by the relevant canons of construction.

> "The starting point for any issue of statutory interpretation ... is the language of the statute itself." "In that regard, we must first determine whether the language at issue has a plain and unambiguous meaning with regard to the particular dispute ... and our inquiry must cease if the statutory language is unambiguous and the statutory scheme is coherent and consistent." "We determine the 'plainness or ambiguity of statutory language ... by reference to the language itself, the specific context in which that language is used, and the broader context of the statute as a whole.'"

Ignacio v. United States, 674 F.3d 252, 254 (4th Cir.2012) (citations omitted). In interpreting a criminal statute, we must be certain that its language clearly identifies the act which is rendered a trespass of the law. "[I]n the interest of providing fair warning of what the law intends to do if a certain line is passed, we will construe ... criminal statute[s] strictly and avoid interpretations not clearly warranted by the text." *WEC Carolina Energy Solutions LLC v. Miller,* 687 F.3d 199, 204 (4th Cir.2012) (internal quotation marks and citations omitted).

We look first, therefore, to the plain language of the statute. Under § 2320(a) the act made a crime is defined, in relevant part, as "intentionally traffic[king] or attempt[ing] to traffic in goods or services and knowingly us[ing] a counterfeit mark on or in connection with such goods or services" and "intentionally traffic[king] or attempt[ing] to traffic in labels,... boxes, containers, ... or packaging of any type or nature, knowing that a counterfeit mark has been applied thereto, the use of which is likely to cause confusion, to cause mistake, or to deceive." Put succinctly, to obtain a conviction under § 2320(a), the government was required to prove that Cone and Zhao "(1) trafficked or attempted to traffic in goods or services; (2) did so intentionally; (3) used a counterfeit mark on or in connection with such goods and services; and (4) knew the mark was counterfeit." *United States v. Lam,* 677 F.3d 190, 197-98 (4th Cir.2012) (quoting *United States v. Habegger,* 370 F.3d 441, 444 (4th Cir.2004)) (internal quotation marks omitted).

The key issue regarding the material alteration theory is what constitutes a "counterfeit mark" under the statute. A "counterfeit mark" is defined in p.207 § 2320(e)(1) as "a spurious mark." That is, a trademark used in connection with goods or labels, "that is identical with, or substantially indistinguishable from, a [registered] mark ... the use of which is likely to cause confusion, to cause mistake, or to deceive." *Id.* § 2320(e)(1)(A)(i). The statute provides no further definition of what constitutes a "spurious" mark; however, we recently relied on the definition provided by *Black's Law Dictionary* to define the term as "deceptively suggesting an erroneous origin; fake." *Lam,* 677 F.3d at 202 (quoting *Black's Law Dictionary,* 1533 (9th ed. 2009) (brackets omitted)).

In order to subject a defendant to criminal liability under § 2320, the government must therefore show that the defendant knowingly trafficked in goods or labels bearing a *spurious* mark. The requirement of a spurious mark is problematic for the government's "material alteration" theory that Cone and Zhao obtained a genuine Cisco product bearing a genuine mark; modified the product, but not the mark; then sold the modified product bearing the genuine mark. The government's contention is that the modification (the material alteration) of the Cisco product to something other than the exact device Cisco originally manufactured transforms not only the genuine product into a counterfeit product but also the genuine mark into a spurious mark. We do not find that § 2320 can be properly read as the government contends without rewriting the statute: an act the Congress, but not this court, can undertake.

The concept put forth by the government, that product modification can transform an unaltered genuine mark into a spurious one, does not appear in the plain language of § 2320, and is not "clearly warranted by the text" of that statute. *See Crandon v. United States,* 494 U.S. 152, 160, 110 S.Ct. 997, 108 L.Ed.2d 132 (1990). Indeed, Congress could have explicitly criminalized in § 2320 the practice of modifying genuine goods that bear a genuine, unaltered mark, but it did not do so. Rather, Congress made criminal the practice of "using a *counterfeit* mark" in connection with "traffic[king] of goods or services," and "trafficking" in containers and labels with knowledge "that a counterfeit [i.e., fake] mark has been applied thereto." *See* 18 U.S.C. § 2320(a). Congress has simply not criminalized in § 2320 the acts that the defendants are accused of committing under the material alteration theory in this case: altering a product with a genuine mark but not altering the mark.

While we are confident that the text of § 2320(a), standing on its own, does not support the government's material alteration counterfeit theory, our conclusion is significantly bolstered by the existence of the so-called "authorized use" exception found at § 2320(e)(1)(B). That subsection provides that:

> such term ["counterfeit mark"] does not include any mark or designation used in connection with goods or services ... of which the manufacturer or producer was, at the time of the manufacture or production in question, authorized to use the mark or designation for the type of goods or services so manufactured or produced, by the holder of the right to use such mark or designation.

18 U.S.C. § 2320(e)(1)(B).

This subsection makes clear that Congress did not intend to criminalize, in the statute it adopted, the use of genuine and unaltered marks on goods that were manufactured by or for the mark holder. As one commentator has explained, "[a] plain reading and literal interpretation of [the authorized use exclusion] excludes from [the statute's] definition of counterfeit goods those products which have their p.208 genesis in authorized production." Brian J. Kearney, Note, *The Trademark Counterfeiting Act of 1984: A Sensible Legislative Response to the Ills of Commercial Counterfeiting*, 14 Fordham Urb. L.J. 115, 142 n.154 (1986).

Our conclusion rejecting the government's material alteration theory is further underscored by the novelty of the material alteration approach as posited by the government. Indeed, the government cites no case, and we can identify none, where a criminal conviction under the counterfeiting statute has been sustained for the type of "material alteration" conduct alleged here. The cases the government does cite are significantly distinguishable.

The government asks us to follow *United States v. Milstein,* 401 F.3d 53 (2d Cir.2005), a case in which the Second Circuit affirmed the counterfeiting conviction of a defendant accused of purchasing drugs manufactured for foreign markets, repackaging them for sale in the United States without the consent of the manufacturers, and representing to the public that the drugs were FDA approved when they were not. *Id.* at 62. *Milstein,* however, is inapposite because the defendant "obscured the fact that the drugs had been repackaged, and, with his package design, fraudulently conveyed that the foreign drugs had been manufactured as FDA-approved products." *Id.* at 63. The *Milstein* defendant manufactured counterfeit packaging "designed to resemble ... authentic packaging." *Id.* In this case, by contrast, the Cisco mark was and remained a genuine mark. *Milstein,* which involved an actual spurious, i.e., fake mark, provides no support for the proposition that genuine marks can lose their genuine character by virtue of alteration only of the good to which the mark was correctly attached when that good was produced.

The government also relies on *United States v. Farmer,* 370 F.3d 435 (4th Cir. 2004), for the proposition that because after-market alteration removes a measure of quality assurance from the original manufacturer, marketing the altered products as genuine is prohibited under § 2320(a). In *Farmer,* this court upheld the counterfeiting conviction of a defendant accused of "purchasing blank t-shirts and sweatshirts manufactured for companies like Nike and Hilfiger, placing those companies' logos on the shirts without authorization, and then passing along the shirts to the public as brand-name goods." *Id.* at 436. The defendant in that case purchased authentic shirts from authorized manufacturers, and then affixed the unauthorized brand-name mark to represent the good as being brand-name marked.

Farmer, however, is materially different from the case at bar. Critically, the mark that was affixed to the goods at issue was not genuine, being fraudulently affixed by the defendant himself, thereby rendering the mark a "spurious mark." In contrast to the marks genuinely affixed by Cisco to the goods before being acquired by JDC, the placement of the marks in *Farmer* was never authorized by the manufacturer at any time during the manufacture of the goods in question. *See id.* at 440 ("[i]t was Farmer rather than the trademark holder who oversaw the construction of the shirts."). *Farmer* therefore does not support the government's material alteration theory of counterfeiting that genuine marks lose their genuine character solely from product alteration.

Additionally, the government argues that we should adopt, for purposes of the criminal counterfeiting statute, certain trademark applications under the Lanham Act, 15 U.S.C. § 1051 *et seq.,* the statute p.209 governing civil trademark disputes.[7] The government argues that cases under the Lanham Act support the proposition that a genuine mark becomes counterfeit when the product is altered in a way not approved by the original manufacturer. *See Intel Corp. v. Terabyte Int'l, Inc.,* 6 F.3d 614, 620 (9th Cir.1993) ("by the time the Intel markings had been scraped off or printed over, Intel did make the chip but it was no longer the source of the *product* which was being sold.").

As the government correctly notes, we recently stated that, "[b]ecause of the similarity between [the Lanham Act] definition [of counterfeit] and the § 2320 definition of 'counterfeit mark,' we find Lanham Act civil counterfeiting cases helpful to our analysis of criminal counterfeiting cases brought under § 2320(a)." *Lam,* 677 F.3d at 199 n. 8.[8] Helpful though these cases may be, it does not necessarily follow that we import every aspect of civil counterfeiting jurisprudence into the criminal counterfeiting context. Indeed, as we recognized in *Lam,* "the standard may 'be construed more narrowly in a criminal context than in a civil context.'" *Id.* (quoting *United States v. Guerra,* 293 F.3d 1279, 1288 (11th Cir.2002)).

As a number of courts have recognized, § 2320 must be construed more narrowly than the civil law definition of counterfeit acts contained in the Lanham Act. *See United States v. Giles,* 213 F.3d 1247, 1250 (10th Cir.2000) ("[W]e must construe [the criminal counterfeiting statute more] narrowly [than the Lanham Act]."); *United States v. Hanafy,* 302 F.3d 485, 489 (5th Cir.2002) ("Lanham Act precedent is of little value in a § 2320 case because the Lanham Act deals with civil liability.") (citing *Giles,* 213 F.3d at 1250); *Guerra,* 293 F.3d at 1288 ("The 'identical or substantially indistinguishable' standard [in the counterfeit context] is to be construed more narrowly in a criminal context than in a civil context.").

Indeed, even the civil cases to have found Lanham Act liability based on material alteration have acknowledged that such a theory of liability strays from a strict statutory definition of "counterfeit." *See Rolex Watch USA*, 158 F.3d at 826 ("The original ... labels are not themselves 'counterfeits' in the literal sense.") (quoting *Westinghouse Elec. Corp. v. Gen. Circuit Breaker & Elec. Supply Inc.*, 106 F.3d 894, 899 (9th Cir.1997)). In doing so, those courts relied upon a rationale critical in the civil trademark infringement context: "the important test is whether the practice of the defendant is likely to cause confusion, *not whether the defendant duplicated the plaintiff's mark.*" *Westinghouse*, 106 F.3d at 899 (citing *Continental Motors Corp. v. Continental Aviation Corp.*, 375 F.2d 857, 861 (5th Cir.1967) ("Confusion, or the likelihood of confusion... is the real test of trademark infringement.")). In applying a criminal statute, p.210 however, we do not have the freedom to disregard an element of the crime: that the defendant did, in fact, employ a counterfeit mark. *See* 18 U.S.C. § 2320(a).

Moreover, Zhao and Cone have correctly identified a second material difference between the Lanham Act and § 2320: the Lanham Act lacks an authorized use exception. Thus, our conclusion that under the § 2320(e)(1)(B) authorized use exception Congress did not intend to criminalize the use of genuine marks used on goods that were manufactured by or for the mark holder distinguishes this case from those civil cases cited by the government. No court, in interpreting the Lanham Act to allow material alteration liability, has even had the opportunity to opine on whether an authorized use exception (such as that codified at § 2320(e)(1)(B)), would preclude such liability in the civil context of trademark infringement.

For all the reasons just discussed, we find that criminal liability under § 2320 cannot be based on the alteration of a product to which a genuine mark was affixed and the mark itself has not been altered. The Congress can certainly rewrite that statute to cover a material alteration theory, but the statute as now written does not do so.

We must now apply our holding on the scope of § 2320 to the facts of this case and determine what, if any relief is available to Cone and Zhao. Based on our review of the indictment, and the evidence adduced at trial, we first conclude that Zhao's conviction under Count 9, a substantive counterfeiting charge against her, must be vacated.

Count 9 charged Zhao with, "on June 16, 2010, ... intentionally traffic[king] in... a counterfeit Cisco unit." (J.A. 74.) The evidence adduced at trial showed that in 2010 the U.S. Fish and Wildlife Service ("FWS") purchased an "enhanced" Cisco switch from Memorydealers.com, which in turn had purchased the switch from JDC. When the switch arrived, officials at FWS became aware that they had received a "standard" model, rather than the enhanced version they had purchased. The MAC address[9] of the switch was assigned to a standard model, while the serial number on the chassis was assigned to an "enhanced" switch. Thus, the government adduced evidence that a standard model switch was purchased from Cisco, which had a proper and genuine Cisco mark affixed to it. Zhao, through JDC, later upgraded the product to resemble an enhanced model switch, and sold it to Memorydealers.com as an enhanced switch. The mark, however, was genuinely affixed to the good when manufactured by or for Cisco and the mark itself was never altered. That conduct is not, we conclude, criminal counterfeiting because the unaltered genuine mark is not a spurious mark, a required element of the crime under § 2320. Thus, Zhao's conviction for Count 9 cannot stand and must be vacated.

Cone and Zhao argue that their convictions for conspiracy under Count 1 must also be vacated. This is so, they contend, because the jury's verdict was a general one and it is impossible to determine whether the conspiracy convictions rested upon the invalid material alteration theory as opposed to the valid theory of improperly declared goods also charged under Count 1.

p.211 Zhao and Cone are correct to state that "reversal is required when a case is submitted to a jury on two or more alternate theories, one of which is legally (as opposed to factually) inadequate, the jury returns a general verdict, and it is impossible to discern the basis on which the jury actually rested its verdict." *United States v. Moye,* 454 F.3d 390, 400 n. 10 (4th Cir.2006) (en banc) (citing *Yates v. United States,* 354 U.S. 298, 311-12, 77 S.Ct. 1064, 1 L.Ed.2d 1356 (1957)).

In this case, however, the jury returned a special, not a general verdict as to Count 1. Indeed, the jury was given and utilized, without objection, a special verdict form. On that verdict form the jury found Cone and Zhao guilty of conspiracy to traffic in counterfeit goods and labels, *and* separately found them guilty of conspiracy to import and sell improperly declared goods. We recently addressed a similar situation in *United States v. Lawson,* 677 F.3d 629 (4th Cir.2012). In that case, after determining that certain juror misconduct rendered a conviction for conspiracy to violate the Animal Welfare Act invalid, we determined whether the defendants' convictions for a single count of conspiracy could nevertheless be affirmed where the indictment alleged a multi-object conspiracy in the conjunctive. We reasoned that

> in contrast to the general verdict rendered in *Yates,* the verdict in the present case reveals that the jury had two separate bases for convicting the ... defendants of the conspiracy charges. Although the indictment alleged both objects in a single count, the jury's verdict forms with respect to each of the... defendants listed separate guilty verdicts for "Count 1 — Conspiracy (Animal Welfare Act: June 18, 2008 through April 18, 2009)" and "Count 1 — Conspiracy (illegal gambling business: May 2007 through April 18, 2009)." Thus, we are not confronted with a situation in which we are uncertain whether a jury's verdict was solely attributable to an underlying conviction which we have set aside on legal grounds. *Cf. Yates,* 354 U.S. at 311-12, 77 S.Ct. 1064. Accordingly, the conspiracy convictions for the... defendants are supported by a valid and independent legal basis that is apparent from the record, and we therefore affirm those convictions.

Id. at 655. Likewise, the conspiracy convictions in this case are supported by a "valid and independent legal basis," *id.,* because of the separate verdict form, and we accordingly affirm the conspiracy convictions of both Cone and Zhao.[10]

Our review of the presentence investigation report ("PSR") and the record of the sentencing hearing, however, plainly demonstrates that the district court relied on the counterfeiting object of the conspiracy convictions in fashioning the sentences for Cone and Zhao. Because the district court may have utilized what we have now determined would be noncriminal acts under the material alteration theory of counterfeiting conspiracy in arriving at the sentences, we must also vacate the sentences of both Cone and Zhao and remand for resentencing.

B. Sufficiency of the Evidence

i. Counts 8 and 10 against Zhao

In addition to her challenges to Count 1 and Count 9, Zhao also argues that Counts 8 and 10 should be vacated because the p.212 evidence was insufficient, as a matter of law, to prove that she engaged in § 2320 criminal counterfeiting. We agree with Zhao as to Count 10, but not Count 8.

"A defendant challenging the sufficiency of the evidence faces a heavy burden." *United States v. Foster,* 507 F.3d 233, 245 (4th Cir.2007). In a sufficiency of the evidence challenge, we view the evidence on appeal in the light most favorable to the government in determining whether any rational trier of fact could find the essential elements of the crime beyond a reasonable doubt. *United States v. Collins,* 412 F.3d 515, 519 (4th Cir.2005). We review both direct and circumstantial evidence, and accord the government all reasonable inferences from the facts shown to those sought to be established. *United States v. Harvey,* 532 F.3d 326, 333 (4th Cir.2008). We do not review the credibility of the witnesses and assume that the jury resolved all contradictions in the testimony in favor of the government. *United States v. Kelly,* 510 F.3d 433, 440 (4th Cir.2007). We will uphold the jury's verdict if substantial evidence supports it and will reverse only in those rare cases of clear failure by the prosecution. *Foster,* 507 F.3d at 244-45.

With respect to the products at issue in Count 8, four routers seized by CBP in 2010, prosecution expert and Cisco engineer Michael Heidecker opined that the MAC addresses found on the routers matched physically different products manufactured by Cisco. (*See* J.A. 1052-54.) Furthermore, Heidecker opined that the labels applied to the routers were nongenuine. Thus, Heidecker was able to conclude that the routers at issue were not manufactured by or for Cisco and could not be genuinely marked. While Zhao's expert reached a different conclusion, this conflicting evidence was for a jury to weigh. The jury had ample evidence on which to conclude that Zhao was guilty as charged in Count 8.

On Count 10, however, the Government did not carry its burden to show that Zhao engaged in the criminal counterfeiting of marks. Count 10 charges that JDC sold counterfeit Cisco transceivers to Vology, a reseller of network equipment. The government alleges that these transceivers were not made by or for Cisco, but identifies only two pieces of evidence in support of this claim.

First, the government points to testimony from Craig Grant, a Vology manager, who testified that, upon receipt of the transceivers, he was able to tell from his experience that the *packaging* was not genuine. Congress, however, has chosen to bar the government from bringing "a criminal cause of action ... for the repackaging of genuine goods or services not intended to deceive or confuse." 18 U.S.C. § 2320(g). Evidence of repackaging, therefore, is not enough standing alone to prove the goods within that packaging bear a counterfeit mark. The government must come forth with some other evidence that the mark on the actual good is spurious.

To that end, the government's second piece of evidence for Count 10 is that law enforcement seized "additional versions" of the transceivers at issue in Count 10 from Zhao's residence, which Heidecker opined were not made by or for Cisco. However, the Vology transceivers were not introduced at trial, having been returned to JDC and resold. Whatever marks the "additional versions" of the transceivers may (or may not) have borne does not prove the status of the marks on the long gone Vology transceivers. No evidence at trial established what marks were on the Vology transceivers; a burden which fell to the government to bear.

p.213 Heidecker opined only that the packaging of the transceivers found at Zhao's home was inauthentic. (J.A. 1024.) He gave no testimony about the marks on the Vology transceivers.

Since the "repackaging" evidence cannot, under the plain terms of § 2320(g), sustain a conviction under the statute for a counterfeit mark on the goods in the package, and as the government adduced no evidence on the marks on the Vology transceivers, the government failed to prove a violation of § 2320 for the acts charged in Count 10. The evidence was insufficient as a matter of law to sustain Zhao's conviction.

Accordingly, while we find that the government adduced sufficient competent evidence to sustain Zhao's conviction under Count 8, we find that the government did not do so with respect to Count 10, and vacate that count of conviction.

ii. Sufficiency of the Evidence Against Cone

Cone individually challenges his conviction for conspiracy to import misdeclared goods (Count 1) by arguing that the evidence was insufficient and the district court accordingly erred in denying his Rule 29 motion for judgment of acquittal. We review the district court's denial of a Rule 29 motion de novo. *Lam,* 677 F.3d at 198. The legal standard for a sufficiency of the evidence claim is set forth above at p. 22.

In Count 1, the government alleged Cone participated in a conspiracy to violate 18 U.S.C. § 545, which criminalizes "fraudulently or knowingly import[ing] or bring[ing] into the United States, any merchandise contrary to law." *Id.* Cone was alleged to have conspired to import goods without taking reasonable care to ensure that the goods were properly declared, in violation of 19 U.S.C. § 1484(a).

> To establish a conspiracy under § 371, the Government must prove "(1) an agreement between two or more people to commit a crime, and (2) an overt act in furtherance of the conspiracy." *United States v. Ellis,* 121 F.3d 908, 922 (4th Cir.1997). "The existence of a tacit or mutual understanding between conspirators is sufficient evidence of a conspiratorial agreement." *Id.* (internal quotation marks omitted). Proof of the agreement may be established by circumstantial evidence. *Burgos,* 94 F.3d at 857. It is no defense to a conspiracy charge that one's role in the conspiracy is minor. *See United States v. Laughman,* 618 F.2d 1067, 1076 (4th Cir.1980) ("Once the existence of a conspiracy is established, evidence establishing beyond a reasonable doubt a connection of a defendant with the conspiracy, even though the connection is slight, is sufficient to convict him with knowing participation in the conspiracy." (internal quotation marks omitted)).

United States v. Kingrea, 573 F.3d 186, 195 (4th Cir.2009).

With the standards of review in mind, we have little difficulty concluding that the government adduced sufficient evidence from which the jury could properly convict Cone under Count 1. Cone was unquestionably an active participant in the scheme to sell counterfeit, mislabeled, or undeclared Cisco products. The evidence adduced at trial showed that Cone confessed to law enforcement that he was a member of that conspiracy. He acknowledged in his confession that he was aware that Han Tong employees were misdeclaring goods to avoid detection by CBP. Furthermore, when he became estranged from Zhao, he sent e-mails to her demanding his share of proceeds from the conspiracy.

p.214 This is not a case, as Cone suggests, where an innocent spouse is implicated solely by his marriage to a conspirator. *See United States v. Dozie*, 27 F.3d 95, 98 (4th Cir.1994) (vacating conspiracy conviction against co-defendant's spouse who "was never tied to the conspiracy by any of the other persons involved"). Rather, the record contains ample evidence from which the jury could have properly concluded that Cone was an active participant in the conspiracy. We accordingly see no merit to Cone's contention that there was insufficient evidence to support his conviction on Count 1.

iii. Money Laundering

Zhao further contends her convictions for money laundering must be vacated on the basis that the government's incorrect "material alteration" theory may have formed the basis for her money laundering convictions.[11] We agree.

Zhao was convicted of two counts (Count 27 and 28) of "concealment" money laundering. *See* 18 U.S.C. § 1956(a)(2)(B)(i); (a)(1)(B)(i). She was also convicted of Count 29, engaging in a monetary transaction with criminally derived proceeds in violation of 18 U.S.C. § 1957(a) (collectively "the money laundering convictions").

To obtain a conviction under § 1956(a)(1)(B)(i) (Count 28), the government had the burden to prove four elements:

> (1) an actual or attempted financial transaction; (2) *involving the proceeds of a specified unlawful activity;* (3) knowledge that the transaction involves the proceeds of some unlawful activity; and (4) knowledge that the transaction was designed in whole or in part to conceal the nature, location, source, ownership, or control of the proceeds of a specified unlawful activity.

United States v. Richardson, 658 F.3d 333, 337-38 (3d Cir.2011) (internal quotation marks, brackets, and ellipsis omitted) (emphasis added). The elements of a violation of § 1956(a)(2)(B)(i), as charged in Count 27, are similar, with the additional requirement that the government prove an international transaction involving the proceeds of unlawful activity. *See Cuellar v. United States*, 553 U.S. 550, 553, 128 S.Ct. 1994, 170 L.Ed.2d 942 (2008). Finally, as to Count 29, § 1957(a) similarly requires the government to allege (and prove) a transaction involving funds derived from a specified unlawful activity. *See United States v. Cherry*, 330 F.3d 658, 668 (4th Cir.2003).

In this case, the district court instructed the jury properly as to each offense, observing that, to sustain a conviction under Counts 27, 28, and 29, the government must prove beyond a reasonable doubt that Zhao engaged in monetary transactions that, *inter alia*, involved funds derived from the offense of trafficking in counterfeit goods or labels. (*See* J.A. 2430-37.)

As the Supreme Court has explained,

> Jurors are not generally equipped to determine whether a particular theory of conviction submitted to them is contrary to law-whether, for example, the action in question ... fails to come within the statutory definition of the crime. When, therefore, jurors have been left the option of relying upon a legally inadequate theory, there is no reason to think that their own intelligence and expertise will save them from that error.

p.215 *Griffin v. United States,* 502 U.S. 46, 59, 112 S.Ct. 466, 116 L.Ed.2d 371 (1991). Accordingly, "a verdict [is required] to be set aside in cases where the verdict is supportable on one ground, but not another, and it is impossible to tell which ground the jury selected." *Yates v. United States,* 354 U.S. 298, 312, 77 S.Ct. 1064, 1 L.Ed.2d 1356 (1957). *But see United States v. Hastings,* 134 F.3d 235, 242 (4th Cir.1998) ("If [the] evidence is such that the jury must have convicted the defendant on the legally adequate ground in addition to or instead of the legally inadequate ground, the conviction may be affirmed.").

While it is no doubt correct that the government adduced ample evidence tending to show that Zhao committed "pure" counterfeiting, neither the indictment, nor the evidence adduced at trial allow us to conclude that the jury necessarily convicted Zhao of money laundering based on the government's "pure" counterfeiting theory.

Agent Hilario testified, in support of Count 27, that JDC and Han Tong engaged in a series of wire transfers in June, 2010, designed to conceal the funds' source. The source of these funds was derived largely, if not entirely, from sales, by JDC, of goods purchased from Han Tong. The evidence of these sales, introduced in the form of Zhao's ledgers, simply does not allow us to determine whether the sales were of "pure" counterfeits, or of "materially altered" goods, which, as discussed *supra,* do not constitute counterfeit marks for the purposes of § 2320.

The government's evidence in support of Count 28 consisted solely of testimony from ICE agent Raymond Orzel, a certified fraud examiner. Orzel testified that Zhao purchased a home in 2005 with funds derived from JDC, Han Tong, and related entities. (J.A. 1520-21.) In 2008, Zhao sold the home to an individual named Dan Lou, (an indicted co-conspirator) who rented the home out. However, the government also put forth evidence that the funds Lou used to purchase the home were drawn from Zhao's accounts, and that rent checks made out to Lou were deposited in accounts controlled by Zhao. Once again, the funds at issue were derived from JDC sales of Han Tong goods. We cannot say with any certainty that the jury only considered sales of "pure" counterfeits when convicting Zhao of Count 28.

In support of Count 29, the government adduced evidence that Zhao directed that two $50,000 checks be drawn from JDC accounts to Marcie Wu, an affiliate of Han Tong. The checks represented, in large part, the proceeds of the sales of certain Cisco switches from JDC to Network Hardware Resale ("NHR"). (*See* J.A. 1964-66.) These switches were obtained from Han Tong, and the evidence adduced at trial demonstrated that the switches were manufactured by or for Cisco, and then later altered by Zhao. Because this conduct is not criminal counterfeiting, the jury's verdict of conviction on Count 29 rests on an unsound legal basis.

Thus, the money laundering convictions must be vacated. Count 29 appears to clearly rest on an improper legal basis, and because we cannot say with certainty whether Zhao's convictions on Counts 27 and 28 are based on "pure" counterfeiting, those convictions must be vacated as well.

iv.

Our distinguished colleague in dissent concurs in the foregoing analysis concerning the "material alteration" theory, but suggests that Zhao's conviction on Count 8, a substantive counterfeit charge, should also be vacated. We respect the views of the dissent but do not agree.

The general thesis of the dissent is that, having held that the government's "material p.216 alteration" theory of counterfeiting is without legal basis, we should have vacated Count 8 owing to improper closing argument by the government. However, at oral argument, when asked by the panel what specific counts of the indictment would be affected by our rejection of the "material alteration" theory, counsel for Zhao responded that such a holding would "most clearly" affect substantive Count 9 and Count 1 (conspiracy). Audio Recording of Oral Argument at 1:30. Counsel, of course, could have argued that vacatur of Count 8 was appropriate as well, but chose to focus entirely on Counts 9 and 1. This is not surprising, as the record is conclusively clear that at no point in the district court or this court, did Zhao raise a claim of error under the material alteration theory as to Count 8. This concept arises *sua sponte* for the first time in the dissent.

The representations of Zhao's counsel to the panel at oral argument were entirely consistent with the arguments set forth in her briefs before this Court and the district court. Indeed, although Zhao contends that Count 8 should be vacated, her argument rests entirely on a sufficiency of the evidence basis, which we rejected in section II(A)(ii), above. (*See* Opening Br. of Appellant at 36-38).

The dissent acknowledges as much, but argues that because the government argued a legally incorrect theory to the jury in closing argument, deference to the jury's verdict is not warranted. To reach this result, the dissent analyzes the government's remarks under *United States v. Lighty*, 616 F.3d 321, 361 (4th Cir.2010). Again, a construct appearing for the first time now, *sua sponte*, and which, under our precedent, has long since been waived by Zhao.

Zhao never made the argument that is the lynchpin of the dissenting opinion: that the prosecutor's closing comments, in and of themselves, constitute reversible error. *See Post* at 228 ("A prosecutor's comments *constitute reversible error* if...."). Zhao's briefs on appeal are utterly devoid of any reference to the *Lighty* factors because Zhao does not make a standalone challenge to the government's statements in closing argument. Rather, to the extent that Zhao discusses the prosecutor's closing arguments at all, it is for purposes of the harmless error analysis under Count 1 only.

Zhao's failure to raise this independent assignment of error, either in brief or at oral argument, regarding the government's comments to the jury is fatal to the position advocated by the dissent. *See United States v. Strieper*, 666 F.3d 288, 293 n. 4

(4th Cir.2012) (Floyd, J.) (citing *Edwards v. City of Goldsboro,* 178 F.3d 231, 241 n. 6 (4th Cir.1999)) ("This argument does not appear in [Appellant's] brief, and as such, it is waived."). Granting relief on a basis not advanced by Zhao (and arguably disclaimed at oral argument) is plainly improper for all the reasons the rule of waiver is in force. The government has not had any opportunity to respond to the claim of error advanced by the dissent, nor was it ever placed before the district court for consideration.[12] *See Cavallo v. Star Enterprise,* 100 F.3d 1150, 1152 n. 2 (4th Cir.1995) ("The [Appellants'] omission of the issue from their initial brief denied [Appellee] an opportunity to respond, so considering it p.217 now would be unfair to the appellee and would risk an improvident or ill-advised opinion on the legal issues raised.") (quoting *Hunt v. Nuth,* 57 F.3d 1327, 1338 (4th Cir.1995) (internal quotation marks omitted)).

Additionally, we do not consider the issue of the prosecutor's comments on appeal as they were not preserved by Zhao in the district court. We have long held that the failure to object to a prosecutor's statements made during closing arguments constitutes a waiver of that claim of error. *See United States v. Sawyer,* 347 F.2d 372, 374 (4th Cir.1965) ("[I]f defense counsel does not object during the course of the Government's closing argument he may be said to have waived the point.").

The mere fact that Zhao challenged, as a general matter, the "material alteration" theory presented by the government is insufficient to preserve the claim of error formulated by the dissent. This is so because, as explained above, the dissent's theory is based on a stand alone prosecutorial misstatement claim. Indeed, the dissent acknowledges that the theory presented by the prosecution during closing statements "was even broader than the material alteration theory advanced in the government's' proposed jury instruction." *Post,* at 224. Accordingly, Zhao's pre-trial challenge to the government's proposed jury instructions would not preserve a claim of error as to the prosecutor's unchallenged remarks in closing.

It is for that reason that the dissent's reliance on *Lacy v. CSX Transportation, Inc.,* 205 W.Va. 630, 520 S.E.2d 418 (1999), is unavailing. In that case, as the dissent observes, the court found that an unsuccessful motion in limine was sufficient to preserve a challenge to later closing remarks by the opposing party so long as the argument fell within the scope of the court's earlier ruling on the motion. *Id.* at 427. In this case, though, as the dissent acknowledges, Zhao succeeded in her motion in limine. It makes sense, therefore, that if the prosecutor's closing remarks ran afoul of the district court's prior ruling, Zhao should have timely objected to alert and afford the court an opportunity to correct any error.[13]

The dissent does correctly observe that Zhao's brief on appeal mentions the government's closing arguments. But even a superficial reading of the briefs demonstrates that, far from raising an independent challenge to the prosecutorial statements, Zhao was merely describing what the prosecutor said, or, in one case, noting that any error in the government's theory of prosecution was non-harmless. *See* Appellants' Br. at 39-40. The dissenting opinion goes several steps farther, raising, for the first time, a stand alone challenge to the prosecutorial remarks.

For those reasons, the cases cited by the dissent in favor of its position are, in our view, inapposite. Judge Floyd's dissent in *Lam,* for example, cited twice in the dissenting opinion, observed that "the district court has sustained repeated objections to the [prosecutorial] statement." *Lam,* 677 F.3d at 212. Here, the district court did not sustain any objection because none was made. Thus the government was deprived of the opportunity to make the case that its argument was proper, and the p.218 district court was deprived of the opportunity to correct any purported error. *See United States v. Hargrove,* 625 F.3d 170, 184 (4th Cir.2010) ("Hargrove failed to object... at the time, thus denying the district court the opportunity to consider Hargrove's argument and correct the purported error.").

Accordingly, while we respect the views of the dissent, we do not agree that the claim of error on which the dissent would vacate Count 8 was properly preserved by the Zhao or raised in this court or the district court.

C. Confrontation Clause

Zhao argues that the district court committed reversible error by admitting Cone's out-of-court statements to Agent Hilario into evidence against her. The core of Zhao's claim is that substituting "another individual" for her name made it obvious to the jury that she was the person referenced and thereby violated her Sixth Amendment Confrontation Clause rights.

In *Bruton,* the Supreme Court held: "[A] defendant is deprived of his rights under the Confrontation Clause when his nontestifying codefendant's confession naming him as a participant in the crime is introduced at their joint trial, even if the jury is instructed to consider that confession only against the codefendant." *Richardson v. Marsh,* 481 U.S. 200, 201-02, 107 S.Ct. 1702, 95 L.Ed.2d 176 (1987) (citing *Bruton v. United States,* 391 U.S. 123, 135-36, 88 S.Ct. 1620, 20 L.Ed.2d 476 (1968)). This court reviews de novo an evidentiary ruling implicating the Confrontation Clause. *United States v. Palacios,* 677 F.3d 234, 242 (4th Cir.2012).

In *United States v. Akinkoye,* 185 F.3d 192 (4th Cir.1999), we summarized Supreme Court precedent as holding that "if a redacted confession of a non-testifying codefendant given to the jury (by testimony or in writing) shows signs of alteration such that it is clear that a particular defendant is implicated, the Sixth Amendment has been violated." *Id.* at 197. We further noted that the Supreme Court's precedent did not directly address the situation in that case — "namely, whether redacted statements that refer to the existence of another party who may be the defendant through symbols or neutral pronouns are admissible," and observed that "[t]he Supreme Court has strongly implied that such statements do not offend the Sixth Amendment." *Id.* at 198.

In *Akinkoye,* the co-defendant's confessions were retyped so as to replace "the defendants' respective names with the phrase 'another person' or 'another individual.'" *Id.* The retyped versions were read to the jury, and the jury "neither saw nor heard anything in the confessions that directly pointed to the other defendant." *Id.* Accordingly, we held that the defendants' Confrontation Clause rights were not violated by the redacted statements because use of the neutral phrase "another person" did not facially implicate the defendant. *Id.*

Applying the holding of *Akinkoye* to the case at bar, we readily conclude that substitution of Zhao's name with "another individual" was sufficient to protect Zhao's rights under the Confrontation Clause. The phrase "another individual" does not facially implicate Zhao. Only by reference to other evidence could the jury have arrived at the conclusion that Zhao was the actual subject of Cone's out of court statement. In such circumstances, we have concluded that the Confrontation Clause is not offended, and thus Zhao's claim lacks merit.

D. Introduction of Customer E-Mails

Cone and Zhao last argue that the district court erred in admitting certain e-mails p.219 from JDC customers complaining that JDC products were "counterfeit" and "fake." Although the district court determined that the e-mails were introduced for a non-hearsay purpose, i.e., to show that Zhao and Cone were on notice that they were selling counterfeit goods, the court declined to give a limiting jury instruction to that effect and instead stated that "the e-mails say what they say and the jury will have to decide if they're believable or not. That's their job." (J.A. 1673-74.) Cone and Zhao contend that the court's actions constitute reversible error.

This Court reviews evidentiary rulings for an abuse of discretion and "will only overturn an evidentiary ruling that is 'arbitrary and irrational.'" *United States v. Cloud,* 680 F.3d 396, 401 (4th Cir.2012) (quoting *United States v. Cole,* 631 F.3d 146, 153 (4th Cir.2011)). Evidentiary rulings are subject to harmless error review, such that any error is harmless where we may say "with fair assurance, after pondering all that happened without stripping the erroneous action from the whole, that the judgment was not substantially swayed by the error." *United States v. Johnson,* 617 F.3d 286, 292 (4th Cir.2010).

At the outset, we believe that the district court properly admitted the e-mails for the non-hearsay purpose of showing that Cone and Zhao were on notice as to the counterfeit nature of the goods they sold. *See* 5-801 *Weinstein's Federal Evidence* § 801.11[5][a] (Out of court statement not hearsay when "offered not for [its] truth but to prove the extent of ... a recipient's notice of certain conditions.").

We are troubled, however, by the court's response to counsel's request for a limiting instruction. Indeed, while the e-mails may have been properly admitted for a reason other than their truth, the district court stated just the opposite — that the jury will have to decide "if they're believable or not." In other words, the court erroneously instructed the jury to consider statements contained in the e-mails for the truth of the matter asserted.

The government contends, nonetheless, that the court's statement was not error because the statements in the e-mails could have been admitted under a hearsay exception, namely the business records exception to the hearsay rule, found at Federal Rule of Evidence 803(6). We are not persuaded.

Rule 803(6)(B) allows for the introduction of records that are "kept in the course of a regularly conducted activity of a business." For a record to be admitted as a business record, it must be "(1) made by a regularly conducted business activity, (2) kept in the 'regular course' of that business, (3) 'the regular practice of that business to make the memorandum,' (4) and made by a person with knowledge or from information transmitted by a person with knowledge." *Clark v. City of L.A.,* 650 F.2d 1033, 1036-37 (9th Cir.1981) (quoting Fed. R.Evid. 803(6)).

E-mails, however, present unique problems of recent vintage in the context of the business records exception. As one district court recently explained:

Courts are in disagreement on whether emails can and should fall under the business records hearsay exception. The business records exception assumes that records containing information necessary in the regular running of a business will be accurate and reliable. *See Certain Underwriters at Lloyd's London v. Sinkovich*, 232 F.3d 200, 204-05 (4th Cir.2000). Email, however, is typically a more casual form of communication than other records usually kept in the course of business, such that it may not be appropriate to assume the same degree of accuracy and reliability. As p.220 email is more commonly used to communicate business matters both internally and externally, however, more formal paper records are becoming more unusual.

It's My Party, Inc. v. Live Nation, Inc., No. JFM-09-547, 2012 WL 3655470 at *5 (D.Md. Aug. 23, 2012) (unpublished). The district court in that case excluded the e-mails on the basis that the "more specificity is required regarding the party's recordkeeping practices to show a particular email in fact constitutes a reliable business record." *Id.*

While properly authenticated e-mails may be admitted into evidence under the business records exception, it would be insufficient to survive a hearsay challenge simply to say that since a business keeps and receives e-mails, then *ergo* all those e-mails are business records falling within the ambit of Rule 803(6)(B). "An e-mail created within a business entity does not, for that reason alone, satisfy the business records exception of the hearsay rule." *Morisseau v. DLA Piper*, 532 F.Supp.2d 595, 621 n. 163 (S.D.N.Y.2008). The district court's observation that the e-mails were kept as a "regular operation of the business" is simply insufficient on that basis alone to establish a foundation for admission under Rule 803(6)(B). Accordingly, because the e-mails could not, on this record, be admitted under an exception to the hearsay rule, the district court's failure to give the limiting jury instruction was error.

We conclude, however, that the any error in the court's jury instructions or failure to give an e-mail limiting instruction was harmless. In the context of a twelve-day jury trial in which the government adduced overwhelming evidence of Cone and Zhao's guilt, we cannot conclude that Cone or Zhao were prejudiced by this single error concerning a minute portion of the total evidence against them. As discussed above, the government further introduced physical evidence in the form of counterfeit labels seized from Zhao's home and storage unit. The government also introduced routers seized by CBP, that Heidecker (a Cisco engineer) identified as counterfeit goods.

The government also introduced evidence from Cone and Zhao themselves. In addition to Zhao's confession at the time of her arrest (that she sold "fake" goods in order to make more money), the government introduced incriminating e-mails from Cone to Zhao wherein Cone threatened to reveal the counterfeiting scheme to law enforcement if he did not receive his share of proceeds from the criminal venture. In sum, the government's evidence against Cone and Zhao was more than ample, and we conclude that the district court's jury instruction with respect to certain e-mails from JDC customers was harmless beyond a reasonable doubt.

III.

Because we conclude that the government's material alteration theory of counterfeiting is not encompassed within the § 2320 statutory crime of counterfeiting marks, we vacate Zhao's conviction on Count 9. In light of this holding, we must vacate Zhao's convictions for Counts 27, 28, and 29. We further hold that the evidence was insufficient as a matter of law to sustain Zhao's conviction on Count 10 and also vacate that conviction. We also vacate the sentences of both Cone and Zhao and remand for resentencing in light of our holding today. We affirm the judgment of the district court in all other respects.

AFFIRMED IN PART, VACATED IN PART, AND REMANDED.

p.221 WYNN, Circuit Judge, concurring in part and dissenting in part:

I concur with the majority's conclusion that the government's "material alteration" theory is not supported by the plain language of the criminal trademark counterfeiting statute, 18 U.S.C. § 2320. As a result, I also agree that this Court must reverse Defendant Zhao's conviction on Count 9, which involved a networking switch that the government concedes was manufactured by or for Cisco, and her three money laundering convictions, which were tainted by the material alteration theory. I further concur that the government adduced insufficient evidence to convict Defendant on Count 10 because the government's evidence at most showed that Defendant Zhao repackaged a genuine Cisco product.

However, I cannot join the majority in affirming Defendant Zhao's conviction on Count 8, the remaining trademark counterfeiting conviction potentially tainted by the errant material alteration theory. The government and Defendant Zhao presented conflicting evidence regarding whether the products at issue in Count 8 were manufactured by or for Cisco. In affirming that conviction, the majority considered the evidence adduced at trial in the light most favorable to the government. But such deference is unwarranted because the government argued its legally incorrect alteration theory to the jury and the district court did not provide an adequate instruction to the jury regarding when a product that has its genesis in authorized production can serve as the basis for a trademark counterfeiting conviction. Because we do not know whether the jury properly credited the government's evidence or improperly credited the government's errant legal theory, this conviction also should be reversed.

In addition, I write separately to clarify that in resentencing Defendants Zhao and Cone on their conspiracy convictions the district court should not take into account evidence that Defendants altered one other type of Cisco product, which, like the switch at issue in Count 9, the government concedes was manufactured by or for Cisco. I further emphasize that this panel was not tasked with answering, and thus did not decide, whether the repackaging of an altered, but genuine product in a non-deceptive manner violates Section 2320 as a matter of law.

I.

Before explaining why Defendant Zhao's conviction on Count 8 should be reversed, it is first useful to provide some additional background on Section 2320, the government's material alteration theory, and the district court's instruction on the definition of "counterfeit" under Section 2320.

A.

Section 2320(a) makes it unlawful for anyone to "intentionally traffic[] or attempt[] to traffic in goods or services and knowingly use[] a counterfeit mark on or in connection with such goods or services...." The statute defines a "counterfeit mark" as a "spurious mark that is used in connection with trafficking in any goods [or] services ... that is identical with, or substantially indistinguishable from, a [registered] mark ... the use of which is likely to cause confusion, to cause mistake, or to deceive...." § 2320(e)(1)(A).

Section 2320 includes two provisions that deal with when the resale of an authentic or genuine good can serve as the basis for a trademark counterfeiting conviction: (1) an "authorized use" exception and (2) a "repackaging," or "gray goods," exception. As the majority correctly notes, the authorized use exception excludes from the p.222 definition of "counterfeit mark ... any mark ... used in connection with goods or services ... of which the manufacturer or producer was, at the time of the manufacture or production in question, authorized to use the mark" by the trademark holder. § 2320(f)(1). The second exception bars the government from bringing "a criminal cause of action ... for the repackaging of genuine goods or services not intended to deceive or confuse." § 2320(g). This applies to "gray goods," which are "goods that are authentic and that have been obtained from overseas and imported into the United States." *United States v. Hanafy*, 302 F.3d 485, 488 (5th Cir.2002).

In *Hanafy*, the Fifth Circuit approvingly quoted its district court regarding the relationship between the two exceptions:

> A common denominator of these two exceptions is that the goods to which the mark is attached were manufactured by, or with the permission of, the owner of the mark — that is, the goods themselves are genuine. That Congress saw fit to exempt "gray market" goods and [authorized users] from criminal liability lends support to an interpretation that § 2320 was intended to prevent trafficking in goods that were similar to but different than the goods normally associated with the mark.

Id. (quoting *United States v. Hanafy*, 124 F.Supp.2d 1016, 1023-24 (N.D.Tex.2000)). Thus, the two exceptions jointly indicate that Congress intended generally to exclude from liability under Section 2320 sellers of goods that have their genesis in authorized production. Such an exclusion makes sense — one of the primary rationales for protecting trademarks is that they assist consumers in identifying the source of goods. *OBX-Stock, Inc. v. Bicast, Inc.*, 558 F.3d 334, 339 (4th Cir.2009) ("Trademark law, at a general level ... enabl[es] consumers readily to recognize products and their source and to prevent consumer confusion between products and between sources of products."). Therefore, it would make little sense for Congress to hold a reseller criminally liable for attaching a mark to a product if the mark correctly identifies the source of the product, and does so in a nondeceptive manner.

B.

Prior to trial, the government submitted a lengthy proposed instruction regarding the definition of "counterfeit," which provided, in pertinent part:

[A] defendant cannot purchase genuine products manufactured by or for the registered owner, materially alter those products, and then offer the products for resale as genuine or unaltered products.... Such modifications convert a genuine product into a "counterfeit" product.

J.A. 160. This language was drawn almost entirely from federal district and appellate court decisions in civil actions brought under the trademark counterfeiting provisions in the Lanham Act.

Defendants Zhao and Cone filed a motion in limine seeking an advance ruling on the government's proposed instruction, arguing that the "material alteration" theory was not supported by the plain language of Section 2320 and had never been applied in criminal cases brought under the statute. Defendants requested that the "material alteration" language not be used, and instead proposed that the instruction state, in pertinent part:

A mark is counterfeit if, and only if ... the challenged mark is spurious, which means false or inauthentic....

Because a counterfeit mark must be false or inauthentic, the definition of counterfeit mark does not include any mark used in connection with goods or applied to labels or packaging if, at the p.223 time of manufacture of the goods or production of the labels or packaging, the manufacturer or producer was authorized to use the mark for the type of goods or packaging being made....

The use of an inauthentic mark in the repackaging of genuine goods does not constitute use of a counterfeit mark if it is done without any intent to deceive or confuse as to the authenticity of the goods.

J.A. 132-33. Thus, Defendants' proposed instruction on the definition of "counterfeit" included both the authorized use and repackaging exceptions.

Noting that a material alteration instruction had not previously been given in a criminal trademark counterfeiting case, the district court expressly rejected the government's proposed instruction. Instead, the court elected to use the model instruction set out in 3 Hon. Leonard B. Sand et al., Modern Federal Jury Instructions, Instruction 54A-4. In comments on the model instruction, Sand states that "[f]urther instruction may be required when the prosecution involves goods other than the typical knock-off containing a false label." Sand, *supra*.

Emphasizing that the parties agreed that this was not the typical "knock-off" case, at the conclusion of evidence, the government renewed its request that the court instruct the jury on the material alteration theory. J.A. 2350. Although the government and Defendants agreed that the Sand instruction was inadequate, they could not agree on how it should be modified. Rather than choosing between the government's and Defendants' proposed instructions, the district court modified the Sand instruction by quoting Section 2320's authorized use exception, instructing the jury, in pertinent part:

A counterfeit mark is one that is identical to or substantially indistinguishable from a registered trademark, the use of which is likely to confuse, cause mistake or deceive the public in general....

I instruct you that as a matter of law, the counterfeiting statute in this case... does not criminalize any mark or designation used in ... connection with goods or services ... if the manufacturer or producer was at the time of the manufacture or production in question authorized to use the mark or designation for the type of goods or services so manufactured or produced.

J.A. 2424, 2427-28. Although it quoted the authorized use exception, the district court did not quote or paraphrase the repackaging exception.

II.

With this background in mind, turn with me to Defendant Zhao's conviction on Count 8, which covered four network routers bearing Cisco trademarks sold by JDC.

Defendant Zhao contends her conviction must be reversed because the evidence adduced by the government would only be sufficient to support a trademark counterfeiting conviction under the government's errant material alteration theory, which she contends that the government impermissibly argued to the jury. In particular, Defendants note that after the district court had instructed the jury and despite the fact that the court had rejected the government's proposed material alteration instruction, the government still argued in its closing that altering and then reselling a genuine good constitutes illegal trademark counterfeiting for purposes of Section 2320.

For example, during its initial closing argument, the government argued that Defendants engaged in

p.224 illegal upgrading.... If they were just buying things in China and selling in the U.S., they could have done that. But they were upgrading them. They were changing them. They were making them new products.

J.A. 2481. Similarly, during its rebuttal argument, the government defined "counterfeit" as follows:

[Defendants] were taking one product and converting it to another. They were making a product in Chantilly, Virginia. That's not a Cisco product any more. Cisco has standards for its products, quality control. What they did is they took software ... to change what those products did. They don't know what they actually could do with that software. Maybe it turned it into something unusable. They took that risk and then they packaged it up with a Cisco logo on it and sold it. That's counterfeit. Those are not Cisco products. Once you make that alteration, it's something different.

J.A. 2546. This argument, referred to hereafter as the "alteration theory," was even broader than the material alteration theory advanced in the government's proposed jury instruction because it suggested that any alteration, no matter how minor, to a product manufactured by or for a mark holder and sold under the original mark violates Section 2320.

A.

Before reaching Defendant Zhao's argument that these remarks constitute reversible error, it is first necessary to address whether this issue is properly before us on appeal. Although not disputing the merits of this argument, the majority maintains that Defendant Zhao waived any argument regarding the government's remarks because she did not timely object below and failed to adequately raise the issue on appeal. I disagree.

At the outset, it is worth noting that the general rule is that the government "waives waiver" by failing to argue on appeal that the defendant did not preserve a given argument. *See, e.g., United States v. Quiroz,* 22 F.3d 489, 491 (2d Cir.1994); *United States v. Beckham,* 968 F.2d 47, 54 n. 5 (D.C.Cir.1991). Here, the government did not argue in its briefs or at oral argument that Defendants waived any challenge to the government's closing remarks by failing to contemporaneously object. Appropriately, the same degree of scrutiny for preserving issues on appeal should be applied to the government as the majority seeks to apply to Defendants. If done so here, then we must conclude that the government waived the waiver argument advanced by the majority.

Nonetheless, regarding whether Defendant Zhao preserved this issue below, the majority correctly notes that the general rule is that "counsel for the defense cannot... remain silent, interpose no objections, and after a verdict has been returned seize for the first time on the point that the comments to the jury were improper and prejudicial." *United States v. Socony-Vacuum Oil Co.,* 310 U.S. 150, 238-39, 60 S.Ct. 811, 84 L.Ed. 1129 (1940). An appellate court, however, may consider improper remarks by counsel in "exceptional circumstances" such as if the remarks were "obvious, or if they otherwise seriously affect the fairness, integrity, or public reputation of the judicial proceedings." *Id.* at 239, 60 S.Ct. 811 (quotation omitted). This Court has indicated that exceptional circumstances exist when comments by the prosecution cause "actual prejudice" to a defendant. *United States v. Elmore,* 423 F.2d 775, 780 (4th Cir.1970).

Additionally, this Court has held that motions in limine "preserve issues that p.225 they raise without any need for renewed objections at trial, just so long as the movant has clearly identified the ruling sought and the court has ruled upon it." *United States v. Williams,* 81 F.3d 1321, 1325 (4th Cir.1996). For example, we have held that when a party moves in limine to exclude evidence, the party need not renew its objection when evidence within the scope of the motion is introduced at trial. *United States v. Ruhe,* 191 F.3d 376, 383 n. 4 (4th Cir.1999); *see also* Fed.R.Evid. 103(b). Although we have not previously had occasion to apply this rule in the context of motions in limine to preclude the jury from considering a particular legal theory, the same logic applies: Because counsel is restricted to arguing the law in accordance with the principles espoused in the court's instructions, *United States v. Trujillo,* 714 F.2d 102, 106 (11th Cir.1983), if a party moves in limine to bar the jury from considering a particular legal theory and the court rules on that motion, it need not renew its objection when the opposing party argues the legal theory at trial, *see Lacy v. CSX Transp. Inc.,* 205 W.Va. 630, 520 S.E.2d 418, 427 (1999) ("[T]o preserve error with respect to closing arguments by an opponent, a party need not contemporaneously object where the party previously objected to the trial court's in limine ruling permitting such argument, and the argument subsequently pursued by the opponent reasonably falls within the scope afforded by the court's ruling.").

The majority contends that *Lacy* is inapposite because in that case the party's motion in limine to preclude the jury from considering a particular legal theory was *unsuccessful*, whereas here Defendant Zhao's motion in limine seeking to exclude the material alteration theory was *successful*. But it is paradoxical to argue that a party need not contemporaneously object when an opposing party argues a legal theory that was explicitly accepted by the court but must contemporaneously object — at risk of waiver — when an opposing party argues a legal theory that was explicitly rejected by the court. Such a holding would unfairly reward parties that violate a court's in limine rulings and is contrary to the policy underlying motions in limine, which is to allow a party to exclude from consideration of the jury a prejudicial matter without drawing attention to the matter by having to contemporaneously object to it. *See* Jeffrey F. Ghent, Annotation, *Modern Status of Rules as to Use of Motion In Limine or Similar Preliminary Motion to Secure Exclusion of Prejudicial Evidence or Reference to Prejudicial Matters,* 63 A.L.R.3d 311 § 1(a) (1975).

Here, Defendants did not contemporaneously object to the government's statements during its closing. At the same time, Defendants did not "remain silent" or "interpose no objections" to the government's efforts to get the material alteration theory before the jury. Rather, Defendants repeatedly sought to bar the jury from considering the theory: on two occasions Defendants successfully asked the district court to exclude the government's proposed material alteration instruction; after the government completed its case in chief, Defendant Cone sought to have the trademarking counterfeiting counts dismissed on grounds that the alteration theory is not supported by the plain language of Section 2320; during their closing argument, Defendants sought to diminish the prejudice from the prosecution's statements by arguing that the alteration theory espoused in the government's closing was contrary to the court's instruction; and, after the jury rendered its verdict, Defendants sought to have their convictions set aside on grounds that the government impermissibly argued the alteration theory to the jury. Because the government's p.226 alteration theory was within the scope of Defendants' motion in limine, which the court definitively ruled upon prior to closing arguments, it was unnecessary for Defendants to renew their objection to the theory when, contrary to the court's ruling, the government argued the errant theory to the jury.

The majority maintains that Defendant Zhao's post-verdict motion for acquittal does not argue that the government's closing remarks regarding the material alteration theory were improper and a basis for acquittal. To the contrary, as her brief notes, Appellant's R. Br. at 12, Defendant's Zhao's motion explicitly incorporated all arguments made by Defendant Cone regarding the criminal trademark counterfeiting counts in his motion for acquittal. J.A. 2698. And Defendant Cone's motion for acquittal states:

> The government argued, and the jury considered, the theory that Mr. Cone agreed to materially alter Cisco-manufactured equipment, and that this activity constitutes a violation of § 2320. Because the jury considered an impermissible basis for liability under § 2320 and the Court is unable to determine the basis

for the jury's guilty verdict, Mr. Cone must be granted a new trial pursuant to Rule 33.

J.A. 2748-49. Thus, Defendant Zhao did argue in her motion for post-verdict relief that the government's closing remarks constituted a basis for her acquittal.

But even if Defendants' repeated efforts to preclude the jury from considering the alteration theory were inadequate to preserve the issue, I believe that this is one of those few cases where exceptional circumstances warrant consideration of the government's remarks on appeal. The government's remarks caused Defendant Zhao actual prejudice because they misled the jury into believing that *any* alteration of a good manufactured by or for a mark holder would be sufficient, by itself, to support a conviction under Section 2320. Yet the majority correctly holds that modifying a genuine good, without modifying the mark on the good, does not run afoul of Section 2320. *Ante* at 207. Thus, at a minimum, Defendants were prejudiced by the government's comments because they may have led the jury to incorrectly believe that Defendants could be convicted for modifying a genuine product even if the jury found that Defendants did not alter the mark on the product. *See United States v. Mitchell,* 1 F.3d 235, 241 (4th Cir.1993) (holding that prosecution's appeal to improper legal theory during closing argument constitutes prejudicial plain error); *United States v. Chong Lam,* 677 F.3d 190, 212 (4th Cir.2012) (Floyd, J., dissenting) (stating that a "misstate[ment of] the relevant legal standard" by the prosecution during closing arguments is prejudicial).

The majority also contends that Defendant Zhao failed to adequately raise this issue on appeal, arguing that Zhao has never "raise[d] a claim of error under the material alteration theory as to Count 8" and never argued that the government's closing remarks constitute reversible error. *Ante,* at 215-16. But the majority's position is belied by Defendant Zhao's briefs.

First, after arguing at length that this Court should reject the government's material alteration theory by adopting a narrower interpretation of Section 2320, Defendant Zhao's brief states:

> If the Court adopts the narrower interpretation of Section 2320 that the plain language and the rule of lenity require, two conclusions follow. First, the government failed to prove that Zhao trafficked in counterfeit goods (as charged in Counts 8, 9, and 10). Those convictions p.227 therefore must be reversed, as must the associated money laundering convictions (Counts 27, 28, and 29).

Appellants' Br. at 36. Moreover, during her discussion of Count 8 in particular, Defendant Zhao asserts that the government's "evidence showed, at most ... that a serial number programmed inside a genuine Cisco product was *altered* by someone." Appellants' Br. at 37 (emphasis added). Thus, Defendant Zhao repeatedly contended that the government's errant alteration theory improperly tainted her conviction on Count 8.[*]

Second, Defendant Zhao's opening and reply briefs also repeatedly take issue with the government's closing remarks, referencing them on at least five occasions. Appellants' Br. at 20-21, 28, 32-33, 39-41; Appellants' R. Br. at 18-19. In particular, Defendant Zhao summarizes her argument as follows:

The district court rejected the government's unprecedented [material alteration] instruction. But the court permitted the government to argue a version of the legal theory to the jury, and it denied appellants' motions challenging the theory and the verdicts that resulted. The district court's instructional ruling and its acceptance of the jury's verdicts cannot be reconciled.

Appellants' Br. at 20-21. Therefore, Defendant Zhao unambiguously argued in her opening brief that the government's closing remarks regarding the alteration theory improperly tainted the jury's verdict.

In sum, Defendant Zhao repeatedly argued below and on appeal that both the material alteration theory and the broader alteration theory tainted her trademark counterfeiting convictions because the government improperly argued the theories to the jury. Indeed, Defendant Zhao's challenges to the alteration theory were and are the central issue in this case. The government has repeatedly had the opportunity to respond to Defendant Zhao's objections on the issue, and in each case has argued that the theory is correct and thus her convictions must be affirmed. The majority correctly rejects the government's arguments and vacates or modifies all of Defendant Zhao's convictions that were potentially impacted by the government's errant alteration theory, except for Count 8. Given the centrality of this issue to Defendant's prosecution and her repeated efforts below and on appeal to raise the issue — regardless of how inartful they may have been — whether the government's argument of the alteration theory during its closing constitutes a basis for vacating Defendant Zhao's conviction on Count 8 is properly before us on appeal.

B.

Having established that the government's comments during closing argument are properly before this Court, turn with me now to the issue of whether these comments warrant reversing Defendant Zhao's conviction on Count 8.

It is axiomatic that questions of law are the province of the court, whereas issues of fact are reserved for the jury. *Georgia* p.228 *v. Brailsford,* 3 U.S. 1, 4, 3 Dall. 1, 1 L.Ed. 483 (1794). When underlying legal principles are "undisputed," counsel is entitled to comment on the law to the jury. *United States v. Sawyer,* 443 F.2d 712, 714 (D.C.Cir.1971). But if "counsel's view of the applicable law differs from that of the court, then ... the jury should hear a single statement of law, from the court and not from counsel." *Id.* Consequently, "[i]n arguing the law to the jury, counsel is confined to principles that will later be incorporated and charged to the jury." *Trujillo,* 714 F.2d at 106.

Although noting that a prosecutor's instruction on the law during closing arguments lacks "the same force as an instruction from the court," the Supreme Court has recognized that "prosecutorial misrepresentations may ... have a decisive effect on the jury" and thus can warrant reversing a conviction. *Boyde v. California,* 494 U.S. 370, 384-85, 110 S.Ct. 1190, 108 L.Ed.2d 316 (1990). Consequently, the Supreme Court has admonished the government to abstain from securing convictions by misrepresenting facts or the law:

The United States Attorney ... may prosecute with earnestness and vigor — indeed, he should do so. But, while he may strike hard blows, he is not at liberty to strike foul ones. It is as much his duty to refrain from improper methods calculated to produce a wrongful conviction as it is to use every legitimate means to bring about a just one.

Berger v. United States, 295 U.S. 78, 88, 55 S.Ct. 629, 79 L.Ed. 1314 (1935); *see also Boyde,* 494 U.S. at 384, 110 S.Ct. 1190.

A prosecutor's comments constitute reversible error if they were "(1) improper and (2) prejudicially affected the defendant's substantial rights so as to deprive the defendant of a fair trial." *Chong Lam,* 677 F.3d at 203 (quotation omitted). This Court considers six factors in determining whether a prosecutor's comments prejudiced a defendant's "substantial rights":

(1) the degree to which the prosecutor's remarks ha[d] a tendency to mislead the jury and to prejudice the accused; (2) whether the remarks were isolated or extensive; (3) absent the remarks, the strength of competent proof introduced to establish the guilt of the accused; and (4) whether the comments were deliberately placed before the jury to divert attention to extraneous matters. We also consider (5) whether the prosecutor's remarks were invited by improper conduct of defense counsel, and (6) whether curative instructions were given to the jury.

United States v. Lighty, 616 F.3d 321, 361 (4th Cir.2010). In cases in which a prosecutor erroneously instructs the jury on the law, "[t]he determinative question is whether the prosecutor's remarks cast serious doubt on the correctness of the jury's verdict." *United States v. Holmes,* 406 F.3d 337, 356 (5th Cir.2005) (citation omitted).

C.

Applying this framework to the case at hand, we first must determine whether the government's remarks were improper. *Chong Lam,* 677 F.3d at 203. In light of our conclusion that the alteration theory advanced by the government is not cognizable under Section 2320, the government's closing remarks were an incorrect statement of the law, and thus improper. *Mitchell,* 1 F.3d at 242 (holding that prosecutor's appeal to improper legal theory during closing argument constituted plain error). The remarks also were improper because the government is restricted to arguing legal principles included in the jury charge, *Trujillo,* 714 F.2d at 106, and the district court had repeatedly sustained p.229 Defendants' motions objecting to the material alteration instruction.

The key issue, then, is whether, under the six *Lighty* factors, the government's comments prejudiced Defendants' substantial rights. Here, all of the *Lighty* factors support reversing Defendant Zhao's conviction on Count 8. Regarding the first factor, as I explained previously, the government's remarks misled the jury and prejudiced Defendant Zhao because they incorrectly suggested that she could be convicted for modifying a genuine product even if the jury found that she did not alter the mark on the product. *See United States v. Mandel,* 862 F.2d 1067, 1073 (4th Cir.1988) ("[W]e hold that in a case in which the jury considers alternate theories of liability, we must reverse the convictions if either theory is an improper basis for punishment.").

Relatedly, based on the evidence adduced at trial, it is unclear whether there was sufficient competent evidence to convict Defendants on Count 8, as is required by the third *Lighty* factor. In particular, the government and Defendant Zhao presented conflicting evidence regarding whether the routers were manufactured by or for Cisco. At trial, a Cisco employee described the routers as "counterfeit" for two reasons: (1) they had codes on them that Cisco had assigned to routers with more ports and (2) the packaging for the routers was not Cisco packaging because it included a number of spelling errors. By contrast, an expert witness testifying on behalf of Defendants said that certain unalterable codes "burned into" the routers' memory indicated that they were manufactured by or for Cisco. J.A. 2207 And the Cisco employee called by the government testified that he did not know whether the routers were manufactured by or for Cisco.

As the majority correctly holds, evidence that a product has been repackaged is not, by itself, sufficient to prove that the product is nongenuine for purposes of Section 2320. *Ante,* at 212-13; *see also Hanafy,* 302 F.3d at 489. Moreover, based on the government's closing statement, the jury may have erroneously believed that any alteration of a genuine product — such as changing the codes assigned to the routers — could serve as the basis for a conviction under Section 2320. Consequently, we do not know whether the jury credited the government's evidence — and thus discredited Defendants' evidence — that the routers were not manufactured by or for Cisco, and therefore we do not know whether there was sufficient competent evidence to support Defendant Zhao's conviction. *See United States v. Hastings,* 134 F.3d 235, 241 (4th Cir.1998) (holding that when a jury may have reached a verdict based on an erroneous legal theory, a reviewing court "must attempt to ascertain what evidence the jury necessarily credited in order to convict the defendant under the instructions given. If that evidence is such that the jury must have convicted the defendant on the legally adequate ground in addition to or instead of the legally inadequate ground, the conviction may be affirmed").

The second, fourth, and fifth *Lighty* factors also support vacating the conviction. In particular, the improper appeal to the alteration theory was extensive: not only did the government argue the alteration theory during its closing, the theory also played a key role in the government's opening argument. The pervasive appeal to the alteration theory throughout the trial and the government's repeated unsuccessful requests that the district court instruct the jury on that theory also indicate that the government's remarks were deliberate. *See Chong Lam,* 677 F.3d at 212 (Floyd, J., dissenting) ("Where, however, a p.230 prosecutor continues to make an incorrect statement of the law after the district court has sustained repeated objections to that statement, notifying the prosecutor of the error, the court should, in my opinion, infer some degree of deliberateness."). Further, there is no evidence that improper conduct by the defense invited the remarks by the government. To the contrary, the defense properly sought to bar the government from arguing the theory through its successful motion in limine to prohibit the proposed instruction.

Regarding the sixth and final factor, because we presume juries follow their instructions, even in the absence of a curative instruction, a misstatement of law by counsel generally will not warrant overturning a jury verdict if the court's instruction on the issue correctly stated the controlling law and barred the jury from convicting the defendant based on the erroneous legal theory. *See, e.g., Chalmers v. Mitchell,* 73 F.3d 1262, 1271 (2d Cir. 1996); *United States v. Fierro,* 38 F.3d 761, 771-72 (5th Cir. 1994). Here, the district court did not provide a curative instruction, so the key question is whether the court's instruction on the definition of "counterfeit" foreclosed the jury from deciding this case based on the government's erroneous alteration theory.

As noted previously, the district court elected to use the Sand model instruction and modified it by quoting the authorized use exception. But neither the Sand instruction nor the language of the authorized use exception explicitly addresses whether altering a product that has its genesis in authorized production constitutes trademark counterfeiting. Thus, jurors reasonably could have believed that the court's instruction did not foreclose them from finding Defendant Zhao guilty under the alteration theory improperly argued by the government. Indeed, the district court appears to have believed that its instruction did not foreclose the jury from relying on the government's errant alteration theory: though the court elected not to give the government's proposed material alteration instruction, the district court did embrace the theory in rejecting Defendant Cone's Rule 29 motion for acquittal. J.A. 2345 ("[T]he presentation of an item as new when it has been altered under a mark is likely to cause confusion and lead the consumer to believe the product was made by the genuine owner of the trademark in the fashion in which it left the factory even though it was not.").

Nevertheless, the government argues that the court's instruction was proper and that "the jury was in no way directed to convict if a 'material alteration' had been made." Appellee's Br. at 25-26. But, despite Defendants' request, the court refused to instruct the jury on the repackaging exception because the court did not want to embrace a novel legal theory in its instruction. Given the centrality of the alteration theory to the government's case, the best course of action would have been for the district court to explicitly address the theory in its instructions — as, with the benefit of our holding in this case, future courts should do. At the least, it was incumbent on the court to instruct the jury on *all* statutory provisions addressing when resale of genuine products can give rise to trademark counterfeiting liability, which it did not do.

In sum, the majority of the *Lighty* factors favor vacating Defendant Zhao's conviction on Count 8. Moreover, the government's uncontradicted alteration argument casts significant doubt on the correctness of the jury's verdict by making it impossible for us to determine whether the jury properly credited the government's evidence or improperly credited the government's errant legal theory — although the p.231 jury's conviction of Defendant Zhao on Count 9, when the government conceded that the product at issue was manufactured by or for Cisco, suggests the jury improperly was doing the latter rather than correctly doing the former.

III.

In addition to disagreeing with the majority's decision to affirm Defendant Zhao's conviction on Count 8, I write separately to highlight two important points not explicitly addressed by the majority.

First, it is important to clarify that in resentencing Defendants on their conspiracy convictions under the majority's decision, the district court must not factor into the revised sentences evidence presented at trial that Defendants' upgraded and resold genuine Cisco PIX firewalls. Sales of the upgraded PIX firewalls constituted a substantial portion of JDC's sales, exceeding $1,200,000, and therefore factored into Defendants' sentences. As was the case with the router at issue in Count 9, the government concedes that the PIX firewalls were originally manufactured by or for Cisco. Yet under this Court's holding, merely upgrading a genuine product does not give rise to liability under Section 2320. Therefore, Defendants cannot be punished for trademark counterfeiting related to the PIX firewalls, and their sentences should be modified accordingly.

Second, it should be emphasized that we were not tasked with addressing whether a defendant violates Section 2320 by repackaging a genuine but modified good in a non-deceptive manner. According to the majority, a defendant cannot be held criminally liable under Section 2320(a) for "obtain[ing] a genuine ... product bearing a genuine mark; modif[ying] the product, but not the mark; then s[elling] the modified product bearing the genuine mark." *Ante,* at 207. Although this is a correct statement of law, it should not be read as holding that a defendant who alters a genuine product *and* simultaneously alters an associated mark or packaging *always* violates Section 2320 as a matter of law.

Here, the government did not argue below and does not argue on appeal that the coincidence of altering a genuine product and altering an associated mark gives rise to liability under Section 2320. Rather, the government consistently has argued that altering a genuine product by itself is sufficient to turn the genuine product into a counterfeit — an argument that we reject. Moreover, the government did not introduce evidence that Defendants altered the marks associated with the Cisco products they upgraded. Consequently, we were not tasked with resolving — and therefore did not answer — whether nondeceptively repackaging an altered, genuine product constitutes criminal trademark counterfeiting.

The district court held that as a matter of law altering and then repackaging a genuine good is inherently deceptive. J.A. 2345. But the Fifth Circuit has rejected the argument that the repackaging of genuine goods causes confusion as a matter of law. *Hanafy,* 302 F.3d at 488. And one can easily envision scenarios in which a defendant nondeceptively alters and resells a genuine product. For example, presumably a computer store can upgrade software on a Cisco router and sell it as "Cisco router with upgraded software" without running afoul of the statute. Therefore, whether the repackaging of an altered product constitutes trademark counterfeiting remains an open question and must be answered on a case-by-case basis.

IV.

In sum, although the majority properly rejected the government's material alteration p.232 theory of trademark counterfeiting, it improperly affirmed one of Defendant Zhao's substantive trademark counterfeiting convictions that was tainted by a version of that theory. Therefore, I respectfully dissent.

[1] Based on the jury's verdict, we recite the facts in the light most favorable to the government. *United States v. Cloud,* 680 F.3d 396, 399 n. 1 (4th Cir.2012).

[2] In addition, Zhao was individually indicted on five counts of importation and sale of improperly declared goods in violation of 18 U.S.C. § 545 (Counts 2-6); four counts of trafficking in counterfeit goods and labels in violation of 18 U.S.C. § 2320 (Counts 7-10); three counts of making false statements to federal law enforcement officials in violation of 18 U.S.C. § 1001(a)(2) (Counts 11-13); two counts of false statements in naturalization in violation of 18 U.S.C. § 1425(a) (Counts 14-15); seven individual counts of wire fraud (Counts 18-2, 24-25); three counts of money laundering in violation of 18 U.S.C. § 1956(a) (Count 26-28); and one count of monetary transaction with criminally derived proceeds in violation of 18 U.S.C. § 1957(a) (Count 29).

[3] For purposes of this appeal, only Counts 1 and 9 are affected by the second object of the conspiracy, which we address as the material alteration theory. The first and third objects are not at issue on appeal as part of the material alteration theory challenge. The convictions related to the first object, importation of misdeclared goods (and underlying substantive counts) are unaffected by our analysis of the material alteration theory, and the third object, wire fraud, was dismissed by the district court.

[4] The district court also dismissed Count 15, false statements in naturalization, on the government's motion.

[5] Section 2320 has been amended in 2011 and 2012. We cite to the prior version of the statute which was the version in effect during all times relevant to this appeal.

[6] Zhao and Cone argue, in the alternative, that § 2320 would be unconstitutionally vague if applied to them in the context of material alteration counterfeiting. Because we agree that the material alteration theory of criminal counterfeit lacks statutory foundation, we do not address their alternative vagueness argument.

[7] *E.g., Rolex Watch USA v. Meece,* 158 F.3d 816, 827 (5th Cir.1998) (upholding civil counterfeiting judgment against defendant who modified "new, genuine Rolex watches" with "non-genuine parts to make them resemble more expensive Rolex watches"); *Westinghouse Elec. Corp. v. Gen. Circuit Breaker & Elec. Supply Inc.,* 106 F.3d 894, 896 (9th Cir.1997) (defendant is liable for civil counterfeit where defendant purchased genuine, used Westinghouse Circuit breakers, refurbished them, and reattached genuine labels); *Intel Corp. v. Terabyte Int'l, Inc.,* 6 F.3d 614, 619 (9th Cir.1993) (affirming civil judgment against defendant who purchased "slow" Intel-brand microchips and relabeled them as "fast" and more expensive chips.).

[8] The Lanham Act defines "counterfeit" in a manner similar to the criminal counterfeiting statute: "A 'counterfeit' is a spurious mark which is identical with, or substantially indistinguishable from, a registered mark." 15 U.S.C. § 1127.

[9] A "MAC address" is an identification feature, unique to each item, imprinted by the manufacturer on networking equipment.

[10] While we have determined that the acts charged to Zhao under Count 9, and to both Zhao and Cone under the material alteration portion of Count 1, are not criminal acts under § 2320, nothing in our opinion should be construed to affect their prosecution under any other state or federal statute which may apply to these acts.

[11] Zhao was also charged with a third count of money laundering, Count 26, on which she was acquitted by the jury.

[12] Because the government never had the opportunity to address an appellate challenge to its closing arguments, the dissent's assertion that the government has "waived waiver" is misplaced and a conclusion of pure speculation. Had Zhao raised an independent challenge to the government's closing remarks, the government could have asserted the waiver bar in response, but was never put on notice to do so.

[13] Moreover, contrary to the dissent's suggestion, at 225, Zhao never argues in her post-verdict motion for acquittal that the government's remarks were improper as to the "material alteration" theory. She only argues that the prosecutor made certain statements, unrelated to the present appeal, that were unsupported by the evidence. *See* Zhao's Mot. Judgment of Acquittal 7 n.8, ECF 240. Nowhere in Zhao's motion as to Count 8 does she mention the material alteration theory. *Id.* at 5-7.

[*] The majority also suggests the Defendant Zhao waived any argument that the alteration theory tainted her conviction on Count 8, when at oral argument her counsel said that the alteration theory "most clearly" impacted Count 1 and Count 9. *Ante,* at 215-16. But this comment cannot reasonably be interpreted as unambiguously waiving any argument that the theory tainted her conviction on Count 8. And the majority fails to cite any authority, nor have I been able to find any, supporting the proposition that an appellant can waive an issue through an ambiguous statement made during oral argument, when the issue was raised in the appellant's briefs, as is the case here.

FIFTH CIRCUIT DECISIONS

The Rule Against Hearsay

705 F.3d 518 (2013)
FACTORY MUTUAL INSURANCE COMPANY, Plaintiff-Appellee
v.
ALON USA L.P.; Alon USA GP L.L.C.; Alon USA Refining Incorporated, Defendants-Appellants.
No. 11-11080.
United States Court of Appeals, Fifth Circuit.
January 23, 2013.
Factory Mut. Ins. Co. v. Alon USA LP, 705 F. 3d 518 (5th Cir. 2013)

p.519 Bruce H. Rogers, John Clifton Hart, Brown, Dean, Wiseman, Proctor, Hart & Howell, L.L.P., Fort Worth, TX, for Plaintiff-Appellee.

Jessica Ann Zavadil, Richard Russell Hollenbeck, Thomas Clark Wright, Wright & Close, L.L.P., Houston, TX, for Defendants-Appellants.

Before WIENER, CLEMENT, and PRADO, Circuit Judges.

PRADO, Circuit Judge:

Plaintiff-Appellee, Factory Mutual Insurance Company ("FM"), was awarded damages stemming from an industrial accident that destroyed a waste treatment plant at an oil refinery plant owned by Defendants-Appellants, Alon USA LP, Alon USA GP LLC, and Alon USA Refining Inc. (collectively, "Alon"). Alon appealed the court's damages determination. We AFFIRM.

I

Alon owns and operates an oil refinery in Big Spring, Texas. It relied on the equipment and services of a third party, Veolia North America-West ("Veolia"), for on-site water treatment and waste management. The equipment located in the waste treatment facility ("the Scalfuel plant" or "the Scalfuel facility") was owned and operated by Veolia and insured by FM. On February 18, 2008, a cloud of vapor exploded at the Scalfuel facility, destroying it. Veolia filed a claim with FM in the amount of $6,106,880, which FM paid in accordance with the insurance policy. Thereafter, on February 17, 2010, FM filed a subrogation claim against Alon to recover damages stemming from the explosion, alleging that Alon's negligence both directly and proximately caused the damages at issue.

Before the bench trial began, Alon stipulated to liability, leaving only the issue of damages to be determined. At trial, the parties agreed that damages would be determined by the fair market value of the Scalfuel plant before the explosion, but they fundamentally disagreed as to how fair market value should be calculated in this context. FM contended that it was entitled to the Scalfuel plant's replacement p.520 cost, *i.e.,* the cost of new parts and labor adjusted downward to account for the original plant's depreciation at the time of the explosion, since there is no market for Scalfuel plants that can be used as a measure of value. On the other hand, Alon argued that FM was only entitled to the cost of the Scalfuel plant's component parts. FM sought $6,106,880, whereas Alon claimed FM could only recover $877,882.

The district court found that, even though there is a market for specific used components, there is no market for used Scalfuel systems. Since the sum price of a Scalfuel system's components does not reflect the full value of an operational

Scalfuel plant, the district court found that the fair market value is determined by the replacement cost adjusted for improvements in value beyond the destroyed plant and depreciation reflecting the remaining useful life of the plant before its destruction. Accordingly, the district court found Alon liable for $3,790,391.96, plus interest. To reach this figure, the district court started with an estimate for new equipment, including taxes and shipping, of $2,356,110. Ten percent was added to this amount as a contingency.[1] The combined sum was then multiplied by 2.25 to account for the costs of installation, testing, and startup and the result was then multiplied by 0.65 to account for the original Scalfuel plant's 35% depreciation. Alon timely appealed the district court's judgment, challenging the measure of damages and calculation of fair market value.

II

The district court had jurisdiction pursuant to 28 U.S.C. § 1332, as the parties are diverse and the amount in controversy exceeds $75,000. This Court has jurisdiction pursuant to 28 U.S.C. § 1291, as the district court entered final judgment on October 12, 2011 and Alon timely filed a Notice of Appeal on November 10, 2011.

III

On appeal, Alon challenges both the district court's use of replacement cost to determine the market value of the Scalfuel plant, as well as two figures that went into calculating the replacement cost. Specifically, Alon claims that expert testimony concerning the 35% depreciation figure should have been excluded and that the 2.25 multiplier lacked an underlying factual basis.

A

While the parties agree that fair market value is the measure of damages here, they disagree as to how fair market value should be calculated. If a market exists for the property destroyed, *i.e.,* if willing buyers and willing sellers engage in the sale of the property at issue, then comparable sales are the usual measure of value. If a market does not exist, however, then replacement cost is the appropriate measure of value. Here, the district court found that no market for Scalfuel plants exists based on the evidence presented at trial. Accordingly, the district court utilized replacement cost to calculate FM's damages.

1

This Court reviews the district court's findings of fact for clear error. *Mid-Continent Cas. Co. v. Davis,* 683 F.3d 651, 654 (5th Cir.2012). "A finding is clearly erroneous if it is without substantial evidence to support it, the court misinterpreted the effect of the evidence, or this court is convinced that the findings are against the p.521 preponderance of credible testimony." *Becker v. Tidewater, Inc.,* 586 F.3d 358, 365 (5th Cir.2009) (quoting *Bd. of Trs. New Orleans Employers Int'l Longshoremen's Ass'n v. Gabriel, Roeder, Smith & Co.,* 529 F.3d 506, 509 (5th Cir.2008)). Thus, when the fact finder is faced with two permissible views of the evidence, the choice between them cannot be clearly erroneous. *Davis,* 683 F.3d at 654.

2

"A plaintiff whose property has been destroyed by the tort[ious] acts of another is generally entitled to recover the market value of the property at the time of its loss." *Seminole Pipeline Co. v. Broad Leaf Partners, Inc.,* 979 S.W.2d 730, 754 (Tex.App.-Houston [14th Dist.] 1998, no pet.); *see also Waples-Platter Co. v. Commercial Standard Ins. Co.,* 156 Tex. 234, 294 S.W.2d 375, 376 (1956). The measure of damages is "the difference in its market value immediately before and immediately after the injury, at the place where the damage occurred." *Thomas v. Oldham,* 895 S.W.2d 352, 359 (Tex. 1995). Market value is the amount a willing buyer, who is under no obligation to buy, would pay to a willing seller, who is under no obligation to sell. *Id.* Importantly, however, not all property has a market value. *Id.* "[I]n situations where a market value does not exist, ... replacement value is the means of assessing damages." *Id.* (quotation omitted); *see also Gulf States Utils. Co. v. Low,* 79 S.W.3d 561, 569 (Tex.2002). Such a situation arises when, for example, "comparable sales figures are lacking...." *City of Harlingen v. Estate of Sharboneau,* 48 S.W.3d 177, 183 (Tex.2001).

Here, the district court determined — and the parties do not dispute — that market value is the correct measure of damages. That is, FM is entitled to recover the value of the Scalfuel facility immediately before the explosion, since the facility was worth nothing after the explosion occurred. Whether replacement cost or the estimated price of used component parts constitutes the appropriate measure of value prior to the explosion forms the foundation of the parties' dispute.

This appeal centers on a determination of fact made by the district court in calculating market value, namely that "[t]here is no market for used Scalfuel systems." The court so held because each Scalfuel system is unique and

> includes some standard constituent subsystems and some subsystems that are specifically constructed for the Scalfuel system. While there is a market for some of the used subsystems, the market price of such used subsystems does not reflect the market value of a running Scalfuel system. The price of the used subsystems does not reflect the expense of integrating the parts into a working Scalfuel system. No reasonable person would construct a working Scalfuel system out of used components.

If, as the district court found, "there is no market price for a generic Scalfuel system," then replacement cost — adjusted for betterment and depreciation — is the correct measure of value. On the other hand, if the value of a Scalfuel plant can be measured by pricing the plant's component parts, as Alon argues, then that approach is the appropriate method for measuring damages. As explained below, the district court did not commit clear error in finding that no market for Scalfuel facilities exists. Therefore, replacement cost was an appropriate measure of damages, and we affirm.

Alon argues that the Scalfuel system at issue here was comprised of a number of component parts, many of which were readily procurable on the open market. Because used versions of most Scalfuel system parts could be procured from vendors, Alon asserts that market value is more appropriately measured by pricing p.522 the individual components likely present at the Scalfuel plant before the explosion.[2]

In support of this claim, Alon relies heavily on *Hartford Insurance Co. v. Jiminez*, 814 S.W.2d 551 (Tex.App.-Houston [1st Dist.] 1991, no pet.), a case in which the appellate court affirmed a trial court's finding that there was no evidence as to the amount of damage the plaintiffs sustained, despite their demonstrating that the automobile had been totaled and that the insurance company paid approximately $7,000 as a result. 814 S.W.2d at 552. The court so held because "[w]hat an insurance company paid is not evidence of reasonable market value" and the plaintiffs' evidence of damages consisted solely of proof regarding payment from his insurance company. *Id.* Thus, the court determined that "no evidence whatever was admitted showing [the car's] reasonable market value at the time of the collision." *Id.* Alon, however, relies on *Jiminez* for a much broader proposition than the case supports. Whereas *Jiminez* can at best be read to support the claim that insurance payments may not be used to prove damages, Alon goes so far as to claim that *Jiminez* means "evidence of replacement cost is no evidence of market value damages." To the contrary, while it is a disfavored method, replacement cost can indeed provide a competent measure of damages. *See Gulf States*, 79 S.W.3d at 569.

Furthermore, *Jiminez* is readily distinguishable from this case in two ways. First, unlike in *Jiminez*, FM did not rely on evidence of its payment to Veolia to prove the amount of damages. Instead, FM relied on expert opinions regarding valuation.[3] Indeed, one witness identified some 74% of the equipment initially present at the Scalfuel plant and sought quotations from vendors regarding price. The plaintiff in *Jiminez* merely presented evidence regarding the amount his insurance company paid for the car, 814 S.W.2d at 552, whereas FM utilized the services of an appraiser to determine the value of the Scalfuel facility prior to the explosion. FM did not rely on proof of its payment to Veolia to prove market value.

Second, the automobile in *Jiminez* unequivocally had an ascertainable market value that can be determined using comparable sales in a specific geographic area. *See City of Harlingen*, 48 S.W.3d at 183 (holding that market value using comparable sales is preferable, but that replacement cost may be used when comparable sales are lacking). But unlike an automobile, the Scalfuel facility here is a specialized, integrated set of systems for which no market exists. Scalfuel plants are not regularly bought or sold, each Scalfuel facility has proprietary component parts, and the plant's underlying process is itself patented. Moreover, Alon's estimate was limited to the cost of procuring component parts; the figure given by Alon did not account for installation, on-site engineering, or startup, all of which are critical to the value of a Scalfuel facility.[4] Alon's p.523 expert conceded that his $877,882 figure amounted to equipment that was "sitting on the ground, not assembled." The price for an automobile in *Jiminez* would account for a complete, working vehicle rather than a pile of used parts. Anthony Foster, President of ChemTech Consultants, further stated that it is "unwise" and highly uncommon to build a Scalfuel plant "completely out of used equipment." These characteristics readily distinguish FM's claim from *Jiminez*.

Based on the evidence presented, the district court did not err when it found that no market for Scalfuel systems exist. Ample evidence was presented to support such a finding. Furthermore, Alon never actually addresses the finding that no market exists. Rather, they reiterate their ability to price out component parts, assuming that this fact alone precludes the use of replacement cost as a measure of damages. This position effectively glosses over the substance underlying the district court's conclusion that a market for complete, operational Scalfuel plants does not exist.

While Alon presented evidence that the component parts of a Scalfuel plant could be priced individually, weighed against FM's proffer, the district court was presented with two permissible views of the evidence. In comparing the parties' arguments, the district court gave weight to factors such as labor, layout, and installation because the market value of a fully operational Scalfuel plant is greater than the sum of its component parts. Considering these factors alongside the unique layout, structure, and design of each Scalfuel plant, the district court determined that a market for Scalfuel plants does not exist. In light of the deferential standard of review applicable, no manifest error was committed. It necessarily follows that replacement cost was the appropriate measure of damages. Therefore, we affirm.

B

1

"This Court reviews the admissibility of expert testimony for abuse of discretion." *Primrose Operating Co. v. Nat'l Am. Ins. Co.,* 382 F.3d 546, 561 (5th Cir.2004) (citing *Vogler v. Blackmore,* 352 F.3d 150, 153 (5th Cir.2003)). The district court's discretion will not be disturbed on appeal unless the its decision was manifestly erroneous. *Id.* (citing *United States v. Tucker,* 345 F.3d 320, 326 (5th Cir.2003)).

2

Expert witnesses may base opinions on facts or data that the expert "has been made aware of or personally observed." Fed.R.Evid. 703. If the facts and data relied upon are the sort that experts in that field would reasonably rely on, then those facts "need not be admissible for the opinion to be admitted." *Id.* Accordingly, experts may base their opinions on otherwise-inadmissible information, such as hearsay, so long as the information is the sort reasonably relied upon in the experts' field.

The purpose of this rule is largely practical: experts generally base their opinions on information which, to be admissible in court, would entail "the expenditure of substantial time in producing and examining various authenticating witnesses." Fed.R.Evid. 703 advisory committee's note. Because experts may use their past experience and professional judgment to make critical decisions on the basis of such information outside of court, Rule 703 was p.524 intended "to bring the judicial practice into line with the practice of the experts themselves when not in court." *Id.* Courts nevertheless must serve a gate-keeping function with respect to Rule 703 opinions to ensure "the expert isn't being used as a vehicle for circumventing the rules of evidence." *In re James Wilson Assocs.*, 965 F.2d 160, 173 (7th Cir.1992). Rule 703 "was not intended to abolish the hearsay rule and to allow a witness, under the guise of giving expert testimony, to in effect become the mouthpiece of the witnesses on whose statements or opinions the expert purports to base his opinion." *Loeffel Steel Prods., Inc. v. Delta Brands, Inc.*, 387 F.Supp.2d 794, 808 (N.D.Ill.2005). The rule "was never intended to allow oblique evasions of the hearsay rule." *Id.*

Here, FM presented an expert appraiser, Leslie H. Miles, Jr. ("Miles"), to testify regarding the value of the Scalfuel plant. Part of the testimony offered by Miles dealt with the remaining life of the original Scalfuel plant at the time of the explosion. This testimony was a necessary part of calculating damages because, without adjusting the replacement cost of the new Scalfuel plant downward to account for the original plant's depreciation, FM would reap a windfall in its overall recovery. Since the original equipment was no longer available, Miles met with individuals who were purportedly familiar with the original Scalfuel plant and attempted to educate them regarding "what depreciation is made up of and how you calculate it." This is a method Miles has apparently used in the past.

The Veolia employees estimated that, prior to the explosion, the Scalfuel plant still had 65% of its remaining life; in other words, it was 35% depreciated at the time of the explosion. Based on the information he provided the employees and the discussion he witnessed, Miles deemed the employees' estimate reliable, and even expressed surprise at the "aggressiveness of it...." Miles did not expect the employees to estimate such a low remaining life given his experience with various chemical processing plants. That said, Miles appears merely to have adopted the depreciation number provided by Veolia's employees; it is not clear how he used past experience as an appraiser to deem the employees' estimate reliable. It is on this ground that Alon challenges the district court's admission of Miles's testimony as violative of Rule 703.

Alon argues that the district court abused its discretion by allowing Miles to testify regarding the Scalfuel plant's estimated depreciation because "Miles knew that physical depreciation had occurred... but he did nothing to calculate that depreciation" beyond relying on a figure estimated by Veolia employees. In support of this claim, Alon relies on *United States v. Mejia*, 545 F.3d 179 (2d Cir.2008), for the proposition that experts may not simply transmit hearsay to the jury. 545 F.3d at 197. Specifically, "the expert must form his own opinions by applying his extensive experience and a reliable methodology to the inadmissible materials." *Id.* (internal quotation marks omitted). Otherwise the expert may simply parrot impermissible hearsay evidence, thereby allowing a party to circumvent the rules against hearsay. *Id.* In *Mejia*, the Second Circuit ruled that the district court had abused its discretion in allowing testimony from one of the government's expert witnesses regarding gang structure and operations. *Id.* at 197-98. The court held that some of the expert's testimony ran afoul of Rule 703 because he had merely repeated information gathered from other sources without articulating how he applied his expertise to the underlying information being relayed. *Id.*

Alon also relies on *Loeffel Steel Products v. Delta Brands, Inc.*, for similar reasons. p.525 In *Loeffel*, which involved an expert's testimony regarding economic loss in a steel factory, a magistrate judge determined that the expert's testimony violated

Rule 703 because the numbers he relied upon to determine economic loss "came from the defendants' employees, on whom [the expert] uncritically relied." 387 F.Supp.2d at 807. Furthermore, the expert had little understanding of the underlying industrial processes he was evaluating and broadly "brought no expertise to bear on the underlying assumptions on which his economic loss theory was based...." *Id.* The expert had very little to offer beyond uncritical reliance on figures provided by others.

In response, FM argues that Miles "clearly explained how he arrived at the factors that he used to determine the depreciated value of the Scalfuel plant." This statement is somewhat misleading, though. On the one hand, Miles did clearly articulate what depreciation means and how it is usually calculated. On the other, however, Miles's testimony does not reveal any particular expertise brought to the process of evaluating the number provided by Veolia's employees. Miles *did* provide guidance to the employees regarding depreciation theory, but he relied solely on the employees' estimation, a figure he deemed reliable based on the discussion he observed. There was no way to verify that the Veolia employees competently applied the considerations on which Miles had instructed them, though Miles did state that he was surprised by the "aggressiveness" of the employees' estimate.

That said, Miles also testified that the estimates of others constitute the sort of information reasonably relied upon by appraisers approaching valuation questions. Neither *Mejia* nor *Loeffel* is entirely apposite, and neither is binding upon this Court. Insofar as he educated and interviewed Veolia employees, Miles did more than just repeat information gleaned from external sources. *Cf. Mejia,* 545 F.3d at 198 (The witness "did not analyze his source materials so much as repeat their contents. [He] thus provided evidence to the jury without also giving the jury the information it needed" to consider the reliability of the underlying sources.). Furthermore, Miles demonstrated his familiarity with the appraisal of heavy industrial plants broadly, even if he had little experience with Scalfuel plants in particular. *Cf. Loeffel,* 387 F.Supp.2d at 807 (stating as "undisputed" the fact that the expert witness had no experience with the relevant machinery and was "incapable of assessing the validity of the information provided....").

In light of the deferential standard on appeal, we affirm because the district court did not abuse its discretion. Miles did clearly state that the sort of information relied upon here — the opinions of others — is the sort of information reasonably relied upon by appraisers. Moreover, Miles's investigation must be viewed in light of what was feasible. Since the original Scalfuel plant was destroyed and scrapped after the explosion, there was very little room for investigation of any sort. While Miles could have doubtless come to a more accurate estimate by inspecting records or the equipment itself, neither was available. Miles thus consulted one of the few sources of information available: employees who had worked at or near the Scalfuel facility.[5] In light of p.526 these considerations, the district court was best placed to evaluate whether Miles uncritically relied upon the depreciation figures given to him by Veolia's employees through his testimony.

C

1

This Court reviews the district court's findings of fact for clear error. *Mid-Continent Cas. Co.,* 683 F.3d at 654; *see also* Part III.B.1, *supra.*

2

At trial, the district court heard from multiple experts concerning the propriety of using a multiplier when calculating replacement costs. In this context, a multiplier refers to a number that, when applied to the underlying cost figure, is intended to account for anticipated costs associated with construction, including installation, startup, overhead, and testing. Alon's expert, Dean Harris ("Harris"), would have applied a multiplier of 1.25 or 1.5 at most. FM's witness, Tony Foster ("Foster"), initially recommended a 2.0 multiplier, but later changed his mind and advised that a 2.5 multiplier was more appropriate. Veolia, which has substantial experience in the construction of Scalfuel plants, has apparently encountered multipliers ranging from 1.8 to 3.2. The district court ultimately used a multiplier of 2.25, which is the compromise figure that FM used when evaluating Veolia's claim. On appeal, Alon contends that FM's proffered 2.5 figure and the district court's adopted 2.25 figure lack factual bases. As explained below, clear error was not committed.

First, Alon's attempt at undermining FM's witness testimony is unavailing because it misconstrues the evidence at issue. During trial, Alon pressed Foster regarding a pair of letters that ostensibly recommended a 1.0 multiplier for calculating the cost of a new Scalfuel facility. Specifically, one document stated: "With this design concept in mind, ChemTech believes that a fair Total Installed Cost is 1 × the estimated equipment cost, or $2.6 million equipment plus $2.6 installation." The second letter said: "ChemTech ... recommends a multiplier of 1.0 times the skidded equipment cost shown on the summary sheet at $2.6 million." Alon implied during this line of questioning that FM's own witnesses did not believe a multiplier between 2.0 and 2.5 was warranted. However, Foster claimed in his response that the 1.0 text was a "typo." Both documents in fact recommend doubling the estimated equipment cost to account for concomitant costs associated with installing the equipment. This means applying a 2.0 multiplier, even if FM misused the term in its correspondence. Indeed, a 1.0 multiplier would do no multiplying at all.

The first letter stated that "Total Installed Cost is 1 × the estimated equipment cost, or $2.6 million equipment plus $2.6 million installation." While not a model of clarity, it is difficult to dispute that the final cost figure should be double the estimated cost of equipment. That is, the estimated equipment cost is $2.6 million p.527 and the estimated installation cost should be the same amount, *i.e.,* "1 × the estimated equipment cost", effectively doubling the total installed cost.

The same is true of the second letter, which made the same mistake. It states that "ChemTech ... recommends a multiplier of 1.0 times the skidded equipment cost shown on the summary sheet at $2.6 million." As Foster explained, multipliers can be conceptually understood in numerous ways: "The common thing is you can take a percentage of value, say, a hundred percent of the cost increase. If you bought a wallet for $10, a hundred percent of it would be another $10, you know? ... The other simpler method of doing it is two times" the original amount. The letters clearly convey the opinion that the estimated equipment cost should be doubled to account for installation costs, regardless of how they used the term multiplier. Alon's reliance on these documents is thus misplaced and does nothing to undermine FM's evidence or the district court's conclusion concerning an appropriate multiplier.

Finally, Alon relies on the testimony of Harris, its own expert, who testified that multipliers are generally disfavored for their inaccuracy and should only be used for broad cost estimates. While Harris clearly believed that use of a multiplier was not appropriate in these circumstances, his testimony does not definitively settle the issue. FM's witnesses agreed that multipliers are not ideal, but suggested that they are nevertheless appropriate in cases such as this in which no better information is available. Given the lack of useful records and resources pertaining to this particular Scalfuel plant, it was entirely reasonable to conclude that use of a multiplier was appropriate. As experts for both parties testified, multipliers are best suited for just such a situation.

The district court was clearly presented with two permissible views of the evidence. Few records were available to estimate the cost of rebuilding the Scalfuel plant, which counsels in favor of using a multiplier. Furthermore, the 2.25 multiplier used by the district court is well within the range recommended by the witnesses and is consistent with Veolia's past experiences. Accordingly, the district court did not clearly err, and we affirm.

IV

For the foregoing reasons, the judgment of the district court is AFFIRMED.

[1] Contingency costs generally refer to unforeseeable capital costs that arise during the course of construction.

[2] The measure of value is based on components "likely" present at the time of the explosion because there do not appear to be any documents in existence that comprehensively detail the component parts of the Scalfuel plant prior to the explosion. As a result, the parties' experts were forced to estimate what equipment was present.

[3] Alon's appeal includes challenges to some of those experts' opinions. Those specific contentions are discussed in Parts III.B and III.C, *infra*.

[4] In their brief, appellants claims that their expert "estimated the number of man-hours needed to construct the unit." This is an untrue statement. The testimony Alon cites merely points to Alon's expert estimating the number of man-hours it would take to estimate the cost of completely rebuilding the Scalfuel plant. That is, Alon's expert did not estimate the number of man-hours it would actually take to build a new Scalfuel plant. This distinction is reiterated later in his testimony: "If you're asking me if I have included the cost of installing the plant and getting the plant running in [the damages figure], the answer is, no, I have not."

[5] The parties do not address why it was not possible to directly depose the employees on whom Miles relied for his depreciation figure, though Alon does briefly raise the issue. Indeed, the third case relied upon by Alon, *In re James Wilson Associates*, 965 F.2d 160 (7th Cir. 1992), involved a similar issue. In that case, which centered on estimating the physical deterioration of a building for valuation purposes, the testimony of an architect was deemed violative of Rule 703 because the architect was merely parroting information given to him by the engineer who had actually inspected the building at issue. 965 F.2d at 173. As the court stated, "The issue was the state of the building, and the expert who had evaluated that state — the consulting engineer — was the one who should have testified." *Id.* The problem was rooted in the fact that the architect was seeking to repeat information on a topic outside of his expertise instead of using "what the engineer told him to offer an opinion within the architect's domain of expertise...." *Id.* This case is distinguishable, however, since Miles sought to use information outside of the employees' expertise to offer an opinion within his own expertise.

706 F.3d 665 (2013)

UNITED STATES of America, Plaintiff-Appellee,

v.

Janice Edwina DEMMITT, Defendant-Appellant.

No. 11-11120.

United States Court of Appeals, Fifth Circuit.

February 1, 2013.

US v. Demmitt, 706 F. 3d 665 (5th Cir. 2013)

p.668 Sonja Marie Ralston, U.S. Department of Justice, Criminal Division, Washington, DC, Nancy E. Larson, Assistant U.S. Attorney, U.S. Attorney's Office, Northern District of Texas, Fort Worth, TX, for Plaintiff-Appellee.

Kevin Joel Page, Federal Public Defender's Office, Northern District of Texas, Dallas, TX, Michael Lowell King, Assistant Federal Public Defender, Federal Public Defender's Office, Northern District of Texas, Lubbock, TX, for Defendant-Appellant.

Before STEWART, Chief Judge, and GARZA and ELROD, Circuit Judges.

CARL E. STEWART, Chief Judge:

A jury convicted Defendant-Appellant Janice Edwina Demmitt of conspiracy to launder monetary instruments, wire fraud, and money laundering. The district court sentenced her to seventy months imprisonment, a net term of five years supervised release, and restitution. Demmitt now appeals on the basis of alleged evidentiary errors, an improper jury instruction as to deliberate ignorance, and as to one of the money laundering counts, a fatal variance from the indictment or, alternatively, insufficient evidence to support the conviction. We AFFIRM in part, VACATE in part, and REMAND.

I. BACKGROUND

A. Facts

Demmitt and her son, Timothy Fry ("Fry") lived and ran an insurance annuity business together. They were both licensed agents for Allianz Life Insurance Company ("Allianz"), a legitimate company. Demmitt and Fry secured several clients and set up annuity policies for them with Allianz.

Between 2007 and 2008, Fry began to defraud his customers. He forged letters and e-mails purporting to be from Allianz that promised customers a fifty or one-hundred percent match for opening a new annuity. Fry encouraged clients to come up with this money in a variety of ways, including cashing out their existing Allianz annuities. Fry told clients he needed the money immediately in order to secure the match and that, to save time, the clients should provide cash or write him, not Allianz, a personal check. Each time a client cashed out or borrowed against an existing Allianz annuity, Fry or Demmitt sent a fax from their office to Allianz's Minnesota office. In most instances, whenever a change was made to an Allianz annuity, Allianz sent a letter to Demmitt to inform her of the changes, even if Fry had initiated them. Fry also obtained money from clients in other ways. In one instance, Fry obtained a $30,000 check from a client by reporting that the client's husband, also a client, owed him the money.

In many cases, Fry deposited the fraudulently-obtained checks into his individual p.669 bank accounts or joint bank accounts he owned with Demmitt. In some instances, Fry cashed the checks and then gave cash to Demmitt, who deposited it into her individual or joint bank accounts. Demmitt used the funds to cover business and personal expenses, including frequent purchases from QVC and payments to an interior decorator who was helping her set up a call center in a warehouse that required significant renovations. Fry and Demmitt both bought new vehicles.

Fry also funneled some of his clients' money into an E*TRADE account that he used to fund his investment activities. Fry's discussions of his trading successes were convincing enough that his brother, Tad Fry ("Tad"), who lived in Colorado and periodically sent money to help with Demmitt and Fry's household expenses, requested that some of his money be invested in the E*TRADE account. In fact, Fry lost a significant amount of the money in the account, including fraudulently-obtained client money.

In the summer of 2008, some of Tad's logging equipment began to break down, and he asked Fry and Demmitt to send him money from the E*TRADE account. Tad believed Fry and Demmitt would send him his own money. Instead, they wired Tad money that was ultimately traced to client funds. For example, on August 21, 2008, Demmitt wired Tad $3,000 in client funds from one of her bank accounts.

Meanwhile, both Demmitt and Fry experienced significant cash flow problems of which Demmitt was aware. Because the business only had a handful of clients, annuity commissions alone were insufficient to cover business expenses, let alone personal expenses. Several people informed Demmitt of financial problems the business and Fry were having. For example, in September 2008, after Tad informed Fry that he needed more money to pay for the equipment, Fry sent Tad a series of checks that were ultimately returned for insufficient funds. Consequently, Tad's bank account became overdrawn by $47,000. Tad informed Demmitt that Fry's checks had been returned for insufficient funds. Demmitt was also informed several times that employee paychecks had been returned for insufficient funds.

In August 2008, clients Georgiann and Donald McCormick filed a complaint with the Amarillo Police Department, alleging that Fry had stolen $450,000 from them. Police Detective Celia Vargas was dispatched to Demmitt and Fry's business office to investigate. When Demmitt opened the locked door, Vargas asked to speak with Fry, but Demmitt reported that he was not present. Upon Demmitt's question, Vargas informed her that she was investigating possible fraud being perpetrated by Fry. When Vargas requested to look around the property, Demmitt called to Fry, who appeared. Demmitt informed Fry that Vargas was there to investigate "financial fraud," thus qualifying Vargas's investigation in a way Vargas had not done.

In total, Fry defrauded over $700,000 from his clients.

B. Procedural History

Demmitt and Fry were each charged with one count of conspiracy to launder monetary instruments, fifteen counts of wire fraud, and eleven counts of money laundering. All of the money laundering counts, except Count 27, were brought under 18 U.S.C. §§ 1957 and 2 and involved amounts over $10,000. Count 27 was brought under 18 U.S.C. § 1956(a)(1)(B)(i) and alleged, *inter alia,* that Demmitt transferred $3,000 to Tad knowing that the transaction was designed to conceal the illegal attributes of the money.

p.670 Fry pleaded guilty, signing a factual resume that, *inter alia,* asserted Demmitt had been involved in the scheme. Demmitt pleaded not guilty, and she was tried before a jury. At trial, Demmitt presented no witnesses or evidence, and she argued that Fry had been the sole perpetrator of the scheme. The jury convicted Demmitt of conspiracy to launder monetary instruments, eight counts of wire fraud, and all of the money laundering counts.

Demmitt now brings this appeal, raising four issues: (1) the district court reversibly erred when it permitted the Government to introduce Fry's factual resume as substantive evidence of Demmitt's guilt; (2) the district court reversibly erred when it permitted the Government to introduce witness Doris Streu's testimony; (3) the district court reversibly erred when it gave the jury a deliberate ignorance instruction; and (4) conviction under Count 27 was improper because the Government's evidence was a fatal variance from the indictment or, alternatively, there was insufficient evidence that Demmitt satisfied the essential elements of the crime.

II. EVIDENTIARY ISSUES

Demmitt raises two evidentiary issues. First, she argues that the trial court erred when it permitted the prosecution to introduce Fry's factual resume as substantive evidence of Demmitt's guilt. Second, she argues that the trial court erred when it permitted the prosecution to introduce Streu's testimony regarding a loan her husband made to Fry.

We first address Demmitt's second argument. As Demmitt has cited no authority in support of her contentions as to the impropriety of admitting Streu's testimony, we hold this argument waived. *See* Fed. R.App. P. 28(a)(9) ("The appellant's brief must contain ... citations to the authorities ...."); *see also Procter & Gamble Co. v. Amway Corp.,* 376 F.3d 496, 499 n. 1 (5th Cir.2004) (collecting citations) ("Failure adequately to brief an issue on appeal constitutes waiver of that argument.").

We now turn to Demmitt's argument that the trial court erred when it permitted the prosecution to introduce Fry's factual resume as substantive evidence of Demmitt's guilt.

A. Standard of Review

Where a party has properly preserved an objection, as is the case here, we review evidentiary rulings for an abuse of discretion, subject to a harmless error analysis. *United States v. Cisneros-Gutierrez,* 517 F.3d 751, 757 (5th Cir.2008) (citation omitted);

United States v. Crawley, 533 F.3d 349, 353 (5th Cir.2008) (citation omitted). "Reversible error occurs only when the admission of evidence substantially affects the rights of a party." *Crawley*, 533 F.3d at 353 (citations omitted).

"A nonconstitutional trial error is harmless unless it had substantial and injurious effect or influence in determining the jury's verdict." *United States v. El-Mezain*, 664 F.3d 467, 526 (5th Cir.2011) (citations and internal quotation marks omitted). "Under this standard, we ask whether the error itself had substantial influence on the jury in light of all that happened at trial; if we are left in grave doubt, the conviction cannot stand." *Id.* (citations and internal quotation marks omitted).

B. Discussion

We now address the merits of Demmitt's contention as to the introduction of the factual resume. Soon after Fry was p.671 sworn in as a witness for the prosecution, the following exchange occurred:

Q [Prosecutor]. And Government's [Exhibit] 17-2, is that the factual resume that provides the factual basis for your plea of guilty that you entered?

A [Fry]. Yes.

Q. And does it bear your signature, along with that of your lawyer?

A. Yes.

[Prosecutor]: The Government offers Government's Exhibit ... W17-2.

[Counsel for Demmitt]: Your Honor, both of these documents are hearsay. They're out-of-court statements that are being offered for the truth of the matter asserted.

The Court: Admitted.

Q (By [Prosecutor]): Did you plead guilty to this on July the 28 of 2011?

A. Yes.

Q. And prior to your — during your plea of guilty, were you sworn in?

A. Yes.

Q. Did you raise your right hand and promise to tell the truth?

A. Yes.

Q. And did you swear that everything contained in the factual resume was true and correct?

A. Yes.

[Prosecutor]: I'll pass the witness.

Fry's factual resume attributes every aspect of the fraud to both himself and Demmitt. On cross-examination, Fry testified that he did not remember most of his fraudulent activities due to heavy medication, but that he did not recall Demmitt's involvement in the fraud. He explained that he did not believe he was representing Demmitt was part of the fraud when he signed the factual resume and that, before he signed the factual resume, he had informed the prosecutor that Demmitt was not involved in the scheme. Fry also stated that he had informed Demmitt that his E*TRADE investments were doing well. However, Fry also conceded Demmitt's awareness of particular aspects of the fraud, such as withdrawals from client annuity accounts.

Demmitt argues that the factual resume was impermissibly admitted hearsay. The Government disputes this characterization, claiming that the factual resume is admissible non-hearsay under Federal Rule of Evidence 801 as an adoption or as a prior inconsistent statement. We disagree with the Government's contentions.

As is well-known, hearsay is a statement, including a "written assertion ... that: (1) the declarant does not make while testifying at the current trial or hearing; and (2) a party offers in evidence to prove the truth of the matter asserted in the statement." Fed.R.Evid. 801(a), (c). Hearsay is not admissible unless a statute or rule provides otherwise. Fed.R.Evid. 802. In some instances, however, a declarant-witness's prior statement is not hearsay. The Government presses two of those non-hearsay situations here: (1) when the declarant adopts the prior statement and (2) when the prior statement is inconsistent with the declarant's testimony. Fed.R.Evid. 801(d).

1. Adoption

"If the witness admits on the stand that he made the statement and that it was true, he adopts the statement and there is no hearsay problem." Fed.R.Evid. 801(d)(1) advisory committee's note; *see also Vanston v. Conn. Gen. Life Ins. Co.,* 482 F.2d 337, 344 (5th Cir.1973) (quoting committee note and recognizing this circuit as having adopted the rule). The Government argues that the direct examination exchange between the prosecutor and Fry, p.672 quoted at the outset of this section, was sufficient to serve as an adoption.

The hearsay rule stands as a bulwark against unreliable testimony, and thus hearsay exceptions and exclusions have been carefully crafted. As made clear in the committee note and our case law, the prior statement must be acknowledged and affirmed *on the stand* in order to be admissible for substantive purposes independent of use as a prior inconsistent statement. As the above exchange illustrates, Fry did acknowledge that he had made the statements in the factual resume. However, he did not admit *on the stand,* in the presence of the jury, that they were true statements, only that he had previously sworn they were true. The prosecutor's careful use of the past tense when asking about the truth of the factual resume — *"did* you swear that everything contained in the factual resume was true and correct?" — is insufficient to establish Fry's affirmation on the stand at Demmitt's trial. *Cf. Cisneros-Gutierrez,* 517 F.3d at 758 (holding that a witness's admission under oath at a plea hearing that a factual resume was "true and correct in every respect" demonstrated sufficient adoption such that the factual resume could be used as a prior inconsistent statement). We thus conclude that Fry did not adopt the factual resume on the stand at Demmitt's trial.

As the factual resume was not adopted on the stand, it was hearsay and should not have been admitted. The trial court erred when it admitted the factual resume, and its error was an abuse of discretion. That, however, does not end our inquiry because we now must assess whether the error was harmless.

2. Harmless Error

Under the Federal Rules of Evidence, when "[t]he declarant testifies and is subject to cross-examination about a prior statement, and the statement ... is inconsistent with the declarant's testimony and was given under penalty of perjury at a trial, hearing, or other proceeding or in a deposition," the statement is not hearsay. Fed.R.Evid. 801(d)(1).

The parties do not dispute that at the time the factual resume was entered into evidence, the document was not yet a prior inconsistent statement. We agree because, as demonstrated by the above testimony, at the time the evidence was admitted, Fry had not yet made any inconsistent statements concerning facts also contained in the factual resume.

Instead, the Government asserts that the factual resume's admission was harmless because it *later* became a prior inconsistent statement under Federal Rule of Evidence 801(d)(1)(A). Specifically, the Government contends that because Demmitt then cross-examined Fry about the factual resume, "by the time of Fry's redirect examination, the factual resume had clearly become a prior inconsistent statement admissible for its truth under [Federal Rule of Evidence] 801(d)(1)(A)." We disagree with the Government's argument, but we nonetheless find the error harmless due to the totality of the evidence adduced at trial.

We first dispense with the Government's argument that the "premature admission of evidence whose foundation is later established is harmless error." Demmitt argues, and the Government implicitly concedes, that Demmitt herself was essentially forced to elicit Fry's inconsistent testimony, thereby correcting the trial court's admission error. After the trial court erroneously admitted the factual resume, Demmitt was left with an unenviable choice: (1) decline to cross examine Fry on the factual resume's contents and hope p.673 that on appeal, Demmitt would prevail on an argument that the document was impermissible hearsay or (2) cross-examine Fry on the document in an attempt to undermine its effectiveness, thereby satisfying Federal Rule of Evidence 801 in the process. Such a prosecution tactic is impermissible, and we decline to endorse it by finding that the trial court's error was ameliorated by *Demmitt's* cross-examination.

However, even though we disagree with the Government's argument about subsequent inconsistency, that does not end our inquiry into the error's harmlessness. Instead, we must consider the admission of the factual resume "not in isolation, but in relation to the entire proceedings." *United States v. Williams,* 957 F.2d 1238, 1244 (5th Cir.1992) (citation and internal quotation marks omitted). Our examination is "fact-specific and record-intensive, requiring a close review of the entire trial proceedings." *El-Mezain,* 664 F.3d at 526. "[W]e must judge the likely effect of any error in the case before us based on the totality of the circumstances in this trial." *Id.* "Unless there is a reasonable possibility that the improperly admitted evidence contributed to the conviction, reversal is not required." *Id.* (citation and internal quotation marks omitted) (alterations omitted). "It is well established that error in admitting evidence will be found harmless when the evidence is cumulative, meaning that substantial evidence supports the same facts and inferences as those in the erroneously admitted evidence." *Id.* (collecting citations).

After carefully reviewing the record, we conclude that the erroneous admission of the factual resume does not require reversal. Although the case against Demmitt was circumstantial, in light of the volume of evidence presented by the prosecution that supports the same facts and inferences as those in the factual resume, we conclude the admission was harmless.

The factual resume stated that Demmitt was actually involved in the fraud. Other trial testimony could lead to the same conclusion or to the conclusion that she was deliberately ignorant of it, either of which is sufficient basis for conviction. *See Chaney v. Dreyfus Serv. Corp.*, 595 F.3d 219, 240 (5th Cir.2010) ("Deliberate ignorance is the legal equivalent of knowledge."). Broadly defined, there were four types of evidence presented at trial, in addition to Fry's factual resume, that lead to this conclusion.

First, there was ample testimony that Demmitt was made aware of problems with client accounts. For example, Allianz Senior Special Investigator Barbara Krueger testified that Demmitt was copied on letters Allianz sent about changes to client annuities, and Fry testified that he "probably" informed his mother that he was sending faxes to Allianz using her name. There were also several instances in which clients directly informed Demmitt that their money had not been properly deposited in their Allianz annuities. For example, client Richard Burdett informed Demmitt that Fry had personally cashed a check he had written, but the money had not been deposited in Burdett's Allianz account. Burdett testified that Demmitt denied Fry's signature was on the check and claimed that the money had been deposited in Burdett's Allianz account. Burdett testified that he did not think Demmitt believed what she told him. Another client, Dahl Clower, testified that Demmitt accepted checks made out to Fry from Clower's wife, as well as discussed the fake Allianz bonus structure with her. A third client, Georgiann McCormick, testified that Demmitt was aware other clients were complaining that their money had not p.674 been deposited in their Allianz annuities. McCormick further testified that she did not believe Fry acted alone or fooled Demmitt.

Second, there was testimony that Demmitt tightly controlled the business and that Fry frequently consulted Demmitt before he made any decisions. For example, former employee Jan Burchfield testified that only Demmitt and Fry were permitted to answer the business telephone or open the business mail. Fry also testified that Demmitt sometimes opened the mail. Additionally, Burchfield testified that she assisted Demmitt in organizing client files around August 2008, and that Demmitt and Fry shared business decisions. Another former employee, Delores Austin, testified that Demmitt was in charge of the office and that Demmitt prohibited her from standing near the copy machine when Demmitt made copies. Multiple people also testified that Fry frequently consulted Demmitt before making decisions. For example, Austin testified that Fry called his mother to find out how he should pay Austin after she refused to accept a personal check for fear it would be returned for insufficient funds. Streu testified that Demmitt became involved when Streu's husband set up a payment plan for Fry, who was delinquent in repaying the truck loan for which Streu's husband had signed. Demmitt personally delivered Fry's payments and required the Streus to sign a receipt for each. Later, when the Streus decided to repossess Fry's truck after Fry stopped paying on the loan, Demmitt called Streu to attempt to convince her not to repossess the truck.

Third, there was significant evidence that Demmitt's annuity commissions alone could not have supported her business or personal expenses, yet she and Fry made frequent and expensive purchases. For example, Demmitt's bank records show that she often received only about $1 per month in commission from Allianz.

Nevertheless, both Fry and Demmitt purchased new vehicles, and Demmitt made numerous QVC purchases. Demmitt and Fry also made down payments on two houses, and Demmitt made numerous payments to the interior decorator who was working on preparing the warehouse for Demmitt's planned call center.

Finally, there was substantial evidence that Demmitt participated in or that her bank accounts received suspicious financial transactions. Demmitt and Fry had at least one joint account into which client-signed checks were directly deposited. On other occasions, Fry cashed client checks and Demmitt deposited the cash into her accounts in suspicious quantities. For example, at least one of these transactions involved a deposit of one hundred and twenty $100 bills.

We hold that the record shows the Government presented significant evidence, albeit circumstantial, that demonstrated Demmitt was actually involved in Fry's scheme or deliberately indifferent to it. Given that this evidence is cumulative of the factual resume, we hold that the trial court's error in admitting the factual resume was harmless and does not warrant reversal.

III. DELIBERATE IGNORANCE INSTRUCTION

Over Demmitt's objection, the trial court gave the jury a deliberate ignorance instruction. The trial court did, however, agree to include a limiting instruction, which was included as the last sentence in the deliberate ignorance instruction:

> You may find that a defendant had knowledge of a fact if you find that the Defendant deliberately closed her eyes to what otherwise would have been obvious to her. While knowledge on the p.675 part of the Defendant cannot be established merely by demonstrating that the Defendant was negligent, careless, or foolish, knowledge can be inferred if the Defendant deliberately blinded herself to the existence of a fact. This does not lessen the Government's burden to prove, beyond a reasonable doubt, that the knowledge elements of the crimes have been satisfied.

On appeal, Demmitt challenges the propriety of the trial court's deliberate ignorance instruction.

A. Standard of Review

We utilize an abuse of discretion standard when reviewing a district court's jury instructions. *Baisden v. I'm Ready Prods., Inc.,* 693 F.3d 491, 504-05 (5th Cir.2012) (citation omitted). We use a two-part test to review challenges to particular instructions. *Id.* at 505 (citation omitted). First, the appellant "must demonstrate that the charge as a whole creates substantial and ineradicable doubt whether the jury has been properly guided in its deliberations." *Id.* (citation and internal quotation marks omitted). Second, even if a jury instruction were given in error, we will not reverse the district court if, "in light of the entire record, the challenged instruction could not have affected the outcome of the case." *Id.* (citation and internal quotation marks omitted).

When a defendant contends that a jury instruction was inappropriate, we consider whether the charge was both legally accurate and supported by fact. *See United States v. Mendoza-Medina,* 346 F.3d 121, 132 (5th Cir.2003) (citations and internal quotation marks omitted). "In assessing whether the evidence sufficiently supports the district court's charge, we view the evidence and all reasonable inferences that may be drawn from the evidence in the light most favorable to the Government." *Id.* (citations and internal quotation marks omitted). If we determine the charge was erroneous, we review for harmless error. *Id.* (citations and internal quotation marks omitted).

B. Discussion

We first note that Demmitt has not challenged the district court's instruction as an incorrect statement of law. Therefore, our sole ground for review is whether the instruction was supported by fact. We conclude that it was.

Due to concerns that a jury will convict a defendant for what she *should* have known rather than the appropriate legal standard, we have "often cautioned against the use of the deliberate ignorance instruction." *Mendoza-Medina,* 346 F.3d at 132 (citations omitted). It is improper for a district court to instruct a jury on deliberate ignorance "when the evidence raises only the inferences that the defendant had actual knowledge or no knowledge at all of the facts in question." *Id.* at 134 (citation omitted).

We use a two-prong test to determine whether the evidence supports a deliberate ignorance instruction, wherein the evidence presented at trial "must raise two inferences: (1) the defendant was subjectively aware of a high probability of the existence of the illegal conduct and (2) the defendant purposefully contrived to avoid learning of the illegal conduct." *Id.* at 132-33 (citation omitted).

In evaluating the first prong, we have noted that "the same evidence that will raise an inference that the defendant had actual knowledge of the illegal conduct ordinarily will also raise the inference that the defendant was subjectively aware of a high probability of the existence of illegal conduct." *United States v. Conner,* 537 p.676 F.3d 480, 487 (5th Cir.2008) (citation and internal quotation marks omitted).

In discussing the second prong, we have cautioned that

> the *sine qua non* of deliberate ignorance is the *conscious* action of the defendant — the defendant *consciously* attempted to escape confirmation of the conditions or events he strongly suspected to exist. Where the choice is simply between a version of the facts in which the defendant had actual knowledge, and one in which he was no more than negligent or stupid, the deliberate ignorance instruction is inappropriate.

Mendoza-Medina, 346 F.3d at 133 (citations and internal quotation marks omitted). We have held that the second prong can be established where "the circumstances in the case were so overwhelmingly suspicious that the defendant's failure to conduct further inspection or inquiry suggests a conscious effort to avoid incriminating knowledge." *Conner,* 537 F.3d at 486 (citation and internal quotation marks omitted) (alterations omitted).

"Under well-established precedent, the error in giving a deliberate ignorance instruction in the absence of evidence of contrivance is harmless where there is substantial evidence of actual knowledge." *United States v. Delgado,* 672 F.3d 320, 341 (5th Cir.2012) (en banc) (citation and internal quotation marks omitted).

1. Prong One

We hold that the trial testimony raises a strong inference that Demmitt was subjectively aware of the existence of Fry's illegal conduct. Much of the evidence supporting this inference is presented in Sub-section II.B, *supra*. Therefore, we need not reiterate all of the relevant facts, but we highlight a few of the more telling pieces of evidence. First, at least two clients informed Demmitt that they were missing money from their Allianz annuity accounts. Second, Allianz copied Demmitt on letters it sent to clients, confirming changes to their annuity accounts. Finally and most tellingly, Fry deposited client checks directly into bank accounts he jointly owned with Demmitt. Thus, there was ample evidence to support an inference that Demmitt was subjectively aware of Fry's illegal conduct, and the first prong is satisfied.

2. Prong Two

Demmitt contends there is no evidence to show she contrived to avoid learning of the illegal conduct. We disagree. Instead, there is ample evidence that the circumstances were "so overwhelmingly suspicious" that Demmitt's "failure to conduct further inspection or inquiry suggests a conscious effort to avoid incriminating knowledge." *See Conner*, 537 F.3d at 486. Much of this evidence overlaps with that discussed in Prong One.

Perhaps most tellingly, Demmitt frequently deposited large sums of cash that she likely obtained from Fry, often in relatively small bills, into her bank accounts. Second, even though the Allianz commissions were clearly unable to support business and personal accounts, Fry and Demmitt made numerous purchases, totaling thousands of dollars per month. In addition, even after Detective Vargas notified Demmitt that Fry was being investigated for fraud, Fry deposited a $60,000 client check into his and Demmitt's joint bank account. Finally, as discussed above, several clients notified Demmitt that their money had not been deposited into their Allianz annuity accounts. Given all these suspicious facts, Demmitt's failure to conduct further inspection or inquiry suggests a conscious effort to avoid incriminating knowledge.

p.677 Moreover, Demmitt admits on appeal that she "devoted all of her attention to the creation of a call center," and this evidence also was presented to the jury. As the government argues, the jury could have inferred that by doing so, Demmitt purposefully contrived to avoid learning of Fry's illegal conduct associated with the annuity business. Thus, the second prong is satisfied.

Because the evidence adduced at trial satisfies both prongs, we conclude that the district court's deliberate ignorance instruction was proper.[1]

IV. MONEY LAUNDERING CONVICTION

Demmitt challenges her conviction under 18 U.S.C. § 1956(a)(1)(B)(i), which was identified in the indictment as Count 27. She first argues that the difference between the date of the action charged in the indictment and the date about which evidence was presented at trial is a fatal variance from the indictment. She next argues that there was insufficient evidence to satisfy the elements of the statute.

Because we agree that the Government did not present sufficient evidence to support Demmitt's conviction under the statute, we need not reach her fatal variance argument.

A. Standard of Review

We review de novo whether sufficient evidence was presented at trial to support a conviction. *United States v. Brown,* 186 F.3d 661, 664 (5th Cir.1999) (citation omitted). Our review is highly deferential to the verdict. *United States v. Elashyi,* 554 F.3d 480, 491 (5th Cir.2008) (citation and internal quotation marks omitted). We review "whether a rational trier of fact could have found that the evidence established the essential elements of the offense beyond a reasonable doubt." *United States v. Ned,* 637 F.3d 562, 568 (5th Cir.2011) (per curiam) (citation omitted). We consider the evidence in the light most favorable to the Government, and we draw all reasonable inferences and credibility choices in support of the verdict. *Id.* (citation omitted). We assess whether "the trier of fact made a rational decision, rather than whether it correctly determined the defendant's guilt or innocence." *Id.* (citation omitted). The standard of review does not change, even though the evidence in this case was largely circumstantial. *See id.* (citation omitted).

B. Discussion

The statute under which Demmitt was charged in Count 27 is as follows:

> Whoever, knowing that the property involved in a financial transaction represents the proceeds of some form of unlawful activity, conducts or attempts to conduct such a financial transaction which in fact involves the proceeds of specified unlawful activity ... knowing that the transaction is designed in whole or in part (i) to conceal or disguise the nature, the location, the source, the ownership, or the control of the proceeds of specified unlawful activity ... shall be sentenced....

18 U.S.C. § 1956(a)(1)(B)(i). The indictment charged Demmitt with violating the statute when she transferred $3,000 via p.678 wire to her son, Tad. Demmitt argues that the Government did not prove that the wire transfer was "designed ... to conceal or disguise the nature, the location, the source, the ownership, or the control" of the fraudulently obtained money. Despite our demanding standard of review, we agree.

The Supreme Court has interpreted the statute's element requiring a design to mean "purpose or plan; *i.e.,* the intended aim of the [transaction]." *Cuellar v. United States,* 553 U.S. 550, 563, 128 S.Ct. 1994, 170 L.Ed.2d 942 (2008) (interpreting 18 U.S.C. § 1956(a)(2)(B)(i), which prohibits transporting, transmitting, and transferring money when it is designed to conceal or disguise the proceeds in specified ways). We have previously applied *Cuellar*'s statutory interpretation to 18 U.S.C. § 1956(a)(1)(B)(i). *See United States v. Brown,* 553 F.3d 768, 786 n. 56 (5th Cir. 2008).

We have explained *Cuellar* as follows:

> In *Cuellar,* the Supreme Court overturned an en banc decision of this court. The Court first held that the "designed to conceal" element of this statute

does not require the government to prove that a defendant sought to "create the appearance of legitimate wealth," because in this provision of the statute, "Congress used broad language that captures more than classic money laundering." However, the Court limited the statute's breadth somewhat: "[M]erely hiding funds during transportation is not sufficient to violate the statute, even if substantial efforts have been expended to conceal the money."

Brown, 553 F.3d at 786-87 (quoting *Cuellar,* 553 U.S. at 558-59, 563, 128 S.Ct. 1994). The concealment of the unlawfully obtained money must be a purpose — not just an effect — of the money transfers. *Chaney,* 595 F.3d at 240-42. The way in which a transaction is structured may be related to the transaction's purpose, but *"how* one moves the money is distinct from *why* one moves the money. Evidence of the former, standing alone, is not sufficient to prove the latter." *Cuellar,* 553 U.S. at 566, 128 S.Ct. 1994. Thus, the statute's design requirement "distinguishes the crime of money laundering from the innocent act of mere money spending." *United States v. Burns,* 162 F.3d 840, 848 (5th Cir.1998) (citing *United States v. Willey,* 57 F.3d 1374, 1384 (5th Cir.1995)). In *Brown,* we held the government's evidence was sufficient to satisfy *Cuellar's* standard where "defendants intended to and did make it more difficult for the government to trace and demonstrate the nature of these funds," including by employing "classic" money laundering techniques, such as conducting transactions in cash and making deposits below $10,000 to avoid reporting requirements. 553 F.3d at 787.

The evidence presented at trial shows that on August 11, 2008, Fry deposited a cashier's check from Georgiann McCormick into the bank account he jointly owned with Demmitt at Amarillo Community Federal Credit Union. This check had been obtained fraudulently. At the time of the deposit, the account balance was only $175.67. On August 21, 2008, Demmitt sent $3,000 from her account, using this money, via wire to Tad. The wire transfer receipt contains Demmitt's name, address, and account number, as well as Tad's business name. Most importantly, Tad testified that Demmitt sent the money upon Tad's request to help him purchase necessary business equipment. The Government has not suggested that Tad was part of Fry and Demmitt's scheme nor has it suggested that Tad did not need the money for business expenses.

As we noted above, mere spending of fraudulently obtained funds does not by p.679 itself satisfy 18 U.S.C. § 1956(a)(1)(B)(i). At trial, the Government proved only that the wire transfer occurred and that it was connected to fraudulently obtained money, not that Demmitt's actions were designed to conceal the fraudulent aspects of the money. Critically, the Government presented no evidence to rebut Tad's testimony that the purpose of the wire transfer was to provide money for his business expenses. Moreover, the series of transactions that culminated in the wire transfer differs from our precedent where we have upheld convictions that employed classic money laundering techniques. *See, e.g., Brown,* 553 F.3d at 787; *United States v. Powers,* 168 F.3d 741, 748 (5th Cir.1999) (finding important that checks did not reveal on their faces that the defendant or his wife were involved in the transactions).

No such techniques appear to have been used here nor did Demmitt intend to or succeed in making "it more difficult for the government to trace and demonstrate the nature of these funds." *Brown,* 553 F.3d at 787. This is not a case where, for this particular transaction, Demmitt commingled fraudulently obtained funds with legitimate business funds — Demmitt's legitimate business funds were so minuscule that the provenance of the client funds were not concealed when deposited into her account. Instead, Demmitt treated the fraudulently obtained money as her personal spending money, and she sent it to Tad upon his request for help with his business expenses. The Government presented no additional evidence or witnesses to explain how this transaction was designed to conceal the fraudulently obtained money in any of the specified ways.[2]

In sum, this transaction does not demonstrate any indicia of the type of unusualness or concealment that we have previously held to be sufficient to support a money laundering conviction. *See, e.g., Willey,* 57 F.3d at 1385-87 (describing unusual brokerage account transactions, the use of third parties, and "convoluted financial maneuvers" designed to conceal the source of funds).

Accordingly, in light of the evidence in the record, we hold that no rational trier of fact could have found that the evidence established all of the essential elements in 18 U.S.C. § 1956(a)(1)(B)(i) beyond a reasonable doubt. We therefore vacate Demmitt's conviction as to Count 27.

V. CONCLUSION

In light of the foregoing, we AFFIRM Demmitt's conviction except as to Count 27. We VACATE Demmitt's conviction as to Count 27, and REMAND to the district court for proceedings not inconsistent with this opinion.

[1] Even if both prongs of the test were not satisfied and the district court erred in giving the deliberate ignorance instruction, we hold the error harmless because there was substantial evidence that Demmitt was aware of the scheme. *See, e.g., United States v. Peterson,* 244 F.3d 385, 395 (5th Cir.2001) (permitting deliberate ignorance instruction where evidence showed defendants were deliberately indifferent or had actual knowledge that they were engaged in fraud).

[2] One of the Government's witnesses testified that Georgiann McCormick's personal check was negotiated in Nazareth. Even if that is the case, the cashier's check Fry obtained is stamped as deposited into Amarillo Community Federal Credit Union on August 11, 2008, and the check is clearly labeled "Remitter: Georgiann McCormick." This check does not present the case, as demonstrated by some of the other checks, where Fry apparently deposited fraudulently obtained funds into one of his accounts, and then purchased a cashier's check in his own name, which he then deposited into another one of his accounts.

SIXTH CIRCUIT DECISIONS

The Rule Against Hearsay

799 F.3d 554 (2015)

UNITED STATES of America, Plaintiff-Appellee,

v.

Russell Lee COLLINS (12-6263); Eddie Wilburn (12-6512); Richard Brosky (13-6617), Defendants-Appellants.

Nos. 12-6263, 12-6512, 13-6617.

United States Court of Appeals, Sixth Circuit.

Argued: November 19, 2014.

Decided and Filed: August 24, 2015.

US v. Collins, 799 F. 3d 554 (6th Cir. 2015)

p.566 ARGUED: Travis A. Rossman, Jewell & Rossman Law Office, Barbourville, Kentucky, for Appellant in 12-6263. Kevin M. Schad, Office of the Federal Public Defender, Cincinnati, Ohio, for Appellant in 12-6512. Mark A. Wohlander, Wohlander Law Office PSC, Lexington, Kentucky, for Appellant in 13-6617. Daniel Steven Goodman, United States Department of Justice, Washington, D.C., for Appellee. ON BRIEF: Travis A. Rossman, Jewell & Rossman Law Office, Barbourville, Kentucky, for Appellant in 12-6263. Kevin M. Schad, Office of the Federal Public Defender, Cincinnati, Ohio, for Appellant in 12-6512. Mark A. Wohlander, Wohlander Law Office PSC, Lexington, Kentucky, for Appellant in 13-6617. Daniel Steven Goodman, United States Department of Justice, Washington, D.C., for Appellee.

Before: DAUGHTREY, CLAY and COOK, Circuit Judges.

CLAY, J., delivered the opinion of the court in which DAUGHTREY, J., joined, and COOK, J., joined in the result.

OPINION

CLAY, Circuit Judge.

Defendants Russell Lee Collins, Eddie Wilburn, and Richard Brosky appeal from final judgments of the United States District Court for the Eastern District of Kentucky in a methamphetamine manufacturing and distribution conspiracy case. Defendant Collins appeals from the judgment of the district court entered on October 2, 2012, sentencing him to 324 months of incarceration for violation of various statutes including 21 U.S.C. § 846. Defendant Wilburn appeals from the judgment of the district court entered on November 26, 2012, sentencing him to 360 months of incarceration for violation of various statutes including 21 U.S.C. § 846. Defendant Brosky appeals from the judgment of the district court entered on December 2, 2013, sentencing him to 70 months of incarceration for violation of 21 U.S.C. § 846. On appeal, Defendants raise a number of arguments, including challenges to the admissibility and sufficiency of evidence, prosecutorial misconduct, constitutional violations, and the reasonableness of their sentences.

For the reasons that follow, we AFFIRM the judgments of the district court.

BACKGROUND

I. Procedural History

Defendants Russell Lee Collins, Eddie Wilburn, and Richard Brosky, as well as eight other individuals, were named in a superseding indictment filed in the United States District Court for the Eastern District of Kentucky on May 12, 2011, and charged with various offenses related to the manufacture and distribution of methamphetamine. A number of the individuals named in the indictment entered plea agreements and agreed to cooperate with the government.

Defendants proceeded to trial on May 29, 2012. On June 5, 2012, after a six-day trial, the jury entered its verdict. Defendants were all found guilty of one count of conspiring to manufacture a mixture or substance containing a detectable amount of methamphetamine in violation of 21 U.S.C. §§ 841(a)(1) and 846 (Count 1). The jury made a finding regarding the quantity of methamphetamine involved for each defendant, attributing 500 grams or more of methamphetamine to Collins and Wilburn, and attributing less than 50 p.567 grams of methamphetamine to Brosky. The jury also found Collins and Wilburn guilty of conspiring to distribute more than 500 grams of a mixture or substance containing methamphetamine in violation of 21 U.S.C. §§ 841(a)(1) and 846 (Count 2), but found Brosky not guilty of that charge.

In addition to the manufacturing and distribution charges, the jury found Collins and Wilburn guilty of one count of possessing equipment used to manufacture methamphetamine in violation of 21 U.S.C. § 843(a)(6) (Count 5), and one count of conspiring to distribute a mixture or substance containing methamphetamine to persons under the age of twenty-one in violation of 21 U.S.C §§ 841(a)(1), 846, and 859(a) (Count 14). Wilburn was found guilty of one additional count of possessing equipment used to manufacture methamphetamine in violation of 21 U.S.C. § 843(a)(6) (Count 7). Collins was found not guilty of one count of transporting stolen anhydrous ammonia across state lines in violation of 21 U.S.C. § 864(a) and 18 U.S.C. § 2 (Count 6).

The district court sentenced Collins to concurrent terms of 324 months of incarceration on Counts 1, 2 and 14, in addition to a concurrent term of 120 months on Count 5. Wilburn was sentenced to concurrent terms of 360 months of incarceration on Counts 1, 2, and 14, and to concurrent terms of 240 months on Counts 5 and 7. Brosky was sentenced to 70 months of incarceration on Count 1, his sole count of conviction.

II. Factual History

A. Initial Investigation of Collins and Wilburn

On September 22, 2010, following an unrelated search, police officers found what they believed to be a methamphetamine laboratory in the woods near the residential compound where Wilburn and Collins lived. A hazmat technician was summoned and confirmed that the items found by the officers were used to manufacture methamphetamine. One of the officers, Detective Kelly Farris, subsequently searched Wilburn's trailer and discovered additional items typically associated with the manufacture of methamphetamine. Additionally, a tank of anhydrous ammonia, which is used in the manufacture of methamphetamine, was found buried in a creek bed near Wilburn's trailer.

On February 17, 2011, Detective Farris and Special Agent Robert O'Neil conducted a home visit at Wilburn's trailer and found a one-step methamphetamine laboratory in the bathroom. They also found other materials used in the manufacture of methamphetamine both inside the trailer and outside the trailer, and observed that there were surveillance cameras set up on Wilburn's residence pointing to the driveway and towards Collins' trailer. No methamphetamine was found at the residence.

Although the conspiracy for which Defendants were indicted allegedly began in January 2009 and continued until April 2011, Collins and Wilburn were incarcerated on unrelated charges until January 2010 and June 2010, respectively. The government does not contend that these defendants participated in the conspiracy while incarcerated.

B. Initial Investigation of Brosky

On November 16, 2010, Detective Farris conducted an investigation of Brosky's residence following a complaint received by the Knox County Police Department that there was a methamphetamine laboratory on a hill behind Brosky's house. Detective Farris and other officers found a number of items suspected of having been used to manufacture methamphetamine in an orchard p.568 behind Brosky's home. Detective Farris also found a video camera overlooking the apple orchard that was hard-wired back to Brosky's home and to a monitor in his bedroom. No methamphetamine was found at the residence. On the basis of this search, Detective Farris arrested Brosky and his wife.

C. Testimony of Government Witnesses

At trial, the government presented testimony from multiple witnesses, a number of whom were also named in the indictment or were facing other charges and agreed to cooperate with the prosecution. Many of these witnesses were "smurfs" — individuals who claimed to have provided Collins and Wilburn with certain over-the-counter medications in exchange for methamphetamine. The active ingredient of these medications is pseudoephedrine, a precursor necessary for the production of methamphetamine. Government witnesses also testified that Collins and Wilburn had a practice of trading methamphetamine for sex, cash, and valuable items.

Few witnesses provided testimony regarding the total amount of methamphetamine allegedly produced by the conspiracy, though some, including Leya Stapleton and Kimberly Griffith, testified that they would obtain quarter to half grams of methamphetamine from the Defendants with some frequency. Mickey Brown testified that he helped Collins and Wilburn "cook" methamphetamine for approximately seven months of the conspiracy, claiming that he was present on 20 to 30 occasions during which Collins and Wilburn produced anywhere from 16 to 34 grams of methamphetamine each time. Brown and Charles

Skaggs, another government witness, testified that Brosky occasionally cooked methamphetamine with Wilburn and Collins.

Agent O'Neil provided testimony at trial regarding pseudoephedrine purchase records from January 2009 through April 2011 of individuals associated with the conspiracy. These records were created and stored by a company called MethCheck. Agent O'Neil testified that the purchases for this time period equaled 1,335 grams of pseudoephedrine. In his testimony, Agent O'Neil conceded that some portion of the pseudoephedrine represented in these records may have been provided to different methamphetamine "cooks" unrelated to the present conspiracy. Agent O'Neil, who was qualified as an expert, also testified regarding the possible conversion ratios between pseudoephedrine and methamphetamine. Throughout the trial, Defendants raised objections to the admissibility of the pseudoephedrine purchase records and to Agent O'Neil's testimony regarding conversion ratios. These objections were overruled.

Collins made multiple objections throughout the trial concerning the admissibility of evidence that overlapped with evidence previously presented at the trial of an unrelated methamphetamine manufacturing operation. The methamphetamine cooks for that operation, Darlene and Roscoe Smith, were convicted on March 1, 2012 of conspiring to manufacture at least 500 grams of a mixture or substance that contained methamphetamine. Many of the government's witnesses in the Smith case also testified against Defendants, and there was significant overlap between the pseudoephedrine purchase records admitted into evidence at both trials.[1]

<h2>p.569 DISCUSSION</h2>

<h3>I. Brosky's Destruction of Evidence Claim</h3>

This Court has applied an inconsistent standard when reviewing a motion to dismiss a defendant's indictment due to the government's failure to preserve exculpatory evidence. *United States v. Grenier,* 513 F.3d 632, 635 (6th Cir.2008) ("The standard of review to be applied for a motion to dismiss an indictment is somewhat unclear."). We have previously reviewed such motions *de novo* and for clear error. *Compare United States v. Wright,* 260 F.3d 568, 570 (6th Cir.2001) (applying *de novo* review to a district court's denial of a motion to dismiss a defendant's indictment on the ground that the government failed to preserve exculpatory evidence), *with United States v. Cody,* 498 F.3d 582 (6th Cir.2007) (reviewing for clear error a district court's denial of a defendant's motion to dismiss an indictment where the government lost or destroyed exculpatory evidence). Brosky's challenge fails under either standard of review.

Brosky's motion to dismiss is based on the government's alleged destruction of evidence obtained during the November 2010 search of Brosky's residence and a nearby orchard. Under the Due Process Clause of the Fourteenth Amendment, criminal defendants must be afforded "a meaningful opportunity to present a complete defense." *California v. Trombetta,* 467 U.S. 479, 485, 104 S.Ct. 2528, 81 L.Ed.2d 413 (1984). "[T]he Court has developed what might loosely be called the area of constitutionally guaranteed access to evidence" in order to protect this

Fourteenth Amendment right. *Id.* (internal quotation marks omitted). The Supreme Court has established two tests to determine whether a government's failure to preserve evidence amounts to a due process violation. The first test, established in *Trombetta,* applies in cases where the government fails to preserve material exculpatory evidence, while the second test, established in *Arizona v. Youngblood,* 488 U.S. 51, 109 S.Ct. 333, 102 L.Ed.2d 281 (1988), applies in cases where the government fails to preserve "potentially useful" evidence. *Wright,* 260 F.3d at 570.

Under *Trombetta,* to be deemed constitutionally material, evidence "must both possess an exculpatory value that was apparent before the evidence was destroyed, and be of such a nature that the defendant would be unable to obtain comparable evidence by other reasonably available means." 467 U.S. at 489, 104 S.Ct. 2528. In such cases, "[t]he destruction of material exculpatory evidence violates due process regardless of whether the government acted in bad faith." *Wright,* 260 F.3d at 571. Meanwhile, under the *Youngblood* standard, in cases "where the government fails to preserve evidence whose exculpatory value is indeterminate and only potentially useful," the defendant must demonstrate:

> (1) that the government acted in bad faith in failing to preserve the evidence; (2) that the exculpatory value of the evidence was apparent before its destruction; and (3) that the nature of the evidence was such that the defendant would be unable to obtain comparable evidence by other reasonably available means.

United States v. Jobson, 102 F.3d 214, 218 (6th Cir.1996) (citing *Youngblood,* 488 U.S. at 57-58, 109 S.Ct. 333). In order to establish bad faith, "a defendant must prove official animus or a conscious effort to suppress exculpatory evidence." *Id.* (internal quotation marks omitted).

p.570 Brosky argues that government agents impermissibly destroyed equipment suspected of being used to manufacture methamphetamine before that equipment could be tested for fingerprints that might have linked it to an individual named Joseph Ore rather than to Brosky. Joseph Ore had been living with Brosky during 2009 and had previously been arrested for manufacturing methamphetamine. Brosky argues that local law enforcement officers "concealed knowledge about the true ownership of the items discovered" during the search. *Brosky's Br.* at 26. The government contends that any evidence obtained from the equipment could "just as easily" have been considered "inculpatory as exculpatory" and that officers' public health and safety concerns counseled in favor of destroying any materials related to the manufacture of methamphetamine. *Appellee's Br.* at 25.

The district court denied Brosky's motion to dismiss, noting that despite Brosky's focus on Joseph Ore's previous criminal history, "there is nothing about the existence of a methamphetamine lab near his own home that could possibly be favorable to Brosky." (R. 343, Memorandum Opinion and Order, Page ID # 1496.) Having determined that the physical evidence at issue in this motion did not constitute material exculpatory evidence, the district court further held that Brosky "failed to argue that the government acted in bad faith when it destroyed the lab" and that this destruction cannot therefore form the basis of denial of the due process claim for destruction of "potentially useful evidence." (*Id.* at 1497.)

Regardless of whether we apply a *de novo* or clear error standard of review, the district court did not err in denying Brosky's motion to dismiss. First, the *Trombetta* test does not apply in this case since the equipment destroyed by the government does not constitute material exculpatory evidence. The evidence at issue here lacked "exculpatory value that was apparent before the evidence was destroyed." *Trombetta,* 467 U.S. at 489, 104 S.Ct. 2528. Second, Brosky has failed to establish a due process violation under *Youngblood.* In addition to the fact that there is no apparent exculpatory value to the destroyed items, Brosky has not shown that any evidence was destroyed because of "official animus" or a "conscious effort to suppress exculpatory evidence," as required to establish a due process violation under *Youngblood. Jobson,* 102 F.3d at 218. Consequently, the district court did not err by denying Brosky's motion to dismiss his indictment on the ground that law enforcement destroyed exculpatory evidence.

II. Evidentiary and Trial Issues

A. Collins' Impeachment with Evidence of Past Conviction

We review a district court's decision to allow impeachment evidence for abuse of discretion. *United States v. Meyers,* 952 F.2d 914, 916 (6th Cir.1992). "An abuse of discretion exists when the district court applies the wrong legal standard, misapplies the correct legal standard, or relies on clearly erroneous findings of fact." *Geier v. Sundquist,* 372 F.3d 784, 789-90 (6th Cir.2004). A district court that has conducted the necessary probative value versus prejudicial effect inquiry "has broad discretion to admit evidence of prior convictions" under Rule 609(b) of the Federal Rules of Evidence. *United States v. Sloman,* 909 F.2d 176, 181 (6th Cir.1990). Even where the reviewing court "concludes that the district court's ruling was erroneous, the defendant must demonstrate substantial prejudice to be entitled to a reversal." *Id.*

p.571 A defendant who chooses to testify at his criminal trial is subject to impeachment on cross-examination. Under Federal Rule of Evidence 609, the district court must admit evidence of a past criminal conviction for any crime that has as an element a dishonest act or false statement. Fed.R.Evid. 609(a)(2). More stringent limitations apply to the admission of evidence of a past criminal conviction if more than ten years have passed since the witness' conviction or release from confinement. In such circumstances, the evidence of conviction is only admissible if:

(1) its probative value, supported by specific facts and circumstances, substantially outweighs its prejudicial effect; and

(2) the proponent gives an adverse party reasonable written notice of the intent to use it so that the party has a fair opportunity to contest its use.

Fed.R.Evid. 609(b).

Convictions that are more than ten years old "should be admitted very rarely and only in exceptional circumstances." *Sloman,* 909 F.2d at 181 (quoting *United States v. Sims,* 588 F.2d 1145, 1147 (6th Cir.1978)). In order to admit such evidence, "a court must make an on-the-record finding based on the facts that the conviction's probative value substantially outweighs its prejudicial impact." *Meyers,* 952 F.2d at

917. This hearing on the record, which "need not be extensive," should include a consideration of the following factors:

(1) The impeachment value of the prior crime.

(2) The point in time of the conviction and the witness' subsequent history.

(3) The similarity between the past crime and the charged crime.

(4) The importance of the defendant's testimony.

(5) The centrality of the credibility issue.

Sloman, 909 F.2d at 181.

The district court abused its discretion by applying an incorrect legal standard in admitting Collins' past conviction as impeachment evidence. However, this error was harmless in light of the substantial evidence against Collins and the limited prejudicial potential of this past conviction. After Collins announced his intention to testify, the government stated its intention to impeach him with a 15-year-old Class B Misdemeanor for giving a false name to a police officer under Kentucky Revised Statutes § 523.110. Collins' counsel objected to the introduction of this evidence absent prior written notice. The following day, the district court concluded that it would consider the admissibility of Collins' prior conviction despite the lack of written notice, finding that the lack of notice was harmless because Collins' counsel knew about Collins' criminal history.

Rather than applying the Rule 609(b) analysis whereby the court determines whether a stale conviction's probative value *substantially outweighs* its prejudicial impact, the district court erroneously applied Rule 403 of the Federal Rules of Evidence. Under Rule 403, a court will exclude relevant evidence if its probative value *is substantially outweighed by* its unfair prejudicial effect. Fed.R.Evid. 403. Upon undertaking this analysis, the district court concluded that it could not find that the evidence of Collins' prior crime was "so prejudicial that it ought not be allowed," because it is the type of conviction that goes "directly to the witness's v[e]racity and his truthfulness." (R. 703, Transcript of Day 6 of Jury Trial, Page ID p.572 # 8353-4.)[2]

By applying the more permissive Rule 403 standard, the district court failed to undertake the requisite probative value versus prejudicial effect balancing, and in fact turned the Rule 609(b) analysis on its head. Accordingly, the district court abused its discretion by allowing the government to introduce evidence of Collins' prior conviction for the purposes of impeachment.

Nonetheless, the district court's error in applying an incorrect evidentiary rule was harmless. In cases where evidence of the defendant's participation in the crime is overwhelming, we have found that the erroneous admission of a stale conviction is harmless error. *See Sloman,* 909 F.2d at 181. Collins must show "substantial prejudice to be entitled to a reversal." *Id.* There was overwhelming evidence in this case of Collins' involvement in the conspiracy. Moreover, the potential prejudice of admitting this evidence is limited for the same reason that its probative value is limited — it had been 15 years since his conviction and he had had no subsequent similar convictions.

In sum, while Collins' prior conviction may have been inadmissible under a Rule 609(b) analysis, in light of the overwhelming testimony against Collins and the limited prejudicial impact of the conviction, the district court's error in applying a Rule 403 analysis and admitting the conviction into evidence was harmless.

B. Expert Witness Disclosures

We review a district court's admission or exclusion of evidence for abuse of discretion. *United States v. Ganier,* 468 F.3d 920, 925 (6th Cir.2006). Defendants argue that the district court abused its discretion by allowing the government's proposed expert witnesses to testify despite the government's deficient expert witness disclosures. We disagree.

Pursuant to Rule 16(a)(1)(G) of the Federal Rules of Criminal Procedure, the government must, at a defendant's request, "give to the defendant a written summary of any testimony that the government intends to use under Rules 702, 703, or 705 of the Federal Rules of Evidence during its case-in-chief at trial." The summary required by this rule "must describe the witness's opinions, the bases and reasons for those opinions, and the witness's qualifications." *Id.*

Where the government has failed to comply with this disclosure requirement, the district court may:

(A) order that party to permit the discovery or inspection; specify its time, place, and manner; and prescribe other just terms and conditions;

(B) grant a continuance;

(C) prohibit that party from introducing the undisclosed evidence; or

(D) enter any other order that is just under the circumstances.

Fed.R.Crim.P. 16(d)(2). We have previously identified three factors for a reviewing court to consider in determining whether "suppression of evidence is an appropriate remedy to be imposed" for a disclosure violation:

(1) the reasons for the government's delay in producing the materials, including whether it acted intentionally or in bad faith;

p.573 (2) the degree of prejudice, if any, to the defendant; and

(3) whether the prejudice to the defendant can be cured with a less severe course of action, such as granting a continuance or a recess.

United States v. Davis, 514 F.3d 596, 611 (6th Cir.2008) (internal quotation marks omitted).

"Suppression of evidence must be viewed as an undesirable remedy for a discovery violation reserved for cases of incurable prejudice or bad faith conduct demanding punishment by the court." *Id.* (internal quotations marks omitted). Courts should impose "the least severe remedy available to cure prejudice" where a potential Rule 16 violation has occurred. *United States v. Maples,* 60 F.3d 244, 247 (6th Cir.1995).

The government in this case filed its initial disclosure of expert witnesses for three potential witnesses on Friday, May 25, 2012 — five days before the trial was scheduled to begin. Defendants had requested the government's expert disclosures fourteen months earlier but had not received them. In discussing the timing of the government's disclosure, the district judge commented, "I don't know if there's a phrase that captures something later than the 11th hour, but it appears that it would be appropriate to apply that phrase to this case." (R. 680, Partial Transcript of Day 1 of Jury Trial, Page ID # 3231.) The prosecutor admitted that he had simply forgotten to file the disclosures. In addition to the government's significant delay in filing its disclosures, the district court found that the disclosures themselves were substantively deficient because they lacked specificity and included fairly boilerplate language to describe the experts' qualifications.

Based on these deficiencies, Defendants orally moved the court to prohibit the government from introducing the testimony of the three witnesses. Finding the remedy of excluding the testimony to be unnecessarily extreme, the district court sought to "fashion a remedy that addresses the concerns that are raised by the defense in terms of the late and cursory notice that's been given in this case, but something short of disallowing the testimony to occur." (R. 713, Partial Transcript of Day 1 of Jury Trial, Page ID # 8803.) The district court determined that the defense would not be significantly prejudiced by the government's error, noting that the experts' potential testimony related to drug quantities and that "this case is largely about drug quantity ... so it's not surprising that there would be expert testimony as it relates to drug quantity in this case." (*Id.* at 8804.) Determining that a less drastic course of action was possible, the district court denied Defendants' motion to exclude the witnesses and instead required the government to produce complete expert disclosures the following day and to introduce the witnesses later in the week. The district court further explained that, following defense counsel's receipt of the government's complete disclosures, it would entertain motions regarding the adequacy of the district court's proposed schedule. Specifically, the court suggested that it could "recess early one day to give counsel a little bit of [] extra time" and would consider making determinations regarding the order in which the government presented its evidence. (*Id.* at 8817).

The district court weighed the appropriate considerations regarding the nature of the Rule 16 violation and the potential prejudice facing Defendants. In so doing, the district court sought a less extreme solution than excluding the government's expert witnesses altogether and invited Defendants to file additional motions regarding the feasibility of the court's proposed p.574 solution. Defendants chose not to avail themselves of the opportunity to seek further remedies, including a continuance that might have allowed them to prepare rebuttal testimony. Having given Defendants additional time to review the disclosures as well as inviting Defendants to request additional time and/or other accommodations, the district court acted within its discretion in denying Defendants' motion to exclude the government's witnesses on the basis of the government's Rule 16 violation. It was not an abuse of discretion for the district court to apply a less severe remedy to address the government's inadequate expert disclosures.

C. Qualification of Agent O'Neil as an Expert Witness

Preservation of the Issue

Collins failed to preserve his objection to Agent O'Neil's expert witness qualifications for appeal. Collins contends that the objection was preserved by a co-defendant's objection, which he joined, on the first day of jury selection. In a lengthy exchange, Defendants raised concerns regarding the qualifications of Agent O'Neil and one other witness to testify regarding scientific issues, stating: "They want to testify to how much meth could be made from different things, and neither, I believe, none of them are qualified for that." (R. 680, Partial Transcript of Day 1 of the Jury Trial, Page ID # 3206.) The district court determined that Defendants would have an opportunity to question Agent O'Neil about his background and expertise before the court qualified him as an expert witness.

After questioning Agent O'Neil, Defendants failed to assert an objection and actively chose not to object to Agent O'Neil's qualifications when explicitly invited to do so by the district court. Rather, Brosky's attorney stated, "I'd certainly like to make an objection, but I think he's going to be in the ballpark as far as that, [] I think we're going to probably at some point in time ask for a more specific jury instruction [regarding his testimony]." (R. 702, Trial Tr., Page ID # 8108.) Collins' attorney then clarified that defense might ask for a jury instruction regarding the pseudoephedrine conversion ratio to which Agent O'Neil was testifying, "because if — he's qualified as an expert, I think for the purposes of trial, he's pretty close to it." (*Id.*) When the district court then sought confirmation that "there's no objection to moving forward with regard to [Agent O'Neil's qualification]," Collins' attorney failed to object, and Brosky's attorney replied, "I don't think I can. I mean, I've looked at all the case law." (*Id.* at 8108-9.) Following this exchange, the government moved to qualify O'Neil as an expert witness in open court and none of the defense attorneys objected. Therefore, despite the earlier objections raised by defense counsel prior to the initial questioning of Agent O'Neil, Collins did not preserve this issue for appeal.

Standard of Review

We generally review a district court's decision to admit proposed expert testimony for abuse of discretion. *United States v. Semrau,* 693 F.3d 510, 520 (6th Cir.2012). However, because Defendants failed to preserve this issue for appellate review, we review the district court's decision to permit Agent O'Neil to testify as an expert for plain error. *United States v. Smith,* 601 F.3d 530, 538 (6th Cir.2010) ("[T]his court reviews issues involving the admissibility of expert testimony for plain error where no objection was made at trial." (internal quotation marks omitted)). To establish plain error, a defendant must demonstrate:

> p.575 (1) error, (2) that was plain, and (3) that affects substantial rights. If all three conditions are met, an appellate court may then exercise its discretion to notice a forfeited error, but only if (4) the error seriously affected the fairness, integrity or public reputation of the judicial proceedings.

United States v. Johnson, 488 F.3d 690, 697 (6th Cir.2007) (internal quotation marks omitted).

Analysis

The district court did not plainly err by finding that Agent O'Neil was qualified to testify as an expert regarding the manufacture of methamphetamine. The government sought to establish the quantity of methamphetamine involved in

Defendants' conspiracy indirectly by introducing evidence of pseudoephedrine purchases made by Defendants' associates. Pseudoephedrine is a necessary precursor for the manufacture of methamphetamine. Agent O'Neil offered testimony regarding how much methamphetamine can be produced from a given quantity of pseudoephedrine (the "conversion ratio").[3] Collins argues that the district court should not have allowed Agent O'Neil to testify regarding the conversion ratio. While acknowledging Agent O'Neil's expertise in investigating and dismantling methamphetamine laboratories, Collins argues that this experience does not qualify Agent O'Neil as an expert in the chemistry behind methamphetamine production. Citing to no relevant case law, Collins specifically points to Agent O'Neil's lack of college education and formal chemistry training as evidence of his lack of expertise.

Despite Agent O'Neil's lack of formal chemistry instruction, he has significant on-the-job experience and training pertaining to methamphetamine manufacturing. Agent O'Neil testified that he had participated in more than 500 methamphetamine investigations and had dismantled more than 1,000 methamphetamine laboratories. In order to join the Two Rivers Drug Task Force, Agent O'Neil completed advanced methamphetamine training as well as a clandestine drug laboratory course, in which he was required to successfully produce methamphetamine. This course also provided Agent O'Neil with training regarding the conversion of pseudoephedrine to methamphetamine. Agent O'Neil testified that the regular re-certification training he receives specifically covers these conversion ratios.

We "regularly allow[] qualified law enforcement personnel to testify on characteristics of criminal activity, as long as appropriate cautionary instructions are given...." *United States v. Swafford,* 385 F.3d 1026, 1030 (6th Cir.2004). Given Agent O'Neil's experience and relevant training, the district court did not commit error, let alone plain error, by allowing Agent O'Neil to testify as an expert regarding the manufacture of methamphetamine.

D. Agent O'Neil's Reliance on Out-of-Court Statements

Preservation of the Issue

Collins challenges Agent O'Neil's testimony about the conversion ratio on the grounds that the testimony was based on out-of-court statements in violation of the Confrontation Clause and the rule against hearsay. Collins acknowledges that he failed to raise either a hearsay or Confrontation p.576 Clause objection at trial and therefore did not preserve either challenge for appeal.

Standard of Review

Due to Collins' failure to preserve this issue for appeal, we review Collins' hearsay and Confrontation Clause claims for plain error. *United States v. Baker,* 458 F.3d 513, 517 (6th Cir.2006) ("When a party fails to object to evidence at the trial court, his contention on appeal will prevail only if the trial court's evidentiary decision was plainly erroneous, thus affecting his substantial rights and resulting in a miscarriage of justice." (internal quotation marks omitted)). To satisfy plain-error review, "there must be (1) error, (2) that is plain, and (3) that affects substantial rights." *Id.*

(internal quotation marks omitted). "If all three conditions are met, an appellate court may then exercise its discretion to notice a forfeited error, but only if [] the error seriously affected the fairness, integrity or public reputation of the judicial proceedings." *Johnson,* 488 F.3d at 697.

Analysis

The district court did not plainly err by admitting Agent O'Neil's testimony regarding conversion ratios between pseudoephedrine and methamphetamine.

When questioned about possible conversion ratios, Agent O'Neil made reference to information he learned from people he caught manufacturing methamphetamine as the basis for his position that a one-to-one conversion ratio may be possible:

> Q. In regards to that method, based on your training and expertise, what [are] the conversion ratios you've encountered for pseudoephedrine over to methamphetamine?
>
> A. Oh, that I've actually encountered is — you know ... during the interviews of some of these people that I've caught manufacturing meth, a lot of them have told me if you know what you're doing, that you'll get one for one. If you use 2.4 grams of pseudoephedrine, you can pull 2.4 grams of meth. But now what that is, is a mixture of methamphetamine, and your purity level is going to go down.

(R. 702, Transcript of Day 5 of Jury Trial, Page ID # 8146-47.) Collins challenges the admissibility of this testimony on the theory that it violated both the Confrontation Clause and the rule against hearsay. Collins argues that the people to whom Agent O'Neil referred in this testimony have never been identified and that the admission of their views amounts to the admission of testimonial out-of-court statements for the truth of the matter asserted.

1. Confrontation Clause

The Confrontation Clause of the Sixth Amendment "guarantees a criminal defendant the right 'to be confronted with the witnesses against him.'" *United States v. Johnson,* 581 F.3d 320, 324 (6th Cir.2009) (quoting U.S. Const. amend. VI). The Confrontation Clause bars the "admission of testimonial statements of a witness who did not appear at trial unless he was unavailable to testify, and the defendant had had a prior opportunity for cross-examination." *Crawford v. Washington,* 541 U.S. 36, 53-54, 124 S.Ct. 1354, 158 L.Ed.2d 177 (2004). For a statement to be considered "testimonial" under the Confrontation Clause, the declarant must have "intend[ed] to bear testimony against the accused." *United States v. Cromer,* 389 F.3d 662, 675 (6th Cir.2004). This determination "depends on whether a reasonable person in the declarant's position would anticipate his statement being used against the accused in investigating and prosecuting the crime." *Johnson,* 581 p.577 F.3d at 325 (internal quotation marks omitted). There is no evidence that the suspected methamphetamine manufacturers Agent O'Neil questioned throughout his career "intended to bear testimony" against Collins or his co-defendants. Consequently, the admission of Agent O'Neil's testimony did not violate Collins' rights under the Confrontation Clause.

2. Rule Against Hearsay

The rule against hearsay bars the admission of out-of-court statements offered to prove the truth of the matter asserted. Fed.R.Evid. 801(c), 802. Although Agent O'Neil's testimony was based on out-of-court statements made by third parties suggesting that a one-to-one conversion ratio was possible, the government argues that this testimony was not admitted for the truth of the matter asserted because Agent O'Neil later testified that the average conversion ratio was lower than one-to-one. This argument lacks merit. Identification of a correct conversion ratio was a core issue at trial since the amount of methamphetamine produced by Defendants was proven in part by the amount of pseudoephedrine received by Defendants. Agent O'Neil's testimony, in which he made multiple references to out-of-court statements made by unidentified people, was expressly elicited by the government to establish potential conversion ratios to be used in this case. This testimony therefore does violate the rule against hearsay.

Nonetheless, Collins has failed to demonstrate that the court plainly erred by admitting this testimony. In order to establish that a plain error has occurred, Collins must show that the error affected his substantial rights. *Baker,* 458 F.3d at 517. This he cannot do. While Collins contests only the portion of Agent O'Neil's testimony that refers to the possibility of achieving a one-to-one conversion ratio, Agent O'Neil also testified that the maximum conversion ratio is 92 percent, that the average conversion ratio in the region was 50 to 75 percent, and that the ratio in this case may be even lower. Furthermore, in its closing argument, the government specifically referenced the typical conversion rate of 50 to 75 percent, and did not claim that a one-to-one ratio might be possible. Consequently, Collins has not demonstrated that Agent O'Neil's introduction of inadmissible out-of-court statements substantially affected his rights.

In sum, the district court did not commit plain error by admitting portions of Agent O'Neil's testimony that included out-of-court statements made by unidentified individuals. The admission of these statements did not violate the Sixth Amendment's Confrontation Clause and, while these statements constituted inadmissible hearsay, Collins is unable to demonstrate that any of his substantive rights have been affected by this testimony.

E. Relevance of Pseudoephedrine Purchase Records

A district court's relevance determinations are reviewed for abuse of discretion. *United States v. Hanna,* 661 F.3d 271, 288 (6th Cir.2011). Additionally, when reviewing the trial court's decision for abuse of discretion, "[we] must view the evidence in the light most favorable to its proponent, giving the evidence its maximum reasonable probative force and its minimum prejudicial value." *United States v. Copeland,* 321 F.3d 582, 597 (6th Cir. 2003).

Under the Federal Rules of Evidence, "irrelevant evidence is not admissible" at trial. Fed.R.Evid. 402. "Evidence is relevant if: (a) it has any tendency to make a fact more or less probable than it would be without the evidence; and (b) the fact is of p.578 consequence in determining the action." Fed.R.Evid. 401. This Circuit applies an "extremely liberal" standard for relevancy. *United States v. Whittington,* 455 F.3d 736, 738 (6th Cir.2006).

Collins argues that the district court abused its discretion by admitting three categories of irrelevant evidence: (1) wholly irrelevant pseudoephedrine transactions of several witnesses who did not testify; (2) "pseudoephedrine transactions that occurred while Collins was in jail on unrelated charges without an instruction limiting the consideration of these transactions vis-à-vis Collins"; and (3) pseudoephedrine transactions from a rival conspiracy. *Collins' Br.* at 44-52. We disagree.

1. Transactions of Witnesses Who Did Not Testify

The government introduced the pseudoephedrine purchase records of multiple witnesses who did not testify at trial. Collins challenges the introduction of the purchase records of Christina Doss and Sonoma Carson on the ground that their purchases were "tied to the conspiracy with a weak or nonexistent foundation for relevancy." *Collins' Br.* at 48. While Collins also asserts that there were deficient foundations for the introduction of pseudoephedrine purchases made by other witnesses, he provides no support for these conclusory assertions and we do not consider them.

a. Christina Doss

Christina Doss did not testify at trial and was not named in the indictment. Nevertheless, Agent O'Neil testified that she had purchased 44.88 grams of pseudoephedrine, which he included in his calculation of the total amount of pseudoephedrine deemed potentially attributable to the conspiracy. The following references were made to Doss during the trial:

> (1) Charles Skaggs testified on Day 2 of the trial that Doss was a young girl who was present in the company of Collins and Wilburn. When he was asked if he ever saw Doss and her friends give anything to Collins or Wilburn, he testified "I never seen them give them nothing." (R. 699, Transcript of Day 2 of Jury Trial, Page ID # 7519-20.)

> (2) Kelly Farris testified that Doss was present at Wilburn's residence when he performed a search and found incriminating items. (R. 701, Transcript of Day 4 of Jury Trial, Page ID # 7925.)

> (3) Agent O'Neil testified that Doss was present at the residence when the residence was searched and the police found items associated with the manufacture of methamphetamine. (R. 702, Transcript of Day 5 of Jury Trial, Page ID # 8114.)

Despite the lack of direct evidence establishing that Doss traded pseudoephedrine for methamphetamine, the testimony of multiple witnesses placing her in the company of Defendants where methamphetamine was allegedly being manufactured and her significant pseudoephedrine purchase history are enough to satisfy this Circuit's "extremely liberal" relevancy standard. *Dortch v. Fowler,* 588 F.3d 396, 400 (6th Cir.2009).

b. Sonoma Carson

Like Christina Doss, Sonoma Carson did not testify at trial. Agent O'Neil introduced records of her purchase of 24.24 grams of pseudoephedrine during his testimony. Additionally, the government presented evidence that Sonoma Carson had purchased pseudoephedrine that was used in the alleged conspiracy through the p.579 testimony of Leya Stapleton. Stapleton testified that Carson sold her pseudoephedrine, which Stapleton then traded to Wilburn for methamphetamine. Regardless of Stapleton's role as a middle man between Carson's pseudoephedrine and Wilburn's methamphetamine, this testimony is sufficient to establish a basis for the conclusion that Carson's pseudoephedrine is connected to the alleged conspiracy.

The government presented sufficient testimony to tie both Sonoma Carson and Christina Doss to Defendants' conspiracy. Consequently, the district court did not abuse its discretion by permitting the introduction of both individuals' pseudoephedrine purchase records.

2. Pseudoephedrine Transactions That Occurred While Collins Was in Jail

The indictment alleged that Defendants' conspiracy extended from January 2009 to April 2011. Collins was incarcerated from November 2008 until mid-January 2010 on unrelated charges, and Wilburn was in custody until June 25, 2010. Collins argues that "his only opportunity to participate in the conspiracy was from January 14, 2010 until April 2011," and that pseudoephedrine purchases made prior to this period should have been excluded. *Collins' Br.* at 50.

In *United States v. Robinson,* a case involving a conspiracy to distribute marijuana and cocaine, we considered a similar challenge to evidence of activities that occurred prior to a defendant's participation in the conspiracy. 390 F.3d 853, 882 (6th Cir.2004). We rejected the defendant's argument, recognizing that "'[i]t has long been established that a conspirator may join a conspiracy already in progress and be held responsible for actions done in furtherance of the conspiracy before he joined.'" *Id.* (quoting *United States v. Gravier,* 706 F.2d 174, 177 (6th Cir.1983)); *see also United States v. Cimini,* 427 F.2d 129, 130 (6th Cir.1970) ("The rule is that where a conspiracy is already in progress, a late comer who knowingly joins it takes it as he finds it and he may be held responsible for acts committed in furtherance of the conspiracy before he joined it."). Under this precedent, the pseudoephedrine purchases of Collins' co-conspirators that occurred in 2009 may be admissible to establish the existence and nature of the conspiracy, even absent evidence that Collins and Wilburn joined the conspiracy before their respective releases from incarceration.

Collins further argues that since the government's witnesses identified Collins and Wilburn as the "cooks" of the conspiracy, it was impossible that the conspiracy manufactured methamphetamine prior to his release from incarceration in January 2010. Despite Collins' assertion that the conspiracy could not have existed without his participation, the indictment identified a total of eleven people in the conspiracy charges, and pseudoephedrine purchases of Defendants' associates from 2009 are relevant in establishing the existence of the conspiracy. Furthermore, the testimony of government witnesses suggested that other participants in the conspiracy, including Brosky, may have "cooked" methamphetamine as well. Consequently, it was not an abuse of discretion for the district court to admit as relevant pseudoephedrine purchases from 2009.

3. Pseudoephedrine Transactions from a Rival Conspiracy

Collins argues that the government introduced evidence of pseudoephedrine purchases that were irrelevant to the Defendants' conspiracy because they were used in an unrelated conspiracy. At trial, Agent O'Neil testified about the amount of p.580 pseudoephedrine purchased by multiple individuals associated with the Defendants' conspiracy and calculated the sum of these purchases to be 1,335 grams of pseudoephedrine. On direct examination, the government asked Agent O'Neil, with regards to the individuals he had just named, "in the course of your investigations, have you encountered other individuals in Knox County who may have received the pseudoephedrine from these individuals?" (R. 702, Transcript of Day 5 of Jury Trial, Page ID # 8145.) The prosecutor then clarified and asked, with regards to a separate conspiracy known as the Smith conspiracy, "based on your investigation, could they have received some items from the people on this list too?" (Id. at 8145-46.) Agent O'Neil replied, "Yes, they could have." (Id. at 8146.)

During cross-examination by Wilburn's attorney, Agent O'Neil again admitted that some unspecified portion of the total 1,335 grams was provided to the Smith conspiracy, rather than the Defendants' conspiracy:

Q. Okay. And [] do you recall the time frame of the conspiracy in the [Roscoe] and Darlene Smith case?

A. I do not know the exact dates off the top of my head, no, sir.

Q. Would there have been overlap with this case?

A. Yes. There would have been overlap with this case.

Q. And some of the witnesses who testified in this trial supplied seed to [Roscoe] and Darlene Smith?

A. Some of the witnesses that testified in this trial?

Q. Well, let me just — let me just rephrase that. Some of the people that were on your list, some 30 people that you just testified to, did some of those people supply seed to [Roscoe] and Darlene Smith?

A. Yes. Some of the people — the names that I read today did supply pseudoephedrine to [Roscoe] and Darlene Smith as well, yes, sir.

Q. Okay. And were [Roscoe] and Darlene Smith convicted in that case?

A. Yes, they were.

Q. And were they convicted of manufacturing more than 500 grams of methamphetamine?

A. Yes, sir, they were.

Q. Okay. So an unknown portion of this 1,335 grams of [pseudoephedrine] was used in the manufacturing [of] more than 500 grams of methamphetamine by [Roscoe] and Darlene Smith; is that a fair statement?

A. Yes. Some of the people on the list that I read did take pseudoephedrine to [Roscoe] and Darlene Smith as well.

Q. Well, so it's a fair statement that some portion of this 1,335 grams was actually used in manufacturing by [Roscoe] and Darlene Smith, who have been convicted of meth manufacturing more than 500 grams?

A. Yes, sir, that's a fair statement.

Q. Okay. And you really don't know how much of that was actually used by [Roscoe] and Darlene Smith?

A. No, sir, I do not.

(*Id.* at 8161-63.)

Collins' relevancy argument is based on his contention that "[i]t is a mathematical certainty that some of the pseudoephedrine transactions counted against the Smith conspiracy were counted against Collins." *Collins' Br.* at 47. This assertion is false. Even if there was a 100 percent overlap between the pseudoephedrine purchase records admitted in the Smith trial and the records admitted in the present trial, it was possible for the jury to convict Collins without counting any of the p.581 pseudoephedrine purchases necessarily relied upon in the Smith trial against him. The jury was told by Agent O'Neil that the typical conversion ratio was 50 to 75 percent, which was later repeated to them by the prosecution during closing arguments. The application of a 75 percent conversion ratio to 1,335 grams of pseudoephedrine results in 1,001 grams of methamphetamine, which is enough, though just barely, to establish two separate conspiracies involving 500 grams or more of methamphetamine.

There is no question that any pseudoephedrine that was unambiguously used by the rival Smith conspiracy would not be relevant to establishing the quantity of methamphetamine produced by Defendants' conspiracy. However, the challenged pseudoephedrine purchases of Collins' associates were not unambiguously used by the rival Smith conspiracy and are, therefore, still relevant to establishing Defendants' conspiracy.

F. Due Process Claims Related to the Smith Conspiracy

Preservation of the Issue

Collins argues that his due process rights were violated by the admission of evidence that was attributable to the Smith conspiracy and by the fact that his jury pool overlapped with the jury pool in the Smith trial. Collins did not raise these due process arguments below and thereby failed to preserve them for appellate review.

Standard of Review

"Where, as here, a defendant failed to make an objection below, the claim of prosecutorial misconduct is reviewed for plain error." *United States v. Carson,* 560 F.3d 566, 574 (6th Cir.2009). "Plain error review applies even if the forfeited assignment of error is a constitutional error." *Cromer,* 389 F.3d at 672. As has already been stated, plain error occurs when there is an "(1) error (2) that was plain, and (3) that affects substantial rights ... but only if ... the error seriously affected the fairness, integrity or public reputation of the judicial proceedings." *Johnson,* 488 F.3d at 697.

Analysis

The district court did not commit plain error by admitting evidence that was also introduced in the Smith trial, or by allowing jurors who may have been in the Smith trial's jury pool to serve on the jury in this case. Courts have recognized "two species" of due process claims in criminal cases: (1) "State action that 'shocks the conscience' violates the Due Process Clause's substantive component," and (2) "[s]tate action that deprives a defendant of a fundamentally fair trial violates the Due Process Clause's procedural component." *Stumpf v. Robinson,* 722 F.3d 739, 748 n. 8 (6th Cir.2013).

1. Evidence of Pseudoephedrine Purchases Used in the Smith Conspiracy

Collins argues that his due process rights were violated by the prosecutor's admission of evidence of pseudoephedrine transactions that "necessarily occurred in the Smith conspiracy." *Collins' Br.* at 52. Collins claims that by admitting this evidence, the government impermissibly "used the same evidence to convict different sets of defendants in two separate, rival conspiracies in two different trials." *Id.* at 53. Although "inconsistent prosecutorial theories can, in certain circumstances, violate due process rights," the government's introduction of the challenged pseudoephedrine purchase records does not amount to reliance on "inconsistent prosecutorial theories." *Smith v.* p.582 *Groose,* 205 F.3d 1045, 1049 (8th Cir.2000). As was discussed above, the overlapping evidence put forward at both Defendants' trial and the Smith trial does not reflect two inconsistent criminal theories because the pseudoephedrine purchases introduced at both trials could account for enough methamphetamine to establish two separate conspiracies.

Moreover, the government in this case affirmatively solicited testimony from Agent O'Neil that some of the pseudoephedrine purchases he identified could have been traded with other dealers or cooks, including Darlene and Roscoe Smith. This testimony was expanded upon during cross-examination, and some of the witnesses whose pseudoephedrine purchases were entered into evidence testified that they traded pseudoephedrine with multiple people other than Defendants.

The district court did not plainly err by allowing the prosecution to admit evidence that may have overlapped with the Smith conspiracy because the government's introduction of this evidence did not necessarily conflict with its presentation of the evidence in the *Smith* case.

2. Potential Inappropriate Influence on Jurors

Citing to no relevant caselaw, Collins also argues that his due process rights were violated because the jury pool in his case was the same as the jury pool in the Smith trial. During *voir dire,* the district court suggested to counsel that the court should ask the potential jurors whether they had served on the jury in the Smith trial. The court subsequently granted the defense's motion to strike five potential jurors who had served on the Smith jury. Collins argues that although no other potential jurors remembered serving on the Smith jury, some of them "undoubtedly participated in voir[] dire in the Smith case, heard the names of witnesses from that case, and were otherwise prejudiced against Collins." *Collins' Br.* at 53. Collins fails to point to any specific information that would have been discussed at *voir dire* in the Smith trial that might have then prejudiced potential jurors against him. The district court did not plainly err by failing to *sua sponte* identify and dismiss jurors who participated in *voir dire* in the Smith trial.

G. Admission of "MethCheck" Records as Business Records

"In reviewing a trial court's evidentiary determinations, [we] review[] *de novo* the court's conclusions of law and review[] for clear error the court's factual determinations that underpin its legal conclusions." *Baker,* 458 F.3d at 516. However, we have also applied an abuse of discretion standard to our review of a district court's Rule 803(6) admissibility decisions. *United States v. Hathaway,* 798 F.2d 902, 906 (6th Cir.1986) ("[O]n review, we will reverse the district court's decision only if we find a clear abuse of discretion."). We need not resolve this discrepancy since Defendants' challenge fails under either standard of review.

Rule 803(6) of the Federal Rules of Evidence permits records of regularly conducted business activity to be admitted into evidence if the records meet four requirements: 1) they were "created in the course of a regularly conducted business activity," 2) they were "kept in the regular course of that business," 3) they resulted from a "regular practice of the business" to create such documents, and 4) they were "created by a person with knowledge of the transaction or from information transmitted by a person with knowledge." *Yoder & Frey Auctioneers, Inc. v. EquipmentFacts, LLC,* 774 F.3d p.583 1065, 1071-72 (6th Cir.2014); Fed.R.Evid. 803(6). The fulfillment of these conditions must be "shown by the testimony of the custodian or another qualified witness, or by a certification that complies with Rule 902(11) or (12) or with a statute permitting certification." Fed.R.Evid. 803(6)(D).

Brosky argues that the government did not lay the requisite foundation to introduce the pseudoephedrine purchase records created by MethCheck under Rule 803(6) because the officers who first discussed the particular MethCheck records at issue in this case were not "qualified witnesses." *Brosky's Br.* at 21. On the other hand, the government contends that the records were properly introduced because, consistent with Rule 803(6), "prior to the testimony of [the officers], the custodian of records (Acquisto) provided the general foundational testimony of 'the custodian or another qualified witness.'" *Appellee's Br.* at 79 (quoting Fed.R.Evid. 803(6)(D)). We conclude that the district court neither erred nor abused its discretion by admitting pseudoephedrine purchase records as business records under Federal Rule of Evidence 803(6).

MethCheck is a service provided by the NPLEx Project, which is run by Appriss, Inc., a public safety technology company. MethCheck electronically tracks the purchase of precursors for methamphetamine, including Sudafed and other over-the-counter medications, in real time. The government's first witness was James Acquisto, the vice president of government affairs for Appriss. Acquisto testified that Appriss keeps records containing MethCheck entries and that he is the custodian of records for these entries. Acquisto testified at length regarding the process by which MethCheck records are created and stored. In sum, Acquisto explained that when a person goes to a drug store and attempts to purchase a medication that is identified as a methamphetamine precursor, federal and state law require the individual to present the pharmacy employee with government-issued photo identification. The information is then scanned or manually entered into the MethCheck System immediately, and the clerk receives a nearly instantaneous message confirming whether the sale is legal or illegal (based on purchase quantity regulations). This purchase information becomes available to law enforcement in under a minute. Acquisto testified that the entries are automated approximately 75 percent of the time, but that the entries are entered manually in some small independent drug stores. Acquisto further testified that law enforcement officers in Kentucky may apply for access to MethCheck records from the Office of Drug Control Policy. If they are granted access, they receive a secure password and user ID to access the portal through the internet.

Despite obtaining detailed information from Acquisto regarding how MethCheck records are kept, the government did not seek to introduce specific MethCheck records through Acquisto. Instead, the government sought to introduce MethCheck records for specific purchasers through two officers, Detective Farris and Agent O'Neil. These officers testified that they accessed the MethCheck database and retrieved the records for people they suspected of being associated with methamphetamine manufacturing.

When the government sought to introduce specific MethCheck records through the officers, counsel for Brosky objected that the records were not admissible because they had not been authenticated by Acquisto, the custodian of the records. The district court overruled Brosky's objection, concluding that the testimony of the officers, in conjunction with Acquisto's detailed testimony regarding the record p.584 keeping process, was sufficient to authenticate the records.

As has already been stated, the foundation for Rule 803(6) evidence must be "shown by the testimony of the custodian or another qualified witness...." Fed.R.Evid. 803(6)(D). We have previously held that the meaning of "[another] qualified witness should be given the broadest interpretation." *Hathaway,* 798 F.2d at 906 (internal quotation marks omitted). The foundation for admitting evidence under Rule 803(6) "may be laid, in whole *or in part,* by the testimony of a government agent or other person outside the organization whose records are sought to be admitted. The only requirement is that the witness be familiar with the record keeping system." *United States v. Laster,* 258 F.3d 525, 529 (6th Cir.2001) (internal quotation marks and citations omitted) (emphasis added). The qualifying witness does not need to have any personal knowledge of the records' preparation. *Baker,* 458 F.3d at 518.

The government concedes that it never sought to authenticate the MethCheck records through Acquisto alone. Moreover, although both officers testified regarding the process by which they were able to access and retrieve data from the MethCheck system, neither officer provided information regarding the manner in which MethCheck records are kept on the backend. Nonetheless, under our existing precedent, evidence is admissible under Rule 803(6) where, as here, foundation is provided in part by the record custodian and in part by an officer who is familiar with the system and can testify to the process by which information is retrieved. Accordingly, the district court neither erred nor abused its discretion in determining that the foundation provided was adequate to introduce the MethCheck records under Rule 803(6).

H. Confrontation Clause Challenge to Admission of MethCheck Records

Preservation of the Issue and Standard of Review

On appeal, Defendants raise Confrontation Clause challenges to the admission of the MethCheck records. The government contends that none of the Defendants preserved this issue for appeal because they did not raise a specific Confrontation Clause objection at trial. Defendants argue that, "[w]hile the term 'Confrontation Clause' was not used," Collins' counsel launched a lengthy objection to the admission of the MethCheck records, repeatedly raising the fact that no one was present at trial to testify to the transactions and that the records had not been disclosed in a timely manner. *Collins' Reply Br.* at 18-19; *Brosky's Reply Br.* at 4. Although lengthy, Defendants' objection was focused exclusively on the authentication of the records and the lack of relevancy to the alleged conspiracy. (*See, e.g.,* R. 697, Transcript of Day 5 of Jury Trial, Page ID # 6772-73 ("[I]t would be our position that [the records] cannot be authenticated. They are not relevant to this trial because those persons did not come here to testify that they had taken those actions with these particular defendants.").) At trial, Defendants did not raise any concerns regarding the violation of their constitutional right to confront the witnesses against them. Accordingly, Defendants failed to preserve their Confrontation Clause claim adequately for appellate review.

Because Defendants failed to preserve this issue for review, we review their Confrontation Clause claims for plain error. "Plain error review applies even if the forfeited assignment of error is a constitutional error." *Cromer,* 389 F.3d at 672; p.585 *see United States v. Hadley,* 431 F.3d 484, 498 (6th Cir.2005) (reviewing a Confrontation Clause claim for plain error because "Defendant raised only a hearsay objection to [the contested] statements at trial, and did not challenge their admissibility on constitutional grounds").

Analysis

The district court did not commit plain error in violation of the Confrontation Clause by allowing the government to introduce the pseudoephedrine purchase records. The Confrontation Clause of the Sixth Amendment "guarantees a criminal defendant the right 'to be confronted with the witnesses against him.'" *Johnson,* 581 F.3d at 324 (quoting U.S. Const. amend. VI). To that end, the Confrontation Clause bars the "admission of testimonial statements of a witness who did not appear at trial unless he was unavailable to testify, and the defendant had had a prior opportunity for cross-examination." *Crawford,* 541 U.S. at 53-54, 124 S.Ct. 1354 (2004). "Hearsay evidence that is non-testimonial is not subject to Confrontation Clause analysis...." *United States v. Parlier,* 570 Fed.Appx. 509, 517 (6th Cir.2014). For a statement to be considered "testimonial" under the Confrontation Clause, the declarant must have "intend[ed] to bear testimony against the accused." *Cromer,* 389 F.3d at 675. This determination "depends on whether a reasonable person in the declarant's position would anticipate his statement being used against the accused in investigating and prosecuting the crime." *Johnson,* 581 F.3d at 325 (internal quotation marks omitted).

1. Nature of the MethCheck Records

As has been previously described, information is entered into the MethCheck system by pharmacy employees whenever a customer attempts to purchase products containing pseudoephedrine. Acquisto testified that, 75 percent of the time, these entries are made automatically through the scanning or swiping of the customer's identification card. The rest of the time, the pharmacy employee must manually enter the customer's information into the system. Collins and Wilburn argue that "[t]he data inputted from the store clerk is essentially a testimonial declaration that 'this person appeared in front of me on a given date and purchased a given quantity of pseudoephedrine.'" *Collins' Br.* at 56. In making this argument, Collins and Wilburn analogize this case to the Supreme Court's decisions in *Melendez-Diaz v. Massachusetts,* 557 U.S. 305, 129 S.Ct. 2527, 174 L.Ed.2d 314 (2009) and *Bullcoming v. New Mexico,* ___ U.S. ___, 131 S.Ct. 2705, 180 L.Ed.2d 610 (2011).

In *Melendez-Diaz,* the Supreme Court held that the admission of affidavits from forensic analysts who had performed drug analysis on evidence seized from a suspect but did not themselves testify violated the Confrontation Clause. 557 U.S. at 329, 129 S.Ct. 2527. Relying heavily on this decision, the Court in *Bullcoming* held that the Confrontation Clause barred the admission of a blood alcohol level test where the certifying analyst did not testify and the government instead relied on the testimony of another analyst familiar with the forensic procedures. The *Bullcoming* Court determined that the analyst's report, like the affidavit at issue in *Melendez-Diaz,* was testimonial in nature because it was made in aid of a police investigation "solely for an evidentiary purpose." *Bullcoming,* 131 S.Ct. at 2717 (internal quotation marks omitted). The report was made by a state laboratory "required by law to assist in police investigations" on the basis of evidence seized by a law enforcement officer. *Id.* According to Collins, p.586 the "store clerks who inputted the data are analogous to the analyst who certified the forensic test in *Bullcoming.*" *Collins' Br.* at 57.

To the contrary, unlike the forensic report at issue in *Bullcoming* and the affidavit at issue in *Melendez-Diaz,* the MethCheck reports at issue in this case were not made to prove the guilt or innocence of any particular individual, nor were they created for solely evidentiary purposes. Although law enforcement officers may use MethCheck records to track pseudoephedrine purchases, the MethCheck system is designed to prevent customers from purchasing illegal quantities of pseudoephedrine by indicating to the pharmacy employee whether the customer has exceeded federal or state purchasing restrictions. *See United States v. Towns,* 718 F.3d 404, 411 (5th Cir.2013) ("Because the [pseudoephedrine] purchase logs were not prepared specifically and solely for use at trial, they are not testimonial and do not violate the Confrontation Clause."). Furthermore, it is improbable that a pharmacy employee running a standard identification check of a customer would have anticipated that the records of that transaction would later be used against these particular defendants at trial. Because the MethCheck records at issue in this case are not clearly testimonial in nature, the district court did not commit plain error in violation of the Confrontation Clause by allowing their admission at trial.

2. Brosky's Right to Cross-Examine Government Witnesses

Brosky argues that his right to cross-examine government witnesses effectively, as guaranteed by the Confrontation Clause, was violated by the government's late disclosure of certain MethCheck records that were introduced as evidence towards the end of trial. Specifically, Brosky notes that MethCheck records attributed to government witnesses who had already been excused were brought to the Defendants' attention only before the last day of the government's case-in-chief, when they were entered into evidence. As a result, Defendants were unable to cross-examine the relevant government witnesses in order to ascertain how much of the pseudoephedrine they purchased was associated with the alleged conspiracy.

"The main and essential purpose of confrontation is to secure for the opponent the opportunity of cross-examination." *Delaware v. Fensterer,* 474 U.S. 15, 19-20, 106 S.Ct. 292, 88 L.Ed.2d 15 (1985) (emphasis and internal quotation marks omitted). "Generally speaking, the Confrontation Clause guarantees an opportunity for effective cross-examination, not cross-examination that is effective in whatever way, and to whatever extent, the defense might wish." *Id.* at 20, 106 S.Ct. 292 (emphasis omitted). In this case, Brosky availed himself of the opportunity to cross-examine the government's witnesses fully. To the extent that the witnesses testified that they had given Brosky boxes of Sudafed in return for methamphetamine, Brosky had an opportunity to question the witnesses about the amount of Sudafed traded even without referencing the MethCheck records. Additionally, Brosky had the opportunity to cross-examine Agent O'Neil about the MethCheck records when they were introduced. Brosky has not demonstrated that the district court committed plain error in violation of the Confrontation Clause by allowing the government to utilize the additional MethCheck records on the last day of their case-in-chief.

I. Prosecutorial Misconduct

We "review claims of prosecutorial misconduct that were objected to in the p.587 trial court de novo." *United States v. Boyd,* 640 F.3d 657, 669 (6th Cir.2011); *United States v. Henry,* 545 F.3d 367, 376 (6th Cir.2008) ("Allegations of prosecutorial misconduct contain mixed questions of law and fact that we usually review de novo.").

Collins has failed to establish that the prosecutor committed misconduct by knowingly eliciting false testimony from Joseph Ore, a government witness. The "deliberate deception of a court and jurors by the presentation of known false evidence is incompatible with rudimentary demands of justice." *Giglio v. United States,* 405 U.S. 150, 153, 92 S.Ct. 763, 31 L.Ed.2d 104 (1972) (internal quotation marks omitted). "This rule applies to both the solicitation of false testimony and the knowing acquiescence in false testimony." *Workman v. Bell,* 178 F.3d 759, 766 (6th Cir.1998). This Court has "fashioned a three-part test for determining whether there was a denial of due process through the use of false testimony." *Peoples v. Lafler,* 734 F.3d 503, 515 (6th Cir.2013). The defendant must establish that "(1) the statement was actually false; (2) the statement was material; and (3) the prosecution knew it was false." *Id.* at 516. A false statement is material "if the false testimony could in any reasonable likelihood have affected the judgment of the jury." *Brooks v. Tennessee,* 626 F.3d 878, 895 (6th Cir.2010).

At trial, Joseph Ore testified that he transacted with Collins daily, trading Sudafed for methamphetamine, from January 2009 until Ore went to prison in July 2009. However, this testimony was necessarily false, as Collins was incarcerated on unrelated charges during this entire time period. Throughout his testimony, Ore seemed to be somewhat confused about the specific dates at issue. For example, when asked by the prosecutor about the timing of the alleged drug transactions, Ore offered, "I can't remember specific dates, but somewhere in that time frame." (R. 700, Transcript of Day 3 of Jury Trial, Page ID # 7800-7801.) Collins' attorney objected to this testimony on the ground that it is undisputed that Collins was incarcerated for all of 2009 and was only released from prison in January 2010. When questioned by the district court, the Assistant United States Attorney indicated that he did not know "specifically when Mr. Collins was in custody" but that he thought that Collins "got out [in] April of 2009." (*Id.* at 7805.) The district court concluded that "the record is [not] sufficient to suggest that the testimony and the responses that are going to be elicited are knowingly false[,]" and overruled Collins' objection. (*Id.* at 7806.) On cross-examination, Collins' attorney elicited Ore's admission that he had no dealings with Collins while either Collins or Ore were incarcerated. Collins argues that the prosecutor either knew or should have known when Collins was in jail, and thus either knew or should have known that Ore was testifying falsely when he stated that he had traded with Collins in 2009.

The prosecutor's communication with the district judge suggests that he was confused about the dates of Collins' incarceration — and therefore did not know he was eliciting false testimony from Ore. Regardless of this confusion, the prosecutor undoubtedly should have known that Collins was incarcerated until January 2010, given that Collins was on trial for a conspiracy that allegedly began in 2009. *See Foley v. Parker,* 488 F.3d 377, 392 (6th Cir.2007) (stating in dicta that the knowledge requirement is fulfilled if the "prosecution knew or *should have known* that [a witness] was committing perjury" (emphasis added)). Even so, Collins fails to satisfy the materiality prong of the requisite p.588 analysis. While Ore's false statement may have been material if left uncorrected, shortly after providing his false testimony, Ore was cross-examined effectively by Collins' counsel, who clearly refuted Ore's previous assertion. During the cross-examination, Ore admitted that he was not sure about the dates and would not be surprised to hear that Collins had been in jail for all of 2009. He also conceded that he had no dealings with Collins while Collins was incarcerated, and the jury was made aware of Collins' dates of incarceration. Given that Ore's testimony was wholly unbelievable in light of Collins' dates of incarceration, there is no reasonable likelihood that the jury believed Ore's incorrect statements. Therefore, while the prosecutor's conduct was highly troublesome, it did not amount to a denial of due process.

J. Testimony that Collins and Wilburn Traded Methamphetamine for Sex

Preservation of the Issue and Standard of Review

Wilburn concedes that counsel did not object to the challenged testimony during trial. admission of that testimony for reversible plain error. *United States v. Willoughby,* 742 F.3d 229, 236 (6th Cir. 2014). To establish that the admission of contested testimony amounted to plain error, a defendant must show that "(1) there is an error; (2) the error is clear or obvious, rather than subject to reasonable dispute; (3) the error affected the appellant's substantial rights, [meaning that] it affected the outcome of the district court proceedings; and (4) the error seriously affects the fairness, integrity or public reputation of judicial proceedings." *United States v. Marcus,* 560 U.S. 258, 262, 130 S.Ct. 2159, 176 L.Ed.2d 1012 (2010) (internal quotation marks omitted). Where a defendant has failed to object to the disputed testimony at trial, our "review is doubly deferential," and "we must determine, in essence, that the district court obviously abused its discretion when it admitted the [challenged] testimony." *Willoughby,* 742 F.3d at 238.

Analysis

The district court did not plainly err by admitting evidence that Wilburn and Collins traded methamphetamine for sex. Under Rule 403 of the Federal Rules of Evidence, "[t]he court may exclude relevant evidence if its probative value is substantially outweighed by a danger of one or more of the following: unfair prejudice, confusing the issues, misleading the jury, undue delay, wasting time, or needlessly presenting cumulative evidence." We have consistently held that "[a] district court has very broad discretion in making this determination." *Semrau,* 693 F.3d at 523 (internal quotation marks omitted). A district court must "weigh the proper probative value of the evidence against ... its unfairly prejudicial effect." *United States v. Parkes,* 668 F.3d 295, 305 (6th Cir.2012). "Evidence that lacks inflammatory detail... might not be unfairly prejudicial at all." *Sims,* 708 F.3d at 836.

Wilburn argues that the government introduced "significant prejudicial evidence" relating to Wilburn and Collins trading methamphetamine for sex. *Wilburn's Br.* at 16. This testimony, Wilburn contends, "caused the jury to have disdain for Wilburn unrelated to the offenses of conviction" and should have been excluded by the district court. *Id.* Although it lacked inflammatory detail, this testimony was likely prejudicial and harmful to the defendants. However, it also had substantial probative value as it helped to establish the government's conspiracy-to-distribute theory. The district court did not p.589 commit "clear or obvious" error by allowing this testimony to be admitted.

III. Sufficiency Issues

We review a challenge to the sufficiency of the evidence supporting a criminal conviction *de novo. United States v. Pritchett,* 749 F.3d 417, 430 (6th Cir. 2014). A defendant challenging the sufficiency of the evidence "bears a very heavy burden." *United States v. Davis,* 397 F.3d 340, 344 (6th Cir.2005). In evaluating such a challenge, we are tasked with determining "whether, after viewing the evidence in the light most favorable to the prosecution, *any* rational trier of fact could have found the essential elements of the crime beyond a reasonable doubt." *Jackson v. Virginia,* 443 U.S. 307, 319, 99 S.Ct. 2781, 61 L.Ed.2d 560 (1979). When engaging in this analysis, we "neither independently weigh[] the evidence, nor judge[] the credibility of witnesses who testified at trial." *United States v. Howard,* 621 F.3d 433, 460 (6th Cir.2010). Any "issues of credibility" must be resolved in favor of the jury's verdict. *United States v. Salgado,* 250 F.3d 438, 446 (6th Cir.2001).

A. Sufficiency of Evidence Related to Wilburn's Participation in the Conspiracy

The government presented sufficient evidence to allow a rational trier of fact to conclude that Wilburn entered into a conspiracy to manufacture and distribute methamphetamine. The elements that the government needed to prove in order to convict Wilburn under 21 U.S.C. § 846 are: "(1) an agreement to violate drug laws, (2) knowledge and intent to join the conspiracy, and (3) participation in the conspiracy." *Pritchett,* 749 F.3d at 431 (internal quotation marks omitted). "[T]he government need not prove the existence of a formal or express agreement among the conspirators. Even a tacit or mutual understanding among the conspirators is sufficient." *United States v. Gardner,* 488 F.3d 700, 710 (6th Cir.2007) (citations omitted). A defendant's knowledge and intent to join the conspiracy "can be inferred through circumstantial evidence... including evidence of repeated purchases, or evidence of a large quantity of drugs." *United States v. Caver,* 470 F.3d 220, 233 (6th Cir.2006).

Wilburn argues that the government failed to prove that an ongoing agreement existed, or that Wilburn had knowledge of such an agreement and purposefully joined it. To the contrary, the government presented significant witness testimony suggesting that Wilburn had an agreement with Brosky and Collins to manufacture methamphetamine. For example, Hollie Adkins testified that Wilburn joined Collins and Brosky in a "three-way split on a cook" of methamphetamine. (R. 699, Transcript of Day 2 of Jury Trial, Page ID # 7577.) She testified that she had seen Wilburn, Collins and Brosky cook methamphetamine together: "I was there. I [saw] them get the stuff together. I[saw] them bring it back and finish smoking it off. I [saw] them weigh it out, sell it." (*Id.* at 7563.) Additionally, Charles Skaggs testified that Wilburn and Collins would give him methamphetamine in exchange for lithium batteries, which are used to manufacture methamphetamine. Likewise, Mickey Brown testified that he helped Wilburn and Collins cook methamphetamine on the mountain close to Wilburn and Collins' trailers 20 to 30 times. Such testimony was sufficient to allow a rational trier of fact to conclude that all three elements of conspiracy had been met.

Resolving all credibility issues in favor of the jury's verdict, the government presented sufficient evidence to allow a rational p.590 trier of fact to conclude that Wilburn entered into a conspiracy to manufacture and distribute methamphetamine.

B. Sufficiency of Evidence Supporting Drug Amounts

Collins and Wilburn argue that the evidence presented at trial was insufficient to prove that they conspired to manufacture or distribute *500 grams or more* of methamphetamine. The basis of this sufficiency challenge is the amount of methamphetamine rather than the existence of the conspiracy itself. In *Alleyne v. United States,* the Supreme Court held that "facts that increase mandatory minimum sentences must be submitted to the jury." ___ U.S. ___, 133 S.Ct. 2151, 2163, 186 L.Ed.2d 314 (2013). Under 21 U.S.C. § 841(b), if a conspiracy involves 500 grams or more of a mixture or substance containing a detectable amount of methamphetamine, a mandatory minimum is triggered. Therefore, this amount is an element of the offense that must be submitted to the jury and proven beyond a reasonable doubt.

In *United States v. Deitz,* we held that a "reasonable jury could infer" the threshold drug quantity in a drug conspiracy case from witnesses' testimony. 577 F.3d 672, 681 (6th Cir.2009). In so finding, we noted that the defendant's sufficiency challenge regarding drug quantities effectively asked us "to substitute our own evaluation for the jury's conclusion about the weight of the evidence and witness credibility, which we may not do." *Id.* at 682. The same concern is raised by Defendants' argument. In the instant case, the government introduced the testimony of Mickey Brown, who testified that over the course of seven (non-consecutive) months, he was present for 20 to 30 instances in which Collins and Wilburn cooked 16 to 34 grams of methamphetamine. This testimony alone could account for up to 1,020 grams of methamphetamine. While Brown's credibility was called into question by defense counsel, it is not the place of this Court to substitute its credibility assessment for that of the jury.

Under the relevant standard of review, which places a "very heavy burden" on defendants, Collins and Wilburn have failed to demonstrate that it would be impossible for "*any* rational trier of fact" to find that Collins and Wilburn conspired to manufacture and distribute 500 grams or more of methamphetamine. *Jackson,* 443 U.S. at 319, 99 S.Ct. 2781. Such a finding is possible on the basis of Brown's testimony alone, as well as in conjunction with numerous other witnesses who testified to observing the Defendants engaging in distribution and manufacturing activities and the previously discussed pseudoephedrine purchase records. Accordingly, the government presented sufficient evidence to support the jury's findings that Collins and Wilburn conspired to manufacture and to distribute more than 500 grams of a mixture or substance containing a detectable amount of methamphetamine.

IV. Sentencing Issues

A. Prosecutorial Misconduct at Collins' Sentencing

Preservation of the Issue and Standard of Review

Collins did not object to statements made by the prosecutor at the time of sentencing and has failed to preserve this issue for appellate review. "We usually review claims of prosecutorial misconduct *de novo,*" but where "the defendant did not raise the misconduct claim below, we review the record only for plain error." *United States v. Coker,* 514 F.3d 562, 568 (6th Cir.2008). To establish that plain error has occurred, the defendant must prove that: "(1) an error occurred in the p.591 district court; (2) the error was obvious or clear; (3) the error affected the defendant's substantial rights; and (4) this adverse impact seriously affected the fairness, integrity, or public reputation of the judicial proceedings." *United States v. Emuegbunam,* 268 F.3d 377, 406 (6th Cir. 2001).

Analysis

Collins argues that his Sixth Amendment rights were violated when, during his sentencing hearing, the prosecutor quoted a statement made to Collins by his defense counsel in a previous case in state court. *Collins' Br.* at 66. Although we are troubled by the prosecutor's behavior, we find Collins' argument unpersuasive.

The Sixth Amendment guarantees defendants access to a fair adversarial criminal process. *United States v. Cronic,* 466 U.S. 648, 656, 104 S.Ct. 2039, 80 L.Ed.2d 657 (1984). "Where the Sixth Amendment is violated, a serious risk of injustice infects the trial itself." *Chittick v. Lafler,* 514 Fed.Appx. 614, 617 (6th Cir. 2013) (internal quotation marks omitted). "[I]n order to establish a violation of the Sixth Amendment right to counsel ensuing from government surveillance, a claimant must not only show that conversations with an attorney were surreptitiously monitored, but must also show that the information gained was used to prejudice the claimant's defense in his criminal trial." *Sinclair v. Schriber,* 916 F.2d 1109, 1112 (6th Cir.1990). The Supreme Court and the Sixth Circuit have identified a number of factors to consider in determining whether a defendant's Sixth Amendment rights have been violated by an "invasion of the attorney-client privilege," including:

> 1) whether the presence of [an] informant was purposely caused by the government in order to garner confidential, privileged information, or whether the presence of [an] informant was the result of other inadvertent occurrences; 2) whether the government obtained, directly or indirectly, any evidence which was used at trial as the result of the informant's intrusion; 3) whether any information gained by the informant's intrusion was used in any other manner to the substantial detriment of the defendant; and 4) whether the details about trial preparations were learned by the government.

United States v. Steele, 727 F.2d 580, 585 (6th Cir.1984) (citing *Weatherford v. Bursey,* 429 U.S. 545, 554, 97 S.Ct. 837, 51 L.Ed.2d 30 (1977)).

Collins' challenge is based on a statement made by the prosecutor in arguing for a sentence at the upper end of the Guidelines range or an upward departure. The prosecutor stated:

> It is open knowledge within the Knox County Bar Association in regards to the facts laid out in Paragraph 7 as to what happened afterwards. The public defender in that case specifically told Mr. Collins this was his last chance. He told him, "Look, the federal authorities are now looking at you. You need to clean up." He chose not to do so. He chose to proceed full blast. And based on that, there is no confidence he will not commit another crime as soon as he is outside the control of any federal judicial officer, Your Honor.

(R. 678, Sentencing Transcript, Page ID # 3078.) In his appellate brief, Collins suggests that the prosecution must have learned about this comment through surveillance. The government asserts that the comment quoted by the prosecutor may have been made by Collins' previous counsel "in open court, or elsewhere within the earshot of the public." *Appellee's Br.* at 102. Collins puts forward no evidence to suggest that the government engaged in p.592 impermissible surveillance of his interactions with his attorney, but argues that it is an "unlikely scenario" that defense counsel would have made this statement in open court. *Collins' Reply Br.* at 25.

Collins further argues that the statement "greatly prejudiced" him at sentencing because it informed the district court's choice of sentence. *Collins' Br.* at 67. In imposing its sentence, the court referenced the statement at issue, attributing it to state or local authorities:

> But I'm very concerned about needing to promote respect for the law and deter future conduct here because whatever I see happening in your past, whatever we've done in the past, hasn't worked. And as with respect to promoting respect of the law, whatever we've done in the past hasn't worked. It's this representation anecdotally I understand the state authorities and the local authorities are saying, "Mr. Collins, you got a last chance here, you know. You got to clean this up. You got to put it behind you. You got to do something else."

(R. 678, Sentencing Transcript, Page ID # 3089-90.)

Regardless of the source of the disputed statement, it was inadvisable and unprofessional for the prosecutor to rely on gossip about an attorney's conversation with his client at sentencing. Nonetheless, we need not decide whether the prosecutor's conduct rose to the level of misconduct because, notwithstanding the propriety of the government's behavior, Collins has not demonstrated that he was prejudiced by the prosecutor's use of his previous attorney's statement. During the sentencing hearing, the government emphasized Collins' lengthy criminal history (eleven felonies and multiple misdemeanor convictions.) The government also called the district court's attention to Collins' failure to comply with previous court orders and his numerous failures to comply with the terms of his state probation. The challenged anecdote may have further emphasized Collins' criminal history and lack of respect for the law, but it contained no additional information about Collins' history or behavior that was not already before the court.

Collins has failed to demonstrate that the prosecutor "surreptitiously monitored" his interactions with his attorney or that Collins was prejudiced by the introduction of potentially privileged statements during his sentencing hearing. He therefore cannot establish that his Sixth Amendment rights were violated by the prosecutor's behavior.

B. Procedural Reasonableness of Collins' Sentence

We review a district court's sentence for reasonableness under an abuse of discretion standard. *United States v. Mitchell,* 681 F.3d 867, 879 (6th Cir.2012). When reviewing a sentence for procedural reasonableness, we "must determine whether the district court: '(1) properly calculated the applicable advisory Guidelines range; (2) considered the other § 3553(a) factors as well as the parties' arguments for a sentence outside the Guidelines range; and (3) adequately articulated its reasoning for imposing the particular sentence chosen, including any rejection of the parties' arguments for an outside-Guidelines sentence and any decision to deviate from the advisory Guidelines range.'" *United States v. Lumbard,* 706 F.3d 716, 725 (6th Cir.2013) (quoting *United States v. Young,* 553 F.3d 1035, 1054 (6th Cir.2009)). We review a district court's findings of fact for clear error, *United States v. Bazazpour,* 690 F.3d 796, 805 (6th Cir.2012), whereas "[q]uestions involving the interpretation of the guidelines are legal questions that [we] review p.593 *de novo.*" *United States v. Murphy,* 241 F.3d 447, 458 (6th Cir.2001). "[T]he determination of whether specific facts actually constitute an obstruction of justice is a mixed question of fact and law that we review *de novo.*" *Bazazpour,* 690 F.3d at 805.

Furthermore, whether Collins committed perjury is a question of fact to be reviewed for clear error. *See United States v. Canestraro,* 282 F.3d 427, 431 (6th Cir.2002) ("This Court reviews the district court's findings of fact at sentencing for clear error."); *United States v. Lane,* 14 F.3d 603, 1993 WL 533577 at *1 (6th Cir.1993) (unpublished table disposition) ("Whether a defendant committed perjury is a question of fact to be determined by the district court and will be reviewed on appeal for clear error with due regard for the district court's opportunity to make credibility determinations.").

Collins argues that his sentence was procedurally unreasonable because the district court miscalculated his Guidelines range by improperly applying a two-level adjustment to his offense level for obstruction of justice under U.S.S.G. § 3C1.1. He also contends that his sentence was procedurally unreasonable because it was based on a clearly erroneous finding that the conspiracy involved more than 500 grams of methamphetamine. We disagree.

1. Obstruction of Justice Enhancement

The district court imposed a two-level increase to Collins' offense level for obstruction of justice under U.S.S.G. § 3C1.1 on the ground that Collins obstructed justice by providing false testimony under oath regarding the purpose of a trip that Collins took to Seymour, Indiana. In particular, the district court found that Collins' testimony that he "didn't go to Indiana and bring any anhydrous ammonia back," was "contrary to what the evidence ended up showing, which was that that trip was [for] the purpose of stealing and acquiring anhydrous ammonia." (R. 678, Collins Sentencing Transcript, Page ID # 3063, 3070-71.)

Section 3C1.1 of the United States Sentencing Guidelines provides:

> If (1) the defendant willfully obstructed or impeded, or attempted to obstruct or impede, the administration of justice with respect to the investigation, prosecution, or sentencing of the instant offense of conviction, and (2) the obstructive conduct related to (A) the defendant's offense of conviction and any relevant conduct; or (B) a closely related offense, increase the offense level by 2 levels.

U.S.S.G. § 3C1.1. The comments to § 3C1.1 note that "committing, suborning, or attempting to suborn perjury" is an "example[] of the type[] of conduct to which this enhancement applies." *Id.* at § 3C1.1 cmt. 4(B). Perjury is defined as "(1) a false statement under oath (2) concerning a material matter (3) with the willful intent to provide false testimony." *United States v. Watkins,* 691 F.3d 841, 851 (6th Cir.2012). In a recent opinion, we cautioned that, if this sentencing enhancement applied to every defendant who testified and then was convicted, "a defendant's constitutional right to testify on his own behalf could be undermined by the prospect that he would be punished at sentencing for doing so." *United States v. Kamper,* 748 F.3d 728, 747 (6th Cir.), *cert. denied,* ___ U.S. ___, 135 S.Ct. 882, 190 L.Ed.2d 712 (2014). In light of this concern, "the obstruction-of-justice enhancement applies only if the district court '(1) identif[ies] those particular portions of defendant's testimony that it considers to be perjurious; and (2) either make[s] a specific p.594 finding for each element of perjury or, at least, make[s] a finding that encompasses all of the factual predicates for a finding of perjury.'" *Id.* (quoting *United States v. Lawrence,* 308 F.3d 623, 632 (6th Cir. 2002)).

The district court made these obligatory findings. First, as stated above, the district court specifically identified Collins' testimony about the purpose of his trip to Indiana as the relevant perjurious testimony. Second, the district court explicitly addressed each element of perjury. Referring to the testimony about Collins' trip to Indiana, the district judge stated, "I think that the record with regard to that specific part of the testimony was certainly willful. It was material to the matter which deals with the manufacture of methamphetamine. It's false testimony under oath, and I think that[] fits the elements of perjury." (R. 678, Collins Sentencing Transcript, Page ID # 3071.)

Collins argues that the district court's finding of obstruction of justice was clearly erroneous because the jury acquitted him of Count 6, Possession of Stolen Anhydrous Ammonia Transported across State Lines. In *United States v. Zajac,* we "consider[ed] the proper standard of proof to be applied by a sentencing judge in determining whether a defendant has committed perjury and is thus subject to an enhanced sentence for obstruction of justice." 62 F.3d 145, 146 (6th Cir.1995). We held that "a preponderance of the evidence standard continues to be the correct standard for all fact-finding at sentencing." *Id.* at 150. In acquitting Collins of Count 6, the jury applied the higher "beyond a reasonable doubt" standard. Consequently, Collins' acquittal does not establish that the district court was clearly erroneous in finding that a preponderance of the evidence supported its finding of perjury. Moreover, the district court's finding was supported by the record. In particular, Mickey Brown testified that he and Collins went to Indiana "[t]o steal anhydrous ammonia" in order to "make methamphetamine." (R. 699, Transcript of Day 2 of Jury Trial, Page ID # 6027). Accordingly, the district court did not commit clear error in finding that Collins perjured himself by testifying that he did not travel to Indiana to acquire anhydrous ammonia, nor did the court err in applying the obstruction of justice enhancement to Collins.

2. Clearly Erroneous Facts

Collins further argues that "no rational jury" could have determined that "the conspiracy manufactured or distributed more than 500 grams of methamphetamine where [1] the cooks were in jail for the first half of the conspiracy, [2] the conversion ratio was problematic, and [3] pseudoephedrine from another conspiracy was attributed to Collins." *Collins' Br.* at 70-71. Collins concludes that his sentence was therefore procedurally unreasonable because he was "sentenced based on clearly erroneous facts." *Id.* at 71. This argument is effectively a reprise of Collins' other unsuccessful arguments.

"The district court's determination of the quantity of drugs for which a defendant is held responsible is a factual finding that we review for clear error." *United States v. Russell,* 595 F.3d 633, 646 (6th Cir.2010). "A factual finding is clearly erroneous where, although there is evidence to support that finding, the reviewing court on the entire evidence is left with the definite and firm conviction that a mistake has been committed." *United States v. Ware,* 282 F.3d 902, 907 (6th Cir.2002) (internal quotation marks omitted). As has been discussed above, the jury found Collins responsible for conspiring to manufacture or distribute at least 500 grams of methamphetamine after hearing evidence p.595 that included: (1) the typical conversion ratio from pseudoephedrine to methamphetamine, (2) the pseudoephedrine purchase records of individuals associated with the conspiracy, and (3) the testimony of multiple witnesses who observed Collins manufacturing and distributing methamphetamine after his release from incarceration. Collins has failed to demonstrate that, given the evidence presented at trial, the jury's finding of drug quantity and the sentence imposed by the district court were based on clearly erroneous facts.

C. Substantive Reasonableness of Collins' Sentence

We "review a district court's sentencing determination for reasonableness under a deferential abuse of discretion standard." *United States v. Cochrane,* 702 F.3d 334, 343 (6th Cir.2012). Review for substantive reasonableness "'requires inquiry into ... the length of the sentence and the factors evaluated ... by the district court in reaching its sentencing determination.'" *Id.* at 344 (quoting *United States v. Herrera-Zuniga,* 571 F.3d 568, 581 (6th Cir.2009)). Our analysis is guided by the statutory requirement that "[t]he court shall impose a sentence sufficient, but not greater than necessary," to accomplish the sentencing purposes set forth by Congress. 18 U.S.C. § 3553(a).

"A sentence may be considered substantively unreasonable when the district court selects a sentence arbitrarily, bases the sentence on impermissible factors, fails to consider relevant sentencing factors, or gives an unreasonable amount of weight to any pertinent factor." *United States v. Conatser,* 514 F.3d 508, 520 (6th Cir.2008). Our substantive-reasonableness review "'take[s] into account the totality of the circumstances, including the extent of any variance from the Guidelines range.'" *Cochrane,* 702 F.3d at 345 (quoting *United States v. Bolds,* 511 F.3d 568, 581 (6th Cir.2007)). "The sentencing judge may not presume that the guidelines range is reasonable, but must consider all of the relevant § 3553(a) factors...." *Conatser,* 514 F.3d at 520. Where the district court selects a properly calculated within-guidelines sentence, the sentence "will be afforded a rebuttable presumption of reasonableness on appeal." *Id.*

Collins fails to show that his sentence was substantively unreasonable. Collins challenges the substantive reasonableness of his sentence on two grounds: first, he asserts that his sentence is substantively unreasonable because it was based on "the attorney-client privileged communications between Collins and his public defender in state court" and, second, he claims that his sentence of 324 months of imprisonment "is substantially greater than necessary to accomplish the sentencing goals." *Collins' Br.* at 72-73.

1. Statement Made by Collins' Former Attorney

As was already discussed, Collins has not shown that the statement made by his former attorney and repeated by the prosecutor at sentencing (that "this was his last chance") was protected by attorney-client privilege. (R. 678, Collins Sentencing Transcript, Page ID # 3078.) In addition, Collins has failed to demonstrate that the district court based its sentence on this statement. Rather, the district court appears to have based its concern about Collins' lack of respect for the law on Collins' lengthy criminal history as well as his history of violating court orders and the terms of his probation. At sentencing, the district judge explained, "I'm very concerned about needing to promote respect for the law and deter future conduct here because whatever I see happening in your past, whatever we've done in the past, p.596 hasn't worked." (R. 678, Collins Sentencing Transcript, Page ID # 3089-90.) The district court further explained, "[W]e are shaking our heads when we find a defendant who's had so many times in which we've tried to impose a sentence to have you change your direction, and you don't." (*Id.* at 3087-88.) The court merely referred to the statement allegedly made by Collins' public defender as anecdotal in nature, and ultimately based its sentence on an appropriate consideration of the § 3553(a) factors.

2. Duration of Collins' Incarceration

Collins' 324-month sentence is within his Guidelines range and therefore should be "afforded a rebuttable presumption of reasonableness on appeal." *Conatser,* 514 F.3d at 520. Collins has offered no rebuttal to this presumption. The district court engaged in a lengthy discussion of the sentencing factors set forth in § 3553(a) in determining Collins' sentence. *See* 18 U.S.C. § 3553(a)(2) (listing the purposes of sentencing as the need for a defendant's sentence — "(A) to reflect the seriousness of the offense, to promote respect for the law, and to provide just punishment for the offense; (B) to afford adequate deterrence to criminal conduct; (C) to protect the public from further crimes of the defendant; and (D) to provide the defendant with needed educational or vocational training, medical care, or other correctional treatment in the most effective manner"). In particular, the district court discussed: the seriousness of Collins' offense given the devastation caused by methamphetamine; Collins' lack of respect for the law; the need "to protect the public from [Collins'] crimes;" the need for "just punishment" given the "people hurt" and "lives destroyed" by this "serious crime;" and Collins' extensive criminal history. (R. 678, Collins' Sentencing Transcript, 3086-96.). The district court explicitly found that "the following sentence is sufficient, but not greater than necessary, to comply with the purposes of 18 United States Code, Section 3553(a)." (*Id.* at 3095-96.)

Collins' sentence was substantively reasonable. The district court did not base its sentence on an impermissible factor; rather, the district court based its sentence on the relevant 3553(a) factors and imposed a sentence that was sufficient, but not greater than necessary, to accomplish the sentencing goals.

D. Wilburn's Career Offender Status

Wilburn was sentenced as a Career Offender within the meaning of U.S.S.G § 4B1.1 and now argues that the Supreme Court's recent decision in *Johnson v. United States,* ___ U.S. ___, 135 S.Ct. 2551, 192 L.Ed.2d 569 (2015) invalidates this designation because one of his predicate offenses qualified under the now invalidated residual clause. In *Johnson,* the Supreme Court struck down the Armed Career Criminal Act's residual clause as violating defendants' constitutional right to due process, and the Court has since vacated the sentences of individuals who were sentenced under the U.S.S.G.'s identical residual clause, U.S.S.G § 4B1.2(a)(2). *See United States v. Darden,* 605 Fed.Appx. 545, 546 (6th Cir.2015).

At issue is whether Wilburn's 2007 conviction for second degree assault under Kentucky Revised Statutes § 508.020 qualifies as a "crime of violence" for the purposes of determining his Career Offender status. Following *Johnson,* a criminal conviction qualifies as a "crime of violence" if it is a federal or state offense that is "punishable by imprisonment for a term exceeding one year" and "(1) has as an element the use, attempted use, or threatened p.597 use of physical force against the person of another, or (2) is burglary of a dwelling, arson, or extortion, [or] involves use of explosives." § 4B1.2(a)(1), (2). A person is guilty of second degree assault under Kentucky law if:

(a) He intentionally causes serious physical injury to another person; or

(b) He intentionally causes physical injury to another person by means of a deadly weapon or a dangerous instrument; or

(c) He wantonly causes serious physical injury to another person by means of a deadly weapon or a dangerous instrument.

Ky.Rev.Stat. Ann. § 508.020(1)(a)-(c).

We have previously held that crimes which require proof of physical injury necessarily have "'as an element the use, attempted use, or threatened use of physical force against the person of another" and thus qualify as crimes of violence under the "elements" clause of the ACCA. *United States v. Anderson,* 695 F.3d 390, 400-01 (6th Cir.2012) (holding that under Ohio law aggravated assault was a violent felony under the ACCA because it required proof of "serious physical harm" or "physical harm," explaining that "it does not matter that the Ohio statute at issue does not contain a stand-alone physical force element because proof of serious physical injury or pain under the statute necessarily requires proof of violent physical force"). Since second degree assault under Kentucky law requires proof of physical injury or serious physical injury, the same reasoning applies in the present case. Accordingly, the Supreme Court's opinion in *Johnson* does not invalidate Wilburn's sentence. Wilburn has failed to show that the district court erred in considering Wilburn's conviction of assault in the second degree as a crime of violence and in classifying Wilburn as a career offender.

E. Substantive Reasonableness of Wilburn's Sentence

As was stated above, we "review a district court's sentencing determination for reasonableness under a deferential abuse of discretion standard." *Cochrane,* 702 F.3d at 343. Review for substantive reasonableness "requires inquiry into ... the length of the sentence and the factors evaluated ... by the district court in reaching its sentencing determination." *Id.* at 344 (internal quotation marks omitted). "A sentence may be considered substantively unreasonable when the district court selects a sentence arbitrarily, bases the sentence on impermissible factors, fails to consider relevant sentencing factors, or gives an unreasonable amount of weight to any pertinent factor." *Conatser,* 514 F.3d at 520. "A properly calculated within-guidelines sentence will be afforded a rebuttable presumption of reasonableness on appeal." *Id.*

The district court sentenced Wilburn to 360 months' incarceration, reflecting the bottom of his Guidelines range, which was 360 months of incarceration to life. Wilburn argues that his sentence is substantively unreasonable because a shorter sentence would have adequately met the statutory purposes of sentencing.

The transcript reflects that when determining Wilburn's sentence, the district court considered the § 3553(a) sentencing factors in choosing to impose a sentence at the bottom of Wilburn's Guidelines range. The district court found that the sentence needed to "be substantial to reflect how serious this crime is ..., to promote respect for the law, [and to] deter future conduct." (R. 687, Wilburn Sentencing Transcript, Page ID # 4623-24.) The court emphasized p.598 that a substantial sentence was necessary "[to] reflect a measure of needing to protect the public from [Wilburn's] future crimes." (*Id.* at 4624.) Furthermore, the district court justified the sentence on the basis of Wilburn's recidivism and the need to hold Wilburn accountable for "making very bad decisions that have damaged the community over the years...." (*Id.* at 4626.) Acknowledging Wilburn's problem's with addiction, the district court noted that Wilburn was going to receive drug treatment in prison. (*Id.* at 4625.) The court ultimately concluded that a sentence of 360 months incarceration "[wa]s sufficient, but not greater than necessary, to comply with the purposes of 18 United States Code, Section 3553(a)." (*Id.* at 4631.) As the record indicates, the district court based its sentencing decision on a thorough analysis of the factors set forth by Congress in § 3553(a), and Wilburn has failed to demonstrate that this low-end sentence was substantively unreasonable.

F. Brosky's Special Conditions of Supervised Release

Preservation of the Issue and Standard of Review

Brosky concedes that he did not object to the special conditions of supervised release imposed at sentencing and did not, therefore, preserve this issue for appeal. Accordingly, this issue is reviewed for plain error.

Our review of a condition of supervised release includes both procedural and substantive elements. First, procedural reasonableness requires the district court to have stated "its rationale for mandating special conditions of supervised release" in open court at the time of sentencing. *United States v. Carter,* 463 F.3d 526, 528 (6th Cir.2006). Next, the substantive reasonableness inquiry requires us to determine whether the condition of supervised release:

(1) is reasonably related to specific sentencing factors, namely the nature and circumstances of the offense and the history and characteristics of the

defendant, and the need to afford adequate deterrence, [and] to protect the public from further crimes of the defendant...; (2) involves no greater deprivation of liberty than is reasonably necessary to achieve these goals; and (3) is consistent with any pertinent policy statements issued by the Sentencing Commission.

United States v. Zobel, 696 F.3d 558, 573 (6th Cir.2012).

Analysis

At Brosky's sentencing hearing, the district court imposed a three-year term of court added special conditions of supervised release. In addition, the district court added special conditions of supervised release relating to alcohol and substance use without providing an explanation for so doing. These conditions included a prohibition on the use of alcohol. (*Id.*) Brosky argues that the district court plainly erred by imposing such special conditions "without providing any justification for doing so on the record." *Brosky's Br.* at 33.

Brosky claims that the circumstances in this case are comparable to those at issue in *United States v. Inman,* 666 F.3d 1001 (6th Cir.2012). In *Inman,* we found that the district court had erred by failing to provide any explanation for imposing a life-time alcohol ban on a defendant who had been convicted of possession of child pornography and had no history of substance abuse. Unlike Inman, who had no history of alcohol or drug dependence and who was convicted of a crime unrelated to controlled substances, Brosky has a history p.599 of drug abuse and was convicted of a drug-related offense.

It is true that our precedent "clearly requires a district court to state in open court at the time of sentencing its rationale for mandating special conditions of supervised release." *Inman,* 666 F.3d at 1006 (internal quotation marks omitted). However, "[a] district court's failure to explain its reasons for imposing a special condition will be deemed harmless error... if such reasons are clear from the record." *Carter,* 463 F.3d at 529 n. 2. In this case, the rationale for imposing the special conditions, including a ban on alcohol for the duration of Brosky's supervised release, was obvious. Requiring Brosky to remain sober and abstain from addictive and mind-altering substances is reasonably related to his history of drug abuse, the nature of his offense, and the goals of rehabilitation and protection of the public. Consequently, although the district court erred by failing to explain in open court its rationale for imposing the special condition of supervised release, this error was harmless because the reasons for its imposition are clear from the record.

V. Collins' Cumulative Error Claim

"The cumulative effect of errors that are harmless by themselves can be so prejudicial as to warrant a new trial. In order to obtain a new trial based upon cumulative error, defendants must show that the combined effect of individually harmless errors was so prejudicial as to render their trial fundamentally unfair." *United States v. Adams,* 722 F.3d 788, 832 (6th Cir.2013) (internal quotation marks and citations omitted). "This Court has not directly addressed the issue of how (if at all) to incorporate into a cumulative-error analysis, plain errors that do not, standing alone, necessitate reversal." *United States v. Warman,* 578 F.3d 320, 349 n. 4 (6th Cir.2009). The distinction between harmless and plain error is irrelevant in this case, as Collins' claim fails in any event.

Collins argues that we should "reverse [his conviction] based on cumulative error because the combined effect of multiple errors deprived [him] of a fair trial." *Collins' Br.* at 75. With respect to the claims advanced by Collins, we have identified only one harmless error and one error that did not amount to plain error. First, the district court committed harmless error by admitting evidence of Collins' previous conviction pursuant to a Rule 403 analysis; the district court should have applied the more stringent Rule 609(b) analysis. Second, Agent O'Neil's testimony that a near one-to-one conversion ratio of pseudoephedrine to methamphetamine was possible was based on impermissible hearsay. Collins did not preserve his appeal to Agent O'Neil's testimony on this ground and the admittance of his testimony did not amount to plain error. Considering both identified errors together, their combined effect is far from sufficiently prejudicial to render Collins' trial fundamentally unfair, particularly in light of the substantial evidence of Collins' guilt.

CONCLUSION

For the foregoing reasons, we AFFIRM the judgments of the district court.

[1] The Smiths appealed their sentences and convictions. On November 6, 2013, a panel of this Court affirmed their sentences. *United States v. Smith,* Nos. 12-5895, 12-5896 (6th Cir. Nov. 6, 2013) (unpublished).

[2] The court subsequently gave a limiting instruction to the jury, instructing them that the "earlier conviction was brought to your attention only as a way of helping you decide how believable [Collins'] testimony was. You cannot use it for any other purpose." (R. 703, Transcript of Day 6 of Jury Trial, Page ID # 8582.)

[3] Agent O'Neil testified that a nearly 1:1 conversion of pseudoephedrine to methamphetamine may be possible, but stated that a conversion rate of 50 to 75 percent was typical and that the conversion ratio in the present case could have been even lower.

800 F.3d 768 (2015)

UNITED STATES of America, Plaintiff-Appellee,

v.

Keith CHURN, Defendant-Appellant.

No. 14-5720.

United States Court of Appeals, Sixth Circuit.

Argued: August 4, 2015.

Decided and Filed: September 10, 2015.

US v. Churn, 800 F. 3d 768 (6th Cir. 2015)

p.771 ARGUED: Andrew Guy, Kevin Potter, Federal Appellate Litigation Clinic, Ann Arbor, Michigan, for Appellant. David M. Lieberman, United States Department of Justice, Washington, D.C., for Appellee. ON BRIEF: Andrew Guy, Kevin Potter, Federal Appellate Litigation Clinic, Ann Arbor, Michigan, Melissa M. Salinas, Office of the Federal Public Defender, Toledo, Ohio, Dennis G. Terez, Office of the Federal Public Defender, Cleveland, Ohio, for Appellant. David M. Lieberman, Sandra G. Moses, United States Department of Justice, Washington, D.C., for Appellee.

Before: COLE, Chief Judge; GIBBONS and STRANCH, Circuit Judges.

OPINION

COLE, Judge.

In December 2013, defendant Keith Churn was found guilty of seven counts of bank fraud stemming from two schemes in which he received bank loans ostensibly to construct houses, but performed little to no work. The district court sentenced him to 33 months in prison and ordered restitution of $237,950.50. On appeal, Churn argues his conviction should be reversed and that he should receive a new trial because the district court purportedly made various evidentiary errors. He also requests vacatur of a portion of his restitution order, claiming the amount exceeds a statutory maximum, and vacatur of his sentence. Because the district court did not commit any reversible evidentiary errors, entered an appropriate restitution order, and properly sentenced Churn, we affirm the judgment of the district court.

I. BACKGROUND

A. Churn Proposes Two Projects.

Defendant Keith Churn owned C & M Construction Management, a Tennessee construction company specializing in remodeling and rehabilitation, since the late 1990s. Around October 2006, Churn entered a business agreement with Dustin Rief, under which Rief would purchase real property at 2408 Clarksville Pike, Nashville, Tennessee, and Churn would install a modular — or prefabricated — house on the property. Churn would pay Rief rent during the six-to-eight months of construction and would purchase the property from him upon completion. For his efforts, Rief would receive $5,000 initially and an additional $5,000 after Churn's purchase, for a total of $10,000.

Rief financed the purchase and construction of the Clarksville Pike property with a $187,800 construction loan from BancorpSouth Bank ("BSB"). Under the terms of the loan agreement, a portion of the loan would be distributed upfront to purchase the property, and the remaining funds would be distributed in stages to pay for construction. BSB disbursed $66,758.19 for the purchase, leaving $121,041.81 for construction.

The same year, Churn proposed a similar investment to Milton Thomas. Thomas agreed to obtain financing to purchase 956 Green Street, Franklin, Tennessee, and Churn agreed to demolish the existing house and install a modular home. The p.772 two would split any profits. To finance the project, Thomas received a $226,500 loan from BSB, $77,976.83 of which was distributed to fund the property purchase.

BSB distributed the portion of the loan for construction in "draws." For each draw, the bank would transfer money from the loan to Rief's and Thomas's checking accounts, which they could then use to pay contractors. Before approving a draw, the bank might send an inspector to the property, or it might review contractors' receipts, to ensure that the claimed work was actually being performed.

There were four draws made for the Clarksville Pike property: $25,000 on October 31, 2006; $15,000 on December 18, 2006; $30,000 on January 10, 2007, and $4,500 on January 12, 2007. On December 5, 2006, Churn submitted an invoice for $17,733 to BSB for permit fees, disconnecting old utilities, grading, and preparing footings and foundations. Based on the invoice, BSB approved a $15,000 draw on December 18.

On December 22, 2006, Churn submitted a specification sheet and an invoice to BSB, which purportedly showed an order for a modular house from All American Homes of N.C., LLC ("AAH"). The invoice charged a down payment of $33,462, or approximately one-third of the total cost of the modular house. Two weeks later, Churn informed a BSB loan officer, Lisa Campsey, that the house would be set on February 8, 2007. Campsey later approved draws of $30,000 and $4,500. During this period, a site inspector for BSB submitted periodic reports to BSB indicating that demolition of the existing structure had occurred and the lot was cleared.

There were four draws on the loan for the Green Street property: $20,000 on December 15, 2006; $8,000 on January 10, 2007; $12,000 on January 18, 2007; $22,000 on January 23, 2007; and $668.91 on February 1, 2007. On January 17, 2007, Churn submitted a specification sheet and an invoice to BSB, which purportedly showed an order for a modular house from AAH. Like the invoice for the Clarksville Pike property, the invoice charged a down payment of approximately one-third of the total cost of the modular house, or $33,638. Based on the invoice, BSB approved draws of $12,000 and $22,000.

B. Questions Arise About the Projects.

At some point, Campsey grew suspicious about the progress of the projects. For the Clarksville Pike property, although some demolition had been done, Campsey learned that the tasks listed on the December 5, 2006, invoice were not actually completed, including "pulling" the construction permit. Nor was the modular house set on February 8 as Churn said it would be. Similarly, she visited the Green Street property, but found no completed work.

An inspector dispatched by BSB made similar observations. On his first visit to the Clarksville Pike property in October 2006, he noted that the existing structure had been torn down and cleared. But a few months later, on March 23, 2007, the inspector estimated that only 1.2 percent of the construction project had been completed. He later found that no additional work was performed from then through July 17. The inspector also assessed the Green Street property on March 16 and determined that only 1.2 percent of the construction project had been completed; when he returned on July 17, he found that no work had been done since his March 16 visit.

Questions about Churn's invoices arose as well. The invoices he submitted to BSB to support draw requests purportedly reflected p.773 purchases for two "Hot Tamale"-style modular houses. But AAH never received any orders or payments from Churn. AAH also did not prepare the invoices Churn submitted to BSB. While the submitted invoices reflected a one-third deposit on the total purchases, as well as costs associated with installing electrical and plumbing "tie-ins," AAH never required more than a 10-percent deposit — the industry standard. Indeed, AAH was not even able or licensed to provide electrical or plumbing services.

On March 3, 2007, Campsey emailed Churn, stating that an AAH representative told her that it had not received funds from Churn and would not start construction on modular homes until it received the money. She stated that Churn's representations to BSB that he had paid deposits on the houses using the loans "greatly conflicts" with information given by AAH. Since Churn had previously said that he would pay for the purchases through checks, Campsey requested copies of cancelled checks and further information about what charges Churn had paid, but she never received any. She also pointed out to Churn that there was no pad (a part of the foundation) laid on the Green Street property even though Churn told her that it was already installed.

Two days later, Churn told Campsey that she would "have the information that's needed by the end of the business day." Churn also said that BSB's inspector should "go by [the] site at [the] end of this week" and that Churn "will also have in writing this week [a] guarantee from [the] manuf[acturer] that we will have product this month on the sites." (*Id.*) Campsey replied by confirming an inspection date, requesting proof of payment, and asking for a written guarantee from the manufacturer. She never received any of the items. When Campsey later went to the Green Street property, she observed that "nothing had been done since the first time. It was the same every single time...." (Trial Tr., R. 80, PageID 296.)

Campsey later called Churn. He said that the houses were coming, but from IBC instead, a different manufacturer. Churn promised to perform additional work on the properties, but Campsey said that she no longer trusted him.

On March 8, 2007, Churn told Campsey that he "will be moving forward with the work on the projects" and that she was "very wrong about [her] comments." Churn said that he would provide "[a]ll info" to Rief and Thomas, who would "deal with [her] directly." (*Id.*) Campsey, who had been in contact with Rief and Thomas throughout the projects, still never received any documentation.

In early May 2007, BSB sent formal demand letters to Rief and Thomas, requesting written confirmation that modular houses were being completed and verification of the delivery dates. The letters warned that failure to provide the requested documentation or to complete the site and foundation work by May 18, 2007, would result in the loans being payable immediately.

On May 18, Churn sent an email with two attachments to BSB. The first attachment was an invoice from "C & M Construction Managment" [sic] to Rief, stating that the "deposite [sic] has been paid for unit ordered for 2408 [Clarksville Pike] job site," and confirming a $33,463 payment. The second attachment was a photo of modular houses sitting on trailers. Churn told Campsey that the structures depicted would be delivered to the Clarksville Pike property.

Campsey quickly responded that "this information is not sufficient." She again demanded written confirmation from AAH p.774 verifying production of the units and the dates of delivery, site preparation, and foundation work.

Churn responded five days later, on May 23, stating that the units were not from AAH, but that BSB would be getting paperwork from C & M Construction Management directly. BSB never received any paperwork. During its investigation, BSB located the modular houses shown in the photographs. After examining the houses' serial numbers, the bank learned that they were owned by other people, not Churn.

Churn stopped making monthly payments on the loans sometime in April 2007. While Rief attempted to make some payments himself, he was ultimately unable to continue paying, leading to the foreclosure of the Clarksville Pike property and Rief's filing for personal bankruptcy. Thomas also attempted to make some payments himself, but was unable to do so after he lost his job; BSB foreclosed the Green Street property and Thomas also filed for personal bankruptcy.

C. Churn's Explanation.

Churn had a different understanding of events. According to him, he did place orders with AAH, but sometime in mid-February to mid-March, it placed his orders on hold "because of a lot of confusion that they said they were having from the bank." (Trial Tr., R. 82, PageID 629-30.) Churn attempted to contact other manufacturers to provide him with modular houses, but was unable to locate any that would sell him units at a comparable cost. Later, he found some modular houses at a defunct AAH plant; the houses were initially purchased by a nonprofit that eventually had no use for them after a failed land deal. These, Churn claims, were the units in the photograph he sent to BSB: Churn speculates that the bank was confused because the units were associated with what were likely the names of the original buyers and not his.

Churn placed these newfound units "under contract" and met with Chris Marketti of BSB to discuss a deal. (Trial Tr., R. 82, PageID 632.) Churn purportedly detailed a breakdown of expenses for the Clarksville Pike property and tried to negotiate with BSB to pay him, but only after delivery of the unit. BSB, however, "never followed up." (Trial Tr., R. 82, PageID 667.) Had the bank not ceased working with him, Churn believed that he could have completed the deals.

D. Churn Is Indicted.

On May 5, 2010, a grand jury indicted Churn on thirteen counts of bank fraud under 18 U.S.C. § 1344, each count corresponding to a particular bank draw. The Clarksville Pike property is the subject of Counts 1, 2, 3, 7, 8, 9, and 13 in the indictment; the Green Street property is the subject of Counts 4, 5, 6, 10, 11, and 12 in the indictment. The government voluntarily dismissed Counts 1 and 4. The jury convicted Churn on Counts 3, 7, 8, 9, 10, 11, and 12, and acquitted him of the remaining four counts. The district court sentenced him to 33 months in prison and five years of supervised release, and ordered restitution of $237,950.50. Churn appeals, arguing that he is entitled to a new trial, vacatur of his sentence, or vacatur of a portion of the restitution order.

II. DISCUSSION

A. Standard of Review for Evidentiary Rulings.

Churn argues that the district court made several erroneous evidentiary rulings. "Generally, a district court's evidentiary rulings are reviewed for abuse of discretion." *United States v. Chalmers,* p.775 554 Fed.Appx. 440, 449 (6th Cir.2014). If evidence was erroneously admitted, we ask whether the admission was harmless error or requires reversal of a conviction. *United States v. Martinez,* 588 F.3d 301, 312 (6th Cir.2009).

B. Whether an Email About an Order Status Contained Inadmissible Hearsay.

Churn claims that the district court committed reversible error by admitting impermissible hearsay in a printed email. During Campsey's testimony, the government introduced a March 3, 2007, email from her to Churn stating that she had spoken with an AAH representative named "Bob." The email stated that Bob "was not familiar with IBC or a house coming out of Indiana." (*Id.*) The email also reflected that Bob said that "the money needed from [Churn] to start production of the homes was being wired by [Churn] to [AAH's] corporate office yesterday.... [I]f the wire was received by Monday it would take approximately 4 weeks to get the materials then an additional 2 weeks to complete the structure." (*Id.*) Campsey's email stated that the information provided by Churn "greatly conflicts with the information given ... by Bob." (*Id.*) So she asked Churn to submit copies of the wire transfer and the confirmation number, to notify her when he had installed a pad and block (a part of the foundation) at the Green Street property, and to set up a meeting to "straighten out all the confusion." (*Id.*)

Churn's counsel objected that the "statements from Bob" in the email constituted inadmissible hearsay. (Trial Tr., R. 80, PageID 282.) The government responded that it was "not admitting [the email] for the truth of what Bob said, but for [Campsey's] state of mind and her concern over whether or not she was receiving accurate information," leading her to "question these other documents." (*Id.* at 282-83.) The district court overruled the objection, stating that the email illuminated Campsey's "understanding, her state of mind, and her reaction to it." (*Id.* at 283.)

The court then instructed the jury that the email was "being admitted for a limited purpose. Not that what the other person actually said is true or not, but to explain the basis of [Campsey's] state of mind, to explain what [she] was doing." (*Id.*)

On appeal, Churn argues that the district court erred in two ways. First, he claims that it wrongly admitted the evidence to show Campsey's state of mind because the state-of-mind exception under Federal Rule of Evidence 803(3) requires that the statement explain the declarant's, i.e., Bob's, state of mind, not Campsey's. Second, Churn claims that the district court wrongly admitted the evidence to show the basis of Campsey's undeclared mental state rather than the declarant's actual mental state. *See Daniels v. Lafler,* 192 Fed.Appx. 408, 424 (6th Cir.2006) ("Federal Rule of Evidence 803(3) does allow the admission of statements as to the declarant's state of mind, but does not allow the admission of statements as to *why* the declarant has said state of mind.").

The government responds that the district court appropriately admitted the statements to demonstrate their effect on Campsey. The statements, it says, are not being offered to prove the truth of the matters asserted. *See United States v. Boyd,* 640 F.3d 657, 664 (6th Cir.2011) ("Statements offered to prove the listener's knowledge are not hearsay."). Rather, the government claims it was trying to show that while Campsey "readily approved disbursements of loan money [early on] based on invoices and representations from Churn," she quickly grew suspicious p.776 of Churn and demanded verification of his work. The statements in the email were not introduced to prove the truth of Bob's statement, the government contends, but rather to explain Campsey's conversation and why BSB demanded records, assurances, and meetings from Churn. The reasons for BSB's actions, in turn, serve to rebut Churn's allegation that BSB obstructed his dealings with AAH and hindered him from completing his projects. Because Bob's statements are not hearsay, the government argues, they need no exception to be admitted, and the state-of-mind exception under Rule 803(3) is irrelevant.

"A statement that is not offered to prove the truth of the matter asserted but to show its effect on the listener is not hearsay." *Biegas v. Quickway Carriers, Inc.,* 573 F.3d 365, 379 (6th Cir.2009). Such a statement may be admitted to show why the listener acted as she did. *See United States v. Pugh,* 273 Fed.Appx. 449, 456 (6th Cir.2008). If a statement is hearsay, it is inadmissible unless some exception applies. Fed.R.Evid. 802. Federal Rule of Evidence 803(3) provides an exception to the bar against hearsay for "[a] statement of [a] declarant's then-existing state of mind (such as motive, intent, or plan) ... but not including a statement of memory or belief to prove the fact remembered or believed." Fed.R.Evid. 803(3).

The district court did not abuse its discretion in admitting the email because the statements therein are not hearsay. Whether Bob's statements were true or not was irrelevant to what the government was trying to show by introducing the email. As the government explained to the district court, it was "not admitting that [email] for the truth of what Bob said, but for [Campsey's] state of mind and her concern over whether or not she was receiving accurate information." (Trial Tr., R. 80, PageID 282.) It did not matter whether Bob "was [] familiar with IBC or a house coming out of Indiana," whether "the money needed from [Churn] to start production of the homes was being wired by [Churn] to [AAH's] corporate office yesterday," or whether "if the wire was received by Monday it would take approximately 4 weeks to get the materials then an additional 2 weeks to complete the structure." A review of the trial transcript supports the government's assertion that it was simply trying to illustrate why Campsey became suspicious and demanded verification from Churn about his work.

While the district court initially called the statements "hearsay," it later clarified that the statements were "[n]ot [being admitted to show that] what the other person actually said is true or not, but to explain the basis of this witness's state of mind, to explain what this witness was doing." (Trial Tr., R. 80, PageID 283.) The district court thus prudently instructed the jury that the document was "being introduced for a limited purpose." (*Id.*) Accordingly, "because the government did not offer the statements for their truth, the statements fall outside of the definition of hearsay." *United States v. Talley*, 164 F.3d 989, 999 (6th Cir.1999). And because the email's statements were only admitted to "show its effect on the listener," *Biegas*, 573 F.3d at 379, the government did not need to rely on the state-of-mind exception.

C. Whether Campsey's Statement Concerning a County Permit Contained Inadmissible Hearsay.

Churn claims that the district court committed plain error by admitting impermissible hearsay about whether Churn secured a county permit. During Campsey's testimony, the government presented Churn's first invoice submitted to BSB, p.777 which listed expenses for building permit fees, disconnecting utilities, and certain construction work. BSB approved a $15,000 draw based on that invoice. The following exchange occurred:

> [The government]: What work that is indicated on this invoice was actually done?
>
> [Campsey]: Through talking to the county, —
>
> [Defense counsel]: Your Honor, I'm going to object to hearsay.
>
> The Court: Restate your question.
>
> [The government]: I will, Your Honor. Do you know personally what work was done, based on your own observations?
>
> . . .
>
> [Campsey]: My own observation, none of this work was ever completed. And through verification with the county, the permit was never pulled.

(Trial Tr., R. 80, PageID 270.) Churn's counsel did not object at trial to Campsey's question.

Churn now argues that the government introduced Campsey's statement that "through verification with the county, the permit was never pulled" to support the proposition that Churn never used the disbursed money to secure the permit and pay fees. He asserts that the statement was hearsay since no one from the county testified and no exception to the hearsay rule applied. Churn maintains that the remaining evidence could not support his convictions on Counts 3 and 7. He points out that while Campsey testified that "none of this work was ever completed," she later conceded that the house was demolished and the pad cleared. (Trial Tr., R. 80, PageID 270-71; *see also id.* at 215.) Because this statement was the only evidence that he failed to spend the disbursed money on building permits, Churn contends that its erroneous admission directly affected his convictions on Counts 3 and 7 and thus prejudiced him. In addition, Churn argues that "the county's statements ... severely damaged Mr. Churn's credibility for the rest of trial."

Campsey's statement called for hearsay. The content of the county records would fall within an exception to the hearsay rule only if properly authenticated under Federal Rules of Evidence 803(6). The outcome does not depend on whether Campsey learned about the permit "[t]hrough talking to the county," as she said, or whether she herself had checked the records.

Nonetheless, Churn fails to demonstrate that the error affected his substantial rights. *See United States v. Vonner,* 516 F.3d 382, 386 (6th Cir.2008) (en banc). Campsey's uncontroverted testimony, based on her personal observations, was that none of the work that appeared on the invoice was ever completed. (*See* Trial Tr., R. 80, Page ID 268-71.) And the bank relied on the invoice as a whole — not just the reference to the permit — in distributing the draw in December 2006. (*Id.* at 271.) Thus, although the statement was clearly hearsay, Churn is not entitled to relief.

D. Whether the District Court Properly Admitted Evidence of Another Transaction as *Res Gestae.*

Churn argues that the district court abused its discretion and prejudiced him by admitting testimony about a real-estate deal that did not underlie his charged offenses. During Rief's testimony, the government asked him whether Clarksville Pike was the only property in which he invested with Churn. When Rief responded "[n]o" and identified another investment in 1712 North 24th Avenue, Churn's counsel requested a sidebar. (Trial Tr., R. 81, PageID 404.)

p.778 Churn's counsel informed the district court that the government's trial brief stated that the government intended to introduce evidence concerning the North 24th Avenue transaction and that the government suggested it could do so under the *res gestae* exception for background information related to the government's allegations or Federal Rule of Evidence 404(b)'s exceptions to the rule's general prohibition against introducing evidence of other crimes or acts to prove character. He objected, however, stating that the exceptions did not apply and that the prejudice from the evidence would outweigh any probative value it had. The government responded that the deal at issue "occurred at the same time," was "part of the same series of events," and happened in the same manner as the Clarksville Pike and Green Street transactions, and thus testimony about it was admissible, though the government also said that it did not intend to introduce any documentary evidence. (*Id.* at 404-05.) The district court overruled Churn's objection and held that the testimony was "intrinsic evidence" because "it explains the relationship between the witness and the defendant and the nature of their business relationship and the course of their business dealings." (*Id.* at 405-06.) It did not address whether the testimony was admissible under Rule 404(b).

Rief then testified about his agreement with Churn concerning the Clarksville Pike property, and stated that although the North 24th Avenue transaction "was a rehab, [] the deal was set up the same." (*Id.* at 406.) For both projects, Rief was responsible for obtaining financing and Churn was responsible for the construction. Like Clarksville Pike, Rief testified that "nothing happened with the property" — not only was the rehab never completed, "[i]t was never started." (*Id.* at 433.) Similarly, it was foreclosed. The government offered no more testimony about the North 24th Avenue transaction.

On appeal, Churn argues that the district court abused its discretion by ruling that the North 24th Avenue transaction was "intrinsic evidence" and thus admissible as *res gestae.* He contends that the North 24th Avenue transaction cannot fit in this court's definition of intrinsic evidence, which "requires a connection to the charged offense," *United States v. Adams,* 722 F.3d 788, 822 (6th Cir.2013), one involving a "close temporal, spatial, and causal proximity" between the prior act and charged offense, *Chalmers,* 554 Fed. Appx. at 451. Here, Churn says, the North 24th Avenue transaction was "merely background explanation" of Churn and Rief's *relationship,* and does not have any "direct connection" with the Clarksville Pike *deal,* notably because a different financial institution was involved. Churn also asserts that the prejudice from admitting testimony about the North 24th Avenue transaction outweighs its probative value because providing a "better understanding" of Churn and Rief's relationship does not justify the possibility of the jury believing that Churn caused the foreclosure in the North 24th Avenue transaction.

The government responds that because "Churn executed a scheme to defraud banks by inducing individuals to obtain construction loans and the banks to disburse those loans," the North 24th Avenue transaction "falls into this scheme." Since "this transaction evidences 'the very scheme alleged in the indictment,'" the government argues, it is "intrinsic" to that scheme and the district court correctly admitted the testimony. *Id.* at 37 (quoting *United States v. Weinstock,* 153 F.3d 272, 277 (6th Cir.1998)). In addition, the government claims that Churn never raised an objection based on Rule 403 and therefore has waived this argument on appeal. Finally, p.779 the government contends that any error in admitting the testimony is harmless because of the overwhelming evidence of fraud from the two charged offenses.

This court "ha[s] recognized the admissibility of *res gestae,* or background evidence, in limited circumstances when the evidence includes conduct that is 'inextricably intertwined' with the charged offense." *United States v. Clay,* 667 F.3d 689, 697 (6th Cir.2012). "Proper background evidence has a causal, temporal or spatial connection with the charged offense." *Hardy,* 228 F.3d at 748. "[Such] evidence may include evidence that is a prelude to the charged offense, is directly probative of the charged offense, arises from the same events as the charged offense, forms an integral part of the witness's testimony, or completes the story of the charged offense." *United States v. Grooms,* 566 Fed.Appx. 485, 491 (6th Cir. 2014) (internal quotation marks omitted).

Res gestae is sometimes also known as "intrinsic evidence." "Intrinsic acts are those that are inextricably intertwined with the criminal act charged or a part of the criminal activity as opposed to extrinsic acts, which are those that occurred at different times and under different circumstances from the offense charged." *United States v. Stafford,* 198 F.3d 248, at *4 (6th Cir.1999). We have "acknowledge[d] that the distinctions among res gestae, inextricably intertwined evidence, intrinsic evidence, and background evidence [are] far from clear." *Adams,* 722 F.3d at 822 n. 26. But we often treat the various concepts similarly. *See id.*

Res gestae evidence does not implicate Federal Rule of Evidence 404(b), which generally bars evidence of past acts to prove character, but with some exceptions. *Hardy,* 228 F.3d at 748. Notably, this court "allow[s] the trial court to admit evidence regarding a defendant's *unindicted* criminal activity when that activity is 'intrinsic' or 'inextricably intertwined' with charges named in the indictment." *United States v. Potts,* 173 F.3d 430, at *9 (6th Cir.1999) (emphasis added). Even if evidence is *res gestae,* we "must also find that the district court did not abuse its discretion in concluding that the probative value of the evidence was not substantially outweighed by the danger of unfair prejudice pursuant to Federal Rule of Evidence 403." *United States v. Joseph,* 270 Fed. Appx. 399, 406 (6th Cir.2008) (per curiam).

Rief's testimony about the North 24th Avenue transaction was *res gestae* because it was "closely related in both time and nature to the crime charged." *United States v. Vincent,* 681 F.2d 462, 465 (6th Cir.1982) (internal quotation marks omitted). As Rief stated at trial, "the deal was set up the same" as the Clarksville Pike transaction. (Trial Tr., R. 81, PageID 406.) The district court correctly found that the testimony "explains the relationship between the witness and the defendant and the nature of their business relationship and the course of their business dealings." (*Id.* at 405-06.) And as the government proffered, Churn persuaded Rief to invest in both that transaction and the Clarksville Pike transaction around the same time. While Churn attempts to distinguish the two transactions by pointing out that the North 24th Avenue transaction did not involve a loan from a bank, that distinction is immaterial; we only require that the facts are "closely related," not identical. *See Vincent,* 681 F.2d at 465. That Churn was not indicted for the North 24th Avenue transaction is also irrelevant because we have held that even unindicted activity can be "inextricably intertwined" with the actual charges. *Potts,* 173 F.3d at *9.

p.780 In ruling that the evidence was admissible, the district court correctly concluded that the probative value of the evidence was not outweighed by unfair prejudice. Because the court did not abuse its discretion in admitting the *res gestae* evidence, reversal is unwarranted.

E. Whether the Cumulative Weight of Evidentiary Errors Warrant Reversal.

Churn argues that the cumulative weight of the district court's erroneous evidentiary rulings prejudiced him and thus reversal is warranted. "Errors that might not be so prejudicial as to amount to a deprivation of due process when considered alone, may cumulatively produce a trial setting that is fundamentally unfair." *Walker v. Engle,* 703 F.2d 959, 963 (6th Cir.1983). Although the court erred in admitting Campsey's testimony about verifying county permit records, that error was harmless and thus did not affect his substantial rights. Accordingly, there is no basis for reversal based on cumulative error.

F. Whether the District Court Imposed an Erroneous Sentence.

Churn argues that the district court improperly based its sentence on conduct underlying charges for which he was acquitted. "This court reviews a constitutional challenge to a defendant's sentence *de novo* wherever the defendant preserves the claim for appellate review." *United States v. Copeland,* 321 F.3d 582, 601 (6th Cir.2003).

Churn argues that this court should reverse his prison sentence and remand for resentencing because the district court used dismissed and acquitted conduct to increase his prison sentence to an "unreasonable" level. Nonetheless, Churn acknowledges that this court "currently allows district courts to consider dismissed and acquitted conduct when imposing sentences below the statutory maximum." Indeed, the Supreme Court of the United States, as well as an en banc panel of this court, has held that "a jury's verdict of acquittal does not prevent the sentencing court from considering conduct underlying the acquitted charge, so long as that conduct has been proved by a preponderance of the evidence." *United States v. Watts,* 519 U.S. 148, 157, 117 S.Ct. 633, 136 L.Ed.2d 554 (1997) (per curiam); *United States v. White,* 551 F.3d 381, 383 (6th Cir.2008) (en banc). Churn does not argue that the conduct underlying the acquitted charges was not proven by a preponderance of the evidence. Because the district court correctly applied existing law in determining Churn's sentence, we affirm the sentence imposed by the district court.

G. Whether the District Court Imposed an Erroneous Restitution Order.

Churn argues that the district court violated his right to a jury trial under the Sixth Amendment of the United States Constitution by using facts it found on its own to increase the restitution amount imposed upon him beyond the maximum allowed under the Mandatory Victims Restitution Act ("MVRA"), 18 U.S.C. § 3663A. In his sentencing memorandum, Churn argued that "restitution should only apply to the counts of conviction," and thus he should only be ordered to pay $97,600. (Sentencing Mem., R. 89, PageID 771.) At the sentencing hearing, Churn's counsel objected to the district court's reliance on the four acquitted and two dismissed counts to augment the calculated loss for which restitution was ordered. The district court overruled the objection and ordered restitution of $237,950.50, or p.781 $140,350.50 more than the amount of harm linked to his convicted counts.

On appeal, Churn argues that because restitution is a criminal punishment, and any fact that increases punishment beyond a statutory maximum must be found by a jury under *Apprendi v. New Jersey,* 530 U.S. 466, 120 S.Ct. 2348, 147 L.Ed.2d 435 (2000), the district court unconstitutionally enhanced his restitution under the MVRA based on judicial factfinding. He also claims that the Supreme Court's decision in *Southern Union Co. v. United States,* ___ U.S. ___, 132 S.Ct. 2344, 183 L.Ed.2d 318 (2012), confirms his position that restitution orders must be based on facts found by a jury.

The government rejects Churn's premise that the MVRA has a statutory maximum and therefore maintains that *Apprendi* does not apply to the statute. Thus, the government distinguishes *Southern Union,* which involved a punishment scheme with a statutory maximum fine, from this case. Even assuming that the MVRA has a statutory maximum, the government argues that because the statute also has an exception for criminal conduct involving a scheme, conspiracy, or pattern of criminal activity, and Churn was convicted of "knowingly execut[ing], or attempt[ing] to execute, a scheme or artifice" to defraud a bank, 18 U.S.C. § 1344, the district court correctly ordered restitution based on Churn's entire scheme, which included conduct underlying the dismissed and acquitted counts.

"This court reviews a constitutional challenge to a defendant's sentence *de novo* wherever the defendant preserves the claim for appellate review." *Copeland,* 321 F.3d at 601.

Under the MVRA, a district court "shall order" a defendant to make restitution to "an identifiable victim or victims [who] has suffered a[] pecuniary loss." 18 U.S.C. § 3663A(a)(1), (c)(1)(B). "Victim" is defined as:

> [A] person directly and proximately harmed as a result of the commission of an offense for which restitution may be ordered including, in the case of an offense that involves as an element a scheme, conspiracy, or pattern of criminal activity, any person directly harmed by the defendant's criminal conduct in the course of the scheme, conspiracy, or pattern.

18 U.S.C. § 3663A(a)(2).

The Supreme Court of the United States has held that, other than the existence of a prior conviction, "any fact that increases the penalty for a crime beyond the prescribed statutory maximum must be submitted to a jury, and proved beyond a reasonable doubt." *Apprendi,* 530 U.S. at 490, 120 S.Ct. 2348. However, we have noted that "[a]n intra-circuit split exists [in the Sixth Circuit] on the question of whether the MVRA specifies a statutory maximum." *United States v. Winans,* 748 F.3d 268, 272 n. 2 (6th Cir.2014). In *United States v. Sosebee,* this court observed that "we have [] held that restitution orders are not affected by the Supreme Court's ruling in *Apprendi v. New Jersey...* because the restitution statutes do not specify a statutory maximum." 419 F.3d 451, 461 (6th Cir.2005). We also pointed out that the Third, Seventh, Eighth, and Tenth Circuits have held that *Apprendi* does not apply to restitution orders under the MVRA. *Id.*

Six years later, however, this court stated in *United States v. Freeman* that "the restitution statute [MVRA] '*does* set a statutory maximum on the amount of restitution.'" 640 F.3d 180, 193 (6th Cir.2011) (quoting *United States v. Gordon,* 480 F.3d 1205, 1210 (10th Cir.2007) (original emphasis)). That maximum, we said, is "the p.782 amount causally linked to the offense of conviction." *Id.* (internal quotation marks omitted). In making this determination, we did not address *Sosebee*'s contrary statement.

Here, even if the MVRA prescribes a statutory maximum, the district court did not exceed it. Churn was convicted of "knowingly execut[ing], or attempt[ing] to execute, a scheme or artifice to defraud a financial institution" when he was convicted of bank fraud. 18 U.S.C. § 1344(1). Because each count of the indictment corresponded to a particular draw related to the Clarksville Pike or Green Street properties, the district court did not impose a restitution amount greater than the amount of harm directly caused by Churn's "criminal conduct in the course of the scheme, conspiracy, or pattern [of criminal activity]." 18 U.S.C. § 3663A(a)(2). Therefore, the order did not go beyond any maximum specified in the MVRA and did not violate *Apprendi,* even if *Apprendi* applies to the MVRA.

As Churn acknowledges, however, we have already squarely held that "restitution orders are not affected by the Supreme Court's ruling in *Apprendi v. New Jersey* ... because the restitution statutes do not specify a statutory maximum." *Sosebee,* 419

F.3d at 461. We adhere to that principle now. As a published decision, *Sosebee* is controlling authority for all subsequent panels of this court absent a reversal by the Supreme Court or an en banc panel of this court, and *Freeman*'s statement does not alter our conclusion to the extent it conflicts with *Sosebee*. *See Darrah v. City of Oak Park*, 255 F.3d 301, 309-10 (6th Cir.2001). Accordingly, *Apprendi* does not apply to the MVRA and the district court's restitution calculation need not be limited only to Churn's convicted offenses.

Contrary to Churn's argument, *Southern Union* does not cast doubt on the conclusion we reach — if anything, it reinforces our decision. *Southern Union* involved a gas company that was charged with violating the Resource Conservation and Recovery Act, which provides for a maximum criminal fine of $50,000 per day of violation. 132 S.Ct. at 2349. Although the indictment accused the company of violating the statute for 762 days, the court instructed the jury that it could convict based on one day's violation, which the jury did. *Id.* The court set a maximum potential fine of $38.1 million, i.e., $50,000 multiplied by 762 days. *Id.* The defendant appealed, arguing that any fact resulting in a fine over the statutory daily maximum had to be found by a jury. *Id.* The Supreme Court agreed. *Id.* at 2357. But the statute in *Southern Union* had a defined statutory daily maximum. The MVRA does not. Thus, *Southern Union* does not apply here.

The weight of authority supports our conclusion. At least four cases from this court have followed *Sosebee* in the wake of *Freeman* and *Southern Union,* holding that judge-found facts can be used to calculate restitution under the MVRA and that *Southern Union* does not dictate otherwise, whereas there appears to be no case to the contrary. *United States v. Johnson,* 583 Fed.Appx. 503, 510 (6th Cir. 2014) (reaffirming *Sosebee*'s holding "that restitution [under the MVRA] falls outside the bounds of the Sixth Amendment" and rejecting contention that *Southern Union* "calls *Sosebee* into question"); *United States v. Rogers,* 580 Fed.Appx. 347, 352 (6th Cir.2014) (rejecting argument that defendant was entitled to a "jury finding on the loss-amount for restitution purposes," noting that other circuits are in accord, and distinguishing *Southern Union*); *United States v. Jarjis,* 551 Fed.Appx. 261, 261-62 (6th Cir.2014) (per curiam) (same); *see also United States v. Agbebiyi,* 575 Fed.Appx. 624, 632-33 (6th Cir.2014) (holding that *Apprendi* and *Southern Union* do p.783 not require facts underlying MVRA restitution calculations to be found by a jury). Similarly, every circuit court (except the Federal Circuit) has held that *Apprendi* does not apply to the MVRA. *See United States v. Bengis,* 783 F.3d 407, 411-13 (2d Cir.2015); *Jarjis,* 551 Fed.Appx. at 261-62 (citing cases from Fourth, Seventh, and Ninth Circuits); *United States v. Milkiewicz,* 470 F.3d 390, 403-04 (1st Cir.2006) (citing cases from Second, Third, Fifth, Sixth, Seventh, Eighth, Ninth, Tenth, and Eleventh Circuits). Many of these cases have also distinguished *Southern Union* and held that it does not extend *Apprendi*'s rule to restitution. For all these reasons, we conclude that the district court's restitution order was proper.

III. CONCLUSION

Because the district court did not commit any reversible evidentiary errors and properly took account of dismissed or acquitted conduct in sentencing Churn, we affirm its judgment.

786 F.3d 470 (2015)

UNITED STATES of America, Plaintiff-Appellee,

v.

Mauricio GIVENS, Defendant-Appellant.

No. 14-5122.

United States Court of Appeals, Sixth Circuit.

May 15, 2015.

US v. Givens, 786 F. 3d 470 (6th Cir. 2015)

p.471 ON BRIEF: Paul L. Nelson, Federal Public Defender, Grand Rapids, Michigan, for Appellant. Carroll L. Andre III, United States Attorney's Office, Memphis, Tennessee, for Appellee.

Before: BOGGS, SILER, and CLAY, Circuit Judges.

BOGGS, J., delivered the opinion of the court in which SILER, J., joined. CLAY, J. (pp. 474-77), delivered a separate dissenting opinion.

OPINION

BOGGS, Circuit Judge.

On December 7, 2010, Defendant-Appellant Mauricio Givens pled guilty to bank fraud. On April 4, 2011, the court sentenced Givens to 18 months of imprisonment and four years of supervised release. On July 14, 2011, Givens was released and his supervised release began. In November 2013, Givens's probation officer petitioned the court to revoke his supervised release. The officer claimed that Givens attempted to drive his car into Steven Queen. During the revocation-of-release hearing that followed this petition, Givens sought to impeach Queen on the basis of hearsay evidence. The district court refused to admit that evidence and subsequently revoked Givens's supervised release. Givens timely appealed. We affirm the judgment of the district court for the reasons that follow.

"The [district] court may, after considering [certain factors] ... revoke a term of supervised release, ... if the court... finds by a preponderance of the evidence that the defendant violated a condition of supervised release...." 18 U.S.C. § 3583(e)(3). Such district-court revocations of supervised release are discretionary. This court reviews those revocations for an abuse of discretion. *See, e.g., United States v. Stephenson,* 928 F.2d 728, 731-2 (6th Cir.1991); see also *N.L.R.B. v. Guernsey-Muskingum Elec. Co-op., Inc.,* 285 F.2d 8, 11 (6th Cir.1960) (defining an abuse of discretion as "arbitrary action not justifiable in view of" the situation and circumstances affecting the individual case).

Because we review a decision to revoke a prisoner's release for an abuse of discretion, this case does not turn on whether Queen testified accurately that Givens assaulted him. Rather, it turns on whether or not the district court was within its discretion to exclude evidence that might have called Queen's testimony into question. In particular, Givens attacks the district court's exclusion of two reports about Queen: "a police report, and the follow-up Secret Service [report] of Mr. Queen." According to Givens's counsel, the report "talk[ed] about how [Queen has] tried to intimidate people," but the court, looking at the report, concluded that it was a report that a church pastor had called the police to tell them that one of his members said that Queen had harassed her; because it was "just a bunch of hearsay," the court refused to let Givens use it p.472 as impeachment material. Givens's counsel did cross-examine Queen without that report. One question Givens's counsel asked was whether Queen had "ever been charged with harassing anyone" other than Givens.

Our task is to determine whether there was *any* justification for the district court to exclude the hearsay evidence that purportedly concerned Queen's reliability as a complaining witness. There was, as a brief review of the relevant doctrinal history will show.

Prior to 1970, it was not clear that the Constitution demanded *any* trial process in administrative proceedings. In *Goldberg v. Kelly,* 397 U.S. 254, 90 S.Ct. 1011, 25 L.Ed.2d 287 (1970), the Supreme Court applied "the template for adjudication provided by the Federal Rules ... *in some respects* to the administrative context." Judith Resnik, *For Owen M. Fiss: Some Reflections on the Triumph and the Death of Adjudication,* 58 U. Miami L.Rev. 173, 179 (2003) (emphasis added). Despite the costs to the government, *Goldberg* and its sequellae afforded a non-zero but less-than-trial amount of process to participants in administrative proceedings.

The revocation of parole is an administrative proceeding, and the Court applied *Goldberg* to it. *Morrissey v. Brewer,* 408 U.S. 471, 487, 92 S.Ct. 2593, 33 L.Ed.2d 484 (1972). This court, in turn, applied *Morrissey* to revocation-of-supervised-release cases. *United States v. Lowenstein,* 108 F.3d 80, 85 (6th Cir.1997). The *Morrissey* Court clarified "the minimum requirements of due process," including (a) written notice, (b) disclosure of evidence, (c) opportunity to be heard in person and to present evidence, "(d) the right to confront and cross-examine adverse witnesses (*unless the hearing officer specifically finds good cause for not allowing confrontation*)," (e) a neutral and detached arbiter, and "(f) a written statement by the factfinders as to the evidence relied on and reasons for" revocation. *Morrissey,* 408 U.S. at 489, 92 S.Ct. 2593 (emphasis added).

Because *Goldberg* does not turn every administrative process into a full trial, *Morrissey* does not entitle convicts to the full panoply of process due to a criminal accused of a crime in the first instance. *Morrissey,* 408 U.S. at 489, 92 S.Ct. 2593 ("[T]here is no thought to equate ... revocation to a criminal prosecution in any sense."). Rather, the idea of *Morrissey* was to provide *some* process to the would-be prisoner while keeping the cost to the government of such process lower than that of the process due at trial to the accused. The *Morrissey* Court emphasized that it had "not thought to create an inflexible structure for parole revocation procedures." *Id.* at 490, 92 S.Ct. 2593. Such an inflexible structure would too little respect the government's legitimate interest in efficiently revoking the supervised release of convicts who had violated the terms on which their release was conditioned.

To mandate that judges presiding over revocation-of-release hearings allow hearsay evidence that might tend to impeach government witnesses would be to extend *Morrissey* beyond all recognition. In other words, Givens was not due a revocation-of-release process *as* defendant-friendly as a process due to criminals before convictions, let alone a process *more* defendant-friendly.

This historical background shows that *Morrissey* and its sequellae do not require a judge to admit hearsay evidence in a revocation-of-release setting. Although hearsay is admissible under certain conditions, *see, e.g., United States v. Waters,* p.473 158 F.3d 933, 940-41 (6th Cir.1998), the court is not *obliged* to admit such evidence. And the rationale for excluding hearsay from trial suggests why a court, in its discretion, might exclude hearsay from an administrative hearing, too. For one thing, hearsay is unreliable, almost by definition. The court might not consider evidence that it considers more likely to obscure than to develop facts. For another, common intuition reveals that "the events that we know firsthand (that is, of our own personal knowledge) are fewer than those of which we have secondhand knowledge (that is, we know of them only through hearsay)." 30 Wright & Graham, Fed. Prac. & Proc.: Evid. § 6321 at 7 (1997). From this logical rule follows a legal one: courts exclude most hearsay from trials. So, "[t]he power over the admission and exclusion of hearsay is a substantial weapon in the trial judge's arsenal.... [I]f hearsay were freely admissible, the number of potential witnesses in a lawsuit and the amount of testimony each could give would expand dramatically." *Ibid.*

As a structural matter, the court might not consider evidence that slows the proceeding, either concerned for judicial economy (this is the rationale, for example, for the rule of evidence that a litigant cannot introduce extrinsic evidence on a collateral matter only for the purpose of contradicting a witness) or for government interests (interests recognized by *Goldberg* and *Morrissey*).

We can distinguish our cases that seem to hold otherwise. In *United States v. Kokoski,* 435 Fed.Appx. 472 (6th Cir. 2011), the district court revoked the defendant's supervised release and relied, in part, on professional records about him. After opining that the records were, in fact, exceptions from the hearsay exclusions because they were business records, we observed that their admission did not prejudice the defendant and so did not constitute reversible error. *Ibid.* Other revocation-of-release apparently hostile to the exclusion of hearsay evidence *affirm* district-court revocations of release. *See, e.g., United States v. Kirby,* 418 F.3d 621 (6th Cir.2005), *United States v. Shakir,* 574 Fed.Appx. 712 (6th Cir.2014), *United States v. Dobson,* 529 Fed.Appx. 536 (6th Cir.2013), *United States v. Thompson,* 314 Fed.Appx. 797 (6th Cir.2008), and *United States v. Shipman,* 215 F.3d 1328 (6th Cir.2000) (table). Here, Givens, not the government, sought to introduce the alleged hearsay. We affirm the judgment of the district court.

Givens also claims that there was insufficient evidence to revoke his release. The government needed to prove violation of supervised-release terms only by a preponderance of the evidence. It was within the discretion of a district court to consider Queen's testimony—whether or not the proceedings included the hearsay evidence possibly undermining Queen's credibility—sufficient evidence that Givens assaulted Queen.

In short, district courts may or must exclude most hearsay evidence from trials. Although revocation-of-release hearings need not follow the inflexible procedural rules of trials, the flexibility of administrative-hearing procedures, such as those for revoking release, makes following the hearsay rules a safe harbor—not required, but virtually always an appropriate exercise of discretion.

In this case, Queen's testimony may not have been as reliable as Givens's—but that was an evidentiary argument for the adjudicator to consider. *See Taylor v. United*

States Parole Comm'n, 734 F.2d 1152, 1155 (6th Cir.1984) ("Our concern in this case is with the paucity of reliable evidence of petitioner's criminal conduct and not with the hearsay nature of the evidence p.474 which was presented."). The district court did consider the relative trustworthiness of the witness and other sources of evidence, and so fulfilled its statutory and constitutional mandate. For the foregoing reasons, we affirm the judgment of the district court.

CLAY, Circuit Judge, dissenting.

This case is not about an individual on supervised release seeking the "full panoply" of due process rights afforded to a criminal defendant; nor is it about the broad discretion commanded by a district judge in determining whether to revoke supervised release. I concur in the majority's views on both of those points. However, because Givens' revocation sentence was determined by a charge that is not sustainable on the limited evidence before the court and because the district judge mistook the law in this case, I respectfully dissent.

I. Factual Background

A more detailed review of the facts is necessary to illustrate why I view this case differently from the majority. Givens' revocation hearing was initiated due to three distinct charges, only one of which he now disputes—an aggravated assault for allegedly driving his car at another individual. This charge subjected Givens to a substantially higher sentence of imprisonment. The only evidence to support this allegation is the account of Givens' accuser, Steven Queen. These are the undisputed facts. Givens was driving down the street in Queen's neighborhood affixing to each mailbox a flyer for his business. Queen flagged Givens down to inform him, incorrectly, that Givens' actions were in violation of the local homeowners' association rules. Givens initially contended that he had all the appropriate permits to be advertising his business, but he eventually relented in trying to convince Queen and drove away. Queen immediately began taking photographs with his cellphone of Givens' car as Givens departed, and he continued taking photographs until Givens' car had rounded a bend and was no longer in sight. Queen intended to inform the police about Givens' activities and provide them with the photographs he had taken.

At this point, their stories diverge. Givens testified that he circled back in his car so that he could affix flyers to mailboxes on the opposite side of the street. When he came back around the bend, he testified, Queen was in the street continuing to take photographs and blocking his path. Givens admitted that he ultimately got out of his car to confront Queen, at which point he threatened Queen, gesticulating with his hands and arms and saying that Queen needed to stop taking photographs because Givens just wanted to be left alone. Queen, on the other hand, testified that he dropped one of Givens' flyers in the middle of the street (which he intended to take to the authorities), and when he bent over to try to retrieve the flyer, Givens' car violently barreled toward him, forcing him to dive out of the way and into his neighbor's yard. Queen explained that Givens jumped out of his car, began throwing punches, took his phone, and deleted all but one photograph before throwing the phone back at his feet. This photograph, which was introduced as evidence to support the lesser-included charge of assault, shows Givens' arm reaching out in the direction of Queen's cellphone.

Queen suffers from paranoia as the result of his post-traumatic stress disorder that arose following his military service. At the hearing, the prosecution disclosed what it thought was potential impeachment evidence that could be used for Givens' defense. This evidence included a harassment complaint filed against Queen by the p.475 pastor at a local church that he had formerly attended with his now-estranged wife and a report made by the United States Secret Service in response to Queen lodging a frivolous complaint, where ultimately, agents demanded that Queen "not go around saying that people were being investigated by the Secret Service." (R. 149, Revocation Hr., PageID # 319). The district court concluded that this evidence could not be used to impeach Queen because it was not a conviction, stating that a supervisee facing revocation "typically can't ask about other conduct like that" because it is "just a bunch of hearsay." (*Id.* at 300, 302). The district judge was implicitly referring to Rule 608(b), which bars the use of extrinsic evidence to attack a witness' character for truthfulness.[1]

The district judge weighed the evidence and found that the photograph showing Givens' arm reaching out toward the cell phone "support[ed] the proposition that [Givens] grabbed the phone," and therefore committed an assault. (*Id.* at 351-52). The district judge also surmised that Givens' display of anger in a phone call that related to one of the other charges "suggests that he has a got a very short fuse," which further supported Queen's claim. (*Id.* at 353). With respect to the aggravated assault, he found that "[b]ecause the defendant is generally discredited and Mr. Queen's testimony is credible in the case by a preponderance of the evidence, I would also find that [Givens] did attempt to strike [Queen] with the vehicle." (*Id.* at 355). The district judge did not explicitly explain why Givens' testimony was discredited and there is no proof on record of Givens having testified dishonestly.[2] Notably, Queen's testimony did contain certain inconsistencies, which the district judge excused because "[Queen] didn't volunteer for posttraumatic stress disorder." (*Id.* at 353).

II. Legal Analysis

This fact pattern presents two issues that combine to result in a revocation of supervised release based on a proceeding that failed to meet the minimum standards of due process. These issues are the insufficiency of the government's evidence and the district judge's legally erroneous exclusion of admissible hearsay, which only served to highlight the weakness of the government's case with respect to the aggravated assault charge levied against Givens.

A district court, within its discretion, may revoke a defendant's supervised release upon a finding by a preponderance of the evidence that a defendant has violated the terms of his release. *United States v. Stephenson,* 928 F.2d 728, 733 (6th Cir. 1991). This judgment must be based, however, on sufficient, reliable evidence. *Id.* The district judge, relying on Queen's word alone, found that Givens committed an aggravated assault while driving his car by attempting to run Queen down. The problem with the district judge's conclusion is that Queen's testimony, on its face, is incredible, inconsistent, and not supported p.476 by any corroborating evidence.

Even the majority concedes that "Queen's testimony may not have been as reliable as Givens's." Maj. Op. at 473. Unlike the majority, however, I would not afford deference to the district judge in this instance, because no deference is due if the witness' testimony is facially implausible, "contradicted by extrinsic evidence," or "internally inconsistent." *Anderson v. City of Bessemer City,* 470 U.S. 564, 573-74, 105 S.Ct. 1504, 84 L.Ed.2d 518 (1985).

Queen admitted that he intended to report Givens to the police based on Givens' lawful activities prior to any alleged assault. Queen stated at the hearing that he reported to the police this alleged assault on the day that it occurred, when in fact he did not lodge his complaint with the police until two months later. Queen testified that he was wounded by the alleged assault and that the police had taken photographs of the wounds, yet there is no such record of any photographs in the police report. Moreover, Queen could not explain why he initially chose to harass Givens, when confronted with the fact that Queen was not aware of any ordinance that would have actually prohibited Givens' activity.

These patent contradictions in Queen's testimony that bear on his credibility, along with the absence of evidence to corroborate his allegation that Givens tried to run him down, magnify the significance of Givens' inability to present evidence for the purpose of further impeaching Queen. The majority asserts that "Givens was not due a revocation-of-release process *as* defendant-friendly as a process due to criminals before convictions, let alone a process *more* defendant-friendly." Maj. Op. at 472. However, no one has suggested a proposition that is contrary to that assertion. What Givens was due is a level playing field. As highlighted in the majority's own opinion, due process at a revocation hearing must include "the right to confront and cross-examine adverse witnesses (*unless the hearing officer specifically finds good cause for not allowing confrontation*)." *Morrissey v. Brewer,* 408 U.S. 471, 487, 92 S.Ct. 2593, 33 L.Ed.2d 484 (1972); *United States v. Lowenstein,* 108 F.3d 80, 85 (6th Cir.1997). Moreover, due process is not satisfied by merely offering a supervisee the ability to engage in a perfunctory examination of an adverse witness, because "effective cross-examination" is too "vital a constitutional right," *Davis v. Alaska,* 415 U.S. 308, 320, 94 S.Ct. 1105, 39 L.Ed.2d 347 (1974), which cannot be limited to the extent that a supervisee is prevented from presenting relevant evidence that bears on the credibility of a government witness. *Cf. United States v. Garrett,* 542 F.2d 23, 25 (6th Cir.1976).

The federal rules of evidence do not apply to revocation of supervised release proceedings. Fed.R.Evid. 1001(d)(3). Therefore, hearsay evidence is admissible at the discretion of a district judge so long as it is relevant and reliable. *See, e.g., United States v. Kirby,* 418 F.3d 621, 628 (6th Cir.2005). Hearsay evidence that would qualify for an exception to the hearsay rule at trial under the federal rules is deemed presumptively reliable. *United States v. Waters,* 158 F.3d 933, 940 (6th Cir.1998). The Secret Service report falls squarely within this category of presumptively reliable documents as a public record, because it contained a memorialization of the agency's actual knowledge and awareness that Queen had been falsely telling people that they were under investigation by the Secret Service.[3] *See Miller* p.477 *v. Field,* 35 F.3d 1088, 1091 (6th Cir.1994) ("It is well established that entries in a police report which result from the officer's own observations and knowledge may be admitted ....").

Although the district judge was not obligated to admit the report—for example, he may have found good cause for its exclusion—he was obligated to know and apply the correct standard for the admission of Givens' impeachment evidence before he chose to reject it. Instead of considering either reports' relevance or reliability, he inappropriately relied on the rules of evidence, which do not apply, and remarked that both reports were inadmissible simply because they were hearsay and not convictions. That is not the law. And absent any application of the correct legal standard, it is incongruous to suggest that the district judge specifically found "good cause," as required by *Morrissey,* for denying the accused the right to confront with all relevant evidence the sole witness against him, whose testimony accounts for the only evidence of the alleged vehicular assault. Givens should have been afforded the opportunity to meaningfully confront an admittedly paranoid individual with impeachment evidence, showing that individual's penchant for harassing people and fabricating complaints.

The majority insinuates that the district judge's failure to comport with the applicable law of this Circuit is unimportant because government hearsay can be treated more favorably than hearsay offered by a supervisee. But that too is plainly wrong. Due process does not allow a district judge to apply one evidentiary standard for the government and another for the accused. Any such circumstance, which for the supervisee is akin to entering a fight with one hand tied behind his back, is fundamentally unfair and inconsistent with any notion of due process. The district judge may have found good cause for excluding the report, but he failed to indicate it. Because this standard presumes that a district judge will freely exercise his or her discretion within appropriate bounds, the majority's concern with a potential glut of hearsay impeachment is completely unfounded. If the proffered evidence is not proved to be reliable *and* relevant it will appropriately be excluded.

This case would not be a matter of concern if Queen's testimony were not so flawed, or if there was additional evidence to support his claims. And any error might be harmless if Givens was already subject to the same punishment for his other violations of supervised release. But that was not the case. Without the finding that Givens attempted to commit a vehicular assault, his guidelines range would be only 6 to 12 months, far less than the 30-month sentence ultimately imposed as a result of the district judge's patently flawed finding that Givens attempted to run Queen down with his car. Queen suffers from post-traumatic stress disorder and was admittedly paranoid. Although the district judge is correct that those limitations are not Queen's fault, justice cannot be served by simply ignoring those limitations and subjecting a supervisee to an additional term of prison based solely on the incredible and inconsistent testimony of a complaining witness who suffers from paranoia. Because there is insufficient evidence, even by a preponderance of the evidence standard, to support a finding that Givens attempted to commit a vehicular assault, I would remand this case to the district court where Givens could be resentenced without the aggravated assault charge.

[1] The exception to Rule 608(b) is 609, which provides for the admission of criminal convictions.

[2] The district judge, earlier in the hearing, did suggest that Givens falsely denied calling his grandmother to ask that she urge his girlfriend to lie to the authorities regarding his alleged domestic assault. But this denial is not false; Givens did not

deny the call, just the prosecution's interpretation of what he was telling his grandmother to do. From Givens' perspective, he was merely asking his grandmother to urge that his girlfriend recant her version of events, inasmuch as Givens maintains that elbowing her was the accidental result of trying to restrain her with one arm, as they were engaged in animated argument while Givens was driving.

[3] The police complaint lodged by Queen's former pastor would not be presumptively reliable.

SEVENTH CIRCUIT DECISIONS

The Rule Against Hearsay

800 F.3d 783 (2015)

Wayne KUBSCH, Petitioner-Appellant,

v.

Ron NEAL, Superintendent, Indiana State Prison,[1] Respondent-Appellee.

No. 14-1898.

United States Court of Appeals, Seventh Circuit.

Argued February 10, 2015.

Decided August 12, 2015.

Kubsch v. Neal, 800 F. 3d 783 (7th Cir. 2015)

p.787 Marie F. Donnelly, Alan Michael Freedman, Evanston, IL, for Petitioner-Appellant.

Stephen R. Creason, James Blaine Martin, Office of the Attorney General, Indianapolis, IN, Respondent-Appellee.

Before WOOD, Chief Judge, and TINDER and HAMILTON, Circuit Judges.

HAMILTON, Circuit Judge.

Wayne Kubsch appeals the denial of his habeas corpus petition. After being convicted of murdering his wife, her son, and her ex-husband, Kubsch was sentenced to death. Kubsch's three principal arguments on appeal are that his conviction and sentence are unconstitutional because (a) the Indiana trial court excluded evidence of a witness's exculpatory but hearsay statement to police, (b) he was denied effective assistance of counsel in seeking admission of the witness's hearsay statement, and (c) his waiver of counsel and choice to represent himself at the sentencing phase of his trial were not knowing and voluntary.

We reject all three claims. Kubsch argues for a constitutional right to defend himself with otherwise inadmissible hearsay, at least if the hearsay seems sufficiently reliable and is sufficiently important to his defense. See *Chambers v. Mississippi,* 410 U.S. 284, 300-02, 93 S.Ct. 1038, 35 L.Ed.2d 297 (1973). Kubsch's evidence is not sufficiently reliable to fit that narrow constitutional exception and to have required Indiana courts to disregard long-established rules against using *ex parte* witness interviews as substantive evidence at trial. His able trial counsel tried hard to have the statement admitted; they were not successful but also were not constitutionally ineffective.

As for the waiver of counsel claim, the Indiana Supreme Court rejected the claim p.788 in a careful discussion tailored to the facts of this case. Its rejection of the claim was not contrary to or an unreasonable application of clearly established federal law as determined by the Supreme Court of the United States. See 28 U.S.C. § 2254(d)(1); *Harrington v. Richter,* 562 U.S. 86, 102-03, 131 S.Ct. 770, 178 L.Ed.2d 624 (2011).

In addition to the exculpatory hearsay claim, the related ineffective assistance claim, and the waiver of counsel claim that we address in detail, Kubsch raises a number of other arguments on appeal, all of which are challenges to the effectiveness of his counsel. We have considered all of these additional arguments, and we reject them for the reasons Chief Judge Simon explained in his thorough opinion. See *Kubsch v. Superintendent,* No. 3:11CV42-PPS, 2013 WL 6229136 (N.D.Ind. Dec. 2, 2013). Accordingly, we affirm the denial of relief as to both Kubsch's convictions and the death sentence.

I. *Factual and Procedural Background*

A. *Court Proceedings*

The State of Indiana charged Kubsch with murdering Beth Kubsch, Aaron Milewski, and Rick Milewski: his wife, her son, and her ex-husband. The three were murdered in Kubsch's home on September 18, 1998. Kubsch was first tried and found guilty in May 2000. The jury recommended and the judge imposed the death penalty. On direct appeal the Indiana Supreme Court held that the first trial violated Kubsch's constitutional rights when the prosecution used his post-*Miranda* silence as evidence against him. Based on that and other errors, the court vacated the convictions and ordered a new trial. See *Kubsch v. State,* 784 N.E.2d 905 (Ind. 2003).

Kubsch's second trial in March 2005 is our focus. Once more a jury convicted Kubsch of the three murders. There were two big differences in the second trial, in addition to avoiding the errors that had required the new trial. First, Kubsch offered as evidence the videotaped interview of Amanda Buck, a nine-year-old neighbor of Aaron and Rick Milewski. Amanda told a police detective four days after the murders that she had seen both Aaron and Rick alive and well at their home on the day of the murders at a time for which Kubsch has a solid alibi. The judge excluded her recorded statement as hearsay and as having no impeachment value. Second, unlike the first trial, Kubsch decided to waive counsel and represent himself in the sentencing phase of the trial. He also declined to present any mitigating evidence. He told the jury he agreed with the State that no mitigating factors outweighed the aggravating factors supporting a death sentence, but he insisted on his innocence. He ended his brief statement to the jury by saying he did not care what penalty was imposed.

Again the jury's verdict was for death and the judge imposed the death penalty. The state courts affirmed the convictions and sentence on direct appeal, *Kubsch v. State,* 866 N.E.2d 726 (Ind.2007), and on post-conviction review, *Kubsch v. State,* 934 N.E.2d 1138 (Ind.2010).

Kubsch then petitioned for a writ of habeas corpus in federal court, raising many more issues than we address in this opinion. The district court denied relief on all claims, *Kubsch v. Superintendent,* No. 3:11CV42-PPS, 2013 WL 6229136 (N.D.Ind. Dec. 2, 2013), and then denied Kubsch's Rule 59 motion, *Kubsch v. Superintendent,* No. 3:11CV42-PPS, 2014 WL 1260021 (N.D.Ind. March 24, 2014). Kubsch appeals. We review the district court's decision *de novo.* E.g., *Harris v.* p.789 *Thompson,* 698 F.3d 609, 622 (7th Cir. 2012).

B. *The Case Against Kubsch*

Chief Judge Simon aptly described the case against Kubsch as a "slow-moving accumulation of a glacier of circumstantial evidence." 2013 WL 6229136, at *3. A critical factor was that Kubsch's account of his own actions changed dramatically between the night of the murders and his trial testimony, after he knew the constraints imposed by physical and other evidence such as telephone records.

Kubsch lived with his wife Beth in Mishawaka, Indiana. They shared the home with Beth's twelve-year-old son, Anthony Earley. September 18, 1998 was Beth's birthday. She had planned to meet Kubsch for lunch. Beth was supposed to pick up Anthony late in the afternoon after a school dance. When she did not appear, Anthony got a ride home with a friend. At about 5:30, he found Beth's car in the driveway, along with a truck that her ex-husband Rick Milewski was using. The house was locked. Only Wayne, Beth, and Anthony had keys. No one seemed to be home. There was no sign of forced entry.

As Anthony looked around the main floor of the house, though, he saw bloodstains and signs of a struggle. He opened the door to the basement. He saw Rick lying at the foot of the stairs. The handle of a large kitchen knife was sticking out of his chest. Anthony went down the stairs, realized Rick was dead, and also found the body of his eleven-year-old step-brother Aaron lying next to Rick.

Anthony ran for help. Mishawaka police officers arrived about 5:45 p.m. Both Aaron and Rick had multiple stab wounds. The police officers found no sign of gunshot wounds. They also found no sign of Beth. After finding no one else in the house, the police secured the scene until they could obtain a search warrant.

That day Wayne Kubsch had finished work at an area factory shortly before 2:00 p.m. Late in the afternoon, he was returning to Mishawaka from picking up his son in Three Rivers, Michigan. He dropped off his son at Kubsch's grandmother's home. Kubsch arrived home about 6:45 and found the house surrounded by police. Kubsch was told that Aaron and Rick were dead and that no one knew where Beth was.

Kubsch soon went with police officers to the South Bend police department for questioning by detectives. That initial interview was audio-and video-recorded. Kubsch appeared preoccupied and careful, not distraught or frantic. He made no reference to the search for his missing wife, though there were obviously powerful reasons to be worried about her safety. He showed little emotion.

In that first interview on the night of the murders, Kubsch gave the police his first account of his movements and activities that day. Kubsch said that he and Beth had planned to meet for lunch to celebrate her birthday, but that he had called her to cancel because he had been late for work that morning. He also said that he had gotten permission to leave work early for lunch so he could buy Beth a birthday present (something he did not actually do until much later in the day). He told the police that he had gone home at lunch but could not get inside because he had forgotten his house key. He also did not mention that he had gone home a second time — shortly after work — before going to pick up his son in Michigan.

Kubsch ended the interview. His friend Dave Nichols and Nichols' wife testified that Kubsch called them about 8:00 or 8:30 that evening and said two things known to the killer but not yet known to the police. p.790 He told Nichols that Beth was "gone," which Nichols understood to mean that she was dead, not missing.[2] At that time, Beth's body had not yet been found. And while "gone" might be explained away as ambiguous, Kubsch also told Nichols that Rick and Aaron had been stabbed *and shot*. Not until autopsies were done the next day did the police learn that Rick and Aaron, in addition to their multiple stab wounds, had each been shot in the mouth.

At about 9:00 p.m., police officers on the scene discovered Beth's body. She was just a few feet from Rick and Aaron, but she was hidden underneath the staircase behind blankets that young Anthony had hung up as a sort of "fort" or hiding place a few weeks earlier. She had been stabbed eleven times. Her head was almost entirely covered in gray duct tape. Her body was "hog-tied" with the same tape, her wrists and ankles all bound together behind her back. (An autopsy also showed a blow to the back of her head and defensive wounds on her hands and wrists.) The officers quickly told the detectives at the South Bend station that Beth had been found murdered. The detectives then brought Kubsch back for more questioning later that evening. He declined to talk with them at that point, but he gave them permission to search his car.

The investigation of physical evidence turned up no evidence pointing conclusively to Kubsch. The only blood found on the scene belonged to the victims. The police did not find evidence of the victims' blood on Kubsch or his clothing. They also found no DNA or fingerprint evidence that pointed to him or anyone else as the killer.

Various items of physical evidence were consistent with Kubsch's guilt. In isolation none is conclusive. Taken together they point toward Kubsch as the killer, though not definitively. In Kubsch's car the police found the wrapper of a roll of duct tape of the type used to bind Beth. A bloody roll of duct tape at the top of the stairs matched the wrapper and the tape on Beth's body. A cloth fiber from the tape roll matched a fiber from the carpet of Kubsch's car. A receipt for purchase of the duct tape, three days before the murders, was found in Kubsch's car.

The police also found in Kubsch's car a wadded-up receipt from a deposit Beth had made the morning of the murders at the drive-through window of her credit union. The presence of that receipt in Kubsch's car contradicted the account he had given police the evening of the murders. (Even Kubsch's explanation at trial, that he found it next to the home telephone on his first stop at home that day, was improbable if not physically impossible. That explanation would have required Beth to do some improbable backtracking between two related errands.)

Of course, the locked house was also evidence that pointed toward Kubsch. The knife in Rick's chest was from the set of kitchen knives upstairs. A kitchen pan also had Beth's blood on it. As the prosecutor pointed out in closing argument, if the killer had been a stranger, it seems improbable that he would have counted on tools found in the home — the knife, the pan, and the duct tape — to carry out the murders.

Telephone records played an important role in the investigation and at trial. Recall that Kubsch had told police that he returned home at lunch but could not get in without his key. Home telephone records showed that was false. A call had been placed from the home telephone p.791 while Beth was running her errands that morning. Kubsch testified at trial that he had in fact gotten into the house — through the garage — where he said he made the call, smoked part of a marijuana cigarette, and then left to return to work around noon.[3]

Kubsch also made numerous calls with his cell phone on the day of the murders. Records of those calls showed his approximate locations at different times during the day. He left work for the day just before 2:00. Though he told the police the night of the murders that he had then gone directly to Michigan to pick up his son, he later admitted he had first actually returned to his home. He claimed that he had stopped at home for a few minutes between 2:30 and 2:45 and that no one else was home. At 2:51 Kubsch placed a cell phone call from a cell sector near his home. Cell phone records and other evidence showed that Kubsch then drove to Michigan to pick up his son. The State's theory has been that Kubsch had an opportunity to commit the murders in the time between approximately 2:00 and 3:00.

Another important discrepancy in Kubsch's story was that at 12:09 p.m. he called Rick Milewski and, according to Rick's brother, asked Rick to meet him at his house at 3:00 p.m. to help move a refrigerator. That request is hard to understand if Kubsch was planning to be on his way to Michigan by then. (The prosecution's theory was that Kubsch planned to have Rick find Beth's body but that Rick and Aaron showed up too early, before Kubsch had left, so he killed them too.)

Yet another discrepancy in Kubsch's story came from Beth's mother, Diane Rasor. She testified that when she talked with Kubsch on the afternoon of the murders, she mentioned that she had not been able to get in touch with Beth all day (Beth's birthday, recall). Kubsch reassured her, telling her that he had talked with Beth by phone and knew Beth was running a number of errands and was not at home to answer the phone. Several days after the murders, Kubsch told Rasor that he had not talked to Beth the day she was killed and he wished he had.

Kubsch also had a significant financial motive to murder Beth. The prosecution showed that the couple was in deep financial distress in 1998. Their cash flow was consistently negative. Early that year Kubsch had refinanced eight of the rental properties he owned, converting all available equity into cash and substantially increasing the total debt to about $424,000. Several credit cards or lines of credit were near their maximum limits. About three months before the murders, Kubsch had bought a new insurance policy on Beth's life for $575,000, with himself as the sole beneficiary. Kubsch claimed at trial that he had not realized they were in such difficult financial straits, but he also testified that he took care of the couple's bills, as well as their credit cards and lines of credit, and of course he had undertaken all the refinancing earlier that year.

As Chief Judge Simon summarized:

> The case against Kubsch was entirely circumstantial. There was no eyewitness, no DNA evidence, no fingerprint testimony, indeed no forensic evidence at all that linked Kubsch to the murders. There was, however, moderately strong evidence of motive and opportunity. But most damning to Kubsch was a series of lies, inexplicable omissions, and inconsistencies in what Kubsch told the p.792 police and later testified on the witness stand, and these statements — in conjunction with a few pieces of circumstantial evidence — are what almost assuredly got Kubsch convicted.

2013 WL 6229136, at *1.

II. *Exclusion of Exculpatory Hearsay Evidence*

Kubsch argues that he was convicted of the murders through a violation of his federal due process right to present a defense. The trial court did not allow him to introduce as substantive evidence a witness's videotaped interview with a police detective four days after the murders. Nine-year-old Amanda Buck and her mother

Monica were interviewed together by the detective. The Bucks lived across the street from two of the victims, Rick and Aaron Milewski. In the recorded twenty-minute interview, Amanda told the detective that she had seen Rick and Aaron alive and well at their home when she got home from school and daycare, between 3:30 and 3:45 p.m. on the day of the murders, Friday, September 18, 1998.

The date and time are critical. Based on telephone records and other evidence, the State argued at trial that Kubsch murdered the three victims between approximately 2:00 and 3:00 p.m. Kubsch's own testimony placed him at his home between approximately 2:30 and 2:45, though he claimed no one else was there. Cell phone records show that by 3:30 p.m. that day, Kubsch was well on his way to the town of Three Rivers, Michigan to pick up his son for the weekend. He did not return to his home in Mishawaka, Indiana until about 6:45, after the bodies of Rick and Aaron had been discovered there.

The importance of the constitutional evidentiary issue cannot be overstated. If the account given by Amanda in her recorded interview is correct, then Kubsch could not have committed the three murders for which he has been sentenced to death. And apart from Kubsch's own claims of innocence — impeached as they are by his shifting accounts of his movements that day — Amanda's recorded interview is the *only* support for Kubsch's alibi defense.

Kubsch bases his due process claim on *Chambers v. Mississippi*, 410 U.S. 284, 93 S.Ct. 1038, 35 L.Ed.2d 297 (1973), and its progeny. In *Chambers* the Supreme Court reversed a murder conviction on direct appeal. The Court held that the defendant was denied a fair trial when the trial court prevented him from impeaching a witness he had called and excluded hearsay evidence that the same witness had confessed to three different acquaintances that he was the killer. Kubsch relies on the hearsay portion of the *Chambers* analysis and its often-quoted statement that "the hearsay rule may not be applied mechanistically to defeat the ends of justice." 410 U.S. at 302, 93 S.Ct. 1038. The actual holding of *Chambers* is considerably narrower, however, for it depended on the combination of the trial court's limits on cross-examination and its exclusion of the multiple hearsay confessions, and the particular facts and circumstances of the case, which we describe in more detail below. See *id.* at 302-03, 93 S.Ct. 1038.

We address this issue in four steps. Part A explains the details of Amanda's statement and its treatment by the trial court and the Indiana Supreme Court. Part B explains the *Chambers* line of cases and the general constitutional standard for the right to present a defense, as well as its application in cases involving hearsay. Part C considers the factors indicating that Amanda's recorded statement is or is not reliable for purposes of *Chambers*. Part D addresses the issue of our standard of review, which turns out to be rather p.793 involved, and explains our conclusion that Kubsch is not entitled to relief.

A. The Statement in the State Courts

Four days after the murders, Sergeant Mark Reihl interviewed nine-year-old Amanda Buck and her mother Monica Buck together. The interview was in a police station and was audio-and video-recorded. The Bucks lived across the street from Rick and Aaron Milewski, and Sergeant Reihl asked them what they remembered from the day of the murders. Amanda answered most of the questions, but Monica added her own recollections, including specific times. Amanda recalled seeing both Aaron and Rick at their home across the street after she got home from school and daycare, which would have been between 3:30 and 3:45 on the afternoon of the murders.

Amanda's account was specific about many details, including what she was doing and which truck Rick was driving. She specifically recalled seeing Rick go into his kitchen and return with a glass. Her account was specific about the time and date. She recalled that she and Aaron were planning to go on a school field-trip the next day, a Saturday, and that Aaron had not shown up for the trip. Her mother Monica recalled having seen Aaron (but not Rick) when she got home shortly after 4:00 p.m. after going to the bank to deposit her paycheck, which she usually did on Friday.

The interview was disclosed to the defense, but Kubsch did not call Amanda or Monica as witnesses at his first trial, which took place less than two years after they spoke to the police. At the second trial in 2005, though, Kubsch called then sixteen-year-old Amanda as a witness. She testified that she did not remember whether she saw Rick and Aaron on the afternoon of the murders. She also testified that she did not even remember being interviewed by the police seven years earlier. After her brief testimony, and outside the presence of the jury, Amanda reviewed the recording of her interview. That apparently did not refresh her recollection because Kubsch offered no further testimony from her. Kubsch never called Monica to testify.

The real purpose of calling the sixteen-year-old Amanda was to put into evidence the video recording of the nine-year-old Amanda. Kubsch first tried to introduce the recording as substantive evidence. The recording was hearsay, of course. It was an out-of-court statement offered to prove the truth of its content. At trial, Kubsch argued that it should be admitted as a recorded recollection. Indiana Rule of Evidence 803(5), like its federal counterpart, recognizes an exception to the rule against hearsay for a "recorded recollection." Recorded recollections are records of what a witness once knew when her memory was fresh but now no longer recalls. A recorded recollection also "accurately reflects the witness's knowledge." Ind. R. Evid. 803(5)(C); see also Fed. R.Evid. 803(5)(C). Examples might include a diary or journal entry or a memorandum to file, as well as recorded interviews.

This recorded statement does not meet the last requirement of Rule 803(5). Amanda would have needed to "vouch for the accuracy" of the statement for it to qualify as a recorded recollection. *Kubsch v. State (Kubsch II)*, 866 N.E.2d 726, 734 (Ind.2007), quoting *Gee v. State*, 271 Ind. 28, 389 N.E.2d 303, 309 (1979). As the trial court found and the Indiana Supreme Court affirmed, "Buck could not vouch for the accuracy of a recording that she could not even remember making." *Kubsch II*, 866 N.E.2d at 735. The videotaped statement p.794 did not qualify as a recorded recollection under Indiana evidence law. *Id.*[4]

Kubsch next offered the videotaped statement to impeach Amanda's trial testimony with extrinsic evidence of a prior inconsistent statement. See Ind. R. Evid. 613(b). As noted, Amanda testified that she simply did not remember talking to the police and did not remember whether she saw her friend and neighbor Aaron between 3:30 and 3:45 p.m. the day of the murders.

The trial court sustained the State's objection to admitting the statement as impeachment evidence because Amanda "testified to no positive fact that is subject to impeachment." Tr. 3120. The Indiana Supreme Court agreed with respect to Amanda's trial testimony that she did not remember what happened or whom she saw on the day of the murders. *Kubsch II,* 866 N.E.2d at 735. However, Amanda also testified at one point that she "probably didn't see" Aaron at home between 3:30 and 3:45 p.m. on the day of the murders. Tr. 2985. The Indiana Supreme Court held that this testimony was properly subject to impeachment and that the trial court had erred by not allowing the attempted impeachment. *Kubsch II,* 866 N.E.2d at 735.

The Indiana Supreme Court also held, however, that the error was harmless. *Id.* In the debate in the trial court about the recording, the State said that if Kubsch were allowed to use Amanda's recorded statement to impeach her trial testimony, the State would respond with additional evidence impeaching the impeachment. The prosecutor asserted that three days after the recorded interview, Lonnie Buck (Monica's father and Amanda's grandfather) had called Sergeant Reihl and reported that both Amanda and Monica had been mistaken about the day they recalled and that they had described for him not the day of the murders but the day before. Monica had followed up with a later statement saying that she and Amanda had not seen Aaron on the day of the murders. At the time of the 2005 trial, the State was prepared to call both Monica Buck and Sergeant Reihl to impeach the proposed impeachment of Amanda.

The Indiana Supreme Court explained its finding of harmless error:

> Amanda's testimony should have been impeached, but other testimony would have supported hers had she been impeached, and therefore, her testimony likely did not contribute to the conviction. *See Pavey v. State,* 764 N.E.2d 692, 703 (Ind.Ct.App.2002) ("An error in the admission of evidence is not prejudicial if the evidence is merely cumulative of other evidence in the record.").

866 N.E.2d at 735. Just before this passage, the court dropped a footnote rejecting p.795 Kubsch's federal constitutional claim under *Chambers:*

> The availability of this testimony is also the reason why Kubsch's claim that he was denied his federal constitutional right to present a defense fails. *See Chambers v. Mississippi,* 410 U.S. 284, 302, 93 S.Ct. 1038, 35 L.Ed.2d 297 (1973) (protecting defendant's due process right by recognizing an exception to application of evidence rules where evidence found to be trustworthy).

Id. at 735 n. 7.

Unless we keep in mind the difference between substantive evidence and impeachment evidence, which may be considered not for the truth of the matter asserted but only to evaluate the credibility of other evidence, these terse passages finding harmless error may seem mistaken. After all, if Amanda's statement were admissible as substantive evidence to prove that what she said in the interview was true, then the mere fact that there was some contradictory evidence would not justify its exclusion. (The State's proffered impeachment did not include any admission by Amanda herself that she had been mistaken.) Conflicting evidence would simply present an ordinary question for a jury to resolve, as the trial judge recognized, see Tr. 3015, though a question of great importance because the statement would, if believed, exonerate Kubsch.

When we focus, however, as the trial judge did on the limited role of impeachment evidence, the harmless error finding is clearly sound as a matter of state evidence law. The only thing Amanda said in her trial testimony that was subject to impeachment was that she "probably didn't see" Aaron on the afternoon of the murders. As the trial judge pointed out, "She gave no substantive evidence in this case whatsoever." Tr. 3032. Amanda's narrow substantive statement that she "probably didn't see" Aaron on the afternoon of the murders was not inculpatory. It had essentially no probative value for the jury, so there would have been no point in impeaching her, and the exclusion of her statement for impeachment purposes could not have contributed to Kubsch's convictions.

The Indiana Supreme Court's rejection of the distinct *Chambers* claim in footnote 7 is the focus of our scrutiny. In the trial court, Kubsch had not asserted a distinct federal, constitutional claim under *Chambers*. He made that federal argument in his direct appeal, though, and the Indiana Supreme Court elected to decide the issue on its merits rather than find a procedural default. Footnote 7 was quite sensible to the extent that the recording was being offered only to impeach the non-inculpatory "probably didn't see him" portion of Amanda's trial testimony. The problem is that that reasoning seems not to have actually engaged with Kubsch's argument under the federal Constitution that the recording should have been admitted *as substantive evidence*. Again, the mere fact that the State would have offered contradictory evidence would have presented a jury question, not a basis for excluding the evidence in the first place. We explore these issues further in Part D on the standard of our review of the state court's decision.

B. *The Right to Present a Defense*

The exclusion of Amanda's recorded statement was not contrary to Indiana evidence law, as the Indiana Supreme Court decided. That conclusion does not resolve the federal constitutional question, though it informs our answer to that question. In a series of decisions led by *Chambers v. Mississippi,* 410 U.S. 284, 93 S.Ct. 1038, 35 L.Ed.2d 297 (1973), the Supreme Court has held that the accused in a criminal p.796 case has a federal constitutional right to offer a defense. Both the accused and the state "must comply with established rules of procedure and evidence designed to assure both fairness and reliability in the ascertainment of guilt and innocence." *Id.* at 302, 93 S.Ct. 1038. In some circumstances, however, the constitutional right to defend takes precedence over rules of evidence. This can include the hearsay rules, as *Chambers* itself showed.

Chambers is the closest Supreme Court case on its facts, so to understand the scope of this right to defend with hearsay, we consider that case in some detail. Leon Chambers was accused of murdering a police officer in a chaotic disturbance, essentially a small riot, as police were trying to arrest another person. Another man named McDonald had confessed to the murder: "McDonald had admitted responsibility for the murder on four separate occasions, once when he gave the sworn statement to Chambers' counsel and three other times prior to that occasion in private conversations with friends." *Id.* at 289, 93 S.Ct. 1038. McDonald was arrested after confessing to Chambers' counsel, but he was released when he repudiated that confession at his own preliminary hearing. *Id.* at 287-88, 93 S.Ct. 1038.

Chambers called McDonald as a witness at trial. McDonald's written confession was admitted into evidence, but McDonald again repudiated it. 410 U.S. at 291, 93 S.Ct. 1038. Chambers was not allowed to test McDonald's memory or otherwise to challenge his testimony. The state courts relied on the old "voucher" rule under which a party who called a witness was deemed to have vouched for his credibility and so was not allowed to impeach him even if he was actually adverse. The Supreme Court found, however, that the voucher rule was no longer realistic and had been applied to limit unfairly Chambers' examination of a critical witness who was in fact adverse. *Id.* at 295-98, 93 S.Ct. 1038.

After his attempts to impeach McDonald were stymied, Chambers then offered the testimony of three friends to whom McDonald had confessed. Their testimony about McDonald's confessions was excluded as hearsay. *Id.* at 292-93, 93 S.Ct. 1038. The jury convicted Chambers of the murder.[5]

On direct appeal, the Supreme Court reversed based on the combination of the voucher rule's barring impeachment of McDonald and the exclusion of the hearsay confessions. *Id.* at 302-03, 93 S.Ct. 1038. The Court noted that declarations against interest have long been treated as sufficiently reliable to be excepted from rules against hearsay. *Id.* at 298-99, 93 S.Ct. 1038. The Court found that the excluded confessions "bore persuasive assurances of trustworthiness" that brought them "well within the basic rationale of the exception for declarations against interest" and were "critical to Chambers' defense." *Id.* at 302, 93 S.Ct. 1038. The Court concluded: "In these circumstances, where constitutional rights directly affecting the ascertainment of guilt are implicated, the hearsay rule may not be applied mechanistically to defeat the ends of justice." *Id.* The combination of the limits on impeachment and the exclusion of the confessions led the Court to hold that "under p.797 the facts and circumstances of this case the rulings of the trial court deprived Chambers of a fair trial." *Id.* at 303, 93 S.Ct. 1038.

Chambers does not stand alone. It is the key precedent in a line of cases considering constitutional challenges to rules of evidence that restrict the defense of an accused. *See Washington v. Texas,* 388 U.S. 14, 22, 87 S.Ct. 1920, 18 L.Ed.2d 1019 (1967) (rejecting state evidence rule that allowed accused accomplices to testify for prosecution but not for defense); *Green v. Georgia,* 442 U.S. 95, 97, 99 S.Ct. 2150, 60 L.Ed.2d 738 (1979) (per curiam) (vacating death sentence where defendant was barred from using same out-of-court confession that prosecution used to obtain death penalty against declarant); *Crane v. Kentucky,* 476 U.S. 683, 691, 106 S.Ct. 2142, 90 L.Ed.2d 636 (1986) (rejecting state court's wholesale exclusion of testimony about circumstances of defendant's confession); *Rock v. Arkansas,* 483 U.S. 44, 56, 107 S.Ct. 2704, 97 L.Ed.2d 37 (1987) (rejecting state rule excluding all hypnotically refreshed testimony as applied to bar defendant's own testimony); *Montana v. Egelhoff,* 518 U.S. 37, 116 S.Ct. 2013, 135 L.Ed.2d 361 (1996) (upholding state rule barring consideration of evidence of voluntary intoxication in determining *mens rea*); *United States v. Scheffer,* 523 U.S. 303, 118 S.Ct. 1261, 140 L.Ed.2d 413 (1998) (upholding military rule of evidence barring use of polygraph test showing "no deception" in denial of drug use by defendant); *Holmes v. South Carolina,* 547 U.S. 319, 330, 126 S.Ct. 1727, 164 L.Ed.2d 503 (2006) (rejecting state rule barring defendant from introducing evidence of third-party guilt when prosecution has introduced forensic evidence that, if credited, is strong proof of defendant's guilt).

In the *Chambers* line of cases, the Court has balanced competing interests, weighing the interests in putting on a full and fair defense against the interests in orderly procedures for adjudication and use of reliable evidence that can withstand adversarial scrutiny. In striking this balance, the Court has recognized that "State and federal rulemakers have broad latitude under the Constitution to establish rules excluding evidence from criminal trials." *Holmes,* 547 U.S. at 324, 126 S.Ct. 1727 (brackets and internal quotation marks omitted), quoting *Scheffer,* 523 U.S. at 308, 118 S.Ct. 1261. Those rules are then put into practice by trial judges "called upon to make dozens, sometimes hundreds, of decisions concerning the admissibility of evidence" in a criminal trial. *Crane,* 476 U.S. at 689, 106 S.Ct. 2142. The latitude exercised by rulemakers and the trial judges they empower proves that the right to "present a complete defense" is not absolute. *Id.* at 690, 106 S.Ct. 2142, quoting *California v. Trombetta,* 467 U.S. 479, 485, 104 S.Ct. 2528, 81 L.Ed.2d 413 (1984). Nevertheless, "to say that the right to introduce relevant evidence is not absolute is not to say that the Due Process Clause places *no* limits upon restriction of that right." *Montana v. Egelhoff,* 518 U.S. 37, 42-43, 116 S.Ct. 2013, 135 L.Ed.2d 361 (1996) (plurality opinion).

The general constitutional standard can now be stated this way: rules of evidence restricting the right to present a defense cannot be "arbitrary or disproportionate to the purposes they are designed to serve." *Rock,* 483 U.S. at 56, 107 S.Ct. 2704. The most recent in the *Chambers* line of cases explained that the Court has struck down as "arbitrary" those restrictions that "excluded important defense evidence but that did not serve any legitimate interests." *Holmes,* 547 U.S. at 325, 126 S.Ct. 1727. We have applied this constitutional standard to grant habeas relief in strong cases. E.g., *Harris v. Thompson,* p.798 698 F.3d 609 (7th Cir.2012); *Sussman v. Jenkins,* 636 F.3d 329 (7th Cir.2011). We have also denied relief where there was room for reasonable jurists to disagree. E.g., *Dunlap v. Hepp,* 436 F.3d 739 (7th Cir.2006); *Horton v. Litscher,* 427 F.3d 498, 504 (7th Cir.2005).

1. *The Parity Principle*

One way a state rule of evidence may be arbitrary is where it restricts the defense but not the prosecution. Several cases in the *Chambers* line have emphasized this "'parity' principle: a state rule that restricts the presentation of testimony for the defense but not the prosecution will generally be deemed arbitrary." *Harris,* 698 F.3d at 632, citing Akhil Reed Amar, *Sixth Amendment First Principles,* 84 Geo. L.J. 641, 699 (1996). For example, *Washington v. Texas* struck down a state rule allowing alleged accomplices to testify *against* each other but forbidding them from testifying *for* each other. 388 U.S. at 22, 87 S.Ct. 1920. *Green v. Georgia* struck down another violation of the parity principle. In that case state courts excluded hearsay evidence that the defendant tried to introduce in his capital sentencing hearing after the state had used that same hearsay evidence against his accomplice in the accomplice's trial. 442 U.S. at 96-97, 99 S.Ct. 2150.

The parity approach to evaluating reliability enables "defendants to benefit from the balance that the state tries to strike when its own evidence-seeking self-interest is at stake." See Amar, 84 Geo. L.J. at 699. If the rule excluding evidence is in fact the product of a genuine balancing of interests by the state, that weighs in favor of respecting the balance by regarding the evidence as unreliable no matter which side it favors. See *id.*

Nothing in the record indicates that the State would have been able to introduce Amanda's recorded statement if it had been inculpatory rather than exculpatory. Whether inculpatory or exculpatory, Amanda "could not vouch for the accuracy of a recording that she could not even remember making," and her statement would not qualify as a recorded recollection regardless. *Kubsch II,* 866 N.E.2d at 735.

The State thus seems to have struck a genuine balance that excludes hearsay evidence like this no matter whom it benefits. But that is not the end of the matter. The *Chambers* line of cases can also protect the accused from a restrictive evidentiary rule that is disproportionate to its purposes. That leads us to the question of reliability.

2. *Reliability*

Reliability is the core of the hearsay rule and its many exceptions. See Federal Rules of Evidence, Article VIII, Advisory Committee Notes (1972). Our adversarial system relies first and foremost on in-court testimony. In court, a trier of fact may watch and listen to a declarant whose testimony is offered to prove the truth of its contents, and adverse parties may further test such testimony through vigorous cross-examination. "The principal justification for the hearsay rule is that most hearsay statements, being made out of court, are not subject to cross-examination." *Rice v. McCann,* 339 F.3d 546, 551 (7th Cir.2003) (Posner, J., dissenting); accord, Federal Rules of Evidence, Article VIII, Advisory Committee Notes; 30 Wright & Graham, Federal Practice and Procedure § 6325 (1997).

When deciding whether to fashion a hearsay exception, the central question is whether the circumstances and content of an out-of-court statement give the court confidence that the statement is sufficiently reliable to admit as evidence despite the inability to test it directly in court. See, p.799 e.g., *Chambers,* 410 U.S. at 298-99, 93 S.Ct. 1038 ("A number of exceptions have developed over the years to allow admission of hearsay statements made under circumstances that tend to assure reliability and thereby compensate for the absence of the oath and opportunity for cross-examination."); Fed.R.Evid. 807(a)(1) (residual hearsay exception requires "equivalent circumstantial guarantees of trustworthiness").

The hearsay portion of *Chambers* thus turned on whether McDonald's hearsay confessions bore sufficient indications of reliability that a mechanical application of the state hearsay rule violated Chambers' right to defend himself at trial. The *Chambers* Court identified four factors that together provided "considerable assurance" of the reliability of the excluded confessions. First, each confession was made spontaneously to a close acquaintance of the declarant shortly after the murder. Second, each statement was corroborated by other evidence. Third, the statements were against the declarant's own interest. Fourth, the declarant was available at trial for cross-examination. *Id.* at 300-01, 93 S.Ct. 1038.

Green v. Georgia also addressed the exclusion of hearsay testimony. Two men, Green and Moore, participated in a rape and murder. Moore had been convicted and sentenced to death. At his trial and sentencing, the state had used against him his out-of-court confession to a friend that he had fired the fatal shots. Yet when Green was being sentenced and offered the same evidence to show that he was less culpable than Moore, it was excluded as hearsay. 442 U.S. at 96-97, 99 S.Ct. 2150. The Supreme Court reversed, emphasizing the state's use of the evidence against Moore as perhaps the "most important" reason for trusting the reliability of the testimony. *Id.* at 97, 99 S.Ct. 2150. But the Court also made note of other "substantial reasons" to treat the confession as reliable. The confession was made spontaneously to a close friend, it was against Moore's penal interest, there was no reason to believe Moore had any ulterior motive to make it, and there was ample corroborating evidence. "In these unique circumstances," the Court wrote, "the hearsay rule may not be applied mechanistically to defeat the ends of justice." *Id.,* quoting *Chambers,* 410 U.S. at 302, 93 S.Ct. 1038.

C. *Amanda's Statement — Reliable or Not?*

Chambers and *Green* both reversed the exclusion of another person's hearsay confession against penal interest when there were substantial indications that the confession was reliable. The problem posed by Amanda Buck's recorded interview, and specifically by whether she saw Aaron and Rick Milewski on the afternoon of the murders or on another day, is quite different.

Weighing in favor of reliability, the interview was recorded, so there is no doubt about what was said, and the interview took place just a few days after the events in question, when memories were fresh. In addition, Amanda was quite detailed and specific in her account. She had nothing to gain by lying and there is no indication that she did so.

Other factors weigh against her statement's reliability, however. The extent of corroboration was central to the reasoning in *Chambers.* McDonald's four independent confessions corroborated each other. They were also corroborated by the testimony of other witnesses: one who saw McDonald shoot the officer, another who saw him with a gun immediately afterward, and another who knew he had owned a gun like the murder weapon and p.800 later replaced it with another similar gun. *Chambers,* 410 U.S. at 293 n. 5, 300, 93 S.Ct. 1038. Furthermore, in *Green* the Court described the corroborating evidence there as "ample," and of course the state had treated the other man's confession to firing the fatal shots as sufficiently reliable to use it to sentence him to death. 442 U.S. at 97, 99 S.Ct. 2150.

In this case, by contrast, there simply is no corroboration of Amanda's statement on the critical point, which is whether Aaron and Rick were at their home alive and well between 3:30 and 3:45 on the day they were murdered.[6] (No corroboration, that is, other than Monica's initial statement that she also saw Aaron at home that afternoon, a statement that Monica later corrected, that was never offered as evidence, and that could not have been admitted as substantive evidence to corroborate Amanda's statement.) The minimal corroboration for Amanda's recorded statement distinguishes this case from *Chambers* and *Green* and their reasoning. See *Rice,* 339 F.3d at 550 (affirming denial of habeas relief in part because state court found hearsay statements in question were not corroborated).

The availability of cross-examination was also central to *Chambers:* "Finally, if there was any question about the truthfulness of the extrajudicial statements, McDonald was present in the courtroom and was under oath. He could have been cross-examined by the State, and his demeanor and responses weighed by the jury." 410 U.S. at 301, 93 S.Ct. 1038.

In this respect, as well, the evidence here is quite different from the confessions in *Chambers.* Unlike the declarant in *Chambers,* Amanda was essentially unavailable for cross-examination. She took the stand at trial but testified that she did not remember being interviewed by the police or what she said to them. "A declarant is considered to be unavailable as a witness if the declarant ... testifies to not remembering the subject matter." Ind. R. Evid. 804(a)(3); Fed.R.Evid. 804(a)(3).

In addition, during the recorded interview, Amanda was never pushed on the critical details — the date and time she saw Aaron and Rick at their home. The interviewing officer was simply taking her account as she spoke in an interview in the early stages of the investigation. Amanda was not under oath, and Sergeant Reihl did not test her story to see how certain and accurate she might have been. Sergeant Reihl's gentle questioning, which was surely appropriate for his purpose at the time, was not remotely like cross-examination of the alibi witness in a murder trial where the stakes are life and death. There was no cross-examination here; there was not even a mild challenge.

By comparison, when a witness is unavailable, it is clear that even former *testimony* is admissible under the rules of evidence only if it is offered against a party who had both an opportunity and a similar motive to develop that witness's testimony by direct, cross-, or redirect examination. Ind. R. Evid. 804(b)(1); Fed.R.Evid. 804(b)(1).

Moreover, if the recorded statement had been admitted, the State would have been unable to test its accuracy through cross-examination. The prosecutor would have p.801 been stuck questioning a witness who did not even remember making the statement. See Fed.R.Evid. 804(a)(3) advisory committee note ("the practical effect" of lack of memory "is to put the testimony beyond reach"); 2 McCormick on Evidence § 253 (7th ed.) (a declarant who does not remember the subject matter of her testimony "is simply unavailable by any realistic standard").

In the adversarial system of Anglo-American law, we put great trust in the power of cross-examination to test both the honesty and the accuracy of testimony. It is virtually an article of faith that cross-examination is the "greatest legal engine ever invented for the discovery of truth." *California v. Green,* 399 U.S. 149, 158, 90 S.Ct. 1930, 26 L.Ed.2d 489 (1970), quoting 5 Wigmore on Evidence § 1367. Without cross-examination to test "any question about the truthfulness" of Amanda's recorded statement, a powerful assurance of reliability present in *Chambers* is absent here. *Chambers,* 410 U.S. at 301, 93 S.Ct. 1038; see also *Christian v. Frank,* 595 F.3d 1076, 1085 (9th Cir.2010) (reversing grant of habeas relief under *Chambers;* witness's "unavailability contrasts sharply with the availability of McDonald in *Chambers,* which the Supreme Court of the United States stressed greatly enhanced the reliability of the extrajudicial statements in that case").[7]

D. *The Standards of Review and Their Application*

To win a federal writ of habeas corpus, Kubsch must show that he is in custody in violation of the Constitution or laws or treaties of the United States. 28 U.S.C. § 2254(a). Since the Antiterrorism and Effective Death Penalty Act (AEDPA) amended § 2254 in 1996, though, if a state court has adjudicated a federal claim on the merits, it is not enough for the petitioner p.802 to show a violation of federal law. The petitioner must also show that the state court adjudication of the claim "resulted in a decision that was contrary to, or involved an unreasonable application of, clearly established Federal law, as determined by the Supreme Court of the United States," 28 U.S.C. § 2254(d)(1), or "resulted in a decision that was based on an unreasonable determination of the facts in light of the evidence presented in the State court proceeding." 28 U.S.C. § 2254(d)(2). On Kubsch's claim under *Chambers,* our focus is on the state court's legal analysis under subsection (d)(1), not factual findings under (d)(2).

We agree with the district court that the Indiana Supreme Court adjudicated on the merits Kubsch's federal constitutional claim under *Chambers.* Footnote 7 of the state court's opinion made that much clear, see *Kubsch II,* 866 N.E.2d at 735 n. 7, so we must evaluate the decision under § 2254(d)(1). Section 2254(d)(1) has two distinct prongs, the narrow "contrary to" prong and the broader "unreasonable application" prong.

1. *"Contrary to" Federal Law?*

On the first prong, the Indiana Supreme Court's adjudication of the *Chambers* claim was not "contrary to ... clearly established Federal law, as determined by the Supreme Court of the United States." Because no Supreme Court cases "confront 'the specific question presented by this case,' the state court's decision could not be 'contrary to' any holding from" that Court. *Woods v. Donald,* 575 U.S. ___, 135 S.Ct. 1372, 1377, 191 L.Ed.2d 464 (2015) (per curiam) (summarily reversing grant of habeas petition), quoting *Lopez v. Smith,* 574 U.S. ___, 135 S.Ct. 1, 4, 190 L.Ed.2d 1 (2014) (per curiam). Under § 2254(d), clearly established federal law includes only "the holdings, as opposed to the dicta," of Supreme Court decisions. *White v. Woodall,* 572 U.S. ___, 134 S.Ct. 1697, 1702, 188 L.Ed.2d 698 (2014), quoting *Howes v. Fields,* 565 U.S. ___, 132 S.Ct. 1181, 1187, 182 L.Ed.2d 17 (2012).

To note again just the most obvious differences between this case and *Chambers,* Amanda did not make her statement spontaneously to a close acquaintance, her statement was not against interest, her statement was not corroborated, and she was not subject to cross-examination about the statement. Any of those distinctions would be enough to demonstrate that the Indiana Supreme Court did not confront "facts that are materially indistinguishable from a relevant Supreme Court precedent" and arrive at the opposite result. See *Williams v. Taylor,* 529 U.S. 362, 405, 120 S.Ct. 1495, 146 L.Ed.2d 389 (2000).

2. *"Unreasonable Application" of Federal Law?*

The second and broader prong, whether the Indiana Supreme Court's rejection of Kubsch's claim under *Chambers* was, also in the terms of § 2254(d)(1), an "unreasonable application" of clearly established federal law as determined by the

Supreme Court of the United States, poses a more difficult question. The state court's rejection of the *Chambers* claim was at best incomplete and at worst wrong and unreasonably so. That poses a methodological question on which federal law is not settled. We explore that methodological question below but ultimately conclude that Kubsch's claim under *Chambers* fails whether or not we apply deferential review under AEDPA.

The narrow holding of *Chambers,* based on the combination of the restrictions on impeachment and the exclusion of multiple reliable hearsay confessions by a declarant subject to cross-examination, topped off by p.803 the "under the facts and circumstances of this case" qualification, see 410 U.S. at 303, 93 S.Ct. 1038, means that state courts have considerable latitude in interpreting and applying *Chambers.* See *Dunlap v. Hepp,* 436 F.3d 739, 744 (7th Cir.2006), quoting *Yarborough v. Alvarado,* 541 U.S. 652, 664, 124 S.Ct. 2140, 158 L.Ed.2d 938 (2004). Nevertheless, the broader standard that has emerged from *Chambers* and subsequent cases is that courts cannot impose restrictions on defense evidence that are arbitrary or disproportionate to the purposes they are designed to serve. See *Holmes,* 547 U.S. at 325, 126 S.Ct. 1727; *Rock,* 483 U.S. at 56, 107 S.Ct. 2704. The general standard requires a balance of competing interests.

The open texture of that standard and the important factual differences between this case and *Chambers* — lack of corroboration and lack of opportunity for meaningful cross-examination — mean that the Indiana courts *could have* rejected Kubsch's claim under *Chambers* without unreasonably applying clearly established federal law as determined by the Supreme Court of the United States. See 28 U.S.C. § 2254(d)(1); see generally, e.g., *Woods v. Donald,* 135 S.Ct. at 1377 ("where the precise contours of a right remain unclear, state courts enjoy broad discretion in their adjudication of a prisoner's claims"), quoting *White v. Woodall,* 572 U.S. ___, 134 S.Ct. at 1705, quoting in turn *Lockyer v. Andrade,* 538 U.S. 63, 76, 123 S.Ct. 1166, 155 L.Ed.2d 144 (2003). Only rarely has the Supreme Court "held that the right to present a complete defense was violated by the exclusion of defense evidence under a state rule of evidence." *Nevada v. Jackson,* ___ U.S. ___, 133 S.Ct. 1990, 1991-92, 186 L.Ed.2d 62 (2013) (per curiam) (summarily reversing grant of habeas relief on *Chambers* claim: "no prior decision of this Court clearly establishes that the exclusion of this evidence violated respondent's federal constitutional rights").

Thus, when habeas relief has been granted on a *Chambers* claim, the facts were a much closer fit to the Supreme Court precedents. In *Cudjo v. Ayers,* 698 F.3d 752 (9th Cir.2012), for example, the state court had found that the hearsay testimony was "trustworthy and material exculpatory evidence" that should have been admitted under state law but still declined to grant relief under *Chambers.* See *id.* at 763. *Cudjo* thus held that its facts were "materially indistinguishable" from *Chambers.* *Id.* at 767, quoting *Williams,* 529 U.S. at 405, 120 S.Ct. 1495. In discussing the rule that defendants have a constitutional right to present a complete defense, *Cudjo* also commented that "it would be extremely difficult to say that a state trial court engaged in an 'unreasonable application' of this rule when faced with new factual circumstances." *Id.;* cf. *Cudjo,* 698 F.3d at 770-74 (O'Scannlain, J., dissenting).

Accordingly, if the Indiana Supreme Court had announced its rejection of Kubsch's claim under *Chambers* without any explanation at all, then we would affirm the denial of habeas relief without further ado. See *Harrington v. Richter,* 562

U.S. 86, 98, 131 S.Ct. 770, 178 L.Ed.2d 624 (2011) ("Where a state court's decision is unaccompanied by an explanation, the habeas petitioner's burden still must be met by showing there was no reasonable basis for the state court to deny relief.").

But the Indiana Supreme Court was not silent on the point. It rejected Kubsch's claim under *Chambers* in a footnote consisting of one sentence and one citation:

> The availability of this testimony [from Monica Buck and Sergeant Reihl to the effect that Amanda had been mistaken] is also the reason why Kubsch's claim that he was denied his federal constitutional p.804 right to present a defense fails. *See Chambers v. Mississippi,* 410 U.S. 284, 302, 93 S.Ct. 1038, 35 L.Ed.2d 297 (1973) (protecting defendant's due process right by recognizing an exception to application of evidence rules where evidence found to be trustworthy).

866 N.E.2d at 735 n. 7.

This terse footnote shows that the state court was aware of the federal constitutional claim and the governing Supreme Court precedent. It cited the page of the *Chambers* opinion finding that the multiple hearsay confessions by McDonald "bore persuasive assurances of trustworthiness" and should have been admitted because they were so critical to the defense. Keeping in mind the presumption that state courts know and follow the law, see *Woodford v. Visciotti,* 537 U.S. 19, 24, 123 S.Ct. 357, 154 L.Ed.2d 279 (2002) (per curiam), we find it sufficiently clear that the state court found that Amanda's statement was not sufficiently reliable to require its admission under *Chambers.* The state court adjudicated the merits, so its decision requires deference under AEDPA.

The problem is that the only reason actually given by the Indiana Supreme Court — the availability of contradictory testimony from Amanda's mother and Sergeant Reihl — is the weakest reason that might support that result. It was a good reason to treat as harmless the exclusion of the recorded statement as impeachment, but not as substantive evidence. The mere existence of conflicting or impeaching evidence is not a sufficient basis, or even a reasonable basis, for rejecting the statement as substantive evidence. Conflicting evidence would simply present a fact issue for the jury to weigh after hearing all of that evidence. Perhaps the state court also had in mind the stronger reasons for excluding Amanda's recorded statement, especially the lack of corroboration and the lack of an opportunity for cross-examination, but if so it did not mention them.

What is the role of the federal courts when a state court offers such a weak reason for a result that could be a reasonable application of federal law? See *Brady v. Pfister,* 711 F.3d 818, 824-27 (7th Cir.2013) (identifying problem and discussing Supreme Court's limited guidance). We must review the actual reason deferentially. But if that reason was unreasonable, do we proceed to *de novo* review? Or do we, instead of doing *de novo* review, hypothesize reasons the court could have used to see if they are reasonable under AEDPA? See *Stitts v. Wilson,* 713 F.3d 887, 893 (7th Cir.2013) (raising but not answering this question).[8]

We have interpreted *Richter* as instructing federal courts to consider what arguments "could have supported" a state court decision when the state court "gave some reasons for an outcome without necessarily displaying all of its reasoning." *Hanson v. Beth,* 738 F.3d 158, 163-64 (7th Cir.2013) (affirming denial of relief on

Chambers claim based on exclusion of evidence); see also *Jardine v. Dittmann*, 658 F.3d 772, 777 (7th Cir.2011) ("This court must fill any gaps in the state court's discussion by asking what theories 'could have supported' the state court's conclusion."), quoting *Richter*, 562 U.S. at 102, 131 S.Ct. 770.[9]

p.805 The Indiana Supreme Court's stated rationale for rejecting Kubsch's claim can be described fairly as incomplete. So long as we have an obligation under § 2254(d)(1) to fill gaps or to complete the state court's reasoning, the result here is not an unreasonable application of federal constitutional law, and relief must be denied on this claim.[10]

3. *De Novo Review*

There is room to argue, however, that the state court's footnote 7 was not just incomplete but wrong, and unreasonably so. And there is room to argue that where the state court has provided a rationale for its decision, the federal courts should focus their attention on the reasons actually given rather than hypothesize a better set of reasons. See *Wiggins v. Smith*, 539 U.S. 510, 528-29, 123 S.Ct. 2527, 156 L.Ed.2d 471 (2003) (holding state court's rationale unreasonable without considering other possibilities); *Frantz v. Hazey*, 533 F.3d 724, 737-38 & n. 15 (9th Cir.2008) (en banc) (confining analysis to reasons actually given by state court, without hypothesizing alternative rationales); *Oswald v. Bertrand*, p.806 374 F.3d 475, 483 (7th Cir.2004) ("reasonableness of a decision ordinarily cannot be assessed without considering the quality of the court's reasoning," though "ultimate question ... is not whether the state court gets a bad grade for the quality of its analysis but ... whether the decision is an unreasonable application of federal law"). As we explained in *Brady v. Pfister*, when evaluating a state court's reasoning in habeas cases, the Supreme Court has focused on the reasons actually given by state courts without engaging in the exercise of trying to construct reasons that could have supported the same result. See 711 F.3d at 826, citing *Rompilla v. Beard*, 545 U.S. 374, 125 S.Ct. 2456, 162 L.Ed.2d 360 (2005), and *Wiggins v. Smith*, 539 U.S. 510, 123 S.Ct. 2527, 156 L.Ed.2d 471 (2003). So AEDPA deference toward state court decisions that reach defensible results for bad or incomplete reasons is not necessarily settled law at this point.

This debate over methodology under § 2254(d) may be ripening for a resolution. In *Hittson v. Chatman*, 576 U.S. ___, 135 S.Ct. 2126, ___ L.Ed.2d ___ (2015), a short opinion concurring in denial of certiorari reminded circuit and district judges of the Court's decision in *Ylst v. Nunnemaker*, 501 U.S. 797, 111 S.Ct. 2590, 115 L.Ed.2d 706 (1991), in which the Court instructed that when federal habeas corpus courts review an unexplained order from a state appellate court, they should "look through" that unexplained order and focus on the last reasoned rejection of the federal claim. See 501 U.S. at 803-04, 111 S.Ct. 2590. In the *Hittson* concurring opinion, Justice Ginsburg (joined by Justice Kagan) wrote that the *Nunnemaker* "look through" presumption remains valid after *Richter*. See 135 S.Ct. at 2127, discussing *Richter*, 562 U.S. at 99-100, 131 S.Ct. 770, citing *Nunnemaker* with approval; see also *Brumfield v. Cain*, 576 U.S. ___, 135 S.Ct. 2269, 2276, 192 L.Ed.2d 356 (2015) (applying *Nunnemaker* "look-through" approach to evaluate and reverse lower state court's factual findings supporting denial of evidentiary hearing under § 2254(d)(2)); *Johnson v. Williams*, 568 U.S. ___, ___ n. 1, 133 S.Ct. 1088, 1094 n.1,

185 L.Ed.2d 105 (2013) (citing *Nunnemaker* with approval); *Hawthorne v. Schneiderman,* 695 F.3d 192, 199-201 (2d Cir.2012) (Calabresi, J., concurring) (arguing that practice under *Richter* of inventing hypothetical reasons for state court decision promotes neither comity nor efficiency).

Justice Ginsburg's opinion in *Hittson* argued that the *Richter* practice of hypothesizing rationales for state court rejections of federal claims should be limited to cases where no state court explained the rejection, and that where the state court's real reasons can be ascertained, the inquiry under § 2254(d)(1) "can and should be based on the actual 'arguments or theories [that] supported ... the state court's decision." 135 S.Ct. at 2128-29, quoting *Richter,* 562 U.S. at 102, 131 S.Ct. 770. This statement may imply that federal courts should shift to *de novo* review as soon as they find that the reason actually given by a state court was unreasonable, without trying to hypothesize alternative rationales.

Because of this uncertainty in whether we may "complete" the state court's reasoning on this *Chambers* claim, it is prudent for us also to consider Kubsch's *Chambers* claim under a *de novo* standard of review. Even if we conclude that the state court's footnote 7 was an unreasonable application of *Chambers* to reject Kubsch's claim, that would not necessarily entitle Kubsch to habeas relief. He would still need to show on the merits that his constitutional rights were in fact violated, as § 2254(a) requires for a grant of actual relief. See *Brady,* 711 F.3d at 827 (applying *de novo* review in the alternative); p.807 *Mosley v. Atchison,* 689 F.3d 838, 852-54 (7th Cir.2012) (where state court decision was unreasonable under § 2254(d)(1), remanding to district court to determine merits *de novo* under § 2254(a)).

If *de novo* review applies, the issue is closer than under § 2254(d)(1), but we conclude that the exclusion of Amanda's recorded statement as substantive evidence did not violate Kubsch's federal constitutional right to put on a defense. As explained above, Amanda's statement is not corroborated on the critical facts by any other evidence, and she was never subjected to meaningful cross-examination. Even during the recorded interview itself, she was never pushed by the interviewer about the critical day and time, nor about the possibility that her memory had confused events of two different days.

Those facts distinguish this case from *Chambers,* which was, on its face, a very narrow opinion. Recall that the holding in *Chambers* depended on the combination of the limits the "voucher rule" placed on cross-examination and the exclusion of the three hearsay confessions, which were directly corroborated in many ways and had other indications of reliability. 410 U.S. at 302-03, 93 S.Ct. 1038.

Even applying the more general principles from the *Chambers* line of cases, we are not persuaded that the Constitution requires the general rule against hearsay to give way to Kubsch's interest in offering as substantive evidence a recorded, exculpatory interview of a witness who was in effect not available for cross-examination and whose account does not have significant corroboration on the critical points.

A vast literature attempts to explain the complex edifice of American hearsay law. A helpful and authoritative explanation came from the Advisory Committee on the Federal Rules of Evidence, published as an introductory note to the hearsay article in the Rules. A helpful and more detailed survey is available in 30 Wright & Graham, Federal Practice and Procedure §§ 6321-6333 (1997). As noted above, issues of reliability and trustworthiness are front and center in deciding whether to relax the general prohibition on hearsay. Our legal system relies primarily on in-person testimony subject to meaningful cross-examination, the "greatest engine ever invented for the discovery of truth," to test evidence. See *California v. Green,* 399 U.S. 149, 158, 90 S.Ct. 1930, 26 L.Ed.2d 489 (1970), quoting Wigmore on Evidence § 1367; see also *Rice v. McCann,* 339 F.3d 546, 551 (7th Cir.2003) (Posner, J., dissenting) ("The principal justification for the hearsay rule is that most hearsay statements, being made out of court, are not subject to cross-examination.").

Lest this reasoning seem like reflexive devotion at the altar of cross-examination, we draw help from Professors Wright and Graham to explain why this is so important. Their treatise identifies four dangers of hearsay: (1) defects in the declarant's perception; (2) defects in the declarant's memory; (3) defects in narration by both the declarant and the witness; and (4) the declarant's lack of sincerity or honesty. 30 Wright & Graham, Federal Practice and Procedure §§ 6324. Without an opportunity for cross-examination before the trier of fact, it can be difficult to test hearsay for these defects. Most hearsay exceptions have evolved from situations providing circumstantial guaranties of trustworthiness that seem to be sufficient substitutes for that direct scrutiny in a trial. See *id.,* § 6333.

In the case of Amanda's recorded statement, the third and fourth dangers seem minimal. The recording eliminates the risk that Amanda's statement would be p.808 relayed inaccurately, and she had no apparent difficulty describing what she remembered. The nine-year-old Amanda in the interview was also a disinterested witness, old enough to know she should tell the truth and with no apparent reason to deceive the police intentionally.

The first two dangers remain, however, with no meaningful protections under these circumstances. There simply is no way to test directly, by cross-examination or otherwise, the accuracy of the nine-year-old Amanda's memories of the past several days, to test the possibility that she was misremembering what and whom she had seen where and on which days. The accuracy of her memory was not tested or even challenged during the recorded interview itself, nor was the importance of being accurate about the time and date brought to her attention in the interview. Nor is there other evidence corroborating the recorded account as to the critical date and time.

In light of these considerations, it was not arbitrary or disproportionate to enforce the rules of evidence to exclude Amanda's recorded statement as substantive evidence. Accepting Kubsch's theory, on the other hand, would upset a good deal of the rules of evidence developed over generations to find the right balance so that trials can be decided fairly and on the basis of reliable evidence. As the prosecutor said in the trial court here, we could just show juries a series of videotaped, *ex parte* witness interviews, but that is not how we do trials in our legal system. There is no indication in the narrow *Chambers* opinion that such a sweeping result was intended then. Nor do the Supreme Court's later cases in the *Chambers* line endorse such a sweeping result.

Kubsch argues that he seeks only a narrow exception, comparable to the narrow decision in *Chambers.* He tries to limit the rule he seeks to hearsay witness statements that are recorded (ensuring accuracy of transmission), about recent events (fresh in the witness's memory), detailed, and from disinterested witnesses, at least where the evidence would be critical to the defense. With inexpensive recording technology widely available, however, we can expect that such evidence will often be available. Kubsch's theory would thus expand dramatically the availability, at least to the accused, of hearsay evidence that cannot be subjected to meaningful cross-examination. Considering the *Chambers* issue *de novo,* we believe Kubsch is seeking a significant and unwarranted expansion of existing doctrine, unmoored from the critical assurances that corroboration and cross-examination provided in *Chambers* itself.

We do not doubt that hearsay rules sometimes exclude evidence that is in fact accurate. They also exclude a good deal of evidence that is unreliable. Those rules have evolved based on experience to prevent the use of inaccurate and unreliable hearsay in trials. We also must recognize the risk of error in our human and fallible criminal justice system, especially in a death-penalty case. That is why *Chambers* was decided as it was, though the sentence there had been life in prison rather than death. In that exceptional case, the familiar rules of evidence worked arbitrarily to exclude reliable evidence of innocence.

The risk of serious error is not enough, however, to open the gates to all hearsay of this type, especially where it is not corroborated as it was in *Chambers* and where it is not subject to meaningful cross-examination. The unavoidable risk of error may offer a strong argument against the death penalty as a matter of policy, but that is not a choice available to us. See, e.g., *Glossip v. Gross,* 576 U.S. ___, 135 p.809 S.Ct. 2726, 192 L.Ed.2d 761 (2015) (all opinions).

Accordingly, we affirm the district court's denial of relief on the *Chambers* claim. The state court's result on this question was not an unreasonable application of federal law. And even if the state court's incomplete and unsatisfactory rationale had amounted to an unreasonable application of federal law, Kubsch's claim does not prevail on the merits under *de novo* review.

III. *Ineffective Assistance of Counsel for Amanda's Statement*

Kubsch approaches Amanda's statement from a different angle by arguing that even if his stand-alone claim under *Chambers* fails, his trial counsel provided ineffective assistance by failing to do a better job in trying to have the recording admitted into evidence. The Indiana Supreme Court rejected this claim on appeal from the denial of post-conviction relief, finding that it was barred by the doctrine of *res judicata. Kubsch III,* 934 N.E.2d at 1143 n. 2.

Under the controlling standard from *Strickland v. Washington,* 466 U.S. 668, 687, 104 S.Ct. 2052, 80 L.Ed.2d 674 (1984), Kubsch must show (1) that his trial lawyers' performance was deficient, meaning that it fell below an objective standard of reasonableness in light of prevailing professional norms, *id.* at 690, 104 S.Ct. 2052, and (2) that the deficient performance prejudiced his case, meaning that there is a reasonable probability that, but for the lawyers' unprofessional errors, the result of the proceeding would have been different, *id.* at 694, 104 S.Ct. 2052. Kubsch has not made either showing.

The Indiana Supreme Court's *res judicata* holding was reasonable as far as it went. To the extent that Kubsch was arguing that the recorded interview should have been admitted and would have made a difference in the trial, the state court had already decided those questions against Kubsch in the direct appeal. *Kubsch II,* 866 N.E.2d at 734-35. A post-conviction petitioner cannot avoid claim preclusion by merely repackaging an earlier claim. E.g., *Reed v. State,* 856 N.E.2d 1189, 1194 (Ind. 2006).

Kubsch's post-conviction argument on this score was not, however, merely a repackaging of the claim that the recording should have been admitted as evidence. He also argued and tried to offer evidence that if his trial lawyers had taken some additional steps, the interview would have been admitted into evidence and was reasonably likely to change the jury's verdict. The state court's *res judicata* holding did not engage that evidence and argument.

Even if we review this claim *de novo,* however, Kubsch has not shown that his trial lawyers were constitutionally deficient. It is not as though the trial lawyers overlooked the issue. Several months before the second trial, Amanda testified in a deposition where her mother was also present. See Tr. 2983-84; 3013. We do not have that transcript, but the lawyers obviously did. And they had the opportunity to talk to Amanda's mother Monica as well. The lawyers made clear in their post-conviction testimony that they had no real interest in anything Amanda or Monica might say from the witness stand; they wanted the recording in evidence. PCR Tr. 106; Tr. 3028.

The trial transcript shows they worked hard to convince the trial court to admit the recording. See Tr. 2982-90; 3010-35; 3112-23. They were not successful because they could not lay a sufficient foundation to admit the recording under Rule 803(5) as recorded recollection, and as explained p.810 above, the inability to use it to impeach the non-inculpatory "probably didn't see him" portion of Amanda's brief trial testimony was harmless. To change this result, Kubsch needed to come forward in the post-conviction proceedings with evidence or new legal arguments that were available to his trial lawyers, clearly should have been presented, and were reasonably likely to turn the tide. As the district court explained, he failed to do so. *Kubsch,* 2013 WL 6229136, at *39-40.

Kubsch criticizes his trial lawyers for having failed to correct or challenge what he says is misinformation about the reports that Amanda and her mother had been mistaken in their interview with Sergeant Reihl, and argues that they should have investigated in more detail her mother's statement of March 2000 asserting that they had mixed up Thursday and Friday in the videotaped interview. Kubsch has not shown what that further investigation would have uncovered, let alone how it would have helped him.

Contrary to the dissent's assertion, the trial judge did not keep out Amanda's videotaped statement because he thought it would have been easily impeached. When the prosecution and defense were debating the admissibility of the statement before the trial court, the prosecutor argued against admitting the statement "full well knowing that the little girl was mistaken" and that her mother would testify to that effect. Tr. 3015-16. The trial judge immediately responded: "The jury judges that. The jury judges if the girl is right or the mother is right." Tr. 3016. The judge kept the recorded hearsay statement out as substantive evidence because it did not qualify as a recorded recollection, and he kept it out as impeachment because Amanda had said nothing worth impeaching.

In this appeal, the specific criticisms of counsel, by both Kubsch and our dissenting colleague, are based on speculation rather than the sort of evidence needed to support the claim. Kubsch developed the factual record for this claim of ineffective assistance of counsel in a three-day evidentiary hearing in a state trial court in 2008. That is the record before us on this question. See *Cullen v. Pinholster,* 563 U.S. 170, 131 S.Ct. 1388, 1398, 179 L.Ed.2d 557 (2011); 28 U.S.C. § 2254(d)(2) & (e).

Kubsch's new lawyers called both of his trial lawyers as witnesses in the post-conviction hearing. The transcript shows that they were asked a few questions about Amanda's recorded interview and her mother's statement from March 2000, but there simply was no inquiry into the lawyers' supposed "failures" on this score. Nor was there any effort to show what would have happened if the trial lawyers had done what Kubsch's new lawyers argue should have been done. They did not call Amanda or Monica or anyone else to fill in the factual gaps. That proceeding and that hearing were Kubsch's opportunity to make a factual record showing deficient performance that was harmful to his case. He simply did not make that showing.

Our dissenting colleague finds the trial lawyers deficient in some additional ways: for not having asked Amanda if her statements in the interview were accurate, if she was actually the girl shown in the video, and if she would have told the police the truth; and for having failed to challenge Lonnie Buck's account of the correction on the date, to call Monica to corroborate Amanda's answers in the interview, to track down bank records for Monica's deposit of her paycheck, and to pursue corroboration about the school field trip. Post at 828-29. But again, there is no factual record to support such speculation p.811 about what these efforts would have shown. Kubsch's post-conviction lawyers did not question his trial lawyers on the witness stand about these matters, nor did they track down and offer the evidence that the dissent says might have helped.

This is not to suggest that Kubsch's post-conviction lawyers were themselves anything other than highly competent and diligent. Kubsch is now being represented by at least his sixth team of capable and experienced capital defense lawyers. See Ind. R.Crim. P. 24 (qualifications and compensation for trial and appellate counsel in capital cases). The post-conviction lawyers (the fifth team) no doubt investigated this claim as thoroughly as possible. But when the time came to offer actual evidence about the results of the investigation, they simply did not have evidence that the dissent says should have been "easily within reach." We cannot grant relief by filling in the gaps with our own speculation that further investigation would have been sufficiently helpful to Kubsch's defense.

IV. *Waiver of Counsel at the Penalty Phase*

We turn now to Kubsch's third principal claim on appeal. At the penalty phase of the trial, Kubsch waived his right to counsel and represented himself. He chose not to present any mitigating evidence. He did make a statement to the jury in which he said the murders were a "horrific nightmare" for which the death penalty would be appropriate, but he also continued to assert his innocence. On direct appeal and federal habeas review — though not in the intervening state post-conviction proceeding — he has argued that his waiver of counsel was not sufficiently knowing and intelligent because he was not "made aware of the dangers and disadvantages of self-representation." See *Faretta v. California,* 422 U.S. 806, 835, 95 S.Ct. 2525, 45 L.Ed.2d 562 (1975).

The Indiana Supreme Court considered and rejected the claim. *Kubsch II,* 866 N.E.2d at 735-38. That decision was not an unreasonable application of federal law under the circumstances of this case. See 28 U.S.C. § 2254(d)(1). Kubsch made clear that he was waiving counsel because he did not want to present evidence at the sentencing phase of the trial. That decision simplified substantially the challenge of representing himself, so the trial judge's colloquy was sufficient under the circumstances. Neither *Faretta* nor any other Supreme Court decision required the judge to discourage Kubsch from making his decision to waive counsel.

A. *The Constitutional Standard*

We first address the constitutional standard before turning to its application in this case. *Faretta* established that "a defendant in a state criminal trial has a constitutional right to proceed without counsel when he voluntarily and intelligently elects to do so." 422 U.S. at 807, 95 S.Ct. 2525. Though "he may conduct his own defense ultimately to his own detriment, his choice must be honored out of 'that respect for the individual which is the lifeblood of the law.'" *Id.* at 834, 95 S.Ct. 2525, quoting *Illinois v. Allen,* 397 U.S. 337, 350-351, 90 S.Ct. 1057, 25 L.Ed.2d 353 (1970) (Brennan, J., concurring). *Faretta* also cautioned that when "an accused manages his own defense" he forgoes "many of the traditional benefits associated with the right to counsel." *Id.* at 835, 95 S.Ct. 2525. Respect for the value of these "relinquished benefits" is why "the accused must knowingly and intelligently" waive the right to counsel. *Id.* (internal quotation marks omitted), citing *Johnson v. Zerbst,* 304 U.S. 458, 464-65, 58 S.Ct. 1019, 82 L.Ed. 1461 (1938).

p.812 "The determination of whether there has been an intelligent waiver of right to counsel must depend, in each case, upon the particular facts and circumstances surrounding that case, including the background, experience, and conduct of the accused." *Johnson,* 304 U.S. at 464, 58 S.Ct. 1019. Two other relevant "case-specific factors" are "the complex or easily grasped nature of the charge" and "the stage of the proceeding." *Iowa v. Tovar,* 541 U.S. 77, 88, 124 S.Ct. 1379, 158 L.Ed.2d 209 (2004). To determine whether a defendant has knowingly and intelligently waived the right to counsel, "a judge must investigate as long and as thoroughly as the circumstances of the case before him demand." *Von Moltke v. Gillies,* 332 U.S. 708, 723-24, 68 S.Ct. 316, 92 L.Ed. 309 (1948).

Both the Indiana Supreme Court and this circuit consider four factors in the waiver inquiry: "(1) the extent of the court's inquiry into the defendant's decision, (2) other evidence in the record that establishes whether the defendant understood the dangers and disadvantages of self-representation, (3) the background and experience of the defendant, and (4) the context of the defendant's decision to proceed *pro se.*" *Kubsch II,* 866 N.E.2d at 736, quoting *Poynter v. State,* 749 N.E.2d 1122, 1127-28 (Ind.2001), quoting in turn *United States v. Hoskins,* 243 F.3d 407, 410 (7th Cir.2001).

The constitutional standard is flexible, and its application must be adapted to the case. The Supreme Court has not prescribed a list of admonitions that must be given to all defendants who want to waive counsel. See *Tovar,* 541 U.S. at 92, 124 S.Ct. 1379 (reversing state court's finding that waiver was invalid: "In prescribing scripted admonitions and holding them necessary in every guilty plea instance ... the Iowa high court overlooked our observations that the information a defendant must have to waive counsel intelligently will depend, in each case, upon the particular facts and circumstances surrounding that case.") (citation and internal quotation marks omitted); see also *United States v. Moya-Gomez,* 860 F.2d 706, 733 (7th Cir. 1988) ("Although we stress the need for a thorough and formal inquiry as a matter of prudence and as a means of deterring unfounded claims on appeal, we shall not reverse the district court where the record as a whole demonstrates that the defendant knowingly and intelligently waived his right to counsel."); *United States v. Egwaoje,* 335 F.3d 579, 585 (7th Cir.2003) (reaffirming this holding of *Moya-Gomez*). The extent and formality of the waiver colloquy are relevant, but it is the waiver itself, not the waiver colloquy, that is the proper focus of the inquiry.

This constitutional standard does not impose a separate duty to discourage a defendant from representing himself. If a defendant is not already "aware of the dangers and disadvantages of self-representation," then the trial court must educate him so that he is aware of those risks when he decides. *Faretta,* 422 U.S. at 835, 95 S.Ct. 2525. When a defendant wants to take on the challenges of representing himself at trial, including dealing with jury selection, presentation of evidence, and jury instructions, the judge may and usually will try to discourage that option as a means of forcing the defendant to think carefully about unfamiliar risks.

We find no Supreme Court decision, however, requiring a judge to discourage self-representation in all circumstances. If a judge believes, as the trial judge did here, that the defendant is making a knowing and intelligent waiver, then she would commit constitutional error by discouraging that decision too strongly. *Faretta* clearly established the constitutional p.813 right to self-representation. "That right is not honored if judges must depict self-representation in such unremittingly scary terms that any reasonable person would refuse." *United States v. Oreye,* 263 F.3d 669, 672 (7th Cir.2001), quoting *United States v. Hill,* 252 F.3d 919, 928-29 (7th Cir.2001).

When a defendant raises the possibility of representing himself, the trial court is placed "between the Scylla of trammeling the defendant's constitutional right to present his own defense and the Charybdis of shirking its 'constitutional duty to ensure that the defendant only represents himself with full awareness that the exercise of that right is fraught with dangers.'" *United States v. Sandles,* 23 F.3d 1121, 1127 (7th Cir.1994) (citation omitted), quoting *Moya-Gomez,* 860 F.2d at 732. Appellate courts have tried to keep the permissible middle ground between these opposing errors fairly broad, allowing trial judges reasonable leeway to adapt the inquiry to the circumstances of the case without requiring a script or checklist. Trial judges seeking this middle way are not constitutionally bound to discourage every defendant from representing himself no matter the facts and circumstances of the case.

B. *Kubsch's Waiver of Counsel*

With this constitutional standard in mind, we turn to the facts of Kubsch's waiver of his right to counsel for the sentencing phase of his trial. The attorneys who represented Kubsch at the guilt phase of his trial were a veteran team who qualified as a capital defense team under Indiana Rule of Criminal Procedure 24, which sets minimum qualifications for lead and co-counsel in capital cases. During the sentencing phase they served as Kubsch's legal advisors by court appointment. Kubsch could ask them for advice, but they could no longer speak for him in court.

Kubsch represented himself at the sentencing phase of his trial because he did not want to present mitigating evidence. Kubsch was advised by the court and counsel that if his counsel had represented him in the sentencing phase, his counsel would have made the final decision about which witnesses to call. His attorneys planned to offer mitigating evidence, and they named the witnesses they would have called and provided Kubsch a written summary of that evidence. The court asked Kubsch whether he wanted any of those witnesses to be called. Kubsch confirmed that he did not.

The court then told Kubsch what to expect in the sentencing phase of the trial if, as both sides planned, he and the State presented no new evidence. Each side would address the jury, and the court would instruct the jury on the applicable sentencing law, including relevant aggravating and mitigating factors. The court told Kubsch that as his own attorney he would have the right to address the jury directly.

Finally, the court considered the standard advice and warnings given to defendants deciding whether to represent themselves. The court noted that nearly all the advice and warnings concern the challenges of trial, such as selecting jurors and presenting evidence, which can be difficult without legal training and experience. The court pointed out that if the sentencing phase did not include additional evidence, the most difficult obstacles for a *pro se* defendant would not be present. The court then reiterated that Kubsch had the right to make a statement to the jury and allowed his attorneys to withdraw their appearances.

Kubsch now argues that his waiver was not knowing and intelligent because the p.814 court's colloquy was insufficient and because the judge did not attempt to discourage his choice. The Indiana Supreme Court considered these arguments in detail and in light of the circumstances of this case, particularly Kubsch's reasons for wanting to represent himself and the stage of the proceeding, where he would only make a statement to the jury about the appropriate penalty. *Kubsch II,* 866 N.E.2d at 735-38.

The Indiana Supreme Court noted that Kubsch himself "eliminated the need" for almost all of the standard advisements given to defendants deciding whether to represent themselves by confirming that he did not wish to present evidence at the sentencing phase of his trial. *Id.* at 736. Accordingly, the waiver colloquy was "sufficient to apprise the defendant of the dangers he is facing in the particular matter at hand." See *id.* All that remained in the trial, as a practical matter, was a closing argument on whether the death penalty should be imposed.

The stakes were as high as they come in a trial, but they were highest for the man who wanted to speak for himself. The *Faretta* right of self-representation is founded upon respect for the autonomy of the defendant:

> The right to defend is personal. The defendant, and not his lawyer or the State, will bear the personal consequences of a conviction. It is the defendant, therefore, who must be free personally to decide whether in his particular case

counsel is to his advantage. And although he may conduct his own defense ultimately to his own detriment, his choice must be honored out of "that respect for the individual which is the lifeblood of the law."

422 U.S. at 834, 95 S.Ct. 2525.

The state court also noted the trial judge's observation about Kubsch's competence at the end of this three-week trial:

> I want to state for the record, in this case, that the Court observed Mr. Kubsch throughout trial, that during trial he pretty much constantly was able to confer with his attorneys, was able to confer with his factual investigator that interviewed witnesses in this case, that he testified in this case, that the Court found his testimony to be coherent and relevant to the facts of this case, and that the Court has no reason to doubt Mr. Kubsch's competency to represent himself in this matter.

Tr. 3339-40, quoted in *Kubsch II,* 866 N.E.2d at 737. The state court quoted this observation to help show that Kubsch was capable of understanding, and did in fact understand, the decision he was making. It also pointed out that "at the time he chose to represent himself, Kubsch had already participated in two murder trials and one penalty phase." *Kubsch II,* 866 N.E.2d at 738. "In other words, he obviously knew from his own experience of his right to call witnesses, present other evidence, and propose mitigating factors." *Id.*

Finally, the Indiana Supreme Court viewed Kubsch's decision to waive counsel as knowing because it was strategic, intended to prevent his counsel from calling witnesses in the penalty phase of the trial. *Id.,* citing *United States v. Todd,* 424 F.3d 525, 533 (7th Cir.2005). "Choosing to waive counsel because one does not agree with trial strategy is perhaps not the best choice, or even a good choice, but it can be a rational choice." 866 N.E.2d at 738.

Citing John H. Blume, *Killing the Willing: "Volunteers," Suicide and Competency,* 103 Mich. L.Rev. 939 (2005), Kubsch argues now that his decision was not so much strategic as suicidal, calculated to p.815 bring about his own execution and indicating "a pre-existing mental illness." That is indeed one way to understand Kubsch's behavior. Another way to understand Kubsch's behavior, however, is to take at face value his words at the sentencing phase of both trials. At both he articulated a principled opposition to arguing that any mitigating evidence could outweigh the aggravating circumstances of the crimes a jury had convicted him of committing. *Faretta* was decided precisely to protect such principled decisions. Kubsch now apparently regrets his decision to proceed *pro se.* That does not mean his decision was any less principled when he made it or that it was the product of mental illness.

His strategy can also be understood in quite sensible terms. Rather than begging for mercy from the jury that had just convicted him of three brutal murders without any apparent mitigating circumstances, Kubsch told the jury, "I wouldn't even dare try to insult your intelligence by wasting your time by presenting mitigation." Tr. 3372. He instead asserted several times that he is innocent. His approach can be understood as a reminder that the jurors should consider the possibility that they might have made a mistake, so that residual doubt should weigh against the death penalty. That approach is entirely consistent with his defense at trial, even though neither was successful. The state courts did not act unreasonably in viewing the waiver as strategic and knowing. See *United States v. Davis,* 285 F.3d 378, 384-85 (5th Cir.2002) (defendant chose to represent himself at sentencing phase of capital trial for similar strategic reason; appellate court issued writ of mandamus barring district court's appointment of independent counsel to present mitigating evidence over defendant's objection).

Kubsch argues most strenuously that the trial judge had a duty under "the spirit of *Faretta*" to discourage him from waiving his right to counsel. That is not what *Faretta* said or means. *Faretta* held that a defendant has a constitutional right to waive counsel as long as the waiver is knowing, voluntary, and intelligent. The core of *Faretta* is respect for the defendant's autonomy even if he makes a foolish decision. 422 U.S. at 834, 95 S.Ct. 2525; see also *Davis,* 285 F.3d at 384. There is no requirement to discourage the defendant. As noted, we have warned that excessive discouragement, even for a defendant who wishes to handle the entire case, can violate *Faretta.* See *Hill,* 252 F.3d at 929 ("A defendant bullied or frightened into acquiescing in a lawyer that he would rather do without would be in a much better position to say that the choice was not made knowingly or intelligently.").

The basic problem with Kubsch's argument is that most of the specific advice usually given to defendants was unnecessary for him. He planned to present no mitigating evidence and planned only to make a brief statement to the jury. Cf. Federal Judicial Center, Benchbook for U.S. District Court Judges § 1.02 (6th ed.) (warnings focus on procedural and evidentiary challenges before and during trial).

Kubsch responds that this view "shifts responsibility from the trial court to the defendant, making the defendant responsible to inform the court how he wished to proceed, to determine the level of warning the court must give him." The Indiana Supreme Court did not make that mistake. Kubsch's counsel and then Kubsch himself explained his plans to the trial judge. The judge was not required to question Kubsch's strategy, and he did not require Kubsch to provide information. Kubsch volunteered it. The trial judge adapted his approach to the waiver inquiry accordingly.

p.816 In a variation on this argument, Kubsch also argues that the waiver colloquy was actually misleading. At one point, the trial judge said, "In a way I'm saying, your representation would not be as complicated as if you were handling the whole trial by yourself. Do you understand that?" Tr. 3342. Taken in context, this statement was not misleading at all. It was true. Making a statement to the jury was far simpler for Kubsch than representing himself in the guilt phase of his trial would have been. See *Tovar,* 541 U.S. at 88 (explaining that the "information a defendant must possess in order to make an intelligent" waiver depends in part on "the stage of the proceeding").

In sum, the federal Constitution required the trial judge to determine whether Kubsch's waiver of counsel for the last phase of his trial was knowing, voluntary, and intelligent. The Indiana Supreme Court did not apply that clearly established federal law unreasonably by holding that Kubsch's waiver was valid in light of "the particular facts and circumstances surrounding that case, including the background, experience, and conduct of the accused," see *Johnson,* 304 U.S. at 464, 58 S.Ct. 1019, and the stage of the proceeding, see *United States v. Hoskins,* 243 F.3d at 410.

Accordingly, we AFFIRM the district court's judgment denying relief.

WOOD, Chief Judge, dissenting.

My colleagues are prepared to send Wayne Kubsch to his death on the basis of a trial at which the jury never heard critical evidence that, if believed, would have shown that Kubsch was not the man responsible for the horrible murders of his wife Beth, her son, Aaron Milewski, and her ex-husband, Rick Milewski. I am not. They concede that the evidence against Kubsch was entirely circumstantial. While there is nothing wrong with circumstantial evidence, it is impossible to have any confidence in a verdict rendered by a jury that heard only part of the story. In my view, the state courts have reached a result that is inconsistent with, and an unreasonable application of, the United States Supreme Court's decision in *Chambers v. Mississippi*, 410 U.S. 284, 93 S.Ct. 1038, 35 L.Ed.2d 297 (1973). Had the contested evidence been admitted under the *Chambers* exception to the normal rules of evidence, a properly instructed jury may have acquitted Kubsch. It also may have convicted him: I do not argue that the state courts wrongly viewed the evidence as sufficient for conviction. But that is not the question before us. The question is whether Kubsch was able to present his entire case and obtain a reliable jury verdict. Because I believe that he was deprived of this essential protection, I would grant the writ and give the State of Indiana a new opportunity to try him.

I

As required by the Antiterrorism and Effective Death Penalty Act, I rely on the facts used by the Supreme Court of Indiana after Kubsch's second trial, conviction, and sentencing. See *Kubsch v. State*, 866 N.E.2d 726 (Ind.2007) (*Kubsch II*). That opinion summarized the facts that had been developed in earlier appeals. See *Kubsch v. State*, 784 N.E.2d 905 (Ind. 2003) (*Kubsch I*); see also *Kubsch v. State*, 934 N.E.2d 1138 (Ind.2010) (*Kubsch III*) (opinion at post-conviction stage).

Wayne and Beth Kubsch were married in November 1997. It was a second marriage for both: Beth had two sons, Aaron Milewski, from her previous marriage to Rick Milewski, and Anthony Earley; and Kubsch had a son, Jonathan, who lived with his mother, Tina Temple. Aaron lived with Rick in South Bend, Indiana, p.817 while Anthony lived with Kubsch and Beth in nearby Mishawaka. Kubsch owned the family home, and he also owned 11 rental properties in St. Joseph County. They were encumbered by mortgages totaling approximately $456,000 as of mid-1998. Kubsch also had credit-card debt exceeding $16,000. He tried paying that off by refinancing four of his rental properties, but by August 1998 the credit-card debt had reached $23,000, and by September Kubsch was falling behind in his mortgage and tax payments. At about that time, he bought a life insurance policy on Beth, with himself as the sole beneficiary; the policy would pay $575,000 on her death.

The fateful day was September 18, 1998. For ease of reference, I provide a timeline of the events in Appendix A to this dissent. Here I summarize what happened that day and the evidence that pins down where the key actors were located. I rely on the evidence that was admitted at Kubsch's second trial.

That morning, both Wayne and Beth Kubsch were up early. By 6:00 a.m., testimony from Beth's coworker Archie Fobear established that Beth had already left her home on Prism Valley Drive in Mishawaka and was just starting to work at

United Musical Instruments in Elkhart, Indiana, approximately 11 miles away. Cellular telephone records indicated that Kubsch made a call at that time from the sector just adjacent to the one covering the home. He was driving to his place of employment at Skyline Corporation, also in Elkhart; he punched in at 6:50 a.m. Cell records show that Kubsch made a telephone call at 9:11 a.m. somewhere near his workplace, and that he made another call at 10:45 a.m. from Skyline's break room. The latter call was to the home, presumably to Beth, who had finished her shift at 10:00 a.m., returned home, and paged him twice from home around 10:30 a.m.

At 10:48 a.m., a five-minute call was placed from the Kubsch home to the home of Rick Milewski. At that point Beth left the house to run some errands. A security camera at the Teacher's Credit Union shows Beth, along with her dog, in her car at a drive-up window at 11:08 a.m. There is a credit union receipt stamped 11:14 a.m. confirming a completed transaction. A little while later, at 11:52 a.m., Beth was with credit counselor Edith Pipke at the Consumer Credit Counseling Agency in South Bend. No evidence admitted at the second trial indicated where she was after she left the credit union and before she arrived for her appointment.

In the meantime, Kubsch drove back to the Prism Valley house after punching out from his job at 11:13 a.m. Erin Honold, a neighbor, saw him and his car in the driveway between 11:30 a.m. and noon, around the same time when Beth was speaking with the credit counselor. Telephone records from the house indicate that a call was made at 11:37 a.m. to American General Finance; Kevin Putz, an employee of the company, testified that he spoke to Kubsch that morning. Between 12:09 and 12:11 p.m., Kubsch made three more calls using his cellphone, one to the house (implying that he was no longer there) and two to Rick Milewski. He apparently interrupted Rick while Rick was speaking with his brother Dave about an upcoming hunting trip. Dave testified that Rick said that Kubsch was calling to discuss moving a refrigerator at the Prism Valley house.

Beth paged Kubsch again at 12:16 p.m.; cell records indicate that at 12:18 p.m., he called the house for 31 seconds from the vicinity of Osceola, a town between Mishawaka and Elkhart. Kubsch returned to Skyline, although he did not punch back in. He made two phone calls from the break room, one at 12:40 p.m. and the other at 1:17 p.m. Between those calls, Rick called p.818 Beth at 12:46 p.m. Kubsch punched out of work again, this time for the day, at 1:53 p.m. A minute later, he called the house from Elkhart and was on the line for 46 seconds. The next call from Kubsch's cellphone came at 2:51 p.m.; it was from a sector near the house. The state's theory was that these last two calls bracket the time when he committed the murders — between 1:53 and 2:51 p.m.

There are some problems with this theory, at least if it is meant to encompass all three murders, because there is no evidence that Aaron left school early that day. To the contrary, witnesses testified that Aaron was waiting outside Lincoln Elementary School in South Bend and that Rick picked him up there between 2:20 and 2:35 p.m. (The school is now called Lincoln Primary Center; its website indicates that the school day runs from 8:15 a.m. to 2:20 p.m. See LINCOLN PRIMARY CENTER, https:// www.edline.net/pages/Lincoln_Primary_Center (last visited Aug. 10, 2015).) In any event, by 3:15 p.m. or so, Kubsch placed numerous calls to Beth's mother, Diane Rasor; he eventually connected on the 11th try. Cellular records indicate that he was heading north at that point, toward the Michigan border.

Between 4:42 and 4:47 p.m. Indiana time, Kubsch made some calls picked up by the cell tower in Schoolcraft, Michigan, which is about 11 miles north of Three Rivers, Michigan, where Kubsch's son Jonathan lived with his mother. (For the sake of consistency, I use Indiana time throughout this account; in fact, though most of Indiana and most of Michigan are in the Eastern time zone, Indiana in 1998 had not yet adopted Daylight Savings Time; thus Indiana was on Eastern Standard Time in September 1998, while most of Michigan, including Three Rivers and Schoolcraft, was an hour ahead on Eastern Daylight Time.) Around 5:00 p.m., Kubsch picked up Jonathan; he also said hello to his friend Wayne Temple around 5:30 or 5:45 p.m. at the local Kmart store. He then headed back to Osceola with Jonathan, stopping for ten minutes at the home of Constance Hardy, the mother of his friend Brad. At 5:56 p.m., he made a call from the cellular region close to the Prism Valley house.

By this time, however, Anthony had come home and discovered the bodies of Rick and Aaron. This happened at 5:30 p.m. He immediately summoned help, and so by the time Kubsch showed up at the house at 6:45 p.m., police were there and it was taped off as a crime scene. (Beth's body had not yet been discovered.) The police took Kubsch to the station, interviewed him, and then released him. Around 9:00 p.m., they discovered Beth's body concealed in the basement. They brought Kubsch back in for a second interview. He did not appear surprised to learn of Beth's death. Asked several times by the officers to tell them what happened, Kubsch chose instead to invoke his right not to speak without an attorney. The police did not arrest him for the murder immediately. They did so three months later, when a person named Tashana Penn Norman told them that she and her boyfriend overheard a person saying that he had "hurt[] a little boy," and she identified Kubsch as the speaker. He was arrested on December 22, 1998, and charged with all three murders.

II

A

Kubsch was tried twice in this case. The first trial took place in 2000. At its conclusion, the jury convicted him and recommended the death penalty, and the court sentenced him accordingly. The Supreme Court of Indiana reversed that p.819 judgment in *Kubsch I,* and ordered a new trial. 784 N.E.2d at 926. The second trial took place in March 2005. Once again, the jury found Kubsch guilty and recommended the death penalty, and once again, the trial court accepted the recommendation and imposed that sentence. In *Kubsch II,* the Supreme Court of Indiana affirmed. 866 N.E.2d at 740. Kubsch then unsuccessfully sought post-conviction relief from the state courts, see *Kubsch III,* 934 N.E.2d at 1154, before turning to the federal court with his current habeas corpus petition, see 28 U.S.C. § 2254.

The State's case, as my colleagues readily admit, was built from various pieces of circumstantial evidence. It pointed to Kubsch's financial problems and the new life insurance policy on Beth as plausible motives for the murders. It attempted to trace his movements through use of the cellular telephone records and the testimony of the people who interacted with Kubsch, Beth, Rick, Aaron, and Anthony throughout that day. It found a fiber on the duct tape used to bind Beth's body that matched a fiber taken from Kubsch's car, and it also noted that the duct tape wrapper in the car matched the brand of tape used on Beth. (It offered nothing to show how common this brand was.) It (as have my colleagues) stressed the fact that Kubsch's account of his own actions during the day was not consistent on key matters, such as whether he went home during the lunch hour, whether he was alone there, and when he headed up to Michigan. These inconsistencies, plus what the district court called a "slow-moving accumulation of a glacier of circumstantial evidence," satisfied both the second jury and all of the reviewing courts so far that Kubsch was properly convicted and sentenced.

B

If the question before this court were simply about the sufficiency of the evidence, I would agree with everyone that Kubsch's challenge fails. Indeed, it would be hard to find fault with the extensive discussion my colleagues have furnished. But that is not the question. It is instead whether the package of evidence that was presented to the jury was complete, and if not, whether the excluded evidence was important and reliable enough to have made a difference.

The critical evidence that was kept from the jury was videotaped testimony by a girl named Amanda ("Mandy") Buck, "who, according to the defense, would have testified that she saw Aaron after 3:30 pm on the day of the murders." *Kubsch II,* 866 N.E.2d at 730. Mandy, who was nine years old at the time, was interviewed immediately after the murders, on Tuesday, September 22, 1998. Because of the importance of what she said, I have included a full transcript of the interview as Appendix B to this dissent. The interviewer was Detective Mark Reihl; the interview took place in what appears to be a room in the police station. Mandy's mother, Monica, was present throughout and volunteered information from time to time.

After establishing some basic information, Detective Reihl confirmed that Mandy was a fourth-grader at Lincoln School, that she lived right across the street from Aaron and his dad Rick, and that she and Aaron were "best friends." She commented that Aaron didn't like Kubsch, because he would get rough and punch too hard "and stuff like that." She saw Aaron frequently: "I always went over to his house. He always came over to my house and like we like used to study for the same spelling words .... And we would help each other on homework and stuff." When Reihl asked her when they got out of school, she replied "two twenty." She p.820 lived close to the school, she said, just a five-minute walk away.

The interview then turned to "last Friday," which was September 18, the day of the murders. On that day, as usual, Mandy was picked up from school by the Alphabet Academy; from there, her mother typically (and that day) picked her up to go home "[b]etween three thirty and quarter to four." At that point Monica interjected that she "waited for [Monica's] mom and dad to get home, and I went and cashed my check and came home." Reihl then asked whether Monica noticed if

Rick was across the street. Monica replied "I didn't pay no attention. All I saw was Aaron." Reihl repeated "You saw Aaron?," and Monica said "[m]mm hmm." She did not remember if Rick's truck was there. Turning back to Mandy, Reihl asked again what time she got home that day. Monica answered instead, repeating "3:30 or quarter to four." Mandy confirmed that she saw Aaron then, and that she also saw "his dad," who "was coming from their living room into the kitchen to get something to drink." She explained that she was able to see this from her own house: "every day when I walk home I always see Rick walk into the kitchen or walk into the restroom or walk into his room." Asked what kind of car Rick drove, Mandy replied "[a] Chevy? He used to drive a Chevy until it broke down." She specified that it was a black, medium-sized, "kinda short" truck. Because his truck had broken down, she added that he was driving a white truck that he had borrowed from his brother on Friday, and that the white truck was at the house when she got home from school.

Reihl next asked whether she saw Rick and Aaron leave that afternoon. She answered, "Um, yeah, like I was on my porch and, and they let me blow bubbles and I was blowin' my bubbles, and I seen Rick pull out and leave." She was not sure what time that was, because she left her watch in her gym bag, but she estimated it was a "medium" time after she got home, and she commented that "it takes a pretty long time to get to [Aaron's] mom's house."

She then went into some detail about Aaron's plans for the weekend. "He said that he was going to his mom's house Friday, 'cause he was gonna stay the night there to go to the field trip Saturday .... You know he was, he — he wanted to go on the field trip bad.... But by the time Saturday when we, when we were on the bus and stuff, he was gonna be in our group, and, um, he never showed up. He wasn't there. And we didn't know why." She went camping after the fieldtrip and told her grandmother that she had not seen Aaron. She learned about the murders after a news crew came to her home while she was at her karate lesson the following Monday, she said.

Reihl then turned back to Monica and confirmed that she cashed her paycheck on Friday, shortly after she came home from work (around 3:50 p.m.). She said again that she had seen Aaron, but not Rick, and that she did not look to see if Rick's truck was there. They discussed what kind of truck Rick drove; interestingly, Mandy knew more about it than her mother — she liked the gold printing that said "Chevrolet" across the back. By then, the interview was winding down. Reihl asked Mandy yet again whether she saw both Aaron and his father, as well as the white truck, in the yard around 3:30 or 3:45 p.m., and she said yes. He asked whether "[t]hese times that you've given me today, uh, these are pretty accurate," and Monica said, "Yeah, 'cause I get off work at quarter after three." This was her daily routine. With that, the interview ended.

p.821 A few days after Mandy's interview, Reihl called Monica's place of employment and then her home, apparently in an attempt to see yet again whether both Mandy and Monica had correctly recounted what happened and when it happened. Reihl spoke to Mandy's grandfather ("Lonnie") and asked him to find out if Mandy and Monica were certain about their story. Lonnie called Reihl back and told him that the events that Mandy and Monica had described had taken place on Thursday, September 17, not on Friday. The prosecutors recounted at Kubsch's trial that Monica told the police that "her father was at her house on that Thursday, and he later reminded her that it was Thursday instead of Friday." She said that she — Monica — had confused the dates because she was so busy; she offered no reason why Mandy would have confused them. Nor was there any effort to explain away Mandy's detailed comments about the timing of the Saturday field trip and her subsequent camping trip, karate lesson, and so on. At that early time, not a week after the field trip, it would have been easy to confirm with the school whether the trip took place on Saturday, September 19, or Friday, September 18. (And even the trial evidence shows Rick picking up Aaron at school between 2:20 and 2:35 p.m. on Friday, strongly suggesting that there was no field trip that day.) In addition, it would have been relatively easy to confirm when Monica was paid and made her deposit, just as evidence had shown when Beth visited her own bank.

Mandy was called to testify at the second trial, but she had almost nothing to say. She claimed to have no memory of talking to the police or being interviewed by them in 1998. When Kubsch's lawyer attempted to use the transcript of the interview to refresh her recollection and later to impeach her, the prosecution objected and the court sustained the objections. The court also refused to permit the use of the videotaped interview as a recorded recollection, despite Mandy's asserted inability to recall anything about the interview.

C

The Supreme Court of Indiana upheld the trial court's rulings. It found that the videotape was not admissible under Indiana's evidentiary rule governing the use of recorded recollection, Ind. R. Evid. 803(5). In 2005 that rule covered:

> [a] memorandum or record concerning a matter about which a witness once had knowledge but now has insufficient recollection to enable the witness to testify fully and accurately, shown to have been made or adopted by the witness when the matter was fresh in the witness's memory and to reflect that knowledge correctly....

(It essentially tracks Fed.R.Evid. 803(5), as it read before the 2011 restyling changes were made.) The court was concerned about the final element, which requires that the recording reflect the witness's knowledge correctly. It found that Mandy's inability to vouch for the accuracy of her prior statement precluded its use. The videotape was not admissible as a prior inconsistent statement, the court added, because Mandy gave no substantive evidence at all in her testimony, and so there was (almost) no prior statement to impeach.

The court conceded, however, that there was one statement that was subject to impeachment. At the trial, Mandy stated that "I probably didn't see [Aaron], because I go straight [from] home to the day care, and then I would go home afterwards." That statement directly contradicts her statement in the video that she saw Rick and Aaron that afternoon from p.822 her porch, and the court acknowledged that "Kubsch should have been allowed to impeach her on this matter." 866 N.E.2d at 735. It found the error harmless, however, because it thought that Mandy's account from the videotape would have been impeached by the call from her grandfather suggesting a mistake in dates. It thought that the prosecutor's ability to put Detective Reihl and Monica on the stand, presumably to support the "mistake" theory, was "also the reason why Kubsch's claim that he was denied his federal constitutional right to present a defense fails. See *Chambers v. Mississippi,* 410 U.S. 284, 93 S.Ct. 1038, 35 L.Ed.2d 297 (1973) (protecting defendant's due process right by recognizing an exception to application of evidence rules where evidence found to be trustworthy)." 866 N.E.2d at 735 n. 7. At a minimum, this passage conclusively shows that the *Chambers* argument was adequately presented to the state courts.

Putting to one side for the moment the niceties of the rules of evidence, one thing is clear: if Mandy was correct in her videotaped interview that the events she was describing had happened on Friday, not on Thursday, and if she had seen both Aaron and Rick as late as 3:45 or 4:00 p.m. that day, then Wayne Kubsch could not have killed them. By that time, he was headed to Michigan to pick up Jonathan. The state has always pegged the time of the murders to midday, from 1:53 to 2:51 p.m. It has never argued that Kubsch arranged for someone else to commit the murders on his behalf, and it is obviously too late in the day to introduce such a radically different theory. And, because the state's theory is that Kubsch killed Aaron and Rick because they stumbled on him as he was murdering Beth, Mandy's testimony undermines the conviction as it relates to Beth, too.

No evidence could be more critical to Kubsch's defense. And the possibility that the state might have been able to impeach the videotaped account cannot cure this problem; that impeachment was itself subject to impeachment from such details as the school's records about the day of the field trip and the date when Monica cashed her paycheck. Under these circumstances, the Supreme Court's decision in *Chambers* overrides the state evidentiary rule that prevented the jury from hearing Mandy's statement. This was evidence that, if believed, might have prompted the jury to acquit on one or more of the counts. As I explain below, the Indiana Supreme Court's decision to the contrary was, in my view, contrary to and an unreasonable application of Chambers, even under the strict standard of review that applies, which my colleagues discuss in such detail despite our agreement on that point.

III

Habeas corpus petitioners come to a federal court of appeals with at least two strikes against them: they already have lost in the state courts (either on the merits or because of one of many procedural hurdles that must be cleared); and they also have failed to convince the federal district court of their entitlement to relief. They face the daunting burden of satisfying the familiar and deliberately demanding standards created in the Antiterrorism and Effective Death Penalty Act (AEDPA), 28 U.S.C. § 2254(d), under which

An application for a writ of habeas corpus on behalf of a person in custody pursuant to the judgment of a State court shall not be granted with respect to any claim that was adjudicated on the merits in State court proceedings unless the adjudication of the claim —

(1) resulted in a decision that was contrary to, or involved an unreasonable p.823 application of, clearly established Federal law, as determined by the Supreme Court of the United States; or

(2) resulted in a decision that was based on an unreasonable determination of the facts in light of the evidence presented in the State court proceeding.

28 U.S.C. § 2254(d); see *Harrington v. Richter,* 562 U.S. 86, 102, 131 S.Ct. 770, 178 L.Ed.2d 624 (2011) ("If this standard is difficult to meet, that is because it was meant to be.").

Kubsch therefore has the burden of showing that the last court in Indiana to speak to his case, see *Ylst v. Nunnemaker,* 501 U.S. 797, 801, 111 S.Ct. 2590, 115 L.Ed.2d 706 (1991), rendered a decision that was either contrary to, or an unreasonable application of, "clearly established Federal law, as determined by the Supreme Court of the United States." 28 U.S.C. § 2254(d)(1). (He has not sought to rely on 28 U.S.C. § 2254(d)(2), which deals with unreasonable determinations of fact, and so I do not discuss that option here.) As we observed in *Lindh v. Murphy,* 96 F.3d 856, 873 (7th Cir.1996) (en banc), reversed on other grounds, 521 U.S. 320, 117 S.Ct. 2059, 138 L.Ed.2d 481 (1997), Congress deliberately restricted the jurisprudence to which a court faced with a habeas corpus petition may resort: only federal law as determined by the Supreme Court is available. This restriction acknowledges that the state supreme courts are equally responsible (along with the lower federal courts) for applying federal law, and that the only federal court whose rulings bind them is the federal Supreme Court.

With that in mind, I turn directly to the Supreme Court decision that controls Kubsch's case: *Chambers v. Mississippi. Chambers* and the line of cases that follow it "clearly establish" (to use AEDPA's term) the fact that a state rule of evidence cannot be used in a way that denies an accused person his right under the Due Process Clause to a fair trial, in which he has a fair opportunity to defend. My detailed look at that case and those that followed it demonstrates why, contrary to the spin my colleagues have tried to place on it, the position I take is not opening up any floodgate for the use of hearsay evidence. Only evidence that satisfies the strict criteria of *Chambers* will be admissible, and to see what that evidence must be like, it is necessary to recall the particulars of the case.

Petitioner Leon Chambers was tried by a jury in Mississippi state court and found guilty of murdering a policeman; he was sentenced to life imprisonment. The story leading up to his conviction was sadly familiar. On a Saturday evening, Woodville (Mississippi) police officers Forman and Liberty went to a local bar to execute an arrest warrant for a young man named Jackson. With the help of a hostile crowd and some 20 to 25 men, Jackson resisted arrest. Forman then radioed for assistance, while Liberty retrieved his riot gun from the squad car. Three deputy sheriffs soon arrived in response to Forman's call, but the situation was still not under control. Shooting broke out while Forman was looking away, but when he turned to check on Liberty, he saw that Liberty had been hit several times in the back. Before Liberty died, he turned and fired toward the place where the shots had come from. His second shot hit a man in the crowd in the back of the head and neck; the injured man turned out to be Chambers.

Forman saw neither who shot Liberty, nor whether Liberty managed to hit anyone. A deputy sheriff later testified that he saw Chambers shoot Liberty, and another deputy sheriff testified that he saw Chambers make a suspicious arm movement shortly before the shots were fired. p.824 At the time, however, the remaining officers were trying to tend to Liberty. They put him in the police car and rushed him to a hospital, but he was declared dead on arrival. Chambers in the meantime was lying on the ground. Returning to the scene, some of his friends discovered that he was still alive and took him to the same hospital, where he was treated and then arrested. Later he was charged with Liberty's murder.

Another man, Gable McDonald, was also in the rowdy group at the bar. A few days later, he left his wife in Woodville and moved to Louisiana, where he found work. Five months later, he returned to Woodville to see an acquaintance, Reverend Stokes. After talking to Stokes, McDonald met with Chambers's attorneys and gave them a sworn confession that he was the one who shot Liberty. He also said that he had told a friend, James Williams, that he was the killer. He admitted that he used a nine-shot, .22-caliber revolver, which according to the autopsy was the murder weapon. McDonald signed the confession, surrendered to the police, and was put in jail.

A month later, at the preliminary hearing, McDonald recanted. His new story was that Stokes had persuaded him to make a false confession; the idea, implausible though it sounded, was that Stokes promised he would not go to jail for the crime and that he would share in the proceeds of a lawsuit Chambers planned to bring against the town. The local justice of the peace accepted the recantation and released McDonald.

Chambers's trial took place the next year. He had two theories of defense: first, he tried to show that there was no evidence indicating that he shot Liberty; second, he wanted to show that the real culprit was McDonald. He was stymied in the latter effort, however, by the confluence of two Mississippi rules of trial procedure. First, because the prosecutor refused to call McDonald as a witness, he was forced to call McDonald himself. This triggered Mississippi's voucher rule, under which the party who calls a witness is forbidden to impeach him. Following that rule, the trial court refused to allow Chambers to treat McDonald as an adverse witness. Second, his effort to use three other witnesses to whom McDonald had confessed was blocked by the hearsay rule. Chambers was prepared to show that each of those three would testify that McDonald unequivocally said that he shot Liberty. Much of their testimony was corroborated.

The Supreme Court found that the combination of these two rules of state procedure resulted in a fundamentally unfair trial for Chambers. The rules rendered him utterly unable to subject McDonald's repudiation and alibi to cross-examination, and they prevented him from putting before the jury the information that would have allowed them to decide whether to believe McDonald. The voucher rule, the Court held, "as applied in this case, plainly interfered with Chambers' right to defend against the State's charges." 410 U.S. at 298, 93 S.Ct. 1038. The Court found no need to decide whether that interference alone would have been enough, because it also found that when one added the effects of the hearsay rule to the mix, there was no doubt that Chambers's constitutional rights were violated. It noted that the hearsay statements "were originally made and subsequently offered at trial under circumstances that provided considerable assurance of their reliability." *Id.* at 300, 93 S.Ct. 1038 (spontaneous, corroborated, independent, against McDonald's penal interest). McDonald was present in the courtroom, under oath, and subject to cross-examination. The Court summarized its holding with these words: "In p.825 these circumstances, where constitutional rights directly affecting the ascertainment of guilt are implicated, the hearsay rule may not be applied mechanistically to defeat the ends of justice." *Id.* at 302, 93 S.Ct. 1038.

The Court did not abandon *Chambers* the minute it was decided in 1973. To the contrary, as my colleagues concede, over the ensuing years the Court has carefully reviewed a substantial number of cases in which *Chambers* arguments have been made. Some decisions have found that state rules must give way to the fundamental dictates of due process, while others have concluded either that the evidence is not so critical, or that the rule as applied does not deprive the defendant of a fair trial. Even in the latter cases, however, the Court has confirmed its continued adherence to *Chambers*.

For example, in *Nevada v. Jackson*, ___ U.S. ___, 133 S.Ct. 1990, 186 L.Ed.2d 62 (2013), the defendant argued in a sexual assault case that a Nevada statute that precludes the admission of extrinsic evidence for impeachment purposes violated the *Chambers* principle. The Court rejected that argument and held that Nevada was entitled to apply its statute. Nevertheless, however, it said:

> [o]nly rarely have we held that the right to present a complete defense was violated by the exclusion of defense evidence under a state rule of evidence. See [*Holmes v. South Carolina,*] 547 U.S. [319], 331, 126 S.Ct. 1727, 164 L.Ed.2d 503 [(2006)] (rule did not rationally serve any discernible purpose); *Rock v. Arkansas,* 483 U.S. 44, 61, 107 S.Ct. 2704, 97 L.Ed.2d 37 (1987) (rule arbitrary); *Chambers v. Mississippi,* 410 U.S. 284, 302-303, 93 S.Ct. 1038, 35 L.Ed.2d 297 (1973) (State did not even attempt to explain the reason for its rule); *Washington v. Texas,* 388 U.S. 14, 22, 87 S.Ct. 1920, 18 L.Ed.2d 1019 (1967) (rule could not be rationally defended).

133 S.Ct. at 1992.

Indeed, only three years before *Jackson* the Court found an application of *Chambers* to be so uncontroversial it addressed the matter in a *per curiam* opinion. *Sears v. Upton,* 561 U.S. 945, 130 S.Ct. 3259, 177 L.Ed.2d 1025 (2010). In that case, evidence of petitioner Sears's cognitive impairments had not been brought to light in state court during his capital sentencing hearing. The Court first found that the state court had not applied the correct standard for ascertaining prejudice for purposes of a Sixth Amendment claim of ineffective assistance of counsel. *Id.* at 946, 130 S.Ct. 3259. It then said that "the fact that some of such evidence may have been 'hearsay' does not necessarily undermine its value — or its admissibility — for penalty phase purposes." *Id.* at 950, 130 S.Ct. 3259 (footnote omitted). In the accompanying footnote, it added this: "Like Georgia's 'necessity exception' to its hearsay rules, ... we have also recognized that reliable hearsay evidence that is relevant to a capital defendant's mitigation defense should not be excluded by rote application of a state hearsay rule." *Id.* at 950 n. 6, 130 S.Ct. 3259.

As the citation to *Holmes* in *Jackson* signals, the Court has not shrunk the *Chambers* principle to one that applies only to sentencing proceedings, in which the normal rules of evidence do not strictly apply. In *Holmes,* the question was "whether a criminal defendant's federal constitutional rights are violated by an evidence rule under which the defendant may not introduce proof of third-party guilt if the prosecution has introduced forensic evidence that, if believed, strongly supports a guilty verdict." 547 U.S. at 321, 126 S.Ct. 1727. Yes, the Court concluded, the defendant's rights are violated by such an p.826 evidence rule, despite the broad latitude that state and federal rulemakers enjoy. It continued as follows:

> Whether rooted directly in the Due Process Clause of the Fourteenth Amendment or in the Compulsory Process or Confrontation Clauses of the Sixth Amendment, the Constitution guarantees criminal defendants a meaningful opportunity to present a complete defense.... This right is abridged by evidence rules that in-fring[e] upon a weighty interest of the accused and are arbitrary or disproportionate to the purposes they are designed to serve.

Id. at 324, 126 S.Ct. 1727 (quotation marks and citations omitted). One of the Court's illustrations of this principle was *Chambers. Id.* at 325, 126 S.Ct. 1727.

Naturally, there are cases in which defendants have contended that they should be entitled to the benefits of the *Chambers* rule and the Court has turned them down. See, *e.g., Fry v. Pliler,* 551 U.S. 112, 127 S.Ct. 2321, 168 L.Ed.2d 16 (2007) (cumulative evidence can be excluded); *Clark v. Arizona,* 548 U.S. 735, 126 S.Ct. 2709, 165 L.Ed.2d 842 (2006) (state entitled to limit issues for which evidence of mental illness and capacity may be used); *Oregon v. Guzek,* 546 U.S. 517, 126 S.Ct. 1226, 163 L.Ed.2d 1112 (2006) (no right to present evidence at sentencing phase that casts "residual doubt" on conviction); *United States v. Scheffer,* 523 U.S. 303, 118 S.Ct. 1261, 140 L.Ed.2d 413 (1998) (permissible to prohibit defendant in a court-martial from relying on polygraph evidence). But it is no surprise that defendants have tried to test the outer limits of *Chambers.* Sometimes the Court has acknowledged the *Chambers* rule but found other reasons why the defendant could not prevail. See *Taylor v. Illinois,* 484 U.S. 400, 108 S.Ct. 646, 98 L.Ed.2d 798 (1988) (stressing nevertheless the importance of ensuring that the jury does not decide based on a distorted record). And, in addition to the cases already discussed, there are others in which defendants have prevailed. See, *e.g., Rock v. Arkansas,* 483 U.S. 44, 107 S.Ct. 2704, 97 L.Ed.2d 37 (1987) (refusing to allow Arkansas to use a *per se* rule excluding all hypnotically refreshed testimony); *Crane v. Kentucky,* 476 U.S. 683, 106 S.Ct. 2142, 90 L.Ed.2d 636 (1986) (exclusion of evidence of physical and psychological circumstances of defendant's confession deprived petitioner of fair trial); *Green v. Georgia,* 442 U.S. 95, 99 S.Ct. 2150, 60 L.Ed.2d 738 (1979) (per curiam) (application of hearsay rule violated due process even though correct as a matter of Georgia law).

Chambers, in short, establishes a rule that binds state and federal courts alike. It ensures the fundamental fairness of a defendant's trial. Its message is especially strong in our case, which, like *Chambers* itself, concerns a defendant's right to demonstrate his innocence on capital charges. Just as in *Chambers,* in Kubsch's case even though the videotaped evidence of Mandy's interview was technically hearsay (the very same rule of evidence at issue in both *Chambers* and *Green*), it was created in a way that provided substantial assurances of its accuracy. It missed qualifying for the "recorded recollection" exception to the hearsay rule by a hair. It included numerous details that were either undisputed (*e.g.,* Mandy was a friend of Aaron's; she lived across the street from him; they went to the same school) or easily subject to corroboration. As I now show, these are precisely the circumstances in which the Court has found that the evidentiary rule must give way to the defendant's due process right to a fair trial.

IV

A

I begin with what may be the strongest reason for admitting the Mandy videotape:
p.827 its quality as a *de facto* recorded recollection. (I say "*de facto*" out of respect for
the Indiana Supreme Court's ruling that it fell short, not because I would
necessarily have come to the same conclusion.) As I noted earlier, at the time of
Kubsch's second trial, Indiana Rule of Evidence 803(5) read as follows:

> The following are not excluded by the hearsay rule, even though the declarant
> is available as a witness: ... (5) Recorded Recollection. A memorandum or
> record concerning a matter about which a witness once had knowledge but
> now has insufficient recollection to enable the witness to testify fully and
> accurately, shown to have been made or adopted by the witness when the
> matter was fresh in the witness's memory and to reflect that knowledge
> correctly.

This rule, along with Indiana's other rules of evidence, had been adopted in 1994.
It was intended to codify the common-law exception to the prohibition against the
use of hearsay evidence for records of past statements about which the witness has
no present memory. By requiring only "insufficient" recollection, the rule as
adopted relaxed Indiana's common-law doctrine, which had required the complete
absence of any memory as a condition of admissibility. INDIANA PROPOSED
RULES OF EVIDENCE 75 (1993); see also FED.R.EVID. 803(5) Committee
Note (the model for the Indiana rule), (discussing "[t]he guarantee of
trustworthiness ... found in the reliability inherent in a record made while events
were still fresh in mind and accurately reflecting them"). The key is that the
circumstances surrounding the preparation of the record make it particularly
reliable. INDIANA PROPOSED RULES OF EVIDENCE 75. The rule itself
does not specify how the accuracy of the recorded version should be proved. The
Indiana Supreme Court in *Kubsch II,* however, took the position that the witness
must somehow vouch for its accuracy. See also 2 McCORMICK ON EVIDENCE
§ 283 (7th ed.2013). That can be difficult, since by definition the witness does not
recall making the statement, but common practice, conformity with other things
the witness knows, or even a statement such as "I would not have lied about that"
typically satisfy the vouching requirement. See generally 30C MICHAEL H.
GRAHAM, FEDERAL PRACTICE AND PROCEDURE § 7046 at 115-16 & n.4
(interim ed.2011).

In applying Rule 803(5), Indiana courts both before and after the various *Kubsch*
opinions have looked to see if the recorded recollection (1) relates to a matter
about which the witness once had knowledge; (2) is one about which the witness
now has insufficient recollection to permit her to testify fully and accurately at trial;
(3) is one that the witness is nonetheless willing and able to adopt or vouch for; (4)
is one made when the matter was fresh on her mind; and (5) correctly reflects the
witness's knowledge at the time of the event. *E.g., Impson v. State,* 721 N.E.2d 1275,
1282-83 (Ind.Ct.App.2000). The final requirement is inevitably awkward, because
there is tension between the ability to vouch and the inability to recall. But Indiana
courts have resolved that tension by adopting a realistic approach to vouching; they

have accepted even a simple statement that the report is accurate. *E.g., A.R.M. v. State,* 968 N.E.2d 820, 827 n. 7 (Ind.Ct.App.2012); see also *Gee v. State,* 271 Ind. 28, 389 N.E.2d 303, 309 (1979) ("At the time of his testimony he may have completely forgotten the event... but at that time he can vouch for the accuracy of the prior writing."). In one case, the court was satisfied when a witness testified that she "told the truth in her videotaped statement." *Horton v. State,* 936 N.E.2d 1277, 1283 (Ind.Ct.App. 2010), *vacated on other grounds,* 949 p.828 N.E.2d 346 (Ind.2011). And at times, the courts have simply assumed that the report in question accurately reflects the witness's knowledge at the time of the report. See, *e.g., Small v. State,* 736 N.E.2d 742, 745 (Ind.2000) (permitting admission of deposition answers because witness could not recall making specific statements in the deposition, but failing to address whether witness affirmed that she was truthful at the time of the deposition); *Smith v. State,* 719 N.E.2d 1289, 1291 (Ind.Ct.App.1999) (stating only that "the report reflected [the witness]'s knowledge correctly" without explaining why).

It is easy to see why an endorsement from the witness would be important for many types of recorded recollection, such as diaries, letters, written reports, memoranda, or data compilations. A witness might be able to authenticate her signature, or her habit of writing every evening in a diary, or her acquaintance with the purpose and recipient of a memorandum, without necessarily remembering what was said as a matter of substance. And this kind of vouching serves an important purpose for those kinds of records, because there is nothing otherwise to ensure that it is *this* witness's recollections that were recorded.

I recognize, however, that it is not up to this court to decide whether the Supreme Court of Indiana correctly interpreted its own rule of evidence. This is so even though that court barely touched on the reason why the videotape was inadmissible. Here is the entirety of its explanation for the conclusion that the final element of Indiana's Rule 803(5) was not satisfied:

> Buck testified twice that she had no memory of being interviewed by the police in 1998. (Trial Tr. at 2985.) As a result, the trial court correctly denied Kubsch the opportunity to read Buck's statement into evidence, because Buck could not vouch for the accuracy of a recording that she could not even remember making.

Kubsch II, 866 N.E.2d at 734-35. This merely describes the fact that this was a matter "about which [the] witness once had knowledge but now has insufficient recollection" to permit full and accurate testimony. Indiana made clear at the time it adopted Rule 803(5) that "insufficient" recollection includes no recollection at all. There is thus no reason to think that the total absence of recollection precludes the use of the rule.

The Indiana Supreme Court did not express any doubt that the other requirements of Rule 803(5) were satisfied. For purposes of *Chambers,* then, we have a situation in which the state hearsay rule was used to block critical evidence. There were, however, just as in *Chambers,* substantial assurances of reliability of this evidence, which I discuss below. This was therefore a situation in which the due process command expressed in *Chambers* should have overridden the state's evidentiary rule.

B

Putting *Chambers* temporarily to one side, the fact that the showing at trial was inadequate to satisfy the letter of Rule 803(5) takes us to one of Kubsch's other theories: that he received ineffective assistance of trial counsel in a number of respects, including "in their attempt to admit Amanda Buck's videotaped statement."[1] p.829 Counsel failed to take any of a number of readily available steps to meet the requirements of Rule 803(5) — steps that were necessary, under *Wiggins v. Smith,* for effective assistance of counsel. Indiana courts require that the witness whose recollection has faded need only tell the finder of fact that her statements in the recording were accurate. Kubsch's attorneys never asked Mandy that question. Instead, they dropped the subject after establishing the fact that she could not recall speaking to the police, which relates to a different requirement of the rule (one that was easily met). They should have asked her whether she would have told the police the truth if such an interview had taken place, but they did not. They could have shown her the beginning of the videotape on the record — the trial transcript indicates they showed Mandy the tape off the record but never put her back on the stand after-ward — and asked her whether she was the girl depicted in the recording. They could have asked Monica or anyone else who knew Mandy well about her reputation for truthfulness. Any of these steps, and certainly all of them taken together, would have met the requirements Indiana courts have set for compliance with Rule 803(5)'s requirement for evidence that shows that the recording reflects the witness's knowledge correctly.

Counsel also could have taken steps to counteract the trial court's assumption that it would have been so easy to impeach Mandy's videotaped account that any error in refusing to allow it as a prior inconsistent statement would have been harmless. The state urged that this was the case based on the telephone call from Mandy's grandfather, Lonnie, a few days after the interview urging the police to disregard her statements because she was supposedly mistaken about the day she was talking about. According to Lonnie, everything Mandy recounted had happened on Thursday, September 17, not on Friday the 18th. But there is no reason to conclude, without any adversarial testing, that Lonnie was correct. No evidence at all indicates how reliable his source of information for that statement may have been. He may have been trying to extricate his granddaughter from involvement in the murder trial, or he may have had some other motive that no one ever explored.

Had counsel for Kubsch been on their toes and complied with their duty to investigate in conformity with *Wiggins,* there are many ways in which they could have rehabilitated Mandy's very clear testimony (see Appendix B) that she was recalling the events of *Friday,* just four days earlier than the interview. Anyone who watches the video can only be impressed by how articulate, bright, and forthcoming Mandy is in it. If there were some concern about the fact that Mandy was nine years old at the time, counsel could have put Mandy's p.830 mother, Monica, on the stand and asked on what day of the week she was paid and whether she possibly could have been depositing her paycheck on a Thursday. Records from Monica's bank could have been subpoenaed to see when that deposit was made, and additional evidence such as security camera footage could have shown the day on which she was there. The school district could have been subpoenaed for records confirming on what day the field trip that Mandy discussed in detail actually took place. Kubsch's counsel did none of these things.

My colleagues dismiss the video as unreliable, but saying so does not make it so. In fact, many factors support the reliability of this video, both for purposes of substantive evidence and for purposes of impeachment:

> • It was created only four days after the events about which both Mandy and Monica were speaking.

> • Because the method of recording the recollection was video, rather than audio or writing, there was no chance that the identity of the speakers nor the content of their statements could be mistaken.

> • Mandy provides an elaborate timeline and describes small details from her direct observations of the victims at their home.

> • Mandy's mother, Monica, was present throughout the interview and provided corroborating details at numerous points.

> • Neither Mandy nor Monica had any personal interest in the case; there was thus no reason to fear that their accounts were slanted one way or the other.

> • Both Mandy and Monica were available at trial to testify after the video was shown, at which point the jury would have been able to weigh their live statements at trial against their recorded statements on the video.

The failure to take steps that would have allowed the videotape to be admitted for all purposes pursuant to Indiana Rule 803(5), and that would also have permitted its use to impeach Mandy's statement at trial that she "probably didn't see" Aaron that afternoon, amounted to insufficient performance for purposes of *Strickland v. Washington,* 466 U.S. 668, 104 S.Ct. 2052, 80 L.Ed.2d 674 (1984). It also severely prejudiced Kubsch. Mandy's videotaped testimony, if believed, would have shown that the murders of at least Rick and Aaron, and probably Beth (on the theory that Rick and Aaron interrupted the assault on Beth), took place at a time when Kubsch was already in or on his way to Michigan to pick up Jonathan. This was easily Kubsch's strongest defense to the charges, and it was swept away by a combination of the trial court's evidentiary rulings and counsel's ineffectiveness.

C

The majority argues that despite the inherently credible nature of the video and Mandy's statements on it, there were three other primary reasons for concluding that it was not reliable enough to meet the *Chambers* standard for use at trial: first, that Mandy's statements were not corroborated; second, that she was "essentially unavailable" for cross-examination; and third, that Detective Reihl "never pushed" Mandy on "critical details" during the 1998 interview, such as whether she had her dates and times correct. *Ante* at 799-801. I begin with the last contention. A review of the transcript at Appendix B shows that this is simply not the case. The majority posits that Reihl "was simply taking [Mandy's] account as she spoke," but Reihl repeatedly stops and "pushes" Mandy to confirm p.831 what she is saying. He asks her over and over whether she is talking about Friday's events. (*E.g.,* "[D]o you remember last Friday?" "And did they pick you up Friday?" "Was that white truck at Rick's house Friday?" "Friday, after you got home, they left just a little bit after when you got home, right?") At the end of the interview, Reihl turns to her mother, Monica, and asks again for assurance: "[t]hese times that you've given me today, uh, these are pretty accurate?" Monica responds that they were, "pretty well," because "sometimes I have to stay a couple minutes after, so, I get home a little later. And that was just so happen [*sic*] to have been one of the days that was a little bit later." It is also clear from the transcript that this was not the first time Monica and Mandy had spoken to Reihl about that past Friday's events. At various points, Reihl indicates that he was following up on a conversation they had previously "at the house." Given these repeated assurances, there was little reason for Reihl a day later to ask the two interviewees yet again "about the possibility that her memory had confused events of two different days," as the majority suggests is necessary to meet the requirements of *Chambers*. *Ante* at 807. For all we know, Reihl did not like what he was hearing and was hoping that they would change their story.

The majority also understates the degree of corroboration for Mandy's account in the videotape (as I have said, corroboration that is just as good as that found in *Chambers* itself). Mandy's own mother interjects corroborating remarks repeatedly during the interview. My colleagues push this to one side because they believe that Monica's subsequent off-the-record, non-testimonial statement to police that she (but not Mandy) had the wrong day effectively erased Monica's own consistent corroboration in the video. The transcript provides no support for this interpretation. To the contrary, Monica is an active participant who provides her own detailed account of her afternoon on that Friday. Like Mandy, Monica herself saw Aaron after school, even though she did not see Rick. (No one thinks that Aaron and Rick took separate cars to the Kubsch house; Aaron was far too young to drive.) And, as I already have pointed out, there was much more corroboration easily within reach.

Last, some precision is necessary with respect to Mandy's availability for cross-examination. She was not "unavailable" in the sense of not being present at trial. She was in the courtroom and she testified; at least one aspect of her testimony, as the Indiana Supreme Court acknowledged, should have been impeached by her statements on the video. She was "unavailable" only because her memory had failed. But that is true of every witness proffered under Rule 803(5). Indiana courts, like others, look for the next-best assurances. Mandy never claimed that she was not the girl on the tape, nor has the state ever argued that the "Monica" on the tape was not Mandy's mother. There was, in short, ample corroboration even on the record that exists to satisfy this aspect of the *Chambers* rule. The majority sees no way to distinguish this hearsay from the ordinary mine-run of hearsay, and it accuses me of throwing the door open to admission of every recorded police interview. Not so. In many cases, the witness will have a good enough recollection of what happened that Rule 803(5) will never come into play. In many cases, the proffered hearsay will be cumulative or relevant only to a peripheral matter. In the great majority of cases, the admission of the hearsay statement will not have life-or-death consequences. The dissent in *Chambers* worried about exactly the same p.832 things the majority here invokes. But the dissent did not prevail, and the Supreme Court has continued to follow *Chambers* in the small group of cases to which it applies. This court should not be second-guessing the Supreme Court, but I fear that is what the majority has done. Under its view, *Chambers* will never apply to allow a defendant to introduce pivotal evidence, if a state rule would block it. By so ruling, it is contravening the Supreme Court's command that "the hearsay rule may not be applied mechanistically to defeat the ends of justice." *Chambers,* 410 U.S. at 302, 93 S.Ct. 1038.

In fact, this case is as close to *Chambers* as anyone is likely to find. My colleagues misapply the Supreme Court's guidance in *Williams v. Taylor,* 529 U.S. 362, 120 S.Ct. 1495, 146 L.Ed.2d 389 (2000) (O'Connor, J.), when they insist on a precise factual match between *Chambers* and the present case. The Court has never insisted on factual identity between its earlier case and the new one. See *id.* at 407, 120 S.Ct. 1495 ("[A] state-court decision also involves an unreasonable application of this Court's precedent if the state court either unreasonably extends a legal principle from our precedent to a new context where it should not apply or *unreasonably refuses to extend that principle to a new context where it should apply.*") (emphasis added). Kubsch's situation, while differing in some details from Chambers's, is close enough to require application of the same principle.

The majority fears that if *Chambers* requires admission of the videotape, then state hearsay rules are out the window. But their gripe is with the Supreme Court, not with me. I have shown why and how the facts cabin this case. In very few matters before the court will the price of insisting on exclusion of evidence that does not fit every technical requirement of the state's hearsay rule be death. That alone should lay to rest any fears that granting Kubsch relief under *Chambers* will produce the "sweeping" result the majority fears. Like defendant Chambers, Kubsch was "thwarted in his attempt to present this portion of his defense by the strict application of certain [state] rules of evidence." *Chambers,* 410 U.S. at 289, 93 S.Ct. 1038. In Kubsch's case, the hearsay problem was compounded by the ineffectiveness of counsel's efforts to get the tape admitted.

In *Chambers* (also a murder trial), the application of the state's rules on vouching for witnesses *and hearsay* prevented the defendant from calling as an adverse witness the person who he said was the real murderer and three witnesses who would have supported that proposition. The state excluded that evidence notwithstanding the fact that it was created "under circumstances that provided considerable assurance of [its] reliability." *Id.* at 300, 93 S.Ct. 1038. Those circumstances included the fact that the confessions of the apparent murderer to which each excluded witness was prepared to testify were "made spontaneously to a close acquaintance shortly after the murder had occurred"; each was corroborated by other evidence in the case; and each was self-incriminatory and against the speaker's interest. *Id.* at 300-01, 93 S.Ct. 1038. The alleged true murderer "stood to benefit nothing by disclosing his role in the shooting," and he was in the courtroom during the trial and so could have been cross-examined by the state and evaluated by the jury. *Id.* at 301, 93 S.Ct. 1038.

Mandy and Monica Buck were not potential suspects in this case, but their videotaped statements bore equally compelling indicia of reliability. The majority downplays these facts, but they overlook the significant ways in which the Supreme p.833 Court itself has confined *Chambers*. Granting the writ to Kubsch under *Chambers* would not abolish the rule against hearsay, any more than *Chambers* abolished hearsay and vouching, the two rules at issue there. A set of very particular circumstances must arise to produce a case like Kubsch's, or like that in *Chambers*. As I already have pointed out, a result in Kubsch's favor would not lead to the admissibility as substantive evidence of "all hearsay of this type [videotapes?]," to use the majority's words, *ante* at 808.

In this case, the operation of Indiana's hearsay rule, coupled with counsel's inadequate efforts with regard to the tape, prevented Kubsch from showing that he could not have been the murderer. Like Chambers, Kubsch also tried to show that someone else was the guilty party — in Kubsch's case, his sometime friend Brad Hardy. There appears to have been significant evidence pointing to Hardy. Indeed, at one point the state had charged him with conspiring with Kubsch to commit the murders and with assisting a criminal (Kubsch). *Kubsch II*, 866 N.E.2d at 731. Hardy wound up testifying against Kubsch in the first trial; interestingly, the state did not drop the charges against him until two years later.[2] The excluded videotaped evidence in Kubsch's case had even greater guarantees of reliability than the evidence before the Supreme Court in *Chambers*. And the exclusion of the videotape drastically undermined Kubsch's ability to demonstrate that someone else must have committed the three murders. The *Chambers* exception exists for just this kind of case. In my view, the Indiana courts' refusal to recognize and apply it amounts to constitutional error that must be recognized, even under the demanding standards of 28 U.S.C. § 2254(d)(1).

V

Wayne Kubsch may be a disagreeable man, as Mandy said in her videotaped statement. His business skills may have been bad, and he may, as of September 1998, been flailing around for a way to solve his financial problems. And a jury with all of the evidence before it may have convicted him for the murders of Beth, Rick, and Aaron, if it had been persuaded that Mandy's videotaped testimony was not worthy of belief for some reason. But a jury with all of the evidence before it may also have concluded that Kubsch, no matter what his other flaws, could not have committed those murders because Rick and Aaron, and perhaps Beth, were still alive at 3:45 p.m., when Kubsch was already far from the house driving to Michigan. We will never know, because my colleagues are unwilling to find either the disregard or incorrect application of *Chambers* here, nor do they perceive ineffective assistance of counsel. I cannot subscribe to that result. I therefore respectfully dissent from the decision to affirm the district court's denial of the writ and the consequent green light for Kubsch's execution.

APPENDIX A

Timeline of events, September 18, 1998

Time Kubsch Beth/Others

p.834 6:00 am Near Mishawaka home (cell Beth is at work in Elkhart record). (United Musical Instruments). 6:50 am At work in Elkhart (Skyline Corp.). 9:11 am Cellphone call near work. 10:00 am Beth finishes shift and goes home. 10:30 am Beth pages Kubsch twice from home. 10:45 am Call to Beth from Skyline break room.

10:48 am Beth makes a call from home to Rick's house. 10:53 am Beth goes out to run errands. 11:08 am Security camera at Teach-er's Credit Union shows Beth with the dog in the car. 11:13 am Kubsch punches out of work. 11:14 am Beth's credit union receipt shows transaction completed. 11:30 am to noon Kubsch at home (seen by Erin Honold). 11:37 am Call from home to American General Finance. 11:52 am Beth meets with credit counselor Edith Pipke in South Bend. 12:09 to 12:11 pm Kubsch makes 1 call to house and 2 calls to Rick (cellphone). 12:16 pm Beth pages Kubsch again. 12:18 pm Kubsch calls the house (31 seconds) from Osceola (toward Elkhart). 12:40 pm Kubsch calls house from break room at Skyline. 12:46 pm Rick calls Beth at home. 1:17 pm Kubsch calls house from break room at Skyline. 1:52 pm Kubsch punches out again and does not return. 1:53 pm Kubsch calls home from Elkhart area (46 seconds). 2:20 to 2:35 pm Rick picks up Aaron from school in South Bend. 2:51 pm Kubsch makes call from near home (cell records). 3:15 pm Kubsch calls Beth's mother from Elkhart (after 10 tries). Cell sectors indicate he is heading toward Michigan. 3:45 to 4:15 pm Approximate time when Mandy saw both Aaron and Rick at their South Bend home.

p.835 4:42 to 4:47 pm Kubsch makes calls near Schoolcraft, MI. 5:00 pm Kubsch picks up son Jonathan in Three Rivers, MI. 5:30 to 5:45 pm Kubsch sees Wayne Temple at Kmart in Three Rivers. 5:30 to 6:30 pm Kubsch and Jonathan stop in Osceola at home of Constance Hardy. 5:30 pm Anthony discovers the bodies of Rick and Aaron Milewski at the house. 5:56 pm Kubsch makes phone call on network close to the house. 6:45 pm Kubsch returns home; police are there; he goes to station for first interview. 9:00 pm Police discover Beth's body in basement; they bring Kubsch back to the station. After 9:00 pm Kubsch interviewed second time by police; he invokes *Miranda* rights.

APPENDIX B

Transcript of Police Interview with Monica and Mandy Buck September 22, 1998

Det. Mark Reihl: [Inaudible] stepped out for a minute. I'll go ahead and start asking you a couple questions. Okay, and the time is now three o'clock PM. And, today is September the twenty-second, nineteen ninety-nine — nineteen ninety-eight. And Mandy, is it M-a-n-d-y?

Mandy: Uh huh.

Reihl: M-a-n-d-y. Buck. B-u-c-k?

Mandy: Uh huh.

Reihl: And you're how old?

Mandy: Nine.

Reihl: Your birthdate is?

Mandy: Ninety-eight. Nineteen ninety-eight. Oh, nineteen eighty-nine.

Reihl: This is nineteen ninety-eight.

Mandy: Nineteen eighty-nine.

Reihl: What month were you born?

Mandy: February.

Reihl: February. What day?

Mandy: Eighth.

Reihl: Nineteen eighty-nine.

Mandy: Yeah.

Reihl: Alright.

Mandy: But you can ask my mommy on that. I think so.

Reihl: Oh, I'm pretty sure, all right? You're pretty intelligent. I think you know.

Mandy: Yeah, I think that, yeah yeah yeah.

Reihl: Mandy was born February the eighth?

Monica: Yeah.

Reihl: Nineteen eighty-nine?

Monica: Mmm hmm.

Reihl: Okay.

Mandy: Cool, I got it right.

p.836 Reihl: See, you got it right. Okay. And your mother's name is Monica?

Mandy: Uh huh.

Reihl: M-o-n-i-c-a? Correct me?

Monica: Yeah.

Reihl: Buck. And you live at thirteen twenty East Indiana in South Bend.

Mandy: Uh huh.

Reihl: And your home phone is two three three, seven seven three seven?

Mandy: Two three three seven seven three seven. Yep.

Reihl: Right. And you go to Lincoln School?

Mandy: Yeah.

Reihl: And you're in which grade? Fourth?

Mandy: Yeah.

Reihl: Okay. How's school this year?

Mandy: Umm, good, even though I have the teacher that, um, is the Wicked Witch of the West, she's fine. She's okay.

Reihl: Well sometimes they gotta be like that so you kids will listen.

Mandy: Yeah.

Reihl: Okay. Well, the reason you're here is that you live right across the street —

Mandy: From Aaron?

Reihl: From Aaron and his dad Rick.

Mandy: Yeah.

Reihl: Okay. And you and Aaron were pretty good friends, huh?

Mandy: Best friends, yeah.

Reihl: Best friends?

Mandy: [Nods head]

Reihl: How long have you known Aaron?

Mandy: I don't know. I think he moved there in like the beginning of May I think. Just beginning. I don't know. I never kept track of it. I don't know. 'Cause he told me one day and then I just forgot.

Reihl: Oh, that's okay.

Mandy: I can't remember I think —

Reihl: Time just goes by so fast, doesn't it? And you said that Aaron used to talk sometimes about things that made him sad?

Mandy: Mmm hmm. [Nods head]

Reihl: Made him upset?

Mandy: Right, and like he, he he wished his mom didn't break up with his dad and like go with Wayne. He was like, he didn't like Wayne.

Reihl: Aaron didn't like Wayne?

Mandy: No.

Reihl: Well how come?

Mandy: Um because, like, he would get rough with him and stuff and punch him too hard and stuff like that.

Reihl: Was it because — did he ever say was it because Wayne was mad at him or were they just playing?

Mandy: He never said, he never said why he didn't like him he just said like, he just said he just didn't like him because Wayne was just like too rough and stuff.

Reihl: Okay. Did he ever say if Wayne ever was rough with his mom?

Mandy: No.

Reihl: You didn't talk about that?

Mandy: No.

Reihl: Okay. What else did you guys talk about?

Mandy: Um, we talked about like, why he moved here and like what we wanted to be when we got older and, um, who are our friends and where we used to live and, like, and I introduced him to my parents; he p.837 introduced me to his dad. Then we just became best friends.

Reihl: That's great.

Mandy: I always went over to his house. He always came over to my house and like we like used to study for the same spelling words. He'd give me my spelling words and I would give him his spelling words. And we would help each other on homework and stuff. We were pretty good friends.

Reihl: That's, that's wonderful.

Mandy: We got along really good.

Reihl: He's a pretty good kid, huh?

Mandy: Mmm hmm. [Nods head]

Reihl: Smart?

Mandy: Uh huh. [Nods head] He knew, he knew his times pretty good. He could, he could just do 'em in a flash. He was pretty good at 'em. He's a lot better than me.

Reihl: Did you, did you say you used to walk to school with him sometimes?

Mandy: Uh no, I never walked.

Reihl: Oh, you never did.

Mandy: No. I see — I seen him walk to school.

Reihl: Uh-huh.

Mandy: I never walked to — I never walked to school or to my house alone.

Reihl: Okay, and how would he get home?

Mandy: Um, usually some, if he wasn't grounded from his bike would ride his bike home. He would walk home. His dad would come and pick him up when he had his truck. Um, Rick would walk to school and pick up Aaron. They would walk back home together.

Reihl: Mmm hmm. And, and you guys get out of school at what time?

Mandy: Two twenty.

Reihl: Two twenty. And how long does it take him to get home do you think?

Mandy: Mmm probably like — we don't live too far from Lincoln. All you gotta do is go straight and turn and you're there.

Reihl: Oh.

Mandy: Probably like five minutes to get there.

Reihl: Uh-huh. Okay.

Mandy: If he was riding his bike it would only take him like two minutes. But if he was walking it would probably take him a pretty long time.

Reihl: Mmm hmm. Now, do you remember last Friday?

Mandy: Yeah.

Reihl: Okay. And you told me earlier that you go to the Alphabet Academy?

Mandy: Uh huh. [Nods head]

Reihl: And that they usually pick you up at school, right?

Mandy: Uh huh. [Nods head]

Reihl: Okay. And did they pick you up Friday?

Mandy: Uh huh. [Nods head]

Reihl: And you went straight to the Alphabet Academy?

Mandy: Uh huh. [Nods head]

Reihl: And say then you what, your mom picks you up from there?

Mandy: Uh huh. [Nods head]

Reihl: Okay. And you said you picked her up about what time?

Monica: Between three thirty and quarter to four.

Reihl: Okay. And you went straight home? Or where'd you go?

Monica: I usually call down there and I watch her walk from there down to our p.838 house. And then I waited for my mom and dad to get home, and I went and cashed my check and came home.

Reihl: Okay, when you got home at three thirty, um, did you notice if Rick was at home across the street?

Monica: I didn't pay no attention. All I saw was Aaron.

Reihl: You saw Aaron?

Monica: Mmm hmm.

Reihl: You don't remember if Rick's truck was there?

Monica: No.

Reihl: Okay. And, then Mandy you were telling me that when you got home that was about what time?

Monica: From day care?

Reihl: Yeah.

Monica: That was around three thirty, quarter to four.

Reihl: Okay, and that's when you saw Aaron?

Mandy: Uh huh. [Nods head]

Reihl: And you saw his dad?

Mandy: Uh huh. [Nods head] His dad, he, his dad was coming from their living room into the kitchen to get something to drink.

Reihl: Did you go over to Aaron's house or you just saw him from your house?

Mandy: I, I, um, when I walked, when I, every day when I walk home I always see Rick walk into the kitchen or walk into the restroom or walk into his room.

Reihl: I mean, did you see him from out-side looking in or did you actually go into the house?

Mandy: No, I um seen it from the out-side 'cause when 'cause I seen him go into the kitchen. When he came back he had a drink in his — he had, um, some um — I don't know what it was. He had a drink in his hand but it was in a cup.

Reihl: Okay.

Mandy: Like usually pop, 'cause they like, they like Storm a lot. So, probably Storm.

Reihl: What, uh, what does Rick drive?

Mandy: A Chevy? He used to drive a Chevy until it broke down.

Reihl: A Chevy what?

Mandy: [Eyes searching, no verbal response]

Reihl: Is it a car or a truck?

Mandy: Truck.

Reihl: What color?

Mandy: Black.

Reihl: Okay.

Mandy: It's like, kinda short. I mean like it — did you see my mom's truck? Um, well, uh my mom's truck, my mom's truck's pretty big. His is probably a medium truck, you know. Kinda short.

Reihl: What was he driving Friday? Did you see that?

Mandy: Um, his truck broke down before that. He was drive — driving a white truck which was his brother's. And his brother had a car so his brother let Rick use the truck.

Reihl: Okay. Was that white truck at Rick's house Friday?

Mandy: Yeah.

Reihl: When you got home from school?

Mandy: Yeah.

Reihl: Okay. And this is about what time again?

Monica: Three thirty, quarter to four.

Reihl: Okay, so between three thirty and quarter to four —

Mandy: Yeah.

p.839 Reihl: You saw —

Mandy: Aaron and Rick.

Reihl: Okay, at the house. Did you ever see 'em leave?

Mandy: Um, yeah, like I was on my porch and, and they let me blow bubbles. And I was blowin' my bubbles, and I seen Rick pull out and leave.

Reihl: Okay. Now how long, how long after — and this might be hard to guess at — 'cause you probably don't wear a watch, do you?

Mandy: Well, until my watch, well, yeah I did but my watch is in my bag and I — 'cause I had to take it off when we had gym. I just take it off.

Reihl: So, about what time do you think they left their house, if you had to guess?

Mandy: Um —

Reihl: I know it's gotta be a hard question.

Mandy: Um —

Reihl: Was it very long after you got home?

Mandy: Mmm, medium. Because his mom lives pretty far away, you know. And you know but I think it was like — I don't know.

Reihl: Okay.

Mandy: It was probably in like medium because you know it takes a pretty long time to get to his mom's house.

Reihl: Well why was he going to his mom's house. I think he told you, didn't he?

Mandy: Um, I guess to just visit her.

Reihl: Okay, did he talk about going to his mom's house?

Mandy: He said that he was going to his mom's house Friday, 'cause he was gonna stay the night there to go to the field trip Saturday. So it was probably why, and Rick probably wanted to stay a little while to talk. You know, he was, he — he wanted to go on the field trip bad. So, they were gonna leave pretty early to get to the school on time to go. But by the time Saturday when we, when we were on the bus and stuff, he was gonna be in our group, and, um, he never showed up. He wasn't there. And we didn't know why. But Saturday — Sunday when we got home with my cousins, um, 'cause we go camp — we went camping after the field trip, we just went, we came back from the field trip, and my mom drove her truck back to the, back up to our house and up to the camper and, and my grandma goes, "Did you see Aaron?" and I'm like, "No, he was supposed to be in our group, he wasn't there." And then Sunday, um, my um, my day care teacher said they showed it on TV but my grandpa didn't get, my grandpa didn't turn it on there because he, he didn't know it was they got murdered Friday night. So, I mean, and then Monday, um, Monday, Monday News Center 16 came to my house, and I was at karate 'cause I, I had practice. When we came home my grandma said News Center 16 just, just came to our house like, probably a while ago.

Reihl: So you didn't get a chance to talk to him then, huh?

Mandy: No.

Reihl: So, Friday, after you got home, they left just a little bit after when you got home, right?

Mandy: Yeah.

Reihl: And you saw 'em leave?

Mandy: Yeah. He pulled out.

Reihl: And they were just together, Rick and Aaron, nobody else with 'em?

p.840 Mandy: No one else was with them, just Aaron and Rick.

Reihl: Okay.

Mandy: 'Cause Rick, cause Aaron's mom — He didn't know if Aaron's mom was home yet so Rick was thinking if his mom's not there, then Wayne's probably not there. So, he said, "I'll just drive you," and they just took off, pulled out and took off.

Reihl: Okay.

Mandy: And —

Reihl: Monica, Monica, I'm sorry.

Mandy: And Fri — and Thur — and when I was playing with them —

Reihl: Mmm hmm.

Mandy: There was, he had some clothes laying on his, laying on his on their swing on the front porch. Um, he had a whole bunch of clothes laying on there and I, I didn't know what they were for. You know, I thought he was gonna spend the night there Saturday and Sunday, come home Monday. Um, Sunday's rolling around and he wasn't there. Saturday, Saturday the field trip, he wasn't there.

Reihl: Monica, you said something back at your house when I was talking to you about um, you said you'd cashed your check.

Monica: Yeah.

Reihl: Friday?

Monica: Yeah.

Reihl: And that was about what time? Was that after you come home from work?

Monica: Shortly after I came home from work.

Reihl: Okay. And, what time do you think that was?

Monica: Let's see. Probably about ten minutes till four.

Reihl: Okay. So then you got home then about — how long were you gone to cash the check?

Monica: Probably about fifteen minutes.

Reihl: Okay, and when you got home, that would have put it a little after four o'clock? And was Rick still at the house then?

Monica: I didn't pay no attention. Like I said, all I saw was Aaron. I really didn't look to see if Rick's truck was there.

Reihl: Well, Aaron was still there when you got back after you cashed your check?

Monica: Yeah.

Reihl: Okay. And you don't remember if that truck was in the —

Monica: Nuh uh, I didn't pay no attention.

Reihl: Okay, um — You said something, too, didn't you about you overheard something one time a couple months ago.

Monica: Yeah. I don't, like I said, I don't know who the woman was. But he was standing, they were standing in their driveway. And, well he was standing in the driveway. She was sitting in the truck. And, uh, I couldn't hear what she was saying, but he was, you know, he was saying the F-word, and F him, he don't scare me, and he was just going on and on and on. And then he, then she left, and he just went into the house.

Reihl: This truck, what did it look like?

Monica: It was a, it was a little black truck.

Reihl: Do you know, do you know your vehicles? Do you know the difference between a —

Monica: Well, the lettering on the back was kinda, on the back of it was kinda like, rusted like, and you couldn't really tell what kind of car it was —

Mandy: Um —

Monica: — what kind of truck.

p.841 Mandy: Aaron's dad's truck had Chevy right there. It was just printed beautifully. It was gold and it was just right on there. You could just read it, so it couldn't have been Aaron, Aaron's dad's truck, 'cause Aaron's dad's truck was, but, it was still there where he, it broke down. I mean Aaron's truck's, dad's truck was just beautiful. The Chevy was just —

Reihl: But was this was this his ex-wife? Was this —

Monica: I don't know.

Reihl: — Elizabeth?

Monica: I don't know who she was. Like I said, all I saw, all I, I never seen the woman. You know, I, I just know that she had blonde hair. Well, I seen her face, but she had blonde hair.

Reihl: Was she a passenger in the truck?

Monica: No. She was driving it.

Reihl: Okay.

Monica: And this was, then I saw her once a little while after that. You know, like a, I don't know, a couple weeks later. And that was the last time I seen her.

Reihl: What was she driving then?

Monica: Same thing.

Reihl: This truck?

Monica: Mmm hmm. I don't know, I don't, like I said I don't know who she was.

Mandy: Aaron's mom's, mom has um, blonde hair.

Reihl: Mmm hmm. I was just trying to see if maybe you could describe this truck. Was there anything, was it, was it a pickup truck where it has the open bed in the back or was it all closed up?

Monica: Uh, let me think. I think it was open. See, 'cause the one that that, ah, Aaron's dad used to drive had the little things that went down the side.

Reihl: Mmm hmm.

Monica: But it wasn't all closed in. It just had like little, I don't know what you'd call 'em, it went from the top all the way to the back of the truck, and it was just a short thing. This one was all open, I believe. I think it was.

Reihl: It was just like a regular pickup truck.

Monica: Yeah.

Reihl: Okay. So it wasn't like a little sport utility vehicle?

Monica: No.

Reihl: Like you see like one of those Suzuki Samurais or something like that?

Monica: No. It was —

Reihl: Kids drive a lot.

Monica: It was pretty rusted.

Reihl: Okay. All right. But you don't know whether or not that was his —

Monica: No I have no idea.

Reihl: His ex-wife Elizabeth or not? All right.

Monica: I just know that he was highly upset that day.

Reihl: Oh.

Monica: And she didn't look too happy, and she left and he went into the house.

Reihl: Okay.

Monica: Yeah, I don't even, I don't know who his ex-wife is. I mean, it could have been her, but I, I don't know.

Reihl: Okay. Was there anything else? I can't remember exactly what all we talked about at the house but, did you say that, uh, I was thinking that you said that Aaron had made some comments to you before, too, about —

Monica: Oh, he just told me the once.

Reihl: Oh.

p.842 Monica: He just told me one time that he doesn't like his stepdad. But, I just figured he was just being a kid.

Monica: You know, "My mom and dad's divorced but I really don't like this guy. I don't want Wayne really to be with my mom. I'd rather, you know, him and my mom be together —"

Reihl: Mmm hmm.

Monica: "— than my stepdad," kinda thing. That's all I thought it was. So I just really didn't pay no attention to it.

Reihl: Okay. Okay. All right. Well, just so I got this right then, Mandy, you got home at about three thirty, quarter of four and you saw Aaron and his dad and that white truck at his house?

Mandy: Yes.

Reihl: And then, Monica, you got home from cashing that check around four o'clock or a little after, and you saw them both at the house, or at least you saw Aaron?

Monica: Yeah, I saw Aaron.

Reihl: Okay. But you never saw 'em leave.

Monica: No. I was in the house by the time they left.

Reihl: Okay, and Mandy, you did see 'em leave, but you don't know exactly when it was that they left?

Mandy: Yeah. I seen 'em leave, but, you know I didn't see no, I didn't see no bags in the truck. And when, when they left, the clothes were still there.

Reihl: Okay. On the swing?

Mandy: Um, yeah. 'Cause when his grandparents were there, they picked up the clothes and just threw 'em in the box.

Reihl: Okay.

Mandy: And we thought that he was moving, like he didn't like the neighborhood so he was moving. What we thought, and I don't know if it, I didn't know if Rick and Aaron Friday were gonna go look for a new house or go to his mom's. I didn't know, I thought they were going to look for a new house and then come back, and you know, and go. Like, then go to his mom's. But, I didn't, I didn't know.

Reihl: Okay. These times that you've given me today, uh, these are pretty accurate?

Monica: Mmm hmm. Yeah, 'cause I get off work at quarter after three. And with the traffic and that, and sometimes the South Shore comes by and you gotta wait for that.

Reihl: Mmm hmm.

Monica: So, yeah, pretty well.

Reihl: It's pretty much a routine that you do every day?

Monica: Yeah.

Reihl: Every day that you work, that is?

Monica: Yeah. Sometimes on, sometimes I have to stay a couple minutes after, so, I get home a little later. And that was just so happen to have been one of the days that was a little bit later.

Reihl: Okay. All right. I, I don't have any more questions that I can think of at the moment. Do you have anything else that you can think of? Maybe I overlooked, that I have overlooked?

Monica: No. Do you?

Mandy: [Shakes head]

Reihl: I thank you very much for coming down. I'll take you back home now. The time is, uh, three twenty PM. [Pause] I told you that would take you about fifteen, twenty minutes.

Mandy: [Pointing to ceiling] Is that your camera?

Reihl: It's up there.

p.843 Mandy: Oh, there it is. I thought it was — it's in that vent right there.

[1] We have substituted as respondent-appellee Ron Neal, the current Superintendent of the Indiana State Prison, for Bill Wilson, the former Superintendent. See Fed. R.App. Pro. 43(c)(2).

[2] Nichols' wife, Gina DiDonato, confirmed his account of the telephone call and in response to a juror's question made clear that Kubsch told them that Beth was dead.

[3] By the time Kubsch testified at trial, of course, he knew about the telephone records and other evidence that contradicted in several key respects the story he had first told the police in his interview the night of the murders.

[4] The recording would also not be admissible under Federal Rule of Evidence 803(5), which is substantially identical to its Indiana counterpart and has the same requirement that the declarant endorse the accuracy of the prior recording. See, e.g., *United States v. Green*, 258 F.3d 683, 689 (7th Cir.2001); *United States v. Schoenborn*, 4 F.3d 1424, 1427-28 (7th Cir.1993). In fact, neither Kubsch nor our dissenting colleague has identified any federal or state decision indicating that the recording of Amanda's interview would have been admissible under the law of any American jurisdiction. See also, e.g., *State v. Perry*, 147 Ohio App.3d 164, 768 N.E.2d 1259, 1264-65 (2002) (under identical recorded recollection rule, affirming exclusion of video recording of interview with eight-year-old child who, when testifying at trial two years later, did not remember the interview and did not testify that the recording correctly reflected her knowledge of events at the time it was made).

[5] The Supreme Court's account of the facts was deliberately terse. It made no mention at all, for example, of the case's racial dimensions and the civil rights boycott at the heart of the events in a small town in rural Mississippi in 1969. For a more complete account that emphasizes the gap between local realities and formal legal recognition of civil rights, see Emily Prifogle, *Law and Local Activism: Uncovering the Civil Rights History of Chambers v. Mississippi*, 101 Cal. L.Rev. 445 (2013).

[6] Kubsch points out that Rick Milewski was driving not his own black truck but a white truck that he had borrowed from his brother. In her statement, Amanda said that Rick was driving a white truck that day. But as Kubsch also acknowledges, Rick had borrowed that truck from his brother a few weeks before the murders. The color of the truck does not corroborate Amanda's statement about which afternoon she saw Rick and Aaron at home.

[7] Our dissenting colleague contends that this case is like *Chambers* because Kubsch, like Chambers, tried to show that someone else committed the murders — Kubsch's long-time friend Brad Hardy. Post at 832-33. We disagree. In *Chambers,* the evidence against McDonald would have exonerated Chambers; there was no evidence that they acted together. Readers of the dissent might think there was a similar either-or dynamic at work here. There was not. The prosecution argued that Hardy had either helped Kubsch or had been set up by Kubsch as his fall guy.

Hardy testified in both of Kubsch's trials, though at the time of the first trial he was charged with conspiring with Kubsch to commit the murders. (The charges were later dismissed.) Kubsch called Hardy on the day of the murders at 9:11 a.m. Hardy and his mother, Constance Hardy, each testified that Constance drove Hardy to Kubsch's workplace two hours later when Kubsch began his early lunch break. Hardy testified that Kubsch then drove him to a parking lot near the Kubsch house and asked him to sneak up to the house from the rear to see if Beth was home. Hardy also testified that the day after the murders Kubsch asked him to lie about their activities the day before. (Kubsch denied Hardy's account.)

Phone records showed that Kubsch again called Brad Hardy on the day of the murders at 4:44 p.m. It is undisputed that Kubsch arrived at Brad and Constance

Hardy's house 45 minutes later and stayed for an hour before going to his home. The defense argued that this visit was for the purpose of "invit[ing] [Brad] out to dinner that night." Tr. at 3301. It is curious that, on the evening of his wife's birthday — when Kubsch claims not to have seen Beth all day and after Beth's mother called him to say that she was concerned about not hearing from Beth — Kubsch would take an hour-long detour to Hardy's house just to extend a dinner invitation, especially when he had spoken to Hardy just 45 minutes earlier. In light of this curious detour, the fact that Beth's credit cards were later found in the woods near Hardy's house could be viewed as implicating Kubsch as much as Hardy. In short, the "significant evidence pointing to Hardy" did not necessarily tend to exonerate Kubsch, as the dissent suggests and in contrast to the evidence related to Gable McDonald in *Chambers*.

[8] In *Stitts* we considered whether to "look through" a state supreme court's ruling to a lower state court's decision. In this case, we cannot "look through" the Indiana Supreme Court's ruling on the *Chambers* claim. The claim was not presented to the trial court, and capital appeals in Indiana go directly to the Indiana Supreme Court.

[9] *Makiel v. Butler,* 782 F.3d 882, 905-06 (7th Cir.2015), presented a related but distinct issue. In *Makiel,* the state court gave two reasons why the exclusion of certain evidence did not violate the petitioner's right to present a complete defense. One reason was flawed but the second was sound. The sound second reason was enough to call for AEDPA deference. Here, by contrast, the state court gave only one reason to reject the constitutional claim, and that reason is flawed.

[10] Most circuits endorse this approach that allows and even requires federal courts to complete or fill the gaps in state courts' reasoning in support of results that are not unreasonable in light of Supreme Court precedent. See *Foxworth v. St. Amand,* 570 F.3d 414, 429 (1st Cir.2009) ("on habeas review, the ultimate inquiry is not the degree to which the state court's decision is or is not smoothly reasoned; the ultimate inquiry is whether the outcome is reasonable"); *Rashad v. Walsh,* 300 F.3d 27, 45 (1st Cir.2002) (where federal courts were troubled by gaps in state court's rationale: "It is not our function, however, to grade a state court opinion as if it were a law school examination."); *Cruz v. Miller,* 255 F.3d 77, 86 (2d Cir.2001) ("deficient reasoning will not preclude AEDPA deference"); *Collins v. Sec'y of Pennsylvania Dep't of Corr.,* 742 F.3d 528, 548 (3d Cir.2014) (while state court adjudication of *Strickland* claim consisted of "admittedly cursory statements, AEDPA requires that we determine what arguments or theories supported... or could have supported, the state court's decision") (citation and internal quotation marks omitted); *Robinson v. Polk,* 438 F.3d 350, 358 (4th Cir.2006) ("In assessing the reasonableness of the state court's application of federal law, therefore, the federal courts are to review the *result* that the state court reached, not whether its decision was well reasoned.") (brackets, citations, and internal quotation marks omitted); *Higgins v. Cain,* 720 F.3d 255, 261 (5th Cir.2013) ("In considering whether the state court's decision constituted an unreasonable application of clearly established federal law, 'a federal habeas court is authorized by Section 2254(d) to review only a state court's "decision," and not the written opinion explaining that decision.'"), quoting *Neal v. Puckett,* 286 F.3d 230, 246 (5th Cir.2002) (en banc); *Holder v. Palmer,* 588 F.3d 328, 341 (6th Cir.2009) ("The law requires such deference to be given

even in cases, such as this one, where the state court's reasoning is flawed or abbreviated."); *Williams v. Roper,* 695 F.3d 825, 831 (8th Cir.2012) ("In reviewing whether the state court's decision involved an unreasonable application of clearly established federal law, we examine the ultimate legal conclusion reached by the court, not merely the statement of reasons explaining the state court's decision.") (citation omitted); *Williams v. Trammell,* 782 F.3d 1184, 1199-1200 (10th Cir.2015) ("uncertainty" regarding rationale for a sparse state court decision "does not change our deference;" federal court still must identify theories that could have supported the decision); *Lee v. Comm'r, Alabama Dep't of Corr.,* 726 F.3d 1172, 1210-14 (11th Cir.2013) (applying AEDPA deference to incomplete state court opinion; state court need not "show its work" by mentioning all circumstances relevant to *Batson* claim); but see *Frantz v. Hazey,* 533 F.3d 724, 737-38 & n. 15 (9th Cir.2008) (en banc) (confining evaluation of "unreasonable application" prong to actual reasons given).

[1] My colleagues attempt to rehabilitate Kubsch's lawyers in this respect, but they are forced to resort to speculation about what a proper investigation would have revealed. As the Supreme Court has made clear, however, it is essential to evaluate the question whether counsel's investigation was constitutionally sufficient. See *Wiggins v. Smith,* 539 U.S. 510, 123 S.Ct. 2527, 156 L.Ed.2d 471 (2003). There the Court faced a case in which the petitioner's claim "stem[med] from counsel's decision to limit the scope of their investigation into potential mitigating evidence." *Id.* at 521, 123 S.Ct. 2527. Quoting from *Strickland,* the Court reaffirmed that "counsel has a duty to make reasonable investigations or to make a reasonable decision that makes particular investigations unnecessary." *Id.* In addition, the Court squarely recognized that it is not enough to gather "*some*" information. *Id.* at 527, 123 S.Ct. 2527. In language that applies with equal force to Kubsch's case, it held that "[i]n assessing the reasonableness of an attorney's investigation, however, a court must consider not only the quantum of evidence already known to counsel, but also whether the known evidence would lead a reasonable attorney to investigate further." *Id.* Just so. Kubsch's lawyers knew about Mandy's videotaped statement, but that evidence would have led a reasonable attorney to investigate further. Their failure to take that step amounted to constitutionally ineffective assistance.

[2] As my colleagues point out, Hardy testified against Kubsch in the second trial. By that time they were surely adverse to one another; indeed, it would not be surprising if Hardy's charges were dropped in exchange for that testimony.

796 F.3d 726 (2015)

Renardo CARTER, Petitioner-Appellant,

v.

Timothy DOUMA, Respondent-Appellee.

No. 13-3312.

United States Court of Appeals, Seventh Circuit.

Argued November 3, 2014.

Decided August 6, 2015.

Carter v. Douma, 796 F. 3d 726 (7th Cir. 2015)

p.729 Leigh Ann Krahenbuhl, Jones Day, Chicago, IL, for Petitioner-Appellant.

Sandra Lynn Tarver, Office of the Attorney General, Wisconsin Department of Justice, Madison, WI, for Respondent-Appellee.

Before WOOD, Chief Judge, and EASTERBROOK and HAMILTON, Circuit Judges.

HAMILTON, Circuit Judge.

Petitioner Renardo Carter challenges his Wisconsin conviction for possessing between five and fifteen grams of cocaine with intent to deliver. At Carter's trial, a police officer testified about his work with an informant who had said Carter was involved in distributing drugs. The officer's testimony relayed the substance of the identification as well as the fact that he requested and heard the informant call Carter to order cocaine. Carter's lawyer did not object to the testimony about the informant's out-of-court statements and actions. During closing argument, the State referred to the informant's statements and actions to support its argument that Carter possessed cocaine with intent to deliver, again without objection from Carter's lawyer.

Carter sought post-conviction relief in state court. He argued that the officer's testimony about his out-of-court conversation with the informant violated his Confrontation Clause right to cross-examine an adverse witness and that his trial counsel was ineffective under *Strickland v. Washington,* 466 U.S. 668, 104 S.Ct. 2052, 80 L.Ed.2d 674 (1984), for failing to object to that testimony. The Wisconsin Court of Appeals rejected both claims, finding no plain error in admission of the evidence and concluding that Carter's lawyer was not ineffective for failing to object. The state court explained that admitting the testimony posed no Confrontation Clause problem because it was offered not to show the truth of what the informant said but to explain why the police investigated Carter as they did.

Carter filed a federal habeas corpus petition under 28 U.S.C. § 2254 asserting the same Confrontation Clause and ineffective assistance theories. The district court denied the petition, and we affirm that denial. While there is a good argument that Carter's trial lawyer should have objected to some of the officer's testimony about the informant and its use during closing argument, we need not determine whether his lawyer rendered constitutionally deficient assistance because Carter has not shown that the failure to object prejudiced him. The evidence shows that Carter possessed at least twelve bags of the sort commonly used to redistribute controlled p.730 substances and that each of those bags would have held at least 1.75 grams of cocaine. Though Carter's dramatic efforts to flee the police and then to dispose of the bags while standing in a river in view of officers prevented the State from proving more definitively what those bags contained, the state court's finding of no prejudice was not unreasonable.

I. *Factual and Procedural Background*

A. *Events Leading to Arrest*

On November 18, 2004, police narcotics investigator Michael Webster went to a motel parking lot to meet a confidential informant with a lead on a person distributing controlled substances. Officer Webster had hoped to get enough information to justify a stop of the suspected man's vehicle or otherwise to secure his arrest. After hearing about this suspicious man, Officer Webster asked the informant to point out the vehicle the man was using. During their conversation, Officer Webster saw that man leave a motel room and walk toward the vehicle. The man was Carter.

At that point, Officer Webster asked the informant to call Carter and say that he wanted to buy cocaine "teeners," one-sixteenth ounce quantities of cocaine. The informant complied, and Officer Webster made sure he could hear what the informant was saying and could observe Carter's actions in response to the informant's requests. He saw Carter pick up his phone when the informant called, and when the informant hung up, so did Carter. Shortly after the conversation ended, Carter drove away.

Officer Webster then enlisted an Officer Starks to follow and stop Carter. Carter refused to stop. This prompted a car chase—involving Officer Starks and later Officer Webster—that ended only when Carter stopped his car and ran into the Wisconsin River near a dam. Officers Webster and Starks pursued Carter on foot. They saw from a distance that Carter was holding a large plastic bag that they thought contained a mixture of powder and crack cocaine. Officer Webster estimated that the bag was about the size of a 14-inch softball and could have contained in excess of two ounces of the powdery substance.

Officers Webster and Starks caught up with Carter in the river and arrested him there. Before they reached him, other officers on top of a nearby dam saw Carter pull small packets of a white, powdery substance out of his pockets, tear the packets open with his teeth, and dump the bags and their contents into the water. When the officers reached Carter, the bag they had seen previously was now empty, and Carter had a white, powdery substance around his mouth. At one point, Carter indicated he had ingested all of the substance, but he later said he had not swallowed any of it. Officer Webster also observed a fair amount of white residue floating on the water. Officer Starks testified that his narcotics-detection dog indicated for the presence of an odor of an illegal substance in the water near Carter.

Beyond seeing traces of the powder, Officer Webster also recovered from the river twelve "baggie corners," a type of bag smaller than the larger bag they previously saw Carter holding. In the officer's experience, people packaging controlled substances often make little bags like these by placing the substance in the corner of a sandwich bag, tying it off, and cutting away the excess bag material. Officer Webster testified that all of these smaller baggies would have fit easily within the larger bag he had seen earlier.

After Carter disposed of the substance in the river, the police were unable to recover much of it for testing. They were not able to test the baggies or powdery residue in the river, but they did test one p.731 rock found in the river and other rocks found in Carter's car. Both samples contained cocaine. The total weight of recovered cocaine was just 0.2 grams.

B. *Trial*

The State charged Carter with possessing between fifteen and forty grams of cocaine with intent to deliver. Carter's actions in the river ensured that the State had little physical evidence at trial, so the State relied primarily on the testimony of Officers Starks and Webster. Then other officers testified about the arrest, including seeing Carter in possession of bags containing a white, powdery substance and trying to dispose of the bags in the river. Officer Webster estimated that Carter had possessed at least 21 grams of cocaine before he disposed of it in the river. Officer. Webster also testified that carrying that many baggie corners is strong evidence of intent to distribute the cocaine to others.

The State had planned to call the informant at trial but had waited until right before trial to disclose the informant's identity. This left Carter little time to investigate the informant's background. At Carter's request, the trial court barred the State from calling the informant as a witness. The trial court said it would permit the State to ask witnesses about their interactions with the informant so long as their testimony complied with hearsay rules.

Officer Webster testified about the informant's role in the investigation. He explained the circumstances of the meeting and said the reason they met was so that the informant could "direct [him] to an individual that was involved in distributing controlled substances." It later came out that the person the informant referred to was Carter. Officer Webster also described what the informant said on the call with Carter and made clear that he heard the informant order "teeners" of cocaine from Carter. At no point did Carter's lawyer object to Officer Webster's discussion of the informant.

Though the State had said it would not use any of the informant's statements for their truth, the State relied on those statements in closing argument:

> Why do I feel that possession with intent has been shown here? It has been shown because you heard the testimony by Investigator Webster of a confidential informant, someone that the officer uses in drug investigations as part of a tactic that they use. I mean they have people out there who are aware of drug activity going on. They don't want to necessarily come here and divulge their name or get involved, because they might be used in continuing investigation, more than one person.

> But with that CI, he was directed to a place where that CI was. The CI came in the vehicle with him, pointed out Mr. Carter; that they went over to Econo Lodge. And as he is pointing him out, the officer said, okay, if what you are saying is true here, order some up for me. So the CI gets on the line, makes the phone call. Mr. Carter is out there answering the phone all observed by the officer. He hears him order four teeners, which he has testified is 1/16 ounce of cocaine. The CI hangs up, the defendant hangs up. He then keeps

surveillance the officer does on the defendant until he becomes mobile after the deal had been set up.

Later the State asked the jury to look at the facts and find that possession with intent to deliver had been shown because:

> You had the officer indicating that the CI said, get me at least four teeners, 16th ounce. You have 12 packages, not that we know that this is all he had, but we have 12 packages that we were able p.732 to find. And the officer said, those could have been packages teeners, eight balls, they could have been higher amounts of cocaine, but I know he ordered teeners. CI ordered teeners, I heard him.

The jury found Carter not guilty of possessing between fifteen and forty grams of cocaine with intent to deliver but convicted him of the lesser offense of possessing between five and fifteen grams of cocaine with intent to deliver.[1]

C. *Post-Conviction Proceedings*

Carter sought post-conviction relief in state court. He argued that Webster's testimony about his conversation with the informant denied him a fair trial. Recognizing that he did not object at trial, he argued the testimony violated his right of confrontation because it was offered for its truth and its admission amounted to plain error. Alternatively, Carter argued that his lawyer's failure to object to the testimony denied him effective assistance of counsel.

To determine whether Carter's trial counsel was ineffective in failing to object, the state trial court held a hearing pursuant to *State v. Machner,* 92 Wis.2d 797, 285 N.W.2d 905 (App.1979). Carter's trial counsel testified that he did not think Officer Webster's testimony that the informant had directed him to a person involved in distributing controlled substances was offered for its truth. He thought this statement served to explain why the officers were interested in investigating Carter. Similarly, the testimony regarding what the informant said on the call to Carter was offered not to prove it was true but to show the effect those statements had on the other party to the drug transaction—Carter—as viewed by Officer Webster. The trial court denied relief, agreeing that the testimony about the informant was not offered for its truth.

Carter appealed to the Wisconsin Court of Appeals. Turning first to whether Carter's counsel was ineffective, the court concluded that "the officer's testimony about what he actually observed and overheard while with the informant was not offered to establish that Carter was selling drugs but, rather, provided background information for the jury to understand why the police tried to stop Carter's vehicle and chased him when he sped away." On this view, admitting the testimony did not violate the Confrontation Clause and the failure to object was not deficient performance by counsel. The court also found that any claimed deficiency would not have resulted in prejudice, finding "no reasonable probability that absent this testimony, the result would have been different." The state appellate court also concluded that admitting the testimony had been neither a plain error nor a reason for a new trial in the interest of justice. In fact, the court was "not convinced that admission of the challenged testimony constituted error, much less plain error." The Wisconsin Supreme Court denied further review.

Carter then filed a federal habeas corpus petition under 28 U.S.C. § 2254 challenging the validity of his state court conviction. The district court denied the petition, concluding that the state court had not unreasonably applied *Strickland* in finding that counsel was not deficient and that Carter was not prejudiced by any possible deficiency. The district declined to issue a certificate of appealability.

p.733 Carter appealed. We granted his request for a certificate of appealability as to: (1) whether Officer Webster's testimony concerning the informant violated the Confrontation Clause; and (2) whether trial counsel was ineffective for failing to object to that testimony. Carter raises both of these grounds on appeal.

II. *Habeas Corpus Review Under 28 U.S.C. § 2254*

Under the Antiterrorism and Effective Death Penalty Act of 1996 ("AEDPA"), Carter must satisfy two statutory requirements to prevail on his federal habeas petition. First, he must establish that "he is in custody in violation of the Constitution or laws or treaties of the United States." 28 U.S.C. § 2254(a). Second, since the state appellate court ruled on the merits of his claims, he must also go further and show that his detention is the result of a state court decision that was (1) "contrary to, or involved an unreasonable application of, clearly established Federal law, as determined by the Supreme Court of the United States; " or (2) "based on an unreasonable determination of the facts in light of the evidence presented in the State court proceeding." 28 U.S.C. § 2254(d).

To prevail in federal court, Carter must show that the state appellate court's ruling on either claim was "objectively unreasonable, not merely wrong; even clear error will not suffice." *Campbell v. Smith,* 770 F.3d 540, 546 (7th Cir. 2014), quoting *White v. Woodall,* 572 U.S. ___, 134 S.Ct. 1697, 1702, 188 L.Ed.2d 698 (2014) (internal quotation marks omitted). That is, the ruling must have been "so lacking in justification that there was an error well understood and comprehended in existing law beyond any possibility for fairminded disagreement." *Harrington v. Richter,* 562 U.S. 86, 103, 131 S.Ct. 770, 178 L.Ed.2d 624 (2011). The district court reviewed these claims under that standard and concluded that the state court's rejection of Carter's claims was not objectively unreasonable. We review that conclusion *de novo.* *Jones v. Basinger,* 635 F.3d 1030, 1040 (7th Cir.2011).

A. *Confrontation Clause*

Carter challenges directly the State's use of the informant's statements on Confrontation Clause grounds. He argues that the state court unreasonably applied *Crawford v. Washington,* 541 U.S. 36, 124 S.Ct. 1354, 158 L.Ed.2d 177 (2004). The State argues that Carter's procedural default, in the form of the failing to object at trial, provides an independent and adequate state law ground for denying relief on this claim. We agree with the State.

If a state court denies relief "by relying on a state law ground that is both independent of the federal question and adequate to support the judgment, federal habeas review of the claim is foreclosed." *Kaczmarek v. Rednour,* 627 F.3d 586, 591 (7th Cir.2010), citing *Coleman v. Thompson,* 501 U.S. 722, 729, 111 S.Ct. 2546, 115 L.Ed.2d 640 (1991). A procedural failure to raise the federal claim as required by state procedural rules, often called a procedural default, is a common example of such an independent and adequate state ground. *Id.* at 591-92.

When the state presents this as an affirmative defense in federal court and the defense is found to apply to a petitioner's claim, the federal court cannot entertain the claim unless the petitioner persuades the federal habeas court to excuse the default. Petitioner can do so by establishing cause for failing to follow the state procedural rules and a resulting prejudice from his failure to do so. See *id.* at 591; *Wrinkles v. Buss,* 537 F.3d 804, 812 (7th Cir.2008), citing *Wainwright v. Sykes,* 433 U.S. 72, 87, 90, 97 S.Ct. 2497, 53 L.Ed.2d p.734 594 (1977). A procedural default may also be excused if a failure to consider the claim would result in a "fundamental miscarriage[ ] of justice" because "a constitutional violation has probably resulted in the conviction of one who is actually innocent." *Wrinkles,* 537 F.3d at 812 n. 3 (alteration in original), quoting *Murray v. Carrier,* 477 U.S. 478, 496, 106 S.Ct. 2639, 91 L.Ed.2d 397 (1986).

The state court declined to give full review to Carter's Confrontation Clause claim because he failed to comply with Wisconsin's contemporaneous objection requirement at trial. See *Kaczmarek,* 627 F.3d at 592 ("A state law ground is independent when the court actually relied on the procedural bar as an independent basis for its disposition of the case."). Under Wisconsin law, a defendant waives an objection—whether based on state law or an alleged violation of a constitutional right—when it is not made at the time the alleged error takes place. See Wis. Stat. § 901.03(1)(a); *State v. Erickson,* 227 Wis.2d 758, 596 N.W.2d 749, 754-55 (1999) (declining to excuse waiver and instead reviewing unobjected-to claim as claim for ineffective assistance of counsel); *State v. Hansbrough,* 334 Wis.2d 237, 799 N.W.2d 887, 896 (App.2011).

Here the state court recognized this failure to object and said that it considered the merits of the Confrontation Clause claim only as a basis for Carter's ineffective assistance claim or under plain-error or interest-of-justice review. That more limited review is not a decision on the merits that allows us to consider the claim on federal habeas review. See *Kaczmarek,* 627 F.3d at 592; *Gray v. Hardy,* 598 F.3d 324, 329 (7th Cir.2010); cf. *Malone v. Walls,* 538 F.3d 744, 756-57 (7th Cir. 2008) (when state court makes clear that it is resolving a federal issue despite procedural problems, federal courts can consider merits). The state court concluded that Carter was not entitled to relief under any of these more limited forms of relief.

In Wisconsin, it is common for state courts to analyze a failure to object as a claim for ineffective assistance of counsel. Doing so does not mean that the state court resolved the merits of the underlying waived claim. See *Erickson,* 596 N.W.2d at 754 ("[T]he normal procedure in criminal cases is to address waiver within the rubric of the ineffective assistance of counsel."); *State v. Hayes,* 273 Wis.2d 1, 681 N.W.2d 203, 223-24 (2004) (Sykes, J., concurring); *State v. Benson,* 344 Wis.2d 126, 822 N.W.2d 484, 489 (App.2012). In Wisconsin, then, there is strong support for what we already presume under federal habeas practice: a state court's rejection of the ineffective assistance of counsel claim does not constitute a decision on the merits of the underlying claim. See *Lewis v. Sternes,* 390 F.3d 1019, 1026 (7th Cir. 2004) ("A meritorious claim of attorney ineffectiveness might amount to cause for the failure to present an issue to a state court, but the fact that the ineffectiveness claim was raised at some point in state court does not mean that the state court was given the opportunity to address the underlying issue that the attorney in question neglected to raise.").

Accordingly, Carter has procedurally defaulted his Confrontation Clause claim. He has not tried to show either "cause and prejudice" or that a failure to consider his Confrontation Clause claim would result in a fundamental miscarriage of justice. Carter is not entitled to relief on that claim.

B. *Ineffective Assistance of Counsel*

In Carter's view, his lawyer's failure to object to use of the informant's out-of-court statements for their truth means that his lawyer rendered ineffective assistance of counsel within the meaning of p.735 *Strickland v. Washington,* 466 U.S. 668, 104 S.Ct. 2052, 80 L.Ed.2d 674 (1984). He argues the State's use of those statements was clearly barred by the rule announced in *Crawford v. Washington,* 541 U.S. 36, 68, 124 S.Ct. 1354, 158 L.Ed.2d 177 (2004), that out-of-court testimonial statements cannot be admitted against a criminal defendant unless the declarant is unavailable and the defendant had a prior chance to cross-examine the declarant. Although this claim is framed in terms of whether Carter's lawyer was ineffective rather than the Confrontation Clause itself, the *Crawford* issue is nonetheless integral to the *Strickland* analysis here. See *Campbell v. Smith,* 770 F.3d 540, 547 (7th Cir.2014) (addressing ineffective assistance of counsel claim based on an embedded constitutional issue). Carter argues that the state court unreasonably applied both *Crawford* and *Strickland* in denying him post-conviction relief.

Under *Strickland's* familiar two-pronged standard, Carter must show both that his counsel's performance was deficient and that he was prejudiced as a result. *Harrington v. Richter,* 562 U.S. 86, 104, 131 S.Ct. 770, 178 L.Ed.2d 624 (2011). Here, the state court decided that counsel's performance was not deficient and that even if it had been, Carter was not prejudiced. Our review of each prong of the *Strickland* analysis is subject to AEDPA's deferential standard of review under § 2254(d)(1). *Sussman v. Jenkins,* 636 F.3d 329, 350-51 (7th Cir.2011). Once AEDPA applies, "[t]he bar for establishing that a state court's application of the *Strickland* standard was 'unreasonable' is a high one, and only a clear error in applying *Strickland* will support a writ of habeas corpus." *Id.* (alteration in original) (citation omitted).

To argue his trial lawyer's performance was deficient, Carter relies on his counsel's failure to object to two portions of Officer Webster's testimony and the prosecution's use of them in closing argument. First, he asserts that Officer Webster should not have been able to testify that he instructed the informant to call Carter to request "teeners" and that the informant did so. This theory has no merit. The officer's instruction and the informant's request for "teeners" were not hearsay because they were not "statements" making any factual assertions. See, e.g., *Schindler v. Seiler,* 474 F.3d 1008, 1010 (7th Cir.2007) ("Statements that constitute verbal acts (e.g., words of contract or slander) are not hearsay because they are not offered for their truth."); *United States v. Moreno,* 233 F.3d 937, 940 (7th Cir.2000). Nor were they testimonial for purposes of the Confrontation Clause. *Crawford,* 541 U.S. at 59 n. 9, 124 S.Ct. 1354. That portion of Officer Webster's testimony merely described verbal acts, his own instruction, and the informant's offer to buy, all of which Webster made and/or saw and heard himself. Such verbal acts are not statements offered to prove the truth of their contents.

If Carter's counsel had objected to this testimony on hearsay or Confrontation Clause grounds, his objection should have been overruled. His performance was not deficient by failing to make a futile objection. See *Lambert v. McBride,* 365 F.3d 557, 564 (7th Cir.2004); *United States v. Neeley,* 189 F.3d 670, 684 (7th Cir.1999) ("Obviously, counsel can not be considered ineffective for failing to make an objection to the introduction of evidence that was properly admitted.").

Carter's second challenge has more substance. He argues that his lawyer should have objected to Officer Webster's testimony that he was investigating Carter because the informant had identified Carter as someone involved in distributing controlled substances. Carter maintains that p.736 the State also impermissibly relied on this testimony during closing argument to establish that he was guilty of possession with intent to distribute cocaine. The prosecutor reminded the jury, albeit obliquely, that the informant had identified Carter as someone involved in drug dealing. The prosecutor asked the jury to infer from the evidence that a deal had been set up and that Carter had teeners on him as the police closed in to arrest him as he stood in the river.

The state court held that counsel's failure to object could not have been deficient performance because introducing this testimony did not violate the Confrontation Clause.[2] See *Lambert,* 365 F.3d at 564; *Neeley,* 189 F.3d at 684. Invoking the "course of investigation" gambit to avoid hearsay rules, it held this testimony was offered only to explain why the police stopped Carter and pursued him.

When the reasons for the police's actions are relevant, a witness can testify about what information prompted those actions. That is, when such a statement is offered only to show the effect it had on the police, it is used for a purpose other than the truth of its contents. E.g., *United States v. Eberhart,* 434 F.3d 935, 939 (7th Cir.2006) (testimony is not for its truth where it is offered "only as an explanation of why the investigation proceeded as it did"). We have applied this "course of investigation" rationale in several cases to permit the government to introduce brief out-of-court statements designed to "bridge gaps in the trial testimony that would otherwise substantially confuse or mislead the jury." See *Jones v. Basinger,* 635 F.3d 1030, 1046 (7th Cir.2011) (collecting cases). This approach is consistent with the Confrontation Clause, which "does not bar the use of testimonial statements for purposes other than establishing the truth of the matter asserted." See *Crawford,* 541 U.S. at 59 n. 9, 124 S.Ct. 1354; *United States v. Gaytan,* 649 F.3d 573, 579 (7th Cir.2011) (testimonial statements of a witness did not violate the Confrontation Clause, because they "were not offered for their truth").

The problem, as we have explained time and again, is that the "course of investigation" gambit is so often abused and/or misunderstood that it is an evidentiary and constitutional minefield. See, e.g., *Jones,* 635 F.3d at 1046; *United States v. Silva,* 380 F.3d 1018, 1020 (7th Cir.2004) ("Allowing agents to narrate the course of their investigations, and thus spread before juries damning information that is not subject to cross-examination, would go far toward abrogating the defendant's rights under the sixth amendment and the hearsay rule."). To convict a defendant, after all, the prosecution does not need to prove its reasons for investigating him. *United States v. Mancillas,* 580 F.2d 1301, 1310 (7th Cir.1978). When the prosecution offers out-of-court statements of non-witnesses on the theory they are being offered to explain "the course of the investigation," it runs a substantial risk of violating both the hearsay rules of evidence and the Confrontation Clause rights of the defendant under the Sixth Amendment. Both defense counsel and trial judges need to be on high alert when the prosecution offers what sounds like hearsay to explain "the course of the investigation."

Under circumstances like these, where the only reason counsel failed to object was his understanding that such testimony was not objectionable—and not p.737 some strategic judgment—counsel runs the risk of rendering performance that falls below the objective standard of reasonableness. See *Barrow v. Uchtman*, 398 F.3d 597, 605 (7th Cir.2005) (noting that a lawyer's failure to act based on his "erroneous understanding of state law" can render his performance deficient); *Gardner v. United States*, 680 F.3d 1006, 1011-12 (7th Cir.2012). Under AEDPA, however, the ultimate question is "whether there is any reasonable argument that counsel satisfied *Strickland's* deferential standard," and we must deny the writ if the state court offered a reasonable argument that counsel behaved competently. *Richter*, 562 U.S. at 105, 131 S.Ct. 770.

We recently addressed the scope of the "course of investigation" theory in *Jones v. Basinger*, 635 F.3d 1030 (7th Cir.2011), when we determined that the state court unreasonably applied *Crawford* in determining that the government's use of out-of-court informant statements fell within the "course of investigation" theory. But that finding does not dictate whether the state court's use of the theory here was reasonable. First, the use of the informant testimony here was much narrower and more limited than in *Jones*, where the government misused the gambit to give the jury a detailed hearsay account that linked the defendant to four murders, explained how the murders were committed, and described what happened to the weapons afterwards. *Id.* at 1036-37. Second, in *Jones*, unlike here, we addressed the Confrontation Clause claim directly and were not encumbered by the need to give deference to counsel under *Strickland*.

We need not resolve whether the failure to object here to the arguably hearsay identification was deficient performance, however. Even if Carter's counsel might have been deficient in failing to object to Officer Webster's testimony about the informant's identification and its use during closing argument, Carter cannot show that the state court unreasonably determined that the problematic testimony did not prejudice him. See *Taylor v. Bradley*, 448 F.3d 942, 948-49 (7th Cir. 2006) (declining to resolve whether deficient performance when clear that no prejudice).

For a petitioner to have been prejudiced by his counsel's deficient performance, he must establish a reasonable probability that the result of the proceeding would have been different had counsel objected to the inadmissible testimony. See *Richter*, 562 U.S. at 104, 131 S.Ct. 770. A reasonable probability is one that undermines confidence in the outcome of the trial. *Strickland*, 466 U.S. at 694, 104 S.Ct. 2052. The likelihood of a different outcome "must be substantial, not just conceivable." *Richter*, 562 U.S. at 112, 131 S.Ct. 770. A guilty verdict that is "overwhelmingly supported by the record is less likely to have been affected by errors than one that is only weakly supported by the record." *Eckstein v. Kingston*, 460 F.3d 844, 848 (7th Cir.2006), quoting *Hough v. Anderson*, 272 F.3d 878, 891 (7th Cir.2001). A state court's application of the prejudice prong of *Strickland* is reviewed under the deferential standard of 28 U.S.C. § 2254(d).

In reviewing Carter's conviction, the state court applied the appropriate standard and pointed to all the evidence of Carter's guilt that made the court confident that the verdict was not affected by the use of hearsay. In light of that evidence, the state court reasonably determined that Carter was not prejudiced by the admission or later use of Officer Webster's testimony about the informant.

The evidence shows that Carter possessed at least some cocaine even if his efforts to dispose of the evidence ensured that only 0.2 grams of cocaine were recovered. p.738 On the disputed points—whether Carter possessed at least five grams of cocaine and whether he actually intended to deliver the cocaine he had—the State offered ample evidence of Carter's guilt. As the state court explained, the police observed Carter holding a large bag containing a substance that looked like a mixture of cocaine and crack cocaine. The officer estimated that the large bag alone might have held a couple of ounces, or over fifty grams.[3] Beyond that, the officers recovered twelve smaller baggies (or bag corners) in the river. Officer Webster testified that the recovered baggies were prepared in such a way that they could be expected to hold either one-sixteenth or one-eighth of an ounce. Even if each contained only the smaller quantity, one "teener," Carter was in possession of well over five grams.

Carter resists using the baggies to infer that he was in possession of well over five grams, emphasizing that none of those baggies contained cocaine at the time of the arrest. But there was ample evidence that they did just before Carter was arrested. After Carter's dangerous and desperate flight from police ended with him standing in the river, Officers Webster and Starks saw him holding a larger bag that contained a substance that looked like cocaine, and also saw that he had a white, powdery substance on his mouth. The little baggies that were recovered are often used to hold controlled substances and are specifically prepared for that purpose. Police officers actually saw him pulling those bags out of his pocket and dumping the bags, along with their white, powdery contents, into the water. He was seen churning the water to disperse the substance. He was not completely successful. A white, powdery residue remained on the water, and a police dog alerted to the presence of narcotics in the water. Carter also argues that absent the informant's testimony there was no evidence that he intended to deliver cocaine. That is not correct. Officer Webster testified that the packaging and quantities indicated intent to distribute.

Given all of the evidence that Carter possessed at least five grams of cocaine and intended to deliver it, the state court did not apply federal law unreasonably in determining there would not have been a reasonable probability of a different result if Carter's attorney had objected to the use of the informant's hearsay identification of him as a person involved in distributing drugs.

The district court's judgment denying Carter's petition for a writ of habeas corpus is AFFIRMED.

[1] Carter was also charged with three other offenses. He was convicted of two (eluding an officer and resisting or obstructing an officer) and acquitted of the third (recklessly endangering safety). Those charges are not at issue in this appeal.

[2] Carter argues in his reply brief that the state court failed to address the testimony regarding the informant's identification of him as a drug dealer, but this is not correct. The state court recognized that this was part of Carter's argument.

[3] An ounce is equivalent to 28.35 grams. A "teener," which is one-sixteenth of an ounce, contains about 1.77 grams. Possession of just three "teeners" would have been sufficient to support the conviction.

782 F.3d 804 (2015)

Mohamed Abdul MATHIN, Plaintiff-Appellant,

v.

John F. KERRY, Secretary of State, Defendant-Appellee.

No. 14-1889.

United States Court of Appeals, Seventh Circuit.

Argued November 13, 2014.

Decided April 7, 2015.

Mathin v. Kerry, 782 F. 3d 804 (7th Cir. 2015)

p.805 Justin R. Burton, Attorney, Kriezelman Burton & Associates, Chicago, IL, for Plaintiff-Appellant.

Craig A. Oswald, Attorney, Office of the United States Attorney, Chicago, IL, Stacey I. Young, Attorney, Department of Justice, Civil Division, Immigration Litigation, Washington, DC, for Defendant-Appellee.

Before POSNER, KANNE, and ROVNER, Circuit Judges.

ROVNER, Circuit Judge.

Mohamed Abdul Mathin claims that he was born in the United States but his request for a United States passport was denied by the State Department after an investigation into his claim of citizenship. He then filed an action in district court under 8 U.S.C. § 1503(a) and 28 U.S.C. § 2201(a) seeking a declaration that he is a United States national for the purpose of obtaining a United States passport. After a trial on the matter, the district court denied his request for declaratory relief, holding that Mathin had failed to establish that he was a United States national. Mathin now appeals that determination to this court.

Pursuant to 8 U.S.C. § 1503, any person who claims a right or privilege as a national of the United States and is denied such right or privilege can institute an action for a judgment declaring him to be a national of the United States. Section 1503 authorizes a *de novo* determination by the district court of the status of the plaintiff as a United States citizen or national. *Hizam v. Kerry,* 747 F.3d 102, 108 (2nd Cir.2014). Because the Government has a "strong and legitimate interest in ensuring that only qualified persons are granted citizenship," the Supreme Court has recognized that "doubts 'should be resolved in p.806 favor of the United States.'" *Berenyi v. District Director, Immigration and Naturalization Service,* 385 U.S. 630, 637, 87 S.Ct. 666, 17 L.Ed.2d 656 (1967); *Bustamante-Barrera v. Gonzales,* 447 F.3d 388, 394-95 (5th Cir.2006).

Mathin's action for a declaration of United States nationality is premised on the claim that his Indian-citizen parents, Mohamed Ziaudeen ("Ziaudeen") and Asiaumma Abdul Majid ("Asiaumma"), traveled to the United States for business while his mother was 8 months pregnant with him, and that he was born prematurely in Chicago on September 23, 1965. The issue, then, is whether the district court erred in determining that Mathin had produced insufficient evidence that he was born in the United States. In this appeal following the bench trial, we review findings of fact for clear error and issues of law *de novo. Cohen Development Co. v. JMJ Properties, Inc.,* 317 F.3d 729, 735 (7th Cir.2003). We will consider a fact finding to be clearly erroneous only if, after reviewing all of the evidence, we are left with a definite and firm conviction that a mistake has been committed. *Id.;*

Anderson v. City of Bessemer City, 470 U.S. 564, 573, 105 S.Ct. 1504, 84 L.Ed.2d 518 (1985).

I.

Mathin maintains that his parents had traveled to the United States and were staying at the home of a friend, Thomas Nielsen, in Chicago, Illinois, when Mathin was born in that home on September 25, 1965. According to Mathin, a midwife, Margaret Roper, was present at the birth, as well as the midwife's 17-year-old niece Judith Roper ("Roper"), Thomas Nielsen ("Nielsen"), and Nielsen's mother Ina Nielsen, along with Mathin's mother and father. Of those individuals, only Mathin's father was still living at the time of the district court trial. Mathin further stated that after his birth, he was taken to Norwegian American Hospital for examination.

There are no contemporaneous records available supporting those events. No birth certificate was filed by his parents, the midwife, or the hospital. Mathin was unable to provide any records from Norwegian American Hospital indicating that he was examined there. Mathin testified that he tried to obtain such hospital records but that the hospital had experienced a flood and fire and his records could not be located. He did not provide any evidence from the hospital confirming that records from that time period had been destroyed, or that it had suffered a flood and fire. Furthermore, although the State Department attempted to verify the trip through the visa or passport records, it was unable to find any record of the trip.

Mathin testified that approximately a month after his birth, his mother returned to India with him. He maintained that he traveled on his mother's passport at that time, and that he continued to travel on his mother's Indian passport until his mother's death when he was 13 years old. At that time, his father obtained an Indian passport for him, which identified India as Mathin's place of birth.

Mathin traveled to the United States numerous times using his Indian passport during the 1990s. He resides in Florida with his wife and two children, all of whom are United States citizens. He applied for United States passports for his children in 1993 and 1995. Each time, he represented that he was born in India. The district court found credible Mathin's testimony that he represented his birthplace as India on the advice of his attorney because of his Indian passport.

Mathin applied for a delayed birth certificate with the State of Illinois in 1996, which was also the year that his five-year _{p.807} visa was set to expire leaving him without immigration status. The Illinois Department of Public Health issued him that delayed birth certificate based on two documents submitted by Mathin—an affidavit from Judith Roper attesting that he was born in Chicago, and his 1988 marriage certificate translated into English which listed his birthplace as the United States. In 1996, 2007 and 2010, Mathin applied for a United States passport. He submitted the delayed birth certificate and the underlying documents in support of his 1996 passport application, which was denied. Mathin applied for a passport again in 2007, and in this application he included affidavits purportedly created by his parents in 1966 regarding the circumstances of his birth. Mathin also included a 2007 letter from a lawyer in India named S. Krishnamurthy indicating that he found the affidavits from Mathin's parents after conducting a search of his warehouse. Mathin subsequently withdrew that 2007 passport application. Finally, Mathin submitted another passport application in 2010 which the State Department denied after an investigation.

Mathin brings this action under 8 U.S.C. § 1503(a) which allows anyone who claims a right or privilege as a national of the United States that has been denied to seek a judgment declaring him to be a national of the United States. Pursuant to 22 C.F.R. § 51.40, Mathin has the burden of demonstrating his citizenship by a preponderance of the evidence.

Mathin acknowledges that the burden of proving citizenship rests with him, and that the primary form of documentary evidence to meet that burden is a contemporaneous official birth certificate, which Mathin lacks. See 22 C.F.R. § 51.42(a). He properly contends, however, that the absence of contemporaneous official birth records is not dispositive, and that secondary evidence can establish his birthplace. Such evidence may include, but is not limited to, "hospital birth certificates, baptismal certificates, medical and school records, certificates of circumcision, other documentary evidence created shortly after birth but generally not more than 5 years after birth, and/or affidavits of persons having personal knowledge of the facts of the birth." 22 C.F.R. § 51.42(b).

In addition to his own testimony, Mathin sought to meet that burden by introducing exhibits including: the delayed record of birth issued by the State of Illinois stating that he was born in Chicago; the affidavits purportedly prepared in 1966 by Mathin's mother and father attesting that he was born in Chicago; an affidavit purportedly by Thomas Nielsen addressed to the Consulate General of India in New York and dated October 15, 1965, stating that Mathin was born in his home in Chicago; and videotaped deposition testimony of his father corroborating that he was born in Nielsen's home in Chicago.

The district court considered all of that evidence and Mathin's testimony, and determined that Mathin had failed to meet his burden of establishing by a preponderance of the evidence that he was born in Chicago and therefore was a United States citizen.

II.

Mathin raises a number of challenges to that determination on appeal. First, Mathin argues that the district court erred in the probative weight that it gave to the evidence. Specifically, he asserts that the delayed birth certificate granted by the State of Illinois should have been given more weight by the court and regarded as primary evidence that he was born in the United States. He further asserts that his testimony and the deposition testimony of his father should have been accorded more p.808 weight by the court, and that the affidavits attesting to his birth were admissible as exceptions to the hearsay rule and should have been given significant probative weight. Finally, he argues that the Investigative Management System Report of Investigation ("IMS Report") from the Diplomatic Security Service of the Department of State ("DSS"), proffered by the government at trial, constituted inadmissible hearsay and should not have been considered.

We need not address Mathin's repeated arguments that the affidavits he presented were admissible under exceptions to the hearsay rule, and that the court erred in refusing to consider them, because those arguments are inconsistent with the district court's holding. The district court noted at the outset that the government had objected to the admission of Mathin's exhibits containing the affidavits and the letters from Nielsen on grounds of authenticity and hearsay. The district court explicitly rejected those challenges to admissibility, noting that those objections might be well taken in another type of case, but that the "affidavits are admissible in this proceeding." Dist. Court Findings of Fact and Conclusions of Law After Trial (March 3, 2014) at 11. The court thus concluded that it would weigh all of the evidence introduced by Mathin, and would resolve any doubts as to authenticity and reliability of the hearsay in light of all the evidence in the case. Because the court held that the documents proffered by Mathin were admissible, we consider only Mathin's challenge on appeal to the court's weighing of the evidence and consideration of authenticity and reliability, as well as his challenge to the IMS Report introduced by the government.

A.

We begin with Mathin's challenge to the government's evidence. Mathin asserts that the court erred in admitting the IMS Report under Federal Rule of Evidence 803(8), which provides that a record or statement of a public office is not excluded as hearsay if "it sets out ... factual findings from a legally authorized investigation... and the opponent does not show that the source of information or other circumstances indicate a lack of trustworthiness."

The IMS report reflected the results of the DSS investigation into Mathin's claim that he was born in the United States. The IMS report included information dating back to the 1996 investigation of his first passport application. As part of that investigation, Special Agent Scott Bultrowicz visited Judith Roper's home based on the affidavit she provided attesting to Mathin's birth. The agent spoke with Roper's roommate, Florence Neel, who told him that Roper was pressured into providing the affidavit, and that when Roper learned her actions were illegal, she experienced a nervous breakdown with physical complications for which she was living in a medical care facility at the time of the agent's visit. Neel also stated that she personally had witnessed Mathin offer Roper $500 in return for her assistance in signing the affidavit. The DSS concluded that the Roper affidavit was obtained through coercion and bribery, and Mathin was arrested in 1996 for passport fraud, although he was not subsequently prosecuted.

The 1996 investigation also determined that the marriage certificate was fraudulent in that the original in India did not list a place of birth but the version submitted by Mathin indicated he was born in the United States. The agent investigating the passport application in 2010, Special Agent Benjamin Hammond, relied on those determinations from the 1996 investigation, p.809 and also determined that the affidavits submitted by Mathin that were purportedly from his parents were false or fraudulent because they were not original documents and could not be independently corroborated.

Mathin argues that the court erred in admitting the IMS Report. He asserts that a report following a government investigation is not automatically trustworthy, and that the person making the report must have observed matters firsthand and acted pursuant to a legal duty. Mathin contends that the factual findings and conclusions made by Agent Hammond in the IMS Report relied upon the opinions and conclusions of Agent Bultrowicz in the 1996 investigation, and faults Agent Bultrowicz for failing to interview Roper personally.

The district court properly rejected that challenge to the admissibility of the IMS Report generally. The public records exception of Federal Rule of Evidence 803(8) constitutes a recognition that information may be passed among multiple public officials before being recorded in a document, and accordingly a report will not be excluded merely because the author did not have firsthand knowledge of the reported matters. *Jordan v. Binns,* 712 F.3d 1123, 1133 (7th Cir.2013). Therefore, the inclusion of information from Agent Bultrowicz was not a bar to admissibility. Mathin has presented no support for his argument that the report was inadmissible because the investigation could have been more thorough. Moreover, the district court properly limited its consideration of the IMS Report to merely the conclusion that the affidavit and the marriage certificate were fraudulent. The court did consider the statements by Neel in the report, as those statements were hearsay within hearsay. *Id.* (Rule 803(8) does not remove the hearsay bar for a statement by a nongovernmental third-party contained in a police report.) Accordingly, we find no error in the court's consideration of the IMS Report.

B.

We turn, then, to Mathin's challenges to the court's consideration of his evidence. Mathin first argues that the delayed certificate of birth from the State of Illinois, although not conclusive, should have been considered to be significant evidence that he was a United States citizen. He asserts that such a birth certificate is not casually issued by the State of Illinois and that it is issued only when warranted by the evidence.

The district court recognized that the issuance of the certificate by Illinois was evidence favorable to Mathin's claim of citizenship. In determining the weight to be given to that evidence, however, the court examined the documents which formed the basis for the issuance of that certificate. Mathin testified that in seeking the delayed certificate of birth, he provided the State with an affidavit from Judith Roper, who was the midwife's niece who was present at his birth, a marriage certificate from India that stated his place of birth as the United States, and affidavits from his father and Nielsen. The delayed certificate of birth issued by Illinois references only two documents, the Roper affidavit and the marriage certificate, and states that the certificate was issued based on those documents. Therefore, in assessing the weight to be given to the delayed certificate of birth, the district court properly considered only those two underlying documents. The court determined that there were credibility problems with both of those documents which cast doubt on the conclusion inherent in the delayed birth certificate that he was born in the United States. We defer to a district p.810 court's credibility determinations unless clearly erroneous, and here the holding by the court is well supported in the record. See *Furry v. United States,* 712 F.3d 988, 993 (7th Cir.2013).

First, the marriage certificate from India that Mathin submitted to the court, which was an English translation of the original, listed his place of birth as the United States, but the DSS investigated Mathin's passport application for fraud and determined that the translated marriage certificate was fraudulent. With assistance from the United States Consulate in Mumbai, India, the State Department determined that the original marriage certificate in India listed no place of birth for Mathin and therefore provided no support for his claim of citizenship. The inclusion of a birthplace in the English "translation" was thus fraudulent, and could properly cause the district court to doubt not just the reliability of the delayed certificate of birth, but also the credibility of Mathin in general.

The Roper affidavit presented credibility concerns as well. The district court noted that Roper's affidavit stated that Mathin was born in the Humboldt Park community, a neighborhood on the northwest side of Chicago, which was inconsistent with Mathin's claim that he was born in the 10900 block of South St. Louis, a southwest side region, and with Mathin's statement in another document that his mother lived at 10733 South St. Louis Avenue one year before his birth. Moreover, the court stated that the timing of the documents was suspicious in that both documents were submitted by Mathin at the time he was applying for a United States passport. Finally, the court considered that the State Department had determined that the Roper affidavit was fraudulent. Mathin argues that the court erred in concluding that the Roper affidavit was inadmissible hearsay, but as we have stated the court in fact held that it was admissible.

In the end, though, the fundamental difficulty with Mathin's argument is that he ultimately seeks a reweighing of the facts from this court, and that is not the province of this court on appeal. It is of no value on appeal to argue that the district court could have found in his favor. We will accept the court's fact findings unless they are clearly erroneous—that is unless we are left with a definite and firm conviction that a mistake has been made. *Buechel v. United States,* 746 F.3d 753, 756 (7th Cir.2014); *Anderson,* 470 U.S. at 573, 105 S.Ct. 1504. "As long as the district court's conclusions are 'plausible in light of the record viewed in its entirety,' we will not disturb them." *Buechel,* 746 F.3d at 756, quoting *Anderson,* 470 U.S. at 573-74, 105 S.Ct. 1504. Mathin fails to present arguments that would approach that burden, and therefore cannot succeed in his challenge.

That problem is apparent as well in his challenge to the court's treatment of his testimony and that of his father. Mathin decries the district court's decision to give little probative value to the testimony of Mathin and his father Ziaudeen, but again ultimately he seeks a reweighing of the evidence that is inappropriate on appeal. For instance, he challenges the court's failure to credit the testimony of his father. Ziaudeen testified that Mathin was born in the home of Nielsen, a family friend, in Chicago, and that Nielsen arranged for the family's travel back to India. Ziaudeen further stated that it was not until Mathin was 18 years old that he informed Mathin that Mathin was born in the United States.

The district court's determination that Ziaudeen lacked credibility is well-supported. Ziaudeen's testimony was inconsistent on a number of critical issues. For instance, evidence was introduced at trial p.811 that a special agent from the Chennai consulate interviewed Ziaudeen, and that he stated that he had traveled with his wife to the United States, but that he had to depart for Hong Kong and left his wife in the care of Nielsen in Chicago, where she prematurely delivered a baby boy. He told the agent that he did not know whether the baby was born at home or in the hospital, and stated that one month later his wife came back to

India with the baby. He further stated that his wife was uneducated and did not register the baby's birth, and that he did not keep in contact with Nielsen. That was inconsistent with his deposition testimony that he was present at Mathin's birth and that they departed for India together. Details such as the presence at the birth of one's child are the type of facts that a person would be expected to remember. It was also inconsistent with Mathin's testimony that Nielsen was a close family friend who kept in touch by sending numerous greetings cards over the years following Mathin's birth.

The district court noted a number of discrepancies in Ziaudeen's testimony such as his explanation as to why he created the 1966 affidavit with his attorney regarding the place of Mathin's birth. Ziaudeen initially testified that he created the 1966 affidavit for Mathin to obtain an Indian passport, but later stated it was to get Mathin into school although Mathin was less than a year old at the time of the affidavit. The district court could properly deem Ziaudeen's testimony incredible in light of the inconsistencies.

Mathin nevertheless asserts that the court erred in finding that Ziaudeen lacked credibility, arguing that Ziaudeen suffered from health problems and the court should have considered that in assessing any inconsistencies. The court heard the testimony regarding those health problems, however, and there is nothing in the record that indicates the court disregarded that in making the credibility determination. Mathin wants us to make a contrary credibility determination, but the finding by the court was not clearly erroneous and it is not our role to reweigh evidence. See *Furry,* 712 F.3d at 993. Moreover, the health issues that Mathin points to as an explanation for the inconsistencies are not the type of issues that would impact memory or the ability to effectively relay information. The only health issues established in the record concern Ziaudeen's difficulties in standing or sitting for long periods of time, and his age of 79. There was no evidence of any issues with memory or mental health that would impact his ability to recall facts. In fact, Mathin acknowledged in his testimony at trial that his father did not have cognitive problems or difficulties with memory generally. Nor is Mathin arguing that a prior recollection is more reliable; Mathin instead is asserting that as to testimony given on the same date, one response should be credited over another. The district court did not clearly err in considering the testimony as a whole, and in light of the circumstances as a whole, determining that Ziaudeen's testimony was not credible.

Similarly, there was no error in the court's failure to credit Mathin's testimony as to where he was born. His knowledge stemmed only from his claims that Ziaudeen and Asiaumma told him that he was born in the United States. Although Mathin argues that his reputation among his family was that he was born in the United States, he did not provide evidence from any of his five living siblings corroborating that fact. Mathin argues that his mother's statement was not inadmissible hearsay because Federal Rule of Evidence 804 allows testimony as to a declarant's family history if the declarant is unavailable as a witness. The district court found that Mathin's testimony, which was p.812 not based on first-hand knowledge but was based on purported statements from his parents, was of little value. We have already discussed the court's credibility determination as to Mathin's father Ziaudeen. As to Mathin's claim that his mother told him he was born in the United States, Mathin's testimony was internally inconsistent on that point. He stated that his mother did not tell him he was born in the United States until he was 13 years old, at which time she told him in the presence of Ziaudeen. Yet Mathin acknowledged that he did not recall her telling him that information, and that his knowledge stemmed solely from Ziaudeen's retelling of the conversation. On cross-examination, Mathin stated that his mother never told him that he was born in the United States. Therefore, the district court did not err in failing to find that testimony probative of his birthplace.

Finally, Mathin asserts that the court erred in failing to credit the 1966 affidavits that he submitted in support of his claim from his mother and father, and from Krishnamurthy. The 2007 letter from Krishnamurthy stated that he had located affidavits from Ziaudeen and Asiaumma upon a search of his warehouse. He also attested that he witnessed the signatures of Ziaudeen and Asiaumma on their affidavits. The affidavits of Ziaudeen and Asiaumma recite that they traveled to the United States where Asiaumma delivered Mathin in Chicago on September 9, 1965. The affidavits from Mathin's parents were purportedly created in 1966, but the district court properly determined that those documents should not be credited.

Under Federal Rule of Evidence 803(16), statements in an ancient document that is at least 20 years old and whose authenticity is established are not excluded as hearsay. The district court noted that it had significant doubts as to the authenticity of the documents under Federal Rule of Evidence 901(b)(8), which provides that an ancient document can be authenticated by showing that it is at least 20 years old, was in a place where, if authentic, it would likely be, and is in a condition that creates no suspicion about its authenticity. The requirement that the document be free of suspicion relates not to the content of the document, but rather to whether the document is what it purports to be, and the issue falls within the trial court's discretion. *United States v. Firishchak,* 468 F.3d 1015, 1021 (7th Cir. 2006); *United States v. Kairys,* 782 F.2d 1374, 1379 (7th Cir.1986); *United States v. Kalymon,* 541 F.3d 624, 632-33 (6th Cir. 2008). "[T]he mere recitation of the contents of documents does not authenticate them or provide for their admissibility." *Firishchak,* 468 F.3d at 1021.

The district court properly held that there was reason to doubt that the affidavits were what they purported to be. Although the affidavits were purportedly created approximately nine months after Mathin's birth, the affidavits lacked any details that might be expected in a document created shortly after such an event, such as precisely where Mathin was born, arrival and departure dates for their travel, and contact information as to Nielsen or other witnesses. Significantly, the affidavits also lacked any declared purpose for their creation. The testimony of Ziaudeen's father as to the purpose of the affidavits was notably inconsistent. Ziaudeen first testified that he did not have any idea as to why he would have created such an affidavit in 1966. Subsequently in the deposition, Ziaudeen testified that he created the affidavit to help Mathin obtain an Indian passport. An affidavit attesting to his birth in the United States, however, could not aid in securing an Indian passport for Mathin. Moreover, Mathin testified p.813 that he traveled on his mother's Indian passport until he was 13 years old, which is also inconsistent with the notion that the affidavit was created in order to secure an Indian passport for Mathin. The court did not err in concluding that the failure to identify any purpose for the affidavit, as well as the dearth of details in the affidavit itself, cast doubt on the claim that it was in fact created by his parents in 1966. The fortuitous timing of Krishnamurthy's discovery of the affidavit in the warehouse further creates doubt as to the legitimacy of the affidavits, as does the court's determination that Ziaudeen's testimony was incredible. Those findings are well-supported in the record, and the court did not err in determining that those affidavits were not reliable evidence as to his birth.

Finally, Mathin presented an affidavit addressed to the Consulate General of India in New York dated October 15, 1965—approximately one month after Mathin's birth—signed by Thomas Nielsen and witnessed by Margaret Roper, Ina Nielsen and Judith Roper, affirming that Mathin was born at Nielsen's house on September 23, 1965. The stated purpose of the affidavit was to obtain a travel permit to travel to India, and Nielsen allegedly discovered the document among his mother Ina Nielsen's possessions upon her death. Mathin also submitted an affidavit from Nielsen dated April 13, 2000 declaring that the 1965 affidavit was true and correct and was provided to the Indian Consulate General to allow Mathin to travel to India. A notary attested that the signature in that April 2000 affidavit was that of Nielsen.

There are myriad problems with this affidavit, including once again difficulties in establishing that the document was in fact created at the stated date. Mathin failed to establish the date of origin, nor was there any basis to conclude that the document was kept in a place where, if authentic, it would likely be. As the district court noted, Mathin failed to explain why Ina Nielsen would have had in her possession an original letter delivered to the Indian Consulate General in 1965. Nor is it conceivable that Nielsen would create and forward such an affidavit to establish the birth, yet not assist Mathin's parents in simply obtaining a birth certificate for Mathin at the time of birth, particularly given Mathin's claim that he was taken for examination to a hospital following his birth. Mathin also failed to produce any evidence that under Indian law in 1965 an undocumented infant could travel on his mother's passport. The insurmountable obstacle to credibility, however, is the uncontested evidence that Nielsen's signature on the April 2000 affidavit which was verified by the notary is starkly different from the signature on the 1965 affidavit. Mathin asserts that signatures may change over time, but the differences in the handwriting are so stark that Mathin acknowledged to the district court that the signatures were in fact different. Mathin submitted three greeting cards that he claimed to have received from Nielsen, and there is no dispute that those signatures were also distinct from the others; in fact the name Nielsen was even spelled differently, as "Nelson," in those cards. The district court properly determined that those disparities created a strong reason to suspect that the Nielsen affidavit was fraudulent. There is no error in that quite reasonable conclusion. In short, although Mathin has presented multiple arguments as to why the district court could have reached different fact findings in this case, he has failed to demonstrate that the district court's findings were clearly erroneous.

The court's determination is well-supported in the record. Accordingly, the p.814 decision of the district court is AFFIRMED.

802 F.3d 884 (2015)

Fedell CAFFEY, Petitioner-Appellant,

v.

Kim BUTLER, Warden, Respondent-Appellee.

No. 13-3454.

United States Court of Appeals, Seventh Circuit.

Argued October 29, 2014.

Decided September 22, 2015.

Caffey v. Butler, 802 F. 3d 884 (7th Cir. 2015)

p.887 Patricia G. Mysza, Attorney, Office of the State Appellate Defender, Chicago, IL, Alan Michael Freedman, Attorney, Evanston, IL, for Petitioner-Appellant.

Leah Myers Bendik, Katherine M. Doersch, Attorneys, Office of the Attorney General, Chicago, IL, for Respondent-Appellee.

Before RIPPLE, KANNE, and SYKES, Circuit Judges.

KANNE, Circuit Judge.

Fedell Caffey is serving a life sentence in Illinois on triple-murder and aggravated kidnapping convictions. Caffey maintains he is innocent. He petitioned the district court for a writ of habeas corpus, claiming that his trial and post-conviction proceedings in state court were marred by numerous violations of his constitutional rights. The district court held an evidentiary hearing, thoroughly reviewed the record, and issued a detailed opinion denying Caffey's petition. We affirm the district court's denial of Caffey's habeas corpus petition.

I. BACKGROUND

On the night of November 16, 1995, Debra Evans was fatally shot and stabbed in her apartment in Addison, Illinois. She was nine months pregnant. The assailants cut open her womb and removed the unborn baby inside, whom Debra had named Elijah. Debra also had three older children — Samantha (age 10), Joshua (age 7), and Jordan (age 2). Samantha was killed in the apartment along with her mother. Elijah and Joshua were taken from the scene. Two-year-old Jordan was left behind, alive, with his dead mother and sister. The next day, police found Joshua's lifeless body in an alley in Maywood, Illinois.

Police arrested Debra's former boyfriend Laverne Ward, who was the father of Jordan and Elijah — the only children who survived. Police also arrested Ward's cousin Jacqueline Annette Williams and her live-in boyfriend Fedell Caffey, the defendant-petitioner in this case. A grand jury indicted Ward, Williams, and Caffey on multiple counts of first-degree murder and aggravated kidnapping. Each defendant was tried separately.

In 1999, a jury found Caffey guilty of the first-degree murder of Debra, Samantha, and Joshua, as well as the aggravated kidnapping of Joshua. Caffey received a sentence of death on the murder convictions and a consecutive thirty-year prison term on the aggravated kidnapping conviction. In 2003, Illinois Governor George Ryan commuted Caffey's death sentence to life without parole.

Caffey claims in this appeal that his trial was fundamentally unfair because certain evidence was excluded or otherwise not presented to the jury. In order to assess his claims, we first have to take stock of the evidence that *was* presented — a lengthy endeavor given the voluminous trial record. In doing so, we walk on well-trodden ground: the state court decisions under review and the district court decision below already provide detailed summaries of the evidence. We assume familiarity with those opinions and highlight only the most relevant facts here. We presume that the state courts' account of p.888 the facts is accurate, unless the petitioner rebuts this presumption "by clear and convincing evidence." 28 U.S.C. § 2254(e)(1); *see also Etherly v. Davis*, 619 F.3d 654, 660 (7th Cir.2010).

A. The Case against Caffey

The State's theory at trial was that Williams faked a pregnancy with Caffey's knowledge, and that Williams, Caffey, and Ward planned to kill Debra Evans, steal her unborn child, and pass the child off as Williams and Caffey's. Williams and Caffey were unable to conceive their own child naturally because Williams had had tubal ligation years earlier in connection with a caesarian birth. And Ward was driven to act, according to the State, because he was angry at Debra for preventing him from seeing his son Jordan.

The State's evidence at trial tended to show the following. James Edwards, who lived with Debra and her children in Addison, left for work around 5:30 p.m. on November 16. When he returned at 2:30 a.m. the next morning, two-year-old Jordan greeted him at the door. Edwards found Debra's and Samantha's bodies and immediately called 911. Several items were missing from the apartment, including Edwards's Grambling State University Tigers Starter jacket.

1. The Testimony of Scott and Pruitt

Williams's friend Patrice Scott and her boyfriend Dwight Pruitt testified that Williams showed up at their apartment in Villa Park, Illinois, around 1 a.m. on November 17 accompanied by a young boy, who turned out to be Joshua Evans. Williams was wearing a Starter jacket and a white sweater spotted with blood. Joshua was wearing a T-shirt, coat, and boots, but no pants or socks. Scott noticed a gray car parked outside. Williams told Scott that the boy's mother had been shot and asked whether he could spend the night at Scott and Pruitt's home. Scott agreed. Williams said she would pick Joshua up in the morning. She also claimed to have just given birth to a baby. (A month earlier, she had told Scott she was pregnant.)

Scott heard Joshua crying during the night. Joshua was still crying in the early morning, when he told Scott that he needed to go home because his younger brother Jordan was there alone, and because Edwards would not know where he (Joshua) was. Joshua explained that four burglars had entered his home and cut his mother and sister. Scott asked who they were, and Joshua answered: "Annette, Levern, and Fedell," and someone Joshua called "Boo Boo." Joshua repeated this statement more than three times. He explained that he was hiding but came out as the burglars left, ran outside, and then bumped into Williams.

Pruitt overheard Joshua's comments from the bedroom, where Pruitt was watching television with the volume lowered. He testified that Joshua said: "Annette"; "Vern"; a name that sounded like "Vedelle", "Adelle", or "Ladelle"; and a fourth name Pruitt could not make out.

Around 9 a.m. on November 17, Williams returned, driving the same gray car that Scott had seen the night before. Scott told Williams what Joshua had said. Williams became angry, cursed at Joshua, and accused him of lying. Joshua insisted he was telling the truth. Williams told Joshua to take his medicine, but he said he did not take any medicine. Williams led him to the kitchen; the boy soon emerged gagging, went to the bathroom, and vomited. Police later found an empty iodine bottle in the kitchen garbage can.

Williams asked Scott to accompany her to the townhouse where Williams and Caffey lived in Schaumburg, Illinois. Williams explained that she wanted to check on her newborn baby, and that she p.889 also had some gifts for Scott's infant daughter Alexis. Scott agreed to go along. She, Williams, and Joshua left the apartment. Scott asked Pruitt to watch Alexis, but he refused, so Scott brought Alexis with her.

While they were gone, Pruitt saw a television report on the Evans murders and recognized Joshua's picture. Pruitt left the apartment looking for a telephone but could not find one that worked. Unsuccessful, he returned home.

When Scott arrived at Williams and Caffey's home, she went upstairs with Williams while Joshua watched Alexis in the living room. Scott testified that she saw Caffey lying on a bed with a "really pale" baby who had "tape across his navel." Scott went back downstairs to feed Alexis. Later, Williams called Scott down to the lower level, where the garage and laundry room were located. Williams asked Scott to bring Joshua downstairs, which she did.

Waiting in the lower-level laundry room were Caffey, Williams, and an unidentified man, who soon left. Scott testified that she heard Caffey ask Williams why she had not taken Joshua "to the projects" as he instructed. Williams explained that Joshua "talked too much" and knew their names. Caffey and Williams then began to strangle Joshua with a white cord. Scott screamed and pushed Williams, forcing her to release her end of the cord. Williams left and returned with a knife. Scott screamed again and asked Williams to take them home. Scott took Joshua upstairs and tried to leave, but the door was locked. Scott went back down to the laundry room with Joshua and Alexis. Caffey warned Scott not to say anything or else he would "get me and my daughters."

Caffey then instructed Williams to take Scott home. They all went to the garage and got into the gray car. Scott was in the front passenger seat with Alexis. Joshua was behind her in the back seat, and Caffey was sitting next to him. Williams was standing along the driver's side and appeared to be holding Joshua. Scott testified that she saw Caffey repeatedly stab Joshua, causing him to gasp and kick the front seat.

Williams then climbed into the driver's seat and drove to Maywood, where she and Caffey took Joshua out of the car, took him to the back of a building, and then returned without him. Williams left Caffey in Maywood and took Scott back to her apartment. They arrived around 12:15 p.m. At Williams's request, Scott gave her cleaning supplies.

Pruitt observed that Scott seemed to be "trying to get rid of [Williams]." Pruitt told Scott to lock the door while he went to call the police. On his way out, he saw Williams cleaning her car. Pruitt called the police from a nearby hair salon. Scott subsequently led them to the location in Maywood where Williams and Caffey had taken Joshua. Police recovered Joshua's dead body in a nearby alley. They then drove to Williams and Caffey's home and arrested them. At the time of arrest, Williams was carrying Elijah, who had a bloody piece of gauze taped over his navel. Caffey was wearing Edwards's Starter jacket, which had blood stains on the right cuff.

2. Physical and Forensic Evidence

The State presented the following physical and forensic evidence. In the Evans apartment, investigators found Williams's bloody fingerprint on a piece of paper. On the sidewalk in front of the apartment, they found a pair of poultry shears covered with Samantha's blood. Police did not find Caffey's fingerprints or DNA in the Evans apartment.

Police searched Williams and Caffey's house. In a garbage bag in the garage, p.890 they found a white coaxial cable with Joshua's blood on it; Scott identified it as the cable used to strangle Joshua. In the dishwasher, police recovered a butcher knife, which Scott identified as the knife that Caffey used to stab Joshua. On the kitchen counter were two counterfeit birth certificates stating that Williams gave birth to a baby, fathered by Caffey, on November 16, 1995. The certificates had been prepared on a typewriter belonging to a woman named Vikki Iacullo. In Williams and Caffey's closet, police found a bedsheet and pillowcase that matched the bloodstained sheet discovered seven blocks from Joshua's body. (The blood was Joshua's.) On the backseat carpet in Williams and Caffey's car, police found Joshua's blood, which had been treated with cleaner.

Iacullo and Dorothy Hale later directed police to a lake in Wheaton, where they found the gun used to shoot Debra Evans. Iacullo invoked her Fifth Amendment privilege and refused to testify. She was later charged with obstruction of justice.

Several doctors testified about the forensic evidence. According to them, the main cause of Debra Evans's death was a gunshot wound to the head. She also had multiple stab wounds, including a thirteen-inch jagged incision across her abdomen consistent with poultry shears. Based on blood spatters around Debra's body and the fact that her baby (Elijah) survived, Debra's obstetrician opined that she was still alive when Elijah was cut from her womb. The doctor opined further that two or three sets of hands would have been necessary to perform such a procedure.

Samantha had defensive wounds on her arms and incisions on her neck, which were also consistent with poultry shears. Joshua's neck bore ligature marks consistent with strangulation and stab wounds consistent with a butcher knife. Joshua's right lung was aspirated, meaning he inhaled his own vomit, causing damage consistent with the ingestion of iodine. His wounds and the lack of defensive marks suggested that he may have been restrained.

3. Other Witnesses' Testimony

Other witnesses provided additional details about the defendants' activities leading up to and on the night of the murders. Dawn Killeen knew Williams and Caffey because she was their neighbor, and because her husband dealt drugs with Caffey and Ward. Killeen testified that she went to Williams and Caffey's house in May 1995 to borrow a vacuum cleaner. Ward stormed in "yelling and screaming that Debbie [Evans] wasn't allowing him to see Jordan." Ward "said he was tired of her shit and he wanted to .... kill the bitch." He punched a hole in the wall. Caffey asked Ward whether he wanted a gun or a knife. Vikki Iacullo was also there. Killeen overheard them talking about a baby.

Williams's cousin John Pettaway saw Williams, Caffey, and Ward together on the day of the murders. Pettaway and Ward were together that afternoon, smoking crack cocaine and driving around Wheaton. They twice encountered Caffey and Williams, and on each occasion Ward got out of the car to speak with them for 15 minutes or so. Ward told Pettaway several times that he (Ward) needed to find Caffey.

Kassandra Turner, Williams's friend, testified that Caffey called her on the evening of November 16 to tell her that he and Williams were going to have the baby. Williams had told Turner months earlier that she was pregnant. The following day, Caffey reported to Turner that Williams had given birth to a "real light skinned" baby boy.

Jacci Sullivan and Tennie Clay lived in Evans's apartment complex. Sullivan testified p.891 that she heard a shot between 8:30 and 9:30 p.m. on November 16. Clay said she heard voices outside around 9:15 p.m., looked out her window, and saw four people talking on a sidewalk. She believed three were African-American and the other was a light-skinned Hispanic. One of them was wearing a dark Starter jacket.

Joy Wilson, age 15, and her aunt Tiffany Wilson, age 16, were babysitting at Tiffany's house on the night of November 16. Tiffany was Ward's and Williams's cousin. Joy and Tiffany testified that Ward entered the house that night carrying a plastic bag stuffed full of what looked like clothing. Joy said she noticed a hole in Ward's pants and blood on his clothes. Ward went to the bathroom and emerged wearing different clothes; the grocery bag appeared fuller. Joy was frightened by the family dog and ran outside. There, she saw a gray car with three people inside: two men in the front and a woman in the back. She later identified two of them as Caffey and Williams. They were honking and calling for Ward. Ward got in the car and they drove off.

Mohammid Siddiqui, a clerk at 7-Eleven in Schaumburg, testified that Caffey and a woman matching Williams's description entered his store on November 17 between 1:30 and 2:00 in the morning. Caffey bought baby wipes and candy. The store register recorded a sale at 1:49 a.m. for one item at $1.99, which is the cost of baby wipes, and one item at $0.99.

Williams called her sister, Tina Martin, around 3:30 a.m. on November 17 and told her the baby had arrived. Tina and her mother drove to Iacullo's house, where they saw Williams, Iacullo, Caffey, and the baby. The baby's complexion was so light that neither Martin nor her mother believed it really was Williams and Caffey's. Tina and her mother left after just a few minutes.

B. Caffey's Defense

Caffey maintained (and still maintains) his innocence. The defense's theory of the case was that Williams was possessive and jealous, so she planned to trap Caffey by faking a pregnancy, stealing Elijah Evans, and then passing him off as their child. Williams allegedly conspired with Ward and Iacullo to pull off her plan.

The defense introduced evidence of Williams's jealousy. She had good reason to be jealous: Caffey began dating Williams in 1994 but continued to have sexual relationships with other women, including his former girlfriend, Katrina Montgomery, with whom he had a child. Williams did not like Caffey's relationship with Katrina, and the two women had physical and verbal altercations from 1994 through 1995. Williams also had a history of feigning pregnancies, according to Caffey and another witness.

In February 1995, Williams told Caffey she was pregnant. Caffey testified that he did not know about Williams's tubal ligation or her inability to conceive any more children. Williams first told him the baby was due in August but then changed the date to mid-October. When that date passed, Caffey stopped believing she was pregnant.

Caffey testified that he was at home in Schaumburg with Williams's children on the night of the murders. Williams went out around 7:15 p.m. on November 16. Shortly after that, Joyce Hotz came over and bought drugs from Caffey. Then Caffey watched New York Undercover with Williams's daughter Christina from 8 until 9 p.m., when the girl went to bed. At 1:30 a.m., Williams still had not come home. Caffey grew worried and went to the nearby 7-Eleven to use a pay phone. He called Martin and asked her to page Williams. Caffey denied buying baby wipes at that time.

p.892 Caffey admitted calling Turner earlier that evening but denied telling her that he and Williams were going to have a baby. According to Caffey, Turner had bought drugs from him the previous day, and he was calling to inform her that her check had bounced. Caffey also admitted to meeting with Ward earlier in the day, but only to sell drugs — not to plan any murders.

Caffey testified that he saw Iacullo's car pull into his driveway around 2:30 a.m. Caffey went outside and saw Williams in the car with a baby. Back inside the house, Iacullo explained that Williams had gone into labor at Iacullo's house. They went to a hospital, where Williams gave birth, but they had to leave because Williams did not have insurance. Caffey was initially skeptical of their story but seeing the baby's umbilical cord bleeding somehow convinced him it was true. They all went to Iacullo's house to get Williams's car. While there, Williams called Martin and gave her the news.

Caffey testified that he and Williams then left Iacullo's house and returned to the 7-Eleven a little before 5 a.m. It was at that time, according to Caffey, that he bought baby wipes. The store register recorded a purchase of an item for $1.99, the cost of baby wipes, at 4:49 a.m. They returned home, and Caffey fell asleep next to the baby. He stayed there most of the day. That night, Caffey, Williams, and the baby went to Iacullo's house, where Iacullo gave Caffey a Grambling Starter jacket as a "Daddy's Day present." When Williams and Caffey returned home, they were arrested.

In addition to presenting Caffey's version of events, the defense attacked the credibility of the State's witnesses and drew out inconsistencies in their testimony. Patrice Scott admitted on cross-examination that she did not contact the police, despite Joshua's naming of the four burglars, Williams's administration of Joshua's "medicine," and other suspicious behavior. Moreover, Scott did not tell any of the investigating officers who initially interviewed her that Joshua had named Caffey as one of the burglars. Scott explained that she was afraid to name Caffey because he had threatened to hurt her and her family.

Pruitt admitted that he was serving a prison sentence for a weapons charge, was a gang member, and had prior convictions. He conceded that he did not initially call the police. And when he did eventually call the police, he did not tell them about the names Joshua had mentioned. Nor did he report that information to the investigating officers who initially interviewed him. Pruitt explained, however, that he was not formally interviewed on those occasions.

The defense theorized that Pruitt and Scott were falsely implicating Caffey in the murders, perhaps to minimize their own culpability. Another possible reason was that Scott feared Bo Wilson, who may have been the fourth burglar, the one Joshua called "Boo Boo." Wilson may also have been the unidentified man who was in the laundry room at Williams and Caffey's house. Scott denied that the man was Wilson. But a detective testified that about a month-and-a-half later, Scott told him Wilson was the man in the laundry room.

The defense elicited testimony to impeach other witnesses too. For example, Kassandra Turner, who testified that Caffey called her on November 16 to say that he and Williams were going to have a baby, did not relay that information to police until more than two months after the crimes. Joy Wilson did not initially tell police that she had seen any specific people in the gray car outside Tiffany's house. And Mohammid Siddiqui, the 7-Eleven p.893 clerk, recalled seeing Caffey in the store only after police showed him a photograph.

Finally, the defense called witnesses whose testimony tended to show that Iacullo supplied the gun for the murders and disposed of it afterward by throwing it in a pond. She burned several documents in one witness's kitchen but saved a birth certificate with Caffey's name on it. The witnesses also implicated Dorothy Hale in these acts.

After deliberating, the jury found Caffey guilty of the first-degree murder of Evans, Samantha, and Joshua, as well as the aggravated kidnapping of Joshua.

C. Post-Conviction Procedural History

In February 2000, Caffey appealed his conviction and sentence to the Illinois Supreme Court. He raised numerous arguments, including that: (1) the trial court improperly excluded hearsay statements made by Ward, Williams, and Iacullo, and thereby deprived Caffey of the ability to mount an effective defense; (2) his trial counsel was constitutionally ineffective for failing to introduce statements by Iacullo and Hale that the trial court had ruled admissible; and (3) the trial court improperly admitted Joshua's hearsay statements naming Caffey as one of the assailants. The Illinois Supreme Court affirmed the trial court's judgment in a detailed opinion. *People v. Caffey*, 205 Ill.2d 52, 275 Ill.Dec. 390, 792 N.E.2d 1163 (2001) ("*Caffey I*"). The U.S. Supreme Court denied Caffey's petition for a writ of certiorari. *Caffey v. Illinois*, 536 U.S. 944, 122 S.Ct. 2629, 153 L.Ed.2d 810 (2002).

In April 2000, while his direct appeal was pending, Caffey filed a petition for post-conviction relief in the Circuit Court of DuPage County. Because Caffey was under a sentence of death, the court appointed counsel to represent him in the post-conviction proceedings. The case was then repeatedly continued. Meanwhile, Caffey served subpoenas, deposed Pruitt, and gathered other evidence. In 2004, Caffey amended his post-conviction petition. He alleged, among other things, that the State violated its obligations under *Brady v. Maryland*, 373 U.S. 83, 83 S.Ct. 1194, 10 L.Ed.2d 215 (1963), by failing to disclose that: (1) Pruitt received special benefits because he knew about drug sales to one of the prosecuting attorneys, Assistant State's Attorney ("ASA") Jeffrey Kendall; (2) ASA Thomas Epach interceded to prevent Cook County from prosecuting Scott for Joshua's murder; and (3) Cara Walker told police that Iacullo sold drugs to Kendall and said that she would reveal this information if charged for the Evans murders. The trial court dismissed Caffey's petition for post-conviction relief. The Illinois Appellate Court affirmed, *People v. Caffey*, No. 2-05-0787, slip op., 379 Ill. App.3d 1081, 354 Ill.Dec. 275, 957 N.E.2d 591 (Ill.App.Ct. Apr. 7, 2008) ("*Caffey II*"), and the Illinois Supreme Court denied Caffey's petition for leave to appeal, *People v. Caffey*, 229 Ill.2d 633, 325 Ill.Dec. 8, 897 N.E.2d 256 (Ill.2008).

In September 2009, Caffey filed a petition for a writ of habeas corpus in the Northern District of Illinois. He renewed the arguments enumerated above from his direct appeal and his post-conviction petition in Illinois. The district court granted an evidentiary hearing to further develop the factual basis for Caffey's *Brady* claims relating to Scott and Iacullo. *Caffey v. Atchison*, No. 09 C 5458, 2012 WL 5230298 (N.D.Ill. Feb. 3, 2012) ("*Caffey III*"). After discovery, Caffey dropped the *Brady* claim concerning Scott, leaving only the claims concerning Pruitt and Iacullo.

On October 7, 2013, the district court denied Caffey's habeas petition on the merits. *Caffey v. Harrington*, No. 09 C p.894 5458, 2013 WL 5529760 (N.D.Ill. Oct. 7, 2013) ("*Caffey IV*"). The court acknowledged, however, that its ruling was "fairly debatable," so it granted a certificate of appealability. *Id.* at *34.

This appeal followed. Caffey renews all of his arguments below, except for the portion of his ineffective-assistance claim concerning Dorothy Hale and his challenge to the admission of Joshua Evans's hearsay statements.

II. ANALYSIS

We review *de novo* a district court's denial of a habeas corpus petition. *Smith v. McKee*, 598 F.3d 374, 381 (7th Cir.2010). A state prisoner is entitled to seek habeas relief on the ground that he is being held in violation of federal law or the U.S. Constitution. 28 U.S.C. § 2254(a). But if a state court has already adjudicated the petitioner's claim on the merits, the Antiterrorism and Effective Death Penalty Act ("AEDPA") precludes habeas relief unless the state court's decision "was contrary to, or involved an unreasonable application of, clearly established Federal law, as determined by the Supreme Court of the United States" or "was based on an unreasonable determination of the facts in light of the evidence presented in the State court proceeding." 28 U.S.C. § 2254(d).

"Clearly established Federal law" refers to the holdings of the Supreme Court that existed at the time of the relevant state court adjudication on the merits. *Greene v. Fisher*, ___ U.S. ___, 132 S.Ct. 38, 44, 181 L.Ed.2d 336 (2011); *Williams v. Taylor*, 529 U.S. 362, 412, 120 S.Ct. 1495, 146 L.Ed.2d 389 (2000). A decision is "contrary to" federal law if the state court applied an incorrect rule — *i.e.*, one that "contradicts the governing law" established by the Supreme Court — or reached an outcome different from the Supreme Court's conclusion in a case with "materially indistinguishable" facts. *Williams*, 529 U.S. at 405-06, 120 S.Ct. 1495. A state court unreasonably applies federal law when it "identifies the appropriate standard but applies it to the facts in a manner with which a reasonable court would disagree." *Etherly v. Davis*, 619 F.3d 654, 660 (7th Cir.2010) (citing *Williams*, 529 U.S. at 413, 120 S.Ct. 1495, and *Williams v. Thurmer*, 561 F.3d 740, 742-43 (7th Cir.2009) (per curiam)). Mere error is not enough to overcome AEDPA deference; instead, the state court's decision must be objectively unreasonable, *Etherly*, 619 F.3d at 660, meaning it is "beyond any possibility for fairminded disagreement," *Mosley v. Atchison*, 689 F.3d 838, 844 (7th Cir.2012) (quoting *Harrington v. Richter*, 562 U.S. 86, 103, 131 S.Ct. 770, 178 L.Ed.2d 624 (2011)).

Where a state court's decision is "contrary to" federal law, or where no state court adjudicated the particular claim on the merits in the first place, AEDPA deference does not apply. *See Ruhl v. Hardy*, 743 F.3d 1083, 1091 (7th Cir.2014); *Mosley*, 689 F.3d at 844. In that event, we review the petitioner's claim under the pre-AEDPA standard of 28 U.S.C. § 2243 and dispose of the matter "as law and justice require," which is essentially *de novo* review. *Eichwedel v. Chandler*, 696 F.3d 660, 671 (7th Cir.2012) (citing *Morales v. Johnson*, 659 F.3d 588, 599 (7th Cir.2011)).

With those principles in mind, we turn to the issues on appeal.

A. Exclusion of Hearsay Statements

Caffey contends, first, that the trial court improperly excluded several hearsay statements by Iacullo, Ward, and Williams. According to Caffey, the Constitution guaranteed him the right to present those statements to the jury. We disagree.

p.895 *1. The Right to Present a Defense*

A criminal defendant has a constitutional right, grounded in the Sixth and Fourteenth Amendments, to "a meaningful opportunity to present a complete defense." *Crane v. Kentucky*, 476 U.S. 683, 690, 106 S.Ct. 2142, 90 L.Ed.2d 636 (1986) (internal quotation marks and citation omitted). That includes the right to present relevant evidence. *United States v. Scheffer*, 523 U.S. 303, 308, 118 S.Ct. 1261, 140 L.Ed.2d 413 (1998). Of course, that right is not unfettered but is instead subject to the states' "broad latitude ... to establish rules excluding evidence from criminal trials." *Id.* In some instances, however, strict application of a state evidentiary rule must yield to the defendant's constitutional rights.

The leading example is *Chambers v. Mississippi*, 410 U.S. 284, 93 S.Ct. 1038, 35 L.Ed.2d 297 (1973), where the Supreme Court vindicated a defendant's right to present reliable, critical evidence that would otherwise have been excluded by a state hearsay rule. Leon Chambers was convicted of murdering a police officer during a melee in a local bar. One witness testified that he saw Chambers shoot the officer. 410 U.S. at 286, 93 S.Ct. 1038. But another man named McDonald had confessed to the murder on several occasions, including in a sworn statement to Chambers's counsel. McDonald was arrested but later repudiated his confession. *Id.* at 287-88, 93 S.Ct. 1038.

Chambers called McDonald as a witness at trial. The court admitted McDonald's written confession into evidence, but McDonald again repudiated it. The court prevented Chambers from cross-examining McDonald and challenging his repudiation based on the common-law "voucher rule" that a party may not impeach his own witness. *Id.* at 295, 93 S.Ct. 1038. Chambers then sought to introduce the testimony of three witnesses to whom McDonald had admitted he was the shooter. The trial court excluded their testimony as hearsay. *Id.* at 298, 93 S.Ct. 1038.

On direct appeal, the Supreme Court reversed. It held that the prohibition on cross-examination of McDonald plus the exclusion of his hearsay confessions violated Chambers's constitutional right to present a defense. *Id.* at 302, 93 S.Ct. 1038. The confessions, although hearsay, bore "considerable assurance of their reliability." *Id.* at 300, 93 S.Ct. 1038. Specifically, the statements were: (1) made spontaneously to a close acquaintance shortly after the shooting; (2) corroborated by other evidence, including McDonald's written confession and the testimony of an eyewitness; and (3) "self-incriminatory and unquestionably against interest," which made the statements more reliable and brought them "well within the basic rationale of the [hearsay] exception for declarations against interest." *Id.* at 300-02, 93 S.Ct. 1038. Moreover, (4) McDonald was present in the courtroom and under oath, so he could have been cross-examined by the prosecution. *Id.* at 301, 93 S.Ct. 1038. The Court emphasized that this final factor "significantly distinguish[ed]" *Chambers* from cases where the declarant was unavailable at trial. *Id.*

The Court also found that the excluded testimony was "critical to Chambers' defense." *Id.* at 302, 93 S.Ct. 1038. The proof at trial excluded the possibility that there was more than one shooter, so McDonald's incriminating confession also tended to exculpate Chambers. *Id.* at 297, 93 S.Ct. 1038. In these circumstances, the Court held, "the hearsay rule may not be applied mechanistically to defeat the ends of justice." *Id.* at 302, 93 S.Ct. 1038.

Chambers is one case in a line of Supreme Court decisions considering constitutional challenges to state evidentiary rules. Sometimes the rule has had to p.896 yield. *See, e.g., Washington v. Texas,* 388 U.S. 14, 22, 87 S.Ct. 1920, 18 L.Ed.2d 1019 (1967) (rejecting rule that accomplices may testify for prosecution but not for defense); *Green v. Georgia,* 442 U.S. 95, 97, 99 S.Ct. 2150, 60 L.Ed.2d 738 (1979) (per curiam) (rejecting exclusion of hearsay confession); *see also Kubsch v. Neal,* No. 141898, 800 F.3d 783, 796-97, 2015 WL 4747942, *10 (7th Cir. Aug. 12, 2015) (collecting cases). But those instances are "rare[]." *Nevada v. Jackson,* ___ U.S. ___, 133 S.Ct. 1990, 1992, 186 L.Ed.2d 62 (2013) (per curiam).

The general standard is that rules of evidence restricting the ability to present a defense cannot be "arbitrary" or "disproportionate to the purposes they are designed to serve." *Scheffer,* 523 U.S. at 308, 118 S.Ct. 1261. The exclusion of hearsay transgresses that standard only where the excluded statements: (1) bear "considerable assurance of their reliability," sufficient to compensate for not being subject to cross-examination or given under oath; and (2) are "critical" to the defense. *Chambers,* 410 U.S. at 299-300, 302, 93 S.Ct. 1038.

The *Chambers* Court identified four factors to help assess reliability, although that list is not exhaustive. *Sharlow v. Israel,* 767 F.2d 373, 377 (7th Cir.1985). We already discussed those four factors above. The Court also clarified what it means by "critical" evidence in *United States v. Valenzuela-Bernal:* evidence is critical if it is "favorable and material," in the sense that "there is a reasonable likelihood that the testimony could have affected the judgment of the trier of fact." 458 U.S. 858, 872-74, 102 S.Ct. 3440, 73 L.Ed.2d 1193 (1982); *see also Scheffer,* 523 U.S. at 308, 118 S.Ct. 1261 (stating that exclusion of evidence is unconstitutional "only where is has infringed upon a weighty interest of the accused"); *Green,* 442 U.S. at 97, 99 S.Ct. 2150 (finding constitutional violation where excluded hearsay was "highly relevant to a critical issue"); *Washington,* 388 U.S. at 16, 87 S.Ct. 1920 (finding violation where evidentiary rule excluded testimony that was "relevant," "material," and "vital" to defense); *Sharlow,* 767 F.2d at 377-78 (recognizing that *Valenzuela-Bernal* standard defines "critical" for purposes of *Chambers* analysis). The *Chambers* "critical" standard is thus the same as the materiality requirement employed in the *Brady* line of cases, as we recognized in *Harris v. Thompson,* 698 F.3d 609, 627-28 (7th Cir.2012).

Deciding whether excluded hearsay is sufficiently reliable and material to trigger a *Chambers* violation in a given case is a fact-intensive inquiry. *Montana v. Egelhoff,* 518 U.S. 37, 52, 116 S.Ct. 2013, 135 L.Ed.2d 361 (1996) (reading *Chambers* as "an exercise in highly case-specific error correction"). It requires balancing the state's legitimate interests against the hearsay statement's trustworthiness and importance to the defendant *See Sharlow,* 767 F.2d at 377 (citing *Chambers,* 410 U.S. at 302, 93 S.Ct. 1038).

2. Iacullo's Statements to the Police

After the police arrested Williams and Caffey, they questioned Vikki Iacullo on November 18, 1995, and several times thereafter. Iacullo gave the following account to the police: Williams arrived at Iacullo's house early on November 17 with a baby. The baby's umbilical cord was bleeding, so Iacullo supplied gauze and tape. Williams had a cut on her hand and blood on her shirt. Iacullo drove Williams home and, once there, presented the baby to Caffey, saying, "Surprise, Baby Fedell Jr." Williams gave Iacullo Edwards's Grambling Tigers Starter jacket and told her to present it to Caffey as a "new daddy present," which Iacullo did. Also, at Williams's behest, Iacullo prepared a p.897 false birth certificate and gave it to Williams outside of Caffey's presence. *See Caffey I,* 275 Ill.Dec. 390, 792 N.E.2d at 1192.

The State charged Iacullo with obstruction of justice for her role in these crimes. She invoked the Fifth Amendment and refused to testify on Caffey's behalf. Defense counsel then sought to introduce Iacullo's out-of-court statements to the police, but the trial court excluded them as inadmissible hearsay under Illinois law.

On direct appeal, the Illinois Supreme Court affirmed their exclusion. *Id.,* 275 Ill.Dec. 390, 792 N.E.2d at 1198. The court acknowledged that state hearsay rules must sometimes yield to a defendant's constitutional right to present a defense under *Chambers*. But the court found that Iacullo's hearsay statements lacked sufficient indicia of reliability: three of the four reliability factors identified in *Chambers* were missing. *Id.*, 275 Ill.Dec. 390, 792 N.E.2d at 1192-95. In particular, the court found that Iacullo's statements were not self-incriminating because "[t]here is no crime in: allowing into one's home a friend who claims to have just given birth; helping to bandage a baby; driving that friend to her home and presenting the baby to the alleged father; or giving someone a jacket." *Id.*, 275 Ill. Dec. 390, 792 N.E.2d at 1194. The court did find the statement regarding the false birth certificate to be "somewhat self-incriminating" but insufficient to satisfy *Chambers. Id.*

The district court below disagreed. It concluded that the Illinois Supreme Court unreasonably applied *Chambers* and *Williamson v. United States,* 512 U.S. 594, 114 S.Ct. 2431, 129 L.Ed.2d 476 (1994), which teaches that "whether a statement is self-inculpatory or not can only be determined by viewing it in context." *Caffey IV,* 2013 WL 5529760, at *17-18. The district court therefore assessed the issue *de novo* and concluded that Iacullo's statements "bore considerable assurances of trustworthiness when assessed in the way that *Williamson* requires." *Id.* Nevertheless, the district court found the statements immaterial because there was no reasonable likelihood that they could have affected the jury's verdict. *Id.* at *18-19. Therefore, the district court ultimately found no *Chambers* violation. *Id.* at *19.

a) Reliability

Unlike the district court, we think the Illinois Supreme Court reasonably applied *Chambers* in finding the excluded statements unreliable, although it is close question. We consider the four *Chambers* factors in turn. The first was missing: these were not spontaneous statements to a close acquaintance, but rather answers given during interrogation by the police.

The second factor, corroboration, was present. Caffey testified that he first encountered the baby when Iacullo presented it to him at 2:30 a.m., and that Iacullo gave him the Starter jacket as a gift. This is some corroboration of Iacullo's statements but not much. Compare *Chambers,* where there was a sworn confession, eyewitness testimony, and other evidence to corroborate McDonald's three hearsay confessions. 410 U.S. at 300, 93 S.Ct. 1038. *See also Kubsch,* 800 F.3d at 799-800, 2015 WL 4747942, at *13 (holding that exclusion of hearsay was constitutional where, among other reasons, there was only "minimal corroboration" for excluded statement).

The third factor — whether Iacullo's statements were self-incriminating — is disputed. We agree with the district court that Iacullo's statements were at least somewhat against her penal interest. There was evidence linking Iacullo to the murders — *e.g.,* showing that she provided and then disposed of the gun used to kill Debra Evans. The police had already arrested p.898 Williams and Caffey, and by the time they were questioning Iacullo, it was apparent they suspected she too was involved. Viewed in this context, Iacullo's statements that she presented the baby to Caffey and gave him the jacket tend somewhat to implicate her, at least in the kidnapping of Elijah Evans, if not in the larger conspiracy.

On the other hand, the statements did not implicate Iacullo in the murders themselves; in that way, they are considerably less self-incriminating than the confessions at issue in *Chambers*. *See* 410 U.S. at 300-01, 93 S.Ct. 1038. Moreover, Iacullo was in custody when she made the statements and likely knew she was a suspect. She may therefore have had a motive to falsify or embellish her testimony to curry favor or gain leverage with the police. Her statements could also be interpreted as a form of damage-control, a way of downplaying her actual role in the crimes, which may have been greater, by admitting to a lesser role. Caffey argues that if Iacullo had really wanted to gain leverage she would have implicated him in the crimes to take the heat off herself. Not necessarily. Perhaps, for example, Iacullo did not want to turn Caffey against her for fear that he would reveal information about her involvement. The fact that she did not implicate him does not bolster the veracity of Iacullo's statements.

Turning to the fourth factor, it is undisputed that Iacullo, having invoked the Fifth Amendment, was unavailable for cross-examination at Caffey's trial. "The availability of cross-examination was ... central to *Chambers*." *Kubsch*, 800 F.3d at 800, 2015 WL 4747942, at *14. But here, that "powerful assurance of reliability," *id.*, was missing.

In these circumstances, we think it is a close question whether Iacullo's hearsay statements were sufficiently reliable to trigger a *Chambers* violation. But for that very reason, we cannot say that the state court's conclusion on this point was objectively unreasonable.

b) Materiality

Additionally, we agree with the district court that Iacullo's statements were not sufficiently material to Caffey's defense to trigger a *Chambers* violation. Because the state supreme court rested its holding on its finding of unreliability, it did not consider the statements' materiality. We therefore review that issue *de novo*.

As a threshold matter, Caffey contends that he does not have to show that Iacullo's statements were *material*, but only that their exclusion had a "substantial and injurious effect" on the jury's verdict. Federal courts generally employ the latter standard, taken from *Brecht v. Abrahamson*, 507 U.S. 619, 113 S.Ct. 1710, 123 L.Ed.2d 353 (1993), to determine whether a constitutional error is harmless or prejudicial in habeas corpus cases under § 2254. *Fry v. Pliler*, 551 U.S. 112, 121-122, 127 S.Ct. 2321, 168 L.Ed.2d 16 (2007). The materiality requirement of *Chambers*, however, is not the same as harmless-error analysis. Caffey's argument wrongly substitutes the latter for the former. *Chambers* materiality sets a higher bar than *Brecht*: Caffey must show a reasonable likelihood that the excluded evidence could have affected the verdict. *Valenzuela-Bernal*, 458 U.S. at 874, 102 S.Ct. 3440.[1]

p.899 Caffey contends that Iacullo's statements constituted the only corroboration for his version events. It is true that her statements, if accepted by the jury, would have supported his explanation of why he was wearing the blood-stained Starter jacket taken from the Evans apartment on the night of the murders — which was one important piece of physical evidence against him. Iacullo's statements also would have corroborated Caffey's story that Williams and Iacullo presented the baby to him at 2:30 a.m., which would tend to support Caffey's claim that he did not know about the baby before then.

Iacullo's statements would not, however, have corroborated the rest of Caffey's story. Nor, crucially, would they have undermined the other powerful evidence against him, including:

• Patrice Scott and Dwight Pruitt's testimony that Joshua identified Caffey as one of the burglars who cut his mother and sister;

• Scott's eyewitness testimony that Caffey strangled and stabbed Joshua, then took him to the alley in Maywood where his body was eventually found;

• The testimony of the 7-Eleven clerk that Caffey and Williams entered his store around 1:30 a.m. and bought baby wipes — an hour before Caffey claims he even knew about the baby's arrival;

• Dawn Killeen's testimony that months before the murders she heard Caffey (perhaps in jest) ask Ward whether he wanted a gun or a knife to kill Debra Evans, and then overhead Caffey, Williams, Ward, and Iacullo talking about a baby;

• John Pettaway's testimony that he saw Caffey with Williams and Ward on the day of the murders, and that Ward said he needed to find Caffey;

• Kassandra Turner's testimony that Caffey called her on the evening of the murders to say that the baby was on its way;

• Tennie Clay's sighting of a light-skinned individual matching Caffey's complexion with three other African-Americans, one of whom had a Starter jacket, on the sidewalk outside the Evans apartment on the night of the murders;

• Joy Wilson's testimony that she saw Caffey in the gray car with Williams and Ward, who had blood on his clothes, on the night of the murders; and

• The implausibility of certain parts of Caffey's testimony — for example, his claim that he did not know about Williams's tubal ligation despite dating her for roughly a year, and his claim that he believed Elijah was his child despite his initial skepticism and even though others who saw the baby thought he was too light-skinned to belong to Williams and Caffey.

Caffey points to weaknesses in the State's case — e.g., prior inconsistent statements by witnesses, possible biases, and motives they may have had to lie. In particular, neither Scott nor Pruitt told the officers who originally questioned them that Joshua had identified Caffey as one of the assailants. The problem with Caffey's argument is that the jury heard all of this impeachment evidence yet still found Caffey guilty beyond a reasonable doubt. Caffey does not claim that the evidence was insufficient to sustain his conviction. Moreover, he has given us no reason to think that the admission of Iacullo's excluded hearsay statements would have changed the jury's evaluation of the evidence or the witnesses, or that it might have tipped the balance in Caffey's favor. In short, there is no reasonable probability that the excluded statements would have altered the outcome of Caffey's trial — we p.900 are confident he still would have been convicted.

The fact that the prosecution in its closing argument emphasized the lack of corroboration for Caffey's story does not change our analysis. The State also argued that the evidence of Caffey's guilt was overwhelming. As we read the record, the jury did not merely opt for the State's theory of the case because Caffey's theory lacked corroboration. No; the prosecution prevailed because it presented strong, positive proof of Caffey's participation in the crimes.[2]

In sum, the Illinois Supreme Court did not "mechanistically" apply its hearsay rule to exclude Iacullo's statements to the police. *Chambers,* 410 U.S. at 302, 93 S.Ct. 1038. Those statements bore insufficient indicia of reliability and lacked the exculpatory significance necessary to support a constitutional claim under *Chambers.* We therefore affirm the denial of habeas relief on this claim. We now turn to Caffey's other *Chambers* arguments, which we can dispose of more quickly.

3. Ward's and Williams's Statements

The trial court excluded (1) John Pettaway's testimony that on the afternoon of the murders Ward said he needed to find Caffey to buy drugs from him; and (2) the testimony of Williams's friend Kimberly Young that Williams said she would fake a pregnancy to keep a man. Caffey contends the first statement supports his claim that he and Ward met only to sell drugs, not to plan murders. Caffey contends the second statement corroborates his testimony that Williams duped him into believing she was pregnant.

The Illinois Supreme Court affirmed the exclusion of both statements. *Caffey I,* 275 Ill.Dec. 390, 792 N.E.2d at 1188-92. It held that no state law hearsay exception applied, and it found further that any error was harmless because the statements were merely cumulative of other evidence. Although the court analyzed the issues under state law rather than *Chambers,* its harmless-error analysis was essentially the same as the *Chambers* materiality inquiry. So the state supreme court's conclusion still deserves AEDPA deference. *See Gilbert v. Merchant,* 488 F.3d 780, 793 n. 2 (7th Cir.2007) (noting that state court need not cite federal cases so long as its analysis is consistent with Supreme Court precedent).

The district court thought the state court's ruling was a reasonable application of federal law. We do too. The jury heard testimony from Pettaway that he and Ward smoked crack together and that Ward bought drugs from Caffey. Caffey also testified that he sold drugs to Ward. Thus, there was already ample evidence from which the jury could draw the inference that Caffey's meetings with Ward concerned drugs. Ward's excluded hearsay statements would not have added anything material to that evidence. Nor would the fact that Ward and Caffey's meetings concerned drugs exclude the possibility that they also concerned the Evans murders.

As for Williams's excluded statement, Caffey presented evidence at trial of Williams's jealousy, and Caffey and other witnesses testified that she had faked pregnancies before. So the jury was already aware of the possibility that Williams would use a sham pregnancy to trap Caffey. The jury simply did not believe that story in light of all the evidence. Williams's hearsay statement would have added nothing material to the defense's p.901 argument. There is no reasonable probability that Williams's excluded statement would have changed the verdict.

For these reasons, we find no *Chambers* violation in the trial court's exclusion of Ward's and Williams's hearsay statements.

B. Ineffective Assistance of Counsel

Before trial Caffey's counsel sought admission, under exceptions to the hearsay rule, of several out-of-court statements that Iacullo made to friends. Ryan Berger would have testified that a few hours before Debra Evans's murder, Iacullo asked him how to clean fingerprints off a gun; and between midnight and 4 a.m. the next day, she asked him how to clean powder burns off her hand.

Patricia Mitchell stated that Iacullo said she found a gun under the front seat of her car and was concerned her fingerprints might be on it.

Dorothy Hale stated that Iacullo told her to get cleaner to wipe fingerprints off a gun, bullets, and a magazine.

David Drenk stated that in the early fall of 1995, Iacullo asked to borrow a gun. A week before the murders, she asked him whether he could obtain a false birth certificate; he said no. On the day of the murders, November 16, 1995, he saw Williams at Iacullo's apartment. On November 17, Iacullo asked Drenk for help getting a birth certificate; the next day she told him how she would go about falsifying a birth certificate herself. A few days later, Iacullo told Drenk she was going to throw the gun into the Fox River.

The trial court ruled that these statements were admissible, but defense counsel did not present them to the jury. Caffey argues that this was an error and that it deprived him of his constitutional right to effective assistance of counsel. We assess ineffective-assistance claims by asking (1) whether counsel's performance fell below an objectively reasonable standard; and (2) whether there is a reasonable probability that, but for counsel's deficient performance, the result of the proceeding would have been different. *Strickland v. Washington,* 466 U.S. 668, 694, 104 S.Ct. 2052, 80 L.Ed.2d 674 (1984). By "reasonable probability" we mean "a probability sufficient to undermine confidence in the outcome." *Id.*

The Illinois Supreme Court rejected Caffey's claim for failure to meet the second prong. *Caffey I,* 275 Ill.Dec. 390, 792 N.E.2d at 1198. The district court below agreed with that conclusion. *Caffey IV,* 2013 WL 5529760, at *20. We afford AEDPA deference to the state court's ruling regarding *Strickland* prejudice, but not regarding the first prong, which the state court did not address.

We do not know why trial counsel decided (assuming it was a decision and not an oversight) not to present Iacullo's statements to the jury. Neither side has identified a strategic reason or given any other explanation. It seems a questionable move, particularly after counsel went to the trouble of obtaining the right to admit the statements into evidence. Counsel might have used Iacullo's statements, for instance, to argue that she was present in the apartment during the murders, which might have cast some doubt on the accuracy of Joshua's statement identifying the four "burglars," because Iacullo was not one of people he named. But even if counsel's conduct was objectively unreasonable (which we do not decide), we find no error in the state court's holding that Caffey suffered no *Strickland* prejudice.

Iacullo's statements tend to show her involvement in the crimes, specifically in obtaining and disposing of the gun and in fabricating birth certificates, though evidence to that effect was already presented at trial. Iacullo's statements could also p.902 be interpreted to show that she participated in the planning of the murders, or perhaps even that she fired the gun. In short, the statements tend to inculpate

Iacullo. But they do not tend to exculpate Caffey, which is what matters here. This is not a case like *Chambers,* where the evidence pointed to only a single participant in the shooting, so that hearsay statements tending to implicate another shooter necessarily also tended to exculpate the defendant. 410 U.S. at 297, 93 S.Ct. 1038. The evidence here shows that several people participated in the Evans murders, the planning, and the cover-up. The fact that Iacullo may have been one of them does not exclude Caffey as another participant — and there was ample evidence that he was. In these circumstances, the state court reasonably applied *Strickland* in finding no prejudice. Therefore, Caffey's ineffective-assistance claim fails.

C. Caffey's Brady Claims

Caffey next argues that the State wrongfully withheld evidence relating to Dwight Pruitt and Vikki Iacullo. The Supreme Court held in *Brady v. Maryland,* 373 U.S. 83, 83 S.Ct. 1194, 10 L.Ed.2d 215 (1963), that due process requires the prosecution to disclose evidence favorable to the defense. *Kyles v. Whitley,* 514 U.S. 419, 432-33, 115 S.Ct. 1555, 131 L.Ed.2d 490 (1995). Both exculpatory and impeachment evidence qualify as "favorable." *Id.* at 433, 115 S.Ct. 1555. Suppression of such evidence violates *Brady,* however, only where the evidence is material, meaning "there is a reasonable probability that, had the evidence been disclosed to the defense, the result of the proceeding would have been different." *Id.* (quoting *United States v. Bagley,* 473 U.S. 667, 682, 105 S.Ct. 3375, 87 L.Ed.2d 481 (1985)). A "reasonable probability" exists where suppression of the evidence "undermines confidence in the outcome of the trial." *Id.* at 434, 115 S.Ct. 1555 (quoting *Bagley,* 473 U.S. at 678, 105 S.Ct. 3375).

1. Benefits Received by Pruitt

In his petition for post-conviction relief in Illinois, Caffey alleged that the State suppressed evidence of two benefits it had given to Dwight Pruitt: favorable treatment in the DuPage County Jail and non-prosecution for his involvement in drug sales to ASA Kendall, one of Caffey's prosecutors. Caffey claims he could have used this evidence at trial to impeach Pruitt's credibility, establish his bias in favor of the prosecution, and show that he may have falsified or embellished his testimony in exchange for the benefits he received.

The state trial court allowed Caffey to develop his claim by taking Pruitt's deposition. Pruitt testified, in relevant part, as follows. Years before Caffey's trial, Pruitt twice drove a man he knew as "Black" to a meeting point to sell cocaine to a buyer who Pruitt later learned was ASA Kendall. Pruitt saw Black and Kendall meet but did not witness hand-to-hand drug transactions. Pruitt later told one of the State's attorneys what he had seen, but the attorney told him "not to worry about it" and to discuss the matter no more. Pruitt was never prosecuted for his role in the drug transactions.

Pruitt further testified that at the time of Caffey's trial, Pruitt was incarcerated on a gun charge in the DuPage County Jail. While there, he believed he received better treatment than the other prisoners. He was allowed to take "off the deck" showers three or four times; he ate "restaurant food" while in the courthouse being interviewed or preparing for trial; he was permitted to smoke and make telephone calls; and he was allowed a personal visit with Scott and his daughter in the courthouse with an attorney for the State p.903 present. When Pruitt was involved in an altercation with a correctional officer, he received no formal discipline, though he was placed in segregation. One of the State's attorneys told Pruitt that he was "getting the VIP treatment."

Pruitt insisted that his testimony at Caffey's trial was "strictly the truth." He said no one in the prosecutor's office ever asked him to lie or promised him anything in exchange for his testimony: "They never asked me to lie. They never told me to make up nothing.... I wasn't paid or nothing."

After reviewing the evidence, the state trial court dismissed Caffey's petition on the merits. The Illinois Appellate Court affirmed, concluding that the undisclosed evidence was immaterial under *Brady*. *Caffey II,* slip op. at 41-52. Giving AEDPA deference to that conclusion, the district court held that it represented a reasonable application of federal law. *Caffey IV,* 2013 WL 5529760, at *33-34. We agree.

To be sure, Pruitt's testimony was important to the prosecution's case. He and Scott were the only witnesses who testified to Joshua Evans's identification of Caffey as one of the assailants who killed Debra and Samantha. But for several reasons, we do not think it reasonably probable that the undisclosed evidence about the benefits Pruitt received would have affected the jury's verdict.

In the first place, Pruitt had only minimal personal knowledge about the drug transactions involving Kendall — he never saw drugs or money change hands. Similarly, Pruitt's benefits in jail were relatively minor. A few good showers, decent food when in court, smoking privileges, telephone calls, one family visit, and reduced discipline — we do not think these are powerful enough incentives to have convinced a jury that Pruitt falsified his testimony, at least not without evidence of some kind of *quid pro quo.*

There was no such evidence. On the contrary, Pruitt testified that he had no deal or understanding with prosecutors to testify in a particular way at Caffey's trial. Pruitt said he testified truthfully. To back up that claim, there was the testimony Pruitt gave during a pretrial hearing on the admissibility of Joshua Evans's hearsay statements. That hearing took place before Pruitt's stint in DuPage County Jail and before Pruitt realized that ASA Kendall was the man involved in the drug transactions — that is, before he received or had reason to expect any benefits from the State. Yet, Pruitt's pretrial testimony was consistent with his later testimony at Caffey's trial. Additionally, Pruitt's testimony was corroborated by Patrice Scott.

Considering all these circumstances together, we conclude that the state court reasonably found the undisclosed evidence concerning Pruitt to be immaterial. Therefore, Caffey's *Brady* claim regarding Pruitt fails.

2. Iacullo's Statements to Cara Walker

Finally, Caffey argues that the State violated *Brady* by not disclosing statements that Vikki Iacullo made to Cara Walker, the mother of Iacullo's daughter's friend. On the weekend of November 18, 1995, Iacullo asked Walker to watch her daughters for a few days. Iacullo explained that she was in a bit of trouble. Walker agreed. During the girls' stay, Walker stopped by Iacullo's home to get them some clothes. While there, Walker spoke with Iacullo. Walker later (but before Caffey's trial) reported to the police what Iacullo had said. According to Walker, Iacullo claimed knowledge of and possibly involvement in the Evans murders. Furthermore, Iacullo said that if she were arrested or charged, she would p.904 reveal that she had knowledge of illegal drug use by DuPage County prosecutors, including Kendall.[3]

Iacullo's statements to Walker were never disclosed to Caffey before or during his trial. He claims that he was entitled to them under *Brady* and that they were material to his defense because they would have bolstered his case for the admission of Iacullo's statements to the police (discussed in section II.A.2 above). The state court did not address this claim on the merits but instead dismissed it on procedural grounds.[4] The district court therefore reviewed the issue *de novo*, held an evidentiary hearing, heard from multiple witnesses, and made factual findings. The district court ultimately rejected Caffey's claim because it regarded the statements at issue as immaterial. *Caffey IV,* 2013 WL 5529760, at *31-32.

We agree with the district court's conclusion and analysis. Iacullo's statements to Walker would have added little to the reliability analysis under *Chambers* and nothing to the materiality analysis. So Iacullo's statements to the police still would have been inadmissible. But Caffey argues that the statements somehow show foul play by the prosecution. Caffey's argument is sketchy, but he seems to suggest that the prosecution procured Iacullo's unavailability at trial, and ensured her silence about Kendall's drug use, in exchange for an agreement not to charge her with murder.

As the district court found, there is no evidence of any such agreement. Nor do the facts plausibly suggest the existence of a tacit agreement or understanding. There is nothing untoward about Iacullo's invocation of her Fifth Amendment privilege; she was, after all, charged with obstruction of justice and may have been guilty of worse. And there is nothing suspicious about the fact that Iacullo was not charged with murder. One of the prosecutors testified before the district court that the State considered bringing such charges but decided not to because it could not place Iacullo at the murder scenes.

We agree with the district court that Iacullo's statements to Walker were immaterial, so we reject Caffey's *Brady* claim regarding Iacullo.

III. CONCLUSION

For the foregoing reasons, we AFFIRM the denial of Caffey's petition for a writ of habeas corpus.

[1] That is why "*Chambers* error is by nature prejudicial." *Fry,* 551 U.S. at 124, 127 S.Ct. 2321 (Stevens, J., concurring in part and dissenting in part). An evidentiary ruling that unconstitutionally excludes critical evidence under *Chambers* is necessarily harmful under *Brecht. Cf. Kyles v. Whitley,* 514 U.S. 419, 435-36, 115 S.Ct. 1555, 131 L.Ed.2d 490 (1995) (making the same observation about *Bagley* error).

[2] Nor are we troubled by the isolated reference in the State's closing argument to Iacullo's race (white), for the reasons given by the Illinois Supreme Court. *See Caffey I,* 275 Ill.Dec. 390, 792 N.E.2d at 1197.

[3] At the hearing before the district court, Kendall testified that he never bought drugs from Iacullo or Pruitt but asserted his privilege against self-incrimination regarding his prior drug use generally. *See Caffey IV*, 2013 WL 5529760, at *30.

[4] The State argues that the state law procedural grounds supply an independent and adequate basis for us to reject Caffey's claim here without even reaching the *Brady* issue. *See Coleman v. Thompson*, 501 U.S. 722, 729-30, 111 S.Ct. 2546, 115 L.Ed.2d 640 (1991). The district court disagreed. *Caffey III*, 2012 WL 5230298, at *12-13. We need not decide this issue because we hold that Caffey's *Brady* claim fails on the merits in any event.

EIGHTH CIRCUIT DECISIONS

The Rule Against Hearsay

756 F.3d 602 (2014)

UNITED STATES of America, Plaintiff-Appellee

v.

Brian Gordon GRAVES, Defendant-Appellant.

No. 13-2356.

United States Court of Appeals, Eighth Circuit.

Submitted: March 13, 2014.

Filed: June 25, 2014.

US v. Graves, 756 F. 3d 602 (8th Cir. 2014)

p.603 Katherine M. Menendez, AFPD, argued, Minneapolis, MN, (Reynaldo A. Aligada, Jr., on the brief), for Appellant.

Jeffrey S. Paulsen, AUSA, argued, Minneapolis, MN, for Appellee.

Before COLLOTON, SHEPHERD, and KELLY, Circuit Judges.

SHEPHERD, Circuit Judge.

A jury convicted Brian Gordon Graves of Assault with a Dangerous Weapon and Domestic Assault by an Habitual Offender. At the trial and over Graves' objections, the district court[1] permitted the government to introduce, as an excited utterance under Federal Rule of Evidence 803(2), statements the alleged victim made to a police officer on the night of the incident. Graves now appeals his conviction, arguing the district court abused its discretion in admitting the statements as an excited utterance because the alleged victim was not under the stress of the incident at the time she made the statements. We affirm.

I.

Graves and his fiancée L.K. were involved in an all-day argument. At some point during the day, Graves left their shared residence. He returned between 10:00 p.m. and 11:00 p.m., kicked in the front door, and confronted L.K. in the back bedroom of the home. During this confrontation, Graves held a loaded shotgun. After 10 to 15 minutes of arguing, Graves left the residence. As he departed, he fired the shotgun five times.

A neighbor called 911 to report the gun shots. Officer Dana Lyons responded. It took Officer Lyons approximately 20 minutes to travel to the residence after being p.604 dispatched.[2] When he arrived, he knocked on the front door, and L.K. answered. Officer Lyons observed that L.K. was shaking and appeared to have been crying. Officer Lyons told L.K. that there had been a report of shots being fired and asked, "What's going on here?" L.K. responded by recalling the details of the fight she had with Graves, including the fact that Graves had pointed the shotgun at L.K. and threatened to shoot her in the head.

Graves was taken into custody. Several days later, he was interviewed by an agent with the Federal Bureau of Investigation where he described the argument he had with L.K., admitted taking the gun into the residence and waving it around, and stated that L.K. had pushed the barrel of the gun away. Graves denied, however, that he ever pointed the gun directly at L.K. or threatened to shoot her.

The government argued that L.K.'s statements to Officer Lyons, made immediately after Officer Lyons encountered L.K., should be admitted as an excited utterance. At an evidentiary hearing, Officer Lyons testified about the night of the incident, stating that he arrived at the residence approximately 30 minutes after the 911 call and that L.K. was shaking when she answered the door. Officer Lyons asked, "What's going on here?" In response, L.K. gave a rapid description of the incident including the statements that Graves had pointed the gun at her and threatened to shoot her. At trial, L.K. testified that she lied to Officer Lyons when she stated that Graves had pointed a gun at her and threatened her.

The district court admitted L.K.'s statements made to Officer Lyons immediately after his arrival at the residence as an excited utterance pursuant to Federal Rule of Evidence 803(2), noting that L.K. was still under the stress of the incident and lacked time for reflection. Despite L.K.'s testimony that she lied to Officer Lyons because she was angry at Graves, the jury found Graves guilty of Assault with a Dangerous Weapon and Domestic Assault by an Habitual Offender. The district court sentenced Graves to 21 months imprisonment.

II.

The sole issue in this appeal is whether the district court abused its discretion in allowing into evidence as an excited utterance L.K.'s statements made to Officer Lyons immediately after Officer Lyons arrived at the residence. *See United States v. Jongewaard,* 567 F.3d 336, 343 (8th Cir.2009) (standard of review). Hearsay — an out of court statement offered in evidence to prove the truth of the matter asserted — is generally not admissible. *See* Fed.R.Evid. 801, 802. "Excited utterances" are excepted from the general rule against hearsay. *See United States v. Bercier,* 506 F.3d 625, 630 (8th Cir.2007) ("Rule 803(2) excepts [from the hearsay rule] an out-of-court statement 'relating to a startling event or condition made while the declarant was under the stress of excitement' caused by the event or condition." (quoting Fed.R.Evid. 803(2))). "The rationale behind this particular exception 'derives from the teaching of experience that the stress of nervous excitement or physical shock stills the reflective faculties, thus removing an impediment to truthfulness.'" *Brunsting v. Lutsen Mtns. Corp.,* 601 F.3d 813, 817 (8th Cir.2010) (quoting *United States v. Sewell,* 90 F.3d 326, 327 p.605 (8th Cir.1996)). In other words, statements made by a declarant while that declarant remains under the stress or shock of an event retains a "'guarantee of trustworthiness'" that is not present when the declarant has the opportunity for reflection and deliberation. *Id.* (quoting *Miller v. Keating,* 754 F.2d 507, 510 (3d Cir.1985)).

Graves does not contest that L.K. experienced a startling event or that L.K.'s statements related to that incident. Instead, Graves argues that L.K. was no longer "under the stress of excitement" caused by the event or condition, and thus her statements to Officer Lyons are not admissible under the "excited utterance" exception to the hearsay rule. *See* Fed. R.Evid. 803(2).

To decide the specific question of whether a declarant remains "under the stress of excitement" caused by the event when the declarant makes the statement, courts consider several factors: "[1] the lapse of time between the startling event and the statement, [2] whether the statement was made in response to an inquiry, [3] the age of the declarant, [4] the physical and mental condition of the declarant, [5] the characteristics of the event, and [6] the subject matter of the statement." *United*

States v. Clemmons, 461 F.3d 1057, 1061 (8th Cir.2006) (quotation marks omitted). Courts also consider "whether the declarant's stress or excitement was continuous from the time of the event until the time of the statements." *United States v. Wilcox,* 487 F.3d 1163, 1170 (8th Cir.2007) (citing *United States v. Marrowbone,* 211 F.3d 452, 455 (8th Cir.2000)). None of these factors is dispositive, and some of the factors may not be relevant in every case. *See United States v. Iron Shell,* 633 F.2d 77, 85-86 (8th Cir.1980).

Outside the presence of the jury, the district court heard testimony from Officer Lyons about his encounter with L.K. After hearing that testimony and arguments from counsel, the district court held that the statements L.K. made to Officer Lyons were not subject to reflection by L.K. because she did not make the call to the police and, thus, was not aware during the approximately 30 minutes from the incident to Officer Lyons' arrival that she was going to be subjected to questioning from a police officer.

In looking at the factors noted above, first the lapse of time in this case — approximately 30 minutes — is seemingly long for the typical application of the excited utterance exception; however, we have previously allowed the inclusion of excited utterances in a similar factual scenario. In *United States v. Phelps,* a victim's boyfriend fired five or six shots in the victim's presence shortly after an argument between the two. 168 F.3d 1048, 1052 (8th Cir.1999). A police officer arrived on the scene 15 to 30 minutes after the incident. *Id.* at 1053. When the officer made contact with the victim, the victim appeared "very upset," "[h] er hands were shaking," and "she ... [was] crying." *Id.* We stated that "[t]he lapse of 15 to 30 minutes between an exciting incident and a statement d[id] not render the statement inadmissible." *Id.* at 1055. We held the district court did not abuse its discretion in admitting the statements as an excited utterance because the victim's statements "occurred only shortly after an exciting event, were made while she was still visibly upset from the shooting, and described the shooting." *Id.* Additionally, *Phelps* cited *Iron Shell,* 633 F.2d at 86, where we allowed admission of statements made between 45 minutes and 1 hour 15 minutes after an assault. 168 F.3d at 1055. Thus, the time lapse of 30 minutes was not so long to render L.K.'s statements inadmissible.

Second, Officer Lyons testified that L.K. was shaking and appeared to have been p.606 crying when she answered the door immediately before giving the statements. L.K.'s state of distress before she gave her statements supports a finding that L.K.'s statements were "spontaneous, excited or impulsive rather than the product of reflection and deliberation." *Iron Shell,* 633 F.2d at 86. Although L.K., who recanted her statements at trial, offered a different explanation for her appearance — that she was subject to hormonal issues pertaining to her pregnancy — the district court acted well within its discretion to find that her "continuous level of stress" from the time of the incident until Officer Lyons appeared supported the application of the excited utterance exception.

Third, L.K. offered her statements to Officer Lyons in response to his general inquiry into what had happened. This question was not the detailed, interrogation-style questioning that might negate the use of the excited utterance exception. *See, e.g., United States v. Elem,* 845 F.2d 170, 174 (8th Cir.1988) (holding statements made by defendant while defendant was in custody and in response to officers' several questions did not qualify for excited utterance exception).

Finally, L.K.'s statements described the argument with Graves, including his placing the gun to her head and threatening to shoot her. The characteristics of such an interaction are the type of event that would cause a reasonable person to experience the type of stress and shock L.K. exhibited.

While Graves may offer alternative explanations for L.K.'s appearance and behavior, those explanations do not undermine the district court's exercise of its discretion in determining that L.K.'s statements bore a "guarantee of trustworthiness" and were not subject to reflection and deliberation. Accordingly, we affirm the district court's admission of the statements as an excited utterance under Federal Rule of Evidence 803(2).

III.

We affirm.

[1] The Honorable Donovan W. Frank, United States District Judge for the District of Minnesota.

[2] According to the trial transcript, the 911 call began at 10:55 p.m., Officer Lyons was dispatched at 11:06 p.m., and Officer Lyons arrived at the residence at about 11:24 p.m. (Trial Tr. at 16-18.)

703 F.3d 1104 (2013)

GENERAL MILLS OPERATIONS, LLC, Plaintiff-Appellee

v.

FIVE STAR CUSTOM FOODS, LTD., Defendant-Appellant

Westland Meat Company, Inc., also known as Hallmark Meat Packing Co.; Hallmark Meat Packing, Inc., Third Party Defendants.

General Mills Operations, LLC, Plaintiff-Appellant

v.

Five Star Custom Foods, Ltd., Defendant-Appellee

Westland Meat Company, Inc., also known as Hallmark Meat Packing Co.; Hallmark Meat Packing, Inc., Third Party Defendants.

Nos. 12-1731, 12-1826.

United States Court of Appeals, Eighth Circuit.

Submitted: November 14, 2012.

Filed: January 7, 2013.

General Mills Operations v. Five Star Custom Foods, 703 F. 3d 1104 (8th Cir. 2013)

p.1106 Meaghan C. Bryan, argued, Peter G. Van Bergen, Andrea E. Reisbord, on the brief, Minneapolis, MN, for Appellant.

Rolf Edward Gilbertson, argued, Christopher R. Paar, Kaisa M. Adams, on the brief, Minneapolis, MN, for Appellee.

Before MURPHY, BENTON, and SHEPHERD, Circuit Judges.

BENTON, Circuit Judge.

General Mills Operations, LLC purchased meatballs from Five Star Custom Foods, Ltd. After delivery and use of the meatballs, Five Star's supplier of ground beef issued a recall. Accordingly, General Mills destroyed its products containing the meatballs. It sued Five Star for breach of contract and breach of warranties. The district court[1] granted summary judgment to General Mills on the breach-of-contract claim, and to Five Star on the breach-of-warranty claims. The parties cross-appeal. Five Star also challenges the award of attorneys' fees to General Mills. Having jurisdiction under 28 U.S.C. § 1291, this court affirms the grant of summary judgment to General Mills and the award of attorneys' fees. General Mills' cross-appeal is dismissed as moot.

I.

Five Star is a manufacturer and supplier of food products. General Mills is a manufacturer of food products that are sold to retail consumers. For over ten years, Five Star sold products to General Mills, including meatballs for Progresso soups.

This case involves two orders for meatballs by General Mills in September 2007. The orders were subject to General Mills' Terms and Conditions (printed on the reverse of the purchase order) and General Mills' Ingredient Specifications. The meatballs were delivered on September 29 and October 5, 2007, and used in Progresso soups.

Five Star purchased some of the beef used to manufacture the meatballs from Westland Meat Company, Inc. In February 2008, Westland voluntarily recalled over 143 million pounds of beef, including p.1107 some used in General Mills' meatballs. Video footage from the Humane Society allegedly showed Westland employees improperly handling cattle designated for slaughter. There were no reports of illness from the beef, but after discussions with the United States Department of Agriculture and the Food Safety Inspection Service, Westland issued the voluntary recall. The USDA issued a Product Recall Recommendation describing the circumstances of the recall, issued a Recall Release to the public, and held a Technical Briefing for members of the industry. The recall reached only the retail level, meaning that end consumers were not required to destroy their products.

Per instructions from the USDA, Five Star notified its customers, providing instructions on destroying affected products. General Mills complied, destroying all of the affected soups. In 2010, General Mills sued Five Star for negligence, breach of contract, breach of express warranties, and breach of the implied warranties of merchantability and fitness for a particular purpose. General Mills voluntarily dismissed the negligence claim. The parties cross-moved for summary judgment. The district court granted summary judgment to General Mills on the breach-of-contract claim, and to Five Star on the breach-of-warranty claims. *General Mills Operations, LLC v. Five Star Custom Foods, Ltd.,* 789 F.Supp.2d 1148, 1160 (D.Minn. 2011). The parties stipulated to $1,473,564 in damages and $150,000 in attorneys' fees.

II.

Five Star argues that the district court should not have granted summary judgment to General Mills on the breach-of-contract claim. This court reviews de novo a grant of summary judgment, construing all facts and making all reasonable inferences favorable to the nonmovant. *Cent. Platte Natural Res. Dist. v. U.S. Dep't of Agric.,* 643 F.3d 1142, 1146 (8th Cir.2011). "The court shall grant summary judgment if the movant shows that there is no genuine dispute as to any material fact and the movant is entitled to judgment as a matter of law." Fed. R.Civ.P. 56(a).

A successful breach-of-contract claim under Minnesota law has four elements: "(1) formation of a contract; (2) performance by plaintiff of any conditions precedent; (3) a material breach of the contract by defendant; and (4) damages." *Parkhill v. Minn. Mut. Life Ins. Co.,* 174 F.Supp.2d 951, 961 (D.Minn.2000). At issue here is the third element — whether Five Star materially breached the contract. Because General Mills accepted the meatballs, it has the burden to establish a breach. Minn.Stat. § 336.2-607(4).

Several contract provisions are at issue in this case. The Terms and Conditions state:

> 5. GOODS: The Goods shall conform in all respects to the description on the face of this Order, and/or [General Mills'] then current specifications furnished to [Five Star]. The Goods, including, without limitation, tools and equipment shall be new, of first class commercial type and of the latest approved design, unless otherwise specified on the face of this Order. Workmanship and materials shall be of the best quality and free from defects that might render the Goods unsuitable or inefficient for the purpose for which it is to be used. [Five Star] warrants and guarantees its Goods for the period of time normally specified for the type of Goods involved. During the warranty period, all Goods or parts disclosing defects in design, material,

and/or workmanship shall be replaced and delivered to the job site by [Five Star] without cost or delay to [General Mills]. This warranty is in addition to and not in lieu p.1108 of, any other warranties or guarantees made by [Five Star] or created or implied as a matter of law. The above warranties, as well as all other warranties contained herein, including, without limitation, the warranties in paragraphs 6, 8, 9, 10, 12, 18, 20, 21, 25 and 26 shall collectively be defined herein as "Warranties."

. . . .

25. COMPLIANCE WITH LAW: [Five Star]'s performance under this Order shall be in compliance with all applicable federal, state, and local laws, ordinances, regulations, rules and statutes ("Laws").

The Ingredient Specifications include:

REGULATORY

. . . .

This ingredient shall be of food grade and in all respects, including labeling in compliance with the Meat Inspection Act of 1906 as amended.

. . . .

Stunning, slaughter, and processing practices must meet or exceed the requirements established by the USDA and the World Animal Health Organization for safe trade in animal products.

These regulations require the meatballs to be of food grade, and for the beef to be procured pursuant to USDA regulations. Five Star contends, however, that there is no admissible evidence establishing the alleged breach of those duties. Even viewing the record most favorably to the nonmovant, the court should not consider statements that are inadmissible hearsay. *Novotny v. Tripp County,* 664 F.3d 1173, 1178 (8th Cir.2011); Fed.R.Civ.P. 56(c)(2). Five Star argues that General Mills relies exclusively on the Recall Release issued by the USDA Public Affairs Office. That release stated: "all beef product produced during the period of time for which evidence indicates such activity occurred had been determined by FSIS to be unfit for human consumption, and is, therefore, adulterated."

Five Star objects that the press release is inadmissible hearsay. General Mills responds that it is not hearsay because it was not offered to prove the truth of the matter asserted. *See* Fed.R.Evid. 801(c)(2); *see also Stevens v. Moore Bus. Forms, Inc.,* 18 F.3d 1443, 1449 (9th Cir. 1994) (press release admissible to prove knowledge), *citing Kunz v. Utah Power & Light Co.,* 913 F.2d 599, 605 (9th Cir.1990) (press release admissible to prove notice). General Mills asserts that the press release is offered to show why it destroyed the beef, not the truth of the matter asserted — that the Westland beef was actually adulterated. There must be some evidence, however, demonstrating that the beef did not comply with the contract. As to that, the press release is hearsay.

Even so, the press release falls within the public-records hearsay exception. The exception provides that a "record or statement of a public office" is not hearsay if it sets out, in a civil case, "factual findings from a legally authorized investigation." Fed.R.Evid. 803(8)(A)(iii). The cases Five Star cites where press releases were inadmissible hearsay do not foreclose admissibility as a public record. In fact, Five Star's only published opinion supports this point. *See Zeigler v. Fisher-Price, Inc.,* 302

F.Supp.2d 999, 1021 n. 10 (N.D.Iowa 2004). Five Star cites *Zeigler* for the proposition that "a press release regarding a product recall was hearsay unless used as an admission by party-opponent under Fed.R.Evid. 801(d)(2)." This ignores the court's statement, "To the extent the press release can be construed as stating conclusions or opinions of the CSPC, it also was admissible under Federal Rule of Evidence 803(8)(c)." *Id., citing Patterson v. Cent. Mills, Inc.,* p.1109 64 Fed.Appx. 457, 462 (6th Cir.2003).[2]

Many press releases are certainly hearsay. Rule 803(8), however, is construed broadly. *Patterson,* 64 Fed.Appx. at 462, *citing Beech Aerospace Servs., Inc. v. Rainey,* 488 U.S. 153, 162, 109 S.Ct. 439, 102 L.Ed.2d 445 (1988). In *Patterson,* the Sixth Circuit addressed statements in "press releases and other publications" of the Consumer Products Safety Commission about defective labeling of t-shirts. *Id.* at 459, 462. The district court required the personal statements of Board members to be redacted (e.g., "as a mother, I hope parents will wisely choose the safer alternative of tight-fitting cotton sleepwear"), but allowed other statements of facts, opinions, and conclusions of the agency. *Id.* at 462. The Sixth Circuit affirmed this approach. *Id.* Similarly here, the press release sets out findings from an investigation pursuant to authority granted by law, and is therefore admissible. *See also Byrd v. ABC Prof'l Tree Serv., Inc.,* 832 F.Supp.2d 917, 921 n. 3 (M.D.Tenn.2011).

Further, as the district court noted, additional evidence supported the conclusion that the meat was procured in violation of regulations and that it was adulterated. *See General Mills,* 789 F.Supp.2d at 1157 n. 12. On the same day the press release issued, the USDA conducted a Technical Briefing about the recall. A transcript of this briefing is in the record. The Undersecretary for Food Safety delivered, *inter alia,* a summary of the investigation:

> First of all, I do want to remind everyone that this is still an ongoing investigation and therefore we may not be able to answer all of your questions today. As a result of the USDA's ongoing investigation, the FSIS, the Food Safety and Inspection Service, just recently obtained evidence that [Westland] had a practice that allowed them to occasionally slaughter cattle that had already passed ante mortem inspection but had become nonambulatory prior to entering the slaughter operation without notifying our public health veterinarian. This practice is not compliant with FSIS regulations.
>
> Therefore, FSIS determined that their products were unfit for human food because the cattle did not receive complete and proper inspection.

This illustrates the same point as the press release. Although Five Star attacks the Technical Briefing as also hearsay, it similarly falls under the exception in Rule 803(8) for the reasons explained. Five Star also asserts that both statements contradict the Product Recall Recommendation. p.1110 It used qualifiers like "allegedly" and "may be adulterated" to describe Westland's situation. In any event, all three documents show that FSIS had evidence of practices that violated regulations. Then, as a result of that ongoing investigation, Westland agreed to recall the beef.

Further, as noted by the district court, Five Star admitted that its understanding was that the beef "had been recalled by the USDA because it didn't meet the USDA's regulations." This admission is in a deposition of Five Star's corporate designee. *See* Fed.R.Civ.P. 30(b)(6). Five Star contends that its designee is not competent to testify about the actual reasons for the recall, because he had no personal knowledge of the events at Westland. *See* Fed. R.Evid. 602. The designee certainly is competent to testify, however, as to Five Star's understanding — that is the precise function of the corporate designee. This admission illustrates that all parties had the same understanding: the recall issued because Westland did not comply with USDA regulations. The admission is particularly relevant because Five Star in turn directed General Mills (albeit at the behest of the USDA) to destroy the meatballs.

Sufficient, admissible evidence established that the beef was procured in violation of USDA regulations, and that it was therefore deemed adulterated. Five Star breached the contract. Five Star correctly notes that contract terms are not read in isolation, rather the contract is read as a whole. *Halla Nursery, Inc. v. City of Chanhassen,* 781 N.W.2d 880, 884 (Minn. 2010). They argue that the regulatory section of the Ingredient Specifications, read as a whole, does not establish liability for Five Star, because Westland was an approved facility with proper procedures in place. Given their plain meaning, the contract terms do not support this argument. *See Brookfield Trade Ctr. v. County of Ramsey,* 584 N.W.2d 390, 394 (Minn. 1998) ("In interpreting a contract, the language is to be given its plain and ordinary meaning."). The terms require "[s]tunning, slaughter, and processing practices [that] meet or exceed the requirements established by the USDA."

Five Star contends that General Mills must prove that the specific product received was adulterated, or procured in a noncompliant manner. This argument is without merit. The cases cited by Five Star support the position that receiving a good that is not in compliance with the contract results in a breach. *Coghlan v. Wellcraft Marine Corp.,* 240 F.3d 449, 451 (5th Cir.2001) (boat hull manufactured of a less durable material than specified in the contract); *US Salt, Inc. v. Broken Arrow, Inc.,* No. 07-1988 (RHK/JSM), 2008 WL 398818, at *4 (D.Minn. Feb. 11, 2008) (salt did not meet specifications in contract for washing, drying, and color). All of the recalled beef was deemed unfit for human food — that is why the recall issued.[3] By the terms of the contract, General Mills ordered meatballs of food grade for use in food products, which is not what it received.

Five Star also argues that this event did not trigger the contract's recall provision, and thus there is no breach of contract. Paragraph 27 says:

> 27. RECALL: [General Mills] shall have the sole right, exercisable in its p.1111 discretion, to initiate and direct the content and scope of a recall, market withdrawal, stock recovery, product correction and/or advisory safety communication (any one or more referred to as "Recall Action") regarding the Goods. At [General Mills]'s option, [General Mills] may direct [Five Star] to, and upon such direction [Five Star] shall, conduct such Recall Action. [General Mills] shall determine in its discretion the manner, text and timing of any publicity to be given such matters in the event a Recall Action is initiated or directed by [General Mills], [Five Star] agrees to fully cooperate and take all such steps as are reasonably requested to implement the Recall Action in a timely and complete manner. Any and all action to be taken in connection with a Recall Action shall be in accordance with FDA policies and other Laws. [Five Star] shall bear the costs associated with any Recall Action which results

from [Five Star]'s negligence or willful misconduct or that the Goods do not comply with [Five Star]'s Warranties under this Order.

Where a contract provides a specific basis for recovery, it excludes additional theories of recovery. *See Art Goebel, Inc. v. N. Suburban Agencies, Inc.,* 567 N.W.2d 511, 515-16 (Minn.1997). Because there was no negligence or willful misconduct by Five Star (and the breach of warranty claims were dismissed by the district court), Five Star contends that it is not liable. However, as the court in *Art Goebel* explained, the contract terms must be read in the context of the entire agreement. *Art Goebel,* 567 N.W.2d at 516; *see also Halla Nursery,* 781 N.W.2d at 884. To make a remedy exclusive, the contract "must clearly indicate the intent of the parties to make the stipulated remedies exclusive." *Cont'l Grain Co. v. Fegles Constr. Co.,* 480 F.2d 793, 796 (8th Cir. 1973), *citing Indep. Consol. Sch. Dist. No. 24 v. Carlstrom,* 277 Minn. 117, 151 N.W.2d 784, 786-87 (1967). Several other provisions in the contract refer to other remedies from a recall. Paragraph 10, for example, states, "[Five Star] shall promptly pay or reimburse [General Mills] for all costs and damages (including lost profits) incurred by [General Mills], including, without limitation, costs for ... recall." Paragraph 27 is not the exclusive recall remedy. Further, even considering just the language of Paragraph 27, it contemplates a recall issued *by* General Mills, not the situation here.

The district court properly granted summary judgment to General Mills on the breach-of-contract claim.

III.

The district court granted summary judgment to Five Star on the breach-of-warranty claims, ruling that General Mills needed to show an actual defect to prove any breach of warranty. *General Mills,* 789 F.Supp.2d at 1155.

The parties stipulated that $1,473,564 is the amount of damages in this case. At oral argument, both parties confirmed that the stipulated damages would be awarded for either breach of contract, breach of warranty, or both. Having found that Five Star breached the contract, this court need not address whether it also breached warranties. General Mills' cross-appeal is therefore dismissed as moot. *See Beachwalk Homeowners Ass'n v. Gen. Star Indem. Co.,* 76 Fed.Appx. 494, 495 (4th Cir. 2003); *Laitram Corp. v. NEC Corp.,* 115 F.3d 947, 955-56 (Fed.Cir.1997); *Abraham v. Pekarski,* 728 F.2d 167, 169 (3d Cir. 1984); *Univ. Computing Co. v. Lykes-Youngstown Corp.,* 504 F.2d 518, 548 n. 44 (5th Cir.1974); *cf. Minnesota ex rel. N. Pac. Ctr., Inc. v. BNSF Ry. Co.,* 686 F.3d 567, 574-75 (8th Cir.2012).

p.1112 Five Star argues that the district court should have treated the breach-of-contract claims identically to the breach-of-warranty claims because the terms of the contract are, in essence, express warranties. As noted, the district court ruled that breach-of-warranty claims require the plaintiff to prove an actual defect in the product. This court makes no statement on the accuracy of that ruling, although the district court correctly said that "evidence of a defect is not an essential element of a breach-of-contract claim." *General Mills,* 789 F.Supp.2d at 1155; *see Parkhill,* 174 F.Supp.2d at 961. Therefore, the district court properly analyzed these claims separately.

IV.

Five Star asserts that the district court erred by awarding attorneys' fees to General Mills. This court reviews de novo the legal issues related to an award of attorneys' fees, and reviews the actual award for abuse of discretion. *Pendleton v. QuikTrip Corp.*, 567 F.3d 988, 994 (8th Cir.2009). In order to award attorneys' fees, there must be a contractual agreement discussing the fees. *Garrick v. Northland Ins. Co.*, 469 N.W.2d 709, 714 (Minn. 1991). The parties stipulated to $150,000 in attorneys' fees.

The clause providing for attorneys' fees is:[4]

   10. AUDIT/INSPECTION:

   . . . .

   (c) [Five Star] shall promptly pay or reimburse [General Mills] for all costs and damages (including lost profits) incurred by [General Mills], including, without limitation, costs for packaging, handling, transportation, recall, destruction, production, and other administrative costs including legal fees, which arise or result from the delivery of Goods by [Five Star] that is not in accordance with the Warranties or any other term in this Order.

Five Star argues on appeal that the doctrine of *ejusdem generis* applies, so that "legal fees" relates only to the administration of the recall. This argument was not raised in the district court, and will not be considered for the first time on appeal. *Lopez v. Tyson Foods, Inc.*, 690 F.3d 869, 875 (8th Cir.2012). As the district court noted: "Five Star does not dispute that the contract provides for attorneys fees; it merely argues that General Mills has no right to such fees because it cannot show that there was any breach." *General Mills*, 789 F.Supp.2d at 1160. The district court properly found that Five Star breached the contract, and appropriately awarded attorneys fees to General Mills.

* * * * * *

The judgment is affirmed. General Mills' cross-appeal is dismissed as moot.

[1] The Honorable Richard H. Kyle, United States District Judge for the District of Minnesota.

[2] None of Five Star's other cases discuss Rule 803(8), nor discuss in detail the admissibility of press releases. *See Smith v. Pfizer, Inc.*, No. 3:05-0444, 2010 WL 1754443, at *1 n. 1 (M.D.Tenn. Apr. 30, 2010) (ruling that the "government's press releases" would be inadmissible hearsay, but not describing the contents of the releases, the purpose for which they were offered, or the grounds on which they were excluded); *Sullivan v. Chesapeake La., L.P.*, No. 09-0579, 2009 WL 3735798, at *2 (W.D.La. Nov. 6, 2009) (noting that "unauthenticated press releases" are inadmissible hearsay, but not mentioning authenticated press releases or releases issued as a result of a government investigation); *Century Colo. Springs P'ship v. Falcon Broadband, Inc.*, No. 05-cv-02295-REB-MJW, 2006 WL 521791, at *3 & n. 3 (D.Colo. Mar. 2, 2006) (ruling that a press release, issued by a business, was hearsay, while denying only the argument that the release was an admission by a party opponent); *Mwani v. Bin Ladin*, No. 99-125(CKK), 2002 U.S. Dist. LEXIS 27826, at *22-23 (D.D.C. Sept. 30, 2002) (ruling that press releases from the State

Department and the President were hearsay, but not discussing the releases' contents or Rule 803(8)); *In re Draganoff's Estate*, 43 Misc.2d 233, 252 N.Y.S.2d 104, 108 (N.Y.Sur.Ct.1964) (stating that a proffered press release was hearsay without discussing its contents).

[3] This case is distinguishable from *Land O'Lakes Creameries, Inc. v. Commodity Credit Corp.*, 185 F.Supp. 412 (D.Minn. 1960), where the issue was how much insect infestation in barrels of dried milk was required to prove that the whole shipment was unfit for human consumption. Here, all of the meat from Westland was deemed to be unfit for human consumption.

[4] General Mills argues that the indemnification clause also provides for attorneys' fees, but as this case does not involve a third-party claim, the indemnification clause is not triggered.

NINTH CIRCUIT DECISIONS

The Rule Against Hearsay

789 F.3d 1107 (2015)
UNITED STATES of America, Plaintiff-Appellee,
v.
Paciano LIZARRAGA-TIRADO, aka Pasiano Lizarraga-Tirado, Defendant-Appellant.
No. 13-10530.

United States Court of Appeals, Ninth Circuit.
Argued and Submitted April 14, 2015.
Filed June 18, 2015.

Roger H. Sigal (argued), Law Offices Roger H. Sigal, Tucson, AZ, for Defendant-Appellant.

Ryan J. Ellersick (argued), Assistant United States Attorney, Robert L. Miskell, Assistant United States Attorney, Appellate Chief, John S. Leonardo, United States Attorney, United States Attorney's Office, Tucson, AZ, for Plaintiff-Appellee.

Before: ALEX KOZINSKI and SUSAN P. GRABER, Circuit Judges, and MICHAEL A. PONSOR,[*] Senior District p.1108 Judge.

OPINION

KOZINSKI, Circuit Judge:

Plotting coordinates on a map used to require a sextant, a compass and quite a bit of skill. Today, anyone can do it with a few clicks of the mouse. This appeal raises a question born of that newfound technological prowess: Are a Google Earth satellite image and a digital "tack" labeled with GPS coordinates hearsay?

I

On January 17, 2003, defendant was arrested near the United States-Mexico border. He was charged with illegal reentry under 8 U.S.C. § 1326 as a previously removed alien who "entered and was found in the United States." At trial, defendant disputed that he had entered the United States before his arrest. He testified that he was still on the Mexico side of the border, waiting for instructions from a smuggler when he was arrested. Because he was arrested on a dark night in a remote location, he insisted that the arresting Border Patrol agents must have accidentally crossed the border before arresting him.

The arresting agents, Garcia and Nunez, testified that they were very familiar with the area where they arrested defendant and were certain they arrested him north of the border. Agent Garcia also testified that she contemporaneously recorded the coordinates of defendant's arrest using a handheld GPS device. To illustrate the location of those coordinates, the government introduced a Google Earth satellite image, attached as Appendix A.

Google Earth is a computer program that allows users to pull up a bird's eye view of any place in the world. It displays satellite images taken from far above the earth's surface with high-resolution cameras. Google Earth superimposes certain markers and labels onto the images, such as names of towns and locations of borders. Relevant here, it also offers two ways for users to add markers of their own. A user can type GPS coordinates into Google Earth, which automatically produces a digital "tack" at the appropriate spot on the map, labeled with the coordinates. A user can also manually add a marker by clicking any spot on the map, which results in a tack that can be labeled by the user.

The satellite image introduced at trial depicts the region where defendant was arrested. It includes a few default labels, such as a nearby highway, a small town and the United States-Mexico border. It also includes a digital tack labeled with a set of GPS coordinates. Agent Garcia testified that the GPS coordinates next to the tack matched the coordinates she recorded the night she arrested defendant. On that basis, she surmised that the tack marked "approximately where [she was] responding to" on the night of defendant's arrest. Because the tack is clearly north of the border, the exhibit corroborated the agents' testimony that defendant was arrested in the United States. Defendant's lawyer cross-examined Agent Garcia about whether she had recorded the GPS coordinates accurately. But he couldn't cross-examine her about the generation of the satellite image or the tack because Agent Garcia hadn't generated them. Indeed, there was no testimony regarding the origin of the satellite image or the tack, and the record doesn't reflect whether the tack was automatically generated or manually placed and labeled. Defense counsel objected to the satellite image on hearsay grounds. The district court overruled that objection and admitted the image.

p.1109 II

Defendant claims that both the satellite image on its own and the digitally added tack and coordinates were impermissible hearsay. The rule against hearsay bars admission of out-of-court statements to prove the truth of the matters asserted. Fed.R.Evid. 801(c)(2), 802; *see also United States v. Arteaga,* 117 F.3d 388, 395 (9th Cir.1997). For hearsay purposes, a statement is defined as "a person's oral assertion, written assertion, or nonverbal conduct, if the person intended it as an assertion." Fed.R.Evid. 801(a). In defendant's view, the satellite image is hearsay because it asserts that it "accurately represented the desert area where the agents worked," and the tack and coordinates are hearsay because they assert "where the agents responded and its proximity to the border."

We first consider whether the satellite image, absent any labels or markers, is hearsay. While we've never faced that precise question, we've held that a photograph isn't hearsay because it makes no "assertion." *See United States v. May,* 622 F.2d 1000, 1007 (9th Cir.1980); *see also United States v. Oaxaca,* 569 F.2d 518, 525 (9th Cir.1978). Rather, a photograph merely depicts a scene as it existed at a particular time. The same is true of a Google Earth satellite image. Such images are produced by high-resolution imaging satellites, and though the cameras are more powerful, the result is the same: a snapshot of the world as it existed when the satellite passed overhead. Because a satellite image, like a photograph, makes no assertion, it isn't hearsay.

The tack and coordinates present a more difficult question. Unlike a satellite image itself, labeled markers added to a satellite image do make clear assertions. Indeed, this is what makes them useful. For example, a dot labeled with the name of a town asserts that there's a town where you see the dot. The label "Starbucks" next to a building asserts that you'll be able to get a Frappuccino there. In short, labeled markers on a satellite image assert that the labeled item exists at the location of the marker.

If the tack is placed manually and then labeled (with a name or GPS coordinates), it's classic hearsay, akin to *Aronson v. McDonald,* 248 F.2d 507, 508-09 (9th Cir. 1957), where we held that hand-drawn additions to a map — there, topography lines — were hearsay. Google Earth allows for the functional equivalent of hand-drawn additions, as a user can place a tack manually and then label it however he chooses. This is like drawing an X on a paper map and labeling it "hidden treasure." That would be an assertion by the person drawing the X that treasure can be found at that location. Similarly, a user could place a tack, label it with incorrect GPS coordinates, and thereby misstate the true location of the tack.

Because there was no evidence at trial as to how the tack and its label were put on the satellite image, we must determine, if we can, whether the tack was computergenerated or placed manually. Fortunately, we can take judicial notice of the fact that the tack was automatically generated by the Google Earth program. By looking to "sources whose accuracy cannot reasonably be questioned" — here, the program — we can "accurately and readily determine[]" that the tack was placed automatically. *See* Fed.R.Evid. 201(b). Specifically, we can access Google Earth and type in the GPS coordinates, and have done so, which results in an identical tack to the one shown on the satellite image admitted at trial.

A tack placed by the Google Earth program and automatically labeled with GPS coordinates isn't hearsay. The hearsay rule applies only to out-of-court *statements,* and it defines a statement as "a p.1110 *person's* oral assertion, written assertion, or nonverbal conduct." Fed.R.Evid. 801(a) (emphasis added). Here, the relevant assertion isn't made by a person; it's made by the Google Earth program. Though a person types in the GPS coordinates, he has no role in figuring out where the tack will be placed. The real work is done by the computer program itself. The program analyzes the GPS coordinates and, without any human intervention, places a labeled tack on the satellite image. Because the program makes the relevant assertion — that the tack is accurately placed at the labeled GPS coordinates — there's no statement as defined by the hearsay rule. In reaching that conclusion, we join other circuits that have held that machine statements aren't hearsay. *See United States v. Lamons,* 532 F.3d 1251, 1263 (11th Cir. 2008); *United States v. Moon,* 512 F.3d 359, 362 (7th Cir.2008); *United States v. Washington,* 498 F.3d 225, 230 (4th Cir. 2007); *United States v. Hamilton,* 413 F.3d 1138, 1142 (10th Cir.2005); *United States v. Khorozian,* 333 F.3d 498, 506 (3d Cir.2003).

That's not to say machine statements don't present evidentiary concerns. A machine might malfunction, produce inconsistent results or have been tampered with. But such concerns are addressed by the rules of authentication, not hearsay. Authentication requires the proponent of evidence to show that the evidence "is what the proponent claims it is." Fed.R.Evid. 901(a). A proponent must show that a machine is reliable and correctly calibrated, and that the data put into the machine (here, the GPS coordinates) is accurate. *See Washington,* 498 F.3d at 231. A specific subsection of the authentication rule allows for authentication of "a process or system" with evidence "describing [the] process or system and showing that it produces an accurate result." Fed.R.Evid. 901(b)(9); *see also United States v. Espinal-*

Almeida, 699 F.3d 588, 612 (1st Cir. 2012) (evaluating whether "marked-up maps generated by Google Earth" were properly authenticated). So when faced with an authentication objection, the proponent of Google-Earth-generated evidence would have to establish Google Earth's reliability and accuracy. That burden could be met, for example, with testimony from a Google Earth programmer or a witness who frequently works with and relies on the program. *See* Charles Alan Wright & Victor James Gold, *Federal Practice & Procedure* § 7114 (2000). It could also be met through judicial notice of the program's reliability, as the Advisory Committee Notes specifically contemplate. *See id.;* Fed.R.Evid. 901 n.9.

But defendant didn't raise an authentication objection at trial, nor does he raise one on appeal. He raised only a hearsay objection, and that objection was properly overruled. Because the satellite image and tack-coordinates pair weren't hearsay, their admission also didn't violate the Confrontation Clause. *See Washington,* 498 F.3d at 231; *United States v. Mitchell,* 502 F.3d 931, 966 (9th Cir.2007) ("The Confrontation Clause does not apply to non-hearsay....").

Defendant also claims that the prosecutor committed misconduct and that the district court erred by admitting evidence of multiple prior removals. We reject those claims for reasons we explain in a memorandum disposition we file concurrently with this opinion.

AFFIRMED.

APPENDIX A

p.1111

[*] The Honorable Michael A. Ponsor, Senior District Judge for the U.S. District Court of Massachusetts, sitting by designation.

784 F.3d 652 (2015)

UNITED STATES of America, Plaintiff-Appellee,

v.

Miguel TORRALBA-MENDIA, Defendant-Appellant.

No. 13-10064.

United States Court of Appeals, Ninth Circuit.

Argued and Submitted February 2, 2015.

Filed April 28, 2015.

US v. Torralba-Mendia, 784 F. 3d 652 (9th Cir. 2015)

p.656 Saji Vettiyil, Vettiyil & Associates, Nogales, AZ, for Defendant-Appellant.

John S. Leonardo, United States Attorney, Robert L. Miskell, Appellate Chief, Bruce M. Ferg (argued), Assistant United States Attorney, United States Attorney's Office, Tucson, AZ, for Plaintiff-Appellee.

Before: RICHARD C. TALLMAN and JOHNNIE B. RAWLINSON, Circuit Judges, and STEPHEN JOSEPH MURPHY III, District Judge.[*]

OPINION

MURPHY, District Judge:

A jury convicted Miguel Torralba-Mendia of conspiring to smuggle undocumented immigrants into the United States, in violation of 8 U.S.C. § 1324(a)(1)(A)(v)(I). Torralba appeals his conviction, contending there was insufficient evidence connecting him to the conspiracy. In addition, he argues the district court incorrectly allowed an expert witness to testify about common practices of alien smuggling organizations. He contends the district court erred in allowing the case agent to offer both lay and expert testimony without giving a curative instruction. And he argues the district court incorrectly admitted redacted I-213 immigration p.657 forms. We have jurisdiction under 28 U.S.C. § 1291, find no prejudicial error, and affirm.

I

A

Between 2007 and 2010, Immigration and Customs Enforcement ("ICE") agents investigated a human smuggling operation near Nogales, Arizona. The investigation revealed that members of the smuggling organization would meet migrants on the Mexican side of the border. Escorts would guide the migrants through the ravines and creek-beds that lie adjacent to Nogales. Once inside the United States, a van or sedan would meet the migrants in the desert and drive them to Geuro Shuttle ("GS"), a company operating out of Tucson. From there, shuttles would drive the migrants to safe houses where they were confined until family members paid for their release.

During the investigation, agents observed Torralba at GS between twenty and twenty-five times. Through intercepted phone calls, agents overheard Torralba coordinate the pick up of migrants and organize their drive north. Agents listened as a person at GS told Torralba to charge $2100 to drive two people to Tucson.

And agents observed Torralba pick up and deliver suspected illegal immigrants to locations in Phoenix.

On one occasion, Torralba picked up several people from GS. Before starting the drive to Phoenix, Torralba did a "heat run" through a local neighborhood: He rapidly accelerated and decelerated, to check if police were following him. He then parked outside a carwash for ten minutes, watching the road. On another occasion, he drove past an unmarked police car with tinted windows parked across from GS. Torralba stopped his car next to the vehicle and tried to look in. He then called GS and told them about the car. Torralba also called GS to tell them that "[t]hey just opened up over here, straight ahead." GS then notified other shuttle drivers that ICE was not operating its checkpoint along the route from Nogales to Tucson.

B

At trial, the government called Agent Burrola as an expert witness. Burrola has more than a decade of law enforcement experience along the border, including three years undercover smuggling undocumented immigrants from Nogales to stash houses in Tucson and Phoenix. He testified about the standard practices of alien smuggling organizations, including how they escorted people over the border, circumvented ICE checkpoints, and utilized safe houses. He explained how to identify undocumented immigrants en route from Mexico, interpreted common code words, and described typical methods and amounts of payment.

The government also called Agent Frazier as both an expert and lay witness. Frazier spent nine years patrolling the border near Nogales. Like Burrola, he explained how smugglers evaded checkpoints and provided ways to distinguish between a guide and a migrant.

After giving expert testimony about the standard practices of alien smuggling organizations, Frazier began to offer lay testimony. The government transitioned from expert to lay testimony by asking, "[a]nd were you eventually assigned to an investigation involving Southern Arizona shuttle companies?" Frazier then testified intermittently over the next few days about his observations in this case. He narrated surveillance videos showing vehicles dropping off and picking up people from GS. He told the jury the duration of time lapses in the videos, pointed out the p.658 vehicles' identifying marks, tied the cars to various conspirators, and counted the number of people exiting and entering different vehicles. He also interpreted phrases in phone calls between shuttle drivers and GS. And he explained which conspirators he thought were the organization's leaders based on evidence that they controlled the migrants, recruited workers, and gave orders to the drivers.

During the trial, the government introduced I-213 immigration forms to prove the migrants detained during the investigation either voluntarily returned to their country of origin or were deported. The admitted forms contained the migrants' photos, fingerprints, physical characteristics, and whether they had been deported or voluntarily returned to their country of origin. The government redacted the agent's narrative detailing how people were apprehended, and all other statements made by the detainee.

II

Torralba challenges the government's use of Agent Frazier as both an expert and lay witness. He contends the district court erred by not instructing the jury on how to evaluate Frazier's dual role testimony, and that much of Frazier's testimony invaded the province of the jury. We hold that, in light of our opinion in *United States v. Vera*, 770 F.3d 1232 (9th Cir. 2014), the district court committed plain error by not instructing the jury on how to properly evaluate Frazier's testimony. Nonetheless, we find that the error was not prejudicial because the government bifurcated Frazier's expert and lay opinion testimony, there was an adequate foundation for Frazier's observations, and sufficient evidence independent of Frazier's testimony linked Torralba to the conspiracy.

A

Torralba argues the district court erred by not instructing the jury on how to properly evaluate Agent Frazier's expert and lay testimony. Because Torralba did not object to the absence of such a jury instruction, we review for plain error. *See United States v. Fuchs*, 218 F.3d 957, 961 (9th Cir.2000); *see also Puckett v. United States*, 556 U.S. 129, 135, 129 S.Ct. 1423, 173 L.Ed.2d 266 (2009) (citing Fed. R.Crim.P. 51(b) & 52(b)).

We have cautioned district courts about the dangers of allowing a case agent to offer both expert and lay opinion testimony. *See Vera*, 770 F.3d at 1242; *United States v. Anchrum*, 590 F.3d 795, 803 (9th Cir.2009); *United States v. Freeman*, 498 F.3d 893, 903-04 (9th Cir.2007). "[A]n agent's status as an expert could lend him unmerited credibility when testifying as a percipient witness, cross-examination might be inhibited, jurors could be confused and the agent might be more likely to stray from reliable methodology and rely on hearsay." *Vera*, 770 F.3d at 1242.

There are several ways to mitigate these concerns. First, the district court should clearly separate the case agent's testimony between lay observations and expert testimony. *See Anchrum*, 590 F.3d at 803. Second, the district court should require an adequately specific foundation, so that the jury has the information needed to evaluate the case agent's testimony. *See Vera*, 770 F.3d at 1243. Third, "the jury must be instructed about what the attendant circumstances are in allowing a government case agent to testify as an expert." *Id.* at 1242 (internal quotation marks omitted). Finally, the court should not allow an officer to "testify based on speculation, rely on hearsay, or interpret unambiguous, clear statements." *Id.*

p.659 In *Vera*, we held that "[i]n light of our Circuit's clearly expressed concerns about case agents testifying in both lay and expert capacities, the district court's failure to give an instruction explaining [the agent's] dual roles was plain error." *Id.* at 1246. We emphasized that, although the defense had not objected to the jury instructions, "the ultimate responsibility for assuring the reliability of expert testimony and for instructing the jury on how to evaluate case agent dual role testimony rests with the district court." *Id.* at 1243.

In the present case, the district court offered to instruct the jury on how to properly evaluate expert and lay testimony. The government also stated it had an instruction that would help the jury evaluate Frazier's dual role testimony. Torralba objected to the government's proposed instruction, however, and failed to offer an instruction of his own. The district court instructed the jury on how to evaluate opinion testimony generally, but did not include any instruction on differentiating between lay and expert testimony. Torralba did not object to the instructions read to the jury.

We hold the district court committed plain error by not instructing the jury on how to evaluate dual role testimony. While there is a small degree of invited error—the district court solicited Torralba to offer an instruction about dual role testimony—our cases make clear that the trial court is ultimately responsible for ensuring the jury understands how to evaluate dual role testimony. *Vera,* 770 F.3d at 1243. Accordingly, the district court committed plain error by not giving a curative instruction, though the error was not prejudicial for the reasons stated in section C.

B

Torralba also argues the district court erred in allowing Frazier to narrate videos, interpret phrases in recorded phone calls, and opine about the role of various conspirators. With a few exceptions, Torralba did not object to Frazier's testimony. We review objected to evidentiary rulings for abuse of discretion, and unobjected to evidentiary issues for plain error. *United States v. Banks,* 514 F.3d 959, 975-76 (9th Cir.2008). For the following reasons, we find Frazier offered proper lay testimony and did not invade the province of the jury.

First, we have previously held that an officer who has extensively reviewed a video may offer a narration, pointing out particulars that a casual observer might not see. In *United States v. Begay,* 42 F.3d 486, 502-03 (9th Cir.1994), an officer narrated a video of a riot. We held the narrative was proper lay testimony. The officer had personal knowledge of the events in the video because he had watched the video nearly a hundred times. And his narration was helpful because he pointed out details a casual observer was likely to miss. Thus, the officer's "testimony concerning which persons were engaged in what conduct at any given moment could help the jury discern correctly and efficiently the events depicted in the video." *Id.* at 503.

Torralba did not object when Frazier narrated videos showing cars arriving and departing from GS. Frazier testified that he had watched each video roughly fifty times, and that he would often watch the video feed live while it was being recorded. The narratives helped the jury understand what they were seeing. For example, Frazier provided the length of time lapses between video clips. He pointed out unique characteristics of the vehicles—like their makes, models, and whether any bodywork had been done to them—that helped the jury identify the same cars in p.660 subsequent videos. He linked the different cars to specific conspirators. He counted the number of passengers exiting or entering the vehicles (a difficult task because the video's angle obscured the view). And he pointed out the particular clothing of certain passengers, to show that a person dropped off in one video was the same person picked up in a later video. Frazier's narratives were based on his repeated viewing of the recordings, and helped the jury understand the import of the videos.

Second, we have held that an officer may give lay testimony about the meaning of ambiguous phrases in recorded calls. The interpretations must be based on the officer's observations in the case, should not rely on hearsay, and must be helpful; i.e., the officer should not interpret clear language. *Freeman*, 498 F.3d at 902, 904-05. For example, in *Freeman*, we found an officer properly interpreted "'[m]an, it's done already' to mean 'he's given the cocaine to Kevin Freeman and that he's received money for it.'" *Id.* at 902. That testimony was based on the witness' personal knowledge of the investigation and was helpful to the jury. To the contrary, in *Vera* we explained that a case agent improperly interpreted the demand that a supplier "'lower the price for you, fool, because tell her that it is a little expensive, fool,' as meaning that 'whatever she is selling it for, Mr. Vera probably feels it's a little more expensive than what he wants to pay for it, so he's trying to negotiate, maybe get the price lowered.'" *Vera*, 770 F.3d at 1246 n. 9. The testimony merely restated the obvious, and was not helpful.

Here, Frazier interpreted multiple recorded phrases. Torralba objected to only two of the interpretations. He objected when Frazier stated the word "radio" referred to a Nextel push-talk phone, arguing the meaning of "radio" was obvious and not helpful to the jury. The government argued that Frazier's interpretation was based on his listening to thousands of recorded phone calls, and the explanation helped the jury put the calls in context. Even if the interpretation was not proper lay testimony—it is unclear why the distinction between a traditional radio and a Nextel push-talk phone is relevant—its admission was harmless for the reasons stated below.

Torralba also objected when the government asked Frazier to interpret Torralba's statement that "it's open straight ahead." At a bench conference, the government stated it expected Frazier to testify that the phrase meant ICE was not operating its checkpoint. After the testimony resumed, Frazier stated it was common for smugglers to tell each other when ICE was not operating the checkpoint. But he did not interpret the phrase "it's open straight ahead," and therefore no error occurred.

Torralba did not object when Frazier interpreted phrases in other recorded phone calls. For example, Frazier stated the words "in the fight" meant the smugglers were trying to guide the migrants around an ICE checkpoint. In support, he explained that he heard that phrase in many phone conversations when the smugglers were transporting people from Nogales to Tucson. According to Frazier, the region south of Tucson contained "a particularly heavy concentration of United States Border Patrol Agents." The district court did not commit plain error in admitting this, and similar, unobjected to testimony: Frazier interpreted arguably ambiguous phrases based on his extensive review of the recorded phone calls, and he consistently explained his reasoning.

p.661 Finally, Torralba argues Frazier invaded the province of the jury when he opined that Chapo Casino, Geuro Pesado, and Alfredo Olea—three men frequently overheard talking on the phone and meeting at GS—led the alien smuggling organization. Torralba objected to this portion of Frazier's testimony at trial. A lay witness may opine about a person's role in an organization when the opinion is based on his own perceptions, is helpful to the jury, and does not require specialized knowledge. *See* Fed.R.Evid. 701; *United States v. Figueroa-Lopez*, 125 F.3d

1241, 1245-46 (9th Cir.1997) (explaining that lay witnesses may testify about the implication of an observation when the "observations are common enough and require such a limited amount of expertise, if any, that they can, indeed, be deemed lay witness opinion").

Frazier testified that Chapo Casino, Geuro Pesado, and Alfredo Olea headed the alien smuggling organization. In support, he pointed to phone conversations in which the men tried to recruit shuttle operators. Furthermore, they referred to the migrants as "mine" or "theirs," and showed control over the undocumented immigrants. They coordinated the shuttles and gave orders to the drivers.

Frazier's testimony was based entirely on his observations in the case. He listened to hours of recorded phone calls, during which he discerned the relationship between the speakers. The phone calls that he based his inferences upon were received as evidence. By knowing the relationship between the speakers, the jury could better understand the meaning and context of the calls. And Frazier's opinion about the members' organizational roles was not based on specialized knowledge or expertise in alien smuggling: Managers in a wide variety of organizations recruit employees, coordinate operations, and give orders to workers.

In short, Frazier offered appropriate lay testimony when he narrated the videos, interpreted ambiguous phrases in recorded phone calls, and stated he thought certain people led the alien smuggling organization.

C

The district court committed plain error when it failed to instruct the jury on how to evaluate Frazier's dual role testimony. We remedy a district court's plain error only when the defendant shows that the error affected his substantial rights. Fed.R.Crim.P. 52(b); *Puckett,* 556 U.S. at 135, 129 S.Ct. 1423. Put differently, there "must be a reasonable probability that the error affected the outcome of the trial." *United States v. Marcus,* 560 U.S. 258, 262, 130 S.Ct. 2159, 176 L.Ed.2d 1012 (2010).

In *Vera,* we held the court's failure to instruct the jury on how to evaluate an agent's dual role testimony prejudiced the defendants. We noted the agent's opinion "comprised the sole evidence" about the quantity of drugs at issue. 770 F.3d at 1246. The district court did not "require an adequately specific foundation" for the agent's opinions. *Id.* at 1243. And the agent testified about the meaning of phone calls "well within the understanding of an ordinary juror," which "may have encouraged the jury to defer to [the agent's] opinions instead of listening to the calls and reaching an independent judgment." *Id.* at 1246.

Here, Torralba has not shown the absence of a curative instruction affected the outcome of the trial. First, the government bifurcated Frazier's testimony between his expert testimony and percipient observations. Frazier's testimony began with his credentials in the field of alien smuggling, his descriptions of how smugglers p.662 circumvented ICE checkpoints, and the common characteristics of undocumented immigrants en route from Mexico. After the completion of his expert testimony, the government transitioned to questions about the instant case, asking "[a]nd were you eventually assigned to an investigation involving Southern Arizona shuttle companies?" From that point forward, Frazier testified about his observations during the investigation of GS. When the government divided Frazier's "testimony into two separate phases it avoided blurring the distinction between Agent [Frazier's] distinct role as a lay witness and his role as an expert witness." *United States v. Anchrum,* 590 F.3d 795, 804 (9th Cir. 2009).

Second, Frazier provided an adequate foundation for most of his observations. Whether he was narrating videos, interpreting phone calls, or opining on the role of various conspirators, he consistently explained his reasoning. And the evidence that he based his testimony on—videos, phone call recordings, still frame photos—was all given to the jury. Thus, the jury had the information it needed to evaluate Frazier's opinions.

Third, a substantial amount of evidence, aside from Frazier's testimony, connected Torralba to the conspiracy. Videos captured him repeatedly picking up suspected illegal immigrants from GS. Recorded phone conversations detailed his efforts to retrieve groups from the desert, as well as the amount of money he intended to charge. And his actions—engaging in counter-surveillance, alerting GS to a suspected police vehicle, and telling GS that ICE was not operating its checkpoint—all support the verdict. Accordingly, while the court committed plain error in not giving a curative instruction, the error was not prejudicial and does not require reversal.

III

Torralba next claims the district court erred in allowing Agent Burrola to offer expert testimony about alien smuggling organizations, arguing the testimony's probative value was greatly out-weighed by unfair prejudice. *See* Fed. R.Evid. 403. We review a district court's decision to admit expert testimony for abuse of discretion. *See United States v. Mejia-Luna,* 562 F.3d 1215, 1218 (9th Cir. 2009).

We have previously held that government agents may testify about the general practices of alien smuggling organizations to establish their modus operandi. In *Mejia-Luna,* we found the district court did not abuse its discretion by admitting expert testimony about "how alien smuggling operations typically operate, the division of responsibility among numerous actors, the methods used, and the manner and method of payment." *Id.* at 1219. Similarly, in *United States v. Lopez-Martinez,* we held the district court did not commit plain error by allowing a government agent to testify "about patterns and methods common among smugglers" in the local area. 543 F.3d 509, 514-15 (9th Cir.2008). We have also found that expert witnesses may testify about the meaning of code words or specialized jargon. *See United States v. Vera,* 770 F.3d 1232, 1241 (9th Cir.2014).

In the present case, Burrola testified about how alien smuggling organizations guide people across the border, evade ICE checkpoints and patrols, and employ safe houses. He pointed out common characteristics of undocumented immigrants en route from Mexico: They were often dirty due to spending several days and nights walking through the wilderness, carried little luggage, and were controlled by guides. He also interpreted common code p.663 words or jargon, and described the amounts and methods of payment.

Burrola's testimony helped the jury understand Torralba's role in the alien smuggling scheme. Based on the common characteristics of migrants en route from Mexico, a jury could determine Torralba knew many of his passengers were not legitimate travelers. Burrola's testimony about the typical smuggling rate is consistent with the amount Torralba stated he would collect to drive two people to Tucson. And Burrola's statements about how guides escort people across the border and around ICE checkpoints helped the jury understand why Torralba coordinated the pick up of groups from remote areas of the desert.

Furthermore, Torralba has not shown the testimony was unduly prejudicial. The only Ninth Circuit precedent he cites were non-conspiracy cases in which we found evidence about the structure of a criminal organization was highly prejudicial and not relevant. *See United States v. Varela-Rivera,* 279 F.3d 1174, 1179 (9th Cir.2002) ("[E]xpert testimony on the modus operandi of drug trafficking organizations is inadmissible in cases where, as here, the defendant is not charged with conspiracy to distribute drugs."); *United States v. Pineda-Torres,* 287 F.3d 860, 864 (9th Cir.2002) (same); *United States v. Vallejo,* 237 F.3d 1008, 1015-17 (9th Cir.2001) (same). Here, by contrast, the government charged Torralba with a conspiracy. Evidence about the smuggling organization's methods helped prove the existence of a conspiracy and put Torralba's actions in context. Accordingly, the district court did not abuse its discretion in admitting Burrola's expert testimony.

IV

Torralba concedes the government proved an alien smuggling organization was operating out of GS, but argues there was no evidence he was aware of, or joined, any conspiracy. "We review de novo the district court's denial of a motion for judgment of acquittal based on insufficient evidence." *United States v. Mincoff,* 574 F.3d 1186, 1191-92 (9th Cir.2009) (citations omitted). When reviewing the sufficiency of the evidence, we "view the evidence in the light most favorable to the prosecution and determine whether any rational trier of fact could have found the defendant guilty of each element of the crime beyond a reasonable doubt." *United States v. Heller,* 551 F.3d 1108, 1113 (9th Cir.2009).

Section 1324 provides criminal penalties for "[a]ny person who ... engages in any conspiracy to commit any of the preceding acts." 8 U.S.C. § 1324(a)(1)(A)(v). To establish an alien smuggling conspiracy, the government must prove an agreement to carry out one of the substantive offenses, and that Torralba had the intent necessary to commit the underlying offense. *See United States v. Herrera-Gonzalez,* 263 F.3d 1092, 1095 (9th Cir.2001) (interpreting a similarly worded drug conspiracy statute); *see also United States v. Shabani,* 513 U.S. 10, 13, 115 S.Ct. 382, 130 L.Ed.2d 225 (1994) (holding conspiracies require an overt act only when explicitly stated in the statute's text).

It is undisputed that a conspiracy to smuggle undocumented immigrants into the United States existed. The only question is whether Torralba was part of the conspiracy and whether he intended to further it. Once the government has established the existence of a conspiracy, "evidence of only a slight connection is necessary to support a conviction of knowing participation in that conspiracy." *United States v. Sanchez-Mata,* 925 F.2d p.664 1166, 1167 (9th Cir.1991). A "slight connection means that a defendant need not have known all the conspirators, participated in the conspiracy from its beginning, participated in all its enterprises, or known all its details." *Herrera-Gonzalez,* 263 F.3d at 1095. But it does require more than a "[m]ere casual association with conspiring people." *United States v. Estrada-Macias,* 218 F.3d 1064, 1066 (9th Cir. 2000) (quoting *United States v. Cloughessy,* 572 F.2d 190, 191 (9th Cir.1977)).

Ample evidence showed that Torralba joined the conspiracy with the intent to further its objectives. For example, in a recorded phone call, Torralba agreed to deliver two people for $2100, an amount consistent with the rates traffickers charge to smuggle people to Tucson. In other calls, Torralba coordinated the pick up and delivery of migrants, and videos showed him transporting suspected illegal immigrants from GS on multiple occasions. Furthermore, many of Torralba's actions are inconsistent with being simply an unsuspecting shuttle driver. He engaged in counter-surveillance techniques to evade police, informed GS of an unmarked police car watching the business, and called GS to tell them the ICE checkpoint was not operating. Based on these facts, a rational juror could find beyond a reasonable doubt that Torralba joined the conspiracy with the intent to further it.

V

The government introduced I-213 immigration forms, which were labeled a "Record of Deportable/Inadmissible Alien." The government introduced the forms to show that many of the passengers detained during the investigation were, in fact, deported. Torralba argues that the forms contained inadmissible hearsay and their introduction violated the Confrontation Clause. We review the district court's rulings on the Confrontation Clause and its construction of the hearsay rules de novo. *United States v. Morales,* 720 F.3d 1194, 1199 (9th Cir.2013). We review decisions to admit evidence under a hearsay exception for abuse of discretion. *Id.*

A

Torralba first argues the forms are inadmissible hearsay. Under Rule 803(8), a record or statement of a public office is admissible as an exception to the hearsay rule if it sets out "a matter observed while under a legal duty to report, but not including, in a criminal case, a matter observed by law-enforcement personnel." Fed.R.Evid. 803(8)(A)(ii).

In *United States v. Lopez* we held the public records exception applied to a "Verification of Removal." 762 F.3d 852, 861 (9th Cir.2014). The verification of removal contained the date, port, and manner of the alien's departure, as well as the alien's photograph, signature and fingerprint, and an officer's signature. *Id.* at 856. We reasoned the officer had a legal duty to fill out the form, explaining that "[r]ecording and maintaining verifications that an individual has been deported falls under the rubric of responsibilities assigned to the Department of Homeland Security; therefore, completing the verification of removal form is appropriate to the function of the agency." *Id.* at 862. Furthermore, we found the documents admissible notwithstanding the general prohibition against admitting records created by law enforcement. We reasoned the law enforcement prohibition's purpose was to "exclude observations made by officials at the scene of the crime or apprehension, because observations made in an adversarial setting are less reliable than observations made by public officials in other situations." *Id.* at 861 (quoting *United States v. Hernandez-Rojas,* 617 F.2d 533, 535 (9th Cir.1980)). p.665 The verification of removal, by contrast, was a "ministerial, objective observation" that merely "records the movement of aliens across the United States border," and was therefore "inherent[ly] reliab[le] because of the Government's need to keep accurate records of the movement of aliens." *Id.* (internal quotation marks and citations omitted); *see also United States v. Loyola-Dominguez,* 125 F.3d 1315, 1317-18 (9th Cir.1997) (finding warrants of removal/deportation were admissible under public records hearsay exception).

The same principles apply here. The admitted record of a deportable alien contains the same information as a verification of removal: The alien's name, photograph, fingerprints, as well as the date, port and method of departure, and the officer's signature. The government redacted all other statements, including the officer's narration explaining how the alien was apprehended, and the alien's statements regarding his country of origin and address. Furthermore, the record of a deportable alien, like a verification of removal, is part of an alien's A-File, filled out and kept by the Department of Homeland Security in its regular course of business. Finally, the admitted forms are a ministerial, objective observation detailing how the aliens were repatriated, and do not implicate the purposes animating the law enforcement exception. Other circuits addressing this issue have found I-213 forms admissible under Rule 803(8). *See United States v. Caraballo,* 595 F.3d 1214, 1226 (11th Cir.2010); *Renteria-Gonzalez v. I.N.S.,* 322 F.3d 804, 817 n. 16 (5th Cir.2003).

Torralba's arguments to the contrary are unavailing. He contends the Court must evaluate whether the aliens' statements independently qualify for a hearsay exception. For example, in *Morales,* we held an I-826 form containing migrants' statements about their country of origin and admissions that they were in the United States illegally did not fall within the public records exception. 720 F.3d at 1201-02. We explained that the aliens did not have a duty to report their immigration status or their place of birth. Here, by contrast, the government has thoroughly redacted the forms. The I-213 forms do not contain any alien statements about their country of origin, or any admission that they were in the United States illegally. Accordingly, there is no need to determine if the aliens' statements qualify for a hearsay exception, as no such statements were included in the forms.

B

Torralba also contends the admission of the I-213 forms violated his confrontation rights. The Sixth Amendment provides, "[i]n all criminal prosecutions, the accused shall enjoy the right ... to be confronted with the witnesses against him." U.S. Const. amend. VI. "[T]he Confrontation Clause bars admission of testimonial statements unless the declarant is unavailable to testify and the defendant previously had an opportunity to cross-examine the declarant." *United States v. Albino-Loe,* 747 F.3d 1206, 1210 (9th Cir.2014). A statement is within the "core class of testimonial statements" when it was "made under circumstances which would lead an objective witness reasonably to believe that the statement would be available for use at a later trial." *Melendez-Diaz v. Massachusetts,* 557 U.S. 305, 310, 129 S.Ct. 2527, 174 L.Ed.2d 314 (2009) (quoting *Crawford v. Washington,* 541 U.S. 36, 52, 124 S.Ct. 1354, 158 L.Ed.2d 177 (2004)).

The Supreme Court has explained that public records are normally non-testimonial because they are "created for the administration of an entity's affairs and not p.666 for the purpose of establishing or proving some fact at trial." *Id.* at 324, 129 S.Ct. 2527. We have repeatedly held that immigration documents contained in an alien's A-file are non-testimonial because they are "not made in anticipation of litigation, and because [they are] simply a routine, objective cataloging of an unambiguous factual matter." *Lopez,* 762 F.3d at 860 (holding verification of removal was non-testimonial); *see also Albino-Loe,* 747 F.3d at 1210-11 (holding notice to appear was non-testimonial); *Morales,* 720 F.3d at 1200 (holding I-826 forms were non-testimonial); *United States v. Orozco-Acosta,* 607 F.3d 1156, 1164 (9th Cir.2010) (holding warrants of removal were non-testimonial); *United States v. Bahena-Cardenas,* 411 F.3d 1067, 1075 (9th Cir.2005) (same).

The same principles apply here. Nothing in the I-213 forms suggest the documents were completed in anticipation of litigation. Rather, the I-213 form "is routinely completed by Customs and Border Patrol agents in the course of their non-adversarial duties, not in the course of preparing for a criminal prosecution." *Caraballo,* 595 F.3d at 1226. As is evident from the form itself, the record of a deportable alien merely collects the alien's biographical information, gives the officer an opportunity to describe how the person was apprehended (which the government redacted), and states whether they were deported or voluntarily returned. Agents complete I-213 forms regardless of whether the government decides to prosecute anyone criminally. *See id.* at 1228 ("[T]he I-213 form is routinely requested from every alien entering the United States, and the form itself is filled out for anyone entering the United States without proper immigration papers."). As with other evidence in an alien's A-file, the documents are prepared for administrative purposes, not as evidence in a later trial. Accordingly, because the documents are not testimonial, their admission did not run afoul of the Confrontation Clause.

VI

There was no reversible error and we therefore affirm.

AFFIRMED.

[*] The Honorable Stephen Joseph Murphy III, District Judge for the U.S. District Court for the Eastern District of Michigan, sitting by designation.

794 F.3d 1053 (2015)

UNITED STATES of America, Plaintiff-Appellee,

v.

Alfonso TORRES, Defendant-Appellant.

No. 13-50553.

United States Court of Appeals, Ninth Circuit.

Argued and Submitted March 5, 2015.

Filed July 22, 2015.

p.1055 Devin Burstein (argued), Warren & Burstein, San Diego, CA, for Defendant-Appellant.

Kyle W. Hoffman (argued), Assistant United States Attorney; Laura E. Duffy, United States Attorney; Bruce R. Castetter, Assistant United States Attorney, Chief Appellate Section, Criminal Division, San Diego, CA, for Plaintiff-Appellee.

Before: MICHAEL R. MURPHY,[*] RONALD M. GOULD, and RICHARD C. TALLMAN, Circuit Judges.

OPINION

TALLMAN, Circuit Judge:

Alfonso Torres appeals his conviction for knowingly transporting seventy-three kilograms of cocaine across the United States-Mexico border concealed in a specially constructed compartment of his pickup truck. *See* 21 U.S.C. §§ 952, 960. At his first trial, which ended in a hung jury, the district court permitted Torres to testify that his friend in Tijuana, Fernando Griese, borrowed his truck on several occasions. During this time, Torres alleged the modifications and concealment could have been made to his truck without his knowledge. On retrial, Torres attempted to testify about other requests made to him by Griese, who Torres claimed was manipulating him into unknowingly carrying drugs across the border by asking him for favors running errands in San Diego. The district court, however, precluded this line of questioning as hearsay and irrelevant.

p.1056 We have jurisdiction under 28 U.S.C. § 1291. We hold that the district court properly excluded Torres's "favors" testimony as hearsay because — although some questions and inquiries may constitute non-hearsay — where the declarant intends the question to communicate an implied assertion and the proponent offers it for this intended message, the question falls within the hearsay definition. But even if the exclusion was error, we find "it is more probable than not that the error did not materially affect the verdict." *United States v. Seschillie,* 310 F.3d 1208, 1214 (9th Cir.2002). Thus, we affirm.

I

A

On August 14, 2012, Alfonso Torres drove his Dodge Ram pickup truck through the Otay Mesa, California, Port of Entry from Mexico into the United States using the Secure Electronic Network for Travelers Rapid Inspection ("SENTRI") lane. A

SENTRI card holder is allowed to use special entry lanes reserved for pre-screened, trusted travelers. Manning the SENTRI lane that day, Customs and Border Protection ("CBP") Officer Rodolfo Sanchez inspected Torres's documents and returned them; Torres paused, gripped the steering wheel, and then hit the gas. The manner in which Torres paused and stared at him seemed abnormal to Officer Sanchez; and as Torres drove away, Officer Sanchez noticed a space discrepancy between the pickup's bed and the chassis underneath the tailgate door. This prompted Officer Sanchez to enter a "forced secondary referral lookout" on Torres's truck in the CBP computer to alert inspectors the next time he crossed.

Two days later, on August 16, 2012, Torres once again drove through the Otay Mesa Port of Entry. Based on the computer alert, he was referred to secondary inspection for closer examination, including an x-ray of his truck. The x-ray produced a "no scan" as a result of Torres stopping only briefly during the scan. CBP officers then instructed Torres to park in the secondary lot for a manual search. Moments later, CBP Officer Benjamin Joseph approached Torres and asked him to turn off the ignition. Officer Joseph testified that as Torres handed over his keys, his hands were shaking.

In secondary, a drug dog alerted to Torres's truck and, after further inspection, officers found a hole and strings leading to packages underneath the truck bed. Because the hole was not big enough to extract the packages, the officers first attempted to pull out the drugs using a crow bar. When this failed, they lifted the truck bed from the chassis and removed an access panel. Still unable to remove all the parcels, CBP officers then instructed a mechanic to cut another access panel. It took CBP officers about two hours to access the compartment. Ultimately, seventy-three kilograms of cocaine were recovered from the well-hidden compartment in Torres's truck.[1] Installation of the compartment had increased the space between the bottom of the truck bed and the chassis of the truck, which Officer Sanchez had noticed two days earlier. The government's auto expert testified that accessing the cocaine bricks in the hidden compartment required either heavy machinery, such as a car lift, or three to four people to lift the truck bed off the chassis.

During Torres's post-arrest interview, he insisted that he had no knowledge of the drugs. Torres stated that he had taken his truck to a mechanic in Tijuana a few months prior to his arrest where modifications p.1057 could have been made without his knowledge.

B

Torres's first trial began on April 9, 2013, but ended in a hung jury. At the first trial, Torres testified that he had left his truck with the mechanic in Tijuana for a month. The mechanic had botched the paint job and then offered to buy the truck from Torres. Torres also testified that he had loaned the truck to his friend, Fernando Griese ("Fernando"), on four different occasions.[2] Torres said that Fernando returned the truck each time meticulously cleaned "inside and out." Fernando last borrowed Torres's truck about a week and a half prior to Torres's arrest. On the day Fernando returned the truck, he asked Torres if he could take Fernando's friend to the D.M.V. near San Ysidro, California, about eight miles from the Otay Mesa Port of Entry. Torres declined. The next day Fernando called making the same request, and Torres declined a second time. Later, Fernando asked Torres to drive his friend to a tire shop in San Diego to pick up some tires. Torres never acted on this request either.

Although at the first trial the Government objected to Torres's testimony as hearsay, at sidebar, Torres argued that he was "not seeking to introduce this for the truth of the matter, but rather for the effect on the listener." The district court overruled the Government's hearsay objection.[3] After further objections, and once it became apparent that Torres declined the favor and never drove to the D.M.V., the district court instructed defense counsel at a second sidebar that "the extent of the examination should be, to the extent it may be permissible, that Fernando asked to take someone to the D.M.V., gave me some instruction, but it didn't happen. That should be it."[4] The trial ended in a p.1058 hung jury after a day and half of deliberations.

C

The second trial began June 4, 2013, and lasted two days. It resulted in a guilty verdict. Prior to the commencement of the second trial, Torres moved to permit the challenged "favors" testimony, but the district court excluded Fernando's requests as hearsay and irrelevant. Because the district court was under the impression that Torres had acted on Fernando's directives, it initially thought the testimony would be admissible under the hearsay exception for the effect on the listener. The district court explained the second time around that after listening to the proffered testimony at the first trial, "the court had the Hobson's choice of directing the jury to disregard that entire batch of testimony from the defendant because [Torres] didn't tie it up [] to acting on that instruction," or admitting it.

However, since Torres never drove to the D.M.V. or the tire shop, the district court found Torres had actually offered his testimony regarding the inquiries "for the assumption of the truth, for the assumption they are true to build a third-party defense...." It concluded, "if [the inquiries] are not presented for the truth of the matter, or if they don't prove or disprove any facts as the defendant suggests, they are not relevant." In other words, "[a]s the statement is not offered to prove any facts or its truth, it's not relevant." However, Torres was permitted to testify that Fernando had borrowed his truck on four occasions leading up to his arrest.

The other major difference between the first and second trial was the testimony of a defense expert witness — Efren Lapuz, a former special agent with the Drug Enforcement Administration. Although the Government did not present drug trafficking organization ("DTO") "structure" or "modus operandi" evidence in its case-in-chief, Lapuz testified for the defense about the value of seventy-three kilograms of cocaine and where DTOs generally purchased the drug. The district court ruled that Torres had opened the door to DTO "modus operandi" evidence, and the Government then impeached Lapuz on cross-examination about prior testimony from an unrelated trial where he had averred that DTOs rarely utilized "blind mules"[5] because drug traffickers preferred straightforward transactions — "I pay you, you take the risk." The Government also elicited helpful testimony from Lapuz that because border crossings were a point of risk, DTOs generally attempted to minimize the number of such crossings with a single load concealed in the vehicle.

On defense re-direct Lapuz testified that drug cartels generally did not care if the courier was unknowing. He testified that cartels like to use a blind mule because it diffuses the risk of compromising the entire organization if he is arrested; it is an inexpensive mode of transporting drugs; and, so long as they can control the transaction on the other side, the cartel has gained something without losing anything. p.1059 On re-cross examination, the Government questioned Lapuz about whether he had ever heard of a blind mule with a wellhidden compartment transporting drugs, as opposed to magnetic compartments on the undercarriage that are easily removable. Lapuz stated he had not personally seen them, but had heard about it in the media.

On June 6, 2013, after deliberating for approximately two and a half hours, the jury found Torres guilty of one count of importation of cocaine under 21 U.S.C. §§ 952 and 960. The district court sentenced Torres to 132 months' imprisonment. This appeal followed.

II

We review the interpretation of the rules of evidence de novo, but a district court's decision to exclude evidence for abuse of discretion. *See United States v. Mitchell,* 502 F.3d 931, 964 (9th Cir.2007); *United States v. Castillo,* 181 F.3d 1129, 1134 (9th Cir.1999). In assessing whether a district court abused its discretion, we first "determine de novo whether the trial court identified the correct legal rule to apply to the relief requested." *United States v. Hinkson,* 585 F.3d 1247, 1262 (9th Cir.2009) (en banc). If so, we then consider "whether the trial court's application of the correct legal standard was (1) illogical, (2) implausible, or (3) without support in inferences that may be drawn from the facts in the record." *Id.* (internal quotation marks and citation omitted). "We review de novo whether an evidentiary error rises to the level of a constitutional violation." *United States v. Pineda-Doval,* 614 F.3d 1019, 1032 (9th Cir.2010) (citation omitted).

A

As a general rule, a party is prohibited from introducing a statement made by an out-of-court declarant when it is offered at trial to prove the truth of the matter asserted. Fed.R.Evid. 801(c), 802. For the purposes of hearsay, a "statement" is defined as "a person's oral assertion, written assertion, or nonverbal conduct, if the person intended it as an assertion." Fed. R.Evid. 801(a). The Advisory Committee Note clarifies that the effect of the "statement" definition is to "exclude from the operation of the hearsay rule all evidence of conduct, verbal or nonverbal, not *intended* as an assertion. The key to the definition [of a statement] is that nothing is an assertion unless intended to be one." Fed.R.Evid. 801 advisory committee's note to Subdivision (a) 1972 Proposed Rules (emphasis added).

Torres alleges that the district court erred in precluding his testimony about Fernando's inquiries because this evidence does not constitute hearsay. We hold that while some questions may constitute non-hearsay, where the declarant intends the question to communicate an implied assertion and the proponent offers it for this intended message, the question falls within the definition of hearsay.

Some of our sister circuits have held that questions or requests are admissible as non-hearsay because questions are not intended to assert anything. *See, e.g., United States v. Lewis,* 902 F.2d 1176, 1179 (5th Cir.1990).[6] In *Lewis,* for example, p.1060 after a defendant's drug-related arrest, his pager or "beeper" went off. *Id.* The police officer who confiscated the pager called the number and impersonated the defendant. *Id.* The unidentified person asked: "Did you get the stuff?" and "Where is Dog?" *Id.* At trial, the district court allowed the officer to testify to the questions asked by the unidentified caller over the defendant's hearsay objections. *Id.* The Fifth Circuit determined that "[t]he questions asked by the unknown caller, like most questions and inquiries, are not hearsay because they do not, and were not intended to, assert anything." *Id.* (citations omitted). Thus, *Lewis* held that the implied assertion contained in the caller's question (i.e., defendant was expecting to receive "stuff") was not hearsay because the definition of "statement" in Rule 801(a) "remov[ed] implied assertions from the coverage of the hearsay rule." *Id.* (citation omitted).

Notwithstanding the Fifth Circuit's broad holding in *Lewis,* we think the issue is more nuanced and context specific. It is widely recognized that the grammatical form of a verbal utterance does not govern whether it fits within the definition of hearsay. *See* 4 Christopher B. Mueller & Laird C. Kirkpatrick, Federal Evidence, § 8.6, at 57 (4th ed. 2013) ("For purposes of the hearsay doctrine [] the term 'assertion' or 'statement' includes questions and imperatives that express or communicate facts or information about acts, events, or conditions in the world. Indeed, such formulations of human expression are as much within the hearsay doctrine as simple declarative sentences."); 4 Clifford S. Fishman & Anne T. McKenna, Jones on Evidence, § 24:13, 168 (7th ed. Supp.2012) ("An utterance that is in the form of a question can in substance contain an assertion of fact." (quotation marks and citation omitted)).

Other circuits have not foreclosed the possibility that questions can be classified as hearsay. *See, e.g., United States v. Summers,* 414 F.3d 1287, 1299-1300 (10th Cir.2005). In *Summers,* police arrested defendant Marvin Thomas along with three co-defendants on bank robbery and aiding and abetting charges. *Id.* at 1293. While being led to a police car, one of the co-defendants inquired of the arresting officer: "How did you guys find us so fast?" *Id.* The codefendant pled guilty, while Thomas proceeded to trial. *Id.* At trial, the district court allowed the police officer to testify about the co-defendant's inquiry under the present-sense impression exception to the hearsay rule. *Id.* at 1298; Fed.R.Evid. 803(1).

On appeal, *Summers* reasoned that, unlike the "innocuous and ambiguous question" in *United States v. Jackson,* 88 F.3d 845 (10th Cir.1996) — where a police officer spoke with an unidentified person paging the defendant's confiscated beeper, who asked "Is this Kenny?" — in Thomas's case the declarant's intent was apparent. *Summers,* 414 F.3d at 1299-1300. "It begs credulity to assume that in positing the question [the co-defendant] was exclusively interested in modern methods of law enforcement, including surveillance, communication, and coordination. Rather, fairly construed the statement intimated both guilt and wonderment at the ability of the police to apprehend the perpetrators of the crime so quickly." *Id.* at 1300. Thus, the p.1061 Tenth Circuit held that "Thomas ha[d] met his burden of demonstrating that by positing the question, 'How did you guys find us so fast?,' [the co-defendant] intended to make an assertion." *Id.*

While we have not previously addressed whether questions constitute hearsay, we think "the term 'matter asserted' as employed in Rule 801(c) and at common law includes *both* matters directly expressed and matters the declarant *necessarily implicitly intended* to assert." 30B Kenneth W. Graham, Jr. & Michael H. Graham, Federal Practice & Procedure § 7001 (2014) (emphasis added). Because there may be instances where a party attempts to admit hearsay by cloaking statements under the guise of a question, the focus of the inquiry should be on what the declarant intended to say, whether implied or directly asserted. *See* Fed.R.Evid. 801 advisory committee's note to Subdivision (a) 1972 Proposed Rules; *cf. Long,* 905 F.2d at 1580 ("[T]he crucial distinction under rule 801 is between intentional and unintentional messages, regardless of whether they are express or implied.").

We hold the district court's application here of Rule 801 is not without support or "illogical." *See Hinkson,* 585 F.3d at 1262. Fernando asked: Can you take my friend to the D.M.V.? Torres said no. Fernando asked a second time: Can you take my friend to the D.M.V.? Torres said no. Fernando asked a third time: Can you take my friend to a tire shop? Torres said no. Fernando's intent in asking for Torres's truck on three separate occasions in the span of a week and a half is apparent: Fernando wanted control of Torres's truck on the U.S.-side of the border. In other words, Fernando intended the implied assertion rather than the express one, and Torres offered the questions for this intended implied message to show it was Fernando who was calling the shots and who unknowingly set him up on the drug importation scheme. Thus, Torres offered the statements for the truth of the defense asserted. We hold the district court did not abuse its discretion in finding that Torres offered Fernando's inquiries for the truth of the matter asserted to prove his third-party culpability defense. Thus, the objections were properly sustained on hearsay grounds.

B

But even assuming that the district court erred, as Torres alleges, a defendant must still prove that the error or defect was prejudicial. *See* Fed.R.Crim.P. 52(a); *see also United States v. Olano,* 507 U.S. 725, 734, 113 S.Ct. 1770, 123 L.Ed.2d 508 (1993) (holding that where the defendant has made a timely objection to an error, Rule 52(a) applies).[7] Under Federal Rule of Criminal Procedure 52(a), we engage in a "harmless error" inquiry to determine whether the error was prejudicial. *Olano,* 507 U.S. at 734, 113 S.Ct. 1770. Torres, however, argues that the district court's exclusion of Fernando's inquiries were not only prejudicial, but constitutional in nature because the trial court prevented him from presenting a complete defense. A constitutional error under Rule 52(a) heightens the government's burden of proof: reversal is warranted unless the error was "harmless beyond a reasonable doubt." *Compare Neder v. United States,* 527 U.S. 1, 7, 119 S.Ct. 1827, 144 L.Ed.2d 35 (1999) (citation and internal quotations marks omitted), *and United States v. Caruto,* 532 F.3d 822, 831 (9th Cir.2008) (analyzing a constitutional error), *with United States v. Gonzalez-Flores,* p.1062 418 F.3d 1093, 1099 (9th Cir.2005) (holding that we reverse a non-constitutional error unless there is a "fair assurance" of harmlessness, i.e., "it is more probable than not that the error did not materially affect the verdict"), *and United States v. Edwards,* 235 F.3d 1173, 1178 (9th Cir.2000) (analyzing a non-constitutional error).

"[T]he Constitution guarantees criminal defendants 'a meaningful opportunity to present a complete defense.'" *Holmes v. South Carolina,* 547 U.S. 319, 324, 126 S.Ct. 1727, 164 L.Ed.2d 503 (2006) (quoting *Crane v. Kentucky,* 476 U.S. 683, 690, 106 S.Ct. 2142, 90 L.Ed.2d 636 (1986)). This right includes, "at a minimum ... the right to put before a jury evidence that might influence the determination of guilt." *Pennsylvania v. Ritchie,* 480 U.S. 39, 56, 107 S.Ct. 989, 94 L.Ed.2d 40 (1987). "When evidence is excluded on the basis of an *improper* application of the hearsay rules, due process concerns are still greater because the exclusion is unsupported by any legitimate state justification." *United States v. Lopez-Alvarez,* 970 F.2d 583, 588 (9th Cir.1992) (emphasis in original) (citing *Crane,* 476 U.S. at 691-92, 106 S.Ct. 2142).

But "not every [evidentiary] error amounts to a constitutional violation." *United States v. Boulware,* 384 F.3d 794, 808 (9th Cir.2004) (quoting *Lopez-Alvarez,* 970 F.2d at 588) (internal quotation marks omitted). As *Boulware* and *Lopez-Alvarez* make clear, a defendant must demonstrate the erroneous exclusion was important to his defense in order to rise to the level of a constitutional violation. *Id.* For example, in *Lopez-Alvarez* we held that — although the district court misapplied the hearsay rule by cutting short defense counsel's line of questioning furthering a defense theory — the exclusion did not amount to constitutional error because the "testimony sought to be adduced would not have added substantially to the knowledge the jury gained during the course of the trial." 970 F.2d at 588.

Torres's reliance on *United States v. Stever* to support his argument that the evidentiary exclusion amounted to constitutional error is misplaced. 603 F.3d 747 (9th Cir.2010). In *Stever,* the defendant was indicted for one count of conspiracy to, and one count of the underlying crime of, manufacture of marijuana. *Id.* at 750. In his defense, Stever sought to prove that the marijuana found on an isolated corner of his mother's 400-acre property was the work of a Mexican DTO that had recently infiltrated rural Oregon. *Id.* The district court barred the Government from arguing that Stever conspired with a DTO to manufacture marijuana since it had denied pre-trial discovery regarding Mexican DTOs, but also ruled *sua sponte* that it would not permit Stever to put on third-party culpability evidence regarding Mexican DTOs or "who else might have been involved." *Id.* at 751. The district court precluded Stever from presenting any defense at all. *Id.* at 752. Defense counsel argued that Stever had no involvement but, given the district court's ruling, proffered no affirmative defense, telling the jury only that the prosecution had the burden of proof. *Id.; see also Pineda-Doval,* 614 F.3d at 1032-33 (finding that the exclusion of the evidence "effectively denied the defendant the only argument that he had").

Here, the district court did not preclude Torres from proffering an affirmative defense. During closing arguments, Torres's counsel argued that Fernando or the mechanic probably planted the drugs in Torres's truck. Indeed, Torres testified that Fernando had previously borrowed his truck on four occasions, that Fernando knew where Torres lived, knew where Torres parked his truck, and had the opportunity to make a spare key. Torres also testified about the Tijuana mechanic who p.1063 kept Torres's pickup for a month and had offered to purchase the truck from Torres after the botched paint job. In other words, additional information about Fernando's requests to take a friend to the D.M.V. or pick up tires from a San Diego tire shop "would not have added substantially to the knowledge the jury gained during the course of the trial." *Lopez-Alvarez,* 970 F.2d at 588. Thus, even assuming the district court erred in sustaining the hearsay objection, we find the exclusion did not amount to constitutional error.

C

Finally, the exclusion of Torres's testimony about Fernando's requests would also have been harmless under the non-constitutional error standard. A non-constitutional error requires reversal unless there is a "fair assurance" of harmlessness, or stated another way, unless "it is more probable than not that the error did not materially affect the verdict." *Seschillie,* 310 F.3d at 1214 (quoting *United States v. Morales,* 108 F.3d 1031, 1040 (9th Cir.1997) (en banc)) (internal quotation marks omitted). "Review for harmless error requires not only an evaluation of the remaining incriminating evidence in the record, but also the most perceptive reflections as to the probabilities of the effect of error on a reasonable trier of fact." *United States v. Bishop,* 264 F.3d 919, 927 (9th Cir.2001) (citation and internal quotation marks omitted); *United States v. Oaxaca,* 233 F.3d 1154, 1158 (9th Cir.2000) (noting "the harmlessness of an error is distinct from evaluating whether there is substantial evidence to support a verdict").

Torres argues that even under the non-constitutional harmless error standard, we should find the error prejudicial simply by comparing what happened in the first trial with Fernando's inquiries (hung jury after a day and a half of deliberations) and what occurred without it in the second trial (guilty verdict in two hours and thirty minutes).[8] But the record shows another major difference between the first and second trial — the testimony of defense expert witness and former DEA special agent, Efren Lapuz.

While the Government did not present DTO "structure" or "modus operandi" evidence in its case-in-chief, the court ruled that Torres opened the door to such evidence in calling Lapuz to testify about the value of seventy-three kilograms of cocaine and how DTOs purchase and import the drugs into the United States. Consequently, the Government was able to cross-examine Lapuz who had testified about the uncommon use of "blind mules" because drug traffickers preferred straightforward transactions — "I pay you, you take the risk."

While Lapuz also testified about the advantages of using a blind mule in importing cocaine, the strategic decision to call an expert witness and then inadvertently open the door to DTO "modus operandi" evidence undercut Torres's defense that he was an unknowing courier in two ways: (1) p.1064 the defense expert's testimony highlighted the rarity of using blind mules in the DTO's importation business; and (2) it allowed the Government to ask the expert witness about a recent case where a DTO had easily attached drugs under the vehicle of an unknowing courier using magnets. The Government effectively contrasted the easily removable magnets with Torres's well-hidden compartment, where the truck bed had to be raised in order to hold the storage box and to extract the drugs. None of this "modus operandi" evidence was before the first jury.

Considering "the probabilities of the effect of error on a reasonable trier of fact" in the context of the remaining incriminating evidence, *Bishop,* 264 F.3d at 927, we find "it is more probable than not that the error did not materially affect the verdict," *Seschillie,* 310 F.3d at 1214. It was undisputed at both trials that CBP officers eventually extracted seventy-three kilograms of cocaine from a truck registered and driven by Torres. Even though it was disputed at trial whether the modifications would have been visible from the rear of the truck to anyone standing behind it, the government proffered sufficient circumstantial evidence of knowledge. To prove knowledge, the Government introduced testimony that Torres's hands were shaking as he handed over the keys during secondary inspection. Two days prior to his arrest, another officer also testified about Torres's "abnormal" behavior. Less weighty but relevant, the Government also introduced evidence that Torres stopped briefly during the x-ray, creating a "no scan," and then inched toward the exit until an officer told him to park his pickup in secondary.

Unique to the second trial, the Government chipped away at Torres's third-party culpability defense because — as Lapuz testified — it was unlikely that a DTO would expose a load of seventy-three kilograms of cocaine to multiple border crossings as this was a point of risk DTOs sought to minimize. Here, because Torres testified that Fernando last borrowed his truck about a week and a half prior to his arrest and Torres crossed the border on three occasions prior to his arrest, but after Fernando returned the truck, Lapuz's testimony about DTOs using blind mules made Torres's third-party culpability defense less credible. The exclusion of Fernando's inquiries, while arguably relevant, became less probative at the second trial with the introduction of the DTO "modus operandi" evidence. Furthermore, the district court could and did properly exclude Fernando's out-of-court statements on hearsay grounds. But even if the district court erred in doing so, any error in excluding Torres's testimony about Fernando's statements was not constitutional and was harmless.

AFFIRMED.

[*] The Honorable Michael R. Murphy, Senior Circuit Judge for the U.S. Court of Appeals for the Tenth Circuit, sitting by designation.

[1] One officer testified that eighty-eight kilograms of cocaine were found in the truck, but both the Government and Torres agreed it was seventy-three kilograms in their closing arguments.

[2] The transcript of the second trial misspells the last name as Gress, however, both parties' briefs refer to Fernando as Griese.

[3] The testimony before and after the Government's initial objection at the first trial was:

Q. When Fernando returned the truck to you that day, a week or a week and a half before your arrest, did he ask you anything?

A. Yes.

Q. What did Fernando want?

[Government]: Objection. Hearsay.

The Court: Sustained. Sustained.

[Defense Counsel]: Your Honor, may I speak?

The Court: Sidebar.

(Sidebar reported; not transcribed herein.)

The Court: One second. The objection is overruled. You may proceed.

[Defense Counsel]: I'll just ask my question again.

Q. What did Fernando want when he returned a week and a half before your arrest?

A. He asked me if I could do a favor for him. He asked that if I could pick up a friend, a friend of his. He wanted me to take him to the D.M.V. because the person did not know where [the] D.M.V. was. And he asked me if there was like a D.M.V. near San Ysidro, or in San Diego, and I said that, yes, I did know. So he asked me if I could do him a favor, if I could take a friend of his. He told me something like he wanted to change his license, like change the category, because he wanted to drive another kind of car.

[4] The testimony leading up to the second side bar at the first trial was:

Q. Did Fernando want you to pick up his friend — Where did Fernando want you to pick up his friend?

[Government]: Objection. Hearsay.

The Court: Sustained. Sustained.

Q. In your mind, where would you be picking up his friend?

The Court: Sustained, counsel.

[Government]: Objection.

The Court: Move on to the reason for the effect on the listener.

Q. Where was the D.M.V. that you were planning to go to?

A. It's close to Brown Field ... [¶]

. . .

Q. So when Fernando asked you to take his friend to the D.M.V., did he also ask you for anything else?

[Government]: Objection. Leading and calls for hearsay.

The Court: Sustained.

. . .

Q. In your mind, after you took this person to the D.M.V., did you think you would go anywhere else?

A. Yes. He told me —

[Government]: Objection. Hearsay.

The witness: — that I was going —

The Court: Sustained. Sidebar, counsel.

(Sidebar reported; not transcribed herein.)

[5] A "blind mule" is a person who transports drugs for a DTO without his knowledge or consent.

[6] *See also United States v. Rodriguez-Lopez,* 565 F.3d 312, 314-15 (6th Cir.2009) ("[A] question is typically not hearsay because it does not assert the truth or falsity of a fact." (citation omitted)); *United States v. Thomas,* 451 F.3d 543, 547-48 (8th Cir.2006) ("Questions and commands generally are not intended as assertions, and therefore cannot constitute hearsay."); *Lexington Ins. Co. v. W. Pa. Hosp.,* 423 F.3d 318, 330 (3d Cir.2005) ("Courts have held that questions and inquiries are generally not hearsay because the declarant does not have the requisite assertive intent, even if the question conveys an implicit message or provides information about the declarant's assumptions or beliefs." (citations and quotation marks omitted)); *United States v. Oguns,* 921 F.2d 442, 449 (2d Cir.1990) ("Because a question cannot be used to show the truth of the matter asserted, the dangers necessitating the hearsay rule are not present."); *United States v. Long,* 905 F.2d 1572, 1579-80 (D.C.Cir.1990) ("While [Defendant's] criticism of a rigid dichotomy between express and implied assertions is not without merit, it misses the point that the crucial distinction under rule 801 is between intentional and unintentional messages, regardless of whether they are express or implied.").

[7] Torres also challenges the district court's finding that his testimony relating to Fernando's inquiries was irrelevant. Fed.R.Evid. 401. Because we find the district court's exclusion under the hearsay rule to be dispositive, we need not reach the issue of relevancy.

[8] Torres argues that the improperly excluded evidence "would have bolstered [the] defense" where the "government's case was hardly overwhelming." *United States v. Crosby,* 75 F.3d 1343, 1349 (9th Cir.1996). While it may be true that the inquiries would have added to Torres's defense theory, the Government's case here was stronger than in *Crosby,* especially considering the DTO "modus operandi" evidence introduced at the second trial. *See id.* at 1349-50 (concluding that the victim's testimony that defendant punched her was undercut by the fact that she was inebriated the night of the assault, continuously changed her story, and the government proffered inconclusive blood tests). Furthermore, in *Crosby,* the district court completely precluded a third-party culpability defense when it prevented defendant from introducing evidence of the victim's husband's prior domestic violence. *Id.*

807 F.3d 1128 (2015)

UNITED STAETS of America, Plaintiff-Appellee,

v.

James LLOYD, aka James V. Lloyd, Jr., aka James Vernon Lloyd, Defendant-Appellant. p.1129
United States of America, Plaintiff-Appellee,

v.

James Lloyd, aka James V. Lloyd, Jr., aka James Vernon Lloyd, Defendant-Appellant.
United States of America, Plaintiff-Appellee,

v.

Paul Baker, aka Darwin Stanton Baker, Jr., aka Paul D. Baker, aka Paul Douglas Baker, Defendant-Appellant.
United States of America, Plaintiff-Appellee,

v.

David Nelson, aka David Paul Nelson, Defendant-Appellant.
United States of America, Plaintiff-Appellee,

v.

Albert Greenhouse, aka Albert Michael Greenhouse, Defendant-Appellant.
United States of America, Plaintiff-Appellee,

v.

Robert Keskemety, Defendant-Appellant.

Nos. 12-50499, 12-50500, 12-50509, 12-50514, 12-50526, 12-50566.

United States Court of Appeals, Ninth Circuit.

Argued and Submitted July 8, 2014.

Filed December 4, 2015.

US v. Lloyd, 807 F. 3d 1128 (9th Cir. 2015)

p.1135 Edward M. Robinson (argued), Law Office of Edward M. Robinson, Torrance, CA, for Defendant-Appellant James Lloyd.

John C. Lemon (argued), San Diego, CA, for Defendant-Appellant Paul Baker.

Sean K. Kennedy and Kathryn A. Young (argued), Deputy Federal Public Defenders, Los Angeles, CA, for Defendant-Appellant David Nelson.

Lawrence Jay Litman (argued), Los Angeles, CA, for Defendant-Appellant Albert Greenhouse.

Russell S. Babcock (argued), Law Offices of Russell S. Babcock, San Diego, CA, p.1136 for Defendant-Appellant Robert Keskemety.

André Birotte, Jr., United States Attorney, Central District of California, Robert E. Dugdale, Chief, Criminal Division, Steven A. Cazares and Ellyn Marcus Linsday (argued), Assistant United States Attorneys, Los Angeles, CA, for Plaintiff-Appellee.

Before: MARSHA S. BERZON and RICHARD R. CLIFTON, Circuit Judges and LEE H. ROSENTHAL,[*] District Judge.

OPINION

ROSENTHAL, District Judge.

Five defendants appeal their convictions or sentences for selling unregistered securities. The defendants worked for telemarketing "boiler rooms" in California and Florida, soliciting investments in partnerships to finance the production and distribution of movies. The defendants promised potential investors that the investments would return swift and large profits, with little to no risk.

Approximately 650 individuals—including unsophisticated people who could not afford the financial loss—invested over $23 million. Most of the investors lost it all.

These appeals arise from two indictments issued in the Central District of California on June 15, 2011. The indictment in *United States v. Daniel Toll et al.,* No. 11-cr-543-JFW, charged James Lloyd, who managed a boiler room in Los Angeles, California; telemarketers Paul Baker, David Nelson, and Albert Greenhouse; and eight others, all of whom worked through a California boiler room to sell partnership units in three movies produced (or supposed to be produced) by Cinamour Entertainment, LLC. The indictment in *United States v. James Lloyd,* No. 11-cr-542-JFW, charged Lloyd, who left Cinamour to manage a different boiler room in California, and Robert Keskemety, who managed a Florida boiler room, along with seven others, for selling partnership units in two movies. These movies were produced by Q Media Assets LLC, a company owned by the same person who owned Cinamour. Both indictments charged conspiracy, mail fraud, wire fraud, and securities fraud between 2001 and 2009.

The two boiler room managers, James Lloyd and Robert Keskemety, were convicted after they pleaded guilty. They appeal only their sentences. Two Cinamour telemarketers working in California, David Nelson and Paul Baker, and Albert Greenhouse, a Cinamour telemarketer working in Florida, were tried together. Nelson and Baker appeal their convictions and sentences. The only issue in the Greenhouse appeal is the sentence. We have jurisdiction under 28 U.S.C. § 1291 and 18 U.S.C. § 3742(a).

The number of defendants, the lengthy period involved, and the type of conduct made this a difficult case for any trial court to resolve. The record shows that the district judge competently and fairly resolved many of the innumerable issues that arose in trial and at sentencing. The points on which we disagree with the district p.1137 judge raise issues that are both complex and close.

James Lloyd pleaded guilty to two counts of wire fraud and Robert Keskemety to one count of mail fraud. They appeal their sentences. We affirm Lloyd's sentence, but we conclude that Keskemety's sentence for managing the Florida telemarketing boiler room improperly included fraud losses from the California boiler room that Lloyd managed. We vacate Keskemety's sentence and remand for resentencing.

David Nelson and Paul Baker appeal both the convictions and sentences entered after the jury convicted each of one count of conspiracy to commit mail and wire fraud and to offer and sell unregistered securities, two counts each of mail and wire fraud, and two counts of offering and selling unregistered securities. We reverse Nelson's conviction based on evidentiary rulings, vacate the sentence, and remand. We affirm Baker's conviction due to the overwhelming evidence against him, making the evidentiary errors harmless, but we vacate Baker's sentence and remand for resentencing because of an error in calculating the Guidelines sentence.

Finally, Albert Greenhouse appeals the sentence he received after the jury convicted him of two counts of offering and selling unregistered securities. We find no error, and we affirm.

BACKGROUND

Glen Hartford, a film producer, founded Cinamour in 2000 to make and distribute independent films, and served as its chief executive officer and majority shareholder. Hartford used telemarketing to solicit money from individual investors to finance three movies: *Forbidden Warrior, From Mexico with Love,* and *Red Water 12.* These three movies are the basis of the *United States v. Toll* indictment.

Cinamour began raising money for *Forbidden Warrior* in 2001 out of a telemarketing boiler room in Los Angeles, California. Lloyd and Baker were involved in the *Forbidden Warrior* fundraising. That movie was released in 2005 directly to video distribution and made about $500,000, a commercial failure of large proportions.

From 2004 to 2007, Cinamour used telemarketing to solicit purchases of partnership units to finance *From Mexico With Love.* Cinamour raised approximately $14.2 million from 445 investors nationwide. *From Mexico With Love* grossed about $800,000 from a very limited theatrical release. The investors received no return on the money they sent. Lloyd, Baker, and Greenhouse were involved in soliciting investments in *From Mexico With Love.*

In 2007, Cinamour began telemarketing sales of partnership units in *Red Water.* Cinamour raised approximately $2.8 million from approximately 100 victims nationwide but spent only $23,000 on making the movie. The investors lost everything. Baker and Nelson were involved in soliciting the investments in *Red Water.*

In 2009, after an undercover investigation, the FBI raided Cinamour's Los Angeles offices. Hartford committed suicide days after the raid.

The indictment in *United States v. Lloyd* arose from telemarketed investments in two movies written, directed, and produced by a former Central Intelligence Agency officer, Michael D. Sellers. Sellers retained Joel Lee Craft, Jr., founder and chief executive officer of American Information Strategies, Inc., to help raise capital for the films, *Eye of the Dolphin* and *Way of the Dolphin.* Sellers worked with Craft to set up telemarketing boiler rooms, p.1138 hiring Keskemety in Florida, and later, Lloyd in California, to manage them.

In 2002, Sellers recruited Keskemety to establish and manage the Florida telemarketing office. The goal was to raise money for the two *Dolphin* movies. In 2004, Keskemety began soliciting investments for *Eye of the Dolphin.* Sellers asked Craft to introduce him to other potential boiler-room managers. Through Craft, Sellers met Lloyd and hired him in 2007 to move from managing the Cinamour telemarketing office in Los Angeles to managing an office in the same city to solicit investments in partnership units to finance Sellers's films. Keskemety and Lloyd hired and paid the other telemarketers to raise money for the *Dolphin* films.

When Lloyd began managing the Los Angeles boiler room for Sellers, he had been working for Cinamour for over four years soliciting money for *Forbidden Warrior* and *From Mexico With Love.* He brought the same marketing techniques to selling partnership units in *Eye of the Dolphin* and *Way of the Dolphin.* The California and Florida boiler rooms together raised $9.6 million from 264 investors for the two *Dolphin* movies. Both movies failed. The investors in the first movie, as a group, received only $370,656 of their initial investment. The investors in the second movie lost everything.

The boiler rooms were similar. Less experienced telemarketers served as "fronters," cold-calling potential investors from lists of leads and reading from scripts to pitch the investments. The scripts included assurances to prospective investors of quick and large profits with little to no risk. These promises, and the details supporting them, were false. If the cold-calls led to expressions of interest, "closers"—more experienced telemarketers—would follow up and try to get signed investment documents and a check to close the deal. "Reloaders" would induce some of those who had already invested to put in more.

Many of the defendants had multiple roles, but each of the appellants worked as closers some of the time. Lloyd helped close investments in *Forbidden Warrior* and *From Mexico with Love*. Baker helped close investments in *Forbidden Warrior; From Mexico with Love,* and *Red Water.* Nelson helped close investments in *Red Water.* Greenhouse helped close investments in *From Mexico with Love.* Lloyd and Keskemety were closers for *Eye of the Dolphin* and *Way of the Dolphin.*

Lloyd, Baker, Nelson, and Greenhouse also worked as "reloaders" on the Cinamour films, targeting those who had already invested to persuade them to invest more. Reloaders participated in conference calls with these investors. The calls included telemarketers who pretended to be investors and enthusiastically agreed to commit more money. Lloyd also worked as a reloader on the two *Dolphin* films, but Keskemety did not.

Most of the defendants asserted that they believed the leads they cold-called and persuaded to invest were suitable and accredited individuals who were sophisticated and financially able to risk losing the money. The trial testimony from and about the investors, as well as the information in the presentence reports, tell a different story. Many of the investors had no significant experience in investing and few had significant liquid assets. Many had or were about to retire. At the trial, some of the investors testified that they had told the fronters, the closers, and the reloaders about their limited investment experience, their limited resources, and their life situations. The investors repeatedly testified about the defendants' assurances that the investments were risk free and would be returned with a profit within a short period. The investors briefly p.1139 testified about the effects on them of losing the money.

The scripts the telemarketers used varied depending on the movie they were pitching, but there were many common elements. In initial solicitation cold-calls, the fronters stated that: (1) there was little to no risk in the investment because there were presale distribution contracts for the movies, which guaranteed that the investors would recoup their investments and make a profit; (2) investors would quickly begin to receive returns because the movies were completed or nearing completion and, with the presales contracts, would be distributed in the near future; (3) films previously produced by the same company had yielded good returns for investors; (4) the money invested would be used to make, promote, and distribute the movies, not to pay for fundraising, overhead expenses, or sales commissions; (5) the marketers earned little to no commissions; (6) investors would get their money back and more out of the movie proceeds before the promoters and sellers were paid; and (7) there was a time limit because the units would shortly become unavailable, requiring a quick commitment. These statements were affirmatively and materially false or omitted material information needed to make them true.

The evidence presented at trial and recounted in the presentence reports showed that there were few or no guaranteed presale distribution contracts and no prospects of obtaining them. While some of the movies were finished and failed in distribution, some were not in production and were never made. Prior investors in films produced by the same company had lost money. Most of the money from investors did not go to make or distribute the films, but to pay personnel and promoters. Most of the telemarketers earned 35 percent in commissions, although some earned as little as 12 percent and others as much as 40 percent. There was no time limit on the investments. Lies abounded.

If a fronter's cold-call produced an expression of interest, the potential investor would receive a private placement memorandum. The memorandum contained some cautionary language but repeated many of the same lies. Closers would follow up, making similar promises to get signed investment contracts and checks. Some of the investors were later targeted for reloading through the staged conference calls. In general, the defendants did not contend that the statements they made were true, but rather that they believed what they were told to say.

The first set of issues analyzed below arises from the sentencing appeals of the two defendants who pleaded guilty, Robert Keskemety and James Lloyd. The second set of issues arises from the appeals of the three defendants tried together and convicted.

DISCUSSION

I. Keskemety's and Lloyd's Sentencing Appeals

A. The Standard of Review

We review a district court's sentencing decision for an abuse of discretion. *United States v. Carty,* 520 F.3d 984, 993 (9th Cir.2008) (en banc). A district court abuses its discretion when it improperly calculates the Guidelines range or bases its sentencing decision on clearly erroneous facts. *Id.; United States v. Treadwell,* 593 F.3d 990, 999 (9th Cir.2010). When a defendant does not object at sentencing, we review for plain error. *See United States v. Vargem,* 747 F.3d 724, 727 (9th Cir. 2014). "Under the plain error standard, relief is warranted where the district court committed (1) error that (2) is plain; (3) 'affected substantial rights;' and (4) 'seriously p.1140 affected the fairness, integrity, or public reputation of judicial proceedings.'" *Id.* at 728 (quoting *United States v. Teague,* 722 F.3d 1187, 1190 (9th Cir.2013)).

B. The Guilty Pleas and Sentences

In 2002, Michael Sellers hired Keskemety to set up and run a telemarketing boiler room in Florida to solicit investments in the two *Dolphin* movies. Keskemety would pay for the boiler-room expenses, including buying his own lead lists and paying the telemarketers. Sellers would pay Keskemety 25 to 40 percent of the money raised in the Florida boiler room. Keskemety began running the boiler room in 2004, soliciting investments first for the *Eye of the Dolphin,* then for the *Way of the*

Dolphin. The telemarketers made their solicitation calls using lead lists Keskemety purchased from Craft. Keskemety managed the Florida boiler room from 2004 to 2009. During this period, the telemarketers raised approximately $2 million from victims who invested in making and marketing the two *Dolphin* films.

Lloyd worked as Cinamour's boiler-room manager from 2003 to 2007. Among other things, Lloyd recruited telemarketers and helped prepare scripts that closers used to get signed investment contracts and checks.

In 2007, Sellers hired Lloyd to set up and run a boiler room in Los Angeles to sell partnership units in Sellers's *Dolphin* films. Unlike his arrangement with Keskemety in Florida, Sellers paid the overhead for the Los Angeles-based boiler room that Lloyd managed. Lloyd convinced many of the telemarketers who worked with him at Cinamour as closers, including Allen Agler, to join him and do the same kind of telemarketing solicitation for Sellers's *Dolphin* films that they had been doing for Cinamour.

From 2007 to 2009, the California and Florida boiler rooms together sold partnership units in the *Dolphin* movies to 264 victims, raising $9.3 million. Keskemety contends that his Florida boiler room raised $1.5 to $2 million of this amount. There is no controverting information. Based on this, Lloyd's California boiler room raised approximately $7.3 million. The number of victims attributable to each location is unclear.

The June 2011 indictment arising from the *Dolphin* movies, *United States v. Lloyd, et al.,* No. 11-cr-542, charged Keskemety with conspiracy under 18 U.S.C. § 371, two counts of mail fraud under 18 U.S.C. § 1341, and offering and selling unregistered securities under 15 U.S.C. §§ 77e and 77x and aiding and abetting under 18 U.S.C. § 2.[1] On March 2, 2012, Keskemety pleaded guilty without a plea agreement to one count of mail fraud.

The same indictment charged Lloyd with one count of conspiracy under 18 U.S.C. § 371, seven counts of mail fraud under 18 U.S.C. § 1341, seven counts of wire fraud under 18 U.S.C. § 1343, eight counts of offering and selling (or aiding and abetting the offer and sale of) an unregistered security under 15 U.S.C. §§ 77e and 77x and 18 U.S.C. § 2, and two counts of engaging in monetary transactions in property derived from illegal activity under 18 U.S.C. § 1957. Lloyd was also named in *United States v. Toll, et al.,* No. 11-cr-543, arising from the Cinamour film telemarketing. This indictment charged Lloyd with one count of conspiracy under 18 U.S.C. § 371, four counts of mail fraud under 18 U.S.C. § 1341, four p.1141 counts of wire fraud under 18 U.S.C. § 1343, three counts of offering and selling (or aiding and abetting the offer and sale of) an unregistered security under 15 U.S.C. §§ 77e and 77x and 18 U.S.C. § 2, and one count of engaging in monetary transactions in property derived from illegal activity under 18 U.S.C. § 1957.[2]

In February 2012, Lloyd pleaded guilty to one count of wire fraud in *United States v. Lloyd;* in April 2012, he pleaded guilty to one count of wire fraud in *United States v. Toll.* The two actions were consolidated for sentencing.

Neither Keskemety nor Lloyd appeals his conviction. Both appeal their sentences. Keskemety received an 80-month prison sentence, well below the 121 to 151 month Guidelines range, and was ordered to pay $8,628,733.93 in restitution. The offense level and restitution amount were based on the victims' losses in both the

Florida boiler room Keskemety managed between 2004 and 2009 and the Los Angeles boiler room Lloyd managed between 2007 and 2009. Keskemety agrees that he is properly held accountable for the fraud losses from the Florida boiler room while he worked there, but he challenges including the Los Angeles boiler-room fraud losses in his relevant conduct.

Lloyd received a 156-month sentence and had to pay $22,258,489.04 in restitution. He challenges the sentence length as both procedurally flawed and substantively unreasonable.

C. Keskemety's Sentencing Appeal

The district court largely adopted the revised presentence report and overruled Keskemety's objections, including his objections to the fraud loss. The court calculated the Guidelines range based on a 20-level increase in offense level under § 2B1.1(b)(1)(K) for $9,304,929.62 in intended fraud losses and a 6-level increase for over 250 victims. These amounts included both the California and Florida victims and their losses. The court calculated restitution the same way, including the 242 investors solicited by the California and Florida boiler rooms who could be identified by name. With a 2-level increase for the vulnerability of some of the victims and a 3-level reduction for acceptance of responsibility, the result was an offense level of 32, which produced a sentencing range of 121 to 151 months. Citing Keskemety's military service, age, and poor health, the district court sentenced him to serve 80 months in prison and ordered him to pay $8,628,733.93 in restitution.

Keskemety does not dispute that he is accountable for Guideline-calculation purposes for the amount raised from telemarketers' solicitations in the Florida boiler room during the time he managed it, a fraud loss of $1.5 to $2 million. Nor does he dispute that he must pay restitution to the identifiable investors solicited from the Florida boiler room. He does dispute that his relevant conduct includes the fraud losses generated by the Los Angeles telemarketing office that James Lloyd managed during the same period; that the number of victims of the Florida office exceed 250; and that he owes restitution to the identifiable investors solicited by the Los Angeles as well as the Florida operation. p.1142 Kesketmy agrees that he knew that the California boiler room existed and what it was doing, but he disputes that this knowledge is enough to include the fraud losses from the California boiler room in his own relevant conduct.

"[I]n the case of jointly undertaken criminal activity," a defendant is responsible for "all reasonably foreseeable acts and omissions of others in furtherance of the jointly undertaken criminal activity, that occurred during the commission of the offense of conviction, in preparation for that offense, or in the course of attempting to avoid detection or responsibility for that offense." U.S.S.G. § 1B1.3(a)(1)(B). The defendant is accountable for the conduct of others that was both: "'(i) in furtherance of the jointly undertaken criminal activity; and (ii) reasonably foreseeable in connection with that criminal activity.'" *United States v. Blitz*, 151 F.3d 1002, 1012 (9th Cir.1998) (quoting U.S.S.G. § 1B1.3, cmt. n. 2). "[W]e have held that a district court may not automatically hold an individual defendant responsible for losses attributable to the entire conspiracy, but rather must identify the loss that fell within the scope of the defendant's agreement with his co-conspirators and was reasonably foreseeable to the defendant." *United States v. Treadwell,* 593 F.3d 990, 1002 (9th Cir.2010). Although a district court need not "proceed item-by-item through a complete list of all losses attributed to a criminal conspiracy and . . . then make an individualized determination whether or not each item was within the scope of the defendant's 'joint undertaking' and was 'reasonably foreseeable' to that defendant," *id.* at 1002-03, the court must make particularized findings about "'the scope of the criminal activity the particular defendant agreed to jointly undertake,'" *Blitz,* 151 F.3d at 1012-13 (quoting U.S.S.G. § 1B1.3, cmt. n. 2).

"In determining the scope of the criminal activity that the particular defendant agreed to jointly undertake (i.e., the scope of the specific conduct and objectives embraced by the defendant's agreement), the court may consider any explicit agreement or implicit agreement fairly inferred from the conduct of the defendant and others." U.S.S.G. § 1B1.3, cmt. n. 2. The example of jointly undertaken criminal activity in the Application Notes is a street-level drug dealer who pools resources and shares profits with four other street-level drug dealers. The first dealer is engaged in jointly undertaken criminal activity and is accountable for all the drugs he and the four other dealers sell during the time he works with them. Their sales are in furtherance of the first dealer's jointly undertaken criminal activity and reasonably foreseeable to him. *Id.,* cmt. n. 2, Illustration (c)(6). By contrast, a dealer who sells to his own customers, in his own territory, and does not share information, other resources, or profits with other dealers who have their own territories and customers, is not engaged in jointly undertaken drug dealing with the other dealers and is not accountable for the drugs they sell. That is true even if the first dealer knows about the other dealers and who they are and knows that the drugs come from the same supplier. Similarly, even if the first street-level drug dealer knows that the person who recruited him to sell drugs also recruited the other dealers for the same purpose, the first dealer is generally accountable only for the drugs he sells. U.S.S.G. § 1B1.3, cmt. n. 2, Illustration (c)(7). The dealers are doing the same kind of criminal activity at the same time, but it is not a jointly undertaken criminal activity. U.S.S.G. § 1B1.3, cmt. n. 2, Illustration (c)(6).

Knowledge of "another participant's criminal acts is not enough to hold p.1143 the defendant responsible for those acts," *United States v. Studley,* 47 F.3d 569, 575 (2d Cir.1995), and knowledge of a conspiracy's overall objectives does not make the defendant accountable for all the coconspirators' acts furthering those objectives. In the telemarketing context, "the scope of a joint undertaking for sentencing purposes depend[s] on whether the telemarketers 'worked together,' 'relied on one another to make a sale,' attended the same sales meetings, and 'depended on the success of . . . the operation as a whole for their financial compensation.'" *Treadwell,* 593 F.3d at 1005 (quoting *Blitz,* 151 F.3d at 1013). If two defendants, working together, design and execute a scheme to sell fraudulent stocks in a telephone boiler-room operation, each is accountable for all the fraud losses that result. The conduct of each is in furtherance of their jointly undertaken criminal activity and is reasonably foreseeable in connection with that criminal activity. U.S.S.G. § 1B1.3, cmt. n. 2, Illustration (c)(2). To determine a defendant's fraud-loss amount and resulting offense level, a district court must consider that defendant's role in the overall scheme. *See Treadwell,* 593 F.3d at 1005; *Studley,* 47 F.3d at 576.

The district court made the following statements about the scope of the criminal activity Keskemety agreed to jointly undertake:

> [T]hat the losses of that amount [$9,304,929.62] to those [264] victims were sustained during the period of, the relevant period of [Keskemety's] participation in the scheme and also that they do include relevant conduct with respect to Mr. Lloyd, and they were clearly foreseeable and therefore properly attributable to [Keskemety].

The court appeared to base this conclusion on Keskemety's knowledge about Lloyd's operations and Sellers's overall objectives and goals:

> Although [Kesketemy] was in Florida, he was fully aware of all the major facets of the scheme, knew others who were raising money from the [*Dolphin*] movies, [sic] ran his own boiler room operation that employed several closers who worked for him.

The district court did not identify additional facts supporting its conclusion that the solicitation and sales activities in Lloyd's Los Angeles boiler room were within "the scope of the criminal activity [Keskemety] agreed to jointly undertake." U.S.S.G. § 1B1.3, cmt. n. 2.

There is evidence that Lloyd and Keskemety were engaged in the same type of activity. Both used similar scripts and materials obtained from Craft's American Information Strategies. But Lloyd and Keskemety did not pool customers, information, or other resources. In this respect, Keskemety was like the drug dealer who gets the drugs he sells from the same source as other dealers and knows about their work, but does not share drugs, customers, or information with them. Keskemety and Lloyd both got lead lists and scripts from Craft, but they did not share information with each other.

At sentencing and on appeal, the government made a number of arguments to show that Keskemety was properly held accountable for the fraud losses from the Los Angeles as well as the Florida boiler room. The government cited evidence that Keskemety received a commission check when Lloyd reloaded Keskemety's investors, even after Keskemety had stopped actively soliciting investments himself. The district court properly rejected this argument because the government could not show that Keskemety "knew that Lloyd . . . [was] reloading his investors other than the fact that he continued p.1144 to get paid[.]" The district court was "not convinced that there [was] sufficient evidence that [Keskemety] was aware of . . . the [reloading] conference calls." The district court expressly rejected the statement in the revised PSR that Keskemety profited from the conference calls Lloyd used to reload investors:

> I don't see any evidence in this record that would support this defendant profited from the conference calls or that he provided his investor client list to . . . Lloyd for reloading.

The record shows that Keskemety did not benefit from the solicitations and sales made in Lloyd's Los Angeles boiler room and did not share the proceeds of his boiler-room solicitations with Lloyd.

The government argues that Keskemety and Lloyd were "acting in concert for the same purported goal: to raise money for Sellers." The fact that Keskemety and Lloyd independently worked for Sellers does not mean that Keskemety and Lloyd jointly undertook their criminal activity. Similarly, the government urges that because "all [telemarketers] used the same materials to sell the deal," all were engaged in jointly undertaken criminal activity. As Keskemety points out, using the same marketing materials does not tie Keskemety's compensation to Lloyd's solicitations and sales such that the California fraud losses should be included in Keskemety's relevant conduct. The fact that Keskemety dealt with some investors who complained and "lulled" them does not show that he did so for Lloyd's investors or that Lloyd shared in the benefits of this work. Evidence that Keskemety eventually "went to a salary plus bonus payment plan that was equal to the commissions he would have earned," does not tie Keskemety's compensation to Lloyd's solicitations and sales sufficiently to include the California fraud loses in Keskemety's relevant conduct.

The government cites evidence that Keskemety had an acting role in one of the *Dolphin* movies, but this does not show that he had an interest in the success of the operation as a whole that would justify including the fraud losses from the Los Angeles boiler room in his own relevant conduct. Keskemety had a very small role in the film, and there is no evidence that it contributed to making the money Lloyd raised through the California boiler room.

In sum, the record support for holding Keskemety accountable for Lloyd's similar criminal activity appears limited to Keskemety's knowledge of Lloyd's operations and of Sellers's overall objectives and goals. That is not enough, given the evidence that Keskemety operated the Florida boiler room independently from Lloyd's California boiler room and did not share information, resources, or profits.

The government contends that *United States v. Blitz,* 151 F.3d at 1012, supports holding Keskemety accountable for the losses attributable to the Los Angeles-based boiler room. The telemarketing scheme in *Blitz* was different from the scheme the record discloses here. In *Blitz,* the "[d]ialers and closers strongly relied on one another to make a sale," "[a]ll employees attended sales meetings," and the "employees did not work on a pure commission basis" and instead "received a salary," thus making them "depend[ ] on the success of the [fraudulent] operation as a whole for their financial compensation." 151 F.3d at 1013. In holding the individual telemarketers accountable for the money raised by the other telemarketers as reasonably foreseeable jointly undertaken criminal activity, the *Blitz* court distinguished *Studley,* in which the court refused to hold one telemarketer accountable for the other telemarketers' intended p.1145 fraud losses. In *Studley,* the defendant "did not design or develop the fraudulent scheme; did not work in any way to further the scheme outside of his own sales efforts; was paid on a pure commission basis, receiving no profits from the overall operation; did not assist other representatives with their sales, but rather competed with them for commissions; did not pool resources with other telemarketers; and had no interest in the success of the operation as a whole." *Blitz,* 151 F.3d at 1013.

The record shows that Keskemety is much closer to the defendant in *Studley* than to the telemarketers in *Blitz.* Keskemety did not design or develop the overall scheme; Sellers did. Lloyd joined the conspiracy to raise money for the *Dolphin* movies long after Keskemety. Keskemety's efforts to further the scheme related to the boiler room he managed. He did not pool resources with Lloyd's boiler room, and he was paid commissions based on the proceeds from the Florida boiler room's sales.

The other cases the government cites do not change the analysis. In *United States v. Treadwell,* 593 F.3d 990 (9th Cir.2010), "[b]oth defendants described themselves as 'founders' of the investment companies they were asking investors to support with funds," "[b]oth defendants led conference calls with the companies' nationwide sales force," "[b]oth defendants traveled around the country selling their companies' investment strategy," "[b]oth defendants misrepresented the investments made by their companies," and "both defendants profited from the mutual efforts of their coconspirators in selling non-existent investments." *Id.* at 1005. In this case, by contrast, the district court did not make similar particularized findings of jointly undertaken criminal activity.[3] Instead, the district court did not find, and the present record does not show, that the solicitations made and money obtained from Lloyd's Los Angeles boiler room were within the scope of the criminal activity that Keskemety agreed to undertake for Sellers.

We reverse the district court's judgment on the amount of fraud loss, vacate the restitution order, and remand for resentencing. We need not and do not address Keskemety's other arguments about substantive reasonableness or restitution.

D. Lloyd's Sentencing Appeal

Lloyd pleaded guilty to one count of wire fraud in each of the two cases naming him as a defendant, and he does not challenge his convictions. He does challenge the 156-month sentence the district court imposed as both procedurally flawed and substantively unreasonable.

"Procedural errors include, but are not limited to, incorrectly calculating the Guidelines range, treating the Guidelines as mandatory, failing to properly consider the [18 U.S.C.] § 3553(a) factors, using clearly erroneous facts when calculating the Guidelines range or determining the sentence, and failing to provide an adequate explanation for the sentence imposed." *United States v. Armstead,* 552 F.3d 769, 776 (9th Cir.2008). The district court's 156-month sentence was a downward variance from the Guidelines range of 210 to 262 months. Lloyd asserts—for p.1146 the first time on this appeal—that the district court failed adequately to explain why it did not impose an even lower below-Guidelines sentence. His argument is without merit.

The district court thoroughly explained its reasons for the sentence in over 20 pages of transcript. A careful review of the record satisfies us that the sentence was procedurally sound and that the district court did not abuse its discretion, much less plainly err, in the below-Guidelines sentence imposed and the explanation provided.

Lloyd's argument that the district court erred in not departing further goes to substantive reasonableness. *See United States v. Ellis,* 641 F.3d 411, 421 (9th Cir.2011). The record shows that the 156-month sentence, well below the bottom of the Guidelines range, was substantively reasonable in light of the 18 U.S.C. § 3553(a) sentencing factors and the totality of the circumstances. *See Gall v. United States,* 552 U.S. 38, 51, 128 S.Ct. 586, 169 L.Ed.2d 445 (2007).

We affirm.

II. The Appeals from the Convictions: Baker and Nelson

A. The Indictments

Baker, Nelson, and Greenhouse were indicted in *United States v. Daniel Toll, et al.*, No. 11-cr-543, for soliciting investments in the Cinamour movies. Baker was charged with one count of conspiracy under 18 U.S.C. § 371, two counts of mail fraud under 18 U.S.C. § 1341, two counts of wire fraud under 18 U.S.C. § 1343, and two counts of offering and selling (or aiding and abetting the offer and sale of) an unregistered security under 15 U.S.C. §§ 77e and 77x and 18 U.S.C. § 2. Nelson was charged with one count of conspiracy under 18 U.S.C. § 371, two counts of mail fraud under 18 U.S.C. § 1341, two counts of wire fraud under 18 U.S.C. § 1343, and two counts of offering and selling (or aiding and abetting the offer and sale of) an unregistered security under 15 U.S.C. §§ 77e and 77x and 18 U.S.C. § 2. Greenhouse was charged with one count of conspiracy under 18 U.S.C. § 371, three counts of mail fraud under 18 U.S.C. § 1341, and two counts of offering and selling (or aiding and abetting the offer and sale of) an unregistered under 15 U.S.C. §§ 77e and 77x and 18 U.S.C. § 2. The three defendants were tried together.

Baker worked from his home in California as a closer from 2004 to 2009, soliciting investments in *From Mexico with Love* and in *Red Water*. Nelson worked in Cinamour's Sherman Oaks and Encino, California, offices as a fronter and closer from October 2007 to May 2009, soliciting investments in *Red Water*. Greenhouse worked from his home in Florida from 2005 to 2007, soliciting investments in partnership units for *From Mexico with Love*.

The jury convicted Baker and Nelson on all the counts submitted against them. The jury acquitted Greenhouse of conspiracy and mail fraud but convicted him for offering and selling unregistered securities and aiding and abetting and causing those sales, in violation of 15 U.S.C. §§ 77e and 77x and 18 U.S.C. § 2.

At sentencing, the district court calculated a 292 to 365 month Guidelines range for Baker but varied downward, imposing a 194-month prison term and a $12,043,678.25 restitution obligation. The district court calculated a 97 to 121 month Guidelines range for Nelson but sentenced him to serve 84 months in prison and to pay $1,860,000 in restitution. Baker and Nelson timely appealed their convictions and sentences. Greenhouse was sentenced to 60 months in prison, below the Guidelines p.1147 range of 63 to 78 months, and to pay $530,000 in restitution. He appeals only his sentence.

B. Baker's and Nelson's Challenges to Their Convictions

1. The Trial Evidence Against Baker

In 2001, Hartford hired Baker as an "associate producer" at Cinamour. Baker was working as a telemarketer soliciting money for *Forbidden Warrior* when he was arrested and jailed in March 2003 for a parole violation. Baker went back to working for Cinamour in January 2004 and, with his partner, worked for Cinamour out of their home in Coachella Valley, California until 2009.

In March 2004, Baker and his partner, doing business as Independent Essentials, entered into a written agreement with Cinamour for a 20 percent commission on the money they raised working as telemarketers and closers soliciting investments in *From Mexico With Love*. From January 2005 to January 2007, Baker closed $200,000 in *From Mexico With Love* investments. Baker also earned a commission for the investments that Lloyd closed using Baker's investor list from *Forbidden Warrior*. Lloyd used Baker's investor information to reload those who had sent money for *Forbidden Warrior*, producing more money for *From Mexico With Love*.

In 2007, Cinamour stopped soliciting for *From Mexico With Love* and turned to soliciting money from investors for *Red Water*. Baker and his partner ran the *Red Water* fundraising. Baker hired codefendant Bart Slanaker, who had experience operating telemarketing boiler rooms. Baker's partner managed the money, received investor checks, and paid commissions. Baker gave Slanaker *Red Water* sales materials and paid him a 15 percent commission.

Baker contacted prospective investors from lead lists. Diane Houseknecht testified that in a letter and conversations, Baker told her that investors would receive 90 cents on every dollar the film earned until they got back all the principal they had paid plus 10 percent. Baker also promised her that the return would be fast. He did not reveal that he would earn a 15 to 20 percent commission. Instead, he emphasized that the investors would get paid before the promoters or salespeople received anything and that the invested funds would be used to make and market the movies, not to pay promoters or salespeople. Houseknecht, who had no investment experience, invested $25,000 in *Forbidden Warrior*, $10,000 in cash and $15,000 from her retirement account. She got back $1,000. Lloyd later convinced Houseknecht to invest another $20,000 in *From Mexico with Love*, using $10,000 in cash and $10,000 from her retirement account.

Gary Tranter testified that Baker called him in 2002 to solicit an investment in *Forbidden Warrior*. In the telephone call, Baker compared *Forbidden Warrior* to the well-known and commercially successful film *Crouching Tiger, Hidden Dragon*. Baker stated that a majority of the *Forbidden Warrior* units had already been sold and that Tranter needed to act quickly. Baker told Tranter that *Forbidden Warrior* was ready for release in theaters in the near future; it was not. Baker also said that investors would be paid back first and that promoters and sales personnel would be paid only after the investors. Baker did not disclose the fact or amount of commissions he and others were getting. Tranter worked as a wholesale broker of indoor houseplants and had little financial or investment experience. He invested $10,000 in *Forbidden Warrior* and got back $800. Baker unsuccessfully tried p.1148 to reload Tranter in *From Mexico With Love* but did get him to send another $5,000 for *Red Water*. Tranter never got any of his investment in *Red Water* back.

Another investor, Thomas Beacham, an office manager for a paint shop, testified that Baker cold-called him in 2002 about investing in *Forbidden Warrior*. Baker told Beacham that *Forbidden Warrior* would be a "big moneymaker" because it was comparable to *Crouching Tiger, Hidden Dragon*. When Beacham said that he did not have the money to invest, Baker emphasized that this was a limited-time offer and asked if Beacham had retirement savings he could use. When Beacham pointed out that he did not meet the requirements for an accredited investor—including that his net worth was far below the $1 million minimum—Baker urged him not to "worry about that. It's just in there for formality. We can make an exception in your case."

Beacham invested $5,000 from his retirement account in *Forbidden Warrior*. Baker successfully convinced Beacham to invest another $10,000 from his retirement account in *From Mexico With Love* after Beacham participated in a reloading conference call run by Lloyd and Agler. Beacham lost all the money he invested except "a hundred bucks or so." Beacham testified that he had lost his job in 2008 and had to cash out his retirement account, which was "15 grand shorter than it probably should have been."

FBI Special Agent Sean Sterle, who worked undercover posing as a Florida businessman interested in investment opportunities, also testified. After a cooperating witness introduced Baker to Sterle, five or six telephone conversations followed in which Baker tried to convince Sterle to invest in *Red Water*. Sterle recorded his conversations with Baker and the jury heard them at trial. The recordings included Baker's statements that *Red Water* had secured $5.4 million in presale commitments to distribute the film in 31 countries; that the presales revenues would pay investors a 110 percent return; that Sterle would receive a 110 percent return in eight to ten months, get his full investment back within the year, and triple his money in two years; and that the sales personnel received no commissions.

The evidence showed that the promises Baker repeatedly made were either false or made without any reasonable basis to believe that they were true.

2. The Trial Evidence Against Nelson

David Nelson worked for Cinamour as a fundraising telemarketer from October 2007 to May 2009. Nelson had a sad personal history. He began drinking at age 11. He dropped out of high school. His drinking and drug use lost him job after job. He tried to rehabilitate himself by joining the Marines, which trained him as a software engineer, but even the Marines could not get him to stop drinking. He received a general discharge. Although the training helped him get jobs, he lost them every few months. Nelson became homeless in 2001. In 2005, after four years of living on the streets and jumping from one job to another, Nelson got treatment for his alcoholism at a halfway house that required its clients to have jobs. Nelson found work as a telemarketer selling industrial equipment, but lost this job. Nelson again became homeless, living behind a dumpster. On March 30, 2007, paramedics found Nelson behind the dumpster and took him to the hospital.

Nelson readmitted himself to the halfway house for a third time in 2007 and got another telemarketing job. Nelson's supervisor there, Bart Slanaker, later convinced him to follow him to Cinamour's p.1149 boiler room to work soliciting money for a new movie, *Red Water*.

Several victims testified about talking to Nelson. Melvin Bitikofer was a retired stove salesman who had owned his own store. Nelson cold-called him in October 2007. Nelson described the *Red Water* investment as a once-in-a-lifetime opportunity and promised Bitikofer that he would begin to receive returns as early as the first quarter of 2008. Nelson told Bitikofer that investors would get a 110 percent return, that the movie was already being filmed, that presale distribution contracts worth $5.9 million were already in place, and that nothing could go wrong. Nelson touted Cinamour's previous movie, *From Mexico With Love*, as a proven commercial success that had rewarded its investors well. Nelson omitted his commissions from the discussions and downplayed the investment risks. Bitikofer invested $50,000.

Nelson and his colleagues successfully reloaded Bitikofer several times. In February 2009, Bitikofer participated in a reloading conference call led by Bart Slanaker. Bitikofer testified that the other persons participating in the call appeared to be potential investors and that they enthusiastically endorsed the *Red Water* investment opportunity. These other participants were, in fact, Cinamour telemarketers. During the call, Bitikofer stated that he did not have more money and that any investment would have to come from his wife's IRA. After the call, Nelson and Slanaker persuaded Bitikofer to get $100,000 from his wife's IRA.

Bitikofer and his wife invested a total of $250,000, which they repeatedly told Nelson was from their retirement and IRA funds. They lost all they invested. Bitikofer testified that this loss resulted in a "[t]errible" financial hardship for the couple. They could "hardly keep up with the bills coming in" and faced the prospect of "tak[ing] out bankruptcy."

Richard Clark was a farmer with no investment experience. He wanted a conservative investment that could provide some income to help him stop farming because of its physical demands. Nelson cold-called Clark in April 2009 and solicited him to invest in *Red Water*.[4] Clark told Nelson what he did for a living and that he had no investment experience. Nelson told Clark that very few units were left and that the investment was the "best thing" he had seen in his career. Nelson told Clark that he would start to receive distributions by the summer of 2009. Nelson assured Clark that there were already enough presale contracts to cover production and marketing costs and ensure him a fast profit.

Clark also participated in a conference call with Slanaker, Nelson, and people he understood to be other investors. Clark testified that Nelson actively participated in this call. Clark invested $15,000, which he lost; he described the loss as "a bad lick for me."

Dennis Eliassen was retired when Nelson cold-called him in June 2008. Nelson told him that Cinamour already had $6 million in presale contracts, twice the amount needed to cover all the film production and marketing costs. Nelson sent Eliassen an email assuring him that investment "security is in place through our pre-sales distribution." Nelson told Eliassen that everything was on track to begin filming *Red Water* in December 2008, and that the investors would be paid first and p.1150 quickly. Nelson also told him that *From Mexico With Love* and *Forbidden Warrior* had been successful for the investors. Eliassen invested $50,000 from his IRA and lost it all, a "pretty" big hardship.

Connie Hurd testified that when Nelson cold-called her in early 2008, she told him that she and her husband owned a tool company and had very little investment experience. Nelson assured her that the *Red Water* investment presented minimal risk and that the investors would be paid back everything before the promoters and sales personnel received anything. Nelson assured her that Cinamour already had presale contracts projected to be worth $5.9 million, which guaranteed a secure and profitable investment. Nelson did not disclose the existence or amount of his or others' commissions. Hurd lost her $5,000 investment.

The jury heard from Stephanie Alarcon, a Cinamour telemarketer hired by Slanaker to work as a fronter cold-calling potential investors and passing the names of those expressing interest to closers, who would follow up to finalize the sale. She made the calls from a lead list and read a script. Nelson listened to make sure she did it properly and gave her tips. Nelson asked her to write down personal information potential investors gave her in the calls for him to use in his closing pitches. Alarcon followed this instruction. For example, when she talked to Richard Clark, she noted that he was a Christian and that Nelson should emphasize "Christian things" in trying to finalize his investment. Alarcon's account of what she was told to say when she called potential investors was consistent with their testimony about what they were promised.

Nadav Shimoni, another fronter, testified that he participated with Nelson in some of the reloading conference calls. Nelson would read a sales pitch from a script, and Shimoni would pretend that he was an investor who had decided to invest more money. His testimony was consistent with what the investors who participated in these calls described.

Nelson testified and told the jury about his background. He testified that in April 2007, just after he became sober, he got a job as a telemarketer working under Bart Slanaker. Nelson testified that Slanaker was so domineering and abusive that Nelson feared him and was intimidated into doing whatever Slanaker told him to do. His fear of losing yet another job contributed to his unquestioning obedience.

Nelson testified that when he began working at Cinamour, he believed it was legitimate. Slanaker took Nelson to the production location for *From Mexico With Love*. Nelson testified that he recognized Cinamour's logo and some of the actors in the film. Nelson looked at Cinamour's website and saw that it was a production and distribution company working in film and television. Nelson read that the Better Business Bureau rated Cinamour Triple A, with no complaints. Nelson learned that Cinamour was raising money for *Red Water*. In October 2007, Nelson followed Slanaker to Cinamour and began soliciting investments in *Red Water*.

Nelson testified that Slanaker prohibited him from associating with anyone else at Cinamour. The office manager testified that Slanaker often screamed at Nelson, who remained quiet and kept to himself, away from the other telemarketers.

Nelson testified that at Cinamour, he was given lead sheets and a script. If a call was met with interest, Nelson filled out a sheet and gave it to Slanaker, who sent an information package to the potential investor. Nelson would then call and go over the package using a preset script, answer questions, and try to persuade the p.1151 prospect to sign the papers and send a check made out to *Red Water* Films.

Nelson testified that he did not know that the representations he made were false and insisted that he did not intend to defraud investors. He believed that the purpose of the script was to keep the telemarketers honest about what they told potential investors, not to give the telemarketers lies to tell. He also believed that Cinamour had $5.9 million in presale distribution contract commitments. Nelson acknowledged that he was getting paid for the sales he made but testified that he did not lie when he stated that no commissions were being paid, because what he received was a "management fee." Nelson did admit, however, that the *Red Water* private placement memorandum he sent to potential investors provided a misleading description of how and when the promoters and sales people would be paid.

Nelson testified that he thought the conference calls he participated in were to give status reports to people who had already invested. Nelson denied knowing that the calls were to "reload" investors or that Cinamour employees were playing the role of happy investors. Nelson was shown a script for a reloading conference call. The script identified him as the Vice President of Technology at View Partners. Nelson denied having seen or used the script or having read or heard that false description of his job and title, but the script was found on Nelson's office computer at Cinamour. The government pointed out that the script made clear the purpose of the call and the presence of the fake "other investors." The script contained a list of the Cinamour employees who participated in at least one reloading conference call playing the role of investors. The script also had handwritten notes about some of the victims who took part. Nelson denied that the notes were his. But another exhibit, which Nelson admitted to writing, had very similar handwriting. The government argued that the similarity between the two documents provided additional support for inferring that Nelson was lying about his role in the *Red Water* conference calls, about not knowing that Cinamour employees were acting as shills, and about not having seen scripts for the calls.

C. Baker's and Nelson's Challenges to Their Convictions

Baker and Nelson challenge the trial court's evidentiary rulings and jury instructions, the prosecutor's comments at closing, and the sufficiency of the evidence. They contend that if no one error justifies vacating their convictions, the cumulative effect does. We identify several errors, find them harmless as to Baker, but conclude that Nelson's conviction must be reversed.

1. The Challenges to the Evidentiary Rulings

We review the district court's evidentiary rulings for abuse of discretion. *See United States v. Pineda-Doval,* 614 F.3d 1019, 1031 (9th Cir.2010).

a. The Victims' Testimony

Baker and Nelson argue that the district court should not have allowed victims to testify about their financial situations and the impact of losing the money they invested. Baker and Nelson argue that the district court erred in admitting the victims' testimony because the risk of unfair prejudice substantially outweighed the probative value. *See* Fed.R.Evid. 403. We disagree.

Because Nelson objected to Eliassen's testimony, we review its admission as to both Nelson and Baker for an abuse of discretion. *See United States v. Orm* p.1152 *Hieng,* 679 F.3d 1131, 1141 (9th Cir.2012).[5] We review testimony elicited without objection for plain error. *See United States v. Lopez,* 762 F.3d 852, 859 (9th Cir.2014).

"A district court's Rule 403 determination is subject to great deference, because 'the considerations arising under Rule 403 are susceptible only to case-by-case determinations, requiring examination of the surrounding facts, circumstances, and issues.'" *United States v. Hinkson,* 585 F.3d 1247, 1267 (9th Cir.2009) (quoting *R.B. Matthews, Inc. v. Transamerica Transp. Serv., Inc.,* 945 F.2d 269, 272 (9th Cir.1991)). Eliassen's testimony that he told Nelson that he had no cash to invest and would have to use his retirement money was relevant to rebut the defendants' argument that they believed their investor-victims to be accredited investors. Eliassen also testified that losing his investment was a "very big" hardship. Any error in admitting this limited and brief victim-impact testimony was harmless. The thrust of Eliassen's testimony was relevant to show not only what Nelson said, but also what he knew and intended.[6]

For similar reasons, the district court did not plainly err by allowing Bitikofer, Beacham, and Clark to testify about how they described their financial situations to Nelson or Baker. Both Nelson and Baker argued at trial that they believed each person they successfully persuaded to invest in partnership units was a wealthy and experienced investor who could afford to lose the money. The testimony was relevant to rebut this defense, and there was no error, much less plain error, in allowing it. Although these victims also briefly described the impact of losing the money, that limited testimony did not affect the defendants' substantial rights. There was no plain error.

Baker and Nelson contend that Rao's testimony that Greenhouse refused to return the money he and his girlfriend invested, even after Greenhouse was told that it was needed for her cancer treatment, was plain error. Rao's testimony discussed only Greenhouse and Agler and did not mention either Baker or Nelson. At oral argument, Nelson's counsel agreed that this testimony prejudiced only Greenhouse. Baker, however, contends that Rao's testimony "was unfairly prejudicial to all the trial defendants because they were charged in Count One with a conspiracy" and the district court did not specifically instruct the jury to consider the testimony only against Greenhouse. The record shows that any error in failing to give the limiting instruction was not plain and did not affect Baker's or Nelson's substantial rights.

Baker separately argues that because he had no duty to tell potential investors about the commissions he was paid, the district court erred in allowing p.1153 the victims he solicited to testify that they would not have invested had they known about the commissions. Baker relies on cases stating that "[a]bsent an independent duty, such as a fiduciary duty or an explicit statutory duty, failure to disclose cannot be the basis of a fraudulent scheme," *United States v. Ali,* 620 F.3d 1062, 1070 n. 7 (9th Cir.2010) (internal quotation marks omitted), and that "otherwise truthful statements made by [a broker] about the merits of a particular investment are not transformed into misleading 'half-truths' simply by the broker's failure to reveal that he is receiving added compensation for promoting a particular investment," *United States v. Skelly,* 442 F.3d 94, 97 (2d Cir.2006). Baker's argument fails to take into account the evidence that he affirmatively told victims that he, other sales personnel, and promoters would not receive any commissions or other payments until after the investors had received a 110 percent return. Baker's argument also fails to take into account that the *Red Water* private placement memorandum, which Baker sent to Gary Tranter and to the undercover FBI agent posing as an investor, included the false statement that no commissions would be paid until the investors had received a profitable return on their investments. The jury heard recorded conversations of Baker telling the undercover FBI agent posing as an investor that he received no commissions. Baker admitted that he lied to the agent about commissions. "[A] broker cannot affirmatively tell a misleading half-truth about a material fact to a potential investor . . . [because] the duty to disclose in these circumstances arises from the telling of a half-truth, independent of any responsibilities arising from a truth relationship." *United States v. Laurienti,* 611 F.3d 530, 541 (9th Cir.2010).

Baker's affirmative misrepresentations that he would receive no commissions until the investors received a profitable return supported his fraud conviction without the need to prove a fiduciary relationship. *See United States v. Benny,* 786 F.2d 1410, 1418 (9th Cir.1986) ("Proof of an affirmative, material misrepresentation supports a conviction of mail fraud without any additional proof of a fiduciary duty."). The district court did not err in allowing the victims to testify about Baker's representations and omissions about commissions.

b. The Lay Opinion Testimony

Baker and Nelson argue that the district court erred in allowing Allen Bruce Agler,[7] who had worked in several movie telemarketing boiler rooms (including for Cinamour during the fundraising for *From Mexico With Love* between 2005 and 2007), to testify about boiler-room management, activity, and strategy. Agler's testimony included his opinions about the information and knowledge telemarketers have when they cold-call potential investors and when they close a deal. Agler's testimony was not admissible under Rule 702 of the Federal Rules of Evidence because the government did not give the defendants the notice required under Rule 16 of the Federal Rules of Criminal Procedure. *See* Fed.R.Crim.P. 16(a)(1)(G) (requiring, at the defendant's request, pretrial disclosure of expert witnesses and a written summary of their testimony). Baker and Nelson argue that this limit could not be avoided by admitting Agler's testimony as lay opinion testimony under Rule 701.

"The admissibility of lay opinion testimony under Rule 701 is committed to the sound discretion of the trial judge and his decision will be overturned only if it constitutes a clear abuse of discretion." p.1154 *United States v. Gadson,* 763 F.3d 1189, 1209 (9th Cir.2014) (quoting *Nationwide Transp. Fin. v. Cass Info. Sys., Inc.,* 523 F.3d 1051 (9th Cir.2008)). The government contends that plain-error review applies because Baker objected on other grounds, not raised on appeal, before moving to strike Agler's testimony as unnoticed expert testimony, and Nelson did not specifically adopt Baker's objections. But Baker's attorney repeatedly objected to Agler's testimony about whether investors ever read the private placement memoranda they were sent. The objections were that Agler was giving "an expert opinion without foundation," as well as hearsay. "[T]he matter was sufficiently brought to the attention of the district court" through Baker's objections for us to review for abuse of discretion. *Gadson,* 763 F.3d at 1201 n. 3 (quoting *United States v. Orm Hieng,* 679 F.3d 1131, 1141 (9th Cir.2012)).

Under Federal Rule of Evidence 701, a lay witness may testify "in the form of an opinion" if it is "(a) rationally based on the perception of the witness; (b) helpful to a clear understanding of the witness' testimony or the determination of a fact in issue; and (c) not based on scientific, technical, or other specialized knowledge." Fed.R.Evid. 701. "Rule 701(a) contains a personal knowledge requirement." *United States v. Lopez,* 762 F.3d 852, 864 (9th Cir.2014). "In presenting lay opinions, the personal knowledge requirement may be met if the witness can demonstrate firsthand knowledge or observation." *Id.* "A lay witness's opinion testimony necessarily draws on the witness's own understanding, including a wealth of personal information, experience, and education, that cannot be placed before the jury." *Gadson,* 763 F.3d at 1208. But a lay opinion witness "may not testify based on speculation, rely on hearsay or interpret unambiguous, clear statements." *United States v. Vera,* 770 F.3d 1232, 1242 (9th Cir.2014).

Agler testified about his experience in working in telemarketing boiler rooms selling investments. He testified that:

- "[e]verybody that I've ever worked with will always stretch the truth and make out—outright lies especially in certain techniques";

- "[i]n my experience, the vast majority of people who invest do not read the private placement memorandum or if they do they read it on a limited basis, and they have no idea what it says";

- this was "absolutely" a "well-known fact" in the boiler rooms that he worked in; and

- investors relied on what telemarketers told them.

On cross-examination, Agler testified that "most investors never gave me an indication that they read the private placement memoranda" and he never brought "the subject up" when "he talked to them." When pressed on the basis for this opinion, Agler testified that he relied on his experience and the assumption that only those investors who asked a lot of questions about a memorandum had read it. On redirect, the government asked whether the fact that "investors did not read" private placement memoranda was "something that was openly discussed among closers that you worked with?" Agler responded, "sure." When asked if "it was a topic of discussion that investors don't read the [private placement memoranda]," he responded, "absolutely."

At the end of Agler's testimony, the prosecutor asked whether, "in all your own personal experience and all the closers who have worked in these rooms that you've spoken to, have you ever heard of any investor making any money on any of p.1155 these investments?" Agler responded, "[n]o, I have not."

Baker and Nelson argue that Agler's testimony impermissibly opined on what the telemarketers who solicited and closed investments, including themselves, knew about what they were selling and about what the investors were doing and thinking. They argue that to the extent Agler expressed a lay opinion, he relied on speculation and hearsay, and to the extent he expressed an expert opinion based on specialized knowledge gained from working in boiler rooms, the government failed to give the notice required under Rule 702 of the Federal Rules of Evidence and Rule 16 of the Federal Rules of Criminal Procedure.

Agler had extensive personal experience working as a telemarketer in boiler rooms soliciting and closing investments, including in Cinamour films. But his testimony that investors did not understand the risks, that all telemarketers knew of and took advantage of this ignorance, and that telemarketers knew that investors never made any money, was largely based on statements he heard from unidentified telemarketers and investors, well beyond his own personal experience with investors. Our cases make clear that Rule 701 prohibits opinions based on such a foundation. *See, e.g., United States v. Freeman,* 498 F.3d 893, 904 (9th Cir.2007) ("If Shin relied upon or conveyed hearsay evidence when testifying as a lay witness or if Shin based his lay testimony on matters not within his personal knowledge, he exceeded the bounds of properly admissible testimony.").[8]

Agler's testimony is different from the lay testimony that we have permitted law-enforcement officers to give. *See, e.g., Gadson,* 763 F.3d at 1208; *United States v. Simas,* 937 F.2d 459 (9th Cir.1991). In those cases, the officers did not base their lay opinions on hearsay statements made by unidentified individuals. *See Simas,* 937 F.2d at 464 (no abuse of discretion in allowing FBI agents to interpret the defendant's own "vague and . . . incomprehensible" statements). In *Gadson,* we held that the district court did not abuse its discretion in admitting lay opinion testimony that the defendant's coconspirator "made these admissions to us [the police]" because the officer "did not testify as to the nature of 'these admissions,' repeat any assertion made by [the coconspirator], or suggest that the jury should consider any admission made by [the coconspirator] to be truthful." 763 F.3d at 1211-12. We emphasized that "an officer's interpretation of intercepted phone calls may meet Rule 701's 'perception' requirement when it is an interpretation 'of ambiguous conversations based upon [the officer's] direct knowledge of the investigation.'" *Id.* at p.1156 1207 (quoting *Freeman,* 498 F.3d at 904-05). Here, by contrast, Agler's opinions that all telemarketers knew that investors rarely—if ever—read any private placement memoranda and never received a return on their investments were based primarily on the statements of unidentified telemarketers and of unidentified investor-victims. And, unlike the record we considered in *Gadson,* Agler testified about the nature of statements by other, unidentified telemarketers and investors. Agler's testimony was not admissible as lay opinion testimony under Rule 701.

During closing argument, the prosecutor urged the jury to consider the statements Agler testified he heard to be truthful and encouraged the jury to rely on them:

> Ladies and gentlemen, do you remember when Allen Agler testified and he told you that he committed fraud in this case and he pled guilty, and he stated that in all his experience as a telemarketer in boiler rooms raising money for movies, and in all his discussions with other people who were boiler room closers, not one single investor that he knew of in a movie investment from cold call telemarketing ever made a cent, not one?
>
> . . . .
>
> Remember, all the closers knew that no investor makes money from an independent movie where the money is raised by cold call telemarketing.

Agler testified that all victims ignored the written materials—including any risk-disclosure statements in the private placement memoranda—and instead relied exclusively on what the telemarketers orally promised in their sales pitches, and that all telemarketers knew and relied on victims following this pattern. Agler based his testimony on taking as true the contents of statements made by unidentified telemarketers and victims. The record is inadequate to allow us to conclude that a hearsay exception or exclusion applies.

The government argues that any error in admitting Agler's testimony under Rule 701 was harmless because he would have qualified as an expert under Rule 702. The government cites *United States v. Mendoza,* 244 F.3d 1037 (9th Cir.2001), and *United States v. Figueroa-Lopez,* 125 F.3d 1241, 1246-47 (9th Cir.1997). Both cases are distinguishable. In *Mendoza,* the defendant was tried and convicted for endangering the safety of an aircraft in flight after he called in a bomb threat to delay a flight so that his girlfriend would not miss it. *See* 244 F.3d at 1042-43. The government had originally given notice that the flight captain would testify but instead presented lay testimony from the first officer to show that the bomb threat endangered the aircraft's safety. *See id.* at 1043, 1047. On appeal, the defendant argued that the first officer was an undisclosed expert witness and that admitting his testimony made the trial unfair. *See id.* at 1046. We found that "the government had given notice that the captain of the flight would testify to emergency procedures, what occurred on [the flight], and endangerment," and "[f]or the purposes of a fair trial it was immaterial that the captain was not available, and that an equally qualified witness who had experienced the same factual circumstances, was substituted." *Id.* Unlike Nelson, the defendant in *Mendoza* had been given notice of the challenged testimony and its basis before trial and could prepare.

In *Figueroa-Lopez,* a special agent with the Drug Enforcement Administration testified about "the means utilized by drug traffickers to detect certain things, . . . and their patterns and other activities." *Figueroa-Lopez,* 125 F.3d at 1247. The officer did not rely on hearsay statements made by unidentified traffickers or others, p.1157 taken as true. The record contained extensive evidence of the officer's training and experience in drug traffickers' methods, a common subject of expert opinion. *Id.* The record in this case, by contrast, provides less support to find Agler qualified as an expert or that his opinions were reliable, and what telemarketers "know" is not a common subject for Rule 702 expert testimony. The record does not present a basis to excuse the failure to provide the defense timely notice of Agler's Rule 702 expert testimony by holding it admissible as lay opinion testimony under Rule 701.

We consider below whether this error and others were harmless in light of the extensive evidence that was properly admitted.[9]

c. The Rule 404(b) Evidence

Nelson testified that he believed Cinamour was a legitimate company, that he never knowingly lied to an investor, and that he would not have worked at Cinamour had he known about the false representations made by others working there. On cross-examination, the government introduced evidence that shortly after law-enforcement agents raided Cinamour, Nelson went to work in a movie telemarketing boiler room for Big Gunn Productions. During his employment there, Nelson received a check from Slanaker with the notation for "leads." The government offered the evidence of Nelson's subsequent employment as a telemarketer for Big Gunn Productions,[10] his work there with Slanaker, and the check from Slanaker, as evidence of subsequent bad acts under Federal Rule of

Evidence 404(b). Outside the jury's presence, the district court found that the evidence was admissible. The court found that the evidence showing that Nelson subsequently worked in a similar boiler room doing very similar work tended to disprove his testimony that he did not know Cinamour's fundraising efforts were fraudulent. The court reasoned that the subsequent employment occurred shortly after the events at issue, involved acts similar to the offense charged, and so supported finding that Nelson had committed the uncharged acts. The court concluded that the evidence was "highly probative of [ ] Nelson's intent and knowledge, and any prejudice [could] be mitigated through the agreed-upon jury instruction."

Evidence of a subsequent bad act is admissible under Rule 404(b) to show "motive, opportunity, intent, preparation, plan, knowledge, identity, absence of mistake, or lack of accident." Fed.R.Evid. 404(b); *see also United States v. Hinostroza,* 297 F.3d 924, 928 (9th Cir.2002) ("[O]ur precedent has squarely resolved in the government's favor the issue that subsequent Rule 404(b) evidence may be relevant and admissible." (citing *United States v. Bibo-Rodriguez,* 922 F.2d 1398, 1400 (9th Cir.1991))). The government must show that "(1) the evidence tends to prove a material point; (2) the other act is not too remote in time; (3) the evidence is sufficient to support a finding that defendant committed the other act; and (4) (in p.1158 certain cases) the act is similar to the offense charged." *United States v. Ramos-Atondo,* 732 F.3d 1113, 1123 (9th Cir. 2013) (internal quotation marks omitted). "[T]he probative value of the evidence must not be 'substantially outweighed by the danger of unfair prejudice.'" *Blitz,* 151 F.3d at 1008 (quoting Fed.R.Evid. 403).

Nelson does not dispute that he began working at Big Gunn less than a year after the FBI raided Cinamour or that he received the check from Slanaker 19 months after the raid. He argues that the government failed to show that Big Gunn was fraudulent or that it hired telemarketers to sell fraudulent or unregistered securities, that he made fraudulent misrepresentations while working for Big Gunn, or that Slanaker paid him for leads. At trial, Nelson testified that he left Big Gunn after he learned that the company was changing the movie's scheduled distribution date, because FBI agents had told him after the Cinamour raid that Cinamour had done the same thing.

Nelson's Big Gunn employment and the check he received from Slanaker were "not too remote in time," *see United States v. Johnson,* 132 F.3d 1279, 1282 (9th Cir.1997), and were "introduced to disprove [Nelson's] claim that he did not know [Cinamour] was a fraud," *Blitz,* 151 F.3d at 1008. But the record does not show "sufficient evidence from which the jury could conclude that [Nelson] was involved in fraudulent telemarketing at [Big Gunn]" to justify admission under Rule 404(b). *Blitz,* 151 F.3d at 1008. The government points to a Form 302 report of an FBI agent's interview with a telemarketer, Amanda Payne, who overlapped with Nelson at Big Gunn.[11] Payne called investors from lead lists to raise money for a movie called *Baby O,* using a script stating that investments in the film would return three to five times the amount invested and omitting any reference to using invested funds to pay the fundraisers. Payne also worked as a secretary, fielding investor follow-up calls, purchasing leads, and doing accounting work. She told the agents that of the 10 to 20 investors she spoke with daily, only a few were disgruntled and most wanted an update on *Baby O's* status. Although Payne testified that she would not recommend that her mother invest in the movie, that was because of some production problems. She would be comfortable having her mother invest in other Big Gunn productions under the right circumstances. Payne told the agents that she did not think that investors had been misled and that those closers who had lied to investors no longer worked for the company. She also told the FBI that Big Gunn's president had stopped taking a salary and had sold personal property to help cover overhead and maximize returns to investors. Payne told the FBI that Slanaker and Nelson worked for Big Gunn for only "a few months." By the time Nelson joined Big Gunn, *Baby O* was already completed and his fundraising work on the movie was limited. The district court repeatedly, and correctly, noted that the Payne interview did not show that Big Gunn was fraudulent. ("Amanda Payne, the problem with her 302 is she concludes by saying that she didn't believe that any of the investors of Big Gun[n] were misled."); ("I don't have the evidence p.1159 in front of me, that there was something fraudulent about the-about the *Baby-O* raise. I don't seem to have that in my notes."); ("I need some better evidence that it was a boiler room and that there was a raise going on for *Baby-O*.").

The government also points to a Form 302 report of the FBI's interview with Leigh Clark, who invested $120,000 in *Baby O* after investing $100,000 in another Big Gunn film. Clark had Nelson's name and contact information on a note in his Big Gunn files, but he could not recall whether he actually spoke with Nelson. To the contrary, Clark thought he talked to someone named "Arnold," not Nelson, before he invested, and Big Gunn's records showed that "Gary/Bart/Dave" closed Clark's investment. Clark did not state that Nelson made any misrepresentations to him or that Big Gunn's solicitation was fraudulent.

Similarly, apart from the check Nelson received from Slanaker with the word "leads" written in the memo line, there was no evidence that Nelson provided Slanaker with leads at Cinamour or at Big Gunn. According to Nelson, the check was to repay a long-outstanding loan. Nelson testified that he wrote the word "leads" in the check at Slanaker's request. When the district court asked the government outside the jury's presence what evidence "other than the existence of the check" showed that Nelson sold Slanaker leads, the government cited "[t]he fact that Slanaker was engaged in unlawful telemarketing, so leads would be an extremely appropriate thing for him to be buying." No evidence showed that Nelson had the means or the ability to generate a lead list.[12] The evidence did not show that Nelson supplied Slanaker or others with leads at Cinamour or Big Gunn.

The government argues that "if [the Big Gunn] scheme was indeed legitimate, [Nelson] cannot assert that it prejudiced the jury, or that it was inadmissible evidence of other bad acts." *United States v. Melvin*, 91 F.3d 1218, 1222 (9th Cir.1996); *see also Blitz*, 151 F.3d at 1008. But in neither *Melvin* nor *Blitz* did the prosecution introduce lay or expert testimony and argue that all companies engaging in a type of business similar to the charged scheme were fraudulent. *See id.* In *Melvin*, the defendant "himself introduced the evidence relating to the [other acts] scheme, in order to highlight its legitimacy as compared to the [charged] schemes." 91 F.3d at 1222 n. 2. And in *Blitz*, "the government presented substantial evidence to establish that the [the business where the uncharged conduct occurred] was engaged in fraudulent telemarketing." 151 F.3d at 1008. It was a "typical scam" in which "victims were told that they were 'guaranteed winners' of a big prize," which they would never receive, "but also were told that in order to quality for it, they had to buy a product, such as cosmetics, perfumes, pens or pencils" and "[t]hose products were sold at grossly inflated prices p.1160 ranging from $250 to a couple of thousand dollars." *Id.* The defendant "conceded that he sold pen sets, vitamins, and makeup for $299 to $999," that "he never heard of a customer who got one of the promised large prizes," and that his prior work included "trying to get money back for people who felt that they had been defrauded by [the other company]." *Id.*

Unlike the record in *Melvin* and *Blitz,* which included specific evidence showing the fraudulent nature of the uncharged scheme, the government here relied heavily on lay opinion testimony based on statements by unidentified telemarketers to show that *all* movie telemarketing operations are fraudulent. The government then used that conclusion as evidence that Big Gunn's telemarketing was fraudulent. When cross-examining Nelson about his telemarketing work for Big Gunn, the prosecutor asked if it was "[j]ust as crooked as Cinamour, just as crooked as all the movie boiler rooms that Mr. Allen Agler told us about, correct?" During closing arguments, the prosecutor told the jury that the "clearest evidence" that Nelson intended to defraud investors at Cinamour was that he went to work at another "movie investment boiler room" shortly after the FBI raided Cinamour's offices. The prosecutor argued that if the jury believed Nelson's testimony that the check was for a loan repayment, then Nelson "accepted money from a fraudulent company that was telemarketing and raising money from investors." Finally, the government told the jury that Slanaker, who took Nelson to Big Gunn, was a "convicted felon in a [prior] movie boiler room case."

We conclude that the district court abused its discretion in admitting this evidence of Nelson's subsequent employment at Big Gunn. We consider below whether this error was harmless. *See Frederick,* 78 F.3d at 1381.

d. The Testimony About Nelson's Involvement in the Conference Calls "Reloading" Prior Investors

Nelson asserts that the district court committed reversible error in admitting Stephanie Alarcon's testimony about conference calls encouraging victims to reload. Alarcon testified not only about reloading conference calls she participated in, but also about conference calls Nelson participated in, even though she was not on those calls or in the room when they occurred. Her information came from what another telemarketer, Verna Capelli, then working as one of the closers, told her about conference calls that she was on with Nelson and Slanaker. Nelson raised a hearsay objection at trial. We review the district court's ruling for an abuse of discretion. *See United States v. Orm Hieng,* 679 F.3d 1131, 1141 (9th Cir.2012).

Alarcon's testimony about what Capelli told her is not hearsay if both Capelli and Alarcon were coconspirators of Nelson's and the statement was offered against him. "A statement is not hearsay if . . . [t]he statement is offered against a party and is . . . a statement by a coconspirator of a party during the course and in furtherance of the conspiracy." *Bourjaily v. United States,* 483 U.S. 171, 173, 107 S.Ct. 2775, 97 L.Ed.2d 144 (1987); *accord* Fed.R.Evid. 801(d)(2)(E). Nelson argues that Alarcon was not his coconspirator because after the FBI and the U.S. Attorney's Office were involved, "the case agent and prosecutors told Alarcon that she was not in trouble and did not have to worry about being arrested." Nelson cites no authority for his argument, and our cases provide no support. "It is not necessary that the statement be made to another member of the conspiracy for it to come p.1161 under [R]ule 801(d)(2)(E)," *United States v. Williams*, 989 F.2d 1061, 1068 (9th Cir. 1993), and "[a] coconspirator's statement is admissible upon proof that it was made in furtherance of a conspiracy," even if "the indictment does not contain a conspiracy count" against that coconspirator, *United States v. Manning*, 56 F.3d 1188, 1197 (9th Cir.1995). "The question is merely whether there was proof of a sufficient concert of action to show the individuals to have been engaged in a joint venture." *Manning*, 56 F.3d at 1197.

Both Capelli and Alarcon were working at Cinamour when Capelli took part in the calls with Nelson and described them to Alarcon. Both Alarcon and Capelli worked as fronters, and Capelli also worked as a closer. Their work as fronters enabled closers, like Nelson, to get potential investors to sign and return the investment agreements to Cinamour with the checks. There is ample evidence that both Alarcon and Capelli were Nelson's coconspirators when Capelli and Nelson took part in reloading conference calls and when Capelli told Alarcon about Nelson's participation in the calls.

The record also supports finding that Capelli's statements kept Alarcon "abreast of an ongoing conspiracy's activities" and were therefore made "in furtherance of" the conspiracy. *See United States v. Yarbrough*, 852 F.2d 1522, 1536 (9th Cir.1988). For example, Capelli told Alarcon about the participants in, and the substance of, the conference calls in which she took part. Capelli explained the strategy behind the conference calls: to "get all the investors together" so that if one decided to invest, the others would be more likely to follow suit "because [of] their egos." And Capelli warned Alarcon that she thought the calls were not "a good idea" and that if the FBI was recording them, the company would be shut down. Although "[m]ere conversations between coconspirators, or merely narrative declarations among them, are not made 'in furtherance' of a conspiracy," the evidence is sufficient to find by a preponderance that Capelli's statements "were made with the intent to keep [Alarcon] abreast of what [Cinamour] had done, was doing, or would do in the future." *See id.* at 1535-36.

The district court did not abuse its discretion in admitting Alarcon's testimony about Nelson's participation in reloading conference calls.

e. The Email Evidence About Baker

Baker asserts that the district court erred in admitting an email containing hearsay statements that he had been warned to stop giving potential investors false information about the investments. The email was admitted during the government's examination of Jennifer Nakamori, Cinamour's Los Angeles office manager during the time Baker worked for that office. Nakamori wrote the email to Glen Hartford in August 2002. It included the following statements:

> Paul [Baker] brings in money because he's giving investors false information. We've given him 5 warning[s] already and he still can't get it right. . . . You [Hartford] are the one who told me that Paul [Baker] would be let go after one more warning. You told me this morning that we are accepting money from

investors who've been given false promises. It sounds like we're just taking money from anyone. How can we make a movie this way? What's going to happen in the future? They may come back and you will be held liable. Paul, Evan, Matt, and everyone else will just walk away happy with their commission monies in their pockets.

Nakamori's information that Baker gave potential investors and victims false information p.1162 came only from "[t]hings I heard in the office" and was "[j]ust rumors that I heard." Nakamori could not remember who said the "things" or spread the "rumors." Hartford told her that he had warned Baker not to give false information or make false promises about the investments. Nakamori could not remember hearing Hartford warn Baker.

Baker objected to the email and Nakamori's testimony about it. His objection was overruled and the email and related testimony were admitted. Baker renews his objection on appeal. We find an abuse of discretion in admitting the email and related testimony. Nakamori had no personal knowledge about whether Baker was making false statements to get victims to invest. Nor did she have personal knowledge about whether Baker had been repeatedly warned not to do this.

The government argues that the email and Nakamori's testimony about it are admissible because they were offered to show Baker's state of mind—his knowledge that what he was telling investors was false—rather than for the truth of the matter stated. The problem is that unless the email contents and related testimony were true, they are not relevant to show Baker's state of mind. The email does not show that Baker knew he was making false representations unless the statements that he was doing so and had been warned about it are accepted as true. The evidence was hearsay.

We consider below whether the error was harmless in light of the other evidence properly submitted to the jury. *See Frederick,* 78 F.3d at 1381.

f. Nelson's Proffered Testimony About His Daughter's Birth

Nelson argues that the district court erred in excluding his testimony about his daughter's birth and the role it played in motivating him to stay sober, law-abiding, and employed. Nelson argues that he followed Slanaker's instructions not because he intended to violate the law, but because he was determined to keep his job. In his opening statement, Nelson's counsel stated:

> [B]ehind [an] alcohol soaked haze, behind [a] dumpster, [Nelson] realized that he was about to be a father. He realized that his girlfriend was about to give birth to his daughter. . . . [he found out] that his girlfriend [was] going to give the baby up for adoption [and that] he's going to lose his parental rights, and there is something that he can do about that, and he does something about that. He was unable to contest the adoption, but he [was] able to somehow retain his parental rights.

The next day, a juror asked to be excused because he "might have a problem being completely objective in regards to the prosecution's case against [Nelson] because of the far-reaching ramifications [another prosecution] had on my own family." The juror remained as an alternate, but the government asked the district court for a limine order excluding evidence about the birth of Nelson's daughter.

The government argued that this evidence was intended only to elicit sympathy, was irrelevant to the legal and factual issues before the jury, and would encourage jury nullification. Nelson responded that the evidence was relevant to show his lack of mens rea.

The court denied the government's limine request in part and granted it in part, allowing Nelson to testify about his history of alcoholism, homelessness, and joblessness. The court allowed Nelson to testify that during this period, "some things [were] happening" that motivated him to become and stay sober, out of jail, p.1163 and employed. The court refused to let Nelson identify those "things" or provide details. The court reasoned that the evidence about Nelson becoming a father and achieving a relationship with his daughter was "designed to improperly appeal to the sympathy of the jury," and concluded that "the probative value is substantially out-weighed by the risks of unfair prejudice."

Nelson argues that the court's ruling prevented him from presenting a complete and meaningful defense, violating the Due Process Clause, *see California v. Trombetta,* 467 U.S. 479, 485, 104 S.Ct. 2528, 81 L.Ed.2d 413 (1984), and Federal Rule of Evidence 401. Nelson contends that this testimony was crucial to explain his "history and state of mind in the time period leading up to his employment at Cinamour." We disagree.

As the experience with the juror who remained as the alternate demonstrates, this testimony carried a high risk of evoking an emotional response. The jury heard undisputed evidence that Nelson stayed sober, out of jail, and employed throughout his time at Cinamour. The jury also heard undisputed testimony that Nelson was so determined to keep his job at Cinamour that he continued to work despite the abuse he took from Slanaker. Given the testimony the jury did hear, the additional testimony about the birth of Nelson's daughter was only marginally relevant to show his mens rea and was cumulative of other evidence. Because the prejudicial impact outweighed the probative value, the district court did not abuse its discretion in excluding this testimony.

2. The Jury Instructions

a. Baker's Claim that the Instructions Constructively Amended the Indictment

"A constructive amendment occurs when the charging terms of the indictment are altered, either literally or in effect, by the prosecutor or a court after the grand jury has last passed upon them." *United States v. Ward,* 747 F.3d 1184, 1190 (9th Cir.2014) (internal quotation marks omitted). The mail-and wire-fraud counts alleged that Baker "knowingly and with the intent to defraud" participated in and executed a scheme "to obtain money from[] investors by means of materially false and fraudulent pretenses, representations, and promises, and the concealment of material facts."

The district court instructed the jury that

> [a] statement or representation is "false or fraudulent" for purposes of mail and wire fraud if known to be untrue, or made *with reckless disregard* as to its truth or falsity, and made or caused to be made with the intent to deceive.

The court gave a similar instruction on Baker's good-faith defense:

> The defendant does not have the burden of proving he acted in good faith. The government must prove beyond a reasonable doubt that the defendant acted with the intent to defraud and did not act in good faith. Proof that a defendant acted *with reckless disregard* as to the truth or falsity of material misrepresentations he may have made is inconsistent with good faith.

Baker argues that the district court constructively amended the indictment by using the term "reckless disregard," which permitted the jury to convict on a lesser mental state than "knowing."

When a defendant makes a constructive-amendment objection at trial, our review is de novo. *Ward,* 747 F.3d at 1190. The government argues that plain-error review applies because although Baker objected to the instruction, it was on the basis of an improper variance, not a p.1164 constructive amendment. Our precedent does not support the government's argument. In *Ward,* we reviewed the defendant's constructive-amendment argument on appeal de novo despite his failure to use specific words, including "the term 'Fifth Amendment,'" when he objected at trial. We reasoned that "the substance of the objection"—the fear that the jury would convict on the basis of conduct not alleged in the indictment—"was patently clear." 747 F.3d at 1189. Similarly, although Baker did not use the words "constructive amendment" in objecting, he did state that "the government in no way alleged a theory of reckless indifference as a mental state on any defendant's part in the indictment." The substance of Baker's objection was clear. Our review is de novo.

"[A] constructive amendment occurs when 'the crime charged [is] substantially changed at trial, so that it [is] impossible to know whether the grand jury would have indicted for the crime actually proved.'" *United States v. Pisello,* 877 F.2d 762, 765 (9th Cir.1989) (quoting *United States v. Von Stoll,* 726 F.2d 584, 586 (9th Cir.1984)). In *United States v. Love,* 535 F.2d 1152 (9th Cir.1976), "the indictment charged [the defendant] with certain fraudulent representations while 'well knowing' that the representations were falsely made." *Id.* at 1157. The defendant appealed, arguing that the district court impermissibly varied from the indictment by instructing the jury that

> [a] statement or representation is false and fraudulent within the meaning of the statute if known to be untrue or made *with reckless indifference* as to its truth or falsity and made or caused to be made with the intent to deceive.

Id. (emphasis added). Applying de novo review, the court rejected the argument, reasoning that in a mail-fraud prosecution, "'[o]ne who acts with reckless indifference as to whether a representation is true or false is chargeable as if he had knowledge of its falsity.'" *Id.* at 1158 (quoting *Irwin v. United States,* 338 F.2d 770, 774 (9th Cir.1964)).[13]

The instruction at issue here was clearer than the instruction in *Love* in that it required the jury to find the statement "known to be untrue, or made with reckless disregard as to its truth or falsity, *and* made or caused to be made with the intent to deceive." An indictment charging that a defendant knowingly participated in a scheme to defraud does not necessarily charge that defendant with making specific false statements. *See United States v. Woods,* 335 F.3d 993, 999 (9th Cir.2003) ("[A] scheme to defraud . . . may or may not involve any specific false statements.").

We conclude that the district court's instruction did not constructively amend the indictment.

b. Nelson's Claim that the District Court Erred in Rejecting His Definition of "Reckless Disregard"

Nelson argues that the district court erred by not including his timely submitted instruction defining reckless indifference. "In reviewing jury instructions, the relevant inquiry is whether the instructions as a whole are misleading or inadequate to guide the jury's deliberation." *United States v. Dixon,* 201 F.3d 1223, 1230 (9th Cir.2000). "A single instruction to a jury may not be judged in artificial isolation, but must be viewed in the context of the overall charge." *Id.* De p.1165 novo review applies to determining "whether the district court's instructions adequately presented the defendant's theory of the case" or "misstate[] the elements of a statutory crime." *Id.; United States v. Frega,* 179 F.3d 793, 807 n. 16 (9th Cir.1999). Review for abuse of discretion applies to the district court's "precise formulation" of the instructions. *Dixon,* 201 F.3d at 1230 (quoting *United States v. Knapp,* 120 F.3d 928, 930 (9th Cir.1997)).

Nelson asked the court to instruct the jury that

> a person acts with reckless indifference as used in these instructions if he consciously disregards a substantial and unjustifiable risk that his statements are false or misleading—that is, if he deliberately closes his eyes to what would otherwise have been obvious to him. The government has the burden of showing reckless indifference beyond a reasonable doubt.

The district court instead told the jury that

> [a] statement or representation is "false or fraudulent" for purposes of mail and wire fraud if known to be untrue, or made with reckless disregard as to its truth or falsity, and made or caused to be made with the intent to deceive.

The court did not define "reckless disregard."

Nelson contends that the district court erred in failing to include the deliberate-blindness or deliberate-ignorance instruction he submitted because leaving the meaning to lay understanding could lead the jury to convict based on negligence. We have repeatedly held that similar "reckless indifference" or "reckless disregard" instructions sufficiently protect against this risk. *See, e.g., United States v. Munoz,* 233 F.3d 1117, 1135-36 (9th Cir.2000), *superseded by statute on other grounds,* 18 U.S.C. § 1341; *United States v. Gay,* 967 F.2d 322, 326-27 (9th Cir. 1992). Recklessness in this context is "within the comprehension of the average juror" and needs no special definition. *United States v. Tirouda,* 394 F.3d 683, 688-89 (9th Cir.2005) ("'[C]riminal recklessness under Alaska law relates essentially to the common-sense definition of recklessness, which the average juror could understand and apply without an instruction.'" (quoting *Walker v. Endell,* 850 F.2d 470, 475 (9th Cir.1987))).

The court's instructions, considered as a whole, clearly told jurors that they could not convict Nelson unless they unanimously found that the government had proven beyond a reasonable doubt that he acted with intent to defraud—the intent to deceive or cheat—and did not act in good faith. The instructions told the jury that they could not convict on the basis of negligence.

We find no basis for reversal on this ground.

c. Nelson's Claim that the District Court Erred in Instructing on the Alleged Securities-Law Violations

Nelson argues that the district court erred in instructing the jury on the counts alleging that he violated 15 U.S.C. § 77e, which forbids the offer or sale of unregistered securities, and § 77x, which punishes "willful[]" violations of the securities laws.

i. The Instruction on Aiding or Abetting the Offer or Sale of Unregistered Securities

The parties agreed to, and the court gave, the following instruction on 15 U.S.C. § 77e and 18 U.S.C. § 2:

> In order for a defendant to be found guilty of the illegal sale or distribution of unregistered securities as charged in the Indictment, the government must prove p.1166 each of the following elements beyond a reasonable doubt:
>
> First, that the securities which the defendant sold were not registered with the [S]ecurities and Exchange Commission;
>
> Second, that the securities sold were required to be registered with the Securities and Exchange Commission— that is, that the transactions were not exempt from registration;
>
> Third, that, knowing the securities were not registered and not exempt, the defendant willfully sold or caused them to be sold to the public; and
>
> Fourth, that the defendant used or caused to be used the mails or the means and instrumentalities of interstate commerce to sell the securities.

Nelson contends that this instruction failed to convey the government's burden to prove that he knew that the unregistered securities he was selling had to be registered. Nelson contends that it was not enough for the government to prove his knowledge that the securities were not exempt from the registration requirement. Because Nelson agreed to the instruction without objection, plain-error review applies. *See United States v. Feldman,* 853 F.2d 648, 652 (9th Cir.1988).

Nelson cites no authority for his argument, and we have found none. In context, the difference between knowing that the law required registering the securities in order to sell them and knowing that the unregistered securities were not exempt from the registration requirement is not material. We find no reversible error.

ii. The Instruction on Willfully Violating the Federal Securities Laws

The court gave the following instruction of "willfully" in instructing the jury on the alleged 15 U.S.C. § 77x violation:

> A person acts "willfully" under the federal securities laws by intentionally undertaking an act that one knows to be wrongful. "Willfully" does not require that the person know specifically that the conduct was unlawful.

Nelson renews the objection he made at trial that the instruction would allow conviction without proof that he knew his conduct violated the securities laws. He contends that because 15 U.S.C. § 77e forbids offering or selling unregistered securities, which is not inherently wrongful, this proof is required to show a "willful[]" violation of 15 U.S.C. § 77x.

We rejected a similar argument in *United States v. Reyes,* 577 F.3d 1069 (9th Cir.2009), an appeal from a conviction for knowingly falsifying "book[s], record[s], and account[s]," in violation of 15 U.S.C. § 78m(b)(5). The defendant argued that because "the knowing falsification of books, records, and accounts is not 'inevitably nefarious,'" she could not be convicted without proof that she knew her conduct violated the law. *Id.* at 1080. We held that her argument was "foreclosed" by *United States v. Tarallo,* 380 F.3d 1174 (9th Cir.2004), and other cases "reject[ing] the argument that, in the context of the securities fraud statutes, willfulness requires a defendant know that he or she was breaking the law." *Reyes,* 577 F.3d at 1080 (citing *Tarallo,* 380 F.3d at 1187-88; *United States v. Charnay,* 537 F.2d 341, 351-52 (9th Cir.1976)). The district court "correctly instructed the jury that it had to find that" the defendant "was aware of the falsification and did not falsify through ignorance, mistake, or accident," but "[t]here is no higher standard for a willful violation of the securities laws." *Id.* (quotation marks omitted).

p.1167 Nelson attempts to distinguish *Reyes* by arguing that it involved "securities fraud" under § 78m, not "regulatory violations" under § 77e that are not "inherently bad acts." But both § 78m and § 77e use the scienter standard under 15 U.S.C. § 77x, which allows conviction if a person "willfully violates" the securities laws. There is no basis in the statutory language or in our cases to read a higher level of scienter into § 77x when the alleged violation is under § 77e. The district court did not commit reversible error in instructing the jury on the counts alleging that Nelson violated the securities laws.

d. The Rule 404(b) Instruction

Nelson argues, without citing authority, that the district court erred in instructing the jury on the Rule 404(b) evidence of his telemarketing work at Big Gunn after the FBI raided the Cinamour office where he worked. Although we find it error to admit the evidence, we find no error in the instruction, which tracked the Ninth Circuit model jury instruction for Rule 404(b) evidence:

> You have heard the evidence that defendant Nelson committed other acts not charged here. You may consider this evidence for its bearing, if any, on the question of defendant Nelson's intent, knowledge, absence of mistake and absence of accident and for no other purpose. You may not consider this evidence against any other defendant on trial.

See Ninth Cir.Crim. Model Jury Instructions § 4.3 (2010 ed.).

According to Nelson, the language "not charged here" implies that the uncharged acts could have been charged. We find that the instruction, considered as a whole, accurately and clearly stated the law. We have recently cited this model instruction with approval. *United States v. Hardrick,* 766 F.3d 1051, 1054, 1056 (9th Cir.2014) (the district court did not abuse its discretion in admitting Rule 404(b) evidence in part because the court "gave a limiting instruction at the close of evidence" describing "'other acts not charged here'" that mirrored the "legally correct model instruction."). The district court did not abuse its discretion in giving the Rule 404(b) instruction.

3. Nelson's Claim of Prosecutorial Misconduct

Nelson asserts that the prosecutor's statements about the victims' testimony, made in closing argument, requires reversal. "To obtain a reversal based on prosecutorial misconduct, [Nelson] must establish both misconduct and prejudice." *United States v. Wright,* 625 F.3d 583, 609-10 (9th Cir.2010), *superseded by statute on other grounds as recognized by United States v. Brown,* 785 F.3d 1337, 1351 (9th Cir.2015). Nelson did not "object[] at trial to acts of alleged prosecutorial misconduct." Our review is for plain error. *See United States v. Hinton,* 31 F.3d 817, 824 (9th Cir.1994).

Nelson argues that the prosecutor intentionally misstated the testimony Melvin Bitikofer gave at trial. Bitikofer testified that Slanaker, not Nelson, asked him to participate in the February 2009 reloading conference call in which he was persuaded to invest another $100,000 in a Cinamour movie, this time using money from his wife's IRA. Bitikofer testified that he did not know if Nelson was on the call or not. During closing, however, the prosecutor told the jury that Nelson "got Mr. Bitikofer on a conference call—look at Exhibit 289—and he took a hundred thousand dollars more." The prosecutor also incorrectly attributed to Melvin Bitikofer the testimony given by another victim, Richard Clark, that "Mr. Nelson told [him] that he p.1168 wasn't just a salesman, but was also involved in the technology aspect of the company as well."

The government concedes that the prosecutor's closing argument contained both statements and that both were wrong. Our review of the record shows no basis for finding that the prosecutor's errors were intentionally made or that they substantially affected Nelson's right to a fair trial. The prosecution accurately described the testimony about the reloading conference call but inaccurately attributed the call to Nelson rather than Slanaker. There was no error in the prosecutor's description of what the victim-witness said, only that Clark, not Bitikofer, was the victim who said it. In context, these mistakes appear to have been inadvertent.

A prosecutor's inadvertent mistakes or misstatements are not misconduct. *See United States v. Del-Toro Barboza,* 673 F.3d 1136, 1153 (9th Cir.2012) (a prosecutor's attribution of one defendant's statement to both defendants was "an honest mistake and not prosecutorial misconduct"); *Downs v. Hoyt,* 232 F.3d 1031, 1038 (9th Cir.2000) (a prosecutor's passing reference to a statement not in evidence was not misconduct when the prosecutor was "confused about which portions of the voluminous medical records had been admitted into evidence"); *United States v. Carrillo,* 16 F.3d 1046, 1050 (9th Cir.1994) (a prosecutor's "misstatement ha[d] earmarks of inadvertent mistake, not misconduct").

Nor were the misstatements "so gross as probably to prejudice" Nelson. *United States v. Navarro,* 608 F.3d 529, 536 (9th Cir.2010). That is particularly so in light of Clark's testimony that Nelson played a substantial role in his conference call and the district court's repeated instructions that the jury's recollections—not the prosecutor's summation—controlled.

The prosecutor's misstatements during closing are not a basis for reversal.

4. Cumulative Error

"Even if no error individually supports reversal, the cumulative effect of numerous errors may support reversal." *United States v. Inzunza,* 638 F.3d 1006, 1024 (9th Cir.2011) (citing *United States v. Frederick,* 78 F.3d 1370, 1381 (9th Cir. 1996)). "Where, as here, there are a number of errors at trial, 'a balkanized, issue-by-issue harmless error review' is far less effective than analyzing the overall effect of all the errors in the context of the evidence introduced at trial against the defendant." *United States v. Frederick,* 78 F.3d 1370, 1381 (9th Cir.1996) (quoting *United States v. Wallace,* 848 F.2d 1464, 1476 (9th Cir.1988)). "In those cases where the government's case is weak, a defendant is more likely to be prejudiced by the effect of cumulative errors." *Id.* "This is simply the logical corollary of the harmless error doctrine which requires us to affirm a conviction if there is overwhelming evidence of guilt." *Id.* (internal quotation marks omitted).

a. Baker

Although the district judge erred in admitting Agler's lay opinion testimony about what telemarketers know and intend, and in admitting the Nakamori email and related testimony, the errors were harmless in light of the overwhelming evidence against Baker. The evidence included voice recordings of Baker's calls with an undercover agent posing as a potential investor in *Red Water.* In the calls, Baker repeatedly lied. He told the agent that Cinamour had already secured $5.4 million presales contracts to distribute the film in 31 countries, guaranteeing a risk-free and profitable investment. He told p.1169 the agent that there was already enough revenue from the presale contracts to guarantee a 110 percent return to the investors. He told the agent that investors would receive the 110 percent return in 8 to 10 months and triple their money in 2 years. He told the agent that the film's promoters and sales personnel would receive no money until the investors had received their money back with a profit, and that none of the fundraisers were receiving commissions. Baker's victims testified that he made the same statements to them. Baker's coconspirators testified about his false statements and role in the conspiracy, including his role in including false statements about commissions in the *Red Water* private placement memorandum. Finally, the jury heard that after the raid, Baker confessed to law-enforcement agents that he had lied in the call with the undercover agent about the presale contracts and the commissions.

In light of the overwhelming admissible evidence against him, the errors we have found do not require reversing Baker's conviction. *See United States v. Ruiz,* 710 F.3d 1077, 1080 n. 1 (9th Cir.2013) ("Finally, since the errors that occurred at trial were isolated, reversal for cumulative error is not warranted."). Baker's conviction is affirmed.

b. Nelson

There was certainly evidence against Nelson, but it was not overwhelming. Nelson's victims testified that he too misrepresented the existence of presale distribution contracts, the resulting profit guarantee and the absence of risk, and the absence of commissions or other payments to promoters and sales personnel.

Although Nelson denied these allegations at trial, he admitted using a script with those statements. Nelson also sent an email to one victim, Eliassen, promising that presales distribution contracts made the investment secure. Nelson testified that some unidentified person at Cinamour had told him at some unidentified time that the presales contracts described in the script did exist. Nelson told his victims that investors in Cinamour's prior movies had been successful even though his coconspirator, Stephanie Alarcon, testified that she and Nelson had talked about the fact that prior investors were unhappy because they had not made money. The evidence showed that Nelson told prospective investors and the victims who invested that filming on *Red Water* had begun or was about to begin. He admitted on the stand that filming had not started and was not about to start. Nelson testified that he did not reveal his 12.5 percent commission to the prospective investors or victims he talked to, and the evidence, including Nadav Shimoni's testimony and scripts, showed that Nelson was involved in the reloading conference calls.

There was also evidence favorable to Nelson's defense theory that he lacked the intent to defraud necessary to show that he willfully violated the securities laws. Nelson joined Cinamour much later than his codefendants, giving him less exposure to the fraudulent practices before the FBI's 2009 raid. He testified that he was only involved in a few reloading conference calls and then only for a brief period, and that he was unaware of the use of "shills" like Shimoni. Although we conclude that there was sufficient evidence to support each count of conviction, *see infra* Part II.C.5, the government has not met its burden to show that the evidentiary errors we have found were harmless. *United States v. Vizcarra-Martinez,* 66 F.3d 1006 (9th Cir.1995) (evidence properly admitted was sufficient to support the conviction but the error in admitting evidence was not harmless, requiring reversal and remand). The inadmissible evidence of Nelson's subsequent employment at Big Gunn and the p.1170 check he wrote to Slanaker, especially when refracted through the lens of Agler's testimony that all movie telemarketing operations are fraudulent and that all fronters and closers knew this, may have "substantially swayed" the jury in concluding that the government had met its burden of proving Nelson's knowledge and intent. *See Freeman,* 498 F.3d at 905.

The risk that the improperly admitted evidence affected the verdict is increased because the government's closing argument repeatedly encouraged the jury to rely on this evidence. The government argued during closing that Nelson, Baker, and Greenhouse "knew" that "there was no way these investors would ever make a dime" and that "they lied in order to get the people to invest their money." The government emphasized Allen Agler's testimony that "all the closers knew that no investor makes money from an independent movie where the money is raised by cold call telemarketing." And the government told the jury that "the clearest evidence" that Nelson had the intent to defraud while working at Cinamour was that he went to work at another "movie investment boiler room"—Big Gunn— after the FBI raided Cinamour.

Our review of the record leaves us without a "fair assurance" that the "jury was not substantially swayed by the error[s]" in convicting Nelson. *See Freeman,* 498 F.3d at 905. We conclude that the errors were not harmless and that they require us to reverse Nelson's conviction, vacate his sentence, and remand.

5. Nelson's Claim that the Evidence Is Insufficient to Sustain His Convictions

Nelson argues that the government presented insufficient evidence to convict him of violating 15 U.S.C. §§ 77e and 77x by selling unregistered securities.[14] We address this question even though we reverse the conviction and remand because a retrial may implicate double jeopardy. "'It has long been settled. . . that the Double Jeopardy Clause's general prohibition against successive prosecutions does not prevent the government from retrying a defendant who succeeds in getting his first conviction set aside, through direct appeal or collateral attack, because of some error in the proceedings leading to conviction." *United States v. Preston,* 751 F.3d 1008, 1028 (9th Cir.2014) (en banc) (quoting *Lockhart v. Nelson,* 488 U.S. 33, 38, 109 S.Ct. 285, 102 L.Ed.2d 265 (1988)). "But the Supreme Court has recognized an exception to the government's right to retry a defendant without offending the Double Jeopardy Clause where the conviction is overturned for insufficient evidence." *Id.* (citing *Burks v. United States,* 437 U.S. 1, 11, 98 S.Ct. 2141, 57 L.Ed.2d 1 (1978)). "This exception recognizes that the 'Double Jeopardy Clause forbids a second trial for the purpose of affording the prosecution another opportunity to supply evidence which it failed to muster in the first proceeding.'" *Id.* (quoting *Burks,* 437 U.S. at 11, 98 S.Ct. 2141). We "must address the sufficiency of the evidence question" on the securities-fraud convictions "even though we are remanding for a new trial." *Id.*

A "two-step inquiry for considering a challenge to a conviction based on sufficiency of the evidence" applies. *United States v. Nevils,* 598 F.3d 1158, 1164 (9th Cir.2010) (en banc). "First, a reviewing court must consider the evidence presented p.1171 at trial in the light most favorable to the prosecution." *Id.* (citing *Jackson v. Virginia,* 443 U.S. 307, 319, 99 S.Ct. 2781, 61 L.Ed.2d 560 (1979)). The reviewing court "may not usurp the role of the finder of fact by considering how it would have resolved the conflicts, made the inferences, or considered the evidence at trial." *Id.* "Rather, when faced with a record of historical facts that supports conflicting inferences," the reviewing court "must presume—even if it does not affirmatively appear in the record—that the trier of fact resolved any such conflicts in favor of the prosecution, and must defer to that resolution." *Id.* (internal quotation marks omitted).

"Second, after viewing the evidence in the light most favorable to the prosecution, the reviewing court must determine whether this evidence, so viewed, is adequate to allow '*any* rational trier of fact [to find] the essential elements of the crime beyond a reasonable doubt.'" *Id.* (quoting and emphasizing *Jackson,* 443 U.S. at 319, 99 S.Ct. 2781). "More than a 'mere modicum' of evidence is required to support a verdict." *Id.* (quoting *Jackson,* 443 U.S. at 320, 99 S.Ct. 2781). "At this second step, however, a reviewing court may not ask itself whether it believes that the evidence at the trial established guilt beyond a reasonable doubt, only whether 'any' rational trier of fact could have made that finding." *Id.* (internal quotation marks and citations omitted).

Nelson argues that the government failed to show that he had the required intent to violate § 77e and § 77x. He points to the statement in the private placement memorandum for *Red Water* that the partnership units were exempt from the registration requirement, and he argues that the evidence failed to show he "had any information to the contrary." The record undercuts his argument.

The evidence included a copy of the private placement memorandum found in Nelson's office. The memorandum clearly stated that "[n]o general solicitation or advertisement in any form may be utilized regarding the offering." The exhibit contained handwritten notes matching a sample of Nelson's known handwriting. A highlighted section discussing the registration exemption clearly stated that if a security was unregistered, solicitations and sales had to be limited to "accredited investors," and handwritten notes on an accompanying subscription document contained annotations about the meaning of that term. Stephanie Alarcon testified that Nelson told her what it meant for an investor to be accredited. There was ample evidence that Nelson knew and understood the accredited-investor limitation on soliciting and selling the unregistered securities and what being an accredited investor meant. There was also ample evidence that Nelson pursued the leads he was provided without any inquiry about whether the investors he successfully solicited were accredited. The evidence showed that he sold units to investors who gave him information showing that they failed to meet the accreditation standards.

Viewing the evidence in the light most favorable to the government, a rational juror could conclude beyond a reasonable doubt that Nelson knew that the securities he was selling had to be registered unless he and others limited offers and sales to accredited investors, and that the investors he solicited—some successfully—included many who were clearly not accredited. The evidence was sufficient for the jury to convict Nelson for violating 15 U.S.C. §§ 77e and 77x.[15] Nelson may be retried p.1172 on these counts, as well as on the counts he does not challenge on the basis of insufficient evidence, without violating the Double Jeopardy Clause.[16]

III. Baker's Sentencing Challenge[17]

The district court calculated Baker's Guidelines range as 292 to 365 months, based on a total offense level of 35 and a criminal history category of VI, and sentenced him to serve a 194-month prison term and pay $12,043,678.25 in restitution. Baker argues that the court committed procedural error in applying a two-level enhancement for targeting vulnerable victims and increasing his criminal history points based on two prior sentences. The increase in points put him in criminal history category VI instead of V.

"Procedural errors include, but are not limited to, incorrectly calculating the Guidelines range, treating the Guidelines as mandatory, failing to properly consider the [18 U.S.C.] § 3553(a) factors, using clearly erroneous facts when calculating the Guidelines range or determining the sentence, and failing to provide an adequate explanation for the sentence imposed." *United States v. Armstead,* 552 F.3d 769, 776 (9th Cir.2008). "We review the district court's interpretation of the [G]uidelines de novo," its "application of the [G]uidelines to the facts for an abuse of discretion," and "the substantive reasonableness of the sentence for an abuse of discretion."[18] *United States v. Hurtado,* 760 F.3d 1065, 1068 (9th Cir.2014).

A. The Vulnerable-Victim Enhancement

A two-level enhancement "applies to offenses involving an unusually vulnerable victim in which the defendant knows or should have known of the victim's unusual vulnerability." U.S.S.G. § 3A1.1(b)(1), cmt. n. 2. A "vulnerable victim" is "a person. . . who is unusually vulnerable due to age, physical or mental condition, or who is otherwise particularly susceptible to the criminal conduct." *Id.,* cmt. n. 2. We review the district court's "findings that the victims were vulnerable . . . for clear error." *United States v. Randall,* 162 F.3d 557, 560 (9th Cir.1998).

Baker contends that the district court erred in applying the vulnerable-victim enhancement because targeting victims for reloading and successfully reloading them did not make them "vulnerable" under § 3A1.1(b)(1). The district court correctly found, and we have twice held, that when, as here, a defendant "reloads" victims by soliciting more money from those who have already proven susceptible p.1173 to an investment fraud, including in the telemarketing context, the vulnerable-victim enhancement is appropriate. *See, e.g., United States v. Ciccone,* 219 F.3d 1078, 1086 (9th Cir.2000) ("[V]ictims of a 'reloading' scheme . . . are vulnerable for the purpose of enhancing a convicted person's sentence."); *Randall,* 162 F.3d at 560 ("[W]hether these persons are described as gullible, overly trusting, or just naive[,] their readiness to fall for the telemarketing rip-off, not once but twice[,] demonstrated that their personalities made them vulnerable in a way and to a degree not typical of the general population." (emphasis original)).

Not only does our precedent make clear that a reloaded investor-victim of a telemarketing scheme is a vulnerable victim, *see, e.g., Ciccone,* 219 F.3d at 1086; *Randall,* 162 F.3d at 560, but the record also shows that Baker intentionally targeted several of his investor-victims for reloading because they had a "track record of falling for fraudulent schemes," *Randall,* 162 F.3d at 560. The district court specifically identified three individuals, Tranter, Beacham and Houseknecht, as vulnerable victims. Baker solicited investments from each for *Forbidden Warrior.* Five years after Tranter's first investment in *Forbidden Warrior,* Baker successfully reloaded him to invest in *Red Water.* Baker tried to reload Beacham to invest in *From Mexico with Love* a few years after convincing him to invest in *Forbidden Warrior.* Although Baker did not initially succeed, his efforts, combined with those of Lloyd and Agler, convinced Beacham to make the additional investment. Beacham was convinced in part because of Baker's representations that he would soon see returns on his earlier investment in *Forbidden Warrior.* Lloyd and Agler had already reloaded Houseknecht when Baker later tried to reload her again, this time without success. Baker received commissions for each successful reloading, including Houseknecht's reloading by Lloyd and Agler. The record amply supports the district court's vulnerable-victim enhancement. There was no procedural error.

B. The Claim of Error in Calculating Baker's Criminal History Category

Baker argues that the district court erred in calculating his criminal history by double-counting the sentences he received when his probation for two prior convictions was revoked. In September 1990, Baker was arrested for forgery, grand theft, and passing bad checks. In January 1991, while on bond for that offense,

Baker was arrested for committing grand theft on five separate occasions. On October 9, 1991, Baker was sentenced on both convictions. In the September 1990 case, Baker was sentenced to serve six months on one count of forgery, to be followed by probation. In the January 1991 case, Baker was sentenced to serve six months on one count of grand theft, to be followed by probation for two additional counts. Baker served the custodial sentence, was released, and violated his probation. In August 1992, his probation was revoked in both cases and he was sentenced to serve two 18-month prison terms, to run concurrently with each other and consecutively to his current term of incarceration.

The district court followed the presentence report's recommendation to increase Baker's criminal history score by six points for the sentences imposed in the September 1990 and January 1991 cases. Baker objected that only three points should have been assessed for the two prior sentences. He objects on appeal as well, but not for the reason he identified at sentencing.

p.1174 At sentencing, Baker pointed to U.S.S.G. § 4A1.2(a)(2) to argue that the September 1990 and January 1991 sentences should have been treated as a single sentence. Because the two sentences were separated by an intervening arrest, the district court reasoned that they counted as two separate sentences under the Guidelines. *See* U.S.S.G. § 4A1.2(a)(2) ("Prior sentences always are counted separately if the sentences were imposed for offenses that were separated by an intervening arrest. . . .").

On appeal, Baker argues that adding six rather than three criminal history points was incorrect under Application Note 11 to U.S.S.G. § 4A1.2(k). The Note provides that "[w]here a revocation applies to multiple sentences, and such sentences are counted separately under § 4A1.2(a)(2), add the term of imprisonment imposed upon revocation to the sentence that will result in the greatest increase in criminal history points." U.S.S.G. § 4A1.2(k), cmt. n. 11. The Note gives the following example:

> A defendant was serving two probationary sentences, each counted separately under § 4A1.2(a)(2); probation was revoked on both sentences as a result of the same violation conduct; and the defendant was sentenced to a total of 45 days of imprisonment. If one sentence had been a "straight" probationary sentence and the other had been a probationary sentence that had required service of 15 days of imprisonment, the revocation term of imprisonment (45 days) would be added to the probationary sentence that had the 15-day term of imprisonment.

Id.

"The effect of this application note would be to add the additional term of incarceration to only one of [the defendant's] first two disputed convictions." *United States v. Flores,* 93 F.3d 587, 592 (9th Cir.1996). Although "'the sentencing court can tack the probation revocation sentence to any one'" of the defendant's underlying sentences, the others would "'remain unaffected.'" *Id.* (quoting *United States v. Streat,* 22 F.3d 109, 111 (6th Cir.1994)).

On appeal, the government concedes that "when multiple probationary sentences are revoked at the same time for the same violation conduct, only one of the new sentences imposed at the revocation hearing can be added to the underlying sentences for purposes of U.S.S.G. § 4A1.2(a)." If Note 11 applies, Baker argues that one of his prior sentences would be 24 months, consisting of 6 months for the original prison term, plus 18 months for the term imposed on revocation. The other prior sentence, Baker contends, would be limited to 6 months under Note 11. Because the revocation applied to both the September 1990 and January 1991 probations, the court would "add the additional term of incarceration to *only one* of [Baker's] first two disputed convictions." *See Flores,* 93 F.3d at 592. One of these two prior sentences would exceed 13 months, and 3 points, not 6, would be added to Baker's criminal history score. *See* U.S.S.G. § 4A1.1(a); § 4A1.2(e). Baker's criminal history category would be V, not VI, and his Guidelines range would be 262 to 327 months, not 292 to 365 months.

The government argues that plain-error review applies because Baker failed to object on the basis of the Application Note during sentencing.[19] But "it is p.1175 claims that are deemed waived or forfeited, not arguments." *United States v. Pallares-Galan,* 359 F.3d 1088, 1095 (9th Cir. 2004) (applying de novo, rather than plain-error, review). Although Baker argued at sentencing that the September 1990 and January 1991 sentences should be treated as a single sentence under U.S.S.G. § 4A1.2(a)(2), and on appeal that Application Note 11 meant that the single revocation triggered only a three-point increase, his argument here is "an alternative argument to support what has been his consistent claim from the beginning." *Pallares-Galan,* 359 F.3d at 1095. The consistent claim is that "for the two sentences imposed on the cases reported in paragraphs 99 and 102 of the Presentence Report, only one 3 point assessment should have been made." "Once a federal claim is properly presented, a party can make any argument in support of that claim; parties are not limited to the precise arguments they made below." *Pallares-Galan,* 359 F.3d at 1095 (quoting *Yee v. Escondido,* 503 U.S. 519, 534, 112 S.Ct. 1522, 118 L.Ed.2d 153 (1992)).

The record does not provide an adequate basis for us to determine whether Baker's criminal history score should be increased by three rather than six points in light of Note 11 to U.S.S.G. § 4A1.2(k). The government argues that because the revised presentence report referred to the revocation sentencing as taking place on both August 21 and August 24, 1992, it was unclear whether he was sentenced for the two revocations at the same time or on two different dates. There is no requirement in either *Flores* or the § 4A1.2(k) Application Note that the underlying revocations be sentenced on the same day, and the record makes clear that there was one motion to revoke and a single revocation, which occurred on August 24, 1992. Read in context, the reference in the presentence report to August 21 is likely a scrivener's error. The report's prior paragraph identifies the revocation sentence as "08/24/92: 18 mos." Two paragraphs in the presentence report refer to the sentencing in the other revocation as taking place on "08/24/92," and that "[o]n August 24, 1992, Baker admitted violating probation and the 18 month prison sentence was imposed."

It is, however, not clear that both of the probation terms imposed for Baker's prior sentences were revoked because of the "same violation conduct." Although the record shows that probation in both cases was revoked and both sentences imposed on the same day, that does not mean that both revocations resulted from the same conduct. *See* U.S.S.G. § 4A1.2(k), cmt. n. 11.

Because the district court understandably did not account for Note 11 in calculating Baker's criminal history score, and because the record does not allow us to determine whether the correct score is based on a three-or a six-point increase, we vacate Baker's sentence and remand to the district court for resentencing, so that the district court can consider whether Note 11 applies, and correctly calculate the criminal history category and Guidelines sentencing range.

IV. Albert Greenhouse's Sentencing Appeal[20]

Greenhouse worked from his home in Florida from 2005 to 2007, soliciting investments p.1176 in partnership units for *From Mexico with Love*. His work succeeded in getting victims to send Cinamour approximately $1,340,000. Greenhouse was indicted on one count of conspiracy under 18 U.S.C. § 371, three counts of mail fraud under 18 U.S.C. § 1341, and two counts of offering and selling (or aiding and abetting the offer and sale of) an unregistered security under 15 U.S.C. § 77e and 77x and 18 U.S.C. § 2. He was tried and convicted on two counts of willfully engaging in the offer and sale of unregistered securities and aiding and abetting and causing those sales. The jury acquitted him on the remaining charges. The district court calculated his Guidelines range as 63 to 78 months, including enhancements under U.S.S.G. §§ 2B1.1 and 3A1.1 for the fraud-loss amount, for the number of victims (10 or more), and for the victims' vulnerability. The court overruled Greenhouse's objections to the enhancements. The government recommended a 78-month sentence and an $8,981,676.68 restitution obligation, based on the total loss for all investors in both the Florida and California boiler rooms during the time Greenhouse was involved. Greenhouse argued for a $10,000 fine and no restitution. The district court sentenced Greenhouse to serve a below-Guidelines 60-month prison term and to pay $530,000 in restitution.

We review Greenhouse's sentencing challenges to the district court's interpretation of the Sentencing Guidelines de novo, to the factual findings during sentencing for clear error, and to the application of the Sentencing Guidelines for abuse of discretion. *United States v. Lynn,* 636 F.3d 1127, 1138 (9th Cir.2011). "The legality of an order of restitution is reviewed de novo, and factual findings supporting the order are reviewed for clear error." *United States v. Brock-Davis,* 504 F.3d 991, 996 (9th Cir.2007) (emphasis removed). "Provided that it is within the bounds of the statutory framework, a restitution order is reviewed for abuse of discretion." *Id.*

Greenhouse first argues that the district court should not have increased the offense level based on the loss amount. Citing no authority, he argues that the district court improperly applied § 2B1.1(b) because it requires a conviction involving fraud or moral turpitude, and he was acquitted of fraud and convicted only of selling unregistered securities. Greenhouse ignores the fact that he was convicted of violating 15 U.S.C. §§ 77e and 77x, which are cross-referenced with § 2B1.1 in the Statutory Index. *See* U.S.S.G.App. A-Statutory Index; U.S.S.G. § 2B1.1, cmt. Statutory Provisions; *United States v. McEnry,* 659 F.3d 893, 897 (9th Cir.2011) ("When deciding which guideline to apply, a district court must determine the guideline section in Chapter Two (Offense Conduct). . . . To do this, the court is to refer to the Statutory Index, Appendix A of the Guidelines, to find the offense of conviction. . . ." (citation omitted)). He also ignores the relationship between the sale of unregistered securities and the absence of disclosures about, or review of, those securities, designed to prevent and address fraudulent misrepresentations. The district court did not err in applying the 16-level enhancement under § 2B1.1(b).

Greenhouse also argues that even if § 2B1.1(b)'s loss enhancement does apply to his securities convictions, the district court erred in concluding that he caused $1,340,000 in investor losses. Greenhouse p.1177 stipulated that he personally solicited $1,340,000 from victims and that they all lost everything they invested. Greenhouse argues that the failure to register the securities and the way they were marketed did not cause these losses. Instead, he asserts, the investors lost money because the movie "bombed at the box office." The district court rejected Greenhouse's argument that he was not responsible for any of the investors' losses. We review the district court's loss-causation finding for clear error. *See Miller v. Thane Int'l, Inc.,* 615 F.3d 1095, 1104 (9th Cir.2010).

The evidence showed that the victims invested after Greenhouse made promises that their money was safely invested, with no risk of loss, and they would get a guaranteed and fast return on their investment. Greenhouse specifically promised victims that the money they invested would go to making and distributing the movie, not to paying the promoters or sales personnel. Contrary to his promises, most of the investments went to pay the telemarketers and promoters and very little went to make or distribute the movie, contributing to the box-office disaster Greenhouse identifies as the only reason for his losses and as unrelated to his acts or omissions. The evidence showed that Greenhouse sold unregistered securities when he "knew or, under the circumstances, reasonably should have known," that "pecuniary harm" was at least "a potential result." U.S.S.G. § 2B1.1, cmt. n. 3(A)(iv). It was reasonably foreseeable to Greenhouse that making these misrepresentations in selling unregistered securities would cause investors to lose their money. These losses were not "caused by the intervening, independent, and unforeseeable criminal misconduct of a third party," *United States v. Hicks,* 217 F.3d 1038, 1049 (9th Cir.2000), or by the vagaries of the movie-watching public. The record supports the district court's conclusion that Greenhouse was a causal factor in his victims' losses and did not err in applying the loss enhancement.

Nor did the district court err in applying either the two-level increase under § 2B1.1(b)(2)(A)(i) for ten or more victims or the two-level increase under § 3A1.1(b)(1) for vulnerable victims, or in imposing $530,000 in restitution as a condition of supervised release. Greenhouse admits that he sold partnership interests in *From Mexico with Love* to ten or twelve investors who lost a total of $1,340,000. Greenhouse admits that he solicited some victims who had already invested money in *From Mexico with Love.* These victims were vulnerable under the applicable law. *Ciccone,* 219 F.3d at 1086; *Randall,* 162 F.3d at 560. Finally, the restitution amount did no more than compensate for the loss caused by the specific conduct that was the basis of Greenhouse's "offense[s] of conviction." *United States v. Batson,* 608 F.3d 630, 636 (9th Cir.2010).

We affirm Greenhouse's sentence.

CONCLUSION

We (1) affirm Lloyd's sentence; (2) vacate Keskemety's sentence and remand for resentencing; (3) reverse Nelson's convictions, vacate his sentence, and remand; (4) affirm Baker's convictions but vacate his sentence and remand for resentencing; and (5) affirm Greenhouse's sentence.

AFFIRMED in part, REVERSED in part, VACATED in part, and REMANDED in part.

[*] The Honorable Lee H. Rosenthal, District Judge for the U.S. District Court for the Southern District of Texas, sitting by designation.

[1] The indictment also charged Craft for his role at American Information Strategies and Agler, Jady Laurence Herrmann, Joseph McCarthy, Matthew Bryan Wellman-Mackin, Morabito, and Robert Ramirez for their roles as closers.

[2] The indictment also charged Daniel Toll for his role as Cinamour's president; Joel Lee Craft, Jr. for his role as head of American Information Strategies, which supplied Cinamour with telemarketers, sales materials, telephone scripts, private placement memoranda, and lists of prospects to cold-call; and Bart Douglas Slanaker, Allen Bruce Agler, Delitha Floyd, Brian Emmanuel Ellis, Daniel Morabito, and Daryl Van Snowden, who were closers.

[3] The government also cites *United States v. Boatner,* 99 F.3d 831 (7th Cir.1996), in which the court held that the defendants, conspirators in an insurance-fraud scheme, were accountable for the entire scheme's fraud losses despite the fact that they had not pooled profits or resources. The court distinguished *Studley* because the *Boatner* defendants "concocted a common story; they feigned injuries together; they lied to the police together; and they retained the same attorney to pursue a fraudulent claim against a single victim." *Id.* at 837. No such evidence is present here.

[4] Clark at first testified that Nelson called him in April 2005 to raise money for *Red Water,* but other evidence and Clark's testimony that he was "a little rusty" about the precise date shows that it was actually April 2009.

[5] Although only Nelson objected to Eliassen's testimony, the government concedes that "[a]buse-of-discretion review applies to [Baker's] claim regarding Eliassen." *See United States v. Orm Hieng,* 679 F.3d 1131, 1141 (9th Cir.2012) (reviewing the defendant's claim of evidentiary error for abuse of discretion even though he did not object because his codefendant did and "the matter was sufficiently brought to the attention of the district court").

[6] The parties do not cite Ninth Circuit case law on using similar victim-impact testimony to show intent to defraud. Other circuits have allowed it under limited circumstances. *See, e.g., United States v. Cloud,* 680 F.3d 396, 402 (4th Cir.2012) (district court did not abuse its discretion in admitting victim-impact testimony because it "met the low bar of relevancy, given [the defendant's] defense that the [victims] were guilty of bank fraud."). The case law also recognizes limits on such testimony. *See, e.g., United States v. Copple,* 24 F.3d 535, 544-46 (3d Cir.1994).

[7] Agler also used the name Paul Kingman.

[8] The government did not argue that Agler's testimony about what other closers had told him was admissible under the coconspirator exception to the hearsay rule

until oral argument in this court. The argument is both untimely and unpersuasive. Agler did not identify the Cinamour closers who made the hearsay statements. Although Rule 801(d)(2)(E) provides that statements made by a "party's coconspirator during and in furtherance of the conspiracy" are "not hearsay," Fed.R.Evid. 801(d)(2)(E), more information about who made the statements would be needed to establish that the persons were coconspirators and that the statements were in furtherance of the conspiracy. *See, e.g., United States v. Mouzin,* 785 F.2d 682, 692 (9th Cir.1986) ("[B]efore a statement is that of a 'coconspirator' there must be independent proof of the defendant's and the declarant's status as members of the same ongoing conspiracy. In order to corroborate or refute this status, the litigants must know the identity of the declarant."). Because Agler's testimony about these other unidentified telemarketers was both vague and general, we cannot conclude on this record that the statements were made by Cinamour coconspirators or in furtherance of the Cinamour conspiracy.

[9] When we find evidentiary error, we typically review for harmlessness before considering other issues, reversing "only if such nonconstitutional error more likely than not affected the verdict." *United States v. Tran,* 568 F.3d 1156, 1162 (9th Cir.2009). But "[w]here, as here, there are a number of errors at trial, 'a balkanized, issue-by-issue harmless error review' is far less effective than analyzing the overall effect of all the errors in the context of the evidence introduced at trial against the defendant." *United States v. Frederick,* 78 F.3d 1370, 1381 (9th Cir.1996) (quoting *United States v. Wallace,* 848 F.2d 1464, 1476 (9th Cir.1988)).

[10] Big Gunn was previously known as First Take Productions.

[11] After FBI agents conduct a formal interview, they "incorporate[]" their handwritten notes "into a more complete report of the interview on the FBI's Interview Report Form FD-302," known colloquially as a "302." *See United States v. Harris,* 543 F.2d 1247, 1249 (9th Cir.1976); *see also United States v. Rewald,* 889 F.2d 836, 866 (9th Cir.1989) ("A 302 report is an FBI agent's formal account of a witness interview filed on the FBI's Interview Report Form FD-302.").

[12] The government responds with an argument that it never made to the district court: the check was admissible to rebut Nelson's purported testimony that he would never be dishonest because it shows he was willing to lie and write "leads" on the check at Slanaker's behest. *See Blitz,* 151 F.3d at 1008 ("[W]hen the evidence of other acts is offered to prove knowledge, the other acts need not be similar to the charged acts as long as they tend to make the existence of the defendant's knowledge more probable than it would be without the evidence."). But Nelson did not testify that he would never be dishonest in his personal dealings. Instead, he testified that he would not lie in the course of his employment, whether to a customer or to an investor. And in any event, the risk of unfair prejudice of submitting the check to the jury substantially outweighed its minimal relevance to impeaching Nelson's claims of honesty.

[13] Although *Love* was a variance challenge, courts have applied its reasoning to constructive-amendment challenges similar to Baker's. *See United States v. Hathaway,* 798 F.2d 902, 911 (6th Cir.1986).

[14] Nelson does not argue that the evidence was insufficient to support his convictions for conspiracy, mail fraud, or wire fraud.

[15] Nelson's reliance on *United States v. Crosby,* 294 F.2d 928 (2d Cir.1961), is unavailing. In that case, the defendants had opinion letters from attorneys stating that the securities they were selling through solicitations were exempt. *See id.* at 939-41. Nelson had no similar opinion or basis for believing that the securities he sold were exempt.

[16] Although we need not consider whether the evidence was sufficient to sustain Nelson's conspiracy, mail-fraud, and wire-fraud convictions because he does not raise that issue on appeal, we note that, viewing the evidence in the light most favorable to the government, a rational factfinder could find the essential elements of those crimes beyond a reasonable doubt.

[17] Nelson also challenges his sentence, but because we reverse his convictions for selling unregistered securities, we need not address that challenge here.

[18] "There is an intracircuit split as to whether the standard of review for application of the Guidelines to the facts is de novo or abuse of discretion." *United States v. Tanke,* 743 F.3d 1296, 1306 (9th Cir.2014). This issue is currently the subject of en banc review. *See United States v. Gasca-Ruiz,* No. 14-50342, ___ F.3d ___, 2015 WL 7067873 (9th Cir. Nov. 12, 2015) (mem.). We would reach the same result under either standard.

[19] The government goes on to argue that any error would be harmless because Baker received a below-Guidelines sentence. A below-Guidelines sentence does not avoid or make harmless an error in the Guidelines calculation. *See United States v. Bonilla-Guizar,* 729 F.3d 1179, 1188-89 (9th Cir.2013); *United States v. Kilby,* 443 F.3d 1135, 1140 (9th Cir.2006).

[20] Greenhouse did not challenge his conviction in his opening brief. In his reply brief, he sought reversal of his conviction based on an SEC proposal to lift the Regulation D ban on general solicitations and advertising in limited certain circumstances. At oral argument, however, Greenhouse abandoned that challenge to his conviction. We consider only his challenge to his sentence.

TENTH CIRCUIT DECISIONS

The Rule Against Hearsay

No cases were selected for publication.

ELEVENTH CIRCUIT DECISIONS

The Rule Against Hearsay

706 F.3d 1321 (2013)

CYNERGY, LLC, as successor in interest to Farmers State Bank, Plaintiff-Appellant,

v.

FIRST AMERICAN TITLE INSURANCE COMPANY, Defendant-Appellee.

No. 12-10495.

United States Court of Appeals, Eleventh Circuit.

January 28, 2013.

Cynergy, LLC v. First American Title Ins., 706 F. 3d 1321 (11th Cir. 2013)

p.1322 Adam William King, Harry D. Revell, Nicholson Revell, LLP, William A. Trotter, III, Augusta, GA, for Plaintiff-Appellant.

Davis A. Dunaway, William James Keogh, III, Hull Barrett, PC, Augusta, GA, for Defendant-Appellee.

Before MARCUS and PRYOR, Circuit Judges, and FRIEDMAN,[*] District Judge.

FRIEDMAN, District Judge:

In this appeal, we are asked to review the district court's interpretation of an exclusion in a title insurance policy issued by the appellee, First American Title Insurance Company, to a Georgia bank, Farmers State Bank, and the district court's decision that First American was entitled to summary judgment based on that exclusion. We affirm the district court in all respects.

I. BACKGROUND

A. Factual Background

This dispute arises from a land development project that failed to go according to plan. The essential facts are as follows. A group of real estate investors formed a company — the Retreat at Lake Thurmond, LLC — to purchase an undeveloped parcel of land in Lincoln County, Georgia, and turn it into a residential subdivision. The Retreat took out a short-term purchase loan from a local institution, Farmers State Bank, to finance only the acquisition of the land; the costs of development were to be funded later from a separate source. The Bank, to protect itself from risks associated p.1323 with the loan it was extending, also obtained personal guarantees from two of the Retreat's principal investors, Tommy Lee and Dean Antonakos, and secured debt on real property owned by individual Retreat investors as additional collateral for the loan. It also took out a title insurance policy with First American Title Insurance Company. Such policies insure "owners of real property or others having an interest in such real property ... against loss by encumbrance, defective titles, invalidity, adverse claim to title, or unmarketability of title by reason of encumbrance or defects not excepted in the insurance contract." Ga.Code Ann. § 33-7-8.

Using the funds it borrowed from the Bank, the Retreat purchased the parcel of land in September 2006. Although it promptly commenced preliminary construction operations, clearing and grading the property, its development plans did not proceed as anticipated. Among the issues with which the Retreat contended was that the property did not abut a public road and lacked dedicated access to any public road. The previous owner, Emily Hester, had accessed the property through a neighboring lot with the permission of its owners. Permissive access was also available via a gravel road situated on adjacent land owned by the United States Army Corps of Engineers, but the property had no legally enforceable right of access. Although the Retreat was aware of this condition before it purchased the property and had intended to obtain an easement across the Army Corps of Engineers land, it abandoned this plan after deeming it too expensive.

The title insurance policy that First American issued to the Bank covered, among other things, loss or damage incurred due to a "lack of a right of access to and from the land." A year after the Retreat purchased the property, it sent a letter to First American purporting to file a claim under this provision of the insurance policy. First American denied the claim because the Bank, not the Retreat, was the insured party.

The Retreat attempted to solve its dedicated access problem by purchasing an adjoining tract of land in 2008 that contained a road leading to the highway. Progress continued to lag, however, due to the Retreat's inability to secure funding for development. Meanwhile, interest on the Retreat's purchase loan from the Bank continued to accrue, while the loan's maturity date approached. In an attempt to reach a mutually beneficial resolution to the Retreat's difficulty in paying back the purchase loan to Farmers State Bank, the Bank and the Retreat began to negotiate about a possible extension of the loan with modified terms. In October 2008, a principal investor behind the Retreat, Dean Antonakos, sent a letter to the Bank acknowledging that while the Retreat originally planned to fund the development of the property through other sources, "due to the financial climate of the over all economy, especially in the banking sector, those original development sources have dried up." Antonakos suggested, among other options, that the Retreat could complete preliminary improvements of the property in tandem with work on the newly purchased adjacent property, with the aim of selling the two together as a single subdivision that could be developed later — an endeavor that would require additional funding from the Bank.

Antonakos wrote to the Bank again the next month, acknowledging an "impasse" in their discussions and suggesting some alternative courses of action. In this letter, Antonakos drew the Bank's attention to its title insurance policy with First American and encouraged the Bank to file a claim under the provision that offered p.1324 coverage for losses incurred due to the lack of a right of access to and from the land.

In March 2009, the Bank's executive vice president, J. Bruce Turner, wrote to Antonakos, declining Antonakos' invitation to make a claim against First American for the insurance proceeds and proposing two options for extending and modifying the loan. In this letter, Turner also stated: "When we originally made this loan, we knew that there was no designated access to the property, but it was in your plans to create one" from the nearby highway.

No agreement was reached with respect to extending the loan. Once the loan went into default, the Bank indicated that it might seek to recover on the personal guarantees that were made at the time of the loan by Antonakos and another Retreat investor, Tommy Lee. To extricate the Retreat from its debt to the Bank, Antonakos, Lee, and others formed a new company — Cynergy, LLC, the appellant here — to raise additional funds from third parties and purchase the

Retreat's promissory note from the Bank. This newly formed company acquired the note at full price in May 2009, essentially purchasing the Bank's loan. Through this transaction, Cynergy became the successor in interest to the Bank under the insurance policy.[1]

Four days after acquiring the Retreat note, Cynergy submitted to First American an insurance claim premised on the Retreat property's lack of dedicated access. First American retained counsel who conducted an investigation into the matter, after the completion of which First American denied the claim. It based this denial on one of the exclusions in the policy, a provision excluding coverage for matters "assumed or agreed to" by the insured. First American explained in its denial letter that, according to the results of its investigation, the Bank extended the loan with full awareness that the land had no dedicated right of access. Therefore, in First American's view, the property's lack of dedicated access was a condition "assumed or agreed to" by the Bank.

After First American refused a subsequent demand for payment, Cynergy filed suit in state court, seeking damages for breach of contract along with bad-faith penalties. First American removed the case to federal court, and the parties filed cross-motions for summary judgment on the issue of First American's liability under the policy.

B. The District Court's Decision

The district court granted summary judgment to First American. The court first agreed with Cynergy's interpretation of the term "right of access" in the title insurance policy, concluding that the policy covers losses resulting from the lack of a *dedicated, legally enforceable* right of access to the property. It rejected First American's argument that the scope of the policy is limited to situations in which the claimant also lacks permissive access. Applying the established principle under Georgia law that ambiguity in insurance contracts should be resolved in favor of coverage, the court construed the phrase "lack of a right of access to and from the land" to mean the lack of legally enforceable access rights, even where, as here, the property owner has never lacked permissive access to the land. The court further found that the Retreat property did not have a legally enforceable right of access. The court therefore determined that Cynergy's p.1325 claim fell within the scope of the insurance policy.

The court then turned to the next question: whether coverage nevertheless was defeated by the policy exclusion negating coverage for losses arising from "defects, liens, encumbrances, adverse claims or other matters" that were "created, suffered, assumed or agreed to by the insured claimant."

Drawing on common definitions of the word "assume," along with the meaning that the word has been given in title insurance policies and in the analogous tort context of assumption of risk, the court concluded that the word, as used in the policy, "means that the Bank must have had actual, subjective knowledge of the access issue and appreciated its effect." No party before us disagrees with that definition.

Applying this standard, the district court found that "the evidence and undisputed facts show that the lack of dedicated access was indeed an 'assumed' condition." In reaching this conclusion, the court relied primarily on the sworn affidavit of George C. Leverett III, the Bank's former president and the officer who personally handled the Retreat loan. In his affidavit, Leverett states that at the time of the loan application, "I was aware that the tract appeared to be landlocked, but I was told by Tommy Lee of Retreat LLC that he was pursuing and expected to obtain an access easement to Highway 378 for their future development plans." The affidavit further explains that because the Bank was not financing the planned development of the property, but was only issuing a short-term loan for the purchase of the land, "obtaining adequate collateral on the loan was more important to [the Bank] than the issue of how the property would be accessed for purposes of Retreat LLC's planned development."

The district court determined that Leverett's affidavit, along with a number of corroborating circumstances lending credence to his statements, demonstrated both the Bank's knowledge of the lack of access and its appreciation of the significance of that condition. It was precisely because the Bank knew that the property lacked dedicated access, Leverett attests, that the Bank "required additional collateral" for the loan beyond the security deed to the property itself, including personal guarantees from Antonakos and Lee as well as security deeds to properties owned by individual Retreat members. The court further observed that the Bank itself never filed an insurance claim with First American based on the property's lack of access, even when pressed to do so by Antonakos — an additional circumstance indicating that the Bank knowingly acquiesced to the lack of dedicated access when it issued the loan. Based on the evidence, the court found, the "only reasonable inference available" was that the Bank "assumed" the Retreat property's lack of dedicated access when it financed the purchase of the property and that "Leverett understood the implications of the issue and accounted for it by securing ample collateral." And Cynergy, the district court stated, presented "no evidence" to rebut this testimony and evidence.

Instead, Cynergy presented two legal arguments. First, Cynergy took issue with the interpretation of the insurance policy and its exclusions summarized above. In Cynergy's view, reading the policy to exclude conditions, like a lack of dedicated access, that were "assumed" by the insured party would "eviscerate" coverage under the policy. The district court quickly dispensed with this argument, which Cynergy revives before this Court and which is discussed below. Second, Cynergy contended that George Leverett's affidavit was inadmissible as hearsay and p.1326 barred from consideration by Rule 56(c)(4) of the Federal Rules of Civil Procedure. The district court, acknowledging the dispositive effect of the affidavit on its ruling, engaged in a lengthy analysis of this point, finding the affidavit to be admissible under Rule 807 of the Federal Rules of Evidence and, contrary to Cynergy's arguments, in no way barred from consideration by Rule 56(c)(4). Having rejected these legal arguments, and finding no genuine issues of material fact in dispute, the court granted summary judgment to First American.

II. JURISDICTION AND STANDARD OF REVIEW

We have jurisdiction over this appeal pursuant to 28 U.S.C. § 1291. This Court reviews a district court's grant of summary judgment *de novo*. *Kernel Records Oy v.*

Mosley, 694 F.3d 1294, 1300 (11th Cir. 2012). Summary judgment is appropriate "if the movant shows that there is no genuine dispute as to any material fact and the movant is entitled to judgment as a matter of law." Fed.R.Civ.P. 56(a). A genuine factual dispute exists only if a reasonable factfinder "could find by a preponderance of the evidence that the plaintiff is entitled to a verdict." *Anderson v. Liberty Lobby, Inc.,* 477 U.S. 242, 252, 106 S.Ct. 2505, 91 L.Ed.2d 202 (1986). "Once the movant adequately supports its motion, the burden shifts to the nonmoving party to show that specific facts exist that raise a genuine issue for trial." *Dietz v. Smithkline Beecham Corp.,* 598 F.3d 812, 815 (11th Cir.2010).

The district court's evidentiary rulings are reviewed for abuse of discretion and will be reversed only "if an erroneous ruling resulted in 'substantial prejudice.'" *Conroy v. Abraham Chevrolet-Tampa, Inc.,* 375 F.3d 1228, 1232 (11th Cir.2004) (quoting *Piamba Cortes v. Am. Airlines, Inc.,* 177 F.3d 1272, 1305 (11th Cir.1999)). This Court will affirm such rulings "unless the district court has made a 'clear error of judgment' or has applied an 'incorrect legal standard.'" *Id.* (quoting *Piamba Cortes,* 177 F.3d at 1306).

III. DISCUSSION

A. Interpretation of the Insurance Policy

Cynergy maintains that the district court's interpretation of the policy exclusion under which it granted summary judgment to First American is unduly broad and inconsistent with Georgia law. As Cynergy reads it, the insurance policy guarantees coverage without exception for losses incurred due to a property's lack of dedicated access. Any knowledge that the Bank may have had about the Retreat property's lack of access is therefore irrelevant in Cynergy's view. We find no merit to Cynergy's arguments.

The title insurance policy covers, among other matters, "loss or damage ... sustained or incurred ... by reason of ... lack of a right of access to and from the land." Among the losses and damages excluded from coverage, however, are those arising from "defects, liens, encumbrances, adverse claims or *other matters*... created, suffered, *assumed* or agreed to by the insured claimant" (emphasis added). As discussed above, the district court construed these provisions as excluding coverage if the insured "assumed" the lack of a right of access, which the court interpreted to mean that the insured was aware of the lack of access when the policy was issued and appreciated its effect. The district court's assumption of risk analogy, quoting *Vaughn v. Pleasent,* 266 Ga. 862, 471 S.E.2d 866, 868 (1996) (emphasis in original), is to the same effect: "In its simplest and primary sense, assumption of the risk means that the plaintiff, in advance, has given his consent to relieve the defendant of an obligation of conduct toward p.1327 him, and to take his chance of injury from a *known risk arising from what the defendant is to do or leave undone.*" Cynergy argues that, properly read, the policy does not actually exclude coverage under this scenario — or, in the alternative, that any such purported exclusion is impermissible under Georgia law.

In support of its position, Cynergy first maintains as a matter of textual interpretation that the phrase "other matters" cannot include the lack of a right of access, because the policy fails to list that specific condition alongside "defects, liens, encumbrances, [and] adverse claims." As Cynergy puts it: "Had First American wanted to list an additional exclusion for lack of access that is assumed, it could have written the policy differently to include that event among those specifically enumerated." But of course, the phrase "other matters" would have no meaning if it did not refer to anything beyond the four examples that precede it. Cynergy's reading of this provision, which would limit the matters covered by the exclusion to the four enumerated examples, therefore is untenable. The plain language of the policy is clear: losses of any type arising from matters that have been "assumed" by the insured claimant are not covered. While these matters include defects, liens, encumbrances, and adverse claims, they are not limited to those examples.

Cynergy next objects that under the district court's interpretation of the exclusion, as Cynergy sees it, the policy purports to cover losses caused by the lack of dedicated access while simultaneously negating coverage for those same losses under the "other matters" exclusion. But that is the nature of an exclusion — to exclude things that otherwise would be covered, when certain conditions are met. The policy does not exclude *all* losses stemming from a lack of dedicated access, merely those that were assumed by the insured. The exclusion therefore does not "eviscerate" coverage under the policy, as Cynergy asserts, and this case is unlike the decisions that Cynergy cites in which exclusions were found to impermissibly subsume a policy's affirmative grant of coverage. Those decisions simply recognize that, under Georgia law, an insurance policy may not purport to offer coverage that inevitably will be defeated by one of the policy's exclusions — in other words, the policy may not offer coverage that is chimerical. *See Hooters of Augusta, Inc. v. Am. Global Ins. Co.,* 272 F.Supp.2d 1365, 1378 (S.D.Ga.2003) ("Read fairly, the Endorsement *completely abrogates* the coverage provided in the same document because *every advertisement would be excluded by it* .... When an exclusion *completely nullifies the coverage provided in a policy,* that exclusion has no effect[.]" (citing *Isdoll v. Scottsdale Ins. Co.,* 219 Ga. App. 516, 466 S.E.2d 48, 50 (1995))) (emphasis added); *Transp. Ins. Co. v. Piedmont Const. Group, LLC.,* 301 Ga.App. 17, 686 S.E.2d 824, 828 (2009) ("Transportation's proposed interpretation of the business-risk exclusion '*would make coverage for such actions merely illusory,* despite the fact that such coverage is expressly provided for in the policy.'" (quoting *Isdoll,* 466 S.E.2d at 50)) (emphasis added). In contrast to the provisions addressed in those cases, this dispute involves a policy exclusion that exempts certain claims from coverage — no more and no less. Cynergy's unhappiness that the exclusion is triggered by the undisputed facts underlying this particular case does not transform the provision into anything else.

Taking a different tack, Cynergy next argues that contrary to the district court's reasoning, the Bank's knowledge and appreciation of the access issue is "irrelevant" to the coverage question, "because First American gave written assurances there was access." What Cynergy appears p.1328 to mean by this is that First American, when issuing the policy, was obliged to comply with a Georgia statute providing that title insurance contracts "shall be written only upon evidence or opinion of title obtained and preserved by the insurer." Ga.Code Ann. § 33-7-8. First American satisfied that obligation, however, by relying on evidence of title supplied by its issuing agent, James Roberts, and the validity of title has never been an issue in this case. Contrary to Cynergy's suggestion, Section 33-7-8 of the Georgia Code speaks only to evidence of *title* and imposes no requirements regarding the accuracy of an insurer's understanding about a property's dedicated access, easements, and other such matters.[2]

Further to its argument under the Georgia Code, Cynergy analogizes this case to a Georgia decision, *Fid. Nat. Title Ins. Co. v. Matrix Fin. Servs. Corp.*, 255 Ga.App. 874, 567 S.E.2d 96 (2002), in which an identical policy exclusion was held inapplicable. The analogy fails. In *Matrix*, a lender sought to recover on a title insurance policy after defects in the title of the property came to light. *Id.* at 99. Among the insurer's many unavailing arguments against coverage was its contention that the lender "assumed, or agreed to" the loss that it incurred. *Id.* at 100. Specifically, the insurer argued that if the lender had "properly investigated" and "performed an adequate property title search," it would have discovered the defects in the title before it closed the loan. *Id.* at 101. According to the insurer, the lender "should never have closed" the loan, and "by doing so, it created its own loss." *Id.* In sum, the insurer contended that the lender "negligently created its own title problems and cannot legally or equitably seek coverage under the policy." *Id.*

The Court of Appeals of Georgia rejected this argument. It stated that the insurer was simply second-guessing the wisdom of the lender's business decisions, and that, regardless of what circumstances may have existed at the time of the loan to raise the lender's suspicions about the title, these circumstances did not affect the insurer's promise to insure the lender's interest in the property. *Fid. Nat. Title Ins. Co.*, 567 S.E.2d at 101. The court went on to note that under Section 33-7-8 of the Georgia Code, the insurer, not the lender, "was responsible for obtaining the evidence to support its title opinion." *Id.* The lender's "failure to discover" the evidence of a title defect before closing therefore had no bearing on the insurer's obligations. *Id.*

Here, by contrast, First American does not allege that the Bank, with proper diligence, would have discovered the property's lack of dedicated access before extending the loan or that the Bank was obligated to undertake such an investigation. Instead, it alleges (and furnishes evidence) that the Bank *actually knew* about the lack of access and fully understood the effect of this fact on the property's value before it made the loan. Although Section § 33-7-8 puts the onus on insurers to obtain evidence of the validity of title before issuing a policy, Cynergy identifies no similar obligation requiring First American to obtain evidence that the land did or did not have a dedicated right of access, or anything prohibiting p.1329 First American from issuing the policy unless such access existed.

The district court correctly interpreted the terms of the title insurance contract. Accordingly, we move on to the question of whether genuine issues of material fact preclude summary judgment in First American's favor.

B. Summary Judgment

As the preceding discussion establishes, First American is not liable under the terms of the title insurance policy if Farmers State Bank was aware of the Retreat property's lack of a dedicated right of access and appreciated its effect when the Bank extended the loan and took out the insurance policy. The district court found that the evidence conclusively demonstrated that the Bank indeed had such knowledge and understood its significance. There being no genuine disputes of fact about this, the court concluded that summary judgment for First American was appropriate. Having reviewed the matter *de novo,* we agree.

1. Admissibility of the Leverett Affidavit

In the district court's reckoning, as in ours, the critical piece of evidence demonstrating that the Bank "assumed" the Retreat property's lack of dedicated access is the affidavit of George C. Leverett III, the Bank's former president and the officer who originated the Retreat loan. Given the significance of the affidavit to the outcome of this case, we must address Cynergy's contention that the affidavit would have been inadmissible at trial and therefore should not have been considered by the district court at summary judgment. As an evidentiary ruling, the district court's determination is reviewed for abuse of discretion and should be affirmed unless the court made a "clear error of judgment" or applied an "incorrect legal standard." *Conroy,* 375 F.3d at 1232 (quoting *Piamba,* 177 F.3d at 1306).

Leverett's affidavit, which was executed at First American's request, was signed on October 1, 2009, at which point First American was investigating Cynergy's policy claim but had not yet denied it. At the time, Leverett was still the Bank's president, but he was undergoing treatment for cancer. He died in early April 2010, before the affidavit was ever produced in discovery for this lawsuit. Cynergy argued to the district court that the affidavit constituted inadmissible hearsay. The court disagreed, concluding after careful analysis that the affidavit was admissible under Rule 807 of the Federal Rules of Evidence. This "catch-all exception to the hearsay rule" permits admission of a hearsay statement "if it is particularly trustworthy; it bears on a material fact; it is the most probative evidence addressing that fact; its admission is consistent with the rules of evidence and advances the interests of justice; and its proffer follows adequate notice to the adverse party." *United States v. Rodriguez,* 218 F.3d 1243, 1246 (11th Cir.2000); *see* Fed.R.Evid. 807.

Cynergy does not challenge any part of the district court's Rule 807 analysis. Instead, Cynergy argues that the court failed to make one of the findings that it was required to make under the Rule — that the affidavit "is more probative on the point for which it is offered than any other evidence that the proponent can obtain through reasonable efforts." Fed.R.Evid. 807(a)(3). This contention is belied by the district court's discussion of the affidavit, during which the court separately addressed each prong of Rule 807(a) and stated that the affidavit speaks "directly and comprehensively" to "a key issue for which very little alternative evidence exists," further observing that "the need for the statements is great because the Bank's knowledge is the fulcrum upon which liability turns, but evidence on this point is scant." We conclude that the district p.1330 court made the necessary finding under Rule 807(a)(3), and we agree that the criterion established by that provision is satisfied here.

Cynergy also maintains that the district court's consideration of the Leverett affidavit violated Rule 807(b), which permits a hearsay statement to be admitted "only if, before the trial or hearing, the proponent gives an adverse party reasonable notice of the intent to offer the statement and its particulars, including the declarant's name and address, so that the party has a fair opportunity to meet it." Fed.R.Evid. 807(b). According to Cynergy, it was impermissible for the district court to consider the affidavit because First American did not provide notice to Cynergy before Leverett's death of its intent to offer the affidavit.[3]

First American disputes Cynergy's interpretation of Rule 807(b), arguing that it supplied notice of its intent to rely on the affidavit well before any "trial or hearing," as required by the Rule, and that First American had no obligation to ensure that such notice was provided before Leverett passed away. Indeed, First American scarcely could have done so, because Leverett was already deceased by the time that Cynergy filed this lawsuit in late April 2010. Cynergy offers no authority (and we are aware of none) precluding the district court's consideration of the affidavit for the purposes of summary judgment based on a lack of notice under these circumstances. Cynergy was provided with the affidavit months before briefing on the dispositive motions took place.[4] The notice requirement "is intended to afford the party against whom the statement is offered sufficient opportunity to determine its trustworthiness in order to provide a fair opportunity to meet the statement." *United States v. Evans*, 572 F.2d 455, 489 (5th Cir.1978) (discussing predecessor Rule 803(24)); *see also United States v. Munoz*, 16 F.3d 1116, 1122 (11th Cir.1994). It does not create a categorical ban on the admission of statements made by deceased persons. Nor does it impose what in this case would be the functional equivalent: a requirement that a defendant supply notice of its intent to offer a statement at trial before the plaintiff has even filed suit.

The district court's conclusion that the affidavit would be admissible at trial was not an abuse of discretion.

2. Genuine Issues of Material Fact

The evidence demonstrates that Farmers State Bank was fully aware of the Retreat property's lack of dedicated access when it extended the purchase loan and took out the insurance policy from First American. No reasonable factfinder could conclude otherwise. Because there are no genuine issues of material fact in dispute, and because First American is entitled to judgment as a matter of law, summary judgment was appropriate.

The sworn affidavit of former Bank president George Leverett leaves no doubt that the Bank understood the Retreat property to lack a dedicated right of access and appreciated the impact of this condition p.1331 on the land's marketability. The statements made in Leverett's affidavit are supported by attendant circumstances surrounding the loan — most notably that the Bank required additional collateral for the loan, beyond the deed to the property itself, to offset the potentially diminished resale value of the land. Leverett's statements derive further credence from overwhelming evidence showing that the principal investors in the Retreat were aware of the lack of access before purchasing the land but — just as Leverett attests — had planned on surmounting this obstacle by obtaining an easement over adjacent property. Leverett's affidavit, supported by these indicia of reliability, is uncontradicted by any other evidence.

The key portion of Leverett's affidavit reads as follows:

> At the application stage of this land acquisition loan, Mr. Tommy Lee made a presentation to me about his future property development plans. At that time I was aware that the tract appeared to be landlocked, but I was told by Tommy Lee of Retreat LLC that he was pursuing and expected to obtain an access easement to Highway 378 for their future development plans.

Cynergy depicts this passage as "vague and equivocal" because it states only that the tract "appeared to be landlocked," but we do not accept this characterization. As the affidavit's next paragraph makes clear, a conclusive determination about the property's access was unnecessary to the Bank, as it was extending only a short-term purchase loan for the land, not for its development:

> FSB was not financing the planned development on the Property; the FSB loan was strictly for the acquisition of the Property. Thus, obtaining adequate collateral on the loan was more important to FSB than the issue of how the property would be accessed for purposes of Retreat LLC's planned development.

What mattered to the Bank, in other words, was not whether or not the property truly lacked dedicated access, as it appeared, but that the Bank obtain adequate security for its loan.

That is exactly what the Bank did. Not satisfied with a promissory note and a deed to the property itself, the Bank required additional security as collateral from the principal investors in the Retreat: personal guarantees from Antonakos and Lee, along with deeds to a residential property owned by Lee and a commercial property owned by other Retreat members. As the district court observed, the Bank's insistence on these terms is an attendant circumstance indicating that the Bank knowingly acquiesced to the property's lack of dedicated access and took the precautions necessary to safeguard its interests in light of this consideration.

Were there any doubt about how to interpret the statements made in Leverett's affidavit, it would be dispelled by notes that the Bank's vice president, Maria Bradford, took to memorialize a telephone conversation she had with Leverett two months before the affidavit was executed. At the time of this conversation, First American was conducting its investigation into Cynergy's policy claim; Leverett, although still the Bank's president, was not coming into the office every day because of his illness, and so Bradford acted as a "messenger" to relay to him the inquiries that were being made about the Retreat loan. Bradford's notes of her conversation with Leverett — which were taken for her own future reference — describe Leverett as saying, in substance, that "since we had other collateral securing this loan and this loan was to be a short term 6 month acquisition loan only, the final outcome of p.1332 public access to the property was not our primary concern."

In her deposition, Bradford explained why the Bank would have been willing to extend the loan despite the property's lack of access: the Bank had "our major collateral... the collateral was Tommy's home, a second mortgage on Tommy Lee's home and acreage. We had other collateral." As the closing attorney for the sale, James Roberts, stated in his own deposition, such an arrangement to secure a loan for land that lacked dedicated access was hardly noteworthy, because banks issue such loans "if they feel that they have adequate collateral."[5]

Further support for Leverett's attestations comes from evidence showing that the investors behind the Retreat — or at least Tommy Lee, who was tasked with responsibility over the matter — were well aware of the property's lack of a right of access before their purchase. Although the knowledge held by the Bank, not the Retreat, is the dispositive issue under the insurance policy, the Retreat's undeniable knowledge lends credence to Leverett's account of having been apprised by Lee both of the access problem and how the Retreat was planning to solve that problem through an easement.

The previous owner of the Retreat property, Emily Hester, has attested to the fact that the primary reason she sold the property was because it lacked a dedicated right of access. She further stated that this issue was discussed among the parties prior to the sale, that the Retreat used this fact during negotiations to obtain a lower purchase price, and that an agent of the Retreat told her before the closing that the lack of access was not an issue because the Retreat could get an easement across the Army Corps of Engineers' adjacent land. The seller's real estate agent, Irma Conrad, likewise testified that she discussed the lack of access with the Retreat's real estate agent, Clay Turner; that the lowered purchase price reflected the property's lack of access; and that the Retreat was not concerned due to its plans to obtain an easement. Clay Turner himself has attested: "I was aware that the Property was landlocked with no road frontage or easement access and discussed this fact with Mr. Lee and Mr. Antonakos when they were considering purchasing the property." Confirming these accounts, Mr. Turner wrote a letter to the seller listing several "obstacles that have to be considered with the purchase of this property" which, according to the letter, justified the price and terms offered by the Retreat. The first of the "concerns" listed in Turner's letter is that "the property is currently land locked with no right of way for access. This is an issue that we feel confident that we could resolve given an appropriate option period of 180 days for which we have asked."

Indeed, Tommy Lee has admitted that he was told by Clay Turner about the property's lack of access and that although p.1333 he had heard "rumors" of an existing easement, no one from the Retreat ever determined before the sale whether or not these rumors were true. Upon being informed by Turner that the property appeared to lack access, however, Lee, in his own words, "told him to use that to try to get the price reduced." This evidence firmly supports Leverett's account of his own understanding, before the loan was made, about the property's lack of dedicated access and of his discussions with Lee about the matter.

All of the evidence in this case tells a consistent story, and in light of this evidence, no reasonable factfinder could doubt that the Bank was aware of the Retreat property's lack of dedicated access and appreciated its significance. The Bank therefore "assumed" that condition, within the meaning of the title insurance policy, and First American is entitled to summary judgment. Because we affirm the district court on the same grounds upon which it relied, we have no need to address First American's many alternative arguments for affirmance.

AFFIRMED.

[*] Honorable Paul L. Friedman, United States District Judge for the District of Columbia, sitting by designation.

[1] We pause to note that Antonakos and Lee therefore appear in this narrative in two different roles. Acting on behalf of the Retreat, they initially secured the loan from the Bank and negotiated the purchase of the land. After that loan went into default, acting on behalf of Cynergy they acquired the loan, stepping into the Bank's shoes.

[2] Cynergy complains that an authorization request form completed by Roberts's firm for First American erroneously indicated that the Retreat property had dedicated access. But Cynergy has not explained how the mistake made by Roberts's firm has any bearing on the validity or interpretation of the exclusions in the title insurance policy. It was not illogical for First American to have issued this policy while knowing that the property lacked dedicated access, so long as the title was valid. Nor has Cynergy pointed to any rule prohibiting First American from doing so.

[3] First American maintains that Cynergy waived this argument by failing to raise it in the district court. But it was not until First American's reply brief in support of its motion for summary judgment that it first suggested, in response to Cynergy's hearsay objection, that the affidavit could be admitted under Rule 807. No hearing was held on the motion for summary judgment during which Cynergy could have countered with its notice argument. We therefore do not regard the argument as waived.

[4] The affidavit was used as an exhibit during the depositions of Antonakos and Lee six months before First American moved for summary judgment.

[5] Additional documentary support for the account set forth in Leverett's affidavit can, perhaps, be found in a letter written under his supervision in March 2009 to Dean Antonakos. In this letter, the Bank's executive vice president, J. Bruce Turner, told Antonakos: "When we originally made this loan, we knew that there was no designated access to the property, but it was in your plans to create one from Highway 378." Cynergy points out, however, that portions of Turner's deposition suggest that Turner was referring here not to the Bank's knowledge about the legal question of whether the property had a dedicated right of access, but rather to the logistical matter of creating a usable entrance to the property, which was being discussed by the Bank and the Retreat as they negotiated an extension of the loan. Because Turner's letter is — at most — simply one additional piece of corroborating evidence confirming the account set forth in Leverett's affidavit, our conclusion would be the same even if we gave no weight to Turner's March 2009 letter.

Made in the USA
Middletown, DE
11 October 2023

40592843R00331